Social Research Methodology

A Critical Introduction

Second Edition

Roger Gomm

First edition 2004
Second edition 2008

Published by
PALGRAVE MACMILLAN
Houndmills, Basingstoke, Hampshire RG21 6XS and
175 Fifth Avenue, New York, N.Y. 10010
Companies and representatives throughout the world

PALGRAVE MACMILLAN is the global academic imprint of the Palgrave Macmillan division of St. Martin's Press, LLC and of Palgrave Macmillan Ltd. Macmillan® is a registered trademark in the United States, United Kingdom and other countries. Palgrave is a registered trademark in the European Union and other countries.

ISBN-13: 978–0–230–22475–9
ISBN-10: 0–230–22475–X

This book is printed on paper suitable for recycling and made from fully managed and sustained forest sources. Logging, pulping and manufacturing processes are expected to conform to the environmental regulations of the country of origin.

A catalogue record for this book is available from the British Library.

A catalog record for this book is available from the Library of Congress.

10   9   8   7   6   5   4   3   2   1
17   16   15   14   13   12   11   10   09   08

Printed and bound in Great Britain by
Cromwell Press Ltd, Trowbridge, Wiltshire

Books are to be returned on or before
the last date below.

Contents

List of Figures

List of Tables

List of Panels

List of Transcripts

List of Activities

Preface to the Second Edition

The first edition gave a high profile to experimental research. This was partly because experiments demonstrate the principle of control so well. But it was also because these days much of the demand for social and behavioural research is precisely for experimental research: that to test the effectiveness of medical, nursing, social, educational or criminological interventions. The demand for such 'evidence-based practice' research has increased since the publication of the first edition so the decision to high-profile experimentation has been vindicated. This second edition strengthens this theme, by including a new chapter on meta-analysis and systematic reviews, and another considering the design and use of data collecting instruments. The two are not unconnected insofar as the possibility of combining the results of many pieces of practice-relevant research via systematic review is greatly facilitated by the use of standard instruments which are well designed for their purpose. The chapter on meta-analysis includes material on the use of Bayesian statistics for judging the level of confidence with which beliefs about the validity of findings can be held. Since the first edition, Bayesian statistics have moved towards mainstream acceptance.

For the first edition, the decision was made not to try to compete with the many excellent statistics texts, now joined by many freely accessible web sites. This decision is retained for the second edition, but I have added more basic information about statistical topics.

Complexity theory is perhaps the most important recent development in science of in the last two decades, and is rather slowly beginning to influence social and behavioural science. To reflect this there is a new chapter on computer simulation as a research method. Computer simulation is not exclusively tied to complexity theorizing. Indeed there is a long history of computer simulation in both economics and demography. However, for complex processes which cannot be subjected to experimental control – which would render them 'non-complex' as it were, or where hundreds, if not thousands, of different outcomes might arise from very similar conditions, computer simulation offers the best hope of studying processes which may be very difficult to observe *in vivo*. The material on the limited generalizability of experimental research, strongly featured in the first edition, is now joined by the observation from complexity theory that similar circumstances may give rise to radically different outcomes. This is an additional warning against the kind of naïve faith in experimentation found in some sections of the evidence-based practice movement.

The examples illustrating methodological points remain mainly drawn from research in health, welfare, education, crime and penal policy. I have only rarely replaced these with more recent examples. Telling examples are often difficult to find, and this is a book about methods and not about substantives. However, where leaving an example unchanged would have given a misleading impression of the current state of knowledge about a particular topic I have either changed the example, or up-dated the commentary and references. A second edition has also allowed for the correction of a number of errors which crept into the first edition, and for a comprehensive updating of the bibliography, particularly the 'further reading' sections.

One of the most strident criticisms of the first edition was that it didn't have enough jokes in it. In response I have doubled the risible content, from one joke to two.

ROGER GOMM

Acknowledgements

The author and publishers wish to thank the following for permission to use copyright material:

American Association for the Advancement of Science, for material from Rosenhan, 'On being sane in insane places', *Science*, 1971 (1973), p. 255 © American Association for the Advancement of Science.

British Journal of Psychiatry, for material from Atkinson, Kessel and Dalgaard, 'The comparability of suicide rates', *British Journal of Psychiatry*, 127 (1975), Table 1, p. 251 © Royal College of Psychiatrists.

Cambridge University Press, for material from Oakley, Rajan and Robertson, 'A comparison of different sources of information about pregnancy and smoking', *Journal of Biosocial Science*, 22 (1990), Table 9, p. 483 © Cambridge University Press.

Elsevier Science Inc., for material from Jadad, Moore, Carroll, Jenkinson, Reynolds, Gavaghan and McQuay, 'Assessing the Quality of Reports of Randomized Clinical Trials: Is Blinding Necessary?', *Controlled Clinical Trials* (1996) 17(1) pp. 10–11 © Elsevier Science Inc.

Wiley-Liss, Inc., for material from Sutton and Smith, 'Bullying as a group process: an adaptation of the Participant Role Scale Approach', *Aggressive Behaviour*, 25 (2) (1999), Table 1, p. 101 © Wiley-Liss, Inc., a subsidiary of John Wiley & Sons, Inc.

School of Education, University of Leicester, for material from Boydell and Jasmin, *The Pupil and Teacher Record: A Manual for Observers* (1987), p. 10 © University of Leicester.

Professor John Gray, co-author, for material from Jesson, Gray and Tranmer (1992), Table 3, p. 28 and Figure 13, p. 29 © University of Sheffield.

Every effort has been made to contact all copyright-holders, but if any have been inadvertently omitted the publishers will be pleased to make the necessary arrangement at the earliest opportunity.

List of Abbreviations

ACASI	Audio Computer-Aided Self-Administered Interview
AI	Artificial intelligence
ASAQ	Audio Self-Administered Questionnaire
CA	Conversation Analysis
CA	Cellular Automota
CAPI	Computer-Aided Personal Interview
CASI	Computer-Aided Self-Administered Interview
CASs	Complex adaptive systems
CATI	Computer-Aided Telephone Interview
CBA	Category-bound analysis
CIs	Confidence intervals
GIS	Geographical information systems
IQ	Intelligence Quotient
MC	Membership category
MCA	Membership categorization analysis
MCD	Membership categorization device
NICRS	National Crime Recording Standards
OLQ	On-line Questionnaire
ORs	Odds ratios
PAPI	Paper and Pencil Personal Interview
PATI	Paper and Pencil Telephone Interview
PIs	Performance indicators
PRS	Participant Roles Scale
PSDs	Problem–solution discourses
QCA	Qualitative comparative analysis
RCT	Randomized controlled trials
SAQ	Self-Administered Questionnaire
SAT	Standardized Achievement Tests
SMRs	Standardized Mortality Ratios
SRPs	Standardized relational pairs
TDE	Telephone Data Entry
VAS	Visual analogue scales

1 Overview of the Book

By the end of this chapter you should have some idea of the contents of this book and of the major themes which run through it:

- The difference between an interest in causality and an interest in meaning
- The trade-off between control and naturalism
- Whether social phenomena are best described in terms of linear or non-linear (complex) dynamics
- The trade-off between finding out a great deal about a few people or a little about a lot of them
- The importance of representativeness
- The difficulties of making generalizations on the basis of research
- The difference between value-neutral and value-led research
- Accountability to research subjects as opposed to accountability to readers
- Research as the production of accountable knowledge.

You will encounter these ideas on and off throughout the book.

1.1   Introduction

Social scientists differ greatly in what they think they are studying, and the purpose of doing this. But, despite this diversity, there is only a limited tool kit for research. Different social scientists choose different tools from the kit, use them in different ways, and interpret the results of using them differently. Nonetheless, there is much which can be learned about social science in general from the tools themselves. The more important tools and the methods of using them are the topic of this book.

1.2   Looking for causes and looking for meanings

Two necessary assumptions for research are that there is something real to study, and that while we might never be sure about the truth, at least we can be fairly sure when we are wrong. This rules out the currently fashionable philosophies of post-modernism (Docherty 1993) as a basis for doing anything which can be called 'research'. Since post-modernist philosophies deny the possibility of there being any means for judging knowledge as being more or less true, they at the same time make research a senseless activity (Hammersley 2008: chapter 7).

Among social scientists who do think that research is a sensible activity there are radically different assumptions about what there is which exists to be investigated. They take very different positions about the nature of reality and about the possibilities of knowing about this. The former topic is often called **ontology**; the latter **epistemology**. However, the term epistemology (the theory of knowledge) is often used to describe both. Nearly all social scientists, and most natural scientists too, take a **phenomenological** position, recognizing that we can never get in touch with raw reality (**noumena**) and can study only **phenomena** which are our perceptions of this (Thines 1987). Confusingly, the term **phenomenology** is usually used in a more limited sense in the social sciences to refer to the study of consciousness. Then it may imply that the most important matter to study is how people experience their lives and make sense of them.

If our perceptions are only a partial glimpse of reality, then the task of the social researcher is to manage perception so as to be able to see reality more clearly. I don't mean anything different in principle here from the example of using a microscope – and using it properly, on the assumption that what is important is very small. As in most fields of science, social scientists use instruments as aids to research: tests and observation schedules, questionnaires and attitude scales. As Gregory (1981) charts for science as a whole, these instruments are not passive and inert but actively shape the pictures of the world that researchers create. Chapter 2 of this book looks at the considerations that guide the construction of research instruments in the human sciences, and this theme reoccurs at various later points in the book.

This book is not the place for an extensive epistemological debate. Instead I will make a simple distinction between those researchers who think of the social reality to be captured as one of *cause and effect*, and those who think of it as a complex of *interpretations and meanings*. Some researchers think of these as mutually exclusive; others as different aspects of the same underlying reality.

1.3   Causal analysis

Causal models

Chapters 3–10 deal mainly with experiments, social surveys, computer simulations and some similar investigative strategies, and Chapter 2 with the instruments used in such research. These strategies are largely used by researchers whose basic question is 'What usually causes what to happen?' The 'usually' is important. Many historians are interested in documenting a unique set of circumstances leading to a unique event. But most social scientists, and some historians, are interested in what often, or generally, causes what. The model which lies behind these approaches is one of a network of **variables** connected together in cause–effect relationships: an electrical circuit or a plumbing system are not bad physical analogies for this. The term 'variable' means something which can vary: male *or* female, working class *or* middle class *or* upper class, percentages of people unemployed. The cause–effect relationship is such that if one variable changes, then other variables will change too. A change in the variable 'unemployment level' will produce changes in the variables, 'family income', 'consumer expenditure', 'average life expectancy' and so on. What is of interest is exactly which down-stream variables do change, and by how much, when an up-stream one changes. For example, what are the 'knock-on effects' of unemployment, or how much change in life expectancy can be attributed to changes in the labour market, including rates of unemployment?

The complexity of causation

Causal investigation like this throws into sharp relief a set of researcher problems associated with the complexity of causation. First, anything previous might be among the causes of anything that comes later. Second, whatever happens is likely to have multiple causes. Third, under normal circumstances, a very large number of things are going on at the same time. All in all, it simply is very difficult to see what is causing what, or which past events are among the causes of some current state of affairs.

Experimental control and the study of cause and effect

Experimentation is one approach to these problems. A controlled experiment, as discussed in Chapter 3, is a simplified working model of reality, designed so that most cause–effect relationships are either insulated off, or are standardized, and only variables of interest are allowed to vary. If you wanted to see whether the gender of an examination candidate was among the causes of the different marks given to candidates by examiners, you might design an experiment where the *only thing* which could cause differences in the marks given would be the responses of the examiners to the gender of the candidates. That would mean excluding all other possibilities.

The term **control** is usually used for such exclusionary strategies. Sometimes people think that control has a sinister implication when applied to human affairs. It might at times, but usually in experiments it means something similar to controlling camera-shake by using a tripod; it means screening out whatever is irrelevant to the question being asked. In the research on gender-bias in exam marking, you might control for the effects of differences in the quality of the scripts, by arranging that for every examiner who got a script with a male name on it there would be another getting *the same* script with a female name on it. You might control for differences between examiners by making sure that there were two groups of them closely matched for age, gender and whatever other characteristics might be relevant, each group receiving the same permutations of scripts and genders. As Chapter 3 discusses, the design of a controlled experiment is one which attempts to exclude from influencing the results anything except that cause–effect relationship which the researcher is interested in investigating.

After the 1940s (Oakley 2000: 163–97) sociologists and anthropologists have rarely conducted controlled experiments of this kind, although they are stock-in-trade for psychologists. But today there is a strong demand for research to determine whether health care, or social work, educational or criminal justice practices are effective or not. The most convincing evidence for this comes from controlled experiments. Chapter 4 includes sections on effectiveness research. The synthesis of many pieces of effectiveness research to create a broader basis for generalization is dealt with in Chapter 15.

More naturalism in experiments

For many topics in the social sciences, controlled experiments are either impracticable, or unethical, or both. Even when they might be conducted, they are vulnerable to the criticism that in producing a simplified environment in which to study cause and effect, experimenters create a situation which is so artificial that, whatever the results, they will have little bearing on what happens under ordinary circumstances. This is sometimes expressed by suggesting that controlled experiments have a low level of **external validity**. This is discussed at the end of Chapter 3 and again in Chapter 4.

Experimenters may attempt to meet this criticism by making their experiments more like real life: for example, by conducting them in settings such as schools or railway stations. Chapter 4 considers more naturalistic experiments. But the more naturalistic an experiment is, the less control the experimenter has over the situation, and the more possibilities there are for the results to be influenced by other factors in a way that might mislead the researcher as to what caused what. This is the first of two important **trade-offs** which you will encounter in this book. The *trade-off between control and naturalism* is between, on the one hand, being able to control the situation so as to draw confident conclusions about cause and effects, but at the cost of producing a result which might not apply outside the experimental situation and, on the other hand, researching naturally occurring situations, but being less able to draw confident conclusions as to what causes what.

Natural experiments

It is important not to confuse **experimentalism** with **experiments**. 'Experimentalism' or 'experimental design' refers to controlling variables, and this may be done for social surveys and other kinds of research as well as in experiments *per se*. The reason why controlled experiments are the topic of an early chapter of this book is because they illustrate the logic of control so well. Other researchers either have to find alternative means to achieve the controls achieved in a controlled experiment or, if they don't, their results may be impossible to interpret with any confidence at all if the topic is a causal one.

If researchers cannot set up the right conditions by mounting a controlled experiment, they may look around for some circumstances where the right conditions crop up naturally, and conduct a **natural experiment**. When astronomers say they are doing an experiment, this means they are either making some strategically planned observations, or adding a twist to their latest computer model. In a natural experiment the kind of control exerted is **statistical control** rather than experimental control. This means analysing data to see what stays the same and what changes when the same data are classified in different ways. Chapter 7 illustrates some natural experiments including twin studies to investigate the relative contribution of heredity and environment and the investigation of what differences it makes for children to go to one school or another. Chapter 8 deals with the use of surveys in natural experiment approaches.

Linear and non-linear dynamics

Traditionally science has operated as if most phenomena obeyed the laws of **linear dynamics,** where outputs are proportional to inputs, where doing the same thing a second time has the same effect and where phenomena are neatly separated off from each other in relatively closed systems. Indeed the controlled experiment can be seen as an attempt to make reality behave like that. For a long time, scientists have known that the world isn't really like this, but have extracted a great deal of understanding of phenomena by making the simplifying assumptions that it is. More recently however, the **non-linearity** of most phenomena has come centre ground in the natural sciences with the development of **complexity theory**, of which the more highly profiled chaos theory is a branch. What 'complexity' means is described in Chapter 5. Here suffice it to say, that in complex phenomena everything prior influences everything subsequent, but not consistently, and that how things turn out depends on how things started – which means they usually turn out differently every time. If this is so then it further undermines claims that experiments conducted under highly controlled conditions can tell us what will happen on another occasion even when what appear to be the same actions are taken. The method of choice for studying complex phenomena is *computer simulation*. A brief introduction to that is also given in Chapter 5.

Surveys and representativeness

Many of the data for natural experiments come from social surveys. So do some of the parameters for computer simulations. Most surveys are **sample surveys,** where data are collected from some people selected to be **representative** of much larger numbers of people. The topic of **representativeness** is an important one for most research, since it is often an issue as to how far what is true for the people studied will be true of other people too. Chapter 6 looks in detail at the means used by sample survey researchers to ensure that the sample selected is *representative of some wider population*, such that the results of the survey can be grossed up and treated as a reasonably accurate estimate of the state of affairs in the larger population.

Chapter 6 also draws attention to the difficulties of making such generalizations where the sample has been small and/or unrepresentative. Small and unrepresentative samples are often characteristic of controlled experiments and of much **qualitative research** (see pp. 7ff) and are among the reasons why it may be difficult to base generalizations on the results of either. There is another trade-off here. This is between collecting a small amount of information from a large number of people, as is in a social survey, and being to make confident generalizations because of the large size of the sample, but at the cost of not gaining any detailed understanding of these people's lives, as against collecting a large amount of information from a small number of people with the chance of gaining a good understanding of them, but at the cost of being uncertain as to how far they represent anyone but themselves. For the same quantum of effort researchers can do only one or the other.

Prospective data

One of the few certainties in research is that something which happened later cannot have caused something which happened earlier. Thus in studying cause and effect it is important to be able to *assign events in time*. In controlled experiments this means that the state of affairs prior to the experiment needs to be investigated and compared with the state of affairs at the end. The chronology of events is rarely a problem in controlled experiments. However, many social surveys give only a snapshot of the state of affairs at one point in time. Then it will not be clear whether, for example, the people who are unemployed were in a worse state of health than others before they became unemployed, or whether becoming unemployed undermined their health. To a point, this problem can be managed by collecting retrospective data: for example, asking people what happened to them at times earlier than the survey date. But **retrospective data** are notoriously unreliable. Human memories are very bad at storing accurate records of the past. Thus, for explaining cause and effect adequately, surveys and similar strategies need to be **longitudinal**, collecting data at various points in time so that what came before what can be clearly established. Taking a longitudinal approach in research is dealt with in Chapter 8.

Administrative data

Social scientists often have to use data collected for bureaucratic purposes – for example, medical records, death certificates, examination results, or police data on arrests. Such information is generated from the routine working practices of doctors, examiners, or police officers. It often tells us more about the way they think and work than about whatever it is that is being classified and counted. If researchers use such data without recognizing this, their results may be very misleading. The use of administrative data for research purposes is discussed in Chapter 9.

Control and naturalism

The route from Chapter 3 to Chapter 8 is the route of the trade-off between control and naturalism (see above). Chapter 3 represents the highly controlled world of the controlled experiment. This excludes nearly everything else in the quest for simplicity but at the risk of creating an entirely artificial picture. By the time we get to Chapters 7 and 8 researchers are again faced with the bewildering complexity of the real world over which they can exert no direct control. They have to rely on what conceptual control they can exercise through making strategic decisions about what data to collect and what potential data to ignore (which is most of them), how to collect data and how to analyse them. While necessary in the pursuit of naturalism, this loss of control is something which is very worrying for researchers concerned with issues of cause and effect and wedded to a linear dynamic view of the world. By contrast, complexity theorists (Chapter 5) take some delight in the surprises which are generated by their computer models. Nonetheless, they still face a 'control versus naturalism' type of problem insofar as there is often a difficulty in bringing off claims that what was simulated by the computer is in some way identifiable with some mechanism which exists 'for real'.

Control versus naturalism issues have been much less worrying for those who believe that the kind of reality which social science should be investigating is one composed of meanings, though it can be argued that it is something they ought to worry more about.

1.4   Research in pursuit of meaning

Qualitative and quantitative

> The language of 'quantitative' and 'qualitative' has always been distinctly unhelpful as a technical guide to research methods, and we would be better off without it.
>
> (Oakley 2000: 303)

It would be fortunate to be able to say that the distinctions 'cause' as against 'meaning' and 'quantitative' as against 'qualitative' mapped onto each other neatly. Unfortunately they do not. If 'quantitative' refers to research which counts things, analyses data statistically and quotes its results in numerical forms then, in psychology in particular, there are many researchers who both consider that their topic is how people make sense of their experience, and who do their research in numbers. Similarly, there are researchers who say that they are studying cause and effect and who do very little counting – for example, many who observe classrooms in order to explain what causes differences in educational achievement between, for example, boys and girls (see Chapter 14, Section 14.4). And, although the idea of cause and effect may be pushed into the background when the central interest is meaning, there is still an issue as to what causes people to make sense of the world in the way they do, and an issue as to what are the effects of their interpreting things this way rather than that way.

Most people who call themselves qualitative researchers are primarily interested in investigating how people experience the world and/or how they make sense of it. This is often indicated by terms such as 'phenomenology', 'interpretivism', 'symbolic interactionism', 'interactionism', 'hermeneutics' and 'ethnomethodology'. Sometimes all of these are grouped together as **interpretive** approaches. Adding in selected elements from psychodynamic psychologies such as Freudian psychoanalytic theory or from socially critical sociology such as Marxism or feminism adds to the diversity. Philosophically speaking, qualitative researchers are much more diverse than quantitative researchers and the diversity is often expressed in arcane philosophical discussions. For this book I will draw a distinction between, on the one hand, the dramaturgical approach of Erving Goffman (Burns 1992) together with ethnomethodological approaches and, on the other hand, all other qualititative approaches (Chapter 11). This marks a gap within qualitative approaches which is at least as large as that between qualitative and quantitative approaches.

Questions in surveys and questions in qualitative interviews

Chapter 10 extends the discussion in Chapter 2 about how instruments shape data; here by looking closely at questions and questioning. Much of the information in both quantitative and qualitative research comes from asking people questions and recording the results. But asking questions to produce numerical data is different from asking questions to produce the kind of data that the researcher will handle as words. Chapter 10 draws a contrast between questioning and answering in experimental and social survey research, on the one hand, and questioning and answering in qualitative interviews, on the other. The former is likely to involve forced choice questions because a major preoccupation will be to make precise point-by-point comparisons between respondents. Treating all the respondents in a similar way will also be an aim. Otherwise differences between their responses might not relate to differences between them, but to differences in the behaviour of the interviewer. In this, and in other ways, interviewing for social surveys shows many similarities with experimental procedures. This is described in Chapter 10, as are the problems which arise when survey researchers depart from these rules.

Just as experiments can be critiqued as artificial and unnatural, so also can the rather formal, structured and impersonal circumstances of a survey research interview. Such a critique backs the policy adopted by qualitative interviewers, who attempt to make the interview more like an ordinary conversation. Instead of adopting the impersonal stance of the survey interviewer they attempt to make more intimate relationships with the respondent. This is on the grounds that only through making such relationships will the researcher learn the important truths about the respondent. In Chapter 10 again we meet the trade-off between control and naturalism, since the qualitative interview is highly vulnerable to criticism that the results may tell us more about the interview*er* than about the interview*ees*.

Two meanings of 'meaning'

The term 'meaning' is a difficult one. I shall suggest two different meanings for 'meaning' here. One of these is that the meaning of what people say or do is what is in their mind when they do so. The other is that the meaning of what people say or do is in whatever it is that they say or do which allows it to be seen as meaningful. The two renderings take analysis in two different directions (Table 1.1).

Two approaches to the meaning of what people say, or otherwise c...

	The mind-reading approach	Dramaturgical a... ethnomethodolo... approaches
What people say is:	Evidence of what people think, feel, experience, how they make sense of and interpret the world	Evidence of hc... (gestures and ... to construct a situa... time when they were used
Behind the words:	There are minds with knowledge, motives, ways of understanding, cognitive structures, interpretive schemes or some such (see below) which are in turn the product of past experiences	There is nothing researchable, the words represent a repertoire these people have for structuring situations.
The analysis of meaning is:	Modelling minds from the evidence of speech (gestures and so on)	Mapping utterances to the situations in which they were spoken

Suppose that we are trying to find the meaning of something someone said. Then the first approach takes us inwards to a private place which is very difficult to know about: the mind of the person who said it. But the second takes us outwards to the public realm, which is much easier to know about. The public question here is 'What is it about that utterance that allows it to be meaningful to the person who uttered it and to the people who hear it?' This must be a public matter because if it was not, communication between people would be impossible. We do not have to do research to know that communication between people is not impossible, though it can be problematic from time to time.

Mind-reading research

The first, 'mind-reading', approach to meaning is the more traditional and more commonsensical. It entails creating a picture of the mind that had to be there to have the experience the researcher says this person had and to contain the reasons which gave rise to the actions or the speech. What all versions of this approach have in common is that they involve constructing a picture of the mind behind the action, using as evidence for this the things that people say or do. But apart from this there is an enormous variety among exponents in their ideas as to what people's minds can be like. In psychology, for example, pictures of people's minds are drawn containing, perhaps some of, but rarely all of, conscious and unconscious sectors, defence mechanisms, complexes, self-serving biases, self-images, motivational sets, representational structures and other components. Sociology and psychology tend to merge into each other in the enterprise of modelling minds. Between them they select from a huge vocabulary of terms for the structure of minds, including actor-theories, attribution sets, folk-theories, sub-cultural ideas, ideologies, perspectives, social theories, interpretive repertoires, typification schemes, schemes of relevance, world views, discourses and more. All of these express much the same idea, which is that people have ways of understanding the world. The object of research then is to produce descriptions of what that understanding is – what is in people's minds. The research usually goes on to explain how people got their minds made up that way, and what are the consequences of people having the minds they do.

There are mind-modellers who believe that minds can be known about by using precisely designed instruments such as attitude scales or various other kinds of questionnaires, or from laboratory experiments generating numerical data for statistical analysis. But those who take the qualitative line would claim that this is a hopeless path to follow. Indeed, they would argue that the kind of questions asked in social survey research not only fail to capture any sense of what it is like to be people going about their daily lives but also grievously misrepresent this. The forced choice questions of the typical questionnaire used in an experiment or a survey are seen to force respondents to answer questions, which may be irrelevant to their lives in words they wouldn't use themselves. On this basis, then, if the qualitative researcher is going to use interviews, he or she prefers them to be discursive and only loosely structured, as described in Chapters 10 and 11.

Thematic analysis

The qualitative interview generates a large amount of verbal data. The mind-reading qualitative researcher then has to analyse all this to find the structure of the mind behind it: the actor-theory, the actor-perspective, the typification scheme, the world view, or what have you. The usual way in which the data from qualitative interviews are analysed for this purpose is by **thematic analysis**. The researcher looks for what comes up in the data commonly and interestingly, calls these 'themes' (or sometimes 'codes') and then uses these as headings for writing up the research report. In some way or other the themes stand for the way ideas are organized in the minds of the people studied. Thematic analysis is illustrated in Chapter 11 with a transcript from a qualitative interview. Just as qualitative interviews are vulnerable to the criticism that they tell us more about the interviewer than about the interviewee, so thematic analysis, based already on the qualitative interview, is vulnerable to the criticism that it tells us more about what was in the mind of the *analyst* than about what was in the mind of the *interviewee*.

Ethnomethodological and similar approaches to meaning

The other approach to meaning in qualitative research (Table 1.1) derives from ethnomethodology and linguistics, or from the inspiration of Erving Goffman. If the data are derived from an interview, then they are not taken to stand for what is in the mind of the respondent, but for what is going on in the interview. What is interesting is how the way people speak makes it clear that this was an interview, and not a chat, or a row, a valedictory oration, a seduction or a lecture. What the people were doing was producing an interview. To do that they must have known how to do 'interview talk'. They must each have known how to produce speech and other communicative action which was meaningful to the other as a contribution to an interview, and not a chat, a row and so on. From this viewpoint there is no need to delve into minds in order to study meanings, since meaning is out in the open for any competent member of a culture to see, including the sociological observer. Thus most British adults know how to recognize a queue when they see one, and know how to do queuing, and hence they know how to co-operate with others in order to organize themselves as a queue. Meaning is social organization and social organization is meaning. Moreover, who someone is (for that moment), and how they are appraised by others, depends on what kind of social organizing is taken to be going on. Queues are also moral orders, and have their own forms of deviance; queue-jumping for example. When queuing, people know that they are likely to be judged by others in terms of abiding by whatever it is that people like them should do in a queue.

Ethnomethodologists are not keen on the idea of rules, but here it will do no harm to say that a meaningful act or utterance is one which complies with some rules which people can follow in producing it, and in interpreting it. This includes finding the meaning of a frown by one person, in another person's queue-jumping. Meaning, of course, is in the minds of people, but equally it is out in the open in their observable doings and hearable sayings. That's where ethnomethodologists, and others of similar ilk, look for meaning.

Conversation Analysis (CA)

These considerations suggest a way of analysing speech which is radically different from that of thematic analysis. Chapter 11, which demonstrates thematic analysis, also subjects the same transcript to the kind of analysis which would be carried out by a **conversation analyst**. Conversation Analysis has its roots partly in ethnomethodology and partly in pragmatic linguistics. Analysing the same data thematically and by the methods of CA leads to two very different sets of conclusions.

From an ethnomethodological point of view, if you conduct interviews you will produce data which tell you about interviews, and perhaps about some more general features of communication and interaction. This is in contradistinction to other researchers who use interviews in order to find out about people's activities and thoughts as they are in circumstances *beyond the interview* situation. Ethnomethodologists take one step further the earlier criticism of experiments or social survey research as being artificial. Any attempt to find out about one kind of situation by interviewing people in an entirely different kind of situation makes no sense. Ethnomethodologists, however, would not use terms such as 'artificial'. Reasonably enough, they would say that any experiment is a real experiment; any interview is a real interview. They are as much part of social life as lying in bed in the morning, or making love in the back of a car. Everything is natural, all research is 'naturalistic' but it is not necessarily in the nature of an interview situation to generate the kinds of thoughts, feelings and interactions that are generated in some other situation which is being discussed as a topic of the interview.

Chapter 13 is on the analysis of written documents. Again it draws a distinction between mind-reading approaches and approaches where what is of interest is how a communication is put together. For writing, the former is an interest in what the writing tells us about the understandings and experiences of the writer, while the latter is an interest in the way pieces of writing are structured. Some of the techniques for analysing writing can be used for analysing speech, but analysis should always take account of the way the data are produced. Speaking and writing are very different kinds of activity and generate data of different kinds (Chapter 13, Section 13.1).

Naturalistic observation

What makes it sensible to conduct interviews for researchers of the mind-reading kind is the idea that people carry around the *same mind* from situation to situation. Thus the person being interviewed is the same person who does whatever it is elsewhere that the researcher asks about, and can 'bring to mind' that other situation. This begs many questions as to how much people actually know about what they do and whether they are able to give accurate accounts of their own doings. And it raises concerns among mind-reading researchers as to whether people give honest accounts. Thus there is an attraction among such researchers for observing people going about their everyday activities. That is a preference for **naturalistic observation**, either as **participant observers**, to some extent acting like an ordinary member of the setting, or by **non-participant observation** – just observing.

Combining naturalistic observation with qualitative interviewing may look like the best of both worlds. The observation shows the researcher what people *actually do*. The interviews are designed to find out what those doings meant to the person concerned, since it would be disruptive of ordinary life for researchers to keep on asking 'what did you mean by that?' or 'what does that mean to you?'. But this pairing of interviews with observation still assumes that what the person says in the interview about what he or she did at some other time was the meaning at the earlier time. For obvious reasons ethnomethodologists also favour observation studies – though, of course, for them an interview is an observation study: an observation of an interview. Chapter 12 deals with naturalistic observation, its problems and its potentials, and some of the differences between naturalistic observers of different kinds.

1.5   Validity and reliability

Together with objectivity (Section 1.8) **validity** and **reliability** are the main criteria by which research is judged. Validity means something like 'truth'. Most researchers accept that we can never know the truth for sure, so in research what is valid is that which hasn't as yet been invalidated, despite attempts to do so. This is the so-called '**falsificationist programme**' following the philosopher Karl Popper (1963) and is given lip service at least by most natural and social scientists. A 'confirmationist programme' would be one in which researchers specifically looked for evidence to prove a favoured theory and ignored evidence which threw doubt on it.

Internal validity refers to the truth of a claim made about the research itself. **External validity** or generalizability (Section 1.6) refers to whether what was found in the research can be generalized to other people, places and times.

Reliability refers to consistency, and applies particularly to research instruments with questions such as 'would this instrument give the same result if measuring the same thing a second time, assuming it hadn't changed in the interim? (Chapter 2, Sections 2.8–2.10).

Validity and reliability are introduced in relation to research instruments in Chapter 2, but they are concepts which appear also in every chapter in the book.

While, or because, validity and reliability are the criteria used in the natural sciences, some qualitative researchers have suggested that they are not appropriate for the study of the social world, which is made of meanings, rather than of materials and forces. Alternative terms have been proposed, for example by Guba and Lincoln (1985). Miles and Huberman (1994) provide a useful translation between the traditional and the alternatives (Table 1.2).

On close inspection, these alternatives do not seem to mean anything very different from the old ones except, of course, that the way qualitative researchers go about collecting and presenting evidence to accomplish, say, internal validity (aka credibility or authenticity) is different from the way in which a quantitative researcher would mobilize evidence to claim internal validity (Hammersley 2000b: Chapter 9). This difference is perhaps best illustrated in the discussion of the differences between social survey interviewing and qualitative interviewing in Chapter 10.

Traditional criteria for judging research compared with some alternatives proposed for qualitative social research TABLE 1.2

Traditional criteria	Alternatives for qualitative research
Internal validity[a]	Credibility or authenticity
Reliability	Dependability or auditability
External validity or generalizability (Section 1.6)	Transferability or fittingness
Objectivity (Section 1.8)	Confirmability
Usefulness	Applicability or action orientation or catalytic validity

Note: [a] Includes ecological validity (see Chapter 12).
Source: After Miles and Huberman (1994: 278).

Generalization

s some historians do not seek to produce generalizable knowledge,
qualitative researchers make only limited claims that what they describe
ir research will apply elsewhere. But most researchers, qualitative and
itative, do make some claims as to the general currency of their ideas.
kinds of generalization can be distinguished.

Empirical or statistical generalization

Empirical or **statistical generalization** refers to the kind of generalizability
aimed for by survey researchers. Here the generalization is the claim that
what is true of the *sample* is true of the *population* from which the sample
was drawn, in some designated ways, and for some limited period of time.
Making it possible to make such generalizations safely is what survey design
is all about, as described in Chapter 6.

Theoretical generalization

Theoretical generalization refers to the applicability to other times, places
and people of some theoretical idea which seemed to explain what happened
in the research. If the interest is in cause and effect then this is researchers
looking for cause – effect **mechanisms**: things that make things happen. The
important mechanisms are the robust ones which make things happen in a
wide range of circumstances. Natural science has many examples such as
gravity, electricity, natural selection, or genes. The social sciences are less
blessed in this regard. The same mechanism may not have the same effects in
different contexts. For example, the mechanism which makes heroin an effective pain killer under one set of circumstances may lead to addiction under
another; or, teacher expressions of disapproval might under some circumstances depress educational performance and under others encourage pupils
to strive harder.

Generalizations along these lines claim that the same mechanism has an
effect in a large number of different circumstances, but the effects may be
different according to the context. The task here is to specify also the *contextual factors* which make a mechanism have a particular effect. The law-like
statements characteristic of the natural sciences both say what does what,
and specify the circumstances under which it will do it: water will freeze at
0 degrees Celsius only if it is of a specified purity, and at a certain baromet-
ric pressure. Social phenomena hardly ever allow for specifications of such
precision. Specification is discussed in Chapter 4, Section 6.

Qualitative researchers have particular problems in deriving generalizations from their research. Given the way they use small and unrepresentative
samples they cannot make empirical generalizations with any confidence at
all. But in practice they actually do make such generalizations, as when they
imply that the 6 teachers they studied in the school stand for, or represent,
another 30 in the same school, or that the one school class they observed
intensely represents other classes as well. More usually qualitative researchers

claim to be making theoretical generalizations, of a weak kind termed 'sensitizing concepts'. These are the kinds of concepts which direct attention to interesting similarities between different aspects of life. For example Goffman's term 'total institution' (Goffman 1968) gathers together under the same heading mental hospitals, boarding schools, military units, monasteries, merchant ships and so on. Looking at these all in the same way does throw interesting commonalities (and differences) into relief. Another concept which does similar work is the idea of a 'career' (Goffman 1968), when applied to criminals, mental patients, school pupils and so on. This implies that the trajectory taken by someone's life is shaped by the assumptions people make about what normally, naturally, ought to be true of someone at that 'stage in their career'. Although ideas like this lack the rigour of the kinds of mechanisms identified in natural science, they nonetheless point us in the direction of interesting features of social life which seem general in that they can be applied to a wide range of settings.

Naturalistic generalization

Some qualitative researchers claim that it is not the purpose of their research to produce generalizations. Rather their purpose is to produce rich, or 'thick' descriptions of social life, so that readers can understand what it would be like to be someone else and experience the world from their point of view (Geertz 1973). This is often the purpose stated for participant observation research as described in Chapter 12. This idea of doing research to provide readers with vicarious experience of other people's lives is often associated with the idea of *naturalistic* generalization (Stake 1994). Here it is not the researcher who does the generalizing, but the readers. The research is presented as a resource for readers to extend their understanding of themselves and other people in the same way as they draw on and learn from direct experience, from plays, films, television documentaries and so on.

Meta-analysis and other syntheses

Chapter 15 is also about generalization in the sense that its topic is that of synthesizing research from different sources in an attempt to provide a broader basis for making generalizations. At this point the idea of generalization (here, theoretical generalization) elides with the idea of external validity (see p. 13).

For a long time social and behavioural scientists have worried that their research endeavours failed to 'add up' into coherent corpuses of knowledge by comparison with the natural sciences. In most English-speaking countries, and in the European Union (EU), there have been government sponsored initiatives to force practitioners in human services to adjust their practices in the light of research evidence: so-called evidence-based practice. Given the paucity of research available for this purpose, this has created a demand to make better use of what research does exist by synthesizing it, as well as to standardize research practices so that new research can be added more easily to old.

Chapter 15 deals with systematic reviews and statistical meta-analysis, which mainly apply to the synthesis of results from randomized controlled experiments. The issues here are causal ones, about the effectiveness of treatments, educational programmes and such like. In terms of the threefold classification above, the kinds of generalizations sought are 'theoretical'; though theoretical in a very practical way.

Though there are many pitfalls, it is relatively easy to synthesize randomized controlled trials (RCTs), because they are very similar to each other. Synthesizing the results of other kinds of research is much more difficult. One approach growing rapidly in popularity is to use Bayesian statistics.

In various other chapters of the book the statistical techniques referred to are **frequentist statistics** (Chapter 2, Panel 2.8; Chapter 3, Panel 3.1; Chapter 6, Sections 6.10 and 6.11; Chapter 15, Section 15.3). These provide estimates of how frequently a result might have occurred by chance, as a benchmark against which to judge whether a result was due to something other than chance: how **statistically significant** it was. 'Result' here might be an experimental result, or the result of taking a population sample in a survey. **Bayesian statistics**, by contrast, provide a measure of how credible knowledgeable judges find some proposition according to the evidence cited in its favour. A brief introduction to Bayesian statistics is given in Chapter 15, Section 15.4.

Chapter 15 also deals with attempts to synthesize qualitative research. This introduces some new vocabulary such as meta-ethnography and qualitative comparative analysis (QCA). But the approaches so named do not seem substantially different from what has long been called 'comparative method' in sociology, anthropology and history, and more particularly, the thematic analysis referred to in Chapter 11.

1.7 Ethics and values

Chapter 14 is about evaluation and evaluation studies, and Chapter 16 is about ethics in research. Both deal with questions about the proper purpose of research, the proper relationships which should obtain between researcher and researched and between researchers and the various audiences for research, and the extent to which the values of the researcher should influence the research.

Value-relevant, value-neutral research

Researchers are pleased if their research has some beneficial outcome. Most would allow that there are no great problems arising from researchers choosing their research topics according to their own moral, political or career interests. It is legitimate then, for research to be **value relevant**. This is Max Weber's term and he is widely quoted in this context (Bruun 1972; Hammersley 2000b: 18–19). Where matters become more controversial is over the issue of **value neutrality**. In Weber's terms, value-neutral research means that, while the topic might be chosen according to the values of the researcher, thereafter the values of the researcher should be excluded from the conduct of the research, except the value of getting at the truth and the values grounding the humane treatment of the people involved in and affected by the research. Value neutrality means not only preventing the personal preferences of the researcher influencing the result, but giving researchers significant freedom from those who employ them or who fund their research. Otherwise these might also exert an influence distorting the research away from the truth.

Chapter 3 describes how the controlled experiment is designed to exclude the influence of both the researchers' and the subjects' hopes, fears, desires and so on from producing misleading results. It draws attention to a large literature showing that people, including researchers, are very likely to see what they want to see. The most obvious way in which this potential for bias is managed in an experiment is through **blinding**: that is, depriving researchers and or subjects of knowledge which, if they had it, would allow their preferences to influence the results. This blinding is only a version of the widespread use of blind decision-making in other fields – for example, anonymizing examination scripts for marking, preventing a jury knowing about previous offences before reaching a verdict, or awarding prizes by lottery. Blinding is not the only device used, and is often impossible. In addition, various means are used to ensure that each subject for the experiment is treated the same. In systematic reviews of medical research, discussed in Chapter 15, blinding is often a quality criterion which determines whether a study is included or ignored, though this cannot be so in those fields where blinding is impossible.

In a similar way, most surveys are conducted so that the researchers' prejudices do not influence who gets selected as a respondent, and efforts are made to ensure that the questions are not written in such a way as to tilt the survey towards producing the results the researcher wanted to get (Chapters 6, 8 and 10).

Pressure groups do conduct 'surveys' which are in effect 'petitions', going out of their way to find the people and record the opinions favourable to their cause. And similarly, charities and other agencies will conduct surveys, and other kinds of research, designed precisely to produce campaign ammunition. This is value-led, rather than value-neutral research. This raises an important issue, and a point of divergence between researchers, and gives two different meanings to the term 'bias' (Hammersley and Gomm 2000).

The more orthodox, mainstream position in the social, as in the natural, sciences, is the Weberian prescription for value-relevant/value-neutral research. Here 'bias' means a deviation from the truth. A particularly powerful source of bias would be the uncontrolled values of politics or commerce impacting on the researcher and his or her own personal values as well. Guarding against these sorts of biases is shown clearly in those journals which require authors to report any 'conflicts of interest', such as sponsorship by an agency which might prefer one account of the truth rather than another, and attempts in systematic reviews to overcome the kind of 'publication bias' which arises, for example, when drug companies have prevented the publication of research conducted for them which does not show their products are effective (Chapter 15, Sections 15.2 and 15.3).

Value neutrality refers to an intention to avoid such bias. This very frequently fails, but failure is taken as a case for trying harder, rather than for abandoning the attempt. It is also part of the Weberian argument that researchers' values, political preferences and so on should be excluded because being a researcher doesn't give anyone any particular expertise in making moral and political judgements.

The working out of this value-neutral position is illustrated by the kinds of evaluation studies explained in the first half of Chapter 14. For example, experimental designs (described in Chapter 3) are frequently used to investigate the **effectiveness** of a medical, social work, or educational intervention. Whether a treatment is effective is a causal issue and the experimental design is the most powerful way of investigating causality (Chapter 3, Chapter 4, Sections 4.4 and 4.5). The experimental design sets up a no-go area for values. If matters are arranged properly, a commercial company piloting the treatment is excluded from influencing the results. Even if it is the researchers themselves who have originated the treatment, the effects of their enthusiasm for it should be controlled through devices such as random allocation, blinding and independent scrutiny described in Chapter 3. The researcher's role as researcher is to decide on the effectiveness of the treatment. It is not to act as advocate for it or to decide whether the treatment should pass into general use. Either that is a decision to be taken by others mandated to make such decisions or, if the researcher is involved in this, it will be on the basis of a position as a doctor, or a social services administrator or some other role which gives someone a mandate for making ethical and political decisions affecting other people. Putting matters around the other way it would be a breach of trust for researchers, as researchers, to allow their desires to change the world, or their personal values or career interests to influence the outcome of the research.

These kinds of considerations raise another criticism of qualitative research: that it has insufficient safeguards for preventing the biases of the researcher influencing the results and that pressures towards bias are likely to arise from the more personal involvement with research subjects that qualitative researchers prefer (Chapter 10, Section 10.6; Chapter 14, Section 14.4).

Value-led or partisan research

However, there is another meaning of the term 'bias'. That is of some ideas or some state of affairs being against, or favouring, the *interests* of someone. Social scientists operate in a world in which it is very obvious that social arrangements favour some people and disadvantage others. It can, and is, argued that this bias extends to the state of knowledge in society, such that current knowledge is biased against women, against poor people, or against members of minority ethnic groups and in favour of white middle-class men and big business and so on. If this is the case it can be argued that what is needed is not 'value-neutral' research, but 'value-led' research where the object is to produce knowledge which redresses the bias.

As Chapter 14 points out, a great deal of social science is socially critical in this way. Varieties of **critical research** include the various Marxisms, the various feminisms, anti-racist research, disability research and queer theory, and various right-wing doctrines too. Researchers of such persuasions regard it as quite proper to 'take sides' and to do research in such a way as to produce knowledge which is favourable to the interests of disadvantaged groups. In a similar way, party political researchers, conducting research to provide ammunition for party campaigns, will also argue that it is in the interests of society that their party is elected, and that for this it is necessary to counter ideas which are biased against them. To adopt such a position researchers must assume that they have a superior expertise in judging what is morally right and what is morally wrong, in discerning who deserves what and what would be to the benefit of which people. Value-neutral researchers do not feel that being a researcher gives them the right or the expertise to decide such matters.

Research ethics

The two positions also predicate different kinds of ethical relationships with the subjects of research, as described in Chapter 16. Researchers who follow the policy of value neutrality largely restrict ethical considerations to avoiding doing any harm to those they research. And they balance violations of privacy or of subjects' rights to make decisions for themselves, against the value of the research findings. Researchers who subscribe to a value-led approach usually believe that research is unethical if it does not do some tangible good to research subjects of selected categories. This leads to research programmes which are designed less to produce knowledge and more to produce change. This might be change in the public reputation of some group where, as it were, researchers act as their public relations consultants. Or it might be change in the way research subjects think and feel about themselves, or tangible changes in their life circumstances. It is often part of such programmes that research subjects are co-opted as partners in research, although the extent of the partnership may vary from one in which they are consulted to one in which they operate as fully fledged researchers themselves. Research of this kind often looks very much more like social work, or counselling or political activism. 'Research methods' which consist of social work skills or the techniques of political mobilization cannot be described in this book.

As discussed in Chapter 16 co-opting vulnerable people as co-researchers leads to another ethical problem, which has to do with the welfare of people encouraged to engage in a programme to change their lives. What are the ethics of researchers encouraging people to take risks with their own lives? What if it all goes horribly wrong? In addition, while professional researchers are usually accountable to university or professional codes of conduct, there are no powerful mechanisms constraining 'lay' co-researchers to behave ethically.

Stake holders for research

There are various groups towards which researchers might be said to be accountable. As noted already, value-neutral researchers try to truncate their accountability towards those who employ them or fund their research. They are willing to take responsibility for doing the research properly but not for producing the results their paymasters would most like to see. Value-led researchers are inclined to say that their prime accountability is towards the subjects of the research. This is potentially in conflict with their accountability towards those who read the research. Readers may feel they have a right to receive an unbiased account. But the subjects of the research may feel that they have a right to determine what other people read about them and to make sure that this depicts them as they would wish to be depicted. In value-led research, subjects often are allowed to vet the research report prior to publication. From a reader's point of view this looks like a conspiracy between researchers and subjects against readers. However, not too much should be made of this. First, the kinds of people who choose to read critical social research are usually those who are pre-disposed to believe it anyway. Second, it is usually abundantly clear as to the partisan nature of such research, and therefore readers can read it with this in mind, just as they do with the output of political spin doctors. The employment title of many people who are called 'spin doctors' is often 'researcher'.

1.8   Research as producing accountable knowledge

Research is about producing knowledge. We usually think of 'knowledge' as something which is stored in the head, in books, or on CD-ROMs. And so it is. But a more useful way of thinking about knowledge is as a kind of claim. If I say I know something, I might be claiming that I can do something, such as ride a bike, or translate from Greek to English. Making such a claim I can be called out and asked to demonstrate that I can indeed do what I claimed. Or alternatively, saying 'I know' might be saying that I will vouch for the truth of this. For example, if I claim that 'Jesus loves me, this I know', I might vouch for this by saying I know 'because the Bible tells me so'. This would be quite appropriate since religious claims need to be vouched for in religious terms, and could never be vouched for by reference to empirical research.

One of the ways of vouching for the verity of knowledge is to say: 'It is known to be so, because research has demonstrated it to be so.' Phrases of this ilk litter social science texts, and you will find them on and off throughout this one too. Saying that 'research has shown that . . .' vouches for some claim, but how does research vouch for itself?

Objectivity

Research can claim to produce knowledge which is superior to other kinds because, and insofar as, and only insofar as, its credentials can be checked. This puts the emphasis on accountability in its traditional place, with the way that researchers make themselves accountable to their readers. This is another way of talking about **objectivity**. Objectivity has various meanings, and various opposites. I am inclined to use it in the ways in which it was used at the birth of modern science in the seventeenth century (Daston 1992), not as the opposite of subjectivity meaning emotionality. My usage is sometimes referred to as **procedural objectivity**. Here objective knowledge primarily means knowledge which is public, open to scrutiny and discussion, auditable or accountable, as opposed to knowledge which is secret, private and requiring to be accepted on trust or having to be accepted on pain of punishment. The historical circumstance in which this meaning was shaped was one in which scientists – or, rather, 'natural philosophers' at the time – saw themselves as emancipating people from an irrational reliance on blind faith and from coercion and manipulation by religious dogmatists. Science, it seemed, allowed for a more 'democratic' way of producing knowledge as well as a more efficient way of getting at the truth: democratic in the sense that knowledge claims were based on evidence which, in principle, anyone could see, and arguments, which, in principle, anyone could follow and disagree with, though at that time 'anyone' was confined to a small male elite. At that time, then, the usual opposite of 'objective' was 'dogmatic'. In addition, however, objectivity also carried the implication that the person making the knowledge claim 'had no axe to grind': that the knowledge was disinterested, personal interests and emotional involvements being seen to bias perception and to be a reason for trying to deceive other people. Researchers are rarely entirely disinterested. But again it is the accountability of the knowledge claim which is supposed to protect people from being misled by the personal interests of others. If the evidence is available to all and the argument followable by all, the influence of such distortions should be easy to detect. The various safeguards against bias built into experimental designs (Chapter 3, and Chapter 15, Sections 15.2 and 15.3), the requirement that researchers give a full account of their methods and the policy of value-neutral research (Chapters 14 and 16) can be seen in this light.

When scientists claim that they produce objective knowledge they do not necessarily mean that the knowledge they produce is true – or, at least, they shouldn't mean this. What they should mean is that it is more likely that knowledge produced by research will be true because it is open to inspection so that any errors it contained are likely to have been detected and corrected. Research knowledge is objective to the extent that the researcher says, honestly:

- Here are the assumptions I made about the nature of reality and how it can be known about
- Here is the question I asked
- Here are the methods I used to collect the data relevant to an answer
- Here are the data I collected
- Here is the way I analysed the data
- This is the answer I came up with
- I think I'm right, but I've given you enough to check all this to see if you come to the same conclusions.

It is relatively easy for quantitative researchers to give an objective account of their research because their procedures are protocol-driven and numerical data isn't particularly weighty. By contrast (Chapters 11 and 12) doing qualitative research is often a hand-to-mouth, flying-by-the-seat-of-your-pants activity, where at the end of the day the researcher may not be very clear what she has done herself. Such researchers will have to make large numbers of *intuitive* analytic decisions on the spot, and it will be difficult to keep track of these, let alone tell other people about them. The sheer bulk of the data from qualitative research means that it can be shared only selectively with readers. It may be difficult for a researcher to persuade readers that data standing against the researcher's interpretations hasn't been conveniently left hidden in the filing cabinet. This problem is discussed in Chapter 15.

Again, the idea of objective knowledge grew up with, and better fits with, the idea of value-neutral research. There are problems in using it where the aims of researchers include changing the moral values or political ideas of their readers, or where the results of the research are crafted to give a favourable impression of some category of person. Being objective about this would rather give the game away in the same way that it would give the game away for an advertiser to draw attention to the persuasive techniques used in an advert (Chapter 13, Section 13.6). These problems are discussed in Chapter 14.

Many, if not most researchers, are careful to report their results objectively, drawing readers' attention to underlying assumptions which have to be taken on trust, and to the shortcomings of the methods used. But these provisions get stripped away as research findings are quoted from source to source and prefaced with the confident phrase: 'research shows that . . .'. Going back to the originals usually shows that research doesn't quite show that. Unpicking the originals, and seeing how they were made, usually shows that alternative interpretations were possible. Paying attention to the methodology of research studies gives the impression that the corpus of social research findings is based on a rather ramshackle foundation. This is not peculiar to social science, however. Go back twenty years in any field of science and, with the benefit of hindsight, you will find many truth claims which today are regarded as erroneous. The same will almost certainly be true twenty years hence. While most scientists would like to discover some eternal and absolute truths, the best any of them can do in practice is to offer up some possibilities for other people's consideration. As the philosopher Daniel Dennett (1995: 380) says, what makes science distinctive, and what makes scientific knowledge superior to other kinds, is that science is a process of making mistakes in public so that they can be corrected.

Further reading

Reading appropriate for most of this chapter will be found at the end of chapters which deal with each issue in more detail. Any standard sociology text book for AS/A2 level or undergraduate use will provide information about the diversity of theories held by social scientists which predispose them to use one investigative approach rather than another. Particularly lucid in this regard are Cuff, Sharrock and Francis (2006). Don't expect too close a match between theories and methods since the choice of method is often determined by what is possible rather than what is theoretically ideal, however Pryke,

Rose and Whatmore (2003) is an interesting discussion of the theory–method linkage. Gomm (2008) is a glossary of research terms.

An overview of causal thinking in social research is Hage and Meeker (1988), but this doesn't really get to grips with the revision of causal ideas associated with chaos and complexity theories. An easy introduction to this, across the sciences, is Buchanan (2000) – although irritatingly he terms complexity theory, 'ubiquity theory'. For complexity in the social sciences specifically, see Byrne (1998), or Eve, Horsfall and Lee (1997).

Gilbert (2001) contains papers on a wide range of research approaches and Hardy and Bryman (2004) is a collection of papers on different methods of data analysis, quantitative and qualitative.

2 Instruments and Instrument Design

> **By the end of this chapter, you will:**
>
> - Be aware of the way in which instruments shape the data collected by researchers and hence shape their findings
> - Know some ways in which the validity and reliability of instruments may be flawed
> - Know some methods for testing instruments for their validity and reliability.
>
> **And you will know the meaning of the following terms:**
>
> Alternate forms test • construct • correlation • culture and gender fairness • data degradation • factor analysis • floor and ceiling effects • Flynn effect • frequency count • indicator • levels of data (nominal, ordinal and interval) • Likert scales • norming • plastic intervals • ranking • rating • reliability as applied to instruments (inter- and intra-rater, internal consistency, test–retest) • research artefact • scales • split-half testing • standard deviation • standardization • validity as applied to instruments (content, construct, criterion (concurrent and predictive), external, face) • z-scores.
>
> At the end of the chapter there is an Activity on devising a truancy counter.

2.1   Introduction

'Instruments' is short for 'data collecting instruments'. These may be called 'tests', 'questionnaires', 'inventories', 'profiles', 'schedules', 'frames', 'grids', 'examinations', 'assessments', 'scales', 'forms', 'records', or even 'instruments'.

They all pose **questions**. Questions may be addressed directly to research subjects: '*What is your date of birth?*', or, in an intelligence test:'*What is the next number in the following sequence?*'. Sometimes they are addressed to the researcher, as in an observation schedule: '*What is the time and which of the following activities is the child doing now?*'(Table 12.2); or in a coding frame for a piece of previously recorded conversation, which asks: '*What kind of utterance is this?*' (see Transcripts 11.1–11.3); or, in a frame for the content analysis of a text: '*How many column centimetres long is this news story?*' (Table 13.1).

The rules for using instruments are usually called '**protocols**'; sometimes '**algorithms**', such as instructions for an interviewer on how to select respondents and how to administer a questionnaire. Once we include such protocols as constituent parts of an instrument, we begin to wonder whether whole research designs, lock stock and barrel, shouldn't be regarded as 'instruments'. Perhaps so, and quantitative research can indeed be regarded as *instrumenting* phenomena so that they generate quantitative data. Think, for example, about the way volcanologists instrument volcanoes by planting strain gauges and thermometers strategically around them. Compare this with the way in which opinion pollsters instrument public opinion by repeatedly conducting surveys about support for political parties or policy options.

Instruments will generate **quantitative** (numerical) or **qualitative** (nonnumerical) data. All instruments which generate quantitative data involve prior qualitative decisions about whether something is an instance of this, or an instance of that. This chapter will concentrate instruments generating quantitative data. Chapter 10 includes more on the kinds of questionnaires and interview schedules used in qualitative research.

The main concerns of this chapter are:

- the design of adequate research instruments
- how the design and use of instruments shapes the pictures of the world produced by research.

2.2 Constructs and indicators

Reality can never be studied directly. All we can know about electricity, for example, are matters such as that it moves the needles and counters on various gauges, illuminates lamps, spreads iron filings in distinctive patterns and so on. We build instruments to show us what electricity does under certain circumstances, and we can draw inferences about the essence of electricity from the way the instruments behave.

Our inferences will be theoretical constructs, or concepts, sometimes, but not always, constituent parts of an academic theory. To be scientifically plausible constructs must be consistent both with what the instruments show, and with other interlocking theoretical constructs, or at least with whatever counts as commonsense at the time.

In short, instruments measure **indicators** which stand for **concepts** or **constructs**. Elaborate and highly abstract and theoretical constructs such as 'self-image' or 'social class' are good examples. But, equally, indicators may stand for far less abstract and more common-sensical constructs such as age, or frequency of library use. It is best to think about constructs as the answer to the question:

How in your mind are you constructing a picture of whatever it is you want an indicator to stand for?

That question in turn raises two others:

Is that the most appropriate way of thinking about what you are trying to research?

And:

Will it be possible to collect accurate data representingt that construct?

Often the construct and the indicator will be developed iteratively. There will be a shuttle backwards and forwards between the definition of the construct and the design of the indicators. Work on the definition influences the design of the indicators: the formulation of the indicators results in revisions to the construct.

2.3 Instrument scales and types of data

Different research instruments will collect information at different levels of measurement, as outlined in Table 2.1.

Some phenomena can be measured only at the nominal or categorical level, or it is only useful to measure them at this level. For most purposes, people are either 'male' or 'female'. The only measurements possible here are a statement of the **mode** to the effect than one gender was the most common or **frequency counts** to the effect that there were so many males and so many females, or that such and such a percentage or proportion of the sample were of a particular gender. But a researcher with a particular interest in masculinity might construct a test asking people questions about themselves yielding a score between 0 and 100, where 100 was most masculine, and zero least masculine. The researcher would probably regard this as producing data at the interval level.

Ordinal level data arises from the operation of ranking, that is putting entities in order – 1st, 2nd, 3rd . . . last – according to some value – for example, importance in a particular context. Table 2.2 illustrates a ranking scale.

Ranking should be distinguished from **rating**. Table 2.3 in an example of a rating scale.

In the ranking scale (Table 2.2) only one entity can be of primary importance while in the rating scale (Table 2.3) all five could be 'very important'. So whichever was used would give different answers to the question: '*What according to customers is the most important aspect of hotel accommodation?*' The ranking scale forces respondents to prioritise among given options, while the rating scale does not. The rating scale is also likely to suffer from *positional bias* which is the reluctance of respondents to use the extreme options on a scale if they have a choice. In addition, in this particular context, it is unlikely that many respondents would use the category 'very unimportant' whereas on the ranking scale they are forced to use the category 5th in importance.

The ranking scale is an obvious example of ordinal data generation. However, if each 1st is given a score of 5, each 2nd a score of 4, and so on, then each aspect of hotel accommodation can be given a numerical score in a way that takes into account all the information made available by the survey. The data then would look like interval-level data, and might well be treated by the researcher as such. But it can hardly be claimed that this was a scale with equal intervals: that, for example, 5 points separating 70 from

TABLE 2.1   Levels of data

Discrete (or discontinuous) data	**Nominal (or categorical) data**	Data classified into categories, such as 'male/female', 'Anglican, Catholic, Methodist, etc., 'White, African-Caribbean, Asian, etc.
	The measurement operation is counting	The categories are mutually exclusive and not ordered in relation to each other. No *mean* (average), nor *median* can be calculated and the only measure of central tendency possible is the *mode*. No standard deviation[a] can be calculated. Only non-parametric statistics[b] can be used. Sometimes expressed as *dummy variables*, for example 'yes' is coded as 1 and 'no' as 0.
May be discrete (or discontinuous) or continuous (or measurable) data	**Ordinal (or ranked) data**	Data classified by rank order, where there are more than 2 ranks, such as '1st, 2nd, 3rd . . . last (place in class)' or 'Most expensive, next most expensive . . . least expensive'. Rank order shows the positional relationship of categories but not how far apart these are. No mean (average) can be calculated, no mode identified and the only measure of central tendency possible is the median. No *standard deviation* can be calculated.[a] Only non-parametric statistics[b] can be used.
	The measurement operation is ranking	
	Interval- and ratio-level data	Data which derive from measurement on a scale, where the intervals on the scale are equal to each other. Allow for the calculation of the *mean, median and mode, the variance and mode, the variance and the standard deviation[a]* and are amenable to analysis using *parametric statistics*.[b] Can also be analysed using non-parametric statistics.[b] The distinction between interval- and ratio-level data rests on the scale having a true zero, and is rarely important in social scientific research.
	The operation measurement operation is measuring in the same sense as measuring with a ruler	

Notes: [a] For standard deviation, see Panel 2.8.
[b] For the distinction between parametric and non-parametric statistics, see Panel 3.1.

TABLE 2.2   *An example of a ranking scale: generating ordinal data*

Please put the following aspects of hotel accommodation in order of importance from 1 to 5 with 1st as the most important to you and 5th as the least. Tick the box which corresponds with your ranking.

	1st	2nd	3rd	4th	5th
Comfortable beds					
Clean rooms					
Friendly staff					
Extensive menu					
Competitive pricing					

TABLE 2.3   *An example of a rating scale: generating plastic interval data*

Please indicate how important to you are the following aspects of hotel accommodation. Tick the answer closest to your own view

	Very important	Important	Neither important nor unimportant	Not important	Very unimportant
Comfortable beds					
Clean rooms					
Friendly staff					
Extensive menu					
Competitive pricing					
Score each tick	5	4	3	2	1

75 were the same as 5 points separating 30 from 35. Equal intervals is a criterion of interval-level data.

In this context Coolican (1994: 193) uses the term 'plastic intervals'. He says this term

> suits the data where you can say: 'Well it *looks* like interval data, but obviously it isn't since we invented the scale, it's not standardised and you can't say the distances at the extremes . . . are the same in size as distances in the middle . . .'

and goes on to say:

> When research produces data which are human estimates, especially if based on an arbitrary scale, it is *safer* to assume that ratings are plastic

interval and should be reduced to an ordinal level . . . then a less sensitive statistical test must be used called 'non-parametric'.

(Coolican 1994: 193)

Where there is any ambiguity, researchers show a distinct bias in treating data as interval or ratio level rather than ordinal. A case in point is college or school examination scores when used in research. Often the actual marks given are better regarded as ranks masquerading as scores. Thus 80% might mean 'among the best', rather than 'twice as good as someone with 40%'.

The example in Panel 15.2 in Chapter 15 is designed to assign scores of 0 to 5 to published accounts of different research studies to assess their credibility. The authors claim it is an interval scale (Moher *et al.* 2001: 420). But it is actually a good example of a 'plastic interval scale' – see p. 28 above. There is no way that the 1s assigned for one reason can have the same value in terms of research quality as the 1s assigned for another reason. Since there are various ways of getting scores of 2 to 4, studies with same score may not 'weigh the same' in research quality as each other. The authors claim that studies using this scale have shown that poorly designed studies are more likely to judge a treatment as effective than well-designed ones. If this so (and that seems likely) then the instrument works for its purpose and it doesn't much matter whether or not it generates data at the interval level. If this claim is not valid, then an instrument generating genuine interval level data probably wouldn't improve matters.

Scales and scaling

The kind of data produced by an instrument depends on the kind of scale it contains. Panel 2.1 gives some question formats in terms of their appearance. Visual analogue scales (VAS) are another possibility. Stars are sometimes used (see the *Amazon* web site, for example), numbers of smiley faces, and sometimes in health contexts, 'thermometers' on which respondents mark the level of their pain, discomfort, dislike or pleasure (Alwin 1997).

The amount of information a scale can capture depends on the number of **intervals** on the scale. At the interval level with continuous measurement this approaches infinity. Having two few divisions may result in important differences being hidden (Table 2.4). Having too many intervals may result in any patterns being invisible. If possible it is best to collect data with a finely graded instrument – this allows the maximum opportunities for statistical analysis, but for reporting the results it may be advisable to '*degrade*' the data by collapsing it into a few categories.

Some kinds of scaling require a great deal of work which is not apparent from the appearance of the scale to the research subject. This is particularly true of Thurston scales and Guttman scales, both of which involve considerable prior research in an attempt to produce scales where the intervals are of the same size. They are mainly used in attitude research.

PANEL 2.1   Question formats

Closed, or forced choice questions – all permissible options are provided for

Dichotomous

Are you male or female?   *Male* ☐   *Female* ☐

Multiple choice

How many cigarettes did you smoke yesterday?

None	*1–5*	*6–10*	*11–20*	*21–30*	*30+*	*Don't know*
☐	☐	☐	☐	☐	☐	☐

Likert scale

How strongly do you agree or disagree with this statement?

Young people these days have no respect for older people

Strongly disagree	*Disagree*	*Don't know*	*Agree*	*Strongly agree*
☐	☐	☐	☐	☐

Semantic differential

Tick the box which is closest to your feelings

Doctors are . . .

Warm ☐☐☐☐☐☐ *Cold*

Wise ☐☐☐☐☐☐ *Foolish*

Rating scale

Please rate the quality of the accommodation as:

Excellent 1 ☐   *Good 2* ☐   *Fair 3* ☐   *Poor 4* ☐   *Very Poor 5* ☐

Open-ended questions

Unstructured (or, better, 'loosely structured')

What does it mean to you to be a woman in a profession dominated by males?

Sentence completion
To me a good day at work means . . . .

Repertory grid technique (Jankowicz 2003)

Can you tell me in what way these two [people] are alike, and unlike this other [person]

In addition, responses can be elicited by asking respondents to complete half-finished stories, or to describe what is shown in a picture or on a video. Instead of answering questions respondents may be asked to put cards in rank order or in piles of different kinds or, in experiments, to press buttons.

TABLE 2.4 *The effect of different scales on the information captured*

Three-point scale	Male (%)	Female (%)	Six-point scale	Male (%)	Female (%)	Continuous scale[b]
Satisfied	32	31	Very satisfied	4	4	For example, the answer to the question: 'Express your satisfaction with the service on a scale of 0 to 100, where 0 means highly dissatisfied and 50 is neither satisfied nor dissatisfied.'
Not satisfied	63	65	Moderately satisfied	14	9	It would be usual to 'degrade the data' and report in, say, six categories. But the continuous scale provides more information for statistical analysis.
			Neutral	59	20	
			Moderately dissatisfied	14	24	
			Very dissatisfied	4	39	
Don't know	5	4	Don't know	5	4	
No statistically significant[a] difference between males and females			A statistically significant difference[a] between males and females			

Notes: [a] For statistical significance, see Panel 3.1.
[b] More correctly, a quasi-continuous scale, since responses will always be in whole numbers.

Floor and ceiling effects

Instruments may discriminate well between subjects in the middle of the range, but badly at the top or the bottom of the range. These are so called *'floor'* or *'ceiling'* effects. An aptitude test may be so easy for most of the subjects that they all score highly and there is little difference to be seen between them, or the questions may be so hard that nearly all the subjects end up at the bottom of the scale.

Floor effects are very common in instruments developed for use in health-related research. They distinguish adequately between degrees of sickness or distress, but lump all those who are a bit under the weather together with those who are in robust health. This reflects the interest in medical practice in sickness rather than health, but is a problem for researchers who are looking for effects of treatment among those who are not seriously ill, or looking for the precursors of serious illness among the not-yet-ill.

Panel 2.2 gives an example of a ceiling effect which was important in a controversy surrounding a major research project.

PANEL 2.2   A ceiling effect in *Progress in Secondary Schools*

Progress in Secondary Schools (Steedman 1980; Steedman, Fogelman and Hutchinson 1980) was a large-scale study of the differences in pupils' progress between selective secondary schools and comprehensive schools. It asked whether children of the same ability at 11 fared better or worse than each other in grammar schools and secondary moderns or in comprehensive schools? Crucial for answering this question were data comparing the highest achievers, because in selective systems they were the ones going to grammar school.

Reading scores at 16 years for top scoring 11 year olds, based on Steedman, Fogelman and Hutchinson (1980: 2)

FIGURE 2.1   *Reading scores at 16 years for top-scoring 11 year olds*

Source: Steedman, Fogelman and Hutchinson (1980: 2).

The graph in Figure 2.1 shows the results on a reading test at 16 of just the children who scored highest on the equivalent reading test at 11 years. A very large percentage scored highly on the later test: nearly one-third scored over

75%. It was possible therefore, that among the highest achievers those who had been in the grammar school had achieved much more than those in the comprehensive school, but that this was hidden by the way the reading test failed to discriminate amongst 'low highs' and 'high highs'. This was seized upon by critics of comprehensive schools to rubbish the report (Cox and Marks 1980). But the reading test scores clumped at a point lower than the maximum possible score, and there was no ceiling effect for the parallel maths testing, which showed that the most able children achieved much the same in both systems of education (Steedman, Fogelman and Hutchinson 1980).

2.4   The validity and reliability of instruments

Validity and reliability, together with objectivity, are the traditional criteria by which scientific research is judged. This is accepted by most quantitative researchers in the social sciences, and by many qualitative researchers too. Some qualitative researchers argue for other criteria (see Chapter 1, Table 1.2), but here the discussion is in terms of the more traditional criteria.

Validity, for an instrument, is about whether it gives accurate measures of what it purports to be measuring. **Reliability** is whether the instrument does this consistently: whether it gives the same results in the same circumstances. After this promising start, validity and reliability dissolve into sub-types that can become confusing (Table 2.5).

The first column of Table 2.5 gives some of the common sub-types suggested for validity and reliability. The definitions of these terms is implied in question form in the second column.

The third column of Table 2.5 provides a better way of looking at things. It is not too difficult to see that all the shortcomings listed, *whatever else they are*, turn out to be different reasons why the data generated by an instrument fail adequately to represent the construct they are supposed to represent. Let's call them 'failures of construct validity'. All the other sub-divisions of validity, reliability and other matters listed in the table, then, appear as different ways in which an instrument may fall short of construct validity, with the partial exception of 10 which is also about the ethics of using the instrument, irrespective of the accuracy of the resulting data (see Chapter 16).

It is much easier to know about *threats to validity* than about the validity that is allegedly threatened. The nearest we ever get to knowing validity is in terms of failing to find any evidence of invalidity (see Chapter 1, Section 1.5). And the quality of that knowledge depends on how hard and how effectively we looked for methodological shortcomings and invalidating evidence.

The fourth column of Table 2.5 refers to ways of testing an instrument to detect if it suffers seriously from these different sources of invalidity. Many of the tests involve calculating **correlations**, which are explained in Panel 2.3.

34

TABLE 2.5 *Criteria for research instruments*

Criterion *Validity criteria in general*	**Defining questions** *Does the instrument measure what it purports to measure?*	**Failure** *The instrument doesn't accurately measure what it purports to measure*	**Test: how failure might be detected**	**Further information in this book**
1 Face validity	Does it *seem* to measure what it is supposed to measure, as judged by appropriate judges?	The claim that it measures what it is supposed to measure is unconvincing to those whose opinions should be respected	Often left to critical reviewers, but might be tested by asking experts Sometimes experts will be research subjects	Chapter 2, Section 2.5
2 Construct validity	Are results from using the instrument consistent with what else is known/theorized about the phenomenon of interest? Are the measures uncontaminated by confounding factors? Do any of the shortcomings listed elsewhere in this table prevent the accurate measurement of this construct?	What is actually measured is something different from what the theory being tested presumes, or different from what the research requires And/or The measurements achieved are seriously contaminated by factors which are no part of the construct And/or Some other shortcoming listed in this table prevents accurate measurement of this construct	No tests specifically for construct validity, but in effect *all* the tests below for other forms of validity and reliability and other desiderata are tests for aspects of construct validity	Chapter 2 as a whole

3 Content validity (coverage/ comprehensiveness/ relevance)	Does it deal with all relevant aspects of what it is supposed to measure?	The measures achieved do not represent the relevant dimensions of the target construct comprehensively: they measure only some aspects of it, possibly giving a misleading picture	Cross-checking instrument items with specifications of the construct Serious checks for content validity usually involve an internal reliability test (see 8 below)	Chapter 2, Section 2.6
4 Criterion validity (concurrent or predictive) (Concurrent validity: and Predictive validity)	**Concurrent validity**: Do the results from using the instrument correlate with the results of using another instruments regarded as 'the gold standard'? Or, if there is no such instrument, with expert opinion? **Note**: the gold standard should itself meet the criteria noted in this table. **Predictive validity**: Do the results of using the instrument accurately predict some later state of affairs?	**Concurrent**: The measures achieved using the instrument are radically different from those which might be achieved by using some other instrument taken to be the 'gold standard' measure The instrument is either measuring something different, or the same thing less accurately **Predictive**: Fails accurately to predict what it was supposed to predict	Statistical tests of correlation or co-variation, measuring the extent of agreement between the results of using this instrument and the results of using another instrument regarded as the 'gold standard' A weak 'criterion test' would be judging the results against expert opinion Or tests measuring the correlation between a prediction made on the basis of the instrument's results and what was predicted	Chapter 2, Section 2.7

TABLE 2.5   continued

Criterion Validity criteria in general	Defining questions Does the instrument measure what it purports to measure?	Failure The instrument doesn't accurately measure what it purports to measure	Test: how failure might be detected	Further information in this book
5 External validity (generalizability, transferability)	Would the instrument produce equivalent measures for a much wider population than it has in fact been used with, and/or over a longer time period?	The instrument, while possibly valid for the population it was used with and, at the time of use, is not more widely valid	Testing instrument for validity and reliability with large representative sample Standardization around the norm for a large population	Raised as an issue with regard to normed instruments – Chapter 1, Section 1.6; Chapter 2, Section 2.12; Chapter 3, Section 3.10; Chapter 4, Section 4.1; see also rows 9 and 15
Reliability in general (dependability, and sometimes replicability)	*Is the instrument consistent in performance?*	*The instrument does not perform consistently – a failure of reliability, hence the instrument does not adequately measure what it purports to measure – a failure of validity*	*See below*	*See below*
6 Stability/ Reproducibility – test–retest reliability	Would it produce the same results with the same subjects on another occasion – assuming the phenomenon of interest hadn't changed between times?	The instrument is erratically or systematically influenced by factors which ought not to influence it It wouldn't give the same result if administered to	Test–retest procedures: Administering the same instrument to the same subjects on a second occasion and statistically comparing the results by correlation	Chapter 2, Section 2.8; for correlation see Panel 2.3

			the same subjects on two different occasions even if there had been no change in the matter of interest	Alternate forms tests	
7 Inter-rater reliability	Where administrators of the test, or analysers of the results make judgements, would they all produce the same results?	Judgements are involved in using the instrument Different people would make these judgements differently		Statistically comparing the results of two or more administrators/analysts and computing the level of agreement by correlation (Panel 2.3)	Chapter 2, Section 2.10
8 Internal consistency	Where several items of the instrument purport to measure aspects of the same phenomenon do the results correlate sufficiently? Where items of the instrument purport to measure different constructs do these measures show absence of correlation?	Items which purport to measure the same construct do not correlate sufficiently and or items which purport to measure different constructs correlate too well (lack discriminant validity)		Testing for internal consistency using Cronbach's alpha test or KR-20, factor analysis or split-half testing	Chapter 2, Section 2.9
Other criteria					
9 Comprehensibility	Do the subjects understand the language and the concepts entailed in the instrument, and what is required of them?	(as a threat to construct validity) Subjects, or significant numbers of them do not understand the words or understand the words or		Interviews with subjects representing respondents asking for their understandings of what the instrument requires	As an aspect of culture-fairness, see Chapter 2, Section 2.12

TABLE 2.5 continued

Other criteria	Defining questions	Failure	Test: how failure might be detected	Further information in this book
		the ideas entailed in the instrument, or don't understand what they are supposed to do, so that the instrument cannot measure what it is supposed to measure, for at least some groups of subject		Chapter 16
10 Acceptability and/ or ethicality	For example, is the instrument non-threatening and inoffensive? Is the time it requires reasonable for the subjects?	For example, the instrument upsets subjects, or fatigues them so that this influences the measurements obtained or is unethical in some way	Pilot test with subjects representing the targets for the instrument (under a range of circumstances if appropriate). See also rows 9 and 10	
11 Appropriateness to context and targets	For example, is it appropriate for this age group? Could it be administered on a bus? See also 4 and 6 in this section of the table	For example, the instrument used was designed for a different age group and this influences the results when age should be irrelevant – similar to comprehensibility (row 9) and acceptability (row 10) Or	Pilot test with subjects representing the targets for the instrument (under a range of circumstances if appropriate). See also rows 9 and 10	

12 Data and data level	Does it produce data in the form at a level appropriate to the best means of statistically analysing the results?	The instrument was designed to be administered with the subject sitting down quietly but was used with people stopped in the street. This influenced the results	The instrument does not produce data at the level appropriate for analysis required. The instrument produces highly skewed data distributions and hence floor or ceiling effects, or otherwise produces data which does not allow for fine discrimination between subjects where this is required (the latter may also be an effect of small samples)	Chapter 2, Section 2.3
13 Usefulness	Is an instrument designed to be of practical use in, say, education (social work, business, etc.) actually useful?	The instrument, while designed to aid practice, does not give results on which sound practical decisions can be based	Most of the tests above but also validating the instrument by monitoring its use under the everyday circumstances of practice	Chapter 3; Chapter 4, Sections 4.4 and 4.5; Chapter 14, Sections 14.3–14.5; see also row 5 above

Note: KR-20 = Kuder–Richardson formula 20.

PANEL 2.3   Correlation and co-variance

Two variables are **correlated** when the value of one changes in step with the value of the other. The relationship can be one of *positive correlation*: a high value on one is associated with a high value on the other, or a low value on one is associated with a low value on the other, as with the relationship between height and weight when measured in a large population; or it can be one of *negative (or inverse) correlation*, as with two ends of a see-saw; when one end goes up, the other goes down.

The strength of correlation is usually judged by calculating a **correlation co-efficient** such as Pearson's product moment co-efficient, or Spearman's Rho. These report values from –1 to +1, where –1 means a perfect negative correlation (two ends of a see-saw), 0 means no correlation at all, and +1 means a perfect positive correlation (two points on a roundabout). Usually a score above 0.3 or below –0.3 is regarded as evidence of correlation. Some tests, however, such as Cronbach's alpha, score only between 0 and 1. This does not distinguish between positive and negative correlations. Scores above 0.6 usually count as correlations. Since correlations can occur by chance co-efficients are meaningless unless they reach a **statistically significant** value. Testing for this is a separate operation (see Chapter 3, Panel 3.1).

Co-variance is another way of describing the association between two variables. It is the extent to which the variance (variety of scores) for one variable is determined by another variable measured through ANCOVA (the analysis of co-variance). For variance, see Chapter 3, Panel 3.1.

2.5   Testing for threats to face validity (Table 2.5, row 1)

Bowling (1997: 132–3) says that face validity

> simply refers to investigators' subjective assessments of the presentation and relevance of the questionnaire: do the questions appear to be relevant, reasonable, unambigous and clear?

The most convincing test of face validity would be one involving experts in the area concerned. This happens *post hoc* in peer review prior to publication (see Chapter 15), but it would be a useful stage in the development of an instrument.

2.6   Testing for content validity (Table 2.5, row 3)

In scholastic examinations, the content validity issue is whether the items on the paper, between them, cover all the important topics featured in the course of instruction. And do they do so in a way that gives each topic an appropriate weight, in terms of time allowed, and/or in terms of opportunities to score marks?

Examinations and other kinds of scholastic tests are often themselves used as research instruments with the above kinds of content validity considerations. In other kinds of research the 'content' to be featured in an instrument will be structured in terms of whatever dimensions the construct to be measured is conceived as having. For example 'intelligence' is usually conceived as being made up of a number of different aptitudes: numerical, visual–spatial, verbal and so on. An intelligence test claiming to test intelligence *as a whole* needs to include items for each dimension and to weight them appropriately.

To judge failures of content validity it is necessary to have a well worked-out specification of the construct(s) to be indicated, against which the instrument can be matched; for example, the learning objectives for a course of instruction or the dimensions of intelligence. Such a test is more credible if it involves judges with some expertise in the field, and is explicitly reported by the researcher. Sometimes an inter-rater reliability test (Section 2.10) might be appropriate. More usually, researchers use a 'face validity' approach (see Section 2.5) to content validity, being satisfied if people qualified to judge, think the content 'looks right'.

2.7   Testing for criterion validity (Table 2.5, row 4)

Criterion validity testing refers to situations where one instrument is tested against another, which is regarded as 'tried and tested'. The latter is then called the 'criterion' and the procedure may be called a test for **concurrent validity**. Or, an instrument is tested by the extent to which results from using it can be used to predict something else, usually something in the future; **predictive validity**. The procedures are logically identical and usually involve some operation of statistical correlation (Panel 2.3), or the same tests as are used for judging internal consistency (Section 2.9) may be deployed. A comparison is made between the results of both instruments used, either with the same subjects, or with groups of subjects who are very similar to each other. Panel 2.4 gives an example of concurrent criterion testing.

PANEL 2.4   Testing intelligence tests for criterion validity

Concurrent criterion testing – this is often done where it is hoped that a new instrument will give similar results to an old one but will be quicker to use, or will be more appropriate for use with some group or in some situation. Sometimes the new instrument is being developed in an attempt to capture the same target constructs more accurately. For example, over the last 100 years (precisely, in 2006) intelligence tests have been developed through a process of testing new versions against old versions and judging whether the new version is superior, in terms of both capturing how current theory conceptualized intelligence, and in characteristics such as ease of administration, culture-fairness, and so on (see also Section 2.12). Intelligence tests score is an important control variable in a wide range of research ventures where there is a need to measure (say) educational achievement, or income, or career success 'after controlling for differences in intelligence' (Chapter 7).

Predictive criterion testing – earlier intelligence tests were validated according to how well they predicted educational achievement (see pp. 42–4).

Chapter 10, Section 10.4 refers to the World Health Organization (WHO) *Angina Questionnaire*, a self-administered questionnaire designed to identify people who have experienced coronary heart disease problems, which is used, in among other ways, as a component of the annual *Health Survey of England* (www.dh.gov.uk/en/Publicationsandstatistics/index.htm). It is used as an alternative to the prohibitively expensive procedure of having survey respondents examined by a doctor. In the development of this instrument the criterion was constituted by the results of doctors conducting physical examinations and taking medical histories. The results of pilot versions of the questionnaire were compared with this, and the items rephrased or replaced with others until the results of the questionnaire corresponded with the results of medical examination with a tolerable degree of error (Rose, McCartney and Reid 1977).

Concurrent criterion testing is a process of validation by prediction. Did the new intelligence test predict the results gained by the same or similar subjects on the old intelligence test? The term **predictive validity** seems to be used mainly to refer to the prediction of future states of affairs. Validation by prediction in this sense seems more often to be an aim of instruments designed to aid practice rather than for use as research tools – though research is required to design the instruments. Thus there has been much interest in designing instruments which predict future violent behaviour from past behaviour, or from psychological and social characteristics, and similarly for instruments which predict re-offending.

Rather than a distinction between concurrent and predictive, it might be more useful to make a distinction between more abstract and more concrete criterion testing. It is almost a joke that, following Boring (1923) some psychometricians define 'intelligence' as 'that which is measured by intelligence tests'. In general, this approach is called 'instrumentalism', once very popular among psychologists (Green 1992). It says there is nothing about intelligence, for example, which is knowable, except what is known from the test used to measure it. A logical problem with this approach is that it implies that there can be no way of deciding between two intelligence tests that give different results (see below).

Such problems are not entirely avoided, but they give rise to different worries if such highly abstract constructs as intelligence are defined by reference to more everyday phenomena. Intelligence tests were originally designed as tests to be given to children to predict their later intellectual development; first with regard to 'mental retardation' by Binet and Simon and then by Terman at Stanford University with the full range of children, and to allocate recruits to ranks in the American military. The criterion testing for the early versions of the Stanford–Binet intelligence test thus involved judging how well intelligence test score (or Intelligence Quotient – IQ) predicted educational achievement, and adjusting the test items, or the scoring (weighting), to improve prediction.

In the first half of the twentieth century, females performed less well than males in the US education system so it is understandable that the tests were designed to reflect this. If the tests showed equal intelligence for males and females, they would have been poorer predictors of educational achievement.

In this regard, it was quite illogical to say that females achieved less well in the educational system *because* they are less intelligent as shown by intelligence tests, when intelligence tests were designed precisely to give boys higher scores than girls in order to match what was happening educationally. The Stanford Binet was revised for its 4th edition in 1986 so that males and females had the same average score, but gender differences remained in that there were more males scoring in the very highest and the very lowest ranges. For mainstream educational selection purposes very low scoring individuals tend to be excluded, thus boosting the average scores of boys in the mainstream population, because more boys are in special educational provision. By 1986 in most English-speaking populations, girls were out-performing boys educationally, though not in all subjects. But girls were rated as of lower average intelligence by intelligence tests. This is mitigated to some extent by quoting intelligence test results as profiles with a score for each of the major sub-scales, rather than as a single score. Males do better on some scales, and females on others but, when consolidated, the average for males is 4 or 5 points higher than for females. Thus intelligence tests now fail a predictive validity test with regard to gender differences *if the criterion is educational achievement*. Within gender groups intelligence tests are still quite good predictors of concurrent and later educational achievement, particularly if differences of socio-economic status are controlled for (Chapter 7, Section 7.3).

In earlier days the construct 'intelligence' was very close to, though not identical with, the idea of 'educability', and the accurate prediction of educational achievement was therefore a crucial test of a good instrument. These days, some psychologists think of intelligence more in terms of neural information processing capacities and are keen to relate intelligence test scores to what is shown by the magnetic resonance imaging of the brain. In this regard, intelligence tests could be accurate predictors of neurological events, without necessarily being accurate predictors of educational achievement.

The use of intelligence test scores for educational selection carries a very high risk of bias against females. Even more unjustifiable are the US Standardized Achievement Tests (SATs) used for university entrance selection. These were designed specifically to measure capacity to benefit from higher education, but females make lower SATs scores on average than males, while they achieve higher marks on average in higher education. The use of SATs for university entrance selection has been subject to various human rights challenges in the US (NCFO 2003).

This discussion of the criterion testing of intelligence tests shows that what criterion-testing means depends upon the construct the instrument is supposed to measure. Thus an alternative way of measuring intelligence, or something very like it, derives from the theories of Piaget. Contemporary research into year 7 maths and science performance in England (Shayer, Ginsburg and Coe 2007) using a test based on this set of constructs suggests a significant *decline* in aptitude underlying the ability to do maths and science over the last 15 years. By contrast, Stanford–Binet and similar intelligence test results, using the sub-scales related to maths and science aptitude, shows an *increase* in ability (see Section 2.12), as does the historical sequence of year

7 (UK) SATs scores. Evidently whether 'intelligence', has increased, or declined, depends on how intelligence is conceptualized and measured. By the same token different conceptualizations will nominate different criteria as appropriate for judging the adequacy of a test.

2.8   Test–retest reliability and alternate form tests (Table 2.5, row 6)

A reliable instrument is one which shows a consistent performance, *where consistency is valid*. The italicized rider is necessary because, for example, a stopped clock is highly consistent, but is an invalid time-keeper. Instruments can be consistently wrong.

Test–retest reliability refers to what is sometimes called '*stability*' or '*reproducibility*'. It requires that an instrument will give similar results when used on a second occasion with the same or similar subjects, assuming that nothing being measured has changed in the meantime. The most stringent test–retest requirement is that a test gives a similar result with the *same subjects* individually. A less stringent test is that it gives a similar result for the *same group* of subjects. For example, at the individual level, polls of voting intention have not been very accurate predictors of how people actually vote. Lots of people change their minds between the poll and the election. But most of the mind changing cancels out so that the poll results are usually quite good predictors of how people vote in aggregate (Himmelweit *et al.* 1985). Similarly Tilburg (1998) found that while interviewees individually changed their estimates of the size of their social networks from one interview to another, the average network size estimate did not change.

An even less stringent test is the requirement of a similar result for a *group of subjects similar* to the first group.

Straightforward test–retest tests with the same subjects are difficult to interpret: the second occasion is never the same as the first. Because it is a second occasion it may give rise to 'here we go again' reactions. This may be unimportant if the measurement is of some unthought phenomenon, such as blood pressure. But it might become so where being asked a question a first time influences the answer on the second occasion. On the one hand, having been asked a question once already may cause people to think about it and change their mind, and their answer, on the second occasion. On the other hand, people self-monitor and often try to appear consistent, so some people who have changed their minds between times may hold to their original response.

In test–retesting, the degree of difference between the two sets of results may be taken as an indication of the test's unreliability, but it is rare that there is any sure way of distinguishing between this and the effects of people really changing their minds. All we know is that the greater the difference in time between the test and retest the bigger the discrepancy in results becomes. This means that for the purpose of establishing reliability, test–retests need to be carried out within a short time span. This is rarely convenient. The appropriate calendar for test–retest may not be the same as the appropriate calendar for base-line and outcome measurement. This is a problem for one-off instruments, custom-made for a particular piece of research. Commonly used instruments will probably have been tested for their test–retest reliability, or for the closely related alternate forms reliability.

Alternate forms tests are attempts to avoid the 'here we go again' problem. They involve pairs of items, developed so that each of them (reliably) produces similar responses from the same or similar subjects. One of each pair then appears in one of a pair of tests. One can then be used as a pre-test or base-line measure, and the other as a post-test or outcome measure without fears that a 'here we go again' reaction will confound the results. There will inevitably be some differences between the results of the two instruments, which can be attributed to the tests themselves, but these can be controlled by randomizing the subjects so that some get one of the alternate forms as a pre-test and some as a post-test and/or randomizing the items so that each subject gets a different combination of pairs before and after (pre- and post-).

2.9 Internal reliability or consistency (Table 2.5, row 7)

Internal reliability or 'consistency' may be tested by using statistical tests designed for the purpose such as the Kuder–Richardson formula 20 (KR-20), or Cronbach's co-efficient alpha, by split-half techniques or by factor analysis.

An example of internal consistency testing is given by a study by Sutton, Smith and Swettenham on bullying in school (Sutton and Smith 1999; Sutton, Smith and Swettenham 1999a, 1999b). This is introduced in Panel 2.5. It is also another illustration of how different ways of theorizing require different instruments to measure different constructs. Conceptualizing bullying as a social activity, requires instruments different from conceptualizing bullying as a character trait.

To discover which roles pupils most often played in bullying, an adaptation of an instrument called the Participant Roles Scale (PRS) was used. Each pupil was asked to characterize his or her own usual action in bullying situations, and the usual actions taken by each class mate. This was done by

---

PANEL 2.5 Measuring pupils' (views on each others') participation in bullying

Sutton, Smith and Swettenham (1999a, 1999b) conceptualized bullying as a social or group-dynamic phenomenon, in which different pupils would play different roles such as Bully, Reinforcer, Assistant, Defender, Victim and Outsider. These seem to exhaust the possibilities and give a plausible content validity (Section 2.6) 'on the face of it' (Section 2.5). The overall aim of the research was to choose between two hypotheses: one that bullies lacked 'social intelligence', and the other that they were highly sensitive to others' feelings and used this to manipulate situations using intimidation. The researchers looked for correlations between the roles played and instruments measuring verbal ability and social cognition. The latter refers to understanding others' feelings and interpretations (for correlation, see Panel 2.3).

affirming or denying given statements about one's own and one's peers' behaviour in bullying situations.

The PRS has sub-scales for each participant role. The researchers found that *within* each sub-scale pupils who got a 'yes' vote on one question were highly likely to get a 'yes' on other items within the same sub-scale, on most sub-scales (see Panel 2.3). The correlation co-efficients (Cronbach's alpha) for items within a sub-scale were as follows (Sutton and Smith 1999: 110):

> Bully sub-scale, 0.85; Reinforcer sub-scale, 0.88; Assistant sub-scale, 0.67; Defender sub-scale, 0.80; Outsider sub-scale, 0.55

A Cronbach alpha score of zero would mean that there was no relationship between responses to one statement on a sub-scale and responses to another. An alpha of 1.00 would mean that any affirmation of any statement in the set was always accompanied by an affirmative on all the others. Thus an alpha over 80.00 represents a high degree of internal consistency.

Each sub-scale seems to hang together internally. When Sutton and Smith deleted one of the statements on an earlier version of the Outsider sub-scale, the correlation co-efficient rose from 0.55 to 0.67. This indicated that the deleted item was not actually measuring outsiderness – whatever that is – and should really be deleted from the instrument. The statement was *'Pretends not to notice what is happening'* and the low alpha comes from affirmatives to this statement not being closely associated with other statements designating an Outsider role, but often being made with regard to pupils designated as playing other roles. An alpha of 0.60 or more is usually regarded as sufficient to warrant inclusion of all the items subjected to the test, though deleting each one in turn and retesting might yield a higher score and a more internally consistent scale.

In comparing two items, an alpha of 1 (or a KR-20 of 1) would indicate that no additional information was gained from using the second one. Usually that would be an indication that one of the items should be deleted as unnecessary. However, in creating an *alternative forms test* (Section 2.8) two items generating an alpha or KR-20 score of near 1.0 would be highly desirable. One could be used in each of the alternative instruments.

A correlation above 0.6, but a less than perfect one, suggests that different aspects of the same construct are being indicated. The responses to items within each sub-scale of the PRS instrument were *not* perfectly correlated, so it can be argued that each of them captures something slightly different about each role.

Factor analysis

For Sutton and his colleagues the internal consistency of the sub-scales was high. But that doesn't necessarily mean that the instrument was discriminating well between participant roles – **discriminant validity**. For this, it is important to look at the correlations between each sub-scale as a set of all possible *pairwise* correlations. The researchers did this using *factor analysis*, shown in Table 2.6. Unlike Cronbach's alpha, these correlation coefficients

An example of a factor analysis matrix: role score correlations   TABLE 2.6

	Bully score	Reinforcer score	Assistant score	Defender score	Outsider score
Reinforcer score	0.75*				
Assistant score	0.62*	0.77*			
Defender score	0.08	0.23*	0.25*		
Outsider score	–0.28*	–0.17**	–0.14**	0.32*	
Victim score	–0.12	–0.01	0.09	0.26*	0.20*

Sutton and Smith (1999: Table 1).
* Statistically significant at 0.05 level (see Chapter 3, Panel 3.1).
** Statically significant at 0.01 level (see Chapter 3, Panel 3.1).

How to read this table
A score higher than 0.3 or lower than –0.3 are considered good correlations. (For Correlation, see Panel 2.3) The positive figures in this table show where scores on one sub-scale are positively correlated with scores on another. This is whether they are high scores on one sub-scale matching high scores on another, or low scores on one sub-scale matching low scores on another, or matching middling scores. For example, pupils scoring high on the bully sub-scale, usually score high on the Reinforcer sub-scale. Pupils scoring low on the Bully sub-scale also scored low on the Reinforcer sub-scale. The shaded cells show a group of roles which correlate with each other positively. The negative figures in this table show where high scores on one sub-scale are associated with low scores on another: for example high scores on the Bully sub-scale with low scores on the Victim scale.

The construct 'Defender' is of a pupil who defends others from bullying. The fact that there are positive correlations between Defender scores and two pro-bullying roles (Reinforcer and Assistant) throws some doubt either on the construct or on the means used to elicit information about it.

score between +1 and –1, allowing for both positive and negative correlations (Panel 2.3).

The matrix in Table 2.6 shows that a high Bully score for a pupils tends to go with a high Reinforcer score and a high Assistant score, and a low Bully score goes with low scores on all these sub-scales. A high score on all of these sub-scales is supposed to indicate roles as perpetrators of bullying, so it is hardly surprising that they are highly correlated. But this means that the PRS does not discriminate well *between* these roles. Perhaps this is a shortcoming of the instrument. But perhaps it is a reflection of reality where different pupils may sometimes play one role, and sometimes another in a bullying situation, but where there is some stability in whether pupils are perpetrators of bullying, or victims or resisters.

It might be wise to rephrase the above to refer not to roles played by the pupils, but to *pupils' expressions of opinion about roles played by the pupils,* because that is what the instrument measures. There is an issue of *construct validity* here – are expressions of opinion about bullying adequate as indicators of roles taken in bullying? A *criterion validity* reference point for resolving this could come from observations of pupil behaviour. Sutton and his colleagues were not able to do this. On another criterion test, the correlations between PRS and teachers' opinions were not very strong.

Factor analysis was being used here to gauge how well an instrument discriminated between different entities. It is also used as a research strategy in its own right where researchers look for variables which seem to hang together and then propose underlying constructs to explain this (Child 2006).

Split-half testing for reliability

Where all items in an instrument, or one of its sub-scales, are purportedly measuring the same construct or aspects of a construct a split-half test may be appropriate. Split-half testing relies on the assumption that if a set of items are all measuring the same construct, albeit different aspects of it, then one half of the items should give a similar result to the other half. For nominal or ordinal level data (Table 2.1) Kuder–Richardson is the appropriate test. For interval-level data Cronbach's co-efficient alpha would be preferable, and other correlation co-efficients might be used.

2.10   Inter-rater and intra-rater reliability testing (Table 2.5, row 2.10)

Some instruments involve the researcher, or an assistant, making judgements which allow considerable discretion. Research on doctors, social workers and police officers at work (see Chapter 9, Section 9.4) shows that their reliability as judges is rarely good. The same appears to be true of psychological researchers according to a vein of research opened up by Richard Rosenthal in the 1960s and confirmed continually since then (Rosenthal 1966; Rosenthal and Fode 1963; Rosenthal and Rosnow 1969; Rosenthal and Rubin 1978). So probably human beings are simply not very good at following rules to reach judgements, or at doing so consistently.

Inter-rater reliability tests provide estimates of how closely different judges agree with each other. The calculation of any correlation co-efficient (Panel 2.3) will serve to provide an estimate of agreement. A statistic called kappa is useful when the data are binary in a format such as 'agree/disagree' (Pett 1997: 237–48). A kappa of below 0.60 should raise worries about the research being flawed by differences in judgements between judges. More rarely, statistical tests of difference are used – measuring the extent of disagreement, rather than of agreement.

It is essential that inter-rater reliability tests are conducted blind because social pressures to agree are very strong. 'Blind' here means that one judge does not know what another judge has decided.

Where there are several researchers, poor levels of inter-rater reliability can be avoided by training people to make their judgements in the same way and or by revising the instructions given to them to make them clearer.

Inter-rater reliability is not only useful when several judges are involved in research. It is also useful when devising an instrument for use by a single observer in order to guarantee that what this observer observes is close to what other observers would observe when following the same instructions: that is, to enhance the *objectivity* ('shareability') of the observations. For

> **PANEL 2.6** Inter-rater reliability testing: an example
>
> Savage and Armstrong (1990) conducted an experiment to see whether patients preferred their doctor to communicate with them in an egalitarian, sharing sort of way or more authoritatively. Richard Savage, a GP, switched from one style to another at random in dealing with his patients. Criteria were drawn up to describe what the two different performances ought to look like and sound like, and a panel of judges was shown a sample of video tapes from the experiment and asked to classify them into the two types, or set them aside as unclassifiable.

example, the researcher might observe something as an act of 'discrimination' (see Chapter 14, Section 14.4). But other observers might observe the same scene and interpret it differently. To reduce the chances of this happening several judges might be assembled to watch video-taped samples and asked to code their observations. Then the results would be tested for inter-rater reliability. If it proved necessary, the criteria for recording an instance of discrimination (say) would be revised. It has been suggested that inter-rater reliability testing of this kind should be practised more widely in qualitative research to improve its rigour (Armstrong *et al.* 1997) (see Panel 2.6).

Avoiding the consequences of unreliable judgement is the reason why blind double-marking (or cross-marking, or masked assessment) and moderation are practised for examinations in educational institutions. In examinations, though, there are standard procedures for deciding disagreements between examiners and reaching a final mark. In research an assumption which may lie unexamined behind inter-rater reliability testing is that the consensus view is the right one. But, of course, it is always possible that the one judge out of line in an inter-rater reliability test is more percipient than the others. The test will not tell which judge this is.

Intra-rater reliability testing is sometimes practised where there is a possibility that a single researcher's judgements might drift from the early research work to the later work, or might differ when interviewing different kinds of people. Here different samples of the single researcher's results will be compared with each other (see also Chapter 10, Section 10.4).

2.11 Other ways in which an instrument may be flawed (Table 2.5, rows 9–13)

Table 2.5 lists some other ways in which research instruments might give misleading results. Some general comments can be made about all of them. Each of them is likely to misrepresent the construct(s) an instrument is supposed to measure and therefore undermine the construct validity of the research; some by under-recording, some by over-recording, some by confusing one category with another and some by introducing research artefacts into the research. Here **research artefacts** means that something happens which would not have happened had the research not been carried out. Since most things that take place in research happen because the research has been

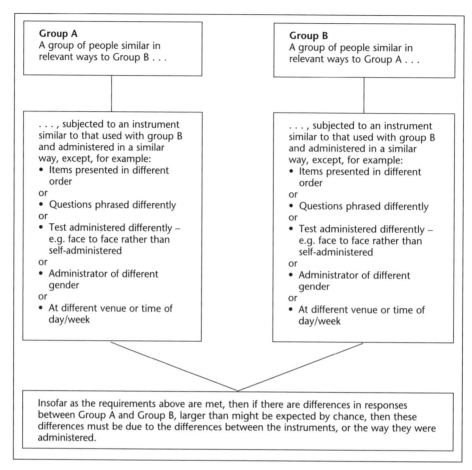

FIGURE 2.2   *A similar-subjects, different-treatments experimental design used to investigate alternatives in the content or the administration of instruments*

carried out, these should perhaps be called *unwanted* research artefacts. An obvious example of an unwanted research artefact is the way that asking for someone's opinions causes people to have opinions about matters they might not otherwise think about.

The approach to detecting such problems involves using experimental designs discussed in Chapter 3 and (as 'natural experiments') in Chapter 7, and when attempts are made to synthesize research from various sources, discussed in Chapter 15. A similar-subjects, different-treatments design as shown in Figure 2.2, will focus on the effects of the instrument. A different-subject similar – treatment design (Chapter 4, Figure 4.1) will focus on different effects for different kinds of subject and might be utilized in the developmental stage of an instrument: for example, in investigating issues such as 'Is this set of questions understood differently by older people as compared with younger people?'

2.12   Standardization and norming

The **standardization** of an instrument means adjusting its items, or adjusting the contributions each item makes to a final score (**weighting**) so that when the instrument is used with a large, randomly selected population, the results shape up as a normal distribution curve. The properties of the **normal distribution** curve are described in greater detail in Panel 2.8, and you might like to look at that now. Standardization in this sense involves recalculating the data so that they are amenable to a 'standard' measure; the **standard deviation**. In a normal distribution there are always roughly the same percentage of subjects or other data points at the same number of standard deviations away from the mean, irrespective of what the data refer to. Textbook normal distributions are usually plotted with a mean of 0 and a standard deviation of 1. But those for intelligence or aptitudes are usually plotted with a mean 100 because it wouldn't make any sense to allow for negative scores for measures of intelligence or aptitude. For intelligence the standard deviation is 15 or16. The score of 'the average person' is 100 and

---

PANEL 2.7   Various meanings of standardization

1 **Proportional comparison**: Expression of differences as proportions, **rates**, **percentages** and **ratios**. For example, death rates are expressed as so many deaths, per time period per 1,000 (or 10,000, or 100,000 and so on) people in the population. A percentage is a rate per 100. Entities compared may be populations (cases per 1,000 people), time periods (events per year), geographical areas (so many per hectare) (Gomm 2000d).

2 **Synonymous with 'control'**: Where two variables are correlated (Panel 2.3) but are in turn influenced by a third variable, standardization is used to control the influence of the third variable. For example, Sutton and his colleagues were interested in the relationship between bullying and social cognition – the latter being the ability to understand other people (see Section 2.9) – and there was an association. But scores on the social cognition test were also correlated with age. Hence in their analysis, Sutton and his colleagues 'controlled for age differences' by age-standardizing the social cognition scores. They did this by recalculating the scores so that they were as if all the pupils were of the same chronological age. This procedure is possible only where there is a *monotonic* relationship between two variables; that is, where for an increase/decrease of *x* points for one, there is *always* approximately, an increase/decrease of *y* points for the other. Age standardization is a common procedure in epidemiology and demography where characteristics of areas are compared after controlling for their different age profiles (see the standardized mortality ratios in Chapter 9, Section 9.4, and Gomm 2000d), but the procedure can be carried out for any two variables at the interval level (Table 2.1).

3 **Standardization of treatment of research subjects**: In both experiments and social survey work, care is taken to treat all subjects in the same way except where the research requires them to be treated differently. This is to avoid irrelevant differences of treatment affecting the outcomes of the research (see Chapter 3 for experiments and Chapter 10 for surveys).

4 **Standardization of a research instrument** (see Section 2.12).

PANEL 2.8 Standardization and the normal distribution

The 'Normal distribution curve' is a family of frequency distributions, to which real data distributions sometimes approximate; also called the *Gaussian distribution*, the *bell curve, z-curve, standard error curve* and *sampling error curve*. Tests of intelligence and aptitude are usually constructed so that the results for all those tested shape up as a normal distribution. Then the percentage of all scores in any sector under the curve can be easily calculated.

Approximately 34% lie between the mean and 1 standard deviation either side of the mean

Approximately 95.5% lie between 2 standard deviations away from the mean either side of the mean

Approximately 99.7% lie between 3 standard deviations away from the mean either side of the mean

If the distribution is anything like 'normal', the **standard deviation** is the best single statistic for describing both the central tendency (the 'middlingness') of the data and their spread. It is also the measure used in calculating how many scores lie within particular sectors under the curve. Intelligence and aptitude tests usually have a mean of 100 and a standard deviation of 15. If the graphs were for an intelligence test, a score of 115 would be 1 standard deviation above average. Someone scoring it would be in the top 16% or at the 84th percentile

Standardizing a data set in terms of the normal distribution, means converting raw scores into z *scores* (or *standard scores*). Z scores report how many standard deviations a score falls above or below the mean.

z = (score – mean)/ standard deviation
   (12 – 11.2)/3.12 = 0.26

From the data (below), a raw score of 12 would equate to a z score of 0.26 standard deviations above the mean. A table called '*Areas under the normal curve*' shows that 10.3% of all scores lie between the mean and this point. 50% of scores lie below the mean, so 60.3% of all scores are at or below this (10.3 + 50), and

39.7% are at or above (100 – 60.3). Use the *population standard deviation* to map the score onto the distribution of scores for the wider population. Here, the result is near enough the same.

Knowing the percentage of scores in each sector under the graph, allows any one score to be placed in relation to all the others; for example as in the 'top 5%' or '2% below average'. For an instrument *normed* on a large representative sample of the population you can estimate the position of any score in relation to the scores each member of the population would have scored had data been collected from them.

Calculating the mean deviation, the variance and the standard deviation
Number of scores = 10

Score	Difference between score and mean of 11.2	Difference squared
7	–4.2	17.64
8	–3.2	10.24
9	– 2.2	4.84
10	–1.2	1.44
10	–1.2	1.44
11	–0.2	0.04
12	0.8	0.64
13	1.8	3.24
15	3.8	14.44
17	5.8	33.64
112/10 = 11.2 mean	sum of squared deviations	87.6

Sample variance = 87.6/ (10–1) = 9.73
[sum of squared deviations/ number of scores minus 1]
Population variance = 87.6/10 = 8.76
[sum of squared deviations/number of scores]
Standard deviation of sample = √9.73 = 3.12
Standard deviation of population (est.) = √8.76 = 2.96

The normal distribution is also the basis for calculating *significance* via *inferential statistics* (see Chapter 3, Panel 3.1) and for calculating *confidence intervals* (see Chapter 6, Panel 6.2: another reason why normal distributions are preferred by researchers.

the average is at one and the same time the mean (or arithmetical average), the median (the middle person) and the mode (the most common score).

The standardization of an instrument can be carried out only with data at the interval level (Table 2.1). There is controversy as to whether intelligence test and aptitude data are truly at this level, but intelligence and aptitude scores are always standardized.

The population used as the criterion to 'norm' an instrument might be the population of a country as a whole, or some sub-group. For example, the most recent version of the Stanford–Binet intelligence test was normed on '*a stratified random sample of 4,800 individuals that matches the 2000 U.S. Census*' (Riverside Publications 2004). For 'stratified random' see Chapter 6, Section 6.8 but, simply put, this means that the sample was cross-checked for its representativeness against the most recent US census. On that basis, it is claimed that the results achieved from the sample of 4,800 would be very close to the results which would be obtained by giving the test to the entire-ity of the US population. A sample of 4,800 is not very large if it is meant to be representative of distribution of test scores within all age groups 2 to 85 and within socio-economic and ethnic groups (see Chapter 6, Section 6.10).

There are two advantages to standardization, the first does not actually require the data to be normed in relation to a known population, the second does:

- Data drawn from a population of data points which are normally distrib-uted can be subjected to virtually all known statistical manipulations (Chapter 3, Panel 3.1)
- If someone is given a score on a scale which is normally distributed *and normed* then you can state that person's position for that attribute in rela-tion to all the other people in the population.

On the latter point you can say, for example, that someone with an intel-ligence test score of 116 is in the top 16% of the the US population for intel-ligence measured this way, or that 84% of the US population are less intelligent than him or her, or that he or she is more intelligent than, roughly 202 million other US citizens and less intelligent than 38 million others. This is what makes normed and standardized tests so attractive for educational and vocational selection purposes.

Very little adjustment to the measurement instrument would be necessary if you wanted a normal distribution curve to derive from measuring (say) the heights of a random sample of males aged 18 years + in the South East of England. But a considerable amount of item swapping, and weighting of the item scores is required to create an intelligence test which generates data in the form of a normal distribution. It is sometimes claimed that intelligence itself is normally distributed within large populations, as is height, or weight (Hernstein and Murray 1996). But this is a cogent claim only if we accept a circular, truistic and instrumentalist definition of intelligence as that which is measured by intelligence tests. We only know about the distribution of intel-ligence *test scores* and this distribution is the result of lots of busy work dedi-cated to mapping them into a bell curve shape.

Problems with norming

There are several problems associated with norming:

- Using instruments with inappropriate norms
- Issues of culture and gender fairness
- The aging of norms.

Inappropriate norms

This is no fault of norming but refers to the use by researchers of normed tests with groups for whom there are no norms, or their assumption that the norms of the criterion population would be valid for some other population. Some major examples of this include the use in the Third World of weight gain standards in child development research and adult height and weight indices developed in America or Europe, or intelligence tests which are normed on US populations and used in the UK or Europe and so on. The WHO *Angina* questionnaire (see p. 42 and Chapter 10, Section 10.4) was normed on a mainly white sample and is less efficient in detecting heart problems with South Asian populations (Fischbaker *et al.* 2000).

Most intelligence tests have norms for different age groups, and most are produced for particular age bands. There have been few intelligence tests suitable for, and normed on, young children, except those designed specifically to diagnose learning difficulties and these have a very strong ceiling effect (see Panel 2.2). There has always been a temptation in research with younger children to use tests normed on older children. Panel 2.9 gives an example of the effects of using a test without appropriate norms. Many of the aptitude and

---

PANEL 2.9 *Pygmalion in the classroom*: an example of using a test without appropriate norms

Rosenthal and Jacobson's Pygmalion experiment (1968, 1992) is widely quoted by people who have evidently never read the original and do not know how flimsy it is as a piece of research. The study purports to show the influence of teachers' (unjustified) expectations on pupils' intellectual development. The teachers were (allegedly) persuaded that some children would bloom intellectually in the future, and others would not. To measure the effect of teachers' expectations it was important to have a base-line measure of ability to begin with. For this, Rosenthal and Jacobson used a paper and pencil intelligence test. There were no norms for the youngest children for this test. This being so it was impossible to score the test according to the originators' instructions. It is far from clear how Rosenthal and Jacobson actually did derive base-line scores for these younger children. It appears that some of them scored hardly any marks at the outset. At that point some would probably have had a difficulty in holding a pencil and would have been unable able to follow the instructions. Not surprisingly, after some months when they were re-tested they had made large gains in 'intelligence'. In fact those who had been bogusly expected to bloom did make greater gains on average than those who had not been so predicted. But since we do not know how to interpret the initial scores it is difficult to know how to interpret this. Such gains were confined to the younger children who had been subjected to an inappropriate test of intelligence, and did not show among the older ones. Attempts to replicate the findings have never been successful and would today be ruled out as unethical (Chapter 16). Jussim and Harber in their review of the large literature on this topic (2005), conclude that teacher expectation effects (enhancing or depressing performance) are typically small and rarely persistent.

personality tests used for vocational recruitment are normed, but are often normed on criterion groups which are different from those an employer is recruiting.

Culture and gender fairness

Norming allows for direct comparisons between individuals in terms of scores on the same instrument. If the normed instrument assumes a certain corpus of cultural knowledge it is unlikely that everyone in the population will possess this to the same degree. This means that sub-groups within the population may then show distributions of scores widely different from the majority; perhaps with a higher mean, or a lower one. This is hardly a problem if the objective is to measure some knowledge or aptitude assumed to be culturally distributed. There would be nothing 'unfair' about an instrument that showed that, say, refugees from a non-English-speaking country scored less well on items assuming knowledge of the English language. By contrast, if the instrument is supposed to be measuring attributes which are independent of cultural experience then a finding that, say, these refugees were 'less intelligent' than their English counterparts might lead to inequities if, in fact their scores were determined in large part by their poor command of the English language. To address this problem there have been many attempts to construct 'culture-fair' aptitude and intelligence tests (see Panel 2.10) including culture-fair driving tests (Elkin *et al.* 2007).

PANEL 2.10 Culture-fair instruments

A culture-fair instrument would be one where cultural differences, *if they should be irrelevant*, would *not* influence the results. Three kinds of issues have given rise to attempts to create culture-fair instruments:

- **Where the measurement process is supposed to be uncontaminated by cultural differences (even though what is being measured may differ between people because of cultural differences).** Most careful researchers try to avoid concepts and vocabularies which would be unfamiliar to some respondents, or use translations or interpreters (see also Chapter 10) or, in the last resort, are careful what they claim in the face of cultural heterogeneity.
- **Where what is being measured is assumed to be independent of cultural differences although the way it is expressed is mediated by cultural factors.** Pain might be an example, or emotion at the level of neurotransmitter chemicals in the brain. In both cases the picture is of something 'real and underlying', which is expressed in a 'distorted' way via a cultural medium. Here a culture-fair instrument would be one which was able, as it were, to strip the culture off of the underlying entity. This assumption is made by some psychometricians with regard to intelligence. Culture-fair tests in intelligence have mainly been in the form of symbols to select between (Ravens Progressive Matrices and other non-verbal reasoning tests) and avoiding all but minimal written or spoken instructions.

- **Where a standard of excellence, or of undesireability which belongs to one cultural group is used as a standard against which to judge others.** For example, it is claimed that the items included in intelligence tests assume a kind of intelligence most valued and more abundantly possessed by white, middle-class Euro-American males. As Gladwin (1971) argued, if they adopted a standard more appropriate for Polynesian Islanders, tests would include items such as how to navigate canoes accurately across hundreds of miles of ocean without navigation aids. Then white middle-class Euro-American males probably wouldn't look so intelligent.

In narrow terms, for the researcher, the problem of cultural bias built into instruments is a problem of inaccuracy – of construct validity. But where the results of using such instrument determine people's life chances or reputations it becomes an important social and political problem which raises ethical issues for researchers (see Chapter 16). Cultural bias in intelligence and other aptitude tests has been an important legal issue in the US (www.fairtest.org).

Mutatis mutandis the remarks in Panel 2.10 apply to gender bias and gender-fair instruments. Issues of culture or gender fairness are not confined to normed instruments, but they tend to be more pernicious where something which is assumed to be the norm in fact is not so.

The aging of norming

It was said above that a score on a normed and standardized test would enable someone to be placed in relation to everyone else 'in the population'. But that population was the criterion population on which the test was normed. The current population may have a different distribution of the feature of interest. The best example of this is the so-called *Flynn Effect* (Flynn 1999). Average intelligence scores on instruments such as the Stanford–Binet, in English-speaking countries, have risen year by year over the 100-year period of intelligence testing, at a rate of about three points per decade. These days, people are on average 30 points 'cleverer' than were people of their age in 1906. Thirty points on an intelligence scale is actually a huge difference: two standard deviations (Panel 2.8). This is not apparent, because intelligence test producers re-norm the test from time to time, reset-ting the average back to 100. It is probable that Flynn-type effects also occur with other measured phenomena such as personality, and certainly attitude, so it is important that if researchers utilize normed tests, they should utilize *recently* normed ones. Of course, the results from instruments normed at an earlier date can be interesting in their own right. For example in studying obesity, normed measures of weight in the past allow for direct comparisons with today's normed measures. The Flynn effect itself is another example.

The aging of the vocabulary of an instrument is a different kind of prob-lem. It happens particularly if attempts are made to make the vocabulary colloquial and 'user-friendly' (see Chapter 10, Section 10.4).

ACTIVITY   A truancy counter

For this activity try devising an instrument which could be used within a school to measure the extent of truancy, and could be used in the same way in many schools to facilitate comparison between them.

Truancy is not absence from school, but *unauthorized* absence from school. You will have to devise a definition of truancy which equates with your construct of this idea, and which could be translated into a set of instructions for school staff to follow in recording all instances of truancy and only truancy as you have defined it. When you have devised the instrument, run it past Table 2.5 to consider what tests for validity and reliability would be appropriate, and how well your instrument would survive them.

A measure of truancy is used as part of the performance management framework for schools in England. You might like to look at the definition and the results on the Children Schools and Families web site (www.dcsf.gov.uk/ performancetables/).

Further reading

As a practical and comprehensive text on designing social science research instruments try Colton and Court (2007), and for psychological tests in particular Kline (2005).

For instruments used in health studies, the two volumes by Ann Bowling (2007a, 2007b) can't be bettered. The National Foundation for Educational Research (NFER) is the major source of instruments used in educational research in the UK (www.nfer-nelson.co.uk) and their site carries information about test construction: about age-standardization, for example. There are hundreds of web sites on personality and aptitude tests, many of them of doubtful quality. The British Psychological Society website has a general introduction to personality testing (www.bps.ac.uk).

Repositories of questionnaires used in previous surveys are given in the *Further reading* for Chapter 10 (pp. 237–8).

Instruments used by UK government researchers are usually meticulously reported, along with details of the way they have been tested (www.statistics. gov.uk/). By contrast with the excellence of government research, government administrative data often leaves much to be desired (see Chapter 9).

The statistical aspects of instrument design are covered in the first two books listed in this section. In addition there are statistics resources listed in the *Further reading* for Chapter 3. Specifically on factor analysis there is Child (2006) which has a linked web site for practising factor analysis, but to use the book fully you need access to the SPSS statistics package. As an alternative, Kline (1993) has stood the test of time well as a relatively simple introduction which is not mathematically very demanding.

3 Controlled Experiments

By the end of this chapter, you will:

- Have an understanding of the way controlled experiments are designed to answer questions about cause and effect by attempting to exclude all those factors which might affect the results, except those of interest
- Be able to list and explain the various kinds of safeguards against confounding which can be built into the design of a controlled experiment, and explain the kinds of problems which might arise if these safeguards are absent or fail
- Know the dangers of bias on behalf of researchers or subjects affecting the results of research
- Understand the problem of external validity for controlled experiments.

And you will know the meaning of the following terms:

Blinding • confounding • control • control group • expectancy effect (experimenter effect, Rosenthal effect) • experimental group • external validity • factorial design • generalizability (or transferability) • internal validity • matched-pairs • placebo • precision-matching • pre-post-test without controls • random allocation • replicability • significant and non-significant results • statistical control • subject reactivity, halo or Hawthorne effect.

At the end of the chapter there is an Activity which will test your understanding about the design of controlled experiments.

3.1 Introduction

Controlled experiments have often been conducted by psychologists but, since the Second World War, rarely by sociologists. But there is a very large demand these days for sociologists to conduct controlled experiments in evaluating the effectiveness of practice in fields such as medicine, nursing, education or criminal justice (see Chapter 4, Section 4.4; Chapter 14, Section 14.8; Chapter 15, Sections 15.1–15.3). By carefully looking at the design of controlled experiments, researchers can understand what is necessary to achieve by other means when controlled experiments are impossible to conduct. The chapter title is a give-away. When studying causality researchers need to be able to achieve **control**. Throughout this

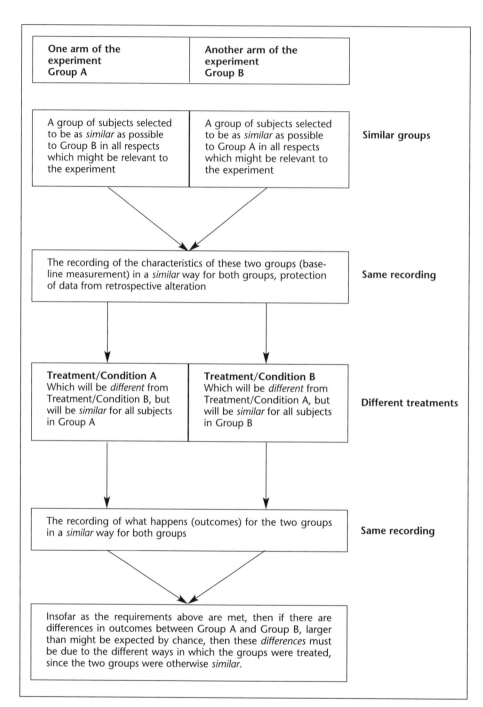

FIGURE 3.1   *The basic structure of a controlled experiment with similar subjects experiencing*
different treatments or conditions

book you will find examples of non-experimental ways of doing this, or of problems which arise when researchers fail adequately to control what they are studying.

The controlled experiment is the most powerful research design for investigating what can cause what to happen. This is because controlled experiments go a long way to solving a major problem in studying cause and effect. This is the problem that everything has a *multitude of causes*. The controlled experiment is a simplified working model of reality. It is designed as an attempt to fix most factors in place, to *control* them, while allowing just a few to vary.

Figure 3.1 gives a picture of the basic structure of a controlled experiment of the similar subjects, different-treatments kind. There is another basic format; a different-subjects, similar-treatments kind which is illustrated in Chapter 4, Figure 4.1.

Figure 3.1 shows the practical problems the experimenter has to solve. The experimenter has to:

- Create two or more comparison groups of people who are similar in all respects which might be relevant to the experiment
- Make sure that all the subjects are treated the same, except in the ways in which they are supposed to be treated differently
- Ensure that the same observations are made of each subject in the experiment in the same way, at least before (pre-) and after (post-).

This list hints at what can go wrong in a controlled experiment. Each of these topics is dealt with in detail in this chapter.

In all research designs, doing one thing well usually means doing something else badly. The well-designed controlled experiment is a splendid way of demonstrating clearly what caused what *under experimental conditions*. But experimental conditions are usually a gross over-simplification of what happens under real-life circumstances. This means that experimental results may not be very enlightening as to what actually happens in the real world. This problem of the **external validity** of experiments is dealt with in Section 3.10 and again in Chapter 4 and Chapter 15, and in a different way in Chapter 5.

3.2 Avoiding confounding

At the end of an experiment there will be a set of results. Imagine, for example, that the experiment involved giving a programme of anti-smoking education to one group of pupils (the experimental or treatment group) and no such programme to another (the control group). And imagine that two years later more pupils in the control group reported that they smoked. It would be tempting to conclude that the anti-smoking education had been successful. But that conclusion would be premature before making a careful check on the design and the execution of the experiment. Many other things might have caused the differences in the result, apart from having or not having experienced the anti-smoking education. **Confounding** means

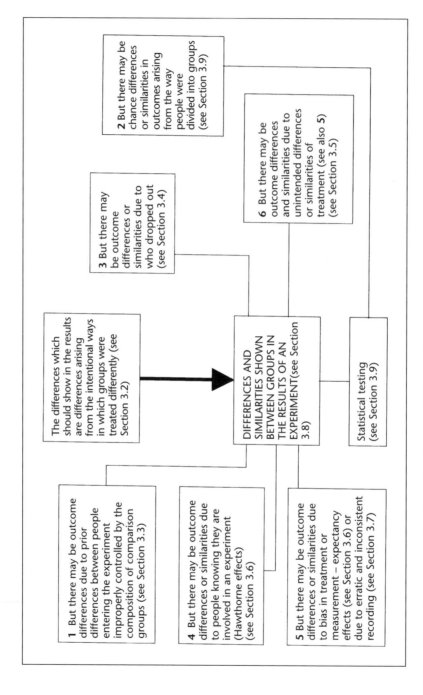

FIGURE 3.2   *The main sources of confounding in controlled experiments*

Source: Based on Gomm (2000a).

drawing the wrong conclusion about the causes of experimental results. It might have been that the pupils who experienced the anti-smoking education were, at the outset, different in important ways from those who did not; less pre-disposed to smoke anyway. Or it might be that something which was happening at the same time as the anti-smoking education, or in the two years after it, influenced one group to smoke more than the other. If either were so then this would confound the results and it would be mistaken to attribute the difference in smoking habits two years later, to the differences in educational treatments.

Figure 3.2 shows the main ways in which the results of experiments can be confounded. In a perfectly conducted experiment the only differences in the results should be those created by treating the subjects differently in the way they should have been treated differently, plus some differences attributable to the play of chance. But no experiments are perfect. You can regard Figure 3.2 as a kind of fault-checker. If you were designing an experiment you should ask 'have I excluded the possibility of that kind of thing happening – 1, 2, 3, 4, 5 and 6?' And if you are reading about someone else's experiment you should ask 'Did they take adequate means to prevent confounding of these kinds?' The remainder of this chapter explains each of the items in Figure 3.2.

3.3 Creating comparison groups to control prior differences between subjects (Figure 3.2, box 1)

It can sometimes appear that the experimental conditions or treatment have had an effect, when really what is being shown is that the people who received one treatment were already different from those who received another. Hence experimenters should arrange things so that people who are going to be treated differently in the experiment are otherwise as similar as possible to each other. This doesn't mean that everyone in an experiment has to be similar to everyone else. It does mean creating groups which *as groups* are similar to each other: for example, that, as groups, they have a similar age profile, ethnic mix, gender ratio, similar mix of educational backgrounds and such like. What is being referred to here is creating 'Group A' and 'Group B' in terms of Figure 3.1, or as many different groups (or 'arms') as the experiment requires. Creating comparison groups can be done in a number of different ways, as described below.

Random allocation to comparison groups

In psychology, and often in medicine, experiments using random allocation are called 'true experiments' and experiments using other means of creating comparison groups are called 'quasi-experiments'. The use of the term 'true' is a mark of how much randomization is valued as a technique. Most experimental research used in testing medical treatments for their effectiveness takes the form of 'randomized controlled trials'. 'Trial' is just another word for an experiment. Putting everyone's name on a card, shuffling the pack and then dealing into two piles is a common way of creating two groups at random.

Why not divide subjects by using what is known about them? The answer is that random allocation gives a better chance that the groups created will be similar for both known *and* unknown characteristics. It would be extremely easy to sort a deck of playing cards into two very similar piles on the basis of their suits and denominations – their known characteristics. But the resulting piles might still be very different in terms of the numbers of dog-eared cards in each, or in terms of the density of finger prints. In experiments with people the important characteristics are often difficult to find out about. For example, people respond differently to the situation of being involved in an experiment, and it is virtually impossible to know these differences in advance. Randomization gives a good chance that for each person who will respond to being an experimental subject in a particular way in one group, there will be a matching person in the other group.

But randomization will work to create similar groups only if the groups are large enough. An *appropriate sample size* for experiments is a complicated issue. It depends on, among other things, how many different characteristics there are which people can have which might influence the results of the experiment, apart from the different treatments they receive. These are the factors which have to be distributed evenly between the groups. Think again of a pack of cards.

If you were interested only in creating two piles each with similar numbers of reds and blacks, then randomly dealing two piles of 10 would give you a good chance of achieving something close to this. But if you were interested in creating two piles with similar numbers of each denomination, then, since there are 13 denominations, two piles of 26 would be too small to do this reliably with a random deal. You will often read that two groups of 20 is around the minimum size for experiments with people. But people are enormously diverse, and some at least of this diversity is likely to be relevant to the experiment. Bald claims that two groups of 20 is enough should be regarded with suspicion.

The cost and effort of conducting an experiment is proportional to the number of subjects involved, so there are strong pressures to use small samples. And there is another way round the problem. If the diversity among people suggests that large and expensive samples are needed, then this can be dealt with by starting with a pool of subjects who are already very similar to each other; thus reducing the sample size needed. For example, biomedical and psychological research with animals usually starts with animals bred to be genetically very similar to each other and raised in very similar conditions. Such researchers still randomize the animals to comparison groups, but the randomization is just balancing out the groups for some rather small differences between animals. Again, in medical research with humans, it is typical to start the experiment with a pool of subjects who are already very similar – for example, of a single gender, within a limited age-range and excluding anyone who has complicating medical conditions. Restricting the diversity in this way solves one problem, but creates another. If the experiment has been conducted with a very narrow range of people, this raises a question about whether the results can be applied to a wider range of people. This is just an aspect of the problem of drawing general conclusions from experimental results, which will be discussed further in Section 3.10 and Chapter 4.

In a meta-analysis (Chapter 15, Section 15.3) of RCTs Schultz and his colleagues (1995) found that failure to randomize adequately can inflate outcome differences between groups, spuriously, by up to 40%. Apart from being an effective means for creating similar groups, randomization has another advantage. Random allocation is automatically *blind* allocation. It means that neither the researcher nor the subjects can influence which subject belongs to which group. Blinding is discussed in Section 3.6. The ethics of randomization is discussed in Chapter 16, Section 16.4.

Alternatives to randomization in creating comparison groups

Intuitively, the most appealing way of creating comparison groups perhaps is a *matched-pairs* design. Here, subjects for the experiment are sorted into pairs, each pair containing two people who are as alike as possible: same age, same gender, same ethnic group and so on. Then members of each pair would be assigned to a different comparison group: perhaps by tossing a coin. This would be called **quasi-randomization**. A matched-pairs design takes a great deal of initial preparation, and may turn out to be a rather messy business with many subjects not finding a match and having to be excluded from the experiment. This creates the same kind of problem as that created by starting with a rather homogeneous pool of subjects for randomization (see above and Section 3.10). In fact for most experiments it is not necessary to match individual by individual. It is usually enough to create two groups with similar profiles for the relevant factors, such as age, gender and so on. Compared with random allocation, matching on the basis of *known characteristics*, or **precision-matching** as it is sometimes called, can produce a better match between the two groups for the characteristics which were used as criteria for selection, but at the cost of producing a worse match between groups for other characteristics.

Sometimes experimenters depart from the simple structure shown in Figure 3.1, by using a **factorial design**. For example, they might not only be interested in the differences caused by treating or not treating, educating or not educating or such like, but also particularly interested in gender differences. In this case a factorial design would mean four comparison groups at minimum: males treated, males untreated, females treated, females untreated. For this purpose it would be necessary to make sure that there were sufficient numbers in each gender. In practical terms all this means is running two experiments together on the Figure 3.1 design, one for males and one for females, using whatever technique is most appropriate or convenient for creating the four groups. Thus the number of males and the number of females would be pre-decided and not left to chance.

There are circumstances in which experimenters cannot organize subjects into comparison groups, but have to use ready-made groups instead. Someone doing experimental research on teaching programmes in schools is unlikely to be able to reorganize the system of school classes. Then the best which can be done will be to select two classes which seem to be composed of similar pupils, and give the educational programme to one of them, and not to the other. If the interest were in whole-school initiative – a multicultural programme, for example – then the experimenter would have to look for two different schools similar to each other, one to implement and the other not to implement the programme. Here we are sliding down a slope. At the top there are the very strong means of controlling the composition of comparison groups via random allocation or matched-pairs designs. Here there is a good chance of creating groups of people similar in all respects relevant to the experiment, and hence of excluding prior differences between the groups from contaminating the experimental results. Selecting two pre-existing school classes for the experiment is a much weaker form of control because there are likely to be some very real prior differences even between school classes which look very similar. There are likely to be even bigger uncontrolled differences between whole schools. An even weaker form of control is sometimes used by health education and mass media researchers where what are compared are the populations of geographical areas – for example, one area which has been targeted for a coronary health campaign (the experimental or campaign area) and another which has not been so targeted (the control area or the reference area) (Tudor Smith *et al.* 1998). Usually this kind of experiment involves a social survey to collect information about health attitudes and behaviours before and after the campaign (see Chapter 6) but the approach is experimental nonetheless. At the bottom of the slope are experiments without comparison groups at all, where something is done to everyone and any change is attributed to what was done to them: so-called **pre-post-test studies without controls**.

There are very good practical reasons why experimental researchers sometimes have to use weaker forms of control at the subject level than those which would be ideal. The important point is that the weaker the form of control used, the more difficult it will be to be confident that differences in outcomes between groups were caused by the different ways in which the groups were treated. In the case of pre-post test studies without controls very little confidence can be had in claims that what was done to the subjects is what caused any changes recorded thereafter.

3.4   Refusals and drop-outs (Figure 3.2, box 3)

An experimenter might be successful at the outset in selecting two or more groups of people similar in ways relevant to the experiment. But some of these may refuse to participate. Some may drop out before the experiment is completed. If people refused or dropped out at random, and in more or less equal numbers from each group, this would not be a problem until there were so few left that no sensible comments could be made about the results. But if the non-participants from one group are different types of people as compared with non-participants from the other, then two groups initially composed to be similar will cease to be so. Thus what look like differences in outcomes caused by differences in treatment may actually be differences caused by differences in the pattern of refusals and drop-outs as between comparison groups.

The problem of initial refusal can be managed to some extent by trying to make sure that people will participate *before* allocating them to groups. That has a downside. It has often been commented that most of the knowledge derived from experimental research relates to the kinds of people who are willing to co-operate with experimenters and leaves us bereft of knowledge about other kinds of people (Suls and Rostow 1988). There are also problems in using incentives to encourage people to participate. Both these latter problems are about the extent to which the results of an experiment can be generalized to other groups of people under non-experimental conditions (see Section 3.10). For example, being paid to participate or being treated as a very important person in an experiment testing a medical treatment may be very different from receiving the same medical treatment in routine general practice.

Among other things, non-participation rates will depend on both the unpleasantness and inconvenience of participation and on the duration of the experiment. Many psychological experiments have durations of a few minutes and can be quite fun and have low drop-out rates. Some experiments designed to test the effectiveness of different forms of criminal rehabilitation can last for years, involve people whose life circumstances are very difficult and may have high drop-out rates. Where there is a reasonable expectation that the drop-out rate will be high, an experimenter will recruit a larger sample to start with. But this solves only the problem of numbers becoming too small, and not the problem of differential non-participation skewing the results. In medical research, in particular, analysis may be on an 'intention to treat' basis. That is to say, even if someone dropped out they remain part of the '100%' for their arm of the experiment.

Experimenters will usually do all they can to reduce refusal and drop-out rates, but they will usually have to fall back on statistical control rather than experimental control. Exerting experimental control means organizing people and the environment so that some things are more likely to happen than others. By contrast, exerting statistical control entails making it possible to analyse the data in an attempt to work out what has happened. Statistical control is dealt with in more detail in Chapter 7. With regard to refusals and drop-outs it is important that there is as much detailed information as possible about each subject *before* the experiment starts and, if possible, data about each subject at various points as it proceeds. This is, first, a cross-check that the comparison groups were indeed similar at the outset, or a warning of important ways in which they were not so. And, second, should people refuse or drop out, what kinds of people they were will be known and this can be taken into consideration in interpreting the results of the experiment.

Non-participation is not all a problem. Sometimes it can be regarded as an experimental result. If far more people drop out of the experimental than the control arm, then that is usually an indication that people find the experimental conditions unpleasant. That may be worth knowing. In some research in community mental health, the object of the research is to discover which kind of service is better at keeping clients 'engaged'. Here difference in drop-out rates between groups is an outcome measure rather than an experimental problem.

3.5 Controlling the experimental situation (Figure 3.2, box 6)

The purpose of controlling the experimental situation is to attempt to ensure that the only differences experienced by the subjects of the experiment are the differences which have been planned for – or, at least, are differences which the experimenter knows about; sometimes this is termed '**fidelity** to the protocol'. Many psychological experiments are brief in duration and it is relatively easy to standardize the experience of subjects where it should be the same, and vary it only where it ought to be varied. Thus is it can be arranged that all subjects meet the same experimenter in the same room and that all those in the same comparison group are subjected to the same set of tasks and given the same standard instructions, perhaps on paper or on audio-tape to minimize differences. It might be worthwhile video-taping the experiment, and then viewing a sample to make sure that the experimenter didn't behave differently to people in different comparison groups in ways other than planned for. It can also be arranged that meetings between the experimenter and the subjects occur so that meetings for members of the two groups are timetabled through the day in the same pattern, and both groups have appointments spread throughout the week. The art of control here lies in drawing on other research, or in making informed guesses as to what might produce the kinds differences which the experimenter wants to exclude.

The limits of experimental control

Even in the kind of situation described above, the experimenter can't control what happened to a subject the previous night or on the bus on the way to the laboratory. With many experiments running over a long period of time, most of the time what happens to subjects is outside of the control of the experimenter, but might still influence the results. If the composition of the comparison groups is similar, and the groups are large enough, then there is a good chance that what happens to someone in one group outside the experimenter's control will be matched by something with a similar effect happening to someone else in the other group – similar things tend to happen to similar people. But experimenters cannot put too much faith in this assumption. A particular difficulty arises where the experiment requires the subjects to do something themselves beyond the observation of the experimenter. Experiments involving diet, for example, rely on subjects sticking to their diets. Putting the results of many dietary experiments together in a systematic review (Chapter 15) shows that diets which are effective when dieting occurs in residential institutions are less so when dieting occurs at home (*Effective Health Care* 1998). The obvious interpretation of this is that many people living at home and involved in dietary experiments don't stick to their dietary regime, while those in residential institutions have less opportunity to cheat. One of the ways in which experimenters attempt to deal with matters which are outside their control is to collect data about such events. In long-running experiments it is common for subjects to complete questionnaires each time they meet the experimenter, detailing what has happened to them in the interim, or sometimes subjects are asked to keep diaries. Both, however, rely on the honesty of the subject. For the diet experiments, not only do many people cheat, many of them almost certainly lie as well.

In the paragraph above you will see something of a dilemma. Controlling people's behaviour and environment in a detailed way gives the experimenter a good chance of isolating causal mechanisms. But doing this creates very unusual circumstances. And each step towards more natural circumstances involves a loss of experimental control and a lowering of confidence in the experimental results. There is also a problem of whether it is wise to believe what people say. This is discussed in more detail in Chapters 5, 6, 9, 10 and 11.

Simple and complex experimental treatments

There are some experimental treatments where it is easy for the experimenter to say 'this is exactly what we did and we did it in exactly the same way each time'. Perhaps the simplest example is where the experiment consists in giving one group of people an active pharmaceutical and another group a pill of an inert substance looking exactly the same – a **placebo**. Actually this isn't quite as simple as it looks since the effect of a medicine may depend on who gives it, how, in what location and when (Moerman 2002). Even the simplest experimental treatments are more complicated than they look at first sight. But there is no doubt that giving someone a medication is a much simpler matter than, say, giving someone a course of counselling, or teaching an educational programme, or setting up property marking projects (see Chapter 4, Section 4.6).

There are two issues here. The first is about treating experimental subjects the same where they should be treated the same and differently where they should be treated differently. There are few inherent problems with simple treatments. But consider a fairly common kind of experiment designed to test whether one kind of psychotherapy is more effective than another, or whether one kind of social work intervention has better results than another. It is in the nature of psychotherapy or social work that what is done is customized to the particularities of each client. Thus it is possible that some clients in the experiment receiving psychotherapy 'Type A' received something very like psychotherapy 'Type B' and vice versa: that there was, on the one hand, much diversity of treatment *within* arms of the experiment and, on the other hand, many similarities of treatment *between* arms of the experiment. In terms of Figure 3.1 this garbles the experiment because what should have been different was not different and what should have been the same was not the same. If this happens, whatever the results they will be impossible to interpret correctly in terms of their being the effects of differences between treatment A and treatment B. In fact most of the experimental research on different kinds of psychotherapy, counselling or social work shows no difference in effectiveness between different kinds (Oakley and Fullerton 1996). This may be because in these experiments the subjects were not actually receiving distinctively different treatments. It might equally be that for these kinds of interventions what is important is not the technique used but something else, such as the demeanour of the practitioner or the rapport between practitioner and client, which isn't specific to an intervention with a particular name. Or it may be that none of the treatments has much greater effect than leaving people to their own devices. But the very complexity of these procedures, and their non-standardized nature, makes it very difficult to resolve this issue. This is a limitation of experimental method, but more so of research in general, because there really is no other kind of research design which would answer questions about the effectiveness of counselling or social work better than an experimental approach could do so (Oakley 2000).

The second issue about complex treatments relates to how an experimenter communicates results. In principle experimental research should be **replicable**. It should be possible for someone to read an experimental research report and repeat the experiment to see whether similar results can be obtained a second time. In practice, experimental researchers do often repeat their own experiments many times. In medical research replication by others is required before a drug is given a licence, but outside this field exact replication is rare. There are more career rewards in producing original work than in checking someone else's work by repeating it. Nonetheless, researchers reading each others' research reports do conduct a sort of replication as a thought experiment and, for this, it is important for them to know exactly what was done to produce the reported results.

Where an experiment features a complex treatment, and especially one which is varied to take account of the differences between individual subjects, it is very difficult for researchers to convey precisely what was done. This becomes an additional problem where the research has a practical application. For example, an experiment showing that 'counselling' was an effective way of reducing criminal recidivism is of not much practical use if the researcher cannot describe in what 'counselling' consisted. Without this, it will be impossible for anyone to do 'the same thing' in order to produce the same results. Similarly, where attempts are made to synthesize the results of different experiments which seem to be addressed to the same question, difficulties arise if it is not precisely clear what happened to the subjects in each of the experiments, as is often the case with complex treatments. Then it may be unclear whether any differences in results were due to differences *between* the experiments in the way the subjects were treated or to some other factor(s). Research syntheses are discussed further in Chapter 15.

In the literature of health, social welfare and education the term 'complex treatment', means more or less what was described above. In science in general however, 'complex' means more than just complicated and refers to the dynamics of interaction between variables. While those who conduct controlled experiments usually assume that similar results will arise from the same intervention under the same circumstances, complexity theorists argue that even tiny differences can cause radically different outcomes. This is discussed further in Chapter 5.

3.6   Expectations, bias and blinding

Expectancy effects (Figure 3.2, box 5)

Much research is conducted under circumstances where there are career rewards for results coming out one way rather than another, and there is a general bias against inconclusive results. There is a general tendency among human being for being rather bad at making accurate judgements and tending to resolve ambiguities in the direction of their desires or their expectations (Gilovich, Griffith and Kahneman 2002), and there is substantial research evidence that what experimenters expect to happen can influence the outcomes of experiments, and so also can what they would prefer to happen. This is sometimes called an **expectancy effect**, sometimes an **experimenter effect** and sometimes a **Rosenthal effect**, after Robert Rosenthal, who conducted pioneering research in this area (Rosenthal 1966; Rosenthal and Rosnow 1969; Rosenthal and Rubin 1978). All three terms mean the same. 'Expectancy effect' has the merits of saying what it means and of being applicable to any kind of research.

There are three main ways in which expectancy effects can confound the results of an experiment. The first is by fraud. Outright fraud is usually described as something different from an expectancy effect. But it is very difficult to make a sharp distinction between someone who sets out to mislead other people, and someone who so wants to produce results of a particular kind that they mislead themselves; self-delusion is certainly a basis for expectancy effects. Whether by intention or self-delusion, fraud is fairly common in scientific research (Broad and Wade 1982), including medical research (*British Medical Journal* 1998). Some researchers simply invent experiments they never conducted, or invent different results for experiments they have conducted. But without going to these lengths it is very easy for a researcher to produce the results he or she wants simply by 'losing' the data for the subjects which skew the results in the 'wrong' direction.

Most fraud reported comes from experimental research. But this gives a misleading picture. First, the areas where the rewards, and the temptations, are greatest are those where experimental research is the most common kind: in medicine, armaments and high-technology applications. Second, it is in experimental research that fraud is most easily detected. This brings us back to the idea of replication. Only if a piece of research is capable of being replicated is it easy to detect fraudulent work. For this reason, if the research is on an important topic, and experimental in kind, the fraud will usually be detected, sooner or later, or the research written off as being wrong for some other reason. Fraud may or may not be widespread in kinds of research other than experimental work but if it is, it is difficult to detect. In a paradoxical sense we should perhaps regard experimental research with more confidence than other kinds precisely because it gives rise to most of the scandals.

The second way in which an expectancy effect can operate is through experimenters inadvertently treating subjects in a way that influences subject responses to produce the results the experimenter expects or wants. One of Rosenthal's best-known experiments on experiments involved telling one group of postgraduate students that the rats they were to train were particularly intelligent, and telling another group that their rats were particularly stupid. In fact all the rats were randomly selected from the same batch (Rosenthal and Fode 1963). The result was that the allegedly intelligent rats, apparently, learned their tasks more quickly than the allegedly stupid ones. It appears that one of the ways that this expectancy effect operated was through the different ways in which the experimenters handled their rats: the 'clever' rats receiving more fondling and were spoken to more. It is not too difficult to imagine that in experiments involving human subjects experimenters' desires and expectations might lead them to treat people in one comparison group differently from those in another, provoking different responses, and thus influencing the results.

In their review of Rosenthal's work, Barber and Silver (1968) suggest that the most important route taken by expectancy effects is not through experimenters influencing the behaviour of experimental subjects, but through biased observation, interpretation and recording. In the experiment above, for example, the experimenters with the 'clever rats' were more likely to regard errors made by the rats as 'false starts', which they didn't record, while those with the 'stupid rats' were more likely to record such errors to stand as evidence of the rats' stupidity. And in other of Rosenthal's experiments there are many examples of experimenters using their discretion in what to record, or how to measure, what statistical test to use and so on, and thus tilting the results one way or another. Panel 4.1 in Chapter 4 lists the conditions under which expectancy effects are most likely to influence results.

Subject reactivity, or Hawthorne effects (Figure 3.2, box 4)

The story usually goes that research conducted in the Hawthorne works of the Bell Telephone Company (Roeslisberger and Dickson 1939) showed that if people know they are subjects of an experiment they will behave differently from normal in such a way as to produce results which would not occur under non-experimental conditions: hence the term **Hawthorne effect**. In fact subsequent re-analysis has demonstrated that the Hawthorne effect was not an important factor in producing the results of the Hawthorne experiments (Franke and Kaul 1978; Gillespie 1991; Jones 1992). It is a tribute to the experimenters that their recording of these large-scale experiments was so thorough that it was possible for other researchers to re-analyse the results to show that the Hawthorne effect was a misnomer.

But misnomer or not, the Hawthorne effect certainly operates sometimes. Experimental subjects do get enthusiastic about being experimental subjects, and sometimes they would prefer the results to come out one way or another. For example, in experiments on para-psychology, complementary medicine, or gender differences it is to be expected that some subjects will be far from neutral. In experimental situations in health and social services, some of the subjects are practitioners who are pleased to be involved in piloting a new form of service. Their enthusiasm for being involved is likely to have an effect independent of whatever the treatment is. '*Halo effect*' is sometimes used as an alternative term where enthusiasm influences subjects' behaviour.

Hawthorne effects may sometimes operate equally across all comparison groups in the experiment. In this case any differences shown in the results will be 'net' of the Hawthorne effect and may really derive from the differences in the way the two groups were treated, just as the experimenter intended. Here there is only a problem of external generalizability. That is a problem that what happened in the experiment may not happen under non-experimental conditions, because under non-experimental conditions people won't feel important and involved (or afraid and alienated) as they did in the experiment (see Section 3.10). But sometimes a Hawthorne effect might affect subjects in only one arm of the experiment. This is particularly likely when one group gets treated in a way that is new and interesting, and another group gets treated in the same boring old way as usual. In this case it is possible that any difference in results between the two groups will be caused by the novelty of one of the treatments, rather than by the treatment itself, and that any or a wide range of novelties would have had the same effect. Here there will be both a problem of external generalizability and a problem of confounding a Hawthorne effect with a treatment effect. Lopsided Hawthorne effects of this sort seem to be particularly common in experiments, and in other research, in the health, welfare, education and criminal justice fields (Chapter 4, Section 4.4).

Blinding

Blinding is the main form of defence against the biases of researchers or of research subjects influencing results in an untoward way. This rather unfortunate term means depriving subjects and or researchers of knowledge which, if they had it, might allow them to influence the experiment to give misleading results. If Rosenthal's students had not been told their rats were intelligent or stupid, this knowledge could not have influenced the results. The term '*double-blinded*' means that both subjects and researchers are deprived of some knowledge. Further than this the term doesn't mean much because it doesn't say what knowledge is being hidden. Table 3.1 shows some forms of blinding and the problems which might arise if blinding is not practised.

The archetype of the double-blinded experiment is the randomized, double-blinded, placebo-controlled trial which is common in testing the effectiveness of pharmaceuticals. Here it is easy to hide to which group subjects have been allocated, since a dummy pill – the placebo – can be made to look, taste and smell exactly like the active drug being tested. The random allocation of subjects to comparison groups is likely to be done by an independent agency so that no one in contact with the patients, nor the patients themselves, know who is getting the drug and who the placebo. This is disclosed only at the end of the experiment, or earlier if there are worries about a particular patient's health. The fact that an experiment is going on is likely to be kept secret from all those caring for the patient except for those who actually need to know. In addition, it is possible that data will be recorded by an independent observer, who not only doesn't know which patient is in which group, but doesn't know which drug is being tested. The ethics of blind allocation are discussed in Chapter 16, Section 16.4.

Blinding to this extent is often impossible. For example, in an experiment about the effects of different styles of communication, the person doing the communicating has to know what kind of communication style to adopt with each subject. And each subject will know they are being communicated with – though since they probably won't know what it is like to be communicated with in the alternative way, they will be blind to this extent.

TABLE 3.1   Kinds of blinding in experimental research

Kinds of blinding	Subjects	Researchers
Blind to the fact of being involved in the experiment	It is usually considered unethical to involve people in experiments without their knowledge and consent (see Chapter 16), and this means that most experiments will be influenced by some degree of Hawthorne effect: people behaving differently because they know they are being researched	Researchers must know who is involved in an experiment
Blind to the purpose of the experiment	The more subjects know about the purpose of the experiment the more possible it will be for them deliberately or inadvertently to influence the results in untoward ways; many experiments in psychology depend on subjects being misled as to the purpose of the experiment: telling them this would often give the game away	Someone among researchers has to know the purpose of the experiment but sometimes the actual conduct of the research is left to someone who doesn't know what its purpose is; then it will be difficult for their expectancies to influence the results
Blind allocation to comparison groups (random allocation is one means of blind allocation: see Section 3.3)	If people can influence which group they belong to this is likely to create important differences between groups; if people know which group they belong to it will be possible for them deliberately or inadvertently to influence the results though their behaviour	If the researcher can choose who is allocated to which group, this presents an opportunity to bias the results through selection, or through influencing drop-out
Blind treatment	Knowing to which comparison group they belong may influence their behaviour; for example, they may believe in the efficacy of some educational or psychotherapeutic treatment and this belief may influence what happens to them	If researchers (or collaborators) know which subject is in which group this knowledge may affect the way they interact with subjects in different groups over and beyond the planned for differences in treatment
Blind recording or measurement of data	Insofar as reports from subjects provide data, subjects knowing which group they are in may influence the responses given	If researchers know which group each subject belongs to this may influence the way they collect and interpret information; using 'blind' independent recorders or judges is common in experimental research

Source: Based on Gomm (2000a: 53).

It may be possible to use independent recorders and observers, but it may not be possible to blind them to which subject is experiencing which set of conditions.

Researcher expectancy effects and subject reactive, or 'Hawthorne' effects can be very powerful forces in influencing the results of experiments – or, indeed, of other research. Where and to the extent that blinding can be used, it will limit the opportunities for the play of these effects. Where blinding is impossible, as it often is, it will be important to consider how these effects might have influenced the results and to interpret the results cautiously in the light of this.

3.7 Reliable observation, recording and measurement (Figure 3.2, box 5)

If different people are involved in collecting information they may interpret the task in different ways, so that for what is really the same situation, different recorders might record something different, or for what is a different situation, different recorders might record the same. This is often tested for using an inter-rater reliability test (Chapter 2, Section 2.10). Using well-designed data collection instruments leaving few opportunities for ambiguity, and training people to use them, is an important part of any experiment involving a number of different people collecting data. The same kind of data collection instrument will also reduce the possibility of the same observer changing the way he or she interprets observations over a period of time, or from case to case. Many experimenters use data collection instruments which have been widely used in the past, and tested for their criterion validity as described in Chapter 2, Section 2.7. This means that the instrument will have been de-bugged previously and if the same instrument is used in different research projects, the results will be directly comparable with each other and this will facilitate synthesis (Chapter 15).

In addition to consistency of recording, it is also important that early recordings are not changed retrospectively. This is the same principle as with police or medical records, for the purpose of preventing later events influencing the record of earlier ones.

3.8 The internal validity of an experiment

At the end of an experiment there will be some results. Either these will show a difference between the groups, or no difference between them. The results might be in terms of, say, percentages of each group re-offending – in an experiment on the rehabilitation of offenders – or percentages of people expressing racially prejudiced attitudes – in an experiment on the influence of some mass media exposure on attitudes – or differences in smoking behaviour – in an experimental evaluation of a health education programme. The experimenter will have tried to design the experiment so that the only factors which *could* cause such similarities or differences were the different ways in which the comparison groups were treated. If this has been successful the results can be regarded as internally valid. 'Valid' means that it is true that any difference in the results were caused by, and only by, the intended differences in treatment, or that any absence of difference in the results was caused by, and only by, the fact that the different treatments had similar effects. 'Internal' means that this is true for this experiment, and would probably be true if it were repeated in the same format. But nothing is being claimed about whether similar results would be obtained under different conditions.

Most of the chapter so far has been about threats to internal validity because, as shown in Figure 3.2, while the results might be due to the intended differences in treatment they might also derive from something about:

- Pre-existing differences between the comparison groups – box 1
- Differences created by the patterns of refusals and drop-outs – box 3
- Unintended differences of treatment – box 6
- Biases on behalf of researchers – box 5
- Subject reactions to being involved in an experiment, over and above their reactions to the experiences arranged for them – box 4
- Unreliable or inaccurate data collection and analysis – box 5.

Thus evaluating whether an experiment has achieved internal validity means judging whether the experimenter has taken adequate measures to avoid the five kinds of confounding listed above. Designing an experiment which will achieve internal validity means building in safeguards to minimize the chances of these kinds of confounding. These safeguards have been discussed above.

3.9   Chance: significant and non-significant results (Figure 3.2, box 2)

There is one more important factor which might influence the results of an experiment. That is chance. If the results of an experiment do show a difference, the question is whether the difference is bigger than might have reasonably been expected to have occurred by chance. This is usually settled by testing the results for their **statistical significance**.

Imagine an experiment consisting of one group of 11 year old pupils receiving a drugs education programme, and another receiving the standard personal health and social education (PHSE) curriculum, with results such as those in Table 3.2.

On the face of it, the drug education seems to have been successful insofar as at age 13–14 there are only half as many pupils reporting themselves as regular smokers in that group compared with the control group where pupils received the standard PHSE curriculum. But could a difference of this size have occurred just by chance? That is what testing for statistical significance is designed to estimate.

A thought experiment might capture the logic of statistical testing. We will ignore the lost subjects for a moment and concentrate on those for whom data are available. In total there are 20 'regular smokers'. Imagine

Outcomes of experimental evaluation of drug education programme delivered at age 11–12, outcomes in terms of smoking behaviour at age 13–14 TABLE 3.2

	Number reporting themselves as regular smokers at age 13–14	Number reporting themselves as not regular smokers at age 13–14	Lost to the experiment owing to change of school or unavailability at date of data collection at age 13–14	Totals
Experimental group (receiving drug education programme at age 11–12)	5	30	3	38
Control group (receiving standard PSE curriculum at age 11–12)	15	20	3	38
Totals	**20**	**50**	**6**	**76**

How to read this table
The totals column (last column, first row) shows that 38 pupils aged 11/12 received a drug education programme including anti-smoking education – the 'experimental group'. A year later an anonymous questionnaire was completed by 35 of them. The third column shows that 3 out of the 38 were unavailable for some reason. Of the 35, five reported themselves as regular smokers, and 30 did not. The second row of the table gives the corresponding results for the 'controls': the 38 pupils who followed a standard Personal and Social Education (PSE) curriculum rather than the drug education programme.

Source: Invented data, but see Hurry and Lloyd (1997).

taking 20 blank cards and writing 'Smoker' on each. In total there are 50 pupils who are not 'regular smokers'. Imagine taking 50 blank cards and writing 'Non-smoker' on each. In your mind, shuffle all the cards together, and then think about dealing them into two decks of 35. Since this is a random deal the single most likely result of doing this would be that there would be 10 'Smokers' in each pile. But chance being what it is, you are rather unlikely to achieve 10 and 10 on a single try. If you did the dealing over and over again you might often achieve 11 and 9, or 9 and 11, or 12 and 8, or 8 and 12: you wouldn't be surprised to obtain 7 and 13 or 13 and 7.

So these are all results which might have occurred by chance. The statistician argues that if a result *might* commonly occur by chance, then it would be unsafe to assume that it actually occurred for any other reason. What testing for statistical significance does is to give an estimate of how likely a particular set of results would occur by chance (Panel 3.1). This is why this tradition of statistics is often called '**frequentist**', because operations entail estimating how frequently a result might have occurred by chance.

PANEL 3.1   Normal distribution: the distribution of chance outcomes and inferential statistics

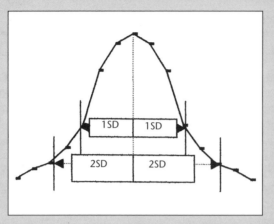

*Approximately 95% of chance outcomes will lie **between** 2 standard deviations away from the mean, either side of the mean. Outcomes in this range are regarded as not significant.*

For standard deviations, see Panel 2.8

FIGURE 3.3   *The normal distribution as a frequency distribution of chance outcomes, or z curve.*

Inferential statistics

(*Fisherian statistics, frequentist statistics*) are dependent on the properties of the normal distribution. The normal distribution curve is the distribution which would arise from measuring the same entity again and again and again, chance errors giving different results each time – hence the term 'error curve'. Or it would arise from taking an infinite number of random samples from the same population and measuring the same feature of each (see Panel 2.8) – hence the term 'sampling error curve'.

Statistical tests of confidence

In one way or another all statistical tests of confidence have a built-in model of the frequency of chance outcomes and mathematically compare actual data to that. What they compare may be numbers, or means, or variances, or standard deviations (see Panel 2.8) or odds ratios (see Panel 15.4).

Parametric statistics: the more powerful tests, but can be used only with interval-/ratio-level data (see Table 2.1) which derives from random samples drawn from a population where the variable of interest approximates a normal distribution.

Non-parametric statistics: can be used with any kind of data, but are the only tests which can be used with nominal and ordinal data (see Table 2.1), and with non-random samples or samples from populations where the variable of interest does not approximate a normal distribution, as with power distributions (see Chapter 5, Panel 5.6).

Statistically significant differences

At the end of an experiment, two groups have different means. Are the differences due to chance factors or is this a *(statistically) significant difference*? To assess this we, in effect, create a model of all the outcomes of the experiment which might have occurred by chance and how likely each of these would be. Here, this is equivalent to taking the results from all the subjects of the experiment together and dividing them at random into two groups, again and again and again. How often would we then get two groups as different as those which were the actual results of the experiment? The chance outcomes will shape up into a normal distribution curve (Figure 3.3). We know what percentage of scores will occur under each sector of the curve (see Panel 2.8), so we know how frequently each chance outcome will happen.

- If two groups with the same or greater differences as those from the experiment would crop up by chance frequently, we would assume the outcome of the experiment was *not* statistically significant.
- If such differences would only rarely occur by chance, then we regard the experiment as having a statistically significant result.

Testing for significance: a worked example using a X^2 test

TABLE 3.3   *Data from Table 3.2 laid out for X^2 calculation*

	O	E	O	E	O	E	Total
Experimentals	5	10	30	25	3	3	38
Controls	15	10	20	25	3	3	38
Totals	20		50		6		76

The O(bserved) figures are what was found. The E(xpected) figures are those most likely by chance, here a fair-shares distribution, so that the experimentals who make up 50% of all pupils, should have 50% of the smokers (10) and so on. The X^2 calculation then compares the O figures with the E figures (by subtraction and division) with squaring to eliminate minuses:

$$\frac{(O-E)^2}{E} + \frac{(O-E)^2}{E} + \frac{(O-E)^2}{E} + \frac{(O-E)^2}{E} + \frac{(O-E)^2}{E} + \frac{(O-E)^2}{E} = X^2$$

$$\frac{(5-10)^2}{10} + \frac{(15-10)^2}{10} + \frac{(30-25)^2}{25} + \frac{(20-25)^2}{25} + \frac{(3-3)^2}{3} + \frac{(3-3)^2}{3} =$$

$$= 2.5 + 2.5 + 1 + 1 + 0 + 0 = 7 = X^2$$

Due to rounding, this result will be slightly different from one calculated electronically.

Tables of critical values

The results of statistical tests may be looked up in tables of critical values appropriate for the test, available in most statistics textbooks. These give some benchmark values for p against which the result of the test can be compared. In our case $X^2 = 7$ (Table 3.3). With 2 degrees of freedom (df), 7 falls between the critical value for $p = 0.10$ and that for $p = 0.05$. The 5% level of significance, $p = 0.05$, is the highest probability allowed for statistical significance, and the result is declared as significant at the 5% level (Table 3.4).

Alternatively, the corresponding p value can be calculated precisely. In this case, $X^2 = 7.0$ gives a p value of 0.03. We would expect a difference of the same size or smaller than shown in the experiment, to occur by chance, 9 times out of 100: within 2 standard deviations of the mean and not statistically significant.

TABLE 3.4   *Extract from table of critical values for X^2*

df	p = 0.50	p = 0.20	p = 0.10	p = 0.05	p = 0.01	p = 0.001
1	0.45	1.64	2.71	3.84	6.64	10.83
2	1.39	3.22	4.60	5.99 7.0	9.21	13.82
3	2.37	4.64	6.25	7.82	11.34	16.27
4	3.36	5.99	7.78	9.49	13.28	18.46

Within 2 standard deviations either side of the mean approximately	Beyond 2 standard deviations from the mean approximately
Not statistically significant	**Statistically significant**

Degrees of freedom (df) are calculated from the original table (Table 3.2) as (rows minus 1) x (columns minus 1) = 2, but there are different calculations for different tests: titles and totals don't count as rows and columns (Table 3.5).

Data transformations

Where data do not appear to be drawn from a population of values approximating a normal distribution, researchers may try to transform the data to achieve a distribution that does. For example they might convert the data to logarithms, or square roots (Pett 1997: 37).This is in order to use parametric, rather than non-parametric statistics (see above). SPSS and various other statistics packages will assess whether a data set comes from a population sufficiently 'normal' to warrant using parametric statistics. But beware: some of the most interesting data are non-normal power distributions. Normalizing these may distort them in a misleading way (see Chapter 5, Section 5.11).

Values of p: the results of tests of statistical significance are reported as values of p for probability; either the precise value for p is cited, or a value which p is less than, as in p < 0.05 (p is less than 0.05)		TABLE 3.5
p < 0.001	p is less than 0.001, there is only 1 chance in 1,000 of a result like this cropping up by chance: the one in one thousand *alpha level*/level of significance.	'Very highly statistically significant' sometimes indicated***
p < 0.01	p is less than 0.01, there is only 1 chance in one hundred of a result like this cropping up by chance: the 1% *alpha level*/ level of significance.	'Highly statistically significant', sometimes indicated**
p < 0.05	p is less than 0.05, there are only five chances in 100 of a result like this cropping up by chance: the 5% *alpha level*/ level of significance. This is the highest value for p which statisticians will accept for a statistically significant results	'Statistically significant', sometimes indicated*
p > 0.05	p is more than 0.05, there is a greater than 5% chance of a result like this cropping up by chance.	'Not statistically significant' – sometimes written NS, or where authors use asterisks indicated by no asterisks at all.

So what about a result of 5 and 15: the actual result of the experiment? How commonly would a result like this occur by chance? If we repeated the card sorting exercise over and over again, then a result of 5 or less and 15 or more, or vice versa, would crop up a little less often than 5 times in one hundred: the so-called 5% *level*. Using a statistical test would give us a similar estimate, though much more conveniently than spending hours dealing cards (see Panel 3.1, Table 3.3, but note that this calculation includes the pupils lost to the experiment, see below).

Conventionally, statisticians regard any results which might occur by chance more often than 5 times in a 100 as statistically non-significant, meaning that whatever caused the results to be as they are, it is safest to regard them as the result of chance (see Panel 3.1, Table 3.5).

So the result 5 and 15 is *statistically significant at the 5% level*, and there are some grounds for regarding the result as being caused by something other than chance. Note that the test won't tell you what actually did cause the results. It won't tell you whether they are the results of differences in intended treatment, or of unintentional or accidental difference, or of comparison groups which were dissimilar at the outset, or of researcher bias or subject enthusiasm, or dislike of being subjects of an experiment. Given the difficulties of conducting experiments in school settings it seems likely that all the kinds of confounding shown on Figure 3.2 and listed in Section 3.8 will have made some contribution to the results, even if only small ones, and even if largely balancing each other out. With this in mind it would be safest not to regard this experiment as showing the effectiveness of anti-smoking education, even though the results were statistically significant. The result 5 and 15 is not statistically significant at the 1% level, meaning that results like this might be expected to crop up by chance more often than once in a hundred times. The result is not *highly significant* (Panel 3.1, Table 3.5).

The result 5 and 15 was significant, but not highly significant. In these circumstances it is worth looking again at an experiment to see if there are any kinds of confounding which might just be tipping the results in favour of being significant. Look, for example, at the 'lost' subjects in Table 3.2. If in reality all the subjects lost to the experimental group were 'regular smokers' and all those lost to control group were 'non-smokers' then the overall result would cease to be statistically significant.

Statistical tests take the *sample size* into consideration. Thus a non-significant result might mean one of two things. First (confounding apart) it might mean that really in the experiment the two different treatments had much the same effect as each other. That would be useful information. But, second, it might mean that a real difference between the effects of the treatments was small, and that the size of the sample was too small for such a small difference to be distinguished from a chance effect. There is more about the relationship between sample size and statistical significance in Chapter 6, Section 6.10, though in relation to surveys.

3.10   External validity, generalizability or transferability

Section 3.8 dealt with internal validity: whether a piece of research is true in its own terms. *External validity* refers to the extent to which what happened in the experiment can be made to stand as an example for things which happen more widely. The external validity of any particular experiment is not something which the experiment itself can decide. Whether the results of a particular experiment have any relevance to anything else has to be decided by previous or further research.

It is often argued that experiments in the social sciences 'must' lack external validity because experimental conditions are so different from those of real life. There have been examples of such differences throughout this chapter. For example, the people who enter an experiment are only rarely a statistically representative sample of the people in some general population. Representativeness is dealt with in detail in Chapter 6. Those entering an experiment are more usually a 'grab' or a 'convenience' sample; the people who were around when the experimenter needed some research subjects. Co-operative people will be over-represented and unco-operative people under-represented. In the corpus of psychological experiments, university students are grossly over-represented as subjects (Suls and Rostow 1988). In medical research people with multiple illness conditions are usually excluded from experiments. In real life most sick people are sick with several conditions at once (Tudor Hart 1993). A very practical issue with regard to generalizing from experiments is that experiments usually report results for a group, whereas a practitioner may want to intervene with an individual who may well not show a response like the group average. Single-subject experiments as a response to this problem are discussed in Chapter 4, Section 4.5.

Again the experimental conditions are likely to vary from real life in the degree of influence that experimenters have in determining what happens. And under experimental conditions there are researchers – who know they are researchers – and subjects – who know they are subjects of an experiment – whereas in real life people play different roles.

The artificiality of the controlled experiment, together with the *context dependency* of outcomes, has been raised several times. There is a practical issue here, especially for complex interventions as to the transferability of experimental findings from one setting to another. Design experiments as a method of custom-building interventions for particular settings is a response to this problem: see Chapter 4, Section 4.5.

It is hardly surprising that experimental circumstances are unlike those of 'real life'. Experiments are designed to overcome a feature of 'real life' which makes it difficult to discern what is causing what, which is that everything has a multitude of causes and everything interacts with everything else. The way the controlled experiment attempts to solve this problem is to simplify things so that under experimental conditions most factors are controlled and only a few are allowed to vary. This is very unlike real life. But it is not the central purpose of experimental research to match real life point by point. What is necessary is to set up situations which allow interesting bits of reality to be investigated, screened off from all the 'noise' created by the multifarious number of things going on at the same time.

A rather more damaging critique of the external validity of controlled experiments arises from questioning the assumptions about causality on which they are based. This is examined further in Chapter 5.

ACTIVITY   Designing a controlled experiment

This activity will test your understanding of much that is in the chapter. The activity asks you:

1 To design a controlled experiment to investigate whether knowing the gender of a student will influence the mark given to an essay by a marker. Use Figure 3.2 as a check list to make sure that, as far as possible, your design avoids the kinds of problems it suggests.

2 Assuming that your experiment was conducted and gave results showing that there were *no* significant differences in the marks given by markers attributable to their knowing the gender of a candidate:
    (a) Which features of your research design would you pinpoint as being the most likely reason to regard this result with caution?
    (b) How would you compare the experiment and its results with marking for real, in order to estimate the external validity of your experiment? There is more about mapping experimental results against real life in Chapter 4, Section 4.5.

Further reading

Most standard psychology texts dealing with research methods give thorough accounts of experimental methods, for example Coolican (2004). A classic, and still excellent text is Campbell and Stanley (1996). Stevens *et al.* (2001) will tell you almost everything you want to know about RCTs. It may be entirely about healthcare but that is where the best research of this kind is done. Baruch (1997) gives a good account of experiments in other applied areas. However, the best way of learning more about experimental methods is to read, analyse and evaluate the results of experimental research. The topic of the research is relatively unimportant. What is important is getting to grips with the *logic of experimentation*. Gomm (2000b) gives advice on what to look for in evaluating experimental research. The references on systematic reviews in Chapter 15 are also relevant.

Most statistical testing these days is done using software packages such as SPSS or MINITAB. Field (2000) is one of several texts explaining statistics using SPSS. Among printed texts which do not assume that you have access to one of the commercial packages, Coolican (2004) is my favourite, but the on-line Statsoft text is a free statistics textbook (www.statsoft.com/textbook/stbasic.html) as is the Hyperstat on-line textbook (http://davidmlane.com/hyperstat/contents.html).

If you don't have access to one of the commercial packages there are various free statistics calculators available on the internet. *Statpages* (http://statpages.org/) is one of several directories making statistics calculators from various sources accessible via hotlinks. Two sites which I quite like are: www.ifigure.com/math/stat/stat.htm (which also gives access to the *Hypertext* textbook), and *BusinessStat* (http://unix.hensa.ac.uk/sites/home.ubalt.edu/ntsbarsh/Business-stat/otherapplets/scientificCal.htm), which also includes 'textbook' screens. If you are already familiar with Excel spreadsheets you might like to invest in one of the statistics up-grades such as *XL Statistics* which will sit on top of your Excel package. Excel add-ons are usually available on 30-day free trial. Check compatibility with your version of Excel.

4 More Naturalism in Experiments

By the end of this chapter, you will:

- Have considered the problems arising from relaxing control in order to make experimental situations more naturalistic as opposed to the problems of adopting rigorous control structures which may make experimental results difficult to generalize from
- Know the main factors to look for in a piece of research to judge the likelihood of its results being biased
- Understand more about the idea of generalization and its relationship to specification
- Have practised analysing a piece of research, to come to a considered judgement as to how far its results might have been an artefact of the research situation
- In the Activity at the end of the chapter, have practised analysing a piece of research to come to a considered judgement as to the specific circumstances of the situations to which its results might be generalized.

And you will know the meaning of the following terms:

Context-dependency • design experiments • effectiveness • intuitive data processing • quasi-experiments as opposed to true experiments • n-of-1 experiments (single-case evalutions) • specification.

4.1 Introduction

Chapter 3 identified a researchers' dilemma: the *trade-off between control and naturalism*. The shape of this dilemma is as follows. Controlled experiments are the best design for investigating causality. They attempt to exert experimental control over all the variables which might have a causal effect on whatever it is that is of interest. If this is done successfully, experiments can achieve a high degree of *internal validity*, which means that they can be successful in identifying what caused what to happen *in the circumstances of the experiment*. Achieving internal validity requires the experimenter to ensure that:

- The subjects for the experiment were really similar in the ways they should have been similar, and different in the ways they should have been different

- The treatments or experimental conditions were really different in the ways they should have been different and similar in the ways they should have been similar
- Any other factors which should have been excluded from influencing the out-turns were successfully excluded from having an influence, or their influence identified and this taken into consideration in interpreting the results.

The problem which arises from exerting strong experimental control is that this creates an artificial situation, so that what happened in the experiment may rarely, or never, happen under real-life conditions. Hence strong experimental control and high levels of internal validity can result in low levels of *external validity*. This means a difficulty in drawing conclusions which can be generalized beyond the experiment. Thus experimenters may be faced with a difficult choice between adopting designs with strong experimental controls and risking producing results which will not have much bearing on what usually happens, or of relaxing control to produce more naturalistic conditions but at the risk of being uncertain as to what actually does cause what to happen. Sometimes experimenters do not so much opt for more naturalism as have it thrust upon them, since there may be practical and ethical reasons why experimental control cannot be imposed on some variables in an experiment (see Chapter 7).

This chapter looks first at four kinds of more naturalistic experiments, **field experiments** (Section 4.2) and **decision-simulation experiments** (Section 4.3), **design experiments**, and **n-of-1 experiments** (Section 4.5) and considers the benefits of relaxing experimental control in pursuit of naturalism and the kinds of problems which arise when experimental control is relaxed. The experiments discussed here are controlled experiments, even though the controls are weak in some regards. They would be termed **quasi-experiments** – not because they are more naturalistic but because **true experiments** always involve creating comparison groups by randomization (Chapter 3, Section 3.3). The remainder of the chapter considers strategies which might be used to judge how naturalistic, or unnaturalistic, an experimental situation was, in order to decide how far its results might apply more widely. In doing this, the chapter will also look at the use of experimental designs in applied social research in evaluating the *effectiveness* of medical, social work, educational or criminal justice interventions.

4.2   Field experiments

There is no definitive meaning of the term 'field experiment'. When I use it I am thinking about the kind of experiment where the researcher injects some control into an otherwise naturally occurring situation – for example, those experiments where two actors playing the role of job applicants with identical CVs, but of different ethnicity, apply for the same real jobs, and covertly record what happens (Brown and Gay 1985). As a major example I shall use part of a famous study by David Rosenhan (1973) which has been reprinted many times (for example, 1996). I have deliberately chosen this because it is a rather flimsy experiment and therefore offers a good illustration of what can go wrong in field experiments.

'I'm looking for a psychiatrist'

David Rosenhan is well known for his 'pseudo-patient experiment' which involved infiltrating 'sane' people into various American mental hospitals as patients, and their observations of what happened to them there. Despite their behaving as sanely as possible they were treated as if they were genuine mental patients and in need of treatment. Since there were no controls, this properly shouldn't be called an experiment. 'Covert participant observation research' would be a more appropriate designation (see Chapter 12). As an adjunct and a follow-up to this, Rosenhan mounted a field experiment. A female assistant was sent to the university hospital precinct. Her task was to approach people who looked like medical staff and ask them for directions. After indicating that she wanted directions she provided the information either that she was 'looking for an internist' (an ordinary doctor), or 'looking for a psychiatrist'. She then went on to attempt to ask another five questions about the hospital. For a third group she just tried to ask the questions without saying she was looking for anyone in particular. Similar procedures were carried out on the university campus, where the same research assistant approached people who looked like university lecturers, asking directions to a non-existent part of the university, and five more questions, but without any reference to doctors or psychiatrists. The control structure here sets up comparisons in the hospital precinct between three groups according to how they were asked for directions, and between all of these and the people asked for directions on the university campus. The results are shown in Table 4.1.

For the hospital precinct the results seem to indicate that when the research assistant was perceived as looking for an ordinary medical doctor, people continued in conversation with her. But when she was perceived to be looking for a psychiatrist people were less likely to do so and overall people spent less time with her in her mental illness role. Rosenhan's interpretation of this was that a label of 'mental illness', here triggered by the reference to the psychiatrist, will intervene in a social relationship such that those who are labelled as 'mentally ill' will be treated differently from others. Although this could not be demonstrated by this experiment Rosenhan drew the further inference from the results that being treated differently from others in this way is likely to cause people who have been labelled as 'mentally ill' to experience themselves as being odd, and hence to contribute to their mental distress.

The issue here is a causal one. The question is whether some intimation of mental illness *causes* people to be treated differently from others. As a causal question it is eminently suitable for experimental treatment. But since the issue is about whether *under ordinary conditions* this happens, it makes sense to conduct the research under as naturalistic conditions as possible. But the fact that these conditions are not under experimental control may give rise to difficulties in interpreting the results, as I discovered in attempting something like a replication of Rosenhan's experiment.

TABLE 4.1   *Responses to requests for directions by researcher in different roles in a university hospital precinct, and on the university campus*

Responses	University campus	University hospital precinct		
		'Looking for an internist'	'Looking for a psychiatrist'	No cues as to who was being looked for
Moves on head averted (%)	0	0	0	0
Makes eye contact (but no more) (%)	0	0	11	0
Pauses and chats (but didn't stop to talk) (%)	0	0	11	10
Stops and talks (%)	100	100	78	90
Mean number of questions answered (out of 6, including the request for directions)	6	4.8	3.8	4.5
Number of Respondents	14	15	18	10

How to read this table

The columns of the table show what happened when the research assistant engaged with people in different places in slightly different ways. For the University campus she approached people who looked like lecturers and asked directions to a non-existent part of the university and five other questions, none of which carried any implications of mental illness. She asked 14 different people and all of them (100%) stopped, talked to her and answered all her enquiries (mean number of questions answered = 6). For the hospital precinct she always asked directions of people who seemed to be staff, but to some (15) she indicated that she was looking for an 'internist' (any kind of doctor), for others (18) that she was looking for a psychiatrist, and with others (10) she gave no indication who she was looking for. In each case she also asked five other questions. The table shows that when she represented herself as looking for a psychiatrist she was less likely to have her request taken seriously. Only 78% stopped and talked, 11% made eye contact but then moved on, 11% paused but did not really stop to talk. When she was 'looking for a psychiatrist' on average the 18 people only answered 3.8 of her questions. The bottom row shows the number of respondents involved. From this, you can work out that the difference in response between 'looking for an internist' and 'looking for a psychiatrist' is accounted for by the negative responses of only 4 people out of 18. Since 18 is the largest set of responses in the table there is a better chance that it will include rarer kinds of response than the smaller sets of responses. Usually, larger samples show more diversity than smaller ones.

Source: After Rosenhan (1973: 255).

As an exercise for student social workers I conducted similar, though not identical experiments, two years running. The locale was a busy district general hospital with general medical and psychiatric facilities. The requests were: 'Excuse me, I've got an appointment with a consultant urologist', or 'Excuse me I've got an appointment with a psychiatrist' and in both cases 'and I don't know where to go'. The targets were anyone with a security badge. Student researchers alternated between the role of a urology patient and the role of a patient for psychiatry.

This wasn't arranged as an exercise in research methodology but as an experiential demonstration that 'mental illness' labels have very powerful effects on social relationships. Having read the research in this area, I simply assumed they did. In this respect the results in the first year were very disappointing. Some students reported that there was no difference in how they were treated whichever kind of patient they represented themselves as being. Some did experience a difference but they 'couldn't put their finger' on what it was. None of the requests for assistance was ignored, even to the extent that a porter left a patient on a trolley to walk the requester part-way to her destination (the psychiatric wing) including a journey in the lift. A doctor running across the car park nonetheless stopped and gave directions – to the department of genito-urinary medicine, in this case.

My first-year version of the experiment improved on Rosenhan's. I had 15 'research assistants' of both genders and various ethnic groups, and far more observations. His version was 'over-controlled' in the sense that there was only one female research assistant. That leaves his results vulnerable to the suggestion that they were produced by something special about her, which might not be true of someone else, and the number of observations in his experiment is perilously few (see Chapter 3, Section 3.9).

In the second year I improved on the design. This time, I sent students out in pairs: one to ask and one to observe and take notes. I provided an observation schedule saying what to look out for. For some students it was agreed between requester and observer that there were no discernible differences in response whichever role was played. For some the observer recorded no differences, but the requester was sure there were some. But for some there were differences agreed between requester and observer in the same direction as in Rosenhan's results (Table 4.1). For these, the observer often reported that the requester behaved differently according to the role he or she was playing. Requesters were often reluctant to accept this but according to observers, requesters who elicited a different response in their differing roles seemed to be 'acting out' a mental patient persona. Eye contact was the most telling difference. In their mental illness roles these requesters did not make prolonged eye contact with those they asked for assistance. There were also differences in tone of voice and their register was less assertive, or so observers claimed.

This was a rather ramshackle experiment and I certainly would not want to claim that the results of Rosenhan's experiment were created by his research assistant behaving differently in the different roles. Ten years and 6,000 miles separates the two so there are many other things which might be different between the two. Nonetheless my experience does suggest that a number of uncontrolled variables might have been at play in both.

As with Rosenhan's experiment so mine also failed to control the selection of targets. Were requesters approaching different kinds of people in their different roles? It was also obvious in my experiment (probably not in Rosenhan's) that physical location was another uncontrolled variable with regard to the duration of encounters. Those offering assistance often walked the requester to a corner before pointing the way, but for some locations this was not necessary. Those in a position to point to a nearby reception desk often did so without giving further directions themselves. It also became apparent that there are two parties influencing how long an encounter lasts. The behaviour of the requesters had a definite influence on this. Sometimes requesters signalled that they were satisfied with a set of directions and thereby ended the encounter; sometimes they asked for further clarification or looked uncertain, and prolonged it. Lastly, my experiment added a problematic element which was not there in Rosenhan's: someone watching what was going on and making notes about it. I can claim that this greatly improved the recording of what happened, but if respondents were aware of being watched, this might have influenced their behaviour.

My version of the experiment, then, illustrates the way variables may be left uncontrolled in the attempt to experiment under more naturalistic circumstances. In summary, there were:

- *Variables at the subject level*: no control over selection of targets for one treatment or the other (Chapter 3, Section 3.3)
- *Variables at the treatment level*: differences in age, gender and ethnicity as between requesters, different behaviour by requesters in their different roles – an expectancy effect (Chapter 3, Section 3.6). Different physical locations of those asked directions (Chapter 3, Section 3.5). Some respondents perhaps realized that they were being observed; others not (maybe a lop-sided Hawthorne effect: Chapter 3, Section 3.6)
- *Variables at the level of observation and recording*: no guarantee that different observers understood or used the observation schedule in the same way (Chapter 3, Section 3.7); possible expectancy effects among some observers (Chapter 3, Section 3.6).

This wasn't a very well-designed experiment. Some of the problems above might have been ameliorated. But apart from standardizing the use of the observation schedule, going too far down the other routes of improving control itself leads to problems. For example, controlling for location of request, by always making the requests in the same location, would lead to results which might be true for that location but no other. Controlling for location of request by selecting a number of different locations would then require an adequate sample of requests made in each location and an experiment on a much larger scale, a flooding of the hospital with researchers and perhaps an undermining of the whole enterprise.

Rosenhan's claim was that people suspected of being mentally ill are treated differently even when they behave *exactly the same* as everyone else. He added the results of his field experiment to other evidence about the power of labelling. Remember that this experiment followed research in which 'sane' people behaved 'normally' in mental hospitals, but were treated as if they were mad. One aspect of this was that often when they spoke to ward staff the pseudo-patients were simply ignored as if they were not there at all. His field experiment seems to cap this nicely since it is apparently another situation in which people who behave sanely are nonetheless treated differently even if, as here, there is only a smidgen of evidence about them that they may be mentally ill. Only when drawn onto a canvas including the way pseudo-patients were treated in mental hospitals do the very small differences shown in Rosenhan's experiment seem interesting. They are certainly not statistically significant (Chapter 3, Section 3.9).

By contrast, my results would bear only the commentary that people suspected of being mentally ill are treated differently when *they themselves* behave *a little bit differently* from others. And my results could also be read as evidence that asking some social work students to pretend to be mental patients causes them more embarrassment than asking them to pretend to be patients of the urology department. As with Rosenhan's interpretation, this one is still suggestive of the power of 'mental illness' labels to affect social interaction, but the causal mechanism suggested is different. In this regard it might have produced misleading rather than enlightening results to control the behaviour of the requesters so that each respondent was confronted with identical behaviour irrespective of the role played by the requester, apart from the destination mentioned. If the important mechanism is in the approach of the requester, then standardization would have eliminated the most interesting feature of the phenomenon of interest. Looked at in this way it seems credible to argue that there was *so little* difference in response to requests made from different roles (Table 4.1), because Rosenhan's research assistant did usually behave in the same way irrespective of the role she was playing.

The experiment didn't disrupt normal goings on very much, and asking directions in a hospital seems an ordinary thing to do. Thus the experiment might be said to have achieved a high degree of naturalism. But because of all the uncontrolled variables it cannot be said with any confidence what it was about the way requests were made which caused differences and similarities of response. Because of its naturalism we might feel comfortable in generalizing the results of the experiment to the normal interaction between requesters and respondents in a hospital. But because of the lack of control it is not at all clear what there is to generalize about.

Thus by comparison with the kind of control which can be achieved in laboratory experiments this one shows considerable shortcomings. But it is important also to make the comparison in another direction; between the field experiment and non-experimental approaches. Assuming the topic was the difference in interaction caused by intimations of mental illness then it might have been approached either through interviews or naturalistic observation. Interviews would tell us how people with some mental illness stigma experienced and interpreted their interaction with others, which would be interesting (for example, see Rogers, Pilgrim and Lacey 1993). But such interviews could not tell us whether their experiences arose from their actually being treated differently from other people, rather than from their assumptions that they were. Observing the ordinary flux of life in the public areas of a hospital would first, give rise to the problem of actually finding and identifying the instances we wanted among the welter of other things going on. One of the reasons for doing experiments is to make something of interest happen frequently when we are around to observe it. Again, the field experiment, as an experiment, already suffered from there being too much diversity between encounters as to the permutations between requesters and respondents in terms of age, gender and ethnicity, in terms of busyness and status of the various responders, location of request and variation in requester behaviour. In the naturalistic observation such diversity would increase by a quantum leap, and it would be even more difficult to make confident statements as to what ingredients in encounters led to people being treated the same, or differently from each other (see also Section 4.7).

4.3 Decision-simulation experiments

All experiments are 'simulations' because they set up simplified simulacra of what might happen. But there are some kinds of experiments which quite explicitly simulate. These are particularly common in the study of the factors which influence decision-making. There are many naturally occurring situations which involve people sitting down at desks, reading and writing documents. These can be simulated with a high degree of naturalism. The Activity at the end of Chapter 3 asked you to design just such an experiment to investigate the causal influence on examination grades of examiner knowledge of candidate gender.

Table 4.2 shows the results of a decision-simulation experiment to judge the extent to which it is sensible to draw conclusions about the causes of suicide from international comparisons of suicide statistics.

In Chapter 3 we were dealing mainly with experiments of the similar-subjects, different-treatments design, used to investigate the causal effects of a particular treatment or set of experimental conditions (see Figure 3.1). The experiment here is an example of the other basic experimental design; a

TABLE 4.2   *Verdicts of five Danish Kredslaege and four English coroners on the same 40 cases*

Verdicts	English coroners				Danish Kredslaege				
	1	*2*	*3*	*4*	*A*	*B*	*C*	*D*	*E*
Suicide	23	21	17	16	32	31	28	27	27
Accident	9	8	10	13	6	5	8	12	6
Open	6	11	13	11	2	3	3	0	6
Natural causes	2	0	0	0	0	1	1	1	1

English mean (average) for suicide verdicts = 19.25; Danish mean = 29.00; the difference is highly statistically significant

How to read this table
The same 40 cases were presented to 4 English coroners (1–4) and 5 of their Danish counterparts (A–E); 4 verdicts were available. The numbers in the cells show the verdicts actually given by each decision-maker. Thus coroner 1 found for suicide in 23 cases, accidental death in 9 and so on. A statistical test was carried out comparing the average number of suicide verdicts for the English and the Danes, respectively (Chapter 3, Panel 3.1). The test suggested that less than once in 1,000 times would a difference of this size be expected to occur by chance and hence that this result was probably not due to chance and probably does reflect a real difference in the way English and Danish functionaries make decisions about cause of death.

Source: After Atkinson, Kessell and Dalgaard (1975).

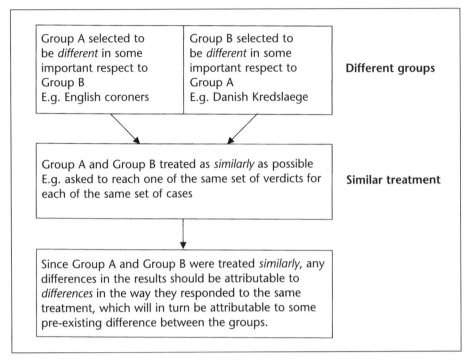

A different subjects/similar treatments experimental design   *FIGURE 4.1*

different-subjects, similar-treatments design, used to investigate the different responses of different kinds of people to the same treatment or set of conditions (Figure 4.1). It is also a design often used in validating research instruments to see whether different kinds of people respond differently to the same instrument (see Chapter 2).

Often this design is used without defining groups initially, identifying groups only at the end of the experiment. Essentially this is what happens with social surveys where everyone receives the same treatment: that is, the same set of questions administered in the same way. In analysing the results the researcher identifies different groups according to their responses (see Chapters 6 and 7).

But in the coroner experiment the comparison groups were defined in advance and the 'same treatment' was the provision of the same sets of evidence about 40 deaths to two different groups of functionaries involved in classifying deaths, asking them to do what they would normally do, which was to reach a verdict on each. The simulation departs from reality in that normally only one functionary would decide on each case, the English coroners would have an option to enrol a jury and all would gather some of their evidence by questioning witnesses. There are excellent studies of coroners actually going about their business (for example, Atkinson 1978), but these cannot tell us clearly whether any differences in verdicts reached by different coroners arise from differences in the cases they dealt with, or from differences in the ways different coroners think and come to conclusions – or, in this example, from differences built into different judicial systems. The experimental design here controls for the differences between cases and allows differences between decision-makers/decision-making systems to show up clearly.

As a group, the Danes were much more likely to reach a suicide verdict than were their English counterparts (Table 4.2). Each of the Danes reached more verdicts of suicide than any of the English. On this basis, Atkinson and his colleagues suggest that the higher national suicide rate in Denmark compared with England may be due to differences in the way decisions on cause of death are made in the two legal systems. In England coroners have to find 'definite proof' of suicide in order to give a suicide verdict, whereas in Denmark it is necessary only to find that 'on balance of probabilities' a death was a suicide in order to apply that verdict: it's just much easier to reach a suicide verdict in Denmark. This explanation sounds credible. Whether it is valid or not, there is certainly evidence here that English and Danish suicide statistics are an unreliable basis for comparing the two countries in terms of how many people deliberately end their own lives.

What the figures in Table 4.2 do not show is that there is almost as much disagreement among individual functionaries *within* a national group as between the two groups. This is something for which an inter-rater reliability test is the best measure (Chapter 2, Section 2.10). Following some analysis of differences in suicide rates emanating from different coroners' courts in London focusing only on poisonings, Atkinson and his colleagues concluded that differences in suicide rates may owe as much to the idiosyncrasies of individual coroners as to differences between the populations and circumstances of the areas in which people do away with themselves. To this extent the problem is recognized in most modern analyses of suicide statistics by the analysis being done with the statistics of suicide *and* those of undetermined deaths combined. This is on the assumption that most disagreements between coroners would concern allocation between these two categories, and that combining them controls for much of coroner disagreement (Charlton *et al.* 1992). However, the research quoted here suggests greater room for disagreement than this. Undetermined deaths are the 'open verdicts' in Table 4.2. In this experiment the 'treatment', in the form of standard stimulus material, was well controlled, except for some problems in producing the same case materials in two different languages for two different legal systems. But control over subject characteristics looks less secure.

In a different-subjects, similar-treatments design, issues about controlling for subject characteristics depend on what the research is about. Here, the research is about the difference between the process of reaching a verdict of suicide in England compared with Denmark. Hence the results might be confounded if, for example the English coroners in the experiment were younger on average than their Danish counterparts. If that were so then the differences between the two groups might be attributable to age differences rather than differences in the two legal systems. Generalizing the results of this experiment to produce an explanation of differences in suicide rates between the two countries relies on the 4 English coroners being representative of all English coroners, and the 5 Kredslaege being representative of all such Danish functionaries. Given that there are only 4 of one and 5 of the other there is a possibility that Atkinson and his colleagues may have been unlucky enough to have selected a set of English coroners more reluctant than their peers to reach suicide verdicts, and/or a set of Kredslaege more gung-ho about giving such verdicts than Kredslaege in general. Except by increasing the number of participants in the experiment it is difficult to think of ways in which experimental control over such differences might be exerted directly. If there were any information that decision-making behaviour in this field varied with some knowable characteristics such as age, rural or urban jurisdiction, or religion, then it might be possible to exert control by restricting all participants to those similar for that characteristic – similar in age, for example, or only urban jurisdictions, or no catholics. However, there seems to be no such information available, and doing that would change the situation from one using participants of unknown representativeness to one using participants known to be unrepresentative but in a particular way. Possibly the best factor for control purposes would be track record, restricting entry to the experiment to those functionaries with a record of giving average-for-nation percentages of suicide verdicts per year.

But research is the art of the possible, and it was probably difficult enough for Atkinson and his colleagues to persuade 9 people to co-operate, let alone being picky about who they should be. Remember also that in each country only a handful of functionaries account for all suicide verdicts nationally: 4 and 5 are quite large numbers in this regard.

In assessing such simulation research, it must always be kept in mind that the subjects will know this is 'not for real' and may behave other than they would in natural conditions; a subject reactive or 'Hawthorne effect', as discussed in Chapter 3, Section 3.6. You probably thought of that in regard to your response to the activity in Chapter 3. However, in this case what is being simulated is decision-making which is normally conducted under highly accountable conditions. The difference between the experiment and the reality it is supposed to represent, may not be very great here as compared with experiments which ask people to do under observation what they would normally do privately and/or informally (Bloor 1994; and see Chapter 9, Section 9.4).

This was a fairly simple example of decision simulation experimentation. But it is possible to elaborate the stimulus material in order to build in variables of particular interest. For example, in researching social workers' decision-making about black children as opposed to white, Owusu-Bempah (1994) used a set of case notes where sometimes a black and sometimes a white ethnicity was written into what were otherwise the same case notes, showing that, without further evidence, social workers interpreted the backgrounds and needs of the children differently according to their ethnicity.

There is more about simulation research in Chapter 5, which deals with computer simulation.

4.4 Experimental designs and effectiveness research

In the 1990s 'evidence-based practice' became a buzz word in health, social work, criminal justice and education. In simple terms, evidence-based practice means basing what is done on the best evidence available, usually meaning research evidence. This has given rise to a growth in applied social research in the form of *effectiveness studies*.

The key question is the 'does it work?' question: 'Is what you are doing effective; does it produce benign effects?' There are two issues here. One is about how it should be judged, and who should judge, whether an effect is worth achieving or not. This is a value decision and the issue of evaluation criteria is discussed further in Chapter 14, Section 14.3. But before evaluation criteria are needed it is necessary to know whether practices have *any* effects and, if so, what they are. This is a causal question and it suggests an experimental approach as the ideal. In medicine, in particular, experimental approaches to the question of effective practice have been regarded as almost the only credible sources of evidence and randomized control trials as the 'gold standard' of evidence among them. As Chapter 3 argues, there are good reasons for regarding well-conducted experiments as the best approach to investigating cause and effect, although there are often good reasons why an experimental approach cannot be used. But if the evidence derived from an experiment is to be the evidence on which routine practice is to be based it becomes particularly important that the results of the experiment will indeed be applicable to routine practice. Here, differences between the artificial circumstances of an experiment and the real world of practice are likely to create serious problems, not just of interpretation but of patient or client welfare.

The bias towards success verdicts in effectiveness studies

A telling form of evidence for the need to take an experimental approach comes from comparing the results of effectiveness studies using experimental approaches of different levels of rigour. It began to become apparent in the 1970s that there was a strong inverse relationship between the extent of experimental control in an evaluation study and the finding that the practice evaluated was effective. Table 4.3 shows the results of one of the earliest of these comparisons, that by Logan in 1972, concerning programmes to reduce crime and delinquency.

Since Logan, similar pictures have been given for other studies of effectiveness in criminology (Lipsey 1995) and in social work (Macdonald, Sheldon and Gillespie 1992; Oakley and Fullerton 1996). In medicine, the same picture had been discovered earlier (Cochrane 1972; see also Moher *et al.* 2001: 418–19). This has led to the increasing use of experimental methods to replace knowledge based on poorly conducted research or other kinds of evidence based on the opinions of doctors or on the unsubstantiated claims of drug companies. Experiments have shown much such knowledge to be ill informed (Oakley 2000).

Studies of effectiveness without any control groups at all are very poorly equipped to provide evidence to determine whether some intervention was the cause of any outcomes recorded. For example, if sick people are given a medical treatment and subsequently get better, without a control group there is no way of knowing whether they got better because of the treatment, or

Experimental control and experimental results: research on programmes to   TABLE 4.3
reduce crime and delinquency

	Number judged successful (%)	Number judged unsuccessful (%)
19 studies with randomized control groups	7 (37)	12 (63)
23 studies with non-randomized control groups	16 (70)	7 (30)
58 studies with no control groups	50 (86)	8 (14)

How to read this table
Logan reviewed 100 studies of programmes designed to reduce criminal behaviour; 58 of these had designs with no control groups – that is, they featured only people receiving the programme, and not anyone receiving any alternative treatment or no treatment at all. The remainder had control groups, 23 with non-randomized control groups and 19 with randomized control groups (see Chapter 3, Section 3.3). The table shows that where there were no control groups the researchers were very likely to judge the programme as a success, and that where there were randomized control groups they were much more likely to judge the programme as a failure.

Source: After Logan (1972: Table 1).

would have got better anyway. Similarly, there is no way of knowing whether they would have got better quicker without the treatment. Or, again, the fact that some groups of people said they liked their experience of counselling provides no evidence as to whether they would have actually liked something other than counselling better, and no evidence that their morale was improved by counselling rather than simply improving with the passage of time, nor indeed whether their morale would have been better had they been left to their own devices. Thus these 'pre-post-tests without control' studies cannot usually be used as a basis for declaring an intervention to be effective without some additional evidence of some kind. Yet, as Table 4.3 shows, these are precisely the kinds of studies where researchers have been most likely to declare an intervention effective. It seems likely that very strong expectancy effects are operating here (Chapter 3, Section 3.6), with researchers being strongly influenced by the faith that practitioners have in favour of the effectiveness of their own practices, in a situation where the hard evidence provided by a control group design is lacking.

At a finer level of detail it seems also to be true that where randomization is used to create control groups, findings of effectiveness are less likely than when control groups are created in other ways (Schultz *et al.* 1995; Kunz and Oxman 1998; Moher *et al.* 2001). The reason for this is that control groups created at random control out more pre-existing differences between groups, while those not created at random let such differences filter through to create a spurious impression of effects caused by the intervention itself (see Figure 3.2). This continues the sequence above, so that the more rigorous the research design, the less likely a practice is to be found effective.

Panel 4.1 gives a list of the conditions which would seem to offer the greatest opportunities for bias of this kind to play a part. The more of these characteristics a particular piece of research has, the more possible it is that any

---

PANEL 4.1   A recipe for bias

There is more room for bias to influence the results of research (experimental or otherwise) when:

- Those who sponsor the research have a considerable financial, emotional or political investment in the results coming out one way rather than another and where those who conduct the research are not independent of the sponsors; sponsors may be government departments, service agencies, commercial companies, political parties, or pressure groups.
- Those who are the subjects of the research have a strong preference for the results coming out one way or another and where those who conduct the research make close sympathetic relationships with the subjects or where the subjects are the sponsors as in participatory research (Chapter 14, Section 14.5).
- For those who conduct the research, there are rewards for the results coming out one way rather than another; for example, where one set of results would be taken as breaking exciting new ground.
- Interested sponsors, and/or interested subjects and/or interested researchers can decide who is included in the research and can influence who drops out.
- The research is broad-based and open-ended, such that preferred findings can be found (and dispreferred ones ignored) (see Chapter 12).
- Interested sponsors and/or interested subjects and/or interested researchers can determine what treatment different subjects get; particularly in an experiment where allocation to comparison groups is not blind and where researchers and subjects are not blinded to the treatment received (Chapter 3, Section 3.6).
- There are no control groups.
- There are no accurate records of the state of affairs prior to the research and establishing a base line relies on memories (see Chapter 8, Panel 8.1).
- Making records of what happens allows considerable discretion.
- It is possible retrospectively to alter data collected at an earlier point in time, or where the situation at an earlier point in time is reconstructed from people's memories (see Chapter 8, Panel 8.1).
- The results are ambiguous and difficult to interpret, allowing researchers to allocate the 'benefit of the doubt' in the preferred direction.
- The results are not made available to other researchers and cannot be audited (for example, where they are regarded as commercially or politically sensitive)
- What gets published is vetted and amended by sponsors or subjects: (Chapter 16, Section 16.8).
- What gets published is determined by publishers' preferences for novel findings, radical critiques, or 'success stories' – publication *bias* (see Chapter 15, Panel 15.3).

---

bias in favour of particular findings will have an influence. You will see that some of the items in the list are those which controlled experimental structures are designed to exclude (see Chapter 3). A particularly important item in the list is the one about 'ambiguous findings, difficult to interpret', for here a researcher's biases have room to allocate the benefit of the doubt in favour of the findings they would prefer. That probably explains a great deal about Logan's (1972) findings and others like them, because studies which claim to show cause and effect relationships, but do not include control groups within the design, always produce results which can be credibly interpreted in different ways, and hence are vulnerable to being interpreted in a biased way.

Sometimes a rigorous experimental approach will mistakenly designate an effective intervention as an ineffective one and the scientific tradition of experimentation is a conservative one, setting high standards of proof before accepting that results are significant (see Chapter 3, Section 3.9). But the overall picture given by studies such as Logan's is so stark that it forces the conclusion that there has been a distinct bias among researchers, many of them practitioners themselves, towards finding that health, social work, criminal justice, or educational interventions are effective. It is important to remember that we are not dealing here with merely academic knowledge but with research findings which, if they are wrong, may result in people being poisoned, or being subjected to hundreds of hours of treatment or education which does them no good, or to investments in ineffectual patterns of service at the cost of non-investment in something else which might be more beneficial to more people.

Effectiveness under ordinary circumstances

But there is a problem in taking a rigorous experimental approach to evaluating effectiveness. It is a problem you are already familiar with. In using a rigorous research design in order to judge effectiveness, a researcher may well be creating a situation most unlike that which occurs in routine practice. Thus what proves effective in the research situation may not work when rolled out into more ordinary circumstances. And, to make matters worse, there is no one such thing as 'routine practice', but rather a wide range of different practice settings, each with its own characteristics, which may alter the effectiveness of the intervention tested by the research.

Most effectiveness research is conducted in naturalistic settings: wards, schools, prisons and so on. If an experimental design is used these might be 'field experiments' in my sense of the term (Section 4.2). But for research purposes the settings and the procedures will be varied from normal practice. For example, in testing medical treatments it is common to select as subjects people who are similar to each other – same gender, similar age perhaps. By reducing the diversity among the subjects the experimenter can get away with using a smaller sample (see Chapter 3, Section 3.3). But this means that the results may not be generalizable to people of a different gender or a different age group. Again in order to simplify the experiment, and to ensure the welfare of the subjects, people with medical complications may be excluded. But as Tudor Hart (1993) comments, this results in situations such as that where 90% of the research on hypertension has been conducted with subjects who suffer from hypertension and nothing else, but 90% of people with hypertension have at least one other medical condition as well. What was true for the subjects of experimental tests of hypertension treatments may not be true for the majority of people presenting to their doctor with hypertension.

Other differences may include that research is conducted where resources are more generous, and where staff are better trained than would be the case elsewhere. It is highly likely that doctors, nurses, teachers, counsellors, prison officers and so on who are involved in the research feel important and interested and behave in a different way from those of their counterparts in non-research situations. Knowing that they are subjects of research, subjects also may feel special and behave in special way. Where blinding is impossible this may affect the results (Chapter 3, Section 3.6). All in all this suggests considerable difficulties in saying with any confidence that because something worked under research conditions it will also work under more usual conditions. There is also the important issue of whether 'ordinary circumstances' should be, or could be, made more like those of the research setting, and in what regards, and what might have to be sacrificed in order to do so. In order to do one thing people usually have to give up doing something else.

A further problem for the practitioner in health care or social work is that experiments usually give results for a group of people, whereas practitioners deal with individuals. Single-case experiments, or n-of-1 experiments, are sometimes used to solve this problem – see Section 4.5.

4.5 Practical responses to the problem of context-dependency

The possibility that doing the same thing under different circumstances, or with different people, might have different effects, is sometimes termed '*context-dependency*'. The problem of transferring findings from research (in one context) to practice (another context) is an aspect of this. Here it is tempting to argue that effectiveness should therefore be investigated in an unobtrusive, non-disruptive way in ordinary circumstances. Some researchers have argued just this (Guba and Lincoln 1989).There are some merits in the suggestion. But this doesn't really solve the problem of transfer. If we studied, say, practice in a children's home by observing it as it usually was, without the research affecting it in any way, we might reach some conclusions as to what was most effective practice there in, say, improving the children's social skills. Given the problems of linking cause and effect under uncontrolled circumstances it would be, or it should be, difficult to be confident about such findings, but at least we might be fairly sure that the findings were not an experimental artefact. But it would still be likely that what was effective practice in one children's home in its normal day-to-day practice would not be effective practice in another children's home in its different normal day-to-day practice.

One approach to the problem above is to custom-build interventions in the situations in which they are to be used, through trial and error 'design experiments' and 'n-of-1' experiments.

Design-experiments

In engineering, design and technology, experimentation often refers to a process of trial and error in which an initial design is tried out, improved, tried out again and so on: the 'research and development (R&D) process'.

This is to create a one-off product for a unique context, or a prototype for later mass production or, as in architecture, the plans and specifications for a building. What has been discovered by basic research usually informs this process.

In applied social science, the term '*design experiment*' is used for this process, although to avoid confusion with controlled experiments the term '*design-based research*' may be used instead. This vocabulary began to be used around the end of the 1980s mainly in relation to the design and testing of teaching programmes (Brown 1992). But it is difficult not to see it as a re-branding of an already well-established tradition described by terms such as '*n*th Phase Evaluation' and 'development though formative evaluation' – 'formative' being used here to indicate that the evaluation is part of the development process and not a final, end-of-project judgement. Clinical Audit, now well entrenched in the British NHS, with its cycles of review and reform, can be regarded as a similar enterprise (Audit Commission 2003).

Among those who practise design experimentation there is a recognition that assigning causality when using this method is fraught with difficulties:

> Complications arise from sustained intervention in messy settings. A single complex intervention (e.g. a 4-week curriculum sequence) might involve hundreds, if not thousands of discrete designer, researcher and teacher decisions – hopefully working in concert – in an attempt to promote innovative practice. In these situations, causality can be difficult to decipher and disambiguate; all possible factors cannot logically be equally pursued: precise replication of an intervention is largely impossible and emergent phenomena regularly lead to new lines of inquiry, informed by current theories or models of phenomena
>
> (Design-based Research Collective 2003: 6)

They see design-based research coupled with controlled experiments, as an ideal way of studying what causes what in teaching and learning. Because design-based research is conducted in naturalistic circumstances, they say, it:

> can generate plausible causal accounts because of its focus on linking processes to outcomes in particular settings, and can be productively linked with controlled laboratory experiments and randomized clinical trials by assisting in the identification of relevant contextual factors, aiding in the identification of mechanisms (not just relationships) and enhancing our understanding of the nature of the intervention itself.
>
> (*Ibid.*)

Hence, it is claimed that hypotheses about the important contextual factors can be generated through design-based research, but tested more rigorously through controlled experiments.

Across all human services, cycles of trial, error and remediation are an important way in which organizational procedures and individual practice develop. What distinguishes design experiments from this is really only the degree of rigour through which a development strategy is planned and evidence collected and analysed. In fields other than education, there are pieces of research which look essentially the same without being named as 'design experiments' or 'design-based research'. They might be called 'action research' (see Chapter 14, Section 14.5) or indeed not even represented as 'research' at all.

n-of-1 experiments

From a practitioner's point of view, a problem with the randomized controlled trial is that it reports a result for a group. If there is no further evidence to go on, then the recommendation is to 'do to your patients/clients/students whatever benefited *most* subjects in the experiment'. But there is rarely any guarantee that the majority of people with whom the practitioner practices will be like the majority in the experiment (Chapter 3, Section 3.10), still less that the particular client, or the particular class or therapy group with which she is dealing at that time, will be either.

n-of-1 experiments are a response to this problem. They are sometimes called 'single-case evaluations' (not to be confused with case study evaluations or evaluation by case study). The 'n' is the statistical abbreviation for number, so the term means 'experiments with one subject'. In most n-of-1 experiments, 1 means one person, though sometimes a large number of n-of-1 experiments are run along side each other. The technique has been mainly used in medicine, nutritional counselling, social work, probation and clinical psychology (Gomm 2000a: 62–8).

In an n-of-1, the single subject (individual or group) is used as its own control, by switching between two conditions. The subject's response to the two conditions is then compared. In medical research one of the conditions can be a placebo, and the subject and the practitioner can be blinded (Chapter 3, Section 3.6), but neither are normally possible in other fields of research. The conditions are usually switched at random and the experiment usually stops when it becomes clear that one condition rather than another suits the subject best. The approach will work only where interventions have transitory effects, and where effects are psychological it may be difficult to know how transitory they are.

It is probably better to see n-of-1 experiments first and foremost as a strategy of practice rather than of research, adopted to ensure that a particular person or group gets the treatment most appropriate for them. But the results of many n-of-1 experiments can be synthesized to add to the knowledge base of a discipline (for example, Marsh *et al.* 1994).

4.6   Specification: cross-mapping for generalization

Design experiments and n-of-1 experiments are practical responses to the problem of the *context-dependency* of cause and effect relationships (Pawson and Tilley 1997). It is a reasonable presumption that some causal mechanisms are more *robust* than others, in the sense that the same mechanism will have the same effects in a wide range of circumstances. Thus the kinds of physiological mechanisms which are triggered by pharmaceuticals are probably more

Topics for which research is more or less likely to produce sound generalizations　　　　*TABLE 4.4*

The characteristics of topics about which research is more likely to produce generalizable knowledge about effectiveness	The characteristics of topics about which research is less likely to produce generalizable knowledge about effectiveness
• Where the entities being studied have robust, reliable and predictable properties, for example; materials, forces, muscles, bones, cells, genes	• Where the entities being studied do not have robust, reliable and predictable properties, for example; emotions, interpretations meanings, human relationships, group dynamics
• Where interventions are simple and standardized and can be much the same irrespective of who carries them out: for example, administering a drug	• Where interventions are complex and differ from client to client, or occasion to occasion and/or where the same named intervention differs according to who carries it out; for example, counselling
• Where there is a strong consensus (or an enforcement) of some criteria of effectiveness.	• Where there are multiple and contradictory criteria of effectiveness
• Where there is little ambiguity as to what evidence counts as meeting the criteria of effectiveness	• Where there is considerable ambiguity as to what evidence counts as meeting the criteria of effectiveness

Source:　　Gomm (2000a: 61).

robust – more consistent in their effects – than the kinds of psycho-social mechanisms which are triggered in group dynamic situations or in consumer behaviour or organizational behaviour. In social science we are usually dealing with mechanisms which are highly context-dependent. Table 4.4 lists some characteristics of topics where research is more, or less likely to produce sound generalizations.

Specification

The term 'generalization' is perhaps a misleading one, because a well-phrased generalization always includes its opposite: a *specification*. A generalization in the field of cause and effect says: 'This happened here under these specific circumstances and it will likely happen *generally* where something like these *specific* circumstances obtain.' The key to producing generalizable knowledge thus lies in identifying the specifications. This is something which is unlikely to be possible within the context of a single research study, of whatever kind it is. Rather it requires a large number of pieces of research conducted in varying circumstances to discover how 'the same thing' has the same or different effects in different circumstances. This is true whether we are dealing with the development of a theoretical science or of applied research. But it is particularly important for applied research since, without the specifications, practitioners will not know whether some intervention will work in *their* circumstances. n-of-1 experiments accomplish specifications on a case-by-case basis, but might do so more generally through the synthesis of many such experiments (Marsh *et al.* 1994). It is the specifications which turn research knowledge into recipes for action (see also Chapter 15).

The natural sciences have been characterized by very successful research programmes identifying the specific circumstances under which something will lead to something else, and the circumstances under which it will lead to something different. Thus it is known, for example, what the circumstances are under which water will freeze at 0 degrees Celsius, and what the circumstances are under which it will become 'super-cooled water'. Success in these regards probably owes much to the inherent robustness of the kinds of phenomena dealt with by natural scientists (see Table 4.4). The social sciences have been much less successful in this regard.

Since there is much less sound information in the social sciences as to the specific circumstances under which something will or will not happen, generalization has to rely, for the time being at least, on *informed speculation*. This is especially true for applied social research where practitioners simply cannot wait for the outcomes of long-term research programmes in order to decide what to do for the best in the here and now.

Some purchase on the problem of transferring research into practice can be gained by **cross-mapping** the circumstances of the research against the circumstances of the locale in which someone might attempt to put the research findings into practice. Table 4.5 illustrates the kinds of dimensions such a cross-mapping might have. Here, the example is for the property-marking of domestic goods: either by etching or by the use of ultra-violet-sensitive markers. This is an area in which there has been considerable research, sometimes showing that this is an effective way of reducing burglaries, sometimes showing it to be ineffectual (Laycock 1985). Table 4.5 shows the kinds of questions which should be asked by someone considering implementing the same kind of project in another area.

Table 4.5 deals with the problem of generalization and specification as a practical problem for those who have to make decisions about community crime control. There have been a large number of property-marking projects. None of these has involved controls more powerful than comparing crime rates in a project area with crime rates in adjoining areas or in areas with similar community characteristics elsewhere over the same time period. Nonetheless, by comparing all the projects and looking at the specificities which are associated with success it has been possible to draw some general conclusions as to how property marking might work to reduce crime, and the circumstances under which it is likely to work. As you might have guessed from reading Table 4.5, property marking seems to work to the extent that burglars are locals, disposing of stolen property locally and where they get to know that property has been marked, which in turn depends on how easily information disseminates through a community.

TABLE 4.5 Cross-mapping local circumstances against a research project

Relevant factors	In the research area where property marking was associated with a reduction in burglaries	Questions for an area considering implementing a similar scheme
The burglary rate	The rate was high	Do we have a similarly high rate of burglaries?
The burglaries	Mainly opportunistic thefts of high-value domestic goods (the kinds which can be property marked)	Is our pattern of burglaries similar?
The burglars	Mainly local young people	Are our burglars similar?
The community	A close community, in which potential burglars would know about property marking	Is our target community similar?
Dissemination	Information about property marking was disseminated through the schools, youth clubs, clubs and other places where young people can be contacted	Are there similar opportunities for dissemination?
The victims	Sufficient numbers of local people were persuaded to adopt property marking	Would this be possible in our target area?
The disposal of stolen property	Most stolen property had been disposed of locally to friends, people in pubs and so on, in ways that made it risky to accept stolen property-marked goods.	Is most stolen property fenced locally, or at a distance?
Displacement of criminal activity	There was no increase in burglaries in surrounding areas greater than the county-wide increase	Might our burglars simply shift their attention to houses outside our target area?
Control	Comparison of burglary rate in the target area with that in adjacent areas of similar socio-economic composition over the same time period	Could we set up a similar control in order to monitor the effectiveness of our project?

TABLE 4.5   *continued*

Relevant factors	*In the research area where property marking was associated with a reduction in burglaries*	*Questions for an area considering implementing a similar scheme*
Resourcing	A high level of funding was put into this demonstration project	Could we/should we invest the same level of funding?
Project personnel	A specially recruited highly enthusiastic team	Could we recruit and enthuse a similar team, or would the project have to be tagged onto someone's existing work?
Outcome measurement	Results measured via changes in levels of crime reported to the police; there was a high level of house contents insurance and hence a high level of reporting (initially the reported level of burglaries increased before declining)	Would people in our area report stolen property in the same way as in the research area? What is the level of house contents insurance in our area?
Duration	The demonstration project lasted 18 months and there is data only for this time period.	Would the project have continued to be successful beyond 18 months? Would a project by us be successful in the longer term?

Source: Based loosely on Laycock (1985); see also Tilley and Laycock (2002).

MORE NATURALISM IN EXPERIMENTS • 107

Where these crucial conditions cannot be met then property marking is unlikely to be effective. Here are the beginnings of a body of useful theory about criminal behaviour and community structure (Pawson and Tilley 1997).

4.7 Specifying variables

The same kind of approach to that above can be taken in designing research or in assessing research conducted by yourself or someone else. It entails thinking of all the important variables which might have made a difference to the research. You can demonstrate this to yourself by doing the following Activity, which builds on your reading of Section 4.2 of this chapter. You will see that the grid in the Activity specifies (Table 4.6) the variables in the experiments. Thus the most confident generalization which could be made about the results of these experiments is that the same would be likely to happen in circumstances with precisely the same constellation of variables. That's not generalizing very far! But we can at least speculate in a disciplined way as to the more general circumstances under which something similar would happen. Although I will not deal with this here, an important resource for such generalizing is other research about similar topics.

ACTIVITY   Specifying the variables which might make a difference to the research outcomes

Rosenhan (Section 4.2) interpreted the results of his field experiment as showing that even when there were minimal intimations of mental illness this could affect social interaction. I interpreted the results of my field experiment as suggesting that where people *both* gave a minimal indication that they might be mentally ill *and* behaved a little oddly this could affect social interaction. In Table 4.6 I have identified some of the major dimensions in both experiments, so that you can think about how changing a variable on these dimensions might have changed the results. You can add to the list if you like.

For the activity:

1 Identify the variables which differ between the two experiments which might be the most important in producing *different results*.
2 Think more expansively and suggest ways in which variables might have been changed to make either or both experiments more widely generalizable.
3 Design another experiment to investigate whether 'behaving a little oddly' is sufficient of itself to affect social interaction, without the necessity for an intimation of mental illness. For this you might want to depart from the field experiment format – for example, to use video-taped stimulus material. When you have designed your experiment, analyse it on the model of Table 4.6 to identity both its weak points and the likely limits to its generalizability.

TABLE 4.6   Grid for comparing Rosenhan's experiment with Gomm's experiment for Activity

Kinds of variable	Rosenhan	Gomm	Your notes
Researchers	1 female researcher	18 researchers, 24–32 years old, male and female, various ethnic groups (differences between these variables were not analysed) Alternating as observers and requesters	
Researcher awareness	Presumably the research assistant knew what the research was designed to investigate	The students knew what the research was designed to investigate; some had strong feelings about the unfair treatment of people with mental illness diagnoses	
Locations	University hospital precinct and University campus West Coast America, 1970s	District general hospital (outside and inside in public areas) various locations therein, England, 1980s	
Time of day and other temporal variables	Unclear, but presumably daytimes	Weekdays 10 a.m. to 2 p.m. The hospital seemed to be in an ordinary state of busyness	
Targets	People looking like medical staff/people looking like University dons Chosen as convenient Exactly who they were is not reported	Anyone wearing a hospital security badge Chosen as convenient but on a strict alternation between request types Exactly who they were was only sometimes recorded	

Requests	Directions varied according to indication of looking for psychiatrist, or internist, or no such indication 5 other questions	*Excuse me I've got an appointment with a psychiatrist/consultant/urologist and I don't know where to go* Other *ad hoc* questions to clarify directions given
Respondent awareness	Respondents were probably not aware that they were subjects of an experiment	Most respondents were probably not aware that they were subjects of an experiment, but we cannot be sure about this
Standardization	Apart from the above the research assistant was supposed to behave similarly towards all targets	Apart from the above the students were supposed to behave similarly towards all targets, but it seems they did not There is no guarantee that different students behaved the same as each other except for the standard requests
Recording	By the research assistant herself of targets' behaviour: in terms of eye-contact made, pausing and chatting, stopping and talking and a number of questions asked Paper and pencil record	By observer, in terms of both requester and respondent behaviour: eye contact, register and assertiveness of request, whether and how directions were given Duration of encounter timed Paper and pencil record
Number of episodes	Between 10 and 18, 57 in total, see Table 4.1	89 and 91 = 180 in total
Any other important variables		

Further reading

What I have called 'decision-simulation experiments' belong to a wider range of research using role-play. Highly recommended is the web site reporting and showing filmed sequences from Zimbardo's Stanford University Prison simulation (Haney *et al.* 1981) where young men screened for their psychological normality were randomly assigned as guards or prisoners in a simulated prison environment: www.prisonexp.org (see also Chapter 16, Section 16.6).

Campbell and Stanley (1996) is a primer on experimental design including the design of quasi-experiments such as those discussed in this chapter and which takes into consideration the difficulties of taking experiments 'into the field' as does Baruch (1997). Oakley (2000) is a justification of the greater use of more rigorous experimental research as applied to social work, health care, counselling, education and similar fields and represents experimentalism as a particularly important recent trend in feminist research. It also contains much interesting information about the history of experimentation in social science. Pawson and Tilley (1997) is an excellent book on evaluation research in general, equally relevant to Chapter 7, with most of its examples drawn from the field of crime control and the rehabilitation of offenders. Its comments on how to interpret the results of different pieces of research alongside each other are particularly helpful and not just relevant to applied research. Gomm, Needham and Bullman (2000) is designed to help practitioners appraise published research on practice covering most major research methods.

The literature under the name of 'design experiments' or 'design-based research' is largely restricted to educational research. The web site of the Design-based Research Collective contains links to representative publications (www.designbasedresearch.org/). In older publications, the index entries for 'formative evaluation' will probably relate to something like 'design-based research' and so also will some kinds of 'action research' (Chapter 14). Though not named as 'design-based research', the practice of clinical audit – now part of 'clinical governance' – is rather similar and can be investigated via the *Clinical Audit Support Centre* web site (www.clinicalauditsupport.com/). For a medical example of n-of-1 trials, try Price and Evans (2002) and for a social work example, see Kasi and Wilson (1996).

5 Computer Simulations and Complexity Theory

By the end of this chapter, you should:

- Understand the difference between a linear dynamic system and a dynamical or complex system and identify features of social phenomena which suggest that they are complex phenomena
- Know what it means to say that a phenomenon is emergent and identify some examples of emergent phenomena
- Know the difference between deterministic and stochastic computer simulations and the uses to which they are put
- Understand the problems of validating computer simulations
- Outline the role computer simulation can play in social research.

And you should know the meaning of the following terms:

Agent (in computing terms) • cellular automata (CAs) • complex adaptive systems (CASs) • complexity (dynamic(al) systems, open systems, dissipative systems, non-linear systems) • deterministic • emergence • genetic algorithms • the Kontiki problem • the Mathew principle • multi-agent simulation • monotonic • neural networks • power laws (including Pareto and Zipf laws) • scale invariance (scale independence) • self-organized criticality • self-similarity (fractal) • sensitivity to initial conditions • small-world networks • stochastic (probabalistic)

At the end of the chapter there is an Activity which will test your understanding about simulating a phenomenon.

5.1 Introduction

Chapter 4 considered redressing the artificiality of controlled experiments by making them more 'natural' – that is, by carrying out experiments in everyday circumstances. This chapter takes us in the other direction, by looking at what can be learned from something even further removed from the ordinary than a controlled experiment – computer simulations.

To simulate means to create a model of something, real or unreal. The model might be acted out in the form of a role play as in a decision-simulation

111

experiment (Chapter 4, Section 4.3), or made out of brass cogs and levers, as in some nineteenth-century models of the economy. It could be a set of algebraic equations, or be in the form of paper or cards with instructions for people to follow, as in *Monopoly*. With powerful and cheap desktop computers and more user-friendly computer languages, the medium for simulation is increasingly computer software.

Although by no means restricted to this, computer simulations are the method of preference for investigating complex phenomena. What 'complexity' means is also dealt with in this chapter.

5.2 Prediction or explanation from simulations

In econometrics and demography the simulation of social processes has a long history going back to the nineteenth century. Today every business school seems to have its own economic model for predicting growth rates, inflation and other economic variables. Models are used to predict the size and shape of future population growth. In these traditional areas of simulation what is of greatest interest is accurate forecasting for economic and social planning. Some of these simulations, such as those which produce population forecasts are merely elaborate calculators: whenever you run them, so long as the inputs are the same, the output will be the same. They are **deterministic**.

Some simulations such as world system models, micro-simulations and multi-level simulations (Gilbert and Troitzsch 2005) include random elements. Up to a point their outcomes are probabalistic, or **stochastic**. But the effects of these random elements tend to balance out so that taking the mean of a large number of runs will give you the most likely outcome, and it is to be hoped the most accurate forecast.

Such simulations are useful aids to social and economic planning, and can be accurate where forecasts are short term, but this chapter will deal mainly with the kinds of simulations where explanation rather than forecasting is the purpose.

If the question is '*would that outcome be caused by that mechanism?*', then the simulation approach is to create a working model of the hypothesized mechanism and its environment, run it and see whether the result is anything like the phenomenon the researcher is trying to explain.

A simulation can quickly generate hundreds, perhaps millions of instances to study, already measured and varied by inputs from the researcher, custom-built with variables in all possible permutations. For some phenomena, actual instances in the real world are too rare to allow for confident generalization. Thus the wars that have actually happened under post-nuclear conditions will not constitute a representative sample of all the wars that could possibly happen. Simulation goes some way towards remedying this problem. Simulation is particularly appropriate where the interest is in *emergent* phenomena which can be treated in terms of complexity theory. These kinds of simulations may have different outcomes every time they are run, some of them surprising to the people who built them. They are highly stochastic, but the differences between runs are not entirely due to chance. Rather they are due to the chance interactions between deterministic mechanisms.

5.3   Emergent phenomena

A traffic jam is an **emergent phenomenon** (Gilbert 2007: 15). While the cars go forward, the traffic jam stays in the same place or goes backwards. Something similar is true of the non-human examples of waves, eddies, or whirlpools which are created by, but different from, the movements of individual water molecules.

Whether they use the term or not, most social scientists regard 'society', 'institutions', 'markets' and 'organizations' as emergent phenomena, which cannot be reduced to the thoughts and actions of individuals.

The more sophisticated methods of simulation allow for the simulation of both emergent phenomena.

The process of simulation   TABLE 5.1

Stage	Example: spread of a rumour through an organization
1 **Select target** – what is to be simulated and for what purpose?	To simulate the spread of a rumour within an organization
2 **Abstraction** – identify what information about the target needs to be built into the simulation?	Information about the ecology of rumours: how they are taken up and passed on, from whom to whom generally
3 **Data collection** – collect data required from target phenomena to set parameters and provide inputs for simulation	Collect data on social networks within the target organization, and characteristics of people most likely to interact with each other
4 **Build model**	See main text
5 **Run simulation to verify and debug**	
6 **Run simulation to generate data**	Multiple runs of basic version of simulation where everyone is equally likely to pass on rumour to everyone else Then change model to simulate different kinds of social network
7 **Real-world data collection** – collect data from target phenomenon to verify simulation	Field experiment (see Chapter 4, Section 4.2) seeding target organization with snippets of information, and social survey (Chapter 6) to discover who heard what from whom. Observations of interaction within organization (Chapter 12)
8 **Validation** – compare data generated by simulation with data collected	Compare data generated by simulation with data collected from target organization The better the match the more accurate the prediction and the better the explanation

Source: Based on Gilbert and Troitzsch (2005).

5.4   The process of simulation

Table 5.1 shows the process of simulation. Because simulations are simplifications 'Selection' (**1**) means identifying just those aspects of some phenomenon relevant to the purpose of the simulation. 'Abstraction' (**2**) means identifying what information about the target needs to be represented in the simulation: typically only a few aspects.

Validation (**8**) usually means comparing data generated by the simulation with data drawn from some instance(s) of the target phenomenon. Some of the difficulties of validating a simulation are shown in Panel 5.1.

Validation seems to be less of a problem if we regard simulation as technological aids to the thought experiments that are always an important part of the development of theories. In this, they are akin to the many kinds of verbal and numerical models which are used in social science – for example the numerical model of 'perfect social mobility' against which actual mobility is measured or, in statistical tests, the models of chance outcomes against which actual outcomes are compared (see Chapter 3, Panel 3.1) or the 'ideal types' pioneered by Max Weber (1949: 90).

There will usually be a way of testing out the ideas generated in simulation using other research techniques, so that simulation functions as a way of generating ideas for empirical research, rather than as a substitute for it.

5.5   Simulation with cellular automata (CA)

Cellular automata are the simplest form of computer simulation which will generate non-trivial emergent phenomena. They consist of an array of identical cells, arranged in a line, a rectangle, or a three-dimensional block. Each cell represents an actor: perhaps an individual, perhaps a country, or a company. Each can be in one of a few states, usually two, such as on or off, alive or dead, knowledgeable or ignorant. The state of a cell is shown by its colour – say, black for 'knowledgeable' and white for 'ignorant'. At each time step in the simulation, the state of each cell is reviewed, and may be changed. The state of each cell is determined by the state of each cell's immediate neighbours, allowing the simulation of individual units influencing each other directly. In this way it allows for the simulation of a wide range of social processes such as those which involve imitation, the spread of fashions, the institutionalization of practices, the diffusion of rumours, the spread of ideas, riots, infection and the development of epidemics, the development of patterns of domination and subservience, or of patterns of residential segregation.

The best known example is Conway's '*Game of Life*' (Berlekamp, Conway and Guy 1982; Dennett 1995: 166–76). This is readily available on-line, with animations, by selecting external links from the *Wikipedia* entry for 'Conway's game of life'. It began as a simulation of biological evolution but it has been pressed into service to represent processes across most domains of science including social and cognitive topics.

Cellular automata are particularly appropriate for simulating diffusion

---

PANEL 5.1   Difficulties in validating simulations

- Simulations are simplifications and are in a medium different from the target phenomenon. There are difficulties in deciding how much difference between target data and simulation data to discount as due to simplification or media difference. This is an external validity problem similar to that raised by controlled experiments (see Chapter 3, Section 3.10). It is also similar to the problem arising from using any kind of conceptual model in sociological theory.
- Where the main purpose of a simulation is producing an accurate forecast, validation is straightforward, but usually too late to be useful.
- In many cases to be faithful to what they are simulating, simulations have to be stochastic and their outputs probabilistic. Therefore it is likely that simulation data will be different from target data. This problem can often be remedied by running simulations a large number of times; even so, the 'real world' may not contain enough examples for comparison.
- Simulation is often adopted to investigate situations which have never arisen in reality, are unavailable to direct empirical research, or happened in the past so that accurate data can't be collected about them. You can't validate the accuracy of a simulation of social conditions post-global warming, before global warming has occurred.
- In validating a simulation it may be the data from the target which is inaccurate: Gilbert and Troizsch (1999: 22) cite the example of simulating the development of social complexity 20,000 years ago and validating it against somewhat speculative archaeological data. Validating simulations of the accumulation of wealth suffer from the effects of tax avoidance and evasion.
- A close match between the simulation data and the target data does not of itself mean that the mechanisms simulated are the mechanisms at work in reality: the 'Kon-tiki problem'. Thor Heyerdahl (1950) successfully sailed a balsa wood raft from South America to Polynesia – he simulated a mechanism. But this doesn't prove that Polynesia was settled by South American raft navigators (indeed nearly all other evidence is against this conclusion).
- Simulation often entails the numerical representation of qualitative characteristics. Thus validation may entail matching quantitative data from a simulation with qualitative data from the target. This is a version of a general problem of quantification throughout social science (Cicourel 1966).

---

processes, such as the spread of ideas. Panel 5.2 gives the program specification for the example in Table 5.1.

Every time the simulation is run, the spread of knowledge through the population will take different routes and the number of time steps taken before the process peters out will vary. The programming in Panel 5.2 can be used to produce a base-line set of displays against which to compare the results of altering the simulation. For example, in this version every unit is equally influential, and equally receptive. But by altering probabilities, cells can be differentiated so that some are much more influential than others, and

PANEL 5.2 Program specifications for a cellular automata simulation of rumour diffusion

1 Let black be the colour of a cell which knows something, and white the colour of a cell which doesn't.
2 Let 'neighbour' mean any of the four cells immediately north, south, east or west (a *Von Neumann* neighbourhood, when all eight neighbours count this is a *Moore neighbourhood*).
3 If the cell is white (ignorant), see if any neighbour is black (knowledgeable). If so, the cell changes to black with a specified probability.
4 Specify the probability.
5 If the cell is black (knowledgeable), the cell remains black (i.e. 'forgetting' is not allowed for).

The product of such a programme is shown in Figure 5.1.

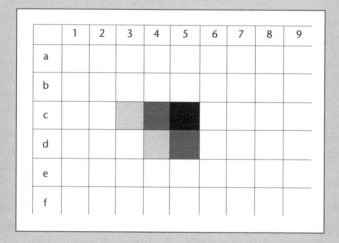

FIGURE 5.1   *An example from the beginning of a diffusion simulation, executed with CA*

How to read this figure
Shades of grey are used for knowledgeable individuals to indicate sequence, but in the simulation all knowledgeable individuals would be shaded the same. The originator of an idea was 5c. Von Neumann neighbours are cells to the immediate North, South, East and West. The probability that the idea will be passed on to a neighbour is 50%. The candidates for receiving the ideas are 4c, 5b, 5d and 6c. A simulated coin toss for each neighbour decides that only 4c and 5d receive the idea. For the next step the candidates are 3c, 4b, 4d, 5e, 6d and 5b and 6c again. Of these only 3c and 4d are chosen. For the next step the candidates are 2c, 3b, 3d, 4b, 4e, 5b, 5e, 6c, 6d. There is a 50% probability that they will acquire the idea: and so on. The landscape of cells is treated as continuous. Cells at the top edge neighbour cells at the bottom edge and similarly with side edge cells.

or some are much more receptive than others. The cells can be differentiated into different kinds and it be arranged that cells are much more likely to be influenced by cells of their own kind. 'Forgetting' can be built in, and the strength of a message can be made to wane from step to step, or be given a boost when taken up by some particularly 'influential' cells. Two different rumours (or ideas, attitudes, fashion accessories, etc.) can be introduced with probabilities ruling when a cell possessing one idea will relinquish it for the other, depending on the state of its neighbours. In one of the earliest forms of cellular automation, Schelling (1971) simulated ethnic residential segregation.

The layout of CA looks as if this restricts simulation to issues where physical location is crucial. But the displays can be regarded as spatial representations of non-spatial phenomena. For example, 'neighbours' could be those most frequently in telephone or e-mail contact, rather than those next door, or who, irrespective of their physical proximity, were proximate because they shared the same self-reference group. There are well-established procedures for measuring social, as opposed to physical distance, usually referred to as *sociometry* (Scott 2000).

CAs behave like human social actors but only in a rather primitive way. Up to a point this is their attraction. If such simple beings can generate something like the phenomena produced by humans, that is presumptive evidence that simple mechanisms underlie human social activity, too. However, there are various modes of simulation which much more adequately represent real people in social interaction with each other. More importantly these more sophisticated simulations, once set going, will themselves evolve so that their operating rules are modified, often in ways that surprise their designers.

5.6 More sophisticated simulation techniques

These forms of simulation include:

- **Multi-agent simulations** Although referring to ant society rather than human societies, Sugarscape (Epstein and Axtell 1996; www.brook.edu/es/dynamics/sugarscape) and MANTA (Drogoul *et al.* 1995; www-poleia.lipb.fr/~drogoul/projects/manta) are good examples of multi-agent simulations. You can experience both of these interactively. Agar and Wilson (2002) reports a multi-agent simulation of epidemics of illicit drug taking (Drugmart) where the important factor is the diffusion between agents of encouraging or discouraging rumours about the 'buzz' a new drug provides.
- **Neural network models** mimic the development of the networks of nerve cells in brains, which is often itself taken for an analogue of other networks (see Section 5.9). The network receives inputs and responds to them with outputs, which are rewarded as better or worse, though the link between output and reward will not be entirely predictable. Those links in the network which make the better responses are strengthened, those which make inappropriate responses wither, and by this the network learns to shape its responses in optimum ways. Artificial neural networks are the stock in trade of applications in artificial intelligence

(AI) and are widely used for purposes other than simulating social or natural processes – for example, in devices which involve visual or auditory pattern recognition.

- **Genetic algorithms** are variants on the basic idea of natural selection where there is reproduction with variation, where some variants are 'fitter' than others and there is a probabilistic mechanism for reducing the chances of reproduction for the least fit and/or increasing the chances of reproduction of the most fit. For science as a whole, natural selection itself has been the target most often simulated. For example, see Chapter 3 of Richard Dawkins' *The Blind Watchmaker* (2006) which describes evolution *in silico* in *Biomorph Land*. It also explains how monkeys really could write *Hamlet*, not quite at random, but through random keystrokes subjected to a selection process. The objects of selection can be individuals (animals or people), species, cities, routes, ideas or strategies. As an example of the latter, Axelrod (1987) and Gilbert and Troitzsch (1999: 220–3) used this kind of model to 'breed' a 'species' of prisoner's dilemma strategies, well adapted to the payoff matrix of the game (see also Lomborg 1996). This is an approach which looks promising as a way of studying the institutionalization of practices, given current interest in sociology in the 'selectionist paradigm' (Runciman 1998), and cultural evolution as a process of reproduction with variation and selection, as in Dawkins' program for memetics (2006: 192 ff.).

Building these kinds of simulations involves computer languages and protocols which some readers would find daunting. I certainly do. No further details will be provided here except in the *Further reading* section. Instead, the remainder of the chapter looks at something much more fundamental which has to do with the very nature of what is to be simulated, and whether the targets for simulation obey the laws of linear or of non-linear dynamics. Computer simulation has become the method of choice for studying non-linear or 'complex' phenomena in the natural sciences and perhaps this is a route which more social scientists should follow (Byrne 1998).

5.7 Linear and non-linear dynamics

Put simply, **linear dynamics** means that outcomes have a *consistent and proportionate relation* to inputs: if you double the force, for example, you double the resistance, which is sometimes phrased by saying that the relationship between an independent and a dependent variable is **monotonic**. Every scientist knows that things are often not as simple as that, but have tended to treat the non-linear, non-monotonic as exceptional. Accompanying this have been simplifying assumptions adopted during research – such as, for example, that phenomena can be regarded as closed systems (even if they rarely are), uninfluenced by factors from outside, together with the practices for excluding 'outside influences' while doing the research, and excluding or controlling other alleged irrelevancies. Chapter 3 showed that classical experimentalism involves a great deal of 'excluding', which solves some problems but creates an issue about the extent to which what happens in the heavily policed and sanitized environment of the experiment would happen in the messy and uncontrolled environment of the 'real world' (Chapter 3, Section 3.10; Chapter 4, Section 4.1).

It is now widely accepted in the natural sciences that all phenomena are in reality organized in a **non-linear** way to some extent. The scientific paradigm dealing with non-linearity is **complexity theory**, of which the more highly profiled '**chaos theory**' is a branch. There is no accepted definition of **complexity theory**. Some equate the term with the use of a particular set of mathematical equations and graphical techniques, including the well-known, if not well-understood, fractal geometry and Mandelbrot plots (Mandelbrot 1983). The mathematics of complexity theory will not be discussed here (but see Section 5.11 and the *Further reading*) for this chapter. '**Dynamical systems**' or '**dynamic systems**', or '**open systems**' are sometimes used as synonyms for '**complexity**' and '**complex**'.

Panel 5.3 gives some general propositions that most people in the complexity field would agree with.

What is written in Panel 5.3 is very similar in essence to the idea of context dependency introduced in Chapter 4, Section 4.5; a different way of looking at the problem of generalizing from what happens in one context to predict would happen in another context, even if it looks similar to the first.

Among natural scientists it is not really an issue as to whether or not phenomena are complex in this sense. Rather, the issue is whether, or how far, it is profitable to adopt simplifying assumptions and study non-linear open systems as if they are components of closed systems with linear dynamics. For example, the successes of space exploration have been accomplished using engineering based on Newtonian physics: a solidly linear complex of ideas.

PANEL 5.3 Some propositions about complex phenomena

- Complex phenomena are usually produced by simple mechanisms.
- Such mechanisms usually involve both indeterminate random elements and deterministic orderly elements.
- Nearly everything prior influences nearly everything else subsequent, but not in a consistent way. (This is often exemplified by the claim that a butterfly flapping its wings on one side of the world can cause a hurricane on the other side. The metaphor is rarely completed as it should be, by noting that this might happen, but probably less than once in the lifetime of the universe.)
- Most processes are **historical processes**, in the sense that what happens next depends on what happened before. This is sometimes expressed as '**sensitivity to initial conditions**' (if that particular butterfly got eaten by a bird, that particular hurricane wouldn't have happened).
- It is impossible in principle to predict the outcome of complex processes except in the very short term (though 'short term' for planets is different from short term for fundamental particles).
- Frequency distributions of complex phenomena often take the form of power distributions and may be scale invariant (or fractal) in character (see Section 5.11).

The behaviour of planets, satellites, materials under various conditions of gravity and heat and so on are sufficiently linear for accurate predictions to be made about what will work in space on a human time scale. The essentially non-linear nature of the universe shows itself mainly over long time periods and vast distances. For example, cosmologists argue that a tiny chance difference in the ratio of matter and anti-matter at the time of the 'Big Bang' led to this being a universe of matter rather than anti-matter (Hawking 1988). Non-linearity kicks in quicker, and more often, in phenomena such as sun-spots, cosmic storms, atmospheric turbulence, signal-noise ratios on telecommunication equipment, metal fatigue and other forms of wear-and-tear, and with the group dynamics of astronauts cooped up in a space-craft (see Table 4.4).

Complexity theorists have found that the precise unfolding of complex phenomena in simulation is unpredictable. But they have, nonetheless, identified some common patterns of emergence which look particularly interesting to social scientists. Three of these emergent patterns are dealt with here. They are not necessarily different from each other and may be different ways of representing the same phenomenon according to how a simulation is designed:

- Self-organized criticality
- Small-world networks
- Aggregation, or condensation patterns.

These are all aspects of **self-organization**, meaning that the internal organization of some system (real or simulated) develops and, for a time, sustains itself without being guided or determined by an outside source. This is an area with no authoritative definitions and the term 'self-organization' may or may not mean the same as other terms such as, **complex adaptive systems (CASs)** (Casti 2001), *dissipative systems* (Prigogine and Stengers 1984), *autopoietic systems* (Luhmann 1990) or, in economics, *callactic systems* (Hayek 1967). Without necessarily using such terms most sociologists and anthropologists have long thought of society as being a self-organizing system. *Sui generis* – self-generating – was a term once often used for this notion.

5.8 Self-organized criticality: the dynamics of avalanches, riots and the spread of warfare

Imagine a device for dropping rice grains one at a time, or a computer simulation of this (Frette *et al.* 1996). The grains will accumulate as a roughly conical pile with a size and spread related to the number of grains and to physical properties which determine the maximum slope on which a grain will rest before sliding downwards. That's the linear dynamics, now for the non-linear elements. From time to time there will be avalanches where one or more grains in the pile will reach such a state of instability that they will fall, bringing with them other grains as well. Regions of potential instability can be identified. But precisely when and where, and how large, an avalanche will be is unpredictable, as with real avalanches of snow, rock or sand, the carving of ice glaciers, or the flow pattern of mud glaciers.

Simulated grains nearing the maximum instability can be identified and marked – for example, by being coloured red. If two reds are neighbours then if one falls so does the other. As the simulation plays out, so networks of red begin to riddle through the pile. The more extensive a network can get before an avalanche happens, the bigger the avalanche will be.

'Tipping-point' simulations (Gladwell 2000) such as this are said to exhibit **'self-organized criticality'** (Bak, Tang and Weisenfeld 1987). The 'criticality' refers to the critical state that the pile is in when poised for an avalanche. The 'self-organized' refers to the way in which grains network with each other to determine the location, size and timing of the avalanche.

Simulations like this (Frette *et al.* 1996; Bak, Tang and Weisenfeld 1987) have been validated as accurate representations of real avalanches and such like, and as getting fairly close to the behaviour of earthquakes and volcanoes (Bak and Tang 1989). They look as if they could capture the essence of social processes such as the outbreak and spread of riots and the escalation of small wars into multinational conflicts. In both cases, a pre-existing state of criticality seems to be a necessary precondition, and how conflict spreads depends on the way agents are networked and communicate with each other. (Buchanan 2000: Chapter 14).

5.9 Small-world and similar networks

Stanley Milgram (1967) conducted a field experiment in which he sent 160 letters to various people in Nebraska and Kansas. Each was told that the letter was ultimately intended for a named stockbroker who lived in the Boston area, whose address was not provided. Recipients were asked to send the letter on to anyone they knew who might have a better chance of sending it on the stockbroker. The results are not quite so impressive as is sometimes reported: 116 letters of the 160 letters disappeared entirely. Those that did arrive at the correct destination made the journey in between 4 and 10 steps (an average of 6), leading sometimes to somewhat misleading statements about everyone in the US being separated by only 6 steps. The 114 letters that didn't arrive suggest something different, but these results do point to something important about the nature of the networks connecting (or not connecting) the subjects of the experiment.

More about such networks was learned by Watts and Strogatz (1998) using the theory of graphs (see Panel 5.4 and Figure 5.2).

Small-world networks (or scale-free networks) typically include a few nodes with a very large numbers of connections, and a very large number of nodes with only a few connections each. Milgram's six steps is explained by this network structure. Presumably messages which arrived at their destination had come via a route which involved some people with large numbers of contacts. Some at least of those messages that got lost were probably bounced around the social networks of people who only knew each other.

Watts and Strogatz tested out their ideas by using an easily available source of information. They found out how closely actors were connected to

PANEL 5.4 Ordered, random and scale-free networks

FIGURE 5.2   *Three kinds of graph: ordered, small-world and random*

How to read the figure
On each graph the dots might be individuals, towns, web sites, or something else. The lines are connections between them. **Graph 1** is an ordered graph. If the maximum step is from node to node it would take a large number of steps to get from one side to the other. **Graph 3** is a random graph. You could get from anywhere to anywhere else in a few steps. Watts and Strogatz (1998) suggest that real social networks are part random, part ordered, and **Graph 2** is this kind of 'small-world' or 'scale-free' network. Only a few 'long-distance' connections are necessary hugely to decrease the number of steps needed to get from one place to another. What best characterizes the small-world/scale-free network is that some nodes have only one connection, while some have a large number: a *power law distribution* (see Panel 5.5).

1 Ordered network
e.g. Crystal lattices, grid-iron town plans

Generative rule:
Join each node to each of its immediate neighbours

2 Small-world or scale free network
e.g. Airline networks, social networks, web site connections

Generative rule:
Select a node at random and join it to another node selected at random but with odds proportionate to how many existing connections it has

3 Random network
e.g. road networks between towns

Generative rule:
Select a node at random and join it to another node selected at random

each other in terms of appearing together in the same film, originating the internet game *The Oracle of Bacon* (www.oracleofbacon.org). In this, for example, Elvis Presley is only two steps away from Kevin Bacon because he played with Walter Matthau in *King Creole*, and Mathau featured alongside Bacon in *JKF*. Overall they found that every actor is linked to every other by around three or four steps. Similar 'small-world' characteristics have been found empirically in other kinds of network, social and otherwise (see Panel 5.4).

So how do small-world networks get established in the first place? Probably through some process which could be simulated using one of the *aggregation, condensation* or *preferential attachment* approaches.

5.10 Aggregation, condensation or preferential attachment patterns, and how it is that the more you have got, the more you get

For unto everyone that hath shall be given, and he shall have abundance, or the '**Matthew principle**' as Robert K. Merton called it (cited in Barabasi and Bonabeau 2003: 55), seems to be a very common pattern of emergence. In nature, it works for crystal growth, icicles and river systems (Buchanan 2000: 53–4) – the bigger they are the bigger they get. It also works for social phenomena such as settlement growth (Makse, Havlin and Stanley 1995) and for the concentration of retail development in particular areas, for the concentration of sectors of the economy into fewer and fewer firms, for the distribution of wealth (Bouchard and Mezard 2000) and, as hinted earlier, for the pattern of social networks where the more contacts someone has, the more new contacts they are likely to acquire and the more existing ones they are likely to retain – see the generation rules in Panel 5.4.

In reality, there are nearly always countervailing mechanisms which stop the concentration process short. Some of these relate to the dependence of 'the

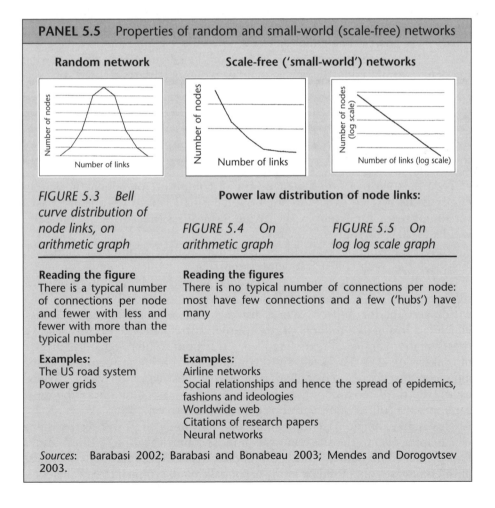

PANEL 5.5   Properties of random and small-world (scale-free) networks

Random network   **Scale-free ('small-world') networks**

FIGURE 5.3   Bell curve distribution of node links, on arithmetic graph

Power law distribution of node links:

FIGURE 5.4   On arithmetic graph   *FIGURE 5.5   On log log scale graph*

Reading the figure
There is a typical number of connections per node and fewer with less and fewer with more than the typical number

Reading the figures
There is no typical number of connections per node: most have few connections and a few ('hubs') have many

Examples:
The US road system
Power grids

Examples:
Airline networks
Social relationships and hence the spread of epidemics, fashions and ideologies
Worldwide web
Citations of research papers
Neural networks

Sources: Barabasi 2002; Barabasi and Bonabeau 2003; Mendes and Dorogovtsev 2003.

great' on the 'lesser', as in predator–prey relationship, or in the dependence of major communication routes on smaller feeder routes. Sometimes the countervailing force will be catastrophic – 'avalanches' again (Section 5.8).

Emergence according to the Matthew principle often produces frequency distributions which are power distributions and may be scale invariant/ independent.

5.11   Power laws, scale invariance and fractals

Rather than the bell-shaped 'normal distributions' (Chapter 2, Panel 2.8; Chapter 3, Panel 3.1; Chapter 5, Panel 5.5) complex phenomena are often characterized by **power law probability distributions** (*power distributions*, for short). This is true of complex phenomena in reality, such as the frequency of earthquakes of a particular magnitude or the highs and lows of stock market indices. And it is also true of the outputs of the more sophisticated simulations such as the rice grain and aggregation/concentration types, and of the nodes in a small-world network (Panel 5.4).

Power distributions are so called because the line on a frequency distribution graph (Figures 5.4 and 5.5; Panel 5.4) corresponds with an equation where one term varies according to the other term when raised (or diminished) by a power. The simplest example would be the equation, height = distance^{power}. If the power were 2, then the height on the graph, showing frequency, would equal distance squared, which generates a curve of ever-increasing steepness upwards on an ordinary arithmetic scaling (Figure 5.4), or a diagonal straight line where log scales are used for both axes (Figure 5.5). However, most power law distributions for complex phenomena are inverse power laws, generating curves of ever-declining steepness downwards on normal graphs and left to right diagonal straight lines on graphs where both scales are log scale (log log graphs).

There are various families of power distributions, of which the **Pareto** family is the best known. The often quoted 80:20 Pareto ratio is a debased version of this – for example, the saying in business that '80% of your sales will be to 20% of your customers'.

Sometimes what is graphed is frequency against rank. In the English language 'the' is the most frequently occurring word. It accounts for nearly 7% of all word occurrences. The second-place word, 'of', accounts for slightly over 3.5% of words followed by 'and' at about 2.8%. Only 135 words account for half the words listed in the *Brown Language Corpus*, which is a listing of a million words in order of frequency of occurrence in a representative sample of texts. Frequency turns out to be roughly the inverse of rank order: thus the second most common word is half as common as the most common word (percentage frequency of most common word, divided by 2), the third most common word is one-third as common as the most common, the fourth one-quarter as common and so on.

This is an example of a **Zipf's law**, another family of power distributions which apply also to the size of towns in most countries (Zipf 1949). A Zipf's law, or something similar, probably applies also to criminal activity where most crimes are committed by a tiny percentage of all criminals (see Panel 5.6).

PANEL 5.6 Normally distributed data compared with power law distributed data

Normally distributed data

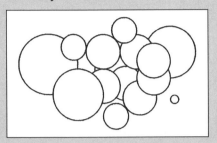

FIGURE 5.6 *A representative data set includes many items with middling values; fewer larger and fewer smaller than this (see Figure 5.3).*

The mean (arithmetic average) is a meaningful indication of the most typical value among items.

The variance is a meaningful measure of the amount of variety in the data set – measured as the distance of each item from the mean (see Panel 2.8).

The standard deviation is a meaningful metric for measuring the dispersion of the data set (see Panels 2.8 and 3.1).

FIGURE 5.8 *Normal distribution: each additional sample added to previous ones will result in less change to the grand mean.*

Power law distributed data/fractal data

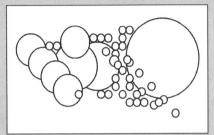

FIGURE 5.7 *With an inverse power law a representative data set has a few very large items with very high values and increasing numbers with increasingly small values (see Figures 5.4 and 5.5).*

The mean (arithmetic average) is not a meaningful indication of the most typical value among items.

The variance is not a meaningful measure of the amount of variety in the data set, which will increase according to how big the data set is. The measure of variety in fractal data is the 'fractal dimension' which quantifies the ratio of small values compared to large values.

The dispersion of the data set will increase according to the size of the sample, so there can be no stable standard deviation.

FIGURE 5.9 *Power law distribution: with an inverse power law, each new sample added to the previous ones will change the grand mean, making it smaller with most samples, and occasionally bigger.*

Source: After Liebovitch and Scheurle (2000: 36).

Although a mode, a mean, or a median can be calculated for a power law distribution there is no point in doing so since none of them express the value most typical of the distribution as a whole. Parametric tests of statistical significance which rely on normally distributed data (Panel 3.1) may give misleading results with power distributions.

For this reason, many statisticians regard power distributions as a bit of a nuisance and dismiss such distributions as 'skewed'. They often use transformations to recast them as something closer to a normal distribution. A 'log normal' transformation is the most usual, which involves transforming each data point by calculating its logarithm; the log values will approximate more closely to the bell curve of the normal distribution (Chapter 3, Panel 3.1). Or perhaps they chop off the tail (sometimes called a 'Pareto tail' or 'an outlier') which contains large values but few instances, and work only with the data concerning smaller values and larger numbers of instances. This can be misleading. For example personal annual incomes in the UK (2006) ranged from zero to just over £50 million, the latter earned by a trader at Goldman Sachs. Large numbers of people earned incomes from zero to £15,000 but thereafter the graph turns into a long curve shaped like that of Figure 5.4, or a straight line like Figure 5.5. It might seem reasonable to ignore the people who earn huge incomes because they are few in number. But they do account for a very large percentage of all income. If we want to see where the income goes, then hiding this minority away misrepresents the enormous disparity in earnings.

Some power distributions are also 'scale invariant' (or 'scale independent'). A good way of thinking about scale invariance is in terms of coastlines with bays and headlands. These are said to show 'self-similarity' or to be 'fractal'. If you focus on a headland, you will find that it in turn is composed of bays and headlands, and if you focus down again, the more smaller bays and headlands you will find. If all headlands from the tiny features around pebbles to the largest scale are measured and graphed as a frequency distribution, then that will be a power distribution. If you just graphed a small segment at the largest scale, that would show the same power distribution. Whatever data you chose at whatever scale, the same power law would apply. This is what is meant by scale invariance or scale independence.

Fractal landscapes like this were not first noted in physical geography but in fluctuations in the price of cotton. Mandelbrot (1983) noticed that the pattern of day-by-day fluctuations looked very similar to that of week-by-week fluctuations and similar again to year-by-year changes. Subsequently this has been found to be true of other commodity prices and of fluctuations of stock exchange share prices, of earthquakes, volcanic eruptions and avalanches graphed by frequency of magnitudes, of the diameter of trunks, twigs and branches of trees, of forest fires by severity, or of human settlements which are shaped as clusters within clusters within clusters, or wars which are small engagements within large ones within larger ones (Buchanan 2000). The almost proverbial Pareto saying that 80% of sales comes from 20% of customers, will usually stop down at least one more level, for within that 20% of customers something like 20% of them will usually account for 80% of sales.

Liebovitch and Scheurle (2000) argue that power distributions, scale invariance and fractal geometry are actually much more common in nature and social life than are normally distributed data, because most phenomena are complex rather than linear. Sometimes it will be reasonable to treat the complex as linear and to transform data which is actually distributed in accordance with a power law, into more normal forms, in order to take advantage of the tool kit of frequentist statistics (see Panels 2.8 and 3.1 and Chapter 15, Section 15.3). But in which instances this can be done is not always clear. Many social and natural phenomena which have hitherto been studied as if data about them were normally distributed will have to be re-examined to see whether it is more enlightening to treat them as complex phenomena with power law data distributions.

ACTIVITY   Simulating a phenomenon

Much can be learned from thinking about how to simulate some phenomenon, without actually building the simulation itself. This Activity asks you to think about simulating the situation in a sports stadium, where the spectators have a choice of sitting down or standing up. But if they sit down while the person in front stands up they may not see what is going on, and if they stand up they may block the view of the people behind. There may be a cost for standing up such as a thump in the back, and tired legs. Plan your simulation by writing a specification for a program for CA along the lines of Panel 5.1. Try simulating this first with spectators of uniform height. What do you think will be the patterns which will emerge? Then think of a simulation where spectators are not of uniform height. How do you think this will differ?

Further reading

For examples of social simulation of different kinds try Gilbert and Conte (1995), including the more deterministic ones hardly dealt with above. The best single source on simulating in the social sciences is Gilbert and Troitzsch (2005). The appendices of this contain many useful references to examples of simulations and to sources of platforms and of ready-made components for simulation and of computer languages for programming. Helpfully, the authors have placed these on the web site for the University of Surrey, Centre for Research in Social Simulation (CRESS) (http://cress.soc.surrey.ac.uk/s4ss/links.html).

Complexity theory is highly generic. Its exponents are less interested in the domain of the phenomena and more interested in their formal properties. Thus what you read about a complex biological or physical phenomenon may be equally apposite to a social or cognitive one. The periodical *Complexity* usually has at least one article per issue of interest to social and cognitive scientists. Buchanan (2000) is an easy-going introduction to complexity theory, though irritatingly he calls it 'ubiquity theory'. Gladwell's *Tipping Points* (2000) makes many links with topics of a social kind, if rather journalistically. More academically, Byrne (1998) locates complexity theory in terms of social theory.

Most of the complexity science terms included in this chapter score hits on the *Wikipedia* web site, giving you access to links to other sites for explanations, animations and research groups. New links are added from time to time which compensates for those which prove abortive.

The mathematics associated with complexity is fairly easy to understand at a very simple level, but suddenly get very difficult. For a relatively simple introduction try the earlier chapters of Byrne (1998) or Hatamian (2001), where at least you will learn about attractors and bifurcations and other features of the graphical depiction of complex phenomena not dealt with above. If you are already proficient in further maths, then you will find much to interest you on the web sites reached from the *Wikipedia* links.

For small-world networks there is an emulation of Milgram's experiment using the internet at http://smallworld.columbia.edu/ and Buchanan (2003) is a popular but sound treatment. The *Scientific American* treatment is short, clear and well illustrated (Barabasi and Bonabeu 2003).

Important areas *not* covered in this chapter include the more deterministic simulations and queue simulations, for which see Gilbert and Troitzsch (2005), and game theoretic approaches, for which Hargreaves Heap and Varoufakis (2004) is an excellent introduction, though Gilbert and Troitzsch (2005) will tell you more about the technology of simulation here.

6 Sample Surveys and Statistical Representativeness

By the end of this chapter, you will:

- Understand the principle of statistical representativeness, the ways samples can be selected to be representative of populations and how survey non-response can impair representativeness
- Know the main considerations in determining the appropriate size for a survey sample
- Know what is meant by confidence intervals, how to calculate these and interpret them in survey research.

And you will know the meaning of the following terms:

Confidence intervals limits • cluster sampling • design factors • grossing up • imputation • maximum diversity sampling • non-response • probability sampling (random and systematic) • quota sampling • sampling error • sampling frame • sensitivity analysis • staged sampling • stratified probability sampling (proportional and disproportional) • weighting (expansion factors).

At the end of the chapter there is an Activity which will test your understanding of the problems of unrepresentativeness in data.

6.1 Introduction

This chapter looks at surveys as attempts to produce accurate estimates of frequency distributions in populations – for example, what proportion of the population suffers from limited and long-standing illness, or whether the percentage of poor people who have had their houses burgled is larger than the percentage of rich people who have experienced this. The use of survey data for theoretical purposes is dealt with in Chapters 7 and 8. The key issue for the current chapter is how researchers can select and sustain **statistically representative samples**. For survey research, the most usual thing to do with a sample of people is to ask them questions. Asking such questions is dealt with in detail in Chapter 10.

Only insofar as a sample is statistically representative can it be claimed with confidence that what was true for the sample will also be true for the population from which it was drawn. Thus statistical representativeness is the basis for an important form of generalization – *statistical* or *empirical generalization* – which is different from the kind of generalization which can be made on the basis of the results of an experiment (see Chapter 3, Section 3.10; Chapter 4, Section 4.6).

6.2   Statistical representativeness

Imagine that you had to pick a representative bunch of flowers from a garden. There are various ways in which you might interpret 'representative'. The most tempting for gardeners, perhaps, would be to select the best blossoms to represent the best of the garden. There are some researchers who behave rather like this, selecting instances to make a convincing case for some theory they have, or to show the worst of some social evil of which they disapprove (see Chapter 14, Section 14.4). Or you could make a selection to show the diversity of flowers in the garden: picking one of each kind. This would be a kind of **purposive sampling**. You would have a scheme of classification in mind – types of flowers – and select one or more to represent each type, irrespective of how common or rare they were. Purposive sampling usually appears in social research in the guise of **theoretical sampling**, where the scheme of classification is a theoretically interesting one. Sampling in qualitative research often takes the form of theoretical sampling (see Chapter 12, Sections 12.5 and 12.6), but it is different from the **statistical sampling** which is the main topic of this chapter.

For statistical sampling you would make a selection to represent the **frequency** with which each kind of flower appeared in the garden. If 95% of all blossoms were forget-me-nots, most of the flowers in the bunch would have to be these. Unless the bunch were to be unmanageably large, it might be necessary to ignore some rarer flowers entirely in favour of those most commonly occurring. It is this selection strategy which uses the principle of **statistical representativeness** used in sample surveys. As you will see, there are ways of making sure that the 'rarer flowers' do get included in a statistically representative sample (Section 6.8).

Censuses, experiments and sample surveys

The 10-year national censuses in the UK attempt to collect data about everyone, and are enormously costly. Experimental researchers attempt to collect data about all their experimental subjects. This is a feasible aim because, typically, the numbers of subjects in an experiment is rather small – though that may give rise to problems in itself (see Chapter 3, Section 3.10).

By contrast, sample surveys collect data from just a selection of people to represent their population. Thus statistical representativeness refers to a sample-to-population relationship such that what was true about *frequencies* in the sample will be true also about *frequencies* in the population from which the sample was drawn. For example, a sample which is representative for gender will have a very similar gender ratio to that in the population from which the sample was selected. The art of choosing such samples is to choose those which will accurately reflect their populations in this way. Given the importance of cost, it is part of the art to choose the smallest sample which will do this adequately.

6.3   A population for sampling: young people in Slegborough

For this chapter we will consider the options and the logistics of taking a statistically representative sample from the population shown in Table 6.1. This shows a population of 14–25 year olds in a town, we'll call it Slegborough. They number 10,796. They divide into two genders, then into three age groups and then into three ethnic groups, though the 'white' category will also include a very small number of people from minority ethnic groups which are neither 'African-Caribbean' nor 'South Asian'. For each category, the numbers and the percentage of the *total population* are given, thus white females 14–17 number 1,503, and make up 14% of the population of young people 14–25.

The sampling will be for a survey on drug use by young people. National and local surveys of this kind became particularly common from the end of the 1990s in connection with the government's *Tackling Drugs Together* strategy. Their purpose is to chart the extent and distribution of illicit drug use and, by repeating much the same survey at different points in time, to identify time trends in drug use. Drug use questions are now a standard item in the regular *British Crime Survey* (Roe and Man 2006), there is a new series of government surveys on smoking, drinking and drug use among young people (Fuller 2005) and drug use features in the longitudinal study of offending behaviour started in 2003 (Pudney 2006) – see Chapter 8 for longitudinal surveys.

To keep things simple, there will be only one question on drug use in our survey for the time being. This will be: *During the last 12 months have you used any of the following drugs?*, with respondents being shown a list of illicit drugs they might have taken, using a variety of names for each. So the survey will actually have *four* questions: one on gender, one on age, one on ethnicity and one on drug use. The final column in Table 6.1 shows what respondents to the survey ought to answer if their answers are accurate and honest. There are no numbers here because we don't know what they would be. Finding out is what the survey is for. In the survey there would also have to be provision for a 'don't know/won't say' response.

The way the population has been divided into categories means that the survey should be able to answer questions about differences in (admitted) illicit drug use as between young people in different age groups, of different genders and different ethnic groups. National surveys on drug use do show that drug use varies with age and gender, though there is no clear relationship with ethnicity except for higher rates among young people of mixed race and a small tendency for Black and minority ethnic youngsters to use drugs less than their white peers, though this may vary from area to area (Aust and Smith 2003). Age, gender and ethnicity are also, as it were, standard 'currency units' for surveys such that if all surveys on a particular topic collect this information, survey results from one area can be compared with

TABLE 6.1   Population for sampling for a survey of illicit drug use by gender, age and ethnicity

Total	Gender	Age	Ethnicity	An accurate and honest response to a question
ALL YOUNG PEOPLE 14–25 10,769 (100%)	FEMALES 14–25 5,341 (49.6%)	Females 14–17 1,656 (15.6%)	White females 14–17 1,503 (14%)	Yes
				No
			African-Caribbean females 14–17 66 (0.6%)	Yes
				No
			South Asian females 14–17 112 (1%)	Yes
				No
		Females 18–21 1,869 (17.4%)	White females 18–21 1,716 (16%)	Yes
				No
			African-Caribbean females 18–21 75 (0.7%)	Yes
				No
			South Asian females 18–21 79 (0.7%)	Yes
				No
		Females 22–25 1,816 (16.9%)	White females 22–25 1,663 (15.4%)	Yes
				No
			African-Caribbean females 22–25 73 (0.6%)	Yes
				No
			South Asian females 22–25 54 (0.5%)	Yes
				No

MALES 14–25 5,428 (50%)	Males 14–17 1,864 (17.1%)	White males 14–17 1,648 (16.2%)	Yes
			No
		African-Caribbean males 14–17 74 (0.7%)	Yes
			No
		South Asian males 14–17 124 (1.1%)	Yes
			No
	Males 18–21	White males 18–21 1,742 (16.2%)	Yes
			No
		African-Caribbean males 18–21 76 (0.7%)	Yes
			No
		South Asian males 18–21 81 (0.75%)	Yes
			No
	Males 22–25	White males 22–25 1,566 (14.5%)	Yes
			No
		African-Caribbean males 22–25 67 (0.6%)	Yes
			No
		South Asian males 22–25 50 (0.5%)	Yes
			No

survey results from another, or local survey results can be compared with national survey results. The age, gender and ethnic structure of a population is also something which can usually be estimated independently of the survey, and these estimates provide benchmarks against which the representativeness of the survey sample can be judged.

As the chapter proceeds we will consider various ways in which a sample might be taken from this population, and the size it would need to be in order accurately to represent the diversity in which a researcher is interested.

Estimating the parameters of the population

Most local authorities and all health authorities maintain a demographic ('population') model of their local populations as a basis for their own planning. Ultimately these are models based on the Census returns for the area, so the models would have been more accurate in 2003 when the results of the 2001 Census were published than in 2002 when the base figures were still those of the 1991 Census. Models are updated by periodic estimates commissioned by the Office for National Statistics (ONS) and available from the ONS web site and by using other data sources such as school rolls, or GP practice lists, or *ad hoc* local surveys. So the figures in Table 6.1 are estimates and they won't be precisely right. One of the reasons we need to have these figures is in order to check that we have indeed selected something like a representative sample: thus the population estimate is for 32 or 33% of the young people 14–25 being in the 14–17 year category. In checking the representativeness of our sample we will be looking to see that the sample selected shows approximately the same percentage. However, except in the period immediately after a Census, if there are discrepancies we will never be quite sure as to whether they show that the sample deviated from representativeness, or that the population estimates for the area were awry. Even up-to-date Census data may be inaccurate. In England, Wales and Scotland its seems that young adult males were likely to be unrecorded in the 1981 and 1991 Censuses to the extent of 20% in some inner urban areas (OPCS 1994; Periera 2002).

6.4 Sampling strategies for statistically representative samples

Panel 6.1 gives a synopsis of the methods available for taking a statistically representative sample.

Most social science survey research uses probability sampling so we will restrict our attention for the time being to this, looking later at quota sampling and other kinds of sampling (Section 6.13).

The principle of probability sampling is that everyone in the population of interest should have an equal chance of being chosen for the sample. It is as if everyone had been given one raffle ticket and it had been arranged to make as many draws in the raffle as were needed to make up the sample.

PANEL 6.1 Statistically representative samples for surveys

There are two basic ways of selecting statistically representative samples and variations on these: probability sampling and quota sampling.

Probability sampling (random and systematic)
(see also Sections 6.5–6.10)

Each person in the population has an as near equal as possible chance of being chosen. This requires some kind of *listing* (or *sampling frame*) from which people can be chosen, which lists everyone in the population of interest. Complete sampling frames are rare so some kinds of people are likely to get excluded at the outset, reducing the representativeness of the sample, or restricting its representativeness to being representative of just those who are in the frame. *Random selection* is usually done with a table of random numbers or a computer programme making random selections. *Systematic selection* is arbitrary selection – for example, every 14th name on a list – 14 would here be the **sampling interval**. As long as there is nothing special about the way people are ordered on the list, systematic selection works as well as random selection to give everyone in the population an equal chance of being selected.

Not all people selected will be contactable. Some may refuse to co-operate. Thus a sample which starts out as representative may become unrepresentative through non-response (Section 6.9).

Very large unmodified (or simple) probability samples are needed to represent diversity within sub-groups or to recruit adequate numbers of people to represent groups which are in a minority in the population. To ensure adequate representation of minority groups stratified probability sampling may be used. *Non-proportional stratified sampling* might mean, for example, collecting samples of the same size from each ethnic group in the population, even though each makes up different percentages of the population: for example, 400 from each ethnic group. *Proportional stratified probability sampling* means selecting the same sampling percentage from each group – say, 10% from each – rather than relying on chance to do this, as in an unmodified probability sample. Either form of stratified sampling may be used to ensure that the sample adequately represents people across geographical areas, where the strata might be wards of a town, or agencies; or cover a diversity of agencies or types of people, where the strata might be ethnic groups or age groups, for example; or types of institutions, where the strata might be types of schools or types of hospital.

Two advantages of probability sampling over *quota sampling* (see below) are that the probability sample is more likely to be representative with regard to previously unknown characteristics (see Chapter 3, Section 3.3) and that the results can be subjected to statistical analysis in ways that the results of quota sampling cannot.

Quota sampling (see also Section 6.13)

Researchers need to have a good knowledge of the structure of the population in advance of doing research. **Quotas** are lists specifying the respondents who need to be recruited in order to build a sample which is a small-scale model of the population. Thus if the population has 5% South Asian males between the ages of 14 and 17, then the instruction will be to find as many South Asian males of this age as needed to make up 5% of the sample. Quotas are filled on a first-found, first-in basis so there is no non-response (see above) but there are problems of deciding who fits the quotas, and strong dangers of over-representing the easily accessible and co-operative people who meet the quota specifications and under-representing others. The problem of representing minorities adequately can be managed by *non-proportional quota sampling* with the same effect as disproportionate probability sampling. Today, quota sampling alone is rarely used for national surveys. Usually random selections of areas are made, and then respondents collected by quota within these.

An advantage of quota sampling over probability sampling is that it requires smaller samples and requires less initial preparation. It is thus cheaper and quicker, and hence it is the method used most often by public opinion polling and market research companies. A major disadvantage is that only a limited amount of statistical analysis is possible with samples which have not been drawn using probability principles.

6.5 Sampling frames for probability samples

The starting point for a probability sample is called a **sampling frame**. It is often a list of some kind. For the population of young people in Slegborough (Table 6.1) school rolls might constitute a sampling frame for 14–16 year olds. But that would exclude young people living in the area being schooled out of area, and include young people from other areas being schooled within it, and it would exclude a minority of young people in the area lost to the school system entirely. A question which arises here is whether the kinds of young people likely to be excluded from the sampling frame are themselves likely to be unrepresentative of the population of young people, in ways relevant to the survey's topic. There is a reasonable expectation that young people of school age, unknown to the authorities, may well have patterns of drug use different from those of their peers. It is also possible that those schooled out of area, or those who come into the area for their schooling, will be distinctive in terms of social class, or in terms or rural or urban residence. Both of these are matters which might be relevant to patterns of illicit drug use.

School rolls are not going to be so much help with those who are 16+. Another, and widely used possibility, is GP listings of patients. Roughly 96% of people are registered with GPs: more in some areas and less in others. But people may be registered with GPs in one area and live in another. The use of school rolls and practice lists as sampling frames raises important issues of confidentiality which have to be solved by using an intermediary to select names and send out postal questionnaires for anonymous return, or an intermediary to ask the person's, or the person's parents'/guardians' permission for the researcher to contact them for face to face interviews (Chapter 16). Both these manoeuvres lead to lower rates of response (see Section 6.9).

The 'out-of-area' problem is an issue when the population of interest is defined in terms of residence in a particular town or health authority area (HAA), or where the area of residence is itself an important characteristic relevant to the research. For example, in a national survey of drug use it might be a matter of interest as to whether respondents lived in areas defined as 'deprived' or 'affluent'. For local surveys, out-of-area problems can be solved by looking for the missing subjects in the listings in surrounding areas, and by deleting in-comers from the sampling frame of the area of interest. But this is extremely time-consuming. A much cheaper response is to cite the population of interest in terms of the sampling frame used. Thus instead of claiming that the survey is of the population of young people living in Slegborough, it might be described as a survey of the young people *registered with a GP* in Slegborough.

A list of residential addresses is another possible sampling frame. The post office maintains a list of all postal addresses – the *postcode address files*, including a 'small-user' sub-set which lists all postal codes receiving on average less than 10 items of mail per day (ONS 2006). This is almost equivalent to being a list of residential addresses, and it will exclude people living in institutions or who are roofless. Given the problem of finding any other sampling frame for the 16–25 year olds in the population in Table 6.1, this may be the best option for a sampling frame. Another address-based approach is to use a street directory or even just a street map as a sampling frame. Telephone directories are another possibility. But these exclude ex-directory subscribers and people without telephones, and with the many telephone companies today there are many directories. Surveys by e-mail will exclude anyone without access to e-mail.

Starting with a list of addresses gives every residential address an (almost) equal chance of being chosen. But the object was to give every 14–25 year old an equal chance. There will be a large number of addresses chosen where there are no 14–25 year olds, so the number of addresses sampled would have to be much bigger than the sample of young people it is intended to recruit. Some households will contain more than one 14–25 year old. If we were to select all 14–25 year olds living in any chosen address then those living together would be over-represented. In practice, it is likely that a survey researcher will make a random decision as to which of several 14–25 year olds at a single address should be selected. The standard device for making random decisions about who in a household to interview is the so-called **Kish grid** (Kish 1975), but in principle the operation is similar to drawing lots to select one of several.

In adopting an address-based approach, survey researchers may use a technique called *focused enumeration*, as in the 4th National Survey of Ethnic Minorities conducted by the Policy Studies Institute (Nazroo 1997) for recruiting systematic samples of minority ethnic respondents:

> This involves interviewers visiting every nth (e.g. 6th) address in a defined area and asking about the ethnic origins of those living both at the address and at the $n-1$ (e.g. 5) addresses on either side of the visited address. Consequently non-visited addresses are asked about at two visited addresses. If positive or uncertain identification [of people being from a minority ethnic group] is made at either of the visited addresses for the non-visited address, the interviewer then goes on to interview them in person.
>
> (Nazroo 1997: 12–13)

This might be a viable option for collecting a sample of young people in Slegborough.

The most important point to take away from this section is that since there are almost never any complete sampling frames for communities, some people are likely to be excluded from the outset, and in this sense the population represented will be a population excluding them, thus creating **sampling bias**. Researchers may devise alternative strategies to contact groups likely to be excluded in this way, creating so-called **booster samples**. In Slegborough, we might parallel an address-based survey with a special investigation in hostels for homeless people, and in the areas where roofless people gather. Since the respondents for this will have been selected in a different way, their responses should not be mixed in with the main sample for statistical analysis. In this regard, survey researchers are much more cautious than experimental ones who do add together the results of experiments where experimental groups have been selected in rather different ways (Chapter 15, Section 15.3). Usually the information gained from the booster samples will be used to estimate the under-recording in the main sample, and to **weight** the main sample to compensate for this (Elliot 1999) (see also Section 6.14).

Complete sampling frames are often available for surveys within organizations, as staff lists, or for members of professional associations, such as doctors or nurses.

6.6 Multi-stage and cluster sampling

The principle of probability sampling is that everyone in the population of interest should have an equal chance of being chosen – well, as equal as possible, anyway. This is less problematic where the population concerned is geographically concentrated, as for our Slegborough population. But following this principle for national surveys means that the people selected will be widely dispersed. There are two problems here. The first is the sampling frame problem already mentioned. It is difficult enough to find an adequate list for a small area. With the exception of the postcode address files or telephone surveys, it is even more difficult to do so for a nation. The second problem is that if people are to be interviewed face to face, or if they have to be found by knocking on doors, a widely dispersed sample incurs a high expense. This is not so with postal surveys or telephone surveys, however.

Staging

In order to reduce the expense of travelling widely, survey researchers often **stage** their sampling. First a sample will be taken of *areas*, then probability samples will be taken of *people* within these areas. Thus the interviews will be geographically clustered. The locations might themselves be chosen on probability principles. For example, all the wards in England together might be treated as a population of wards and a probability sample of these taken to select wards for the survey. Or the locations might be chosen purposively. For example, in the National Survey of Ethnic Minorities referred to earlier, Nazroo and his colleagues (1997) wanted to select a national sample which would be representative of minority ethnic people living in high levels of concentration and in low levels of concentration. They therefore *stratified* their sample of locations into three strata: wards with fewer than 0.5% minority ethnic population, wards with 0.5–10% and wards with 10% +, selecting a sample of wards within each category on probability principles. The data on concentration was taken from the Small Area Census statistics. The next stage was to make a random selection of addresses from the postcode address files for the chosen wards. As you saw earlier, the next stages involved focused enumeration, and the next, where necessary, the random selection of one person within a chosen household to be the respondent. Thus the process of sample selection here was like a series of lotteries, with the 'winners' of one being entered as competitors into the next. The sampling was also adjusted – stratified – in order to ensure adequate numbers of respondents from each minority ethnic group. You can read more about this in Section 6.8. Another possibility would be to use the ranks of affluence/deprivation given by the Index of Multiple Deprivation (www.communities.gov.uk.) as the sampling frame and randomly select from that to give a sample representative of the diversity of socio-economic conditions.

Clustering

Sometimes the most convenient way of making contact with respondents is through naturally occurring clusters of them: as pupils in schools, as patients of a GP practice and so on. **Cluster sampling** is common practice. It may be adopted to avoid the expense of interviewing people in widely dispersed locations. It can achieve economies of scale because making arrangements to interview one person via a school or a clinic costs almost as much as making arrangements to do so for 20. In terms of our Slegborough population most of the 14–17 year olds would be pupils of say, 8 schools. It would be very tempting to select pupils from just 4 schools, rather than 8.

The problem here is that no school is a representative sample of all schools. Starting with a selection of 4 schools is almost certainly starting with a population which is unrepresentative of all the young people of that age in the town. Remember that in this context a 'representative sample' is a sample which shows the *same frequencies as does the population as a whole*, as relevant to the topic of interest: in this case, relevant to percentages of young people admitting to using illicit drugs. If, as seems likely, schools have their own distinctive patterns of drug use, selecting pupils from only some schools is likely to produce results which are seriously unrepresentative for the area: another form of **sampling bias**.

It is very difficult to draw a sharp distinction between multi-stage sampling and cluster sampling. It is better to think of both as 'clustering' the sample. In so doing researchers will inevitably reduce the extent to which the final sample represents diversity within the population. This is because people who live in the same area, or go to the same school, or are registered with the same doctor are more like each other than they are like people elsewhere. Practical considerations of time and money often decide whether researchers use such strategies; and the cheaper the sampling strategy the bigger the sample can be.

They may find themselves faced with the choice of taking a larger clustered and possibly less representative sample because of clustering, but more representative because of larger size, as against taking a smaller more dispersed sample, possibly more representative because of its dispersal through the population, but possibly less representative because of its smaller size.

Design factors

Because staging and clustering reduce the statistical representativeness of a sample, survey researchers sometimes provide an estimate of the effect of this called a 'design factor'. For example, in between censuses the quarterly *Labour Force Survey* is the main regular source of information on the number and characteristics of minority ethnic populations. Its results are regularly published in the magazines *Population Trends* and *Employment Gazette*. For this survey, the sampling unit is the household and unlike the National Survey of Ethnic Minorities mentioned above, all people in the households selected feature in the survey. Some minority ethnic groups typically have larger households than others. If each survey 'hit' is a household, this will mean that the same number of hits for different ethnic groups would recruit different numbers of subjects. Hence simply grossing up the results of the survey to provide estimates for the population as a whole is likely to overestimate the total numbers in the population of people from those minority groups with large households. For the *Labour Force Survey*, estimates of numbers of people in different ethnic groups are adjusted for with a design factor calculated on the basis of average household size for different ethnic groups (Korovessis 2001). This is a **weighting** process (see also Sections 6.9 and 6.14).

6.7   Unmodified (simple) probability sampling

The minority ethnic groups in the population in Table 6.1 make up only a small percentage of all 14–25 year olds. At 8%, this is about the same percentage as for all age groups in England, rather less than for this younger age group (ONS 2003) but four times the percentage found in 80% of local authority areas. As with other numerically small groups, minority ethnic groups tend to get short shrift in national surveys which use an unmodified or simple probability principle to select a sample (see Panel 6.1). For example, the large-scale OPCS, National Psychiatric Morbidity Survey had a sample size in excess of 10,000 (Meltzer *et al.* 1995). It recruited only 460 people from minority ethnic groups of colour. But at 4.6%, the sample was precisely representative of the frequency of such groups in the adult population of Great Britain at that time. Once 460 people are divided into different minority ethnic groups, into genders, age groups, groups of socio-economic status and groups of differing mental health, very little can be said with confidence as to how far the patterns shown in the sample reflect patterns of mental health for minority ethnic groups in the population.

In a simple probability sample, everyone in the population is given an equal chance to be selected. But for the population in Table 6.1 whereas

African-Caribbeans as a group have only 4 chances in 100 of being chosen for the survey, white young people have 82 chances in 100. We don't know how many of these young people have used drugs in the last 12 months: that's what the survey is supposed to find out. But suppose that 50% of African-Caribbean males aged 14–17 should say 'Yes', and the same was true for white males aged 14–17. Then Yes-saying, African-Caribbean males aged 14–17 would have only 3–4 chances in 1,000 of being selected for the sample, while Yes-saying whites of the same age group would have 80 chances in 1,000.

A sample size of 1,000 might sound rather large for the population in Table 6.1. But if it is a sample selected on unmodified probability principles it isn't large enough to produce accurate estimates of drug use within the smaller sub-groups of the sample. If the hypothetical 37 Yes-saying African-Caribbean males aged 14–17 had only 3–4 chances to be selected between them, then none of them might come up at all. With an unmodified probability sample we would not be able to draw any conclusions at this level of detail. We could attempt to solve this problem by simply increasing the sample size overall. But in order to get large enough samples for the smaller sub-groups, we would then be forced to over-recruit numbers from the white majority groups. What we need is a **stratified probability sample**.

6.8 Stratified probability samples

Table 6.2 shows you what a stratified probability sample would look like for the youth population of Slegborough. Section 6.10 will explain how the sample sizes for each sub-group were decided upon. The strata are gender by age by ethnic group, and the simplest way of thinking about stratified sampling is to think of it as doing several surveys at the same time, one for each stratum: in this case 18 surveys alongside each other. Table 6.2 shows a *disproportional* stratified probability sample, since the sample size for each group is not proportional to the percentage it makes up of the population. For example, there is a 20% sample of white females and an 85% sample of African-Caribbean females. The only point in taking a *proportional* stratified sample, with the same percentage from each sub-group, is that this ensures that there is indeed the same percentage of each sub-group, rather than leaving it to chance. The percentage for each sub-group for a proportional stratified sample has to be that required for the smallest group. In our case, that would mean sampling 85% of 'whites' which is not a serious option for us.

The OPCS National Psychiatric Morbidity Survey referred to above used a simple probability sample and recruited only 460 ethnic minority respondents, but the 4th National Survey of Ethnic Minorities, also cited earlier, covered much the same ground as the OPCS survey using a stratified sample consisting of 1,205 Caribbeans, 1,273 Indians, 728 Africans, 1,185 Pakistanis, 591 Bangladeshis and 214 Chinese, with a white sample for comparison. The figures for each minority group are proportional to their size within the total minority ethnic population, but all together the ethnic minority sample was disproportionately large compared to the white

TABLE 6.2 *Disproportional stratified probability sample for the population of young people in Slegborough as shown in Table 6.1: gender, ethnic and age strata*

Age	Females			Males			Totals
	White	African-Caribbean	S. Asian	White	African-Caribbean	S. Asian	
14–17	306	56	87	312	64	94	919
18–21	314	63	66	315	64	67	889
22–25	312	62	47	309	57	44	831
Totals	932	181	200	936	185	205	2,639
(%)	(19)	(85)	(82)	(19)	(85)	(80)	

How to read the table
Each cell in the table represents a stratum defined by age, gender and ethnicity. The figure in each cell gives the sample size needed for this sub-group which would allow estimates to be made with a margin of error plus or minus (±) 5%, which would be accurate 95 times out of 100. Comparing this with Table 6.1, 306 white females aged 14–17, are to be selected on probability principles from a population of 1,503; 56 African-Caribbean females of this age group are to be selected from a population of 66 and so on. Notice that the smaller the sub-group the bigger the sample has to be as a percentage. Thus only about 1 in 5 white females or white males are to be selected (19%) but over 80% of members of minority ethnic groups within genders are to be selected. The total sample size needed for this is 2,639 or there-abouts.

The sample sizes here are set to give accurate estimates ±5%. If you were satisfied with a wider margin of error – say ±10% – then the sample sizes could be smaller.

See also Section 6.10.

sample selected for comparison. Although those are much larger samples than in the OPCS Survey, they were still too small to investigate differences *within* some groups – for example, gender differences within the Chinese group.

6.9 Survey non-response with a probability sample

Survey researchers make great attempts to minimize non-response. This includes making it easy and pleasant for people to participate. Devices include offering incentives for participation, as with many market research surveys conducted by post which use 'prize draws' as an incentive. But, as with paying experimental subjects, this may lead to the over-representation of those who are motivated by gain (Tzamourani 2000; Tzamourani and Lynn 2000). To avoid excluding those whose first language is not English, it may mean producing versions of the survey in several languages and using bi-lingual interviewers (Meadows and Wisher 2000). Once someone has been chosen as a survey respondent, several attempts will usually be made to contact them, if the first approach does not succeed.

An incomplete sampling frame (Section 6.5) may already have skewed a sample away from statistical representativeness if the people excluded from the frame are unlike those included in ways relevant to the survey. There may be further movement away from representativeness though staged sampling or cluster sampling (Section 6.6). Then some people who are chosen for the sample will not be contactable, and some may refuse to cooperate. With postal questionnaires some may not return the questionnaires. At a finer level of detail some people may answer some but not all questions on a questionnaire, or some may terminate an interview before it is completed (de Leeuw 1999). Hence the representativeness of the sample may vary from question to question. Although they occur at different stages, all of these have the same effect of jeopardizing the representativeness of a sample: they are all forms of *sampling bias*. The extent to which this is a problem depends on two factors:

- The absolute numbers of those excluded
- The extent to which those excluded are unlike those included in ways relevant to the survey topic.

The size of the non-response

The first of these relates to the need for statistical purposes to recruit a sample of adequate size. To accommodate for the effect of the absolute size of the non-response, survey researchers often take larger samples than would be necessary with 100% response: for example, larger than those suggested in Table 6.2. You will sometimes read that a 'non-response rate of 20% is acceptable'. But this is extremely misleading. It is not only the size but the shape of the non-response which is important.

The shape of the non-response

The second of the factors above has to do with the shape, or structure, of the group who are initially excluded, or who once selected do not respond. Looking again at Table 6.2 you will realize that 20 non-respondents among white females aged 14–17 will not be such a serious problem as 20 non-respondents among African-Caribbean females aged 14–17. Or if 100 non-respondents were drawn more or less randomly from Table 6.2, this would not matter so much as if all of them were drawn from among South Asians.

For Slegborough we have some estimates of the population parameters for age, gender and ethnicity which are independent of the survey. Apart from the inherent interest of these characteristics in relation to drug use, this gives us an opportunity to compare the sample as it was at the end of the survey with these known characteristics. It is a reasonable assumption that if the sample shows the same age, gender and ethnic distribution as the population, then it will also give an accurate picture of the unknown datum, which in this case is the distribution of illicit drug use in the previous 12 months, subject to the willingness of young people to disclose this information (Pudney 2006). Equally, to the extent that the sample shows deviations from what is known about the population it is a reasonable assumption that it will also deviate with regard to the unknown pattern. This depends, of course, on making some assumptions about the accuracy of the population data.

Sensitivity analysis of non-response

Non-response can make a survey difficult to interpret. Table 6.3 shows what might have been the result of the survey. It shows that females were less likely to report drug use than males, but there were 15% of females and 20% of males who were non-respondents. The non-respondents have a pattern of drug use or non-use. We do not know what it is, but that there are enough

TABLE 6.3   *Survey results*

	Females (%)	Males (%)
'Users' – answered 'yes'	223 (17)	229 (23)
Non-users – answered 'no'	893 (68)	740 (57)
Non-respondents – uncontactable or refused to answer	197 (15)	260 (20)
Totals	1,313 (100)	1,299 (100)

TABLE 6.4   *Sensitivity analysis of survey results shown in Table 6.3: sensitivity of results to combinations of different assumptions about behaviour of survey non-respondents*

	Assumption 1: No non-respondent males used drugs		Assumption 2: Half of all non-respondent males used drugs		Assumption 3: All non-respondent males used drugs	
	Females (%)	Males (%)	Females (%)	Males (%)	Females (%)	Males (%)
Assumption A No non-respondent females used drugs	17	23	17	33	17	43
Assumption B Half of all non-respondent females used drugs	28	23	28	33	28	43
Assumption C All non-respondent females used drugs	33	23	33	33	33	43

How to read this table
The survey showed that 17% of females and 23% of males admitted to having used an illicit drug (Table 6.3). But to accept this as an accurate *population* estimate we have to assume that *none* of the non-respondent females and *none* of the non-respondent males used drugs (as in the first pair of cells in this table). Table 6.4 provides a set of 6 alternative assumptions about the behaviour of the non-respondents, generating 9 combinations. Five of these still leave more males being users than females, but two reverse the picture and one puts males and females as equal.

non-respondents to suggest that the survey results could be different if we did know their answers to the question.

Table 6.4 shows what is sometimes called a *sensitivity analysis*. It is called this because it investigates how sensitive the results were to something or other. In this case, the question is how sensitive were the results to the survey non-response. How different might the results have been had the non-response been different?

This kind of analysis will not provide definitive answers but by disciplined speculation of this kind it is possible to define how big the problem is and how far it should undermine our confidence in the face-value results of a survey. Speculation here can also be linked with other information. For example, if you knew that male non-respondents included a large number of school excludees, whereas female non-respondents did not, then you might have reasonable grounds for suggesting that the non-response actually under-estimated the differences in drug use between males and females. In our survey we would know whether the non-respondents were drawn disproportionately from particular age or ethnic groups, and that might offer some hints on how to interpret the results.

Imputation and weighting

In survey research the term '**imputation**' refers to making estimates of the responses which would have been made by the non-respondents, had they in fact responded: imputing answers to them, even though they didn't give any (Martin 1999). If, for example, young men of a particular ethnic group and social class are under-represented among respondents, then the simplest imputation might be that those who did not respond would have responded with a similar spread of answers to those of the same category who did answer. Imputation differs from **weighting** in that imputation entails changing the results of the sample survey, while weighting affects the way the data in the sample survey is grossed up to refer to the population from which the sample was drawn. Imputation and weighting are obviously risky enterprises, but often can be done with more confidence if there is additional research into the characteristics of the non-respondents. The Census, for example, is followed by a series of follow-up sample surveys designed to estimate both the extent of non-response and the particular characteristics of the non-respondents, in order to form the basis for filling the gaps left by non-respondents (Pereira 2002).

If you are writing up the results of a survey, you should always cite details of the non-response, and you shouldn't believe the results of any survey which omits to do so.

6.10 Sample size for a probability sample

Representativeness is not an all-or-nothing matter. A sample which is large enough to produce an accurate estimate of the ratio of males to females in a population may be too small to provide an accurate estimate of the gender ratios *within* age groups in the population. And a sample big enough for that may be too small to give accurate estimates of gender ratios *within* age groups *within* ethnic or social class groups in the population. The smaller the units or the finer the detail you are interested in, the bigger the sample has to be.

Setting the sample sizes

Table 6.5 is useful for judging the adequacy of a sample size.

I used the same calculations as created Table 6.5 to set the size of strata in Table 6.2. Thus there are 1,503 white females aged 14–17 in the population. Table 6.2 tells me that if I was going to do a survey with just this group asking them to answer a 'yes/no' question, then I would need a sample of 306. So that's the sample size for them. On the same principle, African-Caribbean

TABLE 6.5   *Size of a sample required for various population sizes in order to produce an estimate of a dichotomous variable in a population, accurate to ± 5% or better, with 95% confidence about being right*

Population size	Required sample size	Population size	Required sample size
10	10	800	260
50	44	1,000	278
100	80	1,500	306
150	108	2,000	322
200	132	3,000	341
250	152	4,000	351
300	169	5,000	357
400	196	10,000	370
500	217	50,000	381
700	248	1,000,000 or more	384

How to use this table
You could use this table if you wanted to check whether a sample size in a piece of survey research is adequate for the frequencies being estimated. The heading refers to a 'dichotomous variable' meaning, first and foremost, variables with two modalities such as 'Yes' or 'No' or 'Male' or 'Female'. But remember that any set of results can be reduced to dichotomous variables: for example 'Yes/No/Don't know' can be reduced to 'Yes and No + Don't know'. White, African-Caribbean, South Asian can be reduced to 'white' and 'all other ethnicities'. In terms of the population in Table 6.1, if we wanted an accurate estimate of the population's sex ratio, we would need a sample of between 370 and 381, since the population is 10,769 in total. If we wanted an accurate estimate of the number of males in the population who should say 'Yes' or 'No' to the drug question and the number of females who should say 'Yes' or 'No', then we would need a sample of about 720. This is because we need an adequate sample of males to estimate their 'Yes/No' distribution (say 360), and an adequate sample of females similarly: 360 + 360 = 720. All this is to produce estimates accurate to ± 5% (the *confidence interval*, see Panel 6.2). If you are willing to tolerate a larger margin of error then smaller sample sizes can be used. You might be willing to tolerate a larger margin of error if you were mainly interested in big differences and were prepared to regard figures showing small differences as equivalent to each other.

Source: After Krejcie and Morgan (1970: 608). For an on-line sample size calculator see *Further reading* for this chapter.

females aged 14–17 have a population of 66, and Table 6.2 tells me that I need a sample size of somewhere between 44 and 80. I did a calculation and came up with 56. So that's the sample size for them. I continued doing this for each sub-group, added the results together and ended up with the total sample size of 2,639.

Increasing the response options and increasing the sample size

All this is on the basis that the survey is going to ask just one 'drug question' with 'Yes/No/Don't know' response options. But that would be a rather odd kind of survey. Let's consider the effects of asking more. Now instead of recording the results 'Yes/No/Don't know', we are going to record them in terms of which drugs the young people admitted to taking. This takes us to another level of detail and may require an increase in sample size. Or, at least, it may require an increase in sample size if we want results by gender, by age, by ethnicity and by drug of use. The first three categorizations here have divided the population into 18 groups. Dividing it into users and non-users divides it into 36, as in Table 6.1. Allowing for there being 12 illicit drugs of use would divide it again to create 216 groups, without taking account of the fact that some people might have admitted to using more than one drug. Let's be cautious and just decide to record results in terms of 'cannabis only' and 'all other illicit drugs including or not including cannabis'. Ignoring the 'Don't knows/Won't says' gives us a survey with 54 unique response possibilities. If there are 54 unique response options, then each of these has less of a chance of appearing in the survey than do the representatives of the earlier 36 unique response options. If we go on adding questions or increase the number of response options available for a particular question, sooner or later we will need to increase the sample size, for exactly the same reason as we would need a larger sample size if we divided the population into 4 age groups rather than 3, or cross-classified the 3 ethnic groups by 3 social classes.

Ignoring some diversity to accommodate to a smaller sample size

But, when faced with this problem, what survey researchers usually do instead of increasing sample sizes is to knock out some of the sub-divisions in the analysis. Thus the sample may not be big enough to get accurate estimates of the frequencies with which particular drugs were used by people by gender, by age group, by ethnic group (216 categories). But it might be big enough to give accurate estimates of use and non-use by gender, by age and by ethnicity *irrespective of drug of use* (36 categories) and also to give accurate estimates of main drug of use by ethnicity and gender *irrespective of age* (again 36 categories). It is likely that a survey researcher will present cruder analyses like this rather than increase the sample size.

You will often see surveys which include large numbers of questions but have a rather small sample, with the response to each question being analysed separately without any attempt to relate the answers given on one question to the answers given by the same respondents to another. This is for exactly the same reasons as above. In our case, our sample is large enough to add some more questions without deleting any sub-divisions. This arises from it being a local survey where some of the samples are of a very large percentage size. If you ask questions of 85% of all people in a population, then you can be pretty certain that the pattern of their response will come close to mirroring that for the same category in the population as a whole.

6.11 Statistical testing of survey results and confidence intervals

Statistical significance

Chapter 3, Panel 3.1 gave a brief explanation of the principles underlying the statistical testing of the results of experiments. In testing survey results for their significance, the principle is essentially the same. It aids understanding to think in terms of someone taking the same-sized probability samples again and again and again from the same population. For chance reasons the sample will be different every time; there will be a random sampling error which will map out as a normal distribution curve (see Chapter 3, Panel 3.1). Don't confuse this with *sampling bias*, which is something different (see pp. 138–9). Statistically testing the results of surveys asks the question:

> Are the differences between groups in the survey of such a size that they might be attributed to the chancy business of selecting probability samples (to sampling error), rather than reflecting real differences between groups in the population?

Statistical tests of survey results are presented in the same way as those for experiments, with p or probability values, as shown in Chapter 3, Panel 3.1. Again, statisticians rule that only results less likely to have occurred by chance 5 times out of 100 should be regarded as significant: $p = 0.05$ or less

There is a close relationship between sample size and statistical testing, since the smaller the sample the more it is the prey of chance factors. Statistical tests take sample size into consideration.

Confidence intervals

Confidence intervals (CIs) give a way of appraising results that most people find more meaningful than figures for p. References in Table 6.5 to margins of error of ± 5% were actually references to confidence intervals. You are probably familiar with these from television pathologists who say 'time of death 12 midnight give or take two hours'. The formula for calculating confidence intervals is a useful one and it is not very difficult to use as long as you have a calculator with a square root function. Panel 6.2 shows how to do it.

Confidence intervals really come into their own in providing a graphic display of differences between groups, as shown in Figure 6.1. As you can see, there is no overlap in the confidence limits between males and females in Figure 6.1. You can take this as an indication that the sampling reflects a *real*

PANEL 6.2   Calculating confidence intervals for surveys

The survey found that of females 17% answered 'Yes', 68% answered 'No' and 15% were non-respondents.
   The formula is:

$$1.96 \sqrt{\frac{P \times Q}{N}}$$

Where P = percentage you are interested in – here 'Yes' sayers = 17%
         Q = the percentage the you are not interested in – here 'No' sayers plus non-respondents = 68 + 15 = 83%
         N = the size of the sample = 1,313
   1.96 is a 'magic number', adjusting the calculation to provide 95% confidence that the estimates are right. The formula here is for the *95% confidence interval*. The calculation goes like this:

$$1.96 \sqrt{\frac{17 \times 83}{1,313}}$$

$$1.96 \sqrt{\frac{1414}{1,312}}$$

$$1.96 \sqrt{1.075}$$

The square root of 1.075 is 1.037.

$$1.96 \times 1.037 = 2.03252 = 2.03$$

The confidence interval is **2.03%**.
   This means that 17% yeses can be regarded as an estimate running from 17% – 2.03 = 14.97% to 17% + 2.03 = 19.03%. Thus 14.97% and 19.03% are the *confidence limits*.
   The formula here is for the 95% confidence intervals, giving you odds of being right about these limits of 95 in 100. To raise the odds to 99 in 100 substitute 2.56 for 1.96 in the formula. That will increase the size of the confidence interval. The bigger the margin of error you allow yourself – the less precise your estimate – the less wrong you can be!

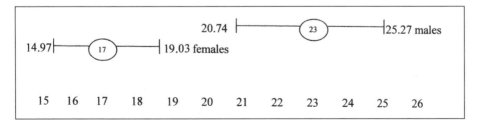

Confidence limits for males and females answering 'Yes' to the survey question (based on figures in Table 6.3)   *FIGURE 6.1*

difference between males and females in the population. You have already seen that some of that difference may be due to a larger percentage of males than females not responding to the survey, and some due to males and females having different patterns of use and non-use. In addition, some of the difference may be due to differential honesty between male and female respondents. The warning here is that differences in results may have a number of causes. Neither statistical testing for significance nor calculating confidence limits will tell you the size of the contributions made by different factors.

You might like to try using the formula in Panel 6.2 to calculate confidence intervals for the sensitivity analysis in Table 6.5. That would tell you just how sensitive the results were to survey non-response.

6.12 Selecting interviewees to 'represent' survey respondents

One of the iron laws of research is that for the same quantum of resources you can find out a little each about a lot of people or a lot each about a few people, but not both. Often researchers try to square the circle by doing a sample survey using a questionnaire collecting numerical data from a large sample and then, from the sample, select some few people to interview in depth. This would be very tempting with our survey of drug use among young people in Slegborough. After all, the survey may tell us about the prevalence and the social distribution of drug use, but it won't give us much information about practices, experiences and meanings of drug use to the young people surveyed. We could ask a lot more survey questions but we would still probably be dissatisfied with survey results as a way of getting to know about the realities of drug use for young people. Having the survey data does provide a kind of sampling frame for selecting a handful of respondents for more intensive interviews.

No doubt the interviews would be interesting. But this practice does raise an important issue about the representativeness of those interviewed in this way: 20 interviews is likely to be the maximum; that means either that 20 people have to represent all the 2,639 people in the sample, who in turn represent 10,796 in the population. Or, more credibly, that the 20 people have to represent some sub-group(s) in the sample and population, for example 100 or so young people in the population who actually used heroin in the last 12 months. As you have seen in this chapter the greater the level of detail a sample is required to represent, the *bigger* the sample has to be. But this interview study is going in the opposite direction. First, this is rather like saying that instead of selecting an adequate sample of 200 South Asian young women, I will select just one or two to interview in depth. Second, in the interview, the interviewer will ask a large number of questions to which the interviewees will give answers. For each answer they give, other uninterviewed people might have given different answers. Hence the deeper the interviews go, the more diversity between people they are likely to uncover and the more unrepresentative a group of 20 interviewees will be.

This is not a case against combining survey work with interviewing in greater depth, but it is warning against regarding the interviewees as being statistically representative of the population for the kinds of questions they are asked in the interviews. It would be difficult to say that the data from the interviews *explained* the patterns shown in the survey results, though this is precisely what some researchers do claim.

6.13 Quota sampling and other sampling techniques

The interviewer in the street who approaches you to ask you questions is probably conducting a *quota survey*. **Quota sampling** has to start from a sound knowledge of the population to be sampled, much as shown by the demographic information in Table 6.1. Then quotas are defined, much like the strata in a stratified probability sample. Quotas are 'shopping lists' which in effect say things like: 'collect responses from 25 African-Caribbean females aged 14 to 17'. The quotas might be proportional, collecting the same percentage of each population sub-category, or dispro-portional, collecting larger percentages from some sub-categories than others – again as with probability sampling, and for the same reasons (see Section 6.8).

Quota sampling is intuitively appealing. If selecting a sample is building a small-scale model of the population, then quota sampling is building the model respondent by respondent. But there are two problems with quota sampling. First, selection is not blind as it is with probability sampling. Quota sampling relies on the judgement of the interviewer as to who to approach and who to include. It is all too easy to avoid recruiting people who are diffi-cult to get at, or who look hostile. Thus quotas tend to get filled with the getatable rather than with the representative. This is a tendency in probabil-ity sampling, too, where there are incomplete sampling frames and/or a high survey non-response (Section 6.9). There is no non-response in quota sampling, since the researcher goes on looking for people until the quotas are filled. This may look like an advantage. But survey non-response leaves a record of gaps, so it can be estimated how it distorted the sample from repre-sentativeness. Something at least is likely to be known about the non-partic-ipants. Because there is no non-response in a quota sample, the extent to which the sample is unrepresentative is unknown if the researcher is success-ful in filling all the quotas. You should see the parallels here between sampling for surveys and composing comparison groups for experiments (see Chapter 3, Section 3.3). The second problem is that because quota sampling is not based on probability principles, there is little guidance available as to how large samples ought to be and no way of estimating confidence intervals for them (Gschwert 2005).

All this said, however, surveys using quota sampling by the top opinion poll companies have been almost as accurate at predicting election results as surveys based on probability samples. Contrary to popular belief, such surveys do give pretty good predictions of electoral out-turns given the small margin there usually is between the two leading parties (Curtis and Sparrow 2002). The level of success achieved with quota sampling by reputable companies such as Gallop, ICM or MORI is due to the way such agencies

PANEL 6.3   Samples other than probability or quota samples

Apart from probability sampling, quota sampling and sampling which approaches 100% of the population of interest, no other methods of sampling can claim to be statistically representative, in the sense that frequencies shown in the sample can be safely generalized to the population from which the sample was drawn.

Snowball sampling

Most usually used in circumstances where nothing like a sampling frame exists and respondents are a group who are difficult to find (Atkinson and Flint 2001). In his study of drug users Gerry Stimson (1972) asked each drug user he met to put him in touch with others, so that he rolled up a 'snowball' sample of drug users in Cheltenham and the surrounding areas. He stopped sampling when contacts were unable, or unwilling, to put him in touch with anyone he didn't know already.

Convenience or 'grab' samples

These are just the people who happened to be around when a sample was needed. Rosenhan's field experiment and my emulation of it (Chapter 4, Section 4.2) used convenience sampling. Who gets into the sample depends very much on the processes which brought people to a place at a time when they were available for being recruited. Being there, then, may, or may not, make them unrepresentative of the population they are supposed to represent. Most experimental work uses convenience samples, which are made more convenient by excluding people who are out of the ordinary – or, in medical research, excluding people who have multiple pathologies, or are very sick. All this adds to the problem of generalizing from experimental results (see Chapter 3, Section 3.10; Chapter 4, Section 4.1).

Self-recruited samples

Newspapers, magazines, radio and TV channels often conduct reader/audience surveys. Some of these are done by reputable survey agencies using probability or quota samples. But some rely on people writing or phoning in. The TV and radio versions often offer respondents the option of ringing one of two telephone numbers, thereby automatically recording an opinion. The populations polled are the readerships or the audience – unrepresentative of the population at large, and an unrepresentative selection of these. No conclusions at all about frequencies in the readership/audience can be drawn from such samples, still less about frequencies in the wider population. The kinds of self-completed evaluation forms which are now common in hospital waiting-rooms are similar. Nearly all sampling has some element of self-recruitment insofar as people can refuse, but the kinds of people eager to engage in long interviews or focus groups are likely to be very unrepresentative in the extent of their co-operativeness. They may be unrepresentative in other ways, too.

Petitions masquerading as surveys

Pressure groups often use what looks like a survey technique to mobilize support for policies they favour or against those they do not. Response will almost certainly be dominated by those who support the aim of the pressure group. It does mean something if 10,000 people register their objection to a by-pass. But this doesn't rule out the possibility that 10,001 others would register their support if given the opportunity.

Theoretical or purposive sampling

For representative sampling the object is to produce a sample which represents the frequencies in the population. Theoretical sampling is used to investigate what is theoretically interesting, irrespective of how frequent it is. For example, a theoretical sample of schools might include large schools, middle-sized schools and small schools, cross-classified by the social class composition of their pupil intake, if the research was about the influence of either or both of school size or social class composition on educational achievement. Frequency of occurrence of each type would not be an issue (see also Chapters 7, Section 7.3; Chapter 12, Sections 12.5 and 12.6).

Maximum diversity sampling

A sample chosen to represent the diversity of the population according to some characteristic(s) of relevance, for example years of marriage, or size of family. This is really a variety of theoretical sampling.

have built up over time a fund of practical knowledge as to which towns and parts of towns and times of day are particularly suitable for filling quotas to get accurate predictions, or due to maintaining carefully selected, semi-permanent panels of people to interview. Agencies like this do essentially similar surveys week in week out. Quota sampling is cheaper because it uses smaller samples, which makes it attractive to commercial polling and market research companies. It is also speedy, which is important if a survey has to be completed and published within a few days, as with public opinion polls. These never claim to be accurate for more than a short time period. They are often designed to measure the impact of a particular event such as a party political conference, or a budget speech.

Panel 6.3 gives a synopsis of other kinds of sampling, none of which can claim to produce statistically representative samples. Hence for none of these could it ever be claimed that what was true about frequencies in the sample would also be true about frequencies in the population from which the sample was drawn; hence they cannot provide a sound basis for empirical or statistical generalization (Section 6.2).

6.14   Generalizing and extrapolating from surveys

Imagine we have conducted our survey of the young people of Slegborough and have a set of results which are frequency estimates within margins of error (confidence intervals). If we selected our sample well, if it was of an adequate size, and if the non-response was not too damaging, then we should be able confidently to generalize the frequencies found in the sample to the frequencies for the population, sometimes called 'grossing up'. If we had selected our sample well, and if there were no non-response, then we could gross up our results by a factor derived from the percentage of the population our sample constituted, in order to get numerical estimates for the population as a whole. For example, if within the sample some group making up 25% of the population, 15% answered 'yes', then we could calculate 15% of 25% for the population as a whole. But things are rarely as simple as that, and in practice to calculate '**expansion factors**' or **weights** we would need to estimate the effect of both design factors (Section 6.6) and non-response (Section 6.9). For example, if we had reason to believe that some group was under-represented by 20%, then their responses should be weighted by a factor or 20%, when grossing up to give the population estimate.

How long generalizations from a sample survey will remain true for a population depends on the kinds of phenomena being studied. Public opinion changes quickly and erratically, the age structure of a population more slowly and more predictably.

Often people want to generalize beyond the population from which the sample was drawn – to apply the results of a survey in one locality to the situation in another, or to apply the results of a national survey to a local population. This is obviously a more hazardous kind of statistical generalization.

The two important questions here are:

- Whether the area to which the survey results are to be extrapolated is similar or different from that in which the survey was conducted, and
- Whether the phenomena of interest are of the kind which are likely to show similar patterns in different areas.

Epidemiology is the study of the geographical and social distribution of illnesses and social problems. Medical epidemiology has demonstrated that a very large number of illnesses has a distribution which is very closely determined by the age and/or gender and/or social class structure of a population. For example if you know the percentage of a population aged 65+, and it is an English population, you can produce very accurate estimates for the prevalence of dementia there (Matthews and Brayne 2005), or if you know the age structure of an area, and how deprived or affluent it is, then you can make a good guess as to its rate of mental illness, or angina, or the number of low-birth-weight babies (see Marmot and Wilkinson, 2000; Doran, Drever and Whitehead 2004; DoH 2006). Something similar is true of crime rates within Britain. Actual crime rates are difficult to predict, but differences between areas are predictable from the number of 15–20 year olds in a population, who commit most of the crimes. The Home Office model has quite a good record of accurately forecasting different rates of property crime area by area (but not whether crime will rise or fall). It assumes a 1% higher level of theft and property crime for every 1% additional size of the male population 15–20 in an area (Dhiri *et al.* 1999: 4). Area deprivation or affluence is also important. With phenomena like this it is possible to take the findings of a national survey, make some adjustments for local differences in age and affluence/deprivation and apply the national survey results to produce reasonable local estimates; and similarly with applying the results of a local survey in one area to the situation in another (Gomm 2000d).

However, it is sensible to do this only when there is a sound body of research demonstrating the age-, gender- or socio-economic-relatedness of a phenomenon. For many phenomena we do not have this knowledge, and for some we have knowledge that local factors other than age or gender or socio-economic factors determine the pattern, though we might not know what these are. It is not quite clear at the moment whether drug use by young people is the kind of phenomenon which shows a consistent pattern nationally (Roe and Man 2006). If it varies systematically according to the age structure populations of young people and according to area affluence or deprivation, then our survey results might been extrapolated to another area after making suitable adjustments for differences in age and deprivation. But it is also possible that drug use by young people has an epidemic pattern, flaring up here, dying down there. Agar and Wilson (2002) created a computer simulation of drug epidemics as if they rose and fell according to rumours about the 'buzz' which could be gained from a new drug or a new way of imbibing an old one. They claim that this produces similar patterns of usage to those actually found by empirical research with drug users. (Chapter 5, Section 5.6). If the simulation is valid, then our survey results from Slegborough are unlikely to travel, and extrapolating from a national survey to Slegborough is unlikely to be accurate.

Another approach to comparing like with like is to use the ONS grouping of areas into 'families' with similar demographic and socio-economic characteristics (Vickers and Rees 2006). This approach is much used when judging the performance of one local government council, or one NHS trust, against another in order to 'level the playing field', of comparison. It is also used in setting up quotas where geographical units are to be sampled, either as the first stage of a survey, where the second-level sampling will be by probability, or by quota selection of individuals.

ACTIVITY   Guarding against unrepresentativeness

Figure 6.2 shows that the outcome from a sample survey will be a set of frequency statements. These might provide accurate estimates for the frequencies in the population from which the sample was drawn. But it also shows that the results might be shaped by other factors as well. Think of a topic which might be researched using a sample survey and define the population of interest carefully – for example, 'people aged 65 years plus, living in residential care in England and Wales', or 'female medical doctors under the age of 35 whether practising or not, and living in Scotland'.

With your chosen population in mind, for each of the numbered boxes in Figure 6.2, jot down what might be done to prevent the sample deviating from statistical representativeness, or to prevent the drawing of misleading conclusions about population frequencies from an unavoidable deviation. (Ignore box **6** for now, it refers to a topic which will be dealt with in Chapter 10).

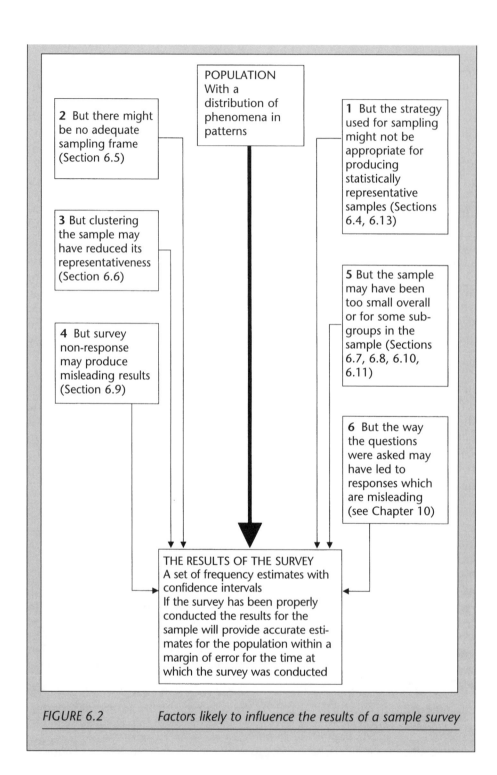

FIGURE 6.2   *Factors likely to influence the results of a sample survey*

Further reading

Survey sampling is a topic which is well provided with textbooks; for example Punch (2003) or Sapsford (2006), which give an overview of both the theory and practice of survey work, or Fink (2003a), which is specifically about sampling decisions. Fink (2005) is step-by-step guide to conducting surveys. de Vaus (2001), Fowler (2001), Fink (2003b) are multi-volume survey research handbooks. Ruddock (1999) is a useful article detailing all the ways in which a survey can depart from representativeness (apart from sampling error).

The design and analysis of surveys is now supported by commercial software packages, such as *Sphinx Survey* (www.sphinxsurvey.com).

For the analysis of survey data, see Fink (2003d), which is particularly helpful in explaining how to interpret computer print-outs from the statistical analysis of surveys. Chambers and Skinner (2003) also explains the statistical models involved in the design and hence analysis of surveys. If you have access to SPSS, Babbie and Halley (2007) is a disk and book kit allowing you to practise the statistical analysis of survey data using the main software in this field. Convenient, free on-line statistics calculators include those listed under Further reading of Chapter 3, but also www.surveysystem.com/sscalc.htm, which will calculate appropriate sample sizes for given confidence intervals, or confidence intervals for given sample sizes.

Quota sampling is usually dealt with best in market research handbooks; for example, Hague, Hague and Morgan (2004). Examples of quota surveys, their sample size and the questions asked can be found on the MORI web site (www.mori.com).

Gomm, Needham and Bullman (2000: 299–305) offer a way of interrogating surveys and case control studies for their quality. For the possibilities of generalizing from the results of surveys in one area to the circumstances in another, or of applying national surveys to local areas, see Gomm (2000d).

For community surveys, census-based data is often the starting point for designing the samples, and provides some benchmarks against which the representativeness of a sample can be judged. A convenient source for these data and commentaries on the methodology of the census and other surveys is the ONS Neighbourhood Statistics Service (http://neighbourhood.statistics.gov.uk).

Further reading on questionnaires and interviews will be found at the end of Chapter 10.

7 Natural Experiments

By the end of this chapter, you will:

- Understand the idea of a 'natural experiment'
- Know what is meant by statistical control
- Understand the use of prediction as a form of explanation
- Know the difference between surveys, case control and population comparison studies
- Be able to state the advantages and disadvantages of a natural experimental approach as compared with controlled experiments.

And you will know the meaning of the following terms:

Ad hocing • age standardization • ascertainment bias • case control studies • interaction effects • internal versus external controls • population control studies • random error • statistical control (standardization).

At the end of the chapter there is an Activity that will test your understanding about controlling variables in explaining reading scores.

7.1 Introduction

An experimental design is the most adequate for investigating cause and effect, but the results of controlled experiments are always vulnerable to the critique that while the experiment might give valid results for the experimental conditions, things would be different in 'real life' (Chapter 3, Section 3.10; Chapter 4). Sometimes a distinction is made between 'experiments' ('true' and 'quasi-') – meaning controlled experiments as described in Chapters 3 and 4 – and observational studies, meaning studies such as surveys asking people questions (Chapters 6 and 8), as well as studies done by observing people going about their everyday affairs (Chapter 12). But when astronomers write about 'experiments', what they usually mean is making some strategic observations of events and entities which would exist whether astronomers existed or not. Of all the sciences, astronomy is the one which has most successfully made such natural experiments its stock in trade. It is **natural experiments** of this kind which are the topic of this chapter and of Chapter 8. Chapter 8 deals with the control of *time* in natural experiments through taking a *prospective* or *longitudinal* approach.

Natural experiments

The term 'natural experiment' is used to refer to the investigation of configurations of factors of the kind which experimenters would create, if they could, where they can't, but which crop up naturally. The interest is in finding out what causes what. Taking this approach is sometimes called 'the comparative method'. Astronomers can't shove stars and galaxies about so, if they want to know what happens when two stellar bodies of particular magnitudes are close together, then they have to look for naturally occurring examples for an answer. Similarly there are often practical – and, in addition, ethical – reasons why social and behavioural scientists cannot, or should not, conduct controlled experiments (Morrison 2001; on research ethics, see Chapter 16). For example, they probably could not, and certainly should not, do a controlled experiment, subjecting a group of children to extreme social and emotional deprivation to see what effects this has on their social and emotional development, compared with a control group of children raised under more benign conditions. But the collapse of the communist regimes in Eastern European countries has made large numbers of orphans available as a natural experiment of this kind (Rutter 1999). Again, we could not divide people among a set of experimental groups and subject some of them to the catholic religion, some to protestant religions, and so on, throughout their lives in order to investigate the effect of religion on suicide rates. But we can analyse the data on suicide to see whether people of one religion rather than another did actually commit suicide more frequently. Durkheim's famous study of suicide at the end of the nineteenth century was an example of a natural experiment of this kind (Durkheim 1952; see Taylor 1982).

Again in their well-known *Affluent Worker* studies, Goldthorpe *et al.* (1968a, 1968b, 1969) chose workers in Luton as their subjects for a natural experiment since they wanted to investigate the notion that manual workers were becoming increasingly middle class, and Luton at the time was a town with cutting-edge industries with manual workers earning wages equivalent to many white-collar workers elsewhere. They reasoned that if manual workers were becoming more middle class, Luton was the kind of place where this trend would be most advanced: a *test case*.

The data for natural experimental research may come from sample surveys, or from routinely collected administrative data such as the registrations of deaths, or the recording of crime (Chapter 9). The practice of 'constant comparison' in qualitative research can also be regarded as conducting natural experiments (Chapter 12, Section 12.6).

Table 7.1 gives a synopsis of the difficulties of studying causality using natural experiments, recapping what was said about controlled experiments in Chapter 3. The table presumes a similar-subjects and different-treatments design (Chapter 2, *Figure 2.2*; Chapter 3, *Figure 3.1*), but the principles are the same for a different-subjects and similar-treatments design. As you can see, there is a trade-off between, on the one hand, being able confidently to say what causes what, but being unsure as to whether anything similar would happen under non-controlled experimental conditions and, on the other,

TABLE 7.1 Controlled experiments and natural experiments compared as ways of studying causality

Requirement for study of causality	Approach adopted in controlled experiments	Difficulties in natural experiments
1 Accurate characterization of the state of affairs before the causal factors of interest have had any impact and after they have had an impact (*prospectivity*) (see Chapter 8)	Controlled experiments are usually *prospective* in that data are recorded prior to the start of the experiment to set a 'base-line' and at the end to measure 'outcomes' Where this is not done the results are less convincing	Researchers often find the right conditions for a natural experiment only *after* the causal factors have had their impact Then they have to collect data about earlier events *retrospectively* It may be difficult to recover accurate data about earlier events Longitudinal designs are sometimes used to avoid this problem; without a longitudinal design it may be difficult to determine direction of effect (see Chapter 8)
2 Existence of two or more comparison groups of subjects (people, situations, events and so on) similar in all respects which might be relevant to the experiment (*Controlling for differences at the subject level*)	Creation of comparison groups by the experimenter which can be subjected to different experiences, creating the groups using one of the means available for creating comparison groups similar in all respects relevant to the experiment (Chapter 3, Section 3.3)	Comparison groups have to be created by the statistical manipulation of data: by *statistical control* It is often difficult to control out important differences between subjects to create groups similar in ways they should be similar and different in ways they should be different as relevant to the research topic The success of statistical control depends on the quality of the data available

3 All the subjects are the same in ways relevant to the research topic, except with regard to the impact of the causal factor(s) of interest (*Controlling for differences at the 'treatment' level*)	As above, and insofar as the experimenter can control what happens to the subjects, it can be arranged that subjects are treated the same where they should be treated the same, and differently where they should be treated differently	What happens to the subjects in a 'natural experiment' happens 'naturally' and is beyond the researcher's control Thus the researcher has to use *statistical control* to separate those to which something happened from those to which it did not happen The success of statistical control depends on the quality of the data available
4 Other factors which might influence what happens are either excluded, or impact equally on all comparison groups (*Controlling out other extraneous variables which might confound the experiment*)	As above, and insofar as experimenters can control what happens to subjects, other factors can be excluded This is where more naturalistic experiments such as field experiments (Chapter 4, Section 4.2) or design experiments (Chapter 4, Section 4.5) often become most problematic	Since natural experiments study what happens naturally, all kinds of other things will have happened to the subjects in addition to what is of interest These other factors cannot be excluded from what happens, and it may be very difficult to identify them and to discount their influence in analysing the data
5 Observations, measurements and so on are made of each subject in the same way (*Controlling for unreliability in data collection*)	This is usually easy to arrange Where it fails, it will be difficult to have confidence in the results of the experiment (see Chapter 3, Sections 3.6 and 3.7)	Often natural experiments utilize data from surveys or from bureaucratic sources (for example, from death certification or crime statistics, see Chapter 9) Any shortcomings in a survey (for example, non-response, Chapter 6, Section 6.9) may undermine the natural experiment
	High degree of control Low degree of naturalism	Low degree of control High degree of naturalism

being sure that what was studied was something that happened under real-life conditions, but being rather uncertain as to what made it happen.

Table 7.1 shows that in controlled experiments, control over variables – *experimental control* – is exerted by organizing people and the environment directly, and that in natural experiments this is replaced with *statistical control*, which involves organizing data from naturally occurring situations into categories and analysing them. The topic raised in row **1** of *Table 7.1* – prospectivity – is dealt with in Chapter 8.

7.2   The idea of statistical control

For social and behavioural scientists, the constellation of variables needed for a natural experiment may occur only rarely and, in addition, may be difficult to find. This can be illustrated by the studies of twins conducted from the 1930s to the 1960s. As well as being important in separating genetic from environmental causes of disease, these are important because they were used as the main prop in an argument that intelligence and some aspects of personality are largely inherited, and that therefore there is a biological basis for social inequality and perhaps for criminality (Kamin 1974). Because identical twins were assumed to have identical genetic endowments the natural experiments constituted by identical twins *reared apart* have been used to study the relative importance of heredity and environment in influencing intelligence and personality. More recently it has become apparent that identical twins do not have identical genetic make-ups (Iordananova 2006), but it is still assumed that they are genetically more similar than non-identical twins.

Table 7.2 shows what 'statistical control' means here. It just means sorting

TABLE 7.2	A statistical control structure for studying the relative influence of heredity and environment on characteristics such as intelligence or personality traits

	Identical twins	Non-identical twins (same gender only)	Non-twin siblings (same gender only)	
Reared apart	Measure of difference in IQ for subjects in this category	Measure of difference in IQ for subjects in this category	Measure of difference in IQ for subjects in this category	Different environment
Reared together	Measure of difference in IQ for subjects in this category Decreasing genetic similarity ⟶	Measure of difference in IQ for subjects in this category	Measure of difference in IQ for subjects in this category	Same environment

subjects into groups of similarity and difference as relevant to the research topic.

Reading from left to right in *Table 7.2*, there are three categories of decreasing genetic similarity. This could be continued with first cousins, second cousins and so on. Reading vertically, there are two states of 'environmental' conditions: 'reared apart' and 'reared together'. You can think of the table as equivalent to three controlled experiments of the similar-subjects and different-treatments kind conducted side by side (Chapter 3, *Figure 3.1*). Taken all together similarities and differences *along the rows* should show the influence of heredity, and similarities and differences *down the columns* should show the influence of environment. And, in principle, at least, if there was more similarity in intelligence between identical twins reared apart, than between non-identical twins reared together, that would be presumptive evidence that heredity was more important than environment in determining measured intelligence. By combining and analysing all the data in all the cells, it is possible to come up with an estimate of the relative importance of heredity, on the one hand, and environment, on the other, in determining IQ *for the people actually studied*. The classic studies always came up with results which showed that heredity was the more important influence.

Representativeness

There are two kinds of problems here, however. One is a problem of statistical representativeness (see Chapter 6). How representative of all twins are the twins in the sample, and how representative are the twins reared apart of all twins reared apart, and so on? Since the twins which appeared in the studies were found mainly by advertising in the mass media and offering a financial reward for participation, it seems unlikely that those found are a representative sample, and identical twins reared apart who did not know they had a twin sibling are excluded. Only if they are representative in the statistical sense (Chapter 6, Section 6.1) can the results be generalized to the population from which the subjects were drawn: all twins. For a researcher to say that intelligence is 75% heredity and 25% environmentally determined is trivial, if this applies only to the small number of people studied and these are not a representative sample of any wider population. It is important only if such an estimate can be generalized to a larger population.

However, even in a small sample there would be something compelling about the demonstration that similarity in IQ always decreased as hereditary difference increased: from identical twins to non-identical twins, to non-twin siblings, to first cousins, to second cousins, and so on. But the problem of representativeness has another twist. Because identical twins reared apart are rare, the sample on which such calculations have been based was drawn from several countries at several different points in time. Think of athletics as a parallel example. Sprinters in 2000AD were running much faster than sprinters in 1900. There is no reason to believe that the genetic endowments of people have changed much in the 100 years, so this must be due to environmental factors – including, in this case, the social processes through which people get to be athletics competitors. Thus the contribution of environmental factors to running speeds as recorded in competitive athletics cannot be of a fixed magnitude and must vary from time to time and place to place; so also must the contribution of genetic factors. Hence any calculation of the relative importance of heredity and environment can refer only to a specified population in its social context at a specified point in time. So it is with IQ. But with twin studies it is far from clear as to just what population the people studied represented in place and time. The Flynn effect (Chapter 2, Section 2.12) is another warning that there cannot be a fixed ratio between environmental and genetic influences; so also is the finding that heritability estimates vary according to socio-economic background (Turkheimer *et al.* 2003).

Statistical control

For statistical control, the more important issue is that of getting the right people into the right cells of a control structure such as *Table 7.2*. There are two axes of difficulty here. First, there used to be a problem of distinguishing identical from non-identical twins. These days, this can be done infallibly with DNA testing. But in the classic twin studies it was done by eye. From DNA tests, we now know that some identical twins are far from identical in appearance, and that some same-gender non-identical twins look very much alike. Second, there is an even worse problem of drawing a line between 'reared together' and 'reared apart'. These are proxies for the idea of 'similar environment/different environment'. But there are many ways in which similar environments can be different for different people, and different environments similar for different people (Horowitz *et al.* 2003; Plass 2005).

There is also a question of *time*: 'how long should twins be reared separately in order to count as having been reared apart?' or 'how short should a period of separation be, not to count as an apartness?' And there is a problem of *timing*: 'Is being separated from the age of 15 years the same as being separated at the age of 15 months?' Re-analyses of the twin studies (Taylor 1980; Kamin 1981) suggest that relatively brief periods of separation were sometimes regarded as instances of being reared apart. Sometimes living in different households next door to each other were counted as being reared apart. A photo of identical twins reared apart and allegedly having just been reunited by the researcher shows two boys in identical suits with identical haircuts, which rather beggars belief. It is not clear whether the 'together/apart' distinctions were made even-handedly with regard to identical and non-identical twins. The data were collected retrospectively by the original researchers, either from bureaucratic records or from interviewing subjects, or their parents and guardians; so it is very difficult to say much with any confidence as to the appropriateness of the 'reared together/reared apart' distinctions actually made. There is more on the problems of retrospectivity in Chapter 8.

Thus in terms of *Table 7.1* (row **2**) the classic twin studies seem to fail in creating comparison groups, which are similar in ways they should be similar and different in ways they should be different – on the genetic axis. And, on the environmental axis, they fail adequately to divide the subjects into groups of pairs who have had similar experiences and to separate these from groups of pairs who have had different experiences from each other (*Table 7.1*, row 3). It is also unlikely that these studies adequately controlled for the host of other things, which might have happened to the subjects which were associated neither with their genetics, nor with their living together, nor living apart: for example, illnesses and accidents. These would probably control themselves out in a large sample by *random error*, since by chance such matters might distribute themselves evenly across all the groups. But here we are talking about a small sample, where a few accidental happenings might have a considerable effect on the overall picture.

Ad hocing and expectancy effects

Not all of these shortcomings would favour results suggesting a hereditarian interpretation. But, in fact, twin studies were for a long time regarded as the definitive proof of the overwhelming importance of heredity in determining intelligence. Wherever data are ambiguous, they offer researchers the opportunity to make *ad hoc* decisions as to where, for example, to locate a case within a statistical control structure, or which data to include or exclude entirely. These are the ideal conditions for expectancy effects (Chapter 3, Section 3.6; and see Chapter 4, *Table 4.4*). Re-analysis of the classic studies (Kamin 1974, 1981; Taylor 1980) suggests that the researchers concerned engaged in *unilateral ad hocing*. That means that they always tended to give the benefit of the doubt to decisions which would favour one interpretation rather than another: in this case, a hereditarian interpretation. For example, Shields (1965) seems to have excluded from his studies identical twins with dissimilar IQs on the grounds that one of them must have misunderstood the test instructions; nor did he note that when he conducted tests himself the IQs of identical twins were more similar than when a research assistant administered tests (Kamin 1981).

Worse than this, the majority of the identical twins reared apart came from the studies of Cyril Burt. It now seems that he invented all or at least some of them (Kamin 1974, 1981; Shipman 1988: 119–21). Despite this fraud being uncovered in the early 1970s, many textbooks published up to 12 years later still cited findings based on Burt's data as the truth, some even despite mentioning the fraud elsewhere in the book or article (Gould 1992). More recent twin studies suggest a much lower degree of heritability for personality and intelligence than was suggested in the past (McGuffin 1999).

The term *standardization* is sometimes used as a synonym for statistical control – see Panel 2.7.

7.3 Measuring the school effect as a natural experiment

Here, I want to illustrate a natural experiment approach with the investigation of 'the school effect' by Jesson, Gray and Tranmer (1992). Do not confuse the school effect with the effect of going to school or not. That would be something different. The school effect is the size of the difference that *attending one school rather than another* can make to the educational achievement of otherwise similar children.

This formulation suggests the outline of a controlled experiment: two or more comparison groups of children selected to be as similar to each other as possible in ways relevant to educational achievement, but treated differently by being sent to different schools (Chapter 3, *Figure 3.1*). Because the groups were similar at the outset any differences between the average achievement scores of the groups at the end should then be due to differences made by attending different schools: the school effect. It would be impossible to perform this controlled experiment, but thinking about it makes it obvious why it is difficult to measure the school effect under naturally occurring circumstances. It is because naturally occurring circumstances are unlike those we would create if we were able to do a controlled experiment. The most important difference here is that, whereas in the experiment we would arrange for the children in each comparison group to be similar to each other, in reality different schools are attended by different groups of children with different combinations of characteristics known to be associated with differences in educational achievement. These are characteristics such as ability, social class, gender, ethnicity, ambition, and so on. In the vocabulary of controlled experiments there is an acute problem here of controlling prior differences at the subject level (*Table 7.1*, row 2). In a controlled experiment, this would be done by creating comparison groups and organizing what was to happen to them. In a natural experiment, it has to be done by statistical control (see Section 7.2).

The technique used by Jesson and his colleagues is a version of multiple regression analysis called multi-level modelling. Many people find the statistics difficult to follow (Goldstein 1987; Schagen 1993). But even if they do, they can still gain from reading this kind of research so long as they understand its underlying logic, which I will explain.

The term 'multi-level' denotes that influences – here, on educational achievement – are conceived of as operating at a number of levels. As *Table 7.3* shows, at a minimum in school studies there are the *pupil-level variables* (equivalent to the subject level of *Table 7.1*, row 2) and the *school-level variables* (equivalent

TABLE 7.3   *Examples of pupil-level and school-level variables*

Pupil-level variables	School-level variables
Gender	Size
Social class	Rural/Urban
Ethnicity	Co-educational/single sex
Poverty/affluence	Single sex – boys
Ability	Single sex – girls
Ambition	Selective/non-selective
Parental interest	Budget per head
Health	Quality of management
	Quality of staff
	Average class size

to the treatment level variables of *Table 7.1*, row 3). Sometimes school-level variables are divided into Local Educational Authority (LEA) variables and school-level variables. Sometimes school-level variables are divided into department-level variables and school-level variables, where the latter are those things that are constant for a school, and the former differ from department to department within a school.

At the school level there are all the differences between schools *except* for differences in the characteristics of their pupils. At the pupil level there are all the differences between all the pupils in all the schools with regard to the kinds of factors which they 'bring to school with them' which might influence their educational achievement *except* for the differences between the schools they attend. I will use the 16+ GCSE examination results as the outcome measure. Statistically speaking, the variation in the results achieved by all the pupils is called the *variance* (Chapter 2, Panel 2.7), and the approach taken is called the *analysis of variance*. Some of this variance will be explained by factors at the pupil level – how schools differ in their intakes – and some will be accounted for at the school level – how schools differ in other respects.

Prediction and explanation

I am going to use the idea of predicting below, so it is important to understand what this means. In research, *prediction* might or might not mean forecasting the future – the term was used in that way in Chapter 5 (Section 5.2). What it will nearly always mean is seeing how accurately you can guess one thing from knowing another. If I know someone's gender then I can make a pretty accurate prediction as to which door they will go through in entering public toilets in the UK, or indeed as to which doors they went through over the previous 12 months. Prediction is often phrased as explanation. Statisticians in particular tend to use the two terms as synonyms. So I might say that in using public loos, gender *explains* why someone goes through one door rather than another. My evidence for this would be that knowing their gender allows me to make accurate *predictions*. Making predictions is at the heart of exerting statistical control.

Imagine that the pupils in a sample of different schools have taken their 16+ examinations and we know the results for each. If we wanted to predict the educational achievement of *any* pupil, not knowing anything else about him or her, then the best bet would be to predict that he or she had achieved the same as the average for all children. Now imagine predicting the result of *each* child in turn. The most sensible bet is still that each one will obtain the average result. So our best prediction is that all children will all score the same, spot on average. Our basis for prediction here is knowing that they all belong to a data set which has an average score. But that isn't a very good basis for a prediction, since looking at the actual results we see that there is a large spread from worst to best and most pupils didn't get the average result. To the extent that this is a poor prediction a statistician says that it leaves a great deal of *unexplained variance*.

We can improve our prediction if we take a factor from the pupil-level variables – gender, for example – and calculate the average score for girls and the average score for boys. Then knowing that a pupil is male, and nothing else, our best prediction is that he will score the average for boys; similarly with girls. If we do this for all boys and for all girls then we will still be wrong for most pupils. But are we less wrong in our predictions than when we made predictions on the basis of the ungendered average for all pupils?

If we make fewer errors by gendering the data and improve our predictions in this way, then we can say that the extent of our improvement is the extent to which gender explains the differences in results between pupils. If that were so then the statistician would say that there is less unexplained variance when the data is gendered than when it was not. In fact, for most educational authorities we would indeed improve our power to predict by knowing the gender of pupils.

The next kind of step is fairly obvious. For example, we could now divide the boys into social class groups and calculate the average scores for boys with fathers with manual jobs, those with routine white-collar jobs and those with professional and managerial jobs, and calculate the average score for each of these sub-groups. We could then use knowledge of boys' membership of such sub-groups to predict that they would gain the average for their group, doing the same for girls. The extent to which this reduced our prediction errors and increased the accuracy of our prediction, over and above using gender groups alone, would be the extent to which the variance was explained by social class, net of gender. And there are other sub-groupings which we could use as well. The logic is shown in Figure 7.1. Sooner or later we will run out of pupil-level variables. When we can't find any more pupil-level variables to improve our predictions we will still be left with some unexplained variance. Inside that there will be the school effect.

The school effect in Nottinghamshire

In studying the school effect in Nottinghamshire schools in 1991 Jesson, Gray and Tranmer (1992) went through a process analogous to that in Figure 7.1, but they started with social class. Social class might be defined by parental occupation, or by the educational level achieved by parents. There is a number of different ways of categorizing by social class (Marshall *et al.* 1988 Chapter 1; Rose and Pevalin 2003). Jesson and his colleagues used father's current or last occupation – or, in the absence of a father, mother's occupation – divided into three categories: manual, intermediate and professional/managerial.

Table 7.4 was created by classifying the 74 Nottinghamshire schools according to the social class compositions of their pupils at age 16. There are nine logical types but for two types there are no examples in Nottinghamshire. Then for each cell, the average school GCSE score is calculated for the schools in the cell. Thus, for the 13 largely middle-class schools in the first cell of the table, the overall average for all 13 schools was 34 points.

This controls only for the social class differences between schools, and there are other pupil-level variables which are known to affect educational achievement. Jesson and his colleagues followed essentially the same procedures to control for gender differences between schools, for 'poverty' as indicated by the

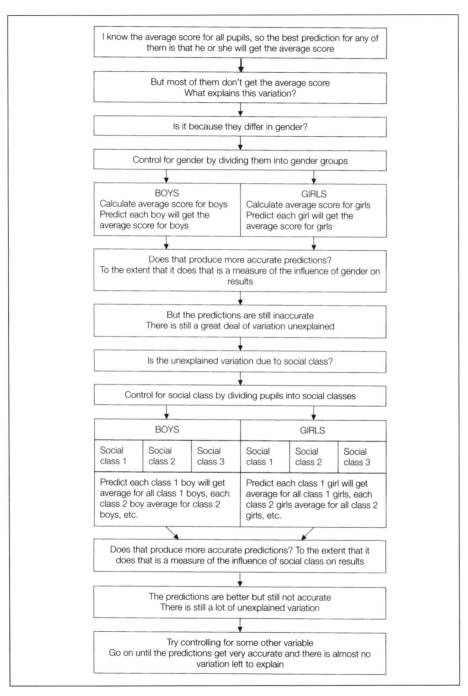

Explaining by reducing prediction errors   *FIGURE 7.1*

TABLE 7.4   The social class composition of schools and their average achievements in 16+ examinations (GCSEs): Nottinghamshire, 1991

| Percentages of pupils with professional/ managerial background | Percentage of pupils with a manual social class background | | | Average exam scores |
	Low (under 28%)	Median (28–60%)	High (above 60%)	
High (above 28%)	13 schools: average score 34	6 schools: average score 28	No examples	33
Median (8–28%)	5 schools: average score 28	26 schools: average score 26	6 schools: average score 25	26
Low (under 8%)	No examples	5 schools: average score 22	13 schools average score 20	20
Average exam score	**33**	**26**	**22**	**26**

How to read this table
Each cell in the table represents a different possible social class composition for a school's pupil body at age 16. The table divides pupils into three social classes, not two. Thus the first cell of the table represents schools where 28% or more of the pupils come from professional/managerial homes, less than 28% come from manual backgrounds and whatever is the remainder in each school come from 'intermediate' backgrounds where a parent is a routine white-collar worker. The first cell in the table then represents the schools with the greatest percentage of middle-class pupils. There were 13 of these in Nottinghamshire in 1991, and the pupil average of all of them together was 34 GCSE points. GCSE scores are calculated on the basis of 7 for an A, 6 for a B and so on, added together for each pupil and divided by the number of pupils in the examination year including those who took no examinations, or gained no passes (this was before the advent of A star grades). The diagonal from the top left-hand cell to the bottom right-hand cell runs from maximum middle-classness, to maximum working-classness: from schools averaging 34 points to schools averaging 20 points. The average for all schools together was 26.

Source: Based on Jesson, Gray and Tranmer (1992: 28).

percentage of pupils receiving free school meals, and for the ethnic mix of schools. This allowed them to draw up the ready-reckoner given as Table 7.5. The figures in Table 7.5 are derived from prediction errors, as suggested in Figure 7.1. Thus if we predicted all pupils to have achieved the average achieved by working-class *girls* not receiving school meals, then we would find that we were wrong about the average for professional managerial *boys* not receiving school meals, by 21.8 – 2.4 examination points. Their average score would be 20.4 + 21.8 – 2.4. Ethnicity is not shown since differences in achievement by different ethnic groups were very small once social class had been controlled for.

With this additional information we could improve on Table 7.4 as a predictor by calculating average scores for schools according to their social

Ready-reckoner for calculating the predicted GCSE scores of pupils from a knowledge of various pupil characteristics

TABLE 7.5

Base score (the pupil is female, from a manual background and does not receive free school meals)	20.5
If the pupil comes from an 'intermediate' background	+10.1
If the pupil comes from a professional/managerial background	+21.8
If the pupil is male	−2.4
If the pupil receives free school meals	−4.4

Source: Jesson, Gray and Tranmer (1992: 27).

class and gender composition and the percentages of children receiving free school meals. Table 7.5 was given only as an illustration here because in practice all this goes on inside the statistical calculations of a multi-level model.

But that's still only some of the pupil-level variables. Why not go on? The reason for not going any further is that diminishing returns from doing so set in quite soon. Note that in the ready-reckoner (Table 7.5) knowing whether a child has free school meals or not doesn't add a great deal to the ability to predict GCSE results. Since the percentage of children having free school meals in each school is rather few, it adds very little to making accurate predictions for the average score of a school. This doesn't mean that poverty is not an important influence on educational achievement. But the procedures adopted, and the order in which they were adopted, have already controlled for social class. This has already mopped up most of the influence that poverty (measured by free school meals) will have. The effect of poverty on lower-class pupils has already been registered and the negative score of 4.4 points in Table 7.5 is created largely by the lower achievements of *higher-class* pupils in poor circumstances. Again, ethnicity would not add much to the ability to predict, since children from ethnic minority groups tend to achieve similar scores on average as white children from the same social class. Nationally, Indian and Chinese children tend to achieve more than white children of the same social class and African-Caribbean and Pakistani and Bangladeshi children a little less, though the pattern varies from areas to area (Gilbourn and Gipps 1996; Demark, Drew and Grimsley 2000).

Ability in terms of either an intelligence test or some measure of prior achievement is the very best predictor for future educational achievement within gender groups. Jesson and his colleagues did not use an ability measure, largely because no convenient measure was available. These pupils had not been tested using national Standardized Achievement Tests (SATs). Future cohorts of pupils will have been, so a convenient measure of ability at an earlier age will be available. When a researcher wants to study the school effect with regard to 18+ examinations, the results of the same students at 16+ can be used as the prior ability measure (for example O'Donaghue *et al.* 1997). There is also a conceptual problem here. Should the ability of pupils be regarded as a pupil-level variable, independent of school influence, or as a school-level variable – as something fostered, or inhibited, by attending a particular school? This can only be resolved arbitrarily. If we are interested only in school effects in the GCSE year, then ability shown in previous years belongs to the pupil level. But if we were interested in the school effect for 5 secondary school years measured in the fifth year, then the problem remains, unless there is a measure of ability for age 11. The use of school SATs and examination scores as performance indicators is featured in the Activity at the end of Chapter 14.

Social class and ability measures for the same pupils usually correlate quite closely, though not exactly. Thus, following the logic of Figure 7.1, if social class is tackled first, followed by ability, then knowledge of pupils' ability does not greatly increase the accuracy of prediction/reduce the remaining unexplained variance. Knowing the pupils' social class will already put them into groups of predicted achievement fairly similar to the groups of predicted achievement they would be put in on the basis of knowledge of their prior ability. And the same is true if ability is taken first and social class second. Using both social class and ability in such an analysis is interesting because it shows the effect of social class net of ability, and of ability net of social class (see, for example, Smith and Tomlinson 1989). Using both measures takes account of higher-achieving pupils of lower social class, and lower-achieving pupils from higher social classes, who are invisible in an analysis based on only social class, or only ability measures.

Figure 7.2 shows what schools in Nottinghamshire actually achieved in 1991 against predictions for their achievement, calculated as described above.

There are two ways of looking at these results. One is to concentrate on the inaccuracies of prediction, the other is to focus on how accurately the predictions were met.

Failure to predict

Failure to predict accurately on the basis of knowledge about one set of factors is taken as evidence about the effects of another set of factors. This is precisely how astronomers identified the presence of planets they could not see, by showing that the orbits of planets they could see could not be accurately predicted from knowledge of the orbits and magnitudes of other known planets. This prediction failure meant there must be some as yet undiscovered body or bodies influencing planetary orbits. Predicting from a knowledge of the characteristics of the pupils in different schools did not result in perfect predictions. Somewhere in this prediction error is the school effect.

We would expect chance factors to prevent the estimates from being perfectly accurate. Jesson, Gray and Tranmer (1992) have allowed for this on the scattergram (Figure 7.2), by marking a zone on either side of the prediction (or regression) line. These are actually the 95% confidence limits (see Chapter 6, Panel 6.2). Within that zone, differences between the results predicted and the results achieved may well be due just to chance. Outside the zone there are 15 schools who show much bigger differences between their predicted and their actual results. Six of these achieved much more than

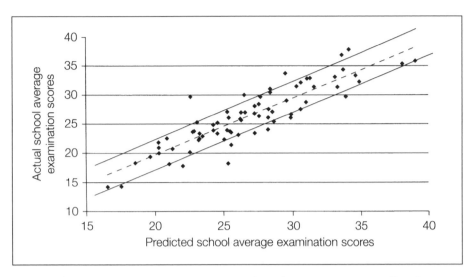

Actual school average examination scores plotted against scores predicted   FIGURE 7.2
from knowledge of school's social class and gender composition and percentages
of pupils receiving free school meals: 74 schools in the state sector,
Nottinghamshire, 1991

How to read this figure
The blocks on the scatter diagram show the average pupil examination score achieved by
each of the schools in Nottinghamshire in 1991. They are plotted in terms of achieving
higher or lower scores than each other against the vertical axis. The most highly achieving
schools are towards the top of the figure. Against the horizontal axis they are plotted in relation to the scores predicted for them. The schools for which high scores were predicted are
towards the right of the figure. The dashed diagonal line shows where schools would lie if
their results were precisely as predicted: the *regression line*. If the plots were all on the line,
each would have scored exactly as predicted from knowledge about their pupils and there
would be no school effect. Thus schools which appear above the line have achieved more
than predicted for them, and schools which appear below the line have achieved less than
predicted for them. The two other diagonal lines mark the boundaries of a zone in which
predictions would be expected to be inaccurate just by chance. For 6 schools which appear
above the top line and 9 which appear below the bottom line it seems unlikely that the differences between the prediction and outcome are just a matter of chance: these are statistically
significant differences (see Chapter 3, Panel 3.1). Since the predictions took account of each
school's social class and gender composition and the percentage of pupils receiving free
school meals, the mismatches between the predictions and the out-turns seem most likely to
be due to:

- A failure to control *adequately* for differences between schools for social class, gender and
  poverty differences
- Some other *uncontrolled factors* at the pupil level: differences in ability not correlated with
  class, gender and poverty would be the most likely
- Differences between schools (other than differences between their pupils) – the *school
  effect*.

Source: Jesson *et al.* (1992: 29).

predicted. It is tempting to suggest that they are particularly *effective* schools. In more everyday terms, these may be the schools which 'do more for their pupils' than others would do for the same pupils. Jesson, Gray and Tranmer (1992) suggest that on average these schools boosted GCSE scores by the equivalent of around 4 points per pupil (equivalent to 1 extra D grade each) with the most effective school among them boosting achievement by a maximum of just over 7 points each: the equivalent of one grade B pass extra for each pupil. This most effective school is one which has a middling GCSE score itself, showing that the most effective schools are not necessarily those which achieve the highest results. Eight of the schools achieved appreciably less than was predicted. It is tempting to regard these as particularly *ineffective* schools. Had their pupils gone to a school outside this group, they would probably have done better. Jesson, Gray and Tranmer (1992) suggest that the disadvantage of attending these schools was equivalent to pupils each gaining on average 4 points (one grade D pass) less.

However, we cannot regard these as precise estimates of the school effect. What has been defined by a process of elimination (Figure 7.1) is an amount of variance where the differences cannot be explained by chance, by gender, by social class (as defined in the study) and by poverty (defined by free school meals): the left-overs when these factors have been controlled for. There are three reasons why this unexplained variance will be bigger than the size of the school effect. First, it is likely that the calculations have not *fully* controlled for social class. Pupils were divided into only three social class groups, and each of these will be heterogeneous with regard to parental income, occupation and parental education. Using a 6-point social class scale and a more elaborate version of Table 7.3 would have improved the accuracy of the estimates. There are also some problems associated with classing pupils according to the information they themselves provided about parental occupation. Since there are only two genders we can probably be certain that the calculations have controlled for gender adequately. We will look a little more at 'controlling for social class' later in this section and at the end of Chapter 8.

Second, some of the gap between prediction and out-turns is also likely to include the effects of some other *uncontrolled factors* at the pupil level. Remarks were made earlier about this study's failure to control for ability except insofar as ability is controlled via controlling for social class. We know that ethnicity has a small effect after social class and free school meals have been accounted for, and so does coming from a one- or a two-parent family. And no doubt there are some other pupil-level factors remaining uncontrolled and influencing the prediction gap. You can consider this possibility in the Activity at the end of the chapter. Controlling also for these factors would alter the relative position of schools right and left of each other in Figure 7.2, since some schools would be affected more than others according to the make-up of their student body.

Third, there are *interaction effects*. The analysis described so far assumes that each of the factors relates to each other in the same way in all circumstances. But in reality this is unlikely to be so. Being female is different in some South Asian communities from being female in a white community.

Being working class in a largely working-class school is different from being working class in a middle-class school. Matters such as the latter have been investigated in other studies, usually under the heading of 'compositional effects' (Gray, Jesson and Sime 1993). For example, do working-class pupils do worse in predominantly working-class schools: is the effect of social class on achievement multiplied according to the percentage of same-class pupils in a school? There is some evidence for a compositional effect with regard to social class. With regard to gender, girls in single-sex schools do seem to achieve more. Complexity theory (Chapter 5) suggests that compositional effects of a large number of kinds are likely. Insofar as such factors might enhance or depress achievement, and are emergent characteristics of the school (Chapter 5, Section 5.3) they would be part of the 'school effect', but unlikely to be amenable to manipulation by staff and management trying to make their school more effective.

Thus the figures cited in the Jesson, Gray and Tranmer (1992) study must be regarded as over-estimates of the differences that school factors make, because some of the unexplained variance will be due to uncontrolled variables at the pupil level and will be an over-estimate of the controllable factors leading to higher or lower attainment.

The implications of accurate predictions

In Figure 7.2, note how accurately the GCSE scores of schools were predicted from a knowledge of the school's social class and gender composition and the percentage of pupils receiving school meals. In fact, simply knowing the social class composition gives pretty accurate predictions alone. You can see this by looking at the ready-reckoner (Table 7.5). The really big figures are those for social class. Compare this with what must be an over-estimate of the school effect. The gap between the most effective and the least effective school was around 12 GCSE points: but the most and the least are only 2 schools out of 74. The overwhelming majority of pupils go to schools which seem more or less equivalent to each other in fostering achievement: the differences between their results might just be a matter of chance. By contrast, the gap between the average for pupils from manual backgrounds and for those from professional and managerial backgrounds is nearly 22 points. Thus social class differences are much more important in explaining educational achievements than are the kinds of factors which are under the control of schools or LEAs. In terms of the logic of this approach the fact that we can better predict a child's educational achievement from knowing his or her social class than from knowing which school they attended is presumptive evidence that social class is more important in determining educational achievement than the influence of the school.

Jesson, Gray and Tranmer (1992) do demonstrate that there is a school effect: that it does make a difference to children's achievements what school a child attends. And they give an (over-)estimate of its size, which turns out to be rather small in comparison with other influences. They identify more and less effective schools. But they do not explain why some schools are more effective than others. To do this they would have to continue the analysis controlling for different school-level variables such as those in Table 7.3. For work of this kind see Teddlie and Reynolds (2000).

Measuring relativities

Jesson, Gray and Tranmer (1992) give an estimate of the size of the school effect. As they themselves point out, that should be taken as an estimate of the size of the school effect *in terms of the way they measured it.* Controlling variables in different ways would have produced different estimates, but probably not very different. But also this study was only for Nottinghamshire in 1991. In fact, their estimates are broadly in line with other local and national studies (Gray, Jesson and Sime 1993; Gray, Goldstein and Jesson 1996). But we would not expect the school effect to be the same size everywhere. There will be some areas where more schools 'do more for' their pupils than in other areas and in other areas there will be more 'failing schools'. In either case there will be a greater school effect, because at base the school effect is a measurement of the distribution of schools above and below an average for all schools in the data set. Changing the schools in the data set will change the average and change the distances by which schools will be below or above average. Changing the boundary of Nottinghamshire LEA in a way that excluded a number of less effective schools would magically reduce the effectiveness of the remaining schools, because some 'weak' competitors would no longer enter into the comparison. But, just as magically, this might increase the effectiveness of all Nottinghamshire schools combined, as against schools in another area. And what schools in Nottingham achieved in 1991 was much less than they achieved in 2007.

Here there is the same kind of problem as arises in making general statements about the relative importance of heredity and environment in determining intelligence test scores (Section 7.2). It is necessary to keep your wits about you when dealing in relativities. The key question is always: 'what exactly is being compared with what, according to what criteria?' or 'who's in the data set to be compared with whom, and who's not counted?'

But what are we controlling for in controlling for social class?

Social class is one of the most widely used concepts in social science, but it is rarely clear exactly what it means (Marshall *et al.* 1988: Chapter 1). In the study discussed above, the working or *operational* definition was achieved by asking pupils about parental occupation and then, on that basis, dividing them into three groups: professional, intermediate and manual. The job one's dad does might have some influence on one's educational achievement in itself, but when sociologists think about the 'influence' of 'social class' they are usually also thinking about the influence of family incomes on the one hand and, on the other, the influence of having parents who have had a particular educational experience themselves. So social class is a hybrid concept: part economic, part cultural. If putting

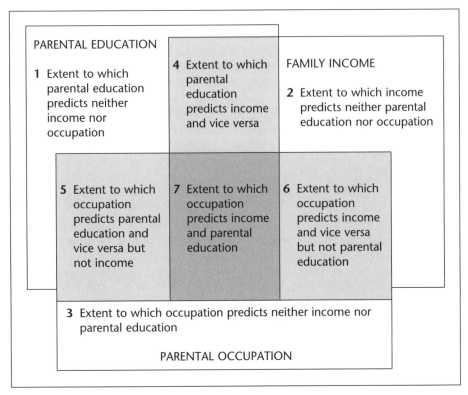

Uncontrolled aspects of 'social class' when social class is defined by occupation   *FIGURE 7.3*

How to read this figure
The zone of maximum overlap (**7**) shows that classing people according to occupation captures something about the relationship between occupation, income and education but not for everyone. Thus if we class people by occupation there will be people with low-status jobs and low incomes but high educational levels and people with high incomes and high-status jobs and low levels of education in sector (**6**), and people with high educational achievements, high-status jobs with low pay in sector (**5**) and so on. Whether we class people according to occupation, income or education some aspect of social class will be left hanging out, and hence uncontrolled (sectors (**1**), (**2**) and (**3**)).

families into 'classes' on the basis of occupation or income or parental education always resulted in the same families being in the same groups there would be no problem. But this isn't so. Thus classing pupils by a parent's occupation will fail to control entirely for 'class-as-income' and will fail to control entirely for 'class-as-educational background', as shown in Figure 7.3.

As you might guess, classing people instead by income, or instead by educational level, would again leave bits of 'social class' hanging out.

In addition pupils usually have two parents, often two parents contribute to family income, and mothers and fathers may themselves have different educational backgrounds. There are schemes for classifying pupils by 'social class' using both mother's and father's occupations, or both mother's and father's educational level. But in practice these are rather difficult to use. The reason is that even if we only defined three classes (however defined) *we would need 16 categories* to accommodate all the possible combinations of mother's and father's 'class' in two-parent families (allowing for either or both parents to be non-employed), and a further 8 to accommodate pupils from single-parent households. We would have converted social class from being a 3-value variable (as in the Nottinghamshire study), into being a variable with 24 values. To make use of this we would need a very large sample (Chapter 6, Section 6.10). Douglas (1964: 69–80) used such a classification but despite having a sample of 5,362 children, he still had to collapse a potential 24-category system into just 4 classes based on combinations of mothers' and fathers' characteristics. However, if we were interested in distinguishing between the effect of mother's social class, and the effect of father's social class, we could follow the logic of Figure 7.1 and see which of the two best predicted a child's educational achievement. Earlier studies suggested that mother's educational achievements were the better predictor.

The general points here are that however social class is operationally defined, it never quite seems to capture everything we mean by 'social class', and that attempts to define it to do so tend to generate more classes than the usual sample size can handle. A more specific point in relation to the school effect study is that, insofar as it failed to control for aspects of social class as shown in Figure 7.4, and for those arising from taking mother's social class into consideration, it will have left some unexplained variance which ought to have been attributed to the pupil level – to diversity between pupils – and will have been wrongly included in the school effect. This a further case for regarding these estimates of the school effect as over-estimates (see also the Activity at the end of Chapter 8 and the discussion of value-added performance measures for schools in the Activity for Chapter 14).

7.4   Case control and population comparison studies

Case control studies

The examples in this chapter so far have used *internal* controls. That means that statistical control groups are created by dividing the subjects in the research into categories and comparing them. But there are also natural experiment approaches which use *external* controls. **Case control** studies are common in medicine and in criminology. Here a researcher usually allows natural processes to assemble a group of subjects with something in common: all suffering from the same disease, all on the doctor's case load, all in prison, put there by the criminal justice process. These are the *cases*. Then the researcher finds a group of people who are in many respects like the cases, but they don't have that disease, or they are not in prison. The cases are compared with the controls and any other differences between them are candidates for being the cause of the difference of interest. There are two main problems with this. The first is **ascertainment bias**. This is mistaking the characteristics which make people into 'known cases' for the causes of their being in the condition in question. With a criminological study there would be a danger of mistaking the factors which increase the chances of being reported, prosecuted, found guilty and being imprisoned, for the factors which made someone likely to commit a crime. This violates the requirement in Table 7.1, row **2**.

Second, there are serious risks of inadequately controlling variables in this way. For example, the study of sudden infant deaths is largely carried out through case control studies (Blair *et al.* 1996). These suggested that parents who smoked were more likely to suffer the sudden death of an infant because there were more smokers among the 'case families' than among the control families recruited to compare them with. But there were also more working-class families among the cases, and working-class people are more likely to smoke. Therefore it is possible that under-recruiting working-class families among the controls created the spurious impression that parental smoking is a cause of sudden infant death (Dwyer and Ponsonby 1996). This is the kind of problem which in a controlled experiment is usually avoided by creating comparison groups at random, though it will occur from time to time (Table 7.1, row 2). The same risks occur when using internal controls from survey data, but they are particularly high with the external controls of case control studies.

Case control studies are usually conducted where the condition of interest is rare. It would take a massive survey sample to collect even a few cases of sudden infant deaths, thereby collecting 'cases' and 'controls' in the same operation. With rare conditions and unusual circumstances the only feasible option is to collect cases and then recruit external controls.

Population comparison studies

An even weaker external control device is **population comparison**. For example, a researcher might have access to a number of young delinquents aged 12–16 and want to investigate what characteristics they have which explain their delinquency. To do this, the researcher might compare the delinquent group with what is known about the population of 12–16 year olds in general. This age group in the population in general becomes the control group. The researcher might be tempted to regard any way in which the delinquent group were uncharacteristic of the population at large as 'causes' of their delinquency. There are many studies like this. Durkheim's suicide study (1952) frequently uses this approach. This usually produces lists of 'risk factors' along the lines, for example, that delinquents are more likely to come from poor homes, more likely to come from single-parent families, more likely to have a parent who has experienced imprisonment and so on. But these studies rarely produce any convincing account of what actually causes what to happen. The major problems here arise from inadequacy of information about the distribution of the characteristics of interest in the population at large which is being used as the control (Table 7.1, rows **2, 3, 4** and **5**). For the example above, unless we know accurately how many 12–16 year olds there are who come from 'poor homes' according to some precise definition, then we cannot know *how much more likely* are the delinquents to come from 'poor homes'. There is also the problem of ascertainment bias again. The control population is likely to contain an unknown number of unknown 'cases' (Table 7.1, row 2). A third problem is that there are rarely any adequate data either for the group being studied or for the control population as to what they were like before they became delinquent, got the disease, got divorced, or whatever is of interest. If they are contemporaneous studies there will be the problems suggested in Table 7.1, row 1, and discussed in more detail in Chapter 8.

Controlling one study against others

Although the term 'control' might not be used, it is in effect what is being done when one researcher compares his or her findings with what has been found in other studies. Thus in the *Affluent Worker* studies referred to earlier (Section 7.1), Goldthorpe and his colleagues had internal comparison groups in the form of both affluent manual workers and white-collar workers from the same industries in the same town at the same time, but no comparison group within the study to represent traditional manual workers. This is important since the heart of the study was about how the well-paid manual workers in the then hi-tech industries in Luton differed from the more traditional, worse-paid manual workers in other industries. For this comparison, they had to rely on other published studies, conducted at other times in other places, using other methods of study. If you look back to Table 7.1, you will see that this introduces the kinds of problems identified in rows 2, 3, 4 and 5, with regard to investigating the causal influence of 'affluence' on workers' life-styles, attitudes and beliefs. These remarks are not so much a criticism of these studies as a recognition, first, that the confidence we can have in the conclusions of a natural experimental study relates closely to how successfully researchers have statistically controlled the important variables; and second, that the naturally occurring circumstances with which the researcher works limit what it is possible to achieve.

Controlling one study against another raises the same problems as does synthesizing the results of several studies, discussed in Chapter 15.

If you look back to Chapter 4, Table 4.6 you will see that the approach of controlling different studies against each other – or, indeed, of using a series of case studies in the same research programme – was what was implied with regard to property-marking projects. The Activity for Chapter 4 took you through the motions of looking for variables which might be the same in different studies or might vary between studies, hence identifying which variables to look for in controlling one study against another.

ACTIVITY   Controlling variables in explaining reading scores

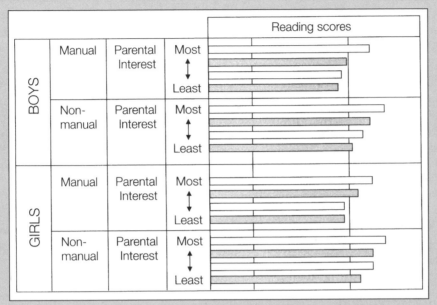

Social class, gender, parental interest and reading scores   FIGURE 7.4

Source: Wadsworth (1996a: 30).

The data for Figure 7.4 came from Douglas' (1964) studies of educational achievement in the primary school.

1 Just check you understand what Figure 7.4 shows by completing the following:

This display shows the relationship between scores on a reading test and: Social class after controlling for gender and parental interest

. . . ., after controlling for . . . ., and . . . .,

. . . ., after controlling for . . . ., and . . . .

2 The caption given to Figure 7.4 in its original form was:

'The power of encouragement: the level of interest shown by parents in their children's progress at school was more important than their gender and social background':

(a)   Parental interest is another 'pupil-level' variable in terms of the study described in Section 7.4.
        What effect do you think controlling for parental interest, in addition to the other pupil-level variables, would have on the size of the 'school effect'?

(b) In the original study, level of parental interest was:

[P]artly based on comments made by the class teachers at the end of the first and at the end of the fourth primary school year, and partly on the records of the number of times each parent visited the school to discuss their child's progress with the Head or class teacher. Parents are said to show a 'high level of interest' if the teachers regarded them throughout the primary school as very interested in their children's work and if they had also taken the opportunity to visit the primary schools at least once a year to discuss their children's progress (Douglas 1964: 83).

I   Do you think that the procedure described above would give an accurate measure of differences in parental interest?

II How far do you think differences in parental interest cause differences in children's educational achievement, and how far do you think that differences in children's educational achievement cause parents to be more or less interested in their children's education?

III How warranted do you think is the original caption for what is shown in Figure 7.4?

Further reading

It is difficult to recommend reading on the design of natural experiments. Each tends to be determined by what is possible under the circumstances, so the best approach is to read the methodological chapters of particular pieces of research. Gerry Rose's *Deciphering Sociological Research* (1982) is a particularly well-written text helping readers to unpick the methods used in a number of studies summarized in his book. Although written for health researchers, Mant and Jenkinson (1997) is a lucid introduction to case control and cohort studies (the latter are dealt with in Chapter 8). For a basic introduction to data analysis, try Marsh (1988). SPSS is the standard software for statistical analysis in social science. If you have access to it SPSS, Foster (2000) is a good text introduction to the use of SPSS. Babbie and Halley (2007) is a book and disk kit which allows you to practise analysing data using SPSS.

Some free on-line statistics calculators are listed in the *Further reading* for Chapter 3.

8 Controlling for Time in Natural Experiments

By the end of this chapter, you will:

- Understand the importance of establishing time sequences for causal analysis
- Know the difficulties of relying on informant memories for reconstructing the past
- Understand longitudinal surveys and cohort studies as ways of doing naturalistic experiments prospectively.

And you will know the meaning of the following terms:

Cohort • contemporaneous or snapshot surveys • correlation • longitudinal/prospective/cohort/panel or follow-up surveys • pre- and post-data • prospective • record-linkage • repeat surveys • retrospective • retrospective or recall bias.

At the end of the chapter there is an Activity which will test your understanding of social class as a variable.

8.1 Introduction

Controlled experiments are *prospective* (Chapter 7, Table 7.1, row **1**). That means that they involve the collection of data *before* the events of interest happen (**pre-data**), then data are collected *after* the event (**post-data**) and the two sets of data are compared to see what effects, if any, the events or conditions of interest had. This enables researchers to establish time sequences of events: to *control for time*. Causality is often difficult to pin down, but one sure rule is that what happened later cannot have caused something which happened earlier. The obverse is not necessarily true. What came earlier will not necessarily be the cause of what came later.

Where there are no trustworthy data on the state of affairs at an earlier point in time it is often difficult to decide what came before what. For example, from studying people at the time of their death we would find that unemployed people tend to die at an earlier age than people in employment. This is a *correlation*: a statement of what is associated with what (Chapter 2, Panel

2.3). The most common cliché in research literature is that 'correlation is not causation'. Cliché this may be, but it is an extremely important principle. Having data only from the time of death we would have no means of knowing whether being unemployed was in some way a cause of early death, or whether being sick was a cause of both unemployment and of early death. It will be difficult to determine direction of effect. We encountered this **direction of effect** problem in relation to parental interest in the Activity at the end of Chapter 7.

There are often difficulties in making natural experiments prospective. One source of difficulty arises from not knowing where and to whom the naturally occurring events are going to happen, until they have. Then it is too late to collect the data about the situation before the events happened. In the classic twin studies (Chapter 7, Section 7.2) what had happened to twins prior to their being discovered by researchers had to be reconstructed by the researchers. Often this was inadequately done with regard to age at separation and length of separation and similarity and difference in environment. Surveys are a common source of data for natural experiments in social research. But most surveys are *contemporaneous*. They are a snapshot about the state of affairs at a particular point in time. They will yield plenty of correlations. But whether the correlations indicate causes and effects and what is the direction of effect, may be difficult to decide.

The Activity at the end of Chapter 7 also illustrated another difficulty with studying cause and effect in natural experiments. In controlled experiments the 'causes' in the form of treatments, or sets of experimental conditions can, as it were, be switched on at the beginning and off at the end, so that at the end of the experiment all that are left are the 'effects'. But under real-life conditions there are *feedbacks* between causes and effects. Thus it is extremely difficult to see whether parents being interested in their children's education is a cause of children doing better at school, or whether children doing well at school is what causes or maintains parents' interest in their child's education.

8.2 Reconstructing the past relying on informant memory

Many surveys actually collect data about circumstances and events which happened before the date of the survey, by asking people questions about the past. But these *retrospective* data may be misleading, partly because people's memories are far from accurate – and, indeed can be strongly influenced by the way they are asked questions about the past. The controversies surrounding false memory syndrome (or implanted memories) in the field of child abuse refer to only the most extreme examples of something more general (www.bfms.org.uk).

Panel 8.1 outlines the difficulties of relying on memories in order to reconstruct the past. It relates mainly to the memories of informants. But researchers may misremember the past as part of an expectancy effect (Chapter 3, Section 3.6; see also Chapter 4, Panel 4.1). This is the reason for the principle of protecting data collected at one point in time from being altered later.

PANEL 8.1   The difficulties of relying on memories to reconstruct the past

The psychology of memory suggests that it is unwise for researchers to rely on the accuracy of what people tell them about experiences and events in the past (Potter and Wetherell 1987). Here are some of the findings:

- People forget a great deal about what happens to them – nearly everything, in fact – but when asked about the past are quite likely to give an answer as if they remembered. This is an aspect of so-called *co-operation bias*. Most respondents try to be helpful to researchers.
- Memory is *re-constructive*. People constantly bring what they remember into line with what has happened to them since. For example, the mothers of children who become delinquent are likely to remember and tell their children's earlier years in ways which are different from the mothers of children who have not become delinquent (West and Farrington 1973). They tell the past in such a way as to provide an explanation for the present. The same seems to be true of parents who have given birth to a child with a disability (Swan, Shaw and Schulman 1992).
- Memory is *conservative*: people tend to remember in a way that confirms continuities between past and present. This is especially true with memories which bear on what kind of person the rememberer thinks they are. The term *self-serving bias* is used for memories which conserve a self-image.
- Memory is *collective*. What people remember and what they believe about the past depends on who they have discussed it with, and memories tend to be shaped by well-established frameworks for telling stories and giving people characters (Douglas 1987; Wertsch 1987; Middleton and Edwards 1990; see Chapter 11, Sections 11.4 and 11.5).
- The telling of memories is shaped by the *immediate circumstances of telling*: for example, by what impression the teller wants to give at the time, what the teller thinks the listener wants to hear, what mood the teller is in and so on (Radley 1990; Shotter 1990; and see Chapter 11, Section 11.4).
- What people remember and how they remember often depends on the *cues given by the person asking them about the past*. Cueing and prompting does not necessarily result in accurate recall and can serve to re-shape what people remember, or at least to shape what they tell (Schwartz 2001; Brandt 2003; Brainerd and Reyna 2005).

All the biases above are sometimes collectively called *retrospective* or *recall bias*.

8.3   Repeat surveys and longitudinal surveys

One advantage surveys have over controlled experiments in studying causality is that they can utilize large statistically representative samples (Chapter 6) while this is difficult in controlled experiments. This means that survey findings can be generalized empirically (Chapter 1, Section 1.6; Chapter 6, Section 6.14) to wider populations with much more confidence than can the results of controlled experiments. With contemporaneous surveys this advantage is usually offset by difficulties in determining direction of effect. By adopting a *longitudinal* approach, survey researchers can combine the advantages of prospectivity with the advantages of representativeness.

Repeat surveys

The weakest way of adopting a longitudinal or prospective approach with surveys is through conducting **repeat surveys**. This means drawing representative samples from a population in the same way at different points in time. This is quite adequate if the objective is simply to chart time trends, without being particularly interested in what causes them. The large-scale repeat government surveys such as the *Expenditure and Food Survey (EFS)* (once the *Family Expenditure Survey (FES)* and the *National Food Survey (NFS)*), the *General Household Survey*, the *British Crime Survey*, *National Survey of Hospital Patients* and other NHS surveys, are primarily designed as time-trend trackers and state-of-the-nation snapshots. The two latter are also part of performance management systems (see the Activity at the end of Chapter 15) for the police and NHS agencies, respectively, as the basis for league tables and financial rewards and penalties. The EFS provides the data on consumer expenditure which is used to compose the 'basket of goods' featured in the calculation of the retail price index (RPI). It is a survey in which respondents are asked to keep diaries, making entries every day. Diarising will produces more accurate data than, for example asking respondents questions at the end of the week. The *Further reading* of this chapter tells you how to access these surveys and their findings and their methodological literature.

If the interest is causal, then repeat surveys suffer from the problem that what is recorded among one group of people at one point in time has to stand as a base-line for changes which occurred among another group of people studied at a later point in time. Nonetheless, where causal matters are of interest, repeat surveys are usually superior to contemporaneous ones.

Longitudinal surveys

The stronger longitudinal design is one which selects a sample of people at one point in time, and then follows these *same people* through time with repeated surveys, or *sweeps*. It is to these that the terms **longitudinal** or **cohort surveys** or **prospective surveys** are applied. ('Cohort' just means a group of people followed through time.) In much American literature, **panel surveys** is the term used. **Follow-up surveys** is yet another term for the same thing.

The best known of these are the national birth cohort studies, which are an important source in the fields of developmental psychology, health, delinquency and educational achievement (Davie 1993; Wadsworth 1996b; Ferrie, Brynner and Wadsworth 2002; Dex and Joshi 2005). These are studies through life of all or a large sample of children born in a particular week in 1946 (5,362 children), 1958 (17,000 children), 1970 (16,000 children) and, with a different kind of sample, 2000–1 (18,818 children). The 1946 cohort had a one-time entry, but for the other three, immigrant children with the same birth date have been identified and added in. The 1946 and the 1958 studies have been extended to study the children of the original children. It was from the 1946 cohort that the data for the Activity at the end of Chapter 7 were drawn. The *Further reading* of this chapter tells you how to access these surveys.

The sampling strategy of all but the last of these studies might be regarded as a kind of *systematic sampling* with a single sampling interval (see Chapter 6, Panel 6.1), or as a form of cluster sample, clustering by time rather than by place (Chapter 6, Section 6.6). Systematic samples are as good as random samples so long as there is an arbitrary relationship between the sampling interval and the data collected. However, there are important differences between children with summer birthdays and children with birthdays elsewhere in the year (Sharp, Hutchinson and Whetton 1994), hence no single week of birth will produce a sample of children representative of all children born that year. Equally, you can see this as a problem of clustering. This is a limitation on the generalizability of these studies, particularly with regard to educational achievement. There is no such problem for the Millennial Cohort, since this is based on a random sample of births occurring over a 12-month period in 2000–1.

These studies together have produced a rich treasure-house of data, but they also illustrate some of the difficulties of adopting a longitudinal approach. A synopsis of these is given in Table 8.1.

Some of the problems of the birth cohort studies arise from the fact that they were open-ended in that they were interested in virtually any differences which might emerge between the children in the sample. At the outset, it was not clear what might cause what interesting differences later in life. Thus it was difficult to decide what data to collect at each stage, though each successive birth cohort study learned from the mistakes of the earlier ones. For designing long-term longitudinal studies it would be nice to have the wisdom of hindsight right at the beginning.

But longitudinal studies can be designed to answer sharply focused questions. Then far less information needs to be collected. Because analysis will entail dividing the sample into only a few sub-groups, smaller samples can be used while retaining statistical representativeness (Chapter 6, Section 6.2). And the duration of a longitudinal survey does not have to be life-long. The standing panels of respondents maintained by many market research and opinion poll firms serve as the subjects of short-term longitudinal surveys. They might be surveyed, for example, before the Chancellor's budget statement and then afterwards to judge the effect of the budget statement on public opinion, using internal statistical control to investigate differences between different kinds of people (Chapter 7, Section 7.2).

Recapping Table 7.1, to be adequate as a basis for a natural experimental approach the researcher needs to collect data of the kinds shown in Table 8.2. For examples of studies something like this see Douglas (1964) or Mortimore *et al.* (1988), though the latter is a cohort *study* rather than a cohort *survey* (see Section 8.4).

TABLE 8.1   *Some of the problems of longitudinal survey designs*

Sample size	Sample size usually has to be larger for longitudinal surveys since each category in the analysis based on data at one point in time will need to be sub-divided according to differences between members of that category at an earlier or a later point in time – this follows the rule that sample size depends on the degree of diversity in which the researcher is interested (Chapter 6, Section 6.10). This is not so much a problem of longitudinal surveys *per se* as of studying causality in detail, where researchers are interested in a wide range of cause and effect relationships. For rare conditions, such as sudden infant death, or Creutzfeldt–Jakob disease (CJD), or the background of serial murderers a longitudinal survey would never have a large enough sample for studying causes: a case control study would be the more feasible option for these topics (Chapter 7, Section 7.4).
Time cluster effect	Choosing a cohort with birth dates in a restricted period of the year means that the cohort will not be representative of children born in other periods of the year, and the cohort may not represent children born in other years. This is avoided in the ONS Longitudinal Study (ex-OPCS Longitudinal Study) Section 8.5, by selecting four birth dates throughout the year and adding in new births and immigrants for each succeeding year, and in the Millennial Cohort by sampling births over a 12-month period.
Sample attrition	The extent of non-response is magnified as more and more subjects become untraceable through time. In another respect non-response via attrition is less of a problem in longitudinal surveys than in contemporaneous surveys, since the characteristics of those lost will be clearly known from previous data collection (Chapter 6, Section 6.9).
Subject reactive or Hawthorne effect	There is a possibility that those involved in a longitudinal study behave differently from the ways they would have behaved if not involved. Some of the birth cohort subjects have themselves become interviewers in similar surveys when grown up (Wadsworth 1996a). But in big samples this is unlikely to have large effects.
Irretrievable errors	Bad decisions made at the beginning of longitudinal research may affect the research for a very long time (see the Activity at the end of Chapter 7).
Unpredicted relevances	As longitudinal surveys unfold, so questions get posed which suggest that other kinds of data should have been collected at an earlier time. But this simply puts the researcher in the position of one conducting contemporaneous research, and forces the use of the same retrospective strategies as a remedy.
Aging of relevance	The findings of the 1946 birth cohort may tell us how the circumstances of childhood in the 1940s led to what happened to people in their 50s at the turn of the twentieth century. But the circumstances of childhood in 2000 are very different. So the 1946 cohort study might not tell us much about people who will be 50 in 2050. This problem varies according to the length and topic of the study. Longitudinal studies such as the OPCS *Longitudinal Study* (OPCS *LS*) (Now the ONS Longitudinal Study, see Section 8.5) deal with this by recruiting an additional younger cohort for each year of the study.
Expense	Long-term longitudinal surveys are expensive. Those who conduct them often have constantly to argue for funds to keep them going.

TABLE 8.2

The kinds of data needed for a longitudinal survey to be adequate as the basis for a prospective natural experiment

Kinds of data	For example, in a study of educational achievement 5–11
To control for prior differences at subject level Base-line data (Table 7.1, row **1**) to divide subjects into comparison groups relevant to what is being investigated (Table 7.1, rows **2** and **4**)	Measure of ability at 5 years, parental social class, parental education, parental aspirations, gender and ethnicity, season of birth
To control for differences at the treatment level Data on what happened to the subjects as relevant to the investigation within duration of study – dividing the comparison groups above yet again Table 7.1, row **3**)	Characteristics of schools attended, streaming/setting/mixed-ability teaching, parental attitudes to education, measures of reading and maths ability at 8 years, health record 5–11, family crises
Outcome data Data on subjects at end of the study period (and or at any interim point) (Table 7.1, row **1**)	Measures of, say, reading and maths ability at 11 years, child's attitudes to school at 11 years

Data of the same kind to be collected from all subjects in the same way (Table 7.1, row **5**).

8.4 Cohort studies

The study of the school effect in Chapter 7, Section 7.3, was contemporaneous. But Smith and Tomlinson's (1989) study of the same topic was longitudinal, collecting data about the same cohort of 3,000 pupils in 20 multi-ethnic inner urban comprehensive schools from entry to secondary school to their 16+ examinations. The schools were not selected by probability. They were chosen purposively (Chapter 6, Panel 6.3) because they had significant numbers of pupils from minority ethnic groups, and ethnicity and education was a major interest of the researchers. In each school the whole year group was studied. Thus this is better called a cohort *study* rather than a cohort or longitudinal *survey*, though often such studies are called surveys (Wall and Williams 1970: 32–7). By contrast with the study by Jesson, Gray and Tranmer (1992) described in Chapter 7, this study allows for children of the same ability at 11, but of different social classes, genders, ethnic groups and schools to be tracked up to their 16+ examinations. And equally it allows children of the same ethnicity but of different ability, social class, genders and schools to be tracked over the same period and so on, with all possible permutations. And hence it allows us to see the school effect over five years in terms of which kinds of pupils, in which schools, made most progress.

However, just as the study of Nottinghamshire schools cannot be generalized to other LEAs, so the results from the schools in the Smith and Tomlinson (1989) study cannot be generalized directly to the secondary education system as a whole. Their study does not represent minority ethnic pupils in schools where they are very much in the minority, or any pupils in schools in more affluent and or in more rural areas. The study which does give a representative picture for the English educational system as a whole is the *Youth Cohort Survey*, which is a longitudinal *survey* with national samples drawn on probability principles of successive cohorts of students. This provides information on class, gender and ethnic differences in educational achievement nationally (for example, Demark, Drew and Grimsley 2000; DfES 2005). But this cannot investigate the school effect, because a nationally representative sample of school students rarely includes more than one student from any one school.

One of the most famous of all cohort studies is that by Doll and Hill (1964), which established the link between smoking, heart disease and lung cancer. This is illustrated in Table 8.3. The study started with a census of doctors rather than a sample, and an incomplete census at that. Doctors cannot be regarded as a representative sample of the wider population, hence

TABLE 8.3   *An example of a medical cohort study: doctors, smoking and death*

| Cause of death | Deaths per 1,000 persons (doctors) per year | | | |
	Doctors smoking more than 25 cigarettes a day	All cigarette smoking doctors	Non-smoking doctors	All doctors in study
All causes	19.7	16.3	12.1	14.1
Lung Cancer	2.2	1.2	0.1	0.7
Coronary Heart Disease	5.0	4.8	3.3	4.0

How to read the table

In 1951 Doll and Hill (1964) sent a questionnaire to all 59,600 doctors on the UK medical register asking about their smoking habits; 68% returned questionnaires. Thereafter the deaths of doctors and the causes of their deaths were monitored, mainly through the death registration process (see Chapter 9). By 1961 there had been 4,963 deaths. These are recorded in Table 8.3 as rates per 1,000. Thus if there were 40,637 doctors in the study and 14.1/1,000 died per year, that is about 500 deaths per year. The table represents a *control structure*, dividing doctors into smokers and non-smokers and distinguishes heavy smokers from among all smokers. The table shows clearly that the risk of death in all three cause categories increases with smoking. The figures show the pattern predicted if smoking is among the causes of death: a so-called *dose relationship* – more smoking, more death. Most deaths were from causes other than lung cancer or CHD (coronary heart disease), so that in terms of actual numbers the differences for deaths from lung cancer and CHD between smokers and non-smokers are quite small, too. They are statistically significant differences (see Chapter 3, Panel 3.1), but that has to be read in relation to the 32% non-response rate (see Chapter 6, Section 6.9). The pattern of deaths shown by doctors dying after 1961, added to those in Table 8.3, provided more convincing evidence (Doll *et al.* 1994).

Source: Doll and Hill (1964).

the results could not be generalized numerically to a wider population with any confidence. Thus this study demonstrates a mechanism – smoking – causing illness, rather than providing an estimate of the size of the effect of this mechanism in the general population. While the initial data were collected by questionnaire, the follow-up data were collected by record-linkage (see Section 8.5). Deaths of doctors in the study were traced through death certificates (see Chapter 9).

Another large-scale longitudinal cohort study is the so-called *Whitehall II Study*, which is a study of the occupational mobility, health and other characteristics of just over 10,000 male government employees recruited from 1985 continuing into retirement and to death (Ferrie 2004). It shows, for example, that there is a close relationship between occupational status, stress, illness and premature death, with the government manual employees having much higher rates of all three. These correlations show in contemporaneous studies (Dreyer, Whitehead and Roden 1996). But as a longitudinal study this one is able to show that differences in health between civil service grades become greater over time, which is presumptive evidence that occupation has an effect in determining health, rather than health determining occupation. This direction of effect is something which cannot be demonstrated so convincingly in a contemporaneous study.

In the Whitehall study, the choice to study civil servants was mainly of convenience and cost. It is easier to conduct such a study where all the subjects have the same employer. For all survey researchers there are costs involved in finding people and travelling to see them. As noted in Chapter 6 these are sometimes reduced by multi-staged sampling and by clustering. In longitudinal surveys these costs are increased by the fact that people have to be surveyed several times. Hence in longitudinal work it is tempting to use convenience samples: doctors, or civil servants rather than the general population. If you like to think of it this way, a cohort *study* is often a longitudinal 'survey' with a convenience sample. The civil service does constitute ideal conditions for a natural experiment insofar as it is a microcosm of the occupational structure. It has workers ranging from low-paid manual workers to highly paid mandarins. But because the civil service excludes the very poor, the very sick, those working in very hazardous conditions and the unemployed, on the one hand, and excludes the very rich, on the other, it under-estimates the extent of class-related inequality in health. There are obviously problems of representativeness here, and hence problems of generalizing from this study to the wider population. As with the Doll and Hill (1964) study, what is demonstrated is the existence of causal mechanisms and their direction of effect, but not the magnitude of these effects in the wider population. Convenience is traded off against representativeness and generalizability. But something is known about how doctors differ from the population at large, and of how the occupational structure of the civil service differs from the wider labour market. Hence any empirical generalizations can be finessed accordingly, and the theoretical generalizations about what kinds of mechanisms cause what kinds of effects seem credible.

8.5   Record-linkage studies

Findings similar to those of the *Whitehall Study* with regard to social class and early death are shown by another longitudinal study: the *ONS Longitudinal Study* (Goldblatt 1990; Harding 1995; Blackwell *et al.* n.d.), once the *Office of Population Censuses and Surveys Longitudinal Study* (*OPCS LS*). This is based on a large representative sample of people, now about 1% of the total population of Great Britain. The study began by selecting from the 1971 Census all those born on one of four birth dates spread throughout the year. It continues by adding in all new births and all officially known immigrants with the same day and month of birth at each new Census. The study is entirely done by *record-linkage*. Data are retrieved about these people from bureaucratic data sets, such as Census returns, birth and infant death registrations (for their children), death certification (for themselves), records of long-stay psychiatric episodes, cancers from the Cancer Registry and so on. Thus the people entered into the survey at the outset can be identified from Census to Census from 1971 to 2001 and onwards, so long as they survived that long, and through various other bureaucratic systems to their death.

Record-linkage is cheaper than interviewing the same number of people. Records will often contain information which subjects themselves could not provide, or might forget. And records of these kinds are taken at the time when events happened and then 'frozen' so that they cannot usually be altered. In these respects administrative records can be very useful in assigning a sequence to events as is necessary for determining direction of effect. But record-linkage studies depend, first, on there being records to link with, and for many topics this is not so. Second, access to records about individuals is often difficult to obtain for reasons of confidentiality and because, unlike most industrial nations, individuals in the UK have as yet no single identity number for bureaucratic purposes. Third, such studies rely on the records being accurate and reliable, which is not always the case. The difficulties of using such data are discussed in Chapter 9.

ACTIVITY   Social class as a variable fixed in time or varying through time

Much social science research treats social class as if it were a variable fixed through time. Thus in the study of the school effect in Chapter 7, Jesson, Gray and Tranmer (1992) divide pupils into three social classes. Yet within each of these social classes there will be pupils who have been in the same social class since birth, and pupils who started life in one social class and were in another at the time they were asked for the information. Presumably educational achievement at 16 is influenced by social class experience *throughout life* and not just at the time when the 16+ examinations were taken. Similarly, the picture given by figures on social class and university entry is of university entrants coming overwhelmingly from middle-class backgrounds. Research by the Sutton Trust claims that by comparison with people born in the 1950s, those born in the 1970s have experienced less upward social mobility (Blanden, Gregg and Machin 2005). This may be so but the research is based on the data from the 1958 and 1970 birth cohorts, which according to Gorard (2005) had by the time of the research experienced enough attrition to make the samples non-representative.

University attendance is an aspect of social mobility, but much research here is based on parental income, residential area or occupation *at the time of University entry*. My own autobiography shows that at birth my father was a manual worker. At the time I entered primary school he was a routine white-collar worker. He was in junior management at the time I entered grammar school, and by the time I entered University a managing director of a medium-sized company. When I graduated he was a managing director of a multinational company. By the time I gained my PhD, he was unemployed. Social mobility on this scale is not the norm, but it is not unusual (Heath and Payne 2000). The question is not so much which 'social class' influenced my own educational achievements, but when. You will see that this adds yet another set of problems to the discussion of controlling for social class in Chapter 7, Section 7.3.

The first part of the Activity assumes that you are a University student, but if you are not you can just imagine doing it and then do the second part of the activity:

1 Conduct a survey among undergraduates as to:

(a) Their social class at birth
(b) Their social class at entry to University.

In both cases use father's occupation (or, in the absence of a father, mother's occupation). Assign occupations to 'Upper Middle', 'Middle' and 'Working Class'. So long as you are consistent in the way you assign occupations to social classes, and these are broadly in line with conventions as to what are higher and what are lower classes, it doesn't matter too much how you do this. But because you will be using your own classification your results will not be directly comparable with anyone else's.

Use a convenience sample for this (Chapter 6, Panel 6.3), unless you are willing to invest the time in taking a probability sample (Chapter 6, Sections 6.4–6.10) and in chasing up the people chosen in order to minimize the non-response (Chapter 6, Section 6.9).

When you have gathered your data, analyse them to discover what percentage of students from upwardly mobile families there are in the higher class categories at time of university entry.

2 If you have conducted the survey, consider the results in the ways below. If not, use your imagination to answer the questions:

(a) What are the implications for sample size of studying social class and University entry using measures of social class at two different times rather than one?
(b) What would be the difficulties of generalizing from the results of the survey above to all undergraduates in British Universities?
(c) What problems are there of relying on subjects for information on parental occupation?
(d) What kinds of problems are introduced by there being 'mature students' in the sample?
(e) What problems did you have/would there be in coding occupations to social classes?

(f) Despite all these problems, what are the merits of taking this more longitudinal approach to investigating the relationship between social class and University entry?

3 Sketch out a feasible design for research which would avoid the problems identified in **(2a)–(2d)** above.

Note that it would not be feasible to use a classification of social class combining mother's and father's social class. Following the logic of the discussion in Chapter 7, Section 7.3, that would turn the social class of students into a variable with 24 × 24 values = 576 (or more if you treated mature students differently). But it might be interesting to see which of mother's or father's social class best predicted University entry (see Figure 7.3).

Further reading

Tarir (2000) and Rispini (2002) are introductory guides to longitudinal research. Hedecker and Gibbons (2006) and Little, Bovaird and Card (2007) deal with the analysis of data collected longitudinally, and with research designs to make best use of longitudinal methods. The University of Sterling Longitudinal Data Analysis for Social Science Researchers web site: (www.longitudinal.stir.ac.uk/index.html) has explanatory text, training activities and links to longitudinal surveys. The use of longitudinal research in criminology is well dealt with by Liberman (2007) and the latest findings from the major British longitudinal study on delinquency is summarized in Farringdon *et al.* (2006) or more extensively in Piquero *et al.* (2007). Information on the Youth Cohort Study is available from the Department for Children, Schools and Families web site (www.dcsf.gov.uk/).

Other major longitudinal studies have their own web sites with both findings and methodological information. These include:

- The White Hall II study
  www.ucl.ac.uk/whitehallII/publications/index.htm
- *The ONS Longitudinal Study (ex-OPCS LS)*
  www.celsius.lshtm.ac.uk/publications/general.html
- *The British Household Panel Survey (BHPS)*
  www.iser.essex.ac.uk/ulsc/bhps/
- *The birth cohort studies*
  www.iser.essex.ac.uk/ulsc/bhps/
- *The Avon Longitudinal Study of Parents and Children*
  www.alspac.bris.ac.uk/welcome/index.shtml

For various repeat surveys:

- *Expenditure and Food Survey (EFS)* – (once the *Family Expenditure Survey (FES)* and the *National Food Survey) (NFS)*
  www.statistics.gov.uk/ssd/surveys/expenditure_food_survey.asp

- *General Household Survey*
  www.statistics.gov.uk/ghs
- *British Crime Survey*
  www.homeoffice.gov.uk/rds/bcs1.html
- *National Survey of Hospital Patients* and other NHS surveys
  www.nhssurveys.org/

9 Using Administrative Data in Research

> **By the end of this chapter, you will:**
>
> - Understand why social researchers often have to use data collected by bureaucratic organizations as part of their routine operations
> - Understand why such data may not be an adequate basis for drawing conclusions
> - Have considered the possibilities of cross-checking such data against alternative sources
> - Have modelled the production of data by a bureaucratic system.
>
> **And you will know the meaning of the following terms:**
>
> Ascertainment bias • construct validity • ethnostatistics • geographical information system • Goodhart's Law • output areas • population at risk • random and systematic error • reliability • standardized mortality ratios • triangulation • validation.
>
> At the end of the chapter there is an Activity which will test your understanding of modelling the production of official statistics.

9.1 Introduction

By necessity, social researchers often have to utilize information which has been collected by the bureaucracies of the state. This may be the only existing record of the past, or the only data available at a cost the research budget can afford. Administrative data have rarely been collected with the needs of academic researchers in mind. Studies of the way bureaucracies produce data are useful in remedying the deficiencies of administrative data, but they are also interesting in their own right as studies of the way in which facts about people are socially produced. That slant is sometimes called **ethnostatistics** (Gephart 2006) although under this term Gephart includes the way sociologists, as well as bureaucrats, construct numerical pictures of people and events.

9.2   Problems of using administrative data in research

The collection of some data by the state does involve rigorous social science methods; for example, the decennial censuses and various repeat surveys or the longitudinal studies referred to in Chapter 8. These are of excellent quality and give rise to relatively few problems when used in secondary analysis. But there are often problems with data collected as a routine part of the way in which state agencies operate in, for example, diagnosing disease and allocating treatments to patients, establishing eligibility for welfare benefits, for deciding what kind of offence has been committed and whether someone is guilty of it, or deciding on the cause of death for legal purposes. Such data are primarily used for internal agency purposes and for the external monitoring of their performance. They are a product of the way such services are organized. They reflect, for example, the way in which clients, conditions, treatments, offences and so on are classified and documented: the decisions made by people to use, or not to use services and decisions which construct this person as a case of this, that person as a case of that, and this person as not a client at all. And they reflect the ways in which people become 'clients', 'patients', 'students', 'offenders', 'claimants', 'unnatural deaths' and so on and flow into, through and out of bureaucratic systems according to complex decision-making processes typically involving quite large numbers of people, often making decisions in rather idiosyncratic ways. In assessing the quality of findings from social science we have to ask: 'by what methods were the findings produced?' In assessing the adequacy and the meaning of administrative data we have to ask a similar question.

Flows, filters and data machine

Figure 9.1 is based on Goldberg and Huxley's (1992) 'filter model' of community mental health. It represents mental health services as machines for generating data which sift and sort clients into different types, send them down different routes, collect some information about them on the way and count which of them end up where. Looking at mental health services in this way, it is difficult to believe that, for example, a count of psychiatric in-patients over a period of a year is a straightforward measurement of the number of people in an area suffering from 'severe mental illness'. Chapter 7, Section 7.4 referred to ascertainment bias, which is the bias arising from treating known cases as statistically representative of all cases. Figure 9.1 gives a picture of the way cases become known, and hence how the conditions for ascertainment bias are created.

Thus data routinely generated from bureaucracies may tell us more about the way the bureaucracies operate than about whatever it is that the data are supposed to stand for: levels of crime, number of children at risk, numbers of homeless people, or episodes of domestic violence.

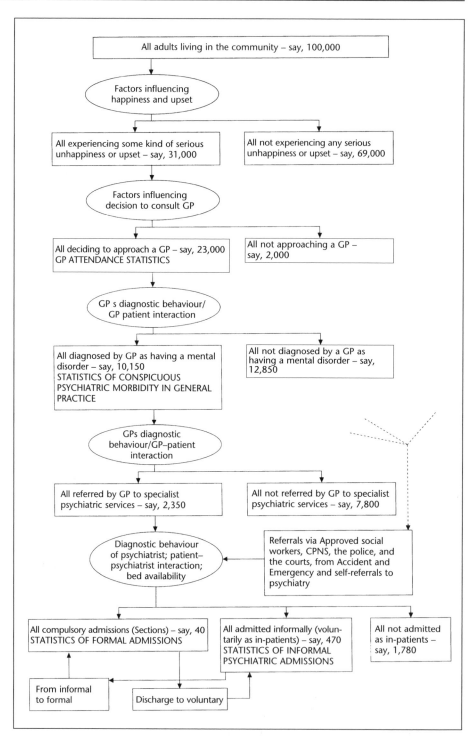

FIGURE 9.1   *Goldberg and Huxley's filter model of mental illness*

Source: Based on Goldberg and Huxley (1992: 4, Table 1).

9.3   Output area muddles and solutions

A common problem with administrative data has been mismatches between **output areas** (geographical areas) for different sets of statistics that a researcher may want to use at the same time. Some data sets refer to political units from the electoral ward upwards to the national scale, some to health authority areas, some to post-code geography, some for police areas and some for legal jurisdictions. Only sometimes do these different divisions match each other. Then there are data where location is important but the data sets do not refer to geographically discrete areas, such as school rolls and GP practice lists. It may happen that if a researcher wants to calculate a rate for, say, a particular illness, then she may have the data on the number of people with the illness for one kind of output area, and the data about the number of people who might catch it (the 100%: **'the population at risk'**), for a different kind of output area. Quite likely the two kinds of data will be for different dates as well. Re-organizations of local authority and health service areas also break historical sequences. Hidden in lots of numerical statements about rates of illness, or rates of crime, are problems like this (Gomm 2000d: 178–80).

Digitization of data, however, now ameliorates this problem. The data for Census 2001 is digitized, and although there is a standard output geography (Martin 1998) it is possible to output Census data for any area chosen by a researcher, so long as it is not so small as to compromise the confidentiality of the people living there. Other government data are slowly coming into line with this. This won't affect older data, but it should be possible to configure new data to output for the old areas to create historical comparisons, and many nineteenth- and twentieth-century data sets are being digitized so that they can be analysed with software packages. An advantage to being able to output data for bespoke neighbourhoods, is that it becomes possible to define a different neighbourhood for every respondent in a survey, according to their social participation, or for every kind of participation; this is useful in the study of social exclusion (Buck 2001).

More and more data collected by local agencies is being handled by **Geographical Information Systems** (GIS), which map events to when and where they happen and allow for their easy spatial and temporal analysis. Most areas, for example, now have GIS for mapping crimes (Chainey and Smith 2006), which can answer such questions as whether putting better lighting in one car park displaces car theft to another area, or what is the 'travel to crime' pattern for, say, burglary. Parsons, Chalkley and Jones (1996) describe the uses of GIS for studying issues about a school and its catchment area.

GIS systems are only as good as the kinds of on-the-spot analyses that people make to decide what to put into the system, and how. Many GIS crime maps, for example, show an intense crime hotspot, which turns out to be the police station, because that's where people get charged with crimes.

9.4 Basing research on administrative data

Sometimes researchers have little choice but to utilize data which are generated by the routine operation of bureaucratic agencies. For example, much epidemiological knowledge is based on data generated by the certification of deaths. Figure 9.2 gives an example of this.

The most telling demonstrations of class inequality in Britain and in other societies are that people of different social classes have different life-expectancies and that poorer people suffer more illness and disability than richer people do. For example, in 2001 men in the least deprived wards in England

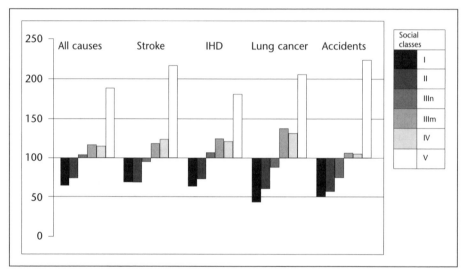

FIGURE 9.2   *Standardized mortality ratios (SMRs) for selected causes of death, by social class (based on occupation), men aged 20–64, England and Wales, 1991–3*

How to read this figure
Standardized mortality ratios (SMRs) are calculated to make comparisons in death rates between different populations or different sections of the population: in this case, between males in different social classes aged 20–64, taking into account that the different groups have different age profiles. The line across the figure set at 100 is the death rate expected for all males in this age group, if each social class had the same age profile. Bars above this line show a death rate higher than the expected death rate, and bars below a lower than the expected death rate. An SMR of 50 would be half the rate for all men, and 200, twice the death rate for all men. Deaths are expressed as a proportion (a rate) of all males in a particular social class in this age group: this figure is derived from up-dated Census data. For the method of calculation, see Gomm (2000d: 181). The causes of death derive from death certification. The social classes are those of the Registrar General's scheme: I – Professional/Managerial; II – Intermediate (e.g. Teachers); IIIn – Routine white-collar workers; IIIm – Skilled manual workers; IV – Semi-skilled manual workers; V – Unskilled manual workers. The figure does not show deaths for a further 'Unoccupied/Other' category. The Registrar General's scheme was largely superceded by the National Statistics Socio-economic Classification (NS SEC) in 2001 (Donkin *et al.* 2002; White *et al.* 2007).

For further details on standardized mortality ratios and a tool for calculating them, see www.lho.org.uk/DataAndMethods/Methods/Age_Standardised_Rates.aspx.

Source: Drever and Bunting (1997) Tables 8.2 and 8.4.

and Wales had a life expectancy of 79.1 years and those in the most deprived wards only 71.5 years. The equivalent figures for women were 82.4 and 77.5, respectively (Rasulo, Madhavi and Yar 2007). A major data source for such findings is the routine certification of deaths by cause (Dreyer, Whitehead and Roden 1996). Figure 9.2 cross-classifies cause of death for males between the age of 20 and 64 with social class. The data for these two addresses come from different procedures. That for cause of death comes from judgements made by a certifying doctor making entries on a death certificate assigning a cause of death. This is then converted into the codes of the International Classification of Diseases (of the World Health Organization (WHO)) by an official in the death registry. In Figure 9.2, these codes have then been translated back into verbal labels such as 'Stroke'.

Michael Bloor realized that only a small number of doctors account for a large percentage of all certificates completed in any health authority area. Idiosyncrasies among this small group would be likely to have large effects on the local data about the cause of death, and that in turn on national patterns. His study of death certification in Scotland (Bloor 1991, 1994) was conducted using a decision simulation experiment on similar principles to that conducted by Atkinson and his colleagues with English and Danish coroners (Chapter 4, Section 4.3). He found that, confronted with the same evidence, on paper, different doctors often reached different conclusions about the cause of death. Bloor also notes, from interviews with the doctors, that they regard death certification as a routine chore, and not something to be done very assiduously. They are much more interested in treating live people than in completing paperwork on dead ones. He also points out that there are only weak mechanisms to hold doctors to account for the accuracy of their assignation of the cause of death. As a GP, Howard Shipman murdered a large number of his elderly patients over a long period of time. His death certificates were accepted without question until an inquiry into one such death was forced by pressure from the deceased's relatives (www.the-shipman-inquiry.org.uk).

There is an important general methodological point to be made here. When researchers involve practitioners in controlled experiments (Chapter 3, Section 3.7), as often happens in health, social work or educational research, they do all they can to make sure that all the practitioners involved make the same judgements in the same way as each other and that each makes judgements in a consistent way each time. That is, they attempt to make practitioners into *reliable* decision-makers, where 'reliable' means 'consistent' (see Chapter 2, Section 2.10). But all research studies of practitioners in normal circumstances show that they are most unreliable judges, different doctors confronted with the same evidence often reaching different diagnoses (Bloor, Venters and Samphire 1978; McPhearson, Strong and Epstein 1981; Dingwall and Murray 1983; Jenkins *et al.* 1985; Sackett *et al.* 1991). Studies of judgements in social work (Dingwall, Eckelaar and Murray 1983; Campbell 1991) and coroners (Atkinson 1978; see Chapter 4, Section 4.3) show the same. In the criminal justice system (Maynard 1989) gives the same impression. The unreliability of judgements in practice is not only a matter of differences between practitioners, but relates also to the general messiness of real-life practice, unlike the more simplified environment of a controlled experiment where judgements are supposed to be made on the basis of a few, well-defined criteria. Practitioners in practice would often fail an inter-rater reliability test (Chapter 2, Section 2.10). Psychology tells us that being poor judges of frequency, quanta, distance and probability are common human characteristics (Gilovich, Griffin and Kahneman 2002), and there is no reason to believe that professionals have better memories than most other people (Chapter 8, Section 8.2).

The other references in Figure 9.2 are to the personal characteristics of the deceased. Gender will rarely be wrongly recorded. Age at death can usually be cross-checked against birth certification for people born in Britain or in another country in which births are certificated and copied forward onto passports or visas. There is some room for error here. A few years either way for occasional cases will not make much difference to the interpretation of the general relationship between social class and early death, though in a study of death rates and ethnicity it might be more important, where many of an ethnic group were born outside the UK. The data from assigning social class are much more problematic.

In the UK this is usually based on information provided to the Registrar of Births Marriages and Deaths by whoever registers the death (Prior 1989). This is usually a kinsperson who is asked to give the current or last occupation of the deceased. Sometimes those who register a death only have a hazy idea as to the occupation of the deceased, when what is needed is some information which can be accurately coded in the registry, first into the 377 occupational categories recognized officially and then into the six categories of the Registrar General's Social Classes (see Figure 9.2). 'He worked for the Council' is not adequate for this purpose. Thus there is bound to be some inaccuracy here, and many people are allocated to a seventh, 'Unoccupied/Other' code. Classing women is particularly problematic since there is an option to class them according to their own or their husband's – or, in the case of young women, their father's – occupation. Research on how deaths are classed through these procedures suggest a general tendency to report occupations higher rather than lower in the social class scale. One aspect of this relates to early retirement. Thus miners, police officers, fisher-folk and people in the military tend to take on less-demanding occupations before their final retirement, but at death are frequently reported according to their earlier more 'notable' occupation. This means, for example, that the records show deaths among miners or police officers disproportionate to number of miners and police officers there are in this age group and thus gives such occupations spuriously high premature death rates (Bloor, Samphire and Prior 1987).

This in turn raises an issue as to what data about death and social class are supposed to show. Recording attempts to tie death and social class to the final pre-retirement occupation of the deceased but it is social class position throughout working life which provides the substrate for the class-related causes of death, not just the final occupation. Most men change their social class by at least one step in the Registrar General's scheme during their lives from birth to death (Heath and Payne 2000). Social class assignation, based on current or last occupation recorded at the time of death, doesn't seem a very adequate way of controlling for the effect of 'social class' on life-expectancy if 'social class' is thought of as a life-time of experience (recall the Activity at the end of Chapter 8).

A further problem with regard to social class and early death raised by Figure 9.2 is that the number of deaths is expressed as a proportion of all people in that social class in that age group at that point in time; the so-called 'population at risk'. This means that the statistics in Figure 9.2 include data from yet another source: from the questions about occupation in the Census. As soon as the Census is conducted, reality begins to depart from what the Census shows, since the occupational and social class structures are constantly in a state of flux. This is the same problem as noted with popula-tion comparison studies in Chapter 7, Section 7.4.

The relationship between social class and premature death is such an important topic, and the system of death certification is such a convenient source of data on this, that there has been much research investigating how far the certification data can be trusted. This research has taken the form of studying how certification data are produced – as with Prior's (1989) study of death certification in the Northern Ireland Registry, J. M. Atkinson's (1978) study of coroners' investigations and decisions, simulation experi-ments as with Bloor's research reported here or M.W. Atkinson's simulation experiment (Chapter 4, Section 4.3) – and by cross-checking samples of certi-fication data against different sources, such as more detailed interviews about the occupation of the deceased with samples of kin who register deaths, or checking cause of death on death certificates against independent post-mortem examinations.

For the relationship between social class and early death, the overall conclusions are, first, that many of the errors are random and simply cancel each other out, which has the paradoxical effect that data which might be inaccurate at the level of individuals are, nonetheless, accurate in aggregate. This is common with **random error** in large samples. Second, that the main direction of **systematic error** in the certification data tends to *under*-report the extent to which lower social class membership is associated with earlier death. This is partly because of the tendency to elevate the occupation of the deceased on registration, and partly because the 'Unoccupied/Other' category is dominated by people from lower social classes, who ought really to be added in as deaths among those of social classes IV and V (Bloor, Samphire and Prior 1987). And it is partly because much of the impact of social class on life-expectancy occurs in childhood and is not captured in the registration procedure for the deaths of adults many years later. Many people who die prematurely from the circumstances of a 'lower-class' childhood will have moved up the social scale before they die: most social mobility is upwards. The same picture of social class conditions causing illness and premature death is given by studies such as the *ONS Longitudinal Study* (*ONS LS*) referred to in Chapter 8, Section 8.5. But that study in turn relies on linkage to death certification to attribute cause of death.

Note the relationship between the precision with which a claim is made and the confidence we can have in it. We can be fairly confident that, for adult males at least, the death certification data give a fairly accurate picture of the relationship between the fact of death between 20 and 64 and having had a manual or a non-manual occupation. It becomes less accurate the more we elaborate these two addresses. Thus on the one hand the more causes of death we allow for, the more disagreements there will be between doctors about the cause of death. And, on the other hand, the more finely we divide people into socio-economic categories – 'classes' – the more errors can be made about these.

9.5   Checking administrative data against alternative sources

The discussion above illustrates something general about what is needed in order to use administrative data for research purposes. Unlike data produced by quantitative social science research, these data may not have a clearly articulated audit trail showing how they were produced. In this regard they are more like the data produced by some forms of *qualitative research* (see Chapter 10, Section 10.6 and Chapter 12). Thus using administrative data requires this deficit to be remedied by studying the process of data production to see what the data actually mean and by checking the data produced against alternative sources.

As discussed in relation to death certification above, a very common kind of research project involves comparing administrativec data with data produced through some alternative means, called either *triangulating between sources* or *validating* (Chapter 13, Panel 13.3). For example, Payne and Saul (1997) used a questionnaire sample survey to estimate the frequency of angina in Sheffield (see Chapter 2, Section 2.7; Chapter 10, Section 10.4). This showed that angina was more common among people living in the poorer wards of the city. By contrast, health service records showed that it was the people living in the more affluent wards who were more likely to be receiving treatment for heart disease. Again, information on the incidence of crime, collected independently of the criminal justice system, is what is needed to check whether some group in society is disproportionately likely to be arrested and charged in relation to their actual level of offending. The only way in which such data can be produced is through self-reporting. The regular *British Crime Survey* is a sample survey which collects information both about whether people have been the victims of crime and whether they have committed crimes themselves. The victimization data show that the majority of crimes go unreported and unrecorded (Salisbury 2003; Walker, Kershaw and Nicholas 2006). A major consideration in reporting crime is whether insurance is involved, since insurance companies often require police authentication for a settlement. That in turn suggests that poorer people, who are less likely to have insurance, are also less likely to report crimes where they are the victims. Again, the fact that the majority of crimes go unreported creates a kind of permanent reservoir from which spurious crime waves can be created, with crime remaining stable but people on occasion becoming more likely to report it. Large increases in the recorded incidence of sexual assault (Harris and Grace 1999), domestic violence (Mirrlees-Black 1999) and racially motivated crime (FitzGerald and Hale 1996) in the 1990s may have been due more to increases in *reporting* than to increases in *commission*.

The *Crime and Justice Survey*, parallel to the *British Crime Survey*, asks people to admit to committing crimes. It seems reasonable to assume that these data are less accurate than those on crime victimization, but they are the only data source which allows rates of commission of crime for particular groups as recorded via the police and the courts to be compared with an independent source of information (Budd, Sharp and Mayhew 2005). One of the problems with self-report data of this kind is that it assumes that different levels of reporting reflect different levels of offending rather than different degrees of self-disclosure in various social groups.

The angina survey used by Payne and Saul, the *British Crime Survey* and the *Crime and Justice Survey* have a further problem. This is that respondents are not 'expert' in classifying their illness, in the one case, or offences, in the others. In practice what 'heart disease' is, what kind it is and what its severity is, is something which will be decided by doctors. The way the *WHO Angina Questionnaire* was designed seems to make it a fairly reliable indicator of the amount of heart disease which would be diagnosed by competent doctors if they examined the people concerned, though with a consistent over-estimate (see Chapter 10, Section 10.4). But it is much more difficult to achieve a similar kind of matching in the crime surveys. This is because the police, the Crown Prosecution Service (CPS) – or, in Scotland, the Procurator Fiscal – and the courts have so much discretion in how to categorize crime into particular types and particular levels of severity, and the discretion seems to be exercised differently in different areas of the country and at different points in time. Asking people what crimes they have committed for which they have not been prosecuted is asking them a question they cannot answer accurately, since the correct answer could be determined only by their being caught and prosecuted. Nonetheless, the exercise does produce a useful point of reference on the extent of crime which is independent of the activities of criminal justice agencies.

These remarks raise important issues about *construct validity*: a question about what a datum is supposed to measure (Chapter 2, Sections 2.4–2.11). Suicide statistics, for example, measure the number of suicide verdicts reached by coroners, not the number of people who intentionally kill themselves. Crime statistics measure reports of crime recorded by the police, or numbers of arrests, or numbers of prosecutions and so on. Only with difficulty can data measuring one kind of phenomenon – say, verdicts – be used as a measure of another kind of phenomenon – say, self-homicides.

One of the effects of the *British Crime Survey* has been to draw attention to the shortcomings of police-collected statistics on crime, particularly differences between police forces. This resulted in the introduction of National Crime Recording Standards (NICRS) in 2002 in an effort to create more consistency in recording. One effect was to increase the crime rate as judged by (police) recorded crimes (Salisbury 2003). The NICRS can be found on the *Home Office* web site. An Audit Commission report (2005) found improvement but still incoherence and inconsistency in some forces. Recording standards have also been introduced into the NHS (www.connectingforhealth.nhs.uk/ systemsandservices/data/) and across local government and most central government agencies, as a step to moving towards e-administration, on the one hand, and management by performance, on the other (see the Activity on performance indication at the end of Chapter 15).

With regard to performance management, the way data are recorded can now have enormous consequences for the funding of agencies paid by results (NHS Trusts, for example), for agencies paid according to some measure of need for their services (services for the homeless, for example) and for the careers of their managers and staff. This creates a pressure to record in such a way as to maximize the benefits to the agency. Goodhart's Law states that when a measurement becomes a target it ceases to be a good measurement (Goodhart 1975, cited in Elton 2004). Elton goes on to say that when Goodhart's Law is applied to social phenomena it becomes a special case of Heisenberg's uncertainty principle (from physics), to the effect that measurement will change what is being measured. From across the public services there are examples of changes in practice in order to maximize a score on a performance indicator which, from some points of view, distort the operation of the agency away from more worthwhile aims: schools cheating on SATs tests, or under-recording truancies, hospitals lying about their waiting lists and police forces maximizing the number of crimes they charge each offender with in order to boost arrest rates (Davie 1999; see also the Activity at the end of Chapter 15).

ACTIVITY   Modelling the production of official statistics on crime

1   Select any kind of crime.
2   Look again at the filter diagram of Figure 9.1, and draw up something similar to show how the official statistics for this particular crime might be produced. Include at least three levels: 'Reported to the police', 'Charged with the offence', 'Found guilty of the offence'.
3   Look at the diagram you have produced:

   (i)   For this crime, two police divisions show radically different levels of reports to the police (after taking into account differences in the size of the population). What alternative kinds of explanation might be given for this?

   (ii) For this crime, there is a very large rise in guilty verdicts from one year to the next. What alternative kinds of explanation might be given for this?

   (iii) For this crime, the statistics from a particular police division show that some sub-group of the population (for example, African-Caribbean males, aged 17–25) are much more likely to be charged with the offence than other people. What alternative kinds of explanation might be given for this?

4   Look up the meaning of 'ascertainment bias' in Chapter 7, Section 7.4. Use your diagram to explain what it means, and note down the problems that this kind of bias might cause in studying crime.

Further reading

Gorard (2006a) is about analysing the kind of data you might get from administrative sources without the use of inferential statistics, while Gilbert (1993) is a lucid introduction to log linear analysis which is particularly appropriate for analysing statistics where all you have are tables of data.

Interpreting Official Statistics (Guy and Levitas 1996) is now out of date in the examples it uses, but nonetheless does identify a wide range of ways in which administrative data may be misleading. Bottomley and Pease (1986) remains a model for how to understand crime statistics: worth looking at after you have completed the Activity of this chapter. The substantive data in their book are out of date, but crime statistics are always 'out of date' because the law, policing and criminal justice procedures change rapidly. What were 'robberies' in 1980 were what were constituted as robberies by the criminal justice system of the 1980s. They cannot be directly equated with 'robberies' of the 2000s, which would have been constituted as such through the criminal justice system of the time. See also Muncie and McLaughlin (2001: Chapter 1). Over the last ten years government has done a great deal to improve the quality of official 'administrative' statistics and the ONS web site contains various publications on this, including GSS (2005).

For GIS there is a good instructional package on the Ordnance Survey web site: www.ordnancesurvey.co.uk/oswebsite/gisfiles/, and the Wikipedia site is also very informative. The Geo-ed web site has a continuously updated GIS resource list: www.geo.ed.ac.uk/home/giswww.html, and Heywood, Cornelius and Carver (2006) is one of the best textbooks. Although mainly about historical research, Gregory (2005) is a good introduction to researching in this medium.

10 Questions and Answers

> **By the end of this chapter, you will:**
>
> - Have a good understanding of the considerations which shape the questioning strategies of researchers conducting social survey research and be able to contrast these with . . .
> - . . . the considerations which shape the questioning strategies of those who conduct the more discursive interviews of qualitative research
> - Know the main factors which might give misleading results from questioning respondents and the measures researchers may take to manage such problems.
>
> **And you will know the meaning of the following terms:**
>
> Acquiescence bias • construct validity • co-operation bias • Delphi group • demand characteristics of an interview • focus group • forced choice (or closed) questions • incorrigibles • interviewer effects • leading questions • modes of administration (ACASI, ASAQ, CAPI, CASI, CATI, OLQ, PAPI, PATI, SAQ,TDE) • open-ended questions • pre-structured data • random error • scaling • self-serving bias • social desirability bias • standardization of administration • systematic error.
>
> At the end of the chapter there is an Activity which asks you to evaluate the fitness for purpose of the kinds of questions which appear in social survey questionnaires. In Chapter 11 you will look at the kinds of responses which arise from the questions asked in qualitative interviews and the Activity at the end of the chapter features a transcript from a focus group.

10.1 Introduction

Many data come from asking people questions and recording their responses. Whether this is experimental research, social survey research or through the longer more discursive interviews of qualitative research (see Chapter 11), in each case the data collected are shaped by the way the questions are posed, and the manner and the context in which they were asked. Much administrative data arises from asking people questions, too (Chapter 9). This chapter examines the implications of data being responses to questions in the circumstances under which the questions were asked.

10.2   Validity and reliability in questioning

Figure 10.1 shows that, at the end of research involving researchers' questions and respondents' answers, there will be a data set for which it will be possible to say that there are these similarities and these differences between

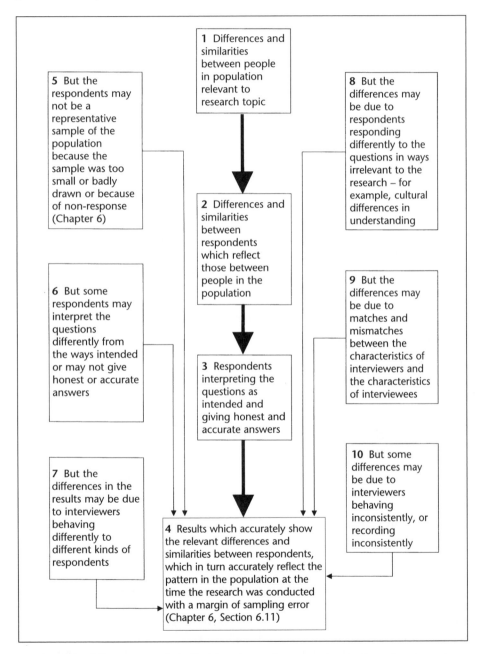

Reasons for differences and similarities shown between respondents in research involving questioning and answering   FIGURE 10.1

respondents. If the research was a controlled experiment (see Chapter 3) then the important differences and similarities would be between members of different comparison groups composed in advance. If it was a sample survey then the interesting differences and similarities are likely to be between categories already provided for in the survey design: between genders, age groups, or ethnicities, perhaps (see Chapter 6). And in some more open-ended research there may have been no prior assumptions as to what groups would emerge as interesting and what would be the differences between them, and the researcher will be looking to discover this in the data (see Chapters 11 and 12). This chapter will concentrate on the differences and similarities in the data *put there through the processes of questioning and answering*.

What the researcher hopes for is that any differences and similarities in the data will accurately reflect something real: that they won't simply be *artefacts* of the way the data were collected: that the research will go straight down the middle of Figure 10.1: Box **1, 2, 3, 4.**

The meaning of validity and reliability is explained in Chapter 2, for research instruments in general including questionnaires and interview prompts. Both concepts relate to the accuracy of the data collected. For some topics it is possible in principle (if not always in practice) to know whether a response is accurate and honest or not, and the use of validity and reliability as criteria for judging the effectiveness of a research method is straightforward. But, there is much of interest in social research where it would be impossible, *in principle*, to find any means of independently verifying what respondents say. These include matters of 'self-knowledge', or incorrigibles ('uncorrectables') such as opinions, attitudes, experiences, intentions, feelings, beliefs, values, ideas and ways of understanding. The problem of **incorrigibles** is discussed further in Chapter 11. But here it is worth noting that distinguishing between accurate and inaccurate answers to incorrigible questions requires evidence of beliefs and motives which is not usually available.

10.3 Two different approaches to eliciting information from respondents

Social research includes three different approaches to interviewing. I shall deal with two of these here: social survey interviewing and qualitative interviewing. The third is that adopted by ethnomethodological researchers, and is discussed in Chapter 11.

Social survey interviewing

This is of a piece with experimental research, and is followed by most researchers doing research using questionnaires with forced choice questions, which is most survey researchers. For convenience I will call this a *social survey approach* to questioning, though it is usual for collecting data in controlled experiments too. Here a premium is placed on **standardization**: on doing as much as possible to make sure that every respondent is asked the same questions in the same way, departing sometimes from this where it seems necessary to cater for major differences between respondents – for example, where it is necessary to translate questions into different languages.

Since they recognize that different respondents will experience the research situation differently, and that differences between interviewers may create misleading effects, researchers may make provision to collect information to judge whether this is happening. For example, they might analyse the results from different interviewers separately and compare them, in the same way as national examination boards analyse results to see if any marker is marking more or less leniently than others. Well-conducted research in this genre, then, involves exerting some statistical control over the research process in order to detect matters such as different responses to the same situation by different kinds of respondents, or differences in performance between different interviewers. In these ways, this approach employs something like the same safeguards against error that were described for experiments in Chapter 3.

Qualitative interviewing

The second approach is to regard standardization of the kind above as itself being a process of distortion. The argument goes that approaching respondents like this creates a thoroughly unnatural situation, so whatever the results they won't have much bearing on what respondents usually think, generally feel, normally experience, or really believe. The criticism here is similar to that sometimes made of experiments (Chapter 3, Section 3.10 and Chapter 4). It is important to note that this criticism is applied particularly in the context of research on matters of 'self-knowledge' (see p. 210). The approach suggested instead is to develop close, friendly, trusting, relationships with respondents, and to vary interviews from respondent to respondent in order that they will make authentic disclosures about their thoughts and feelings. The logical conclusion of this policy is not to conduct interviews with respondents at all, but to share their lives via some kind of participant observation research (Chapter 12) or though some kind of collaborative research activity (Chapter 14). But many people who hold this view do conduct interviews, though interviews which look much more like ordinary conversations. For want of a better term I will call this *qualitative interviewing*, since the users generally identify themselves as qualitative researchers, and the results are usually expressed in non-numerical terms.

The two approaches represent different ideas about the efficiency of different methods for eliciting information from respondents. But, in addition, the positions also entail different ethical ideas about the way researchers ought to treat the subjects of their research. This is discussed further in Chapter 14. For the time being, it is worth keeping issues of expediency separate from ethical issues. Below I will take each of the two approaches in turn.

10.4 Standardization and control in eliciting information in survey or experimental research

Social survey research has a long history. Part of that history is a body of research identifying what can go wrong in a social survey, and suggesting improvements to technique (de Heer, de Leeuw and van der Zouwen 1999; Kalton 2000). In addition, experimentation (in psychology, in particular) has generated a literature explaining why it sometimes happens that when experimenters ask subjects questions, the results prove difficult to interpret, or easy to misinterpret. The lessons taken from both sources are that when it comes to asking people questions what is needed is more rigour, more standardization and more control over confounding variables. Note here the similarities between this approach to collecting information and a 'similar-treatments, different-subjects' experimental design (see Chapter 4, Figure 4.1). In all cases, the aim is to treat the subjects similarly so that any differences in results are attributable to pre-existing differences between them and not to differences in the way the research has dealt with them.

The problems addressed in this genre of research are of a number of kinds. The first of these concerns failures of *representativeness*, including the problem of *non-response* (Figure 10.1, box 5). These were discussed in Chapter 6 and will not be discussed further here. But remember that usually people who are asked questions are being taken to stand for larger groups of people and only if they are representative can what was discovered about them be generalized more widely. Other kinds of problems are those shown in Figure 10.1, which deal primarily with misleading differences or similarities of response patterns between the respondents to the same survey. But there are also issues about how survey responses might have been different from all or some of the respondents had the survey been conducted in a different way, as indicated in Panel 10.1.

PANEL 10.1 How survey responses might have been different

The frequencies of responses might have been different:

- If the questionnaire had been administered differently, for example as a self-completed questionnaire, rather than an interviewer completed questionnaire
- If questions (on the same topic)
  - had been phrased differently
  - had been presented in a different order
  - had been included in a longer or a shorter survey
  - the permissible responses had been different
  - open rather than closed questions had been used
  - responses had been scaled differently.
- If the venue in which the questionnaire was completed had been different as an environment for responding and in terms of people present
- If the time at which the survey was done had been different: in relation to daily activities, time of year, or topicality of relevant events
- If the interviewer had been a different kind of person: male rather than female, black rather than white, formally rather than casually dressed and such like.
- If the survey had been explained to the respondents differently
- If the respondents had/had not been remunerated for their participation (Tzamourani 2000; Tzamourani and Lynn 2000)
- Other factors (Ruddock 1999).

Designing the questions and administering them in survey or experimental research

The different methods of administering questionnaires (Table 10.1) have the different implications for survey non-response noted in Chapter 6 – postal and internet questionnaires having low rates of response and internet and telephone surveys being representative only of those with internet and or telephone access. Some other differences are discussed below.

Computer-assisted/aided interviewing

Increasingly, Computer Aided Personal Interviewing (CAPI), Computer Aided Self-Administered Interviews (CASI) and Computer Aided Telephone Interviewing (CATI) are being used. These methods do seem to be an improvement on paper and pencil recording, as shown in Table 10.2 though it is not clear how far the improvements in terms of ease of administration feed through to produce more accurate data (Nicholls *et al.* 1997).

Social distance between researcher and respondent

The more distance that can be placed between the respondent and the questioner, the more likely respondents are to disclose information embarrassing, or upsetting to them. This has been a robust finding from research into research (de Leeuw *et al.* 1999). Table 10.3, for example, compares the results of three methods of eliciting information about their smoking habits from pregnant women. The greater the distance between the questioner and the respondent, the higher the level of smoking admitted. It seems reasonable in this case to assume that the higher levels are the more accurate ones.

Postal questionnaires promising anonymity seem to win out here, but that advantage is more than offset by the higher non-response rates of postal questionnaires, some of which must derive from respondents not wishing to disclose personal matters. The *British Crime Survey* sometimes uses the CASI mode. With particularly sensitive topics such as domestic violence this generates much fuller responses, and discloses more incidents than face to face interviewing (Walby and Allen 2004) and the more assistance the interviewer gives, the fewer incidents of domestic abuse are disclosed. The *British Crime Survey* researchers assume that more here means more valid. Ruddock (1999) reports the same for surveys asking respondents to disclose the number of their previous sexual partners. Generally, then, the evidence points towards the fullest disclosure occurring where the relationship between respondent and researcher is most distant, but offset by higher non-response rates in the more 'distant' modes.

Researcher control over responses and influence on respondent

Each mode of delivery gives different opportunities for researchers to control the research situation (Table 10.1 column (8)). With a postal questionnaire, the characteristics of an interviewer cannot influence the response except

TABLE 10.1 Modes of administering questionnaires: face to face, by telephone, postal and otherwise

Acronym (1)	Description (2)	f t f (3)	tel (4)	pstl (5)	Other (6)	Control by respondent (7)	Influence of Interviewer (8)
PAPI/PATI	Paper and pencil personal interview – interviewer asks questions and records on paper, f t f or telephone	X	X			Medium	High
SAQ	Paper and pencil self-administered questionnaire; respondent answers on paper	X		X		High	Low if postal/medium if interviewer present
ASAQ	Walkman-administered questionnaire – respondent hears recorded questions through headphones and answers on paper				X	Low	Low
CAPI/CATI	Interviewer reads questions from computer screen and keys in respondent's answers, f to f or telephone	X	X			Medium	Low if telephone/ Medium if Interviewer present
CASI	Computer-assisted self-administered interviews where interviewer hands lap-top to respondent, questions are on screen and respondent keys in responses	*				High	Low
ACASI	As above but questions (also) heard though earphones	*				Medium/	Low Low
TDE	Respondent is read questions over telephone/ hears recording of questions over telephone and responds using telephone keys		X			Medium with interviewer/ Low with recording	Low
OLQ	On-line questionnaires: respondent replies to questions on PC: web-based or e-mailed				X	High	Low
–	Loosely structured interviews (see Section 10.6 and Chapter 11)	X	X			Low to medium	Very high

Notes: * 'Interviewer' may be present to set-up and close down the 'self-administration' and offer help if asked.
f t f = face to face.
tel = telephone.
pstl = postal.

Advantages and disadvantages of computer aided interviewing (CAPI, CASI and CATI) by comparison with paper and pencil-based interviewing

Table 10.2

Advantages	Disadvantages
Routing from filter questions ('if "Yes" go to Q27') and irrelevant questions is automated With a paper questionnaire the interviewer has to search for the next relevant question Interviewers cannot easily miss out questions or ask the wrong questions Questions can be automatically customized as to, say, gender, or household role by answers to earlier questions Calculations can be made automatically The computer can signal inappropriate or inconsistent responses – for example, an age given not within a pre-specified age range.	Many interviews will not follow the expected sequence, because interviewees will want to correct earlier answers, or answer questions refused earlier (see Transcript 10.1) It can be difficult to use the computer aided questionnaire out of sequence – but better software could correct this For those who regard all standardized interviewing as artificial and distorting CAPI, CASI and CATI looks worse than paper and pencil interviewing

Source: Sainsbury, Ditch and Hutton (1993).

Intimacy and anonymity in disclosure: reports of numbers of cigarettes smoked daily at the beginning of pregnancy as reported in hospital records, by mothers interviewed at home and in postal questionnaires

TABLE 10.3

Number of cigarettes smoked daily	Hospital records (%)	Home interviews (%)	Postal questionnaires (%)
1–9	23	21	11
10–19	57	57	42
20 +	20	22	47
Total:	**100**	**100**	**100**
Average	**11.7 cigarettes**	**13 cigarettes**	**16.6 cigarettes**

How to read this table

Information about smoking at the beginning of pregnancy was sought from the same group of 75 women in three different ways. Very similar results were obtained through the two face to face methods, but the anonymous postal questionnaire suggested much higher rates of smoking. Since it is difficult to imagine these women exaggerating their smoking under circumstances of anonymity it seems reasonable to assume that the postal questionnaire gives the more accurate figures. There is evidence to suggest, in addition, that many smokers do not know accurately how many cigarettes they smoke, and that they consistently under-estimate this.

Source: After Oakley, Rajan and Roberson (1990: 483).

through what appears on paper. But nor can the researcher control the circumstances under which a questionnaire is completed, or even who actually completes it. Moreover, the only guidance the researcher can give to the respondents has to be written in advance on the questionnaire. Much the same is true with e-mail questionnaires, though an on-screen 'Help' facility can be provided. Telephone interviewers cannot influence responses by their appearance or gestures, and can offer supplementary guidance as to the meaning of questions – for good or ill. Self-completed computer-aided questionnaires usually require the presence of an administrator, and the possibility of assistance. Face to face interviews may offer considerable opportunities for the interviewer to control the circumstances of the interview, especially if interviews are conducted at a venue chosen by the researcher, though less so if conducted in the respondents' home or work place, and even less so on a busy street. Face to face interviews also offer greater risks that what should be irrelevant characteristics about interviewers will influence responses.

There is some evidence that more the interview process is in the hands of the respondent (Table 10.1, column (7)) particularly its pacing, the more accurate the data generated (Ruddock 1999). Again, the evidence points towards the desirability of minimizing the role of the interviewer.

Question formats in survey or experimental research

Closed-ended or **forced choice** questions are usually preferred by survey researchers (see Chapter 2, Panel 2.1 and the surrounding text in Chapter 2). This is because the object of most survey work is to make point-by-point comparisons between different kinds of people, or between the same kinds of people at different times. This can be done precisely only if the same questions are asked of everyone, and if respondents are restricted to a limited number of responses. The responses from forced choice questions are easily coded into numerical forms. Sometimes researchers begin by designing the tables in which the results are to be expressed, and then devise questions to generate the numbers to fill into the tables. How the researcher intends to analyse the results statistically will also influence the way the questions are framed. Issues of *scaling* are particularly important since the scale determines the kinds of data generated, and hence the kinds of statistical analysis possible (Chapter 2, Section 2.3)

In a survey, **open-ended questions** may sometimes be asked. But if respondents are allowed to use their own words, what these words mean may not be clear to the researchers. And when they analyse the results they will have anyway to reduce the diverse responses to a much smaller number of categories. There is a strong possibility that a large percentage of the responses will end up in the 'miscellaneous' category and not really contribute to the results at all. Probably some respondents will provide more than one answer to a question. If all the answers are counted this will over-represent the responses of the loquacious as against those of the more reticent, thus undermining the representativeness of the sample for this question. Or, if only one of several answers from some respondents is to enter the analysis, then it is difficult to find principles for choosing and excluding responses. In addition, having to analyse the responses to open questions is costly in time and money.

The use of **closed-ended questions** often gives rise to the criticism that these force respondents to express ideas they may not have, in words they would not normally use, and that they are thereby misrepresented. Whether this is an apposite criticism depends on the purpose of the research. Consider, for example, research designed to establish the extent of 'homelessness' and the risk of being 'homeless' among different categories of people, and conducted to influence policy in this field. Here it would produce meaningless results to allow each respondent to define 'homelessness' differently, because the purpose of the research implies that the results should be meaningful in policy terms and meaningful to policy-makers. The most appropriate approach here might be to elicit from respondents the kind of information which a housing officer would ask for in order to determine someone's eligibility for housing: either under a current policy, or according to one the researcher thought should be adopted. Here it would be appropriate to force respondents to use response categories provided for them.

However, in a piece of research designed to capture something of what it was like to experience homelessness it would pre-judge what this experience was to ask respondents closed questions. The results from closed-ended questions might then be meaningless in the sense of not capturing the meaning of 'homelessness' to those experiencing it. It would be better to get them to use their own words, even if it might sometimes turn out to be uncertain as to what they meant. Many surveys include both closed-ended and open-ended questions according to the use to which the resulting information will be put. Research using open-ended questions is often a preliminary for the design of a closed-question questionnaire.

In their studies of what respondents prefer Graham, Lewis and Nicholas (2006) and Graham, Grewal and Lewis (2007) found that, if they were interviewed face to face, what respondents liked were easily flowing interactions between interviewer and interviewee. Respondents were just as likely to report having had this experience when formal questionnaires were used as when more discursive qualitative interviewing was used. This suggests that, in putting the respondent at ease, the social skills of the particular interviewer are as important as the format of the questions.

Different questions, different answers

The use of closed-ended as opposed to open-ended questions can certainly give rise to different answers about the same matters. For example, in a Finnish study of the menopause Hemminki and colleagues (Hemminki, Topo and Kangas 1995) found that when given a list of symptoms to tick, 45% ticked 'tiredness', 41% 'hot flushes' and 35% 'headaches' as symptoms they had experienced in the previous 2 weeks which they associated with the menopause. But when asked an open-ended question only 9% mentioned 'tiredness' and only 4% 'headaches', though about 40% mentioned 'hot flushes'. The first mode of questioning seems likely to have produced the more accurate data on symptoms experienced. The second mode generates responses which are more difficult to interpret.

The use of closed-ended questions is also a response to the problem of collecting data from large numbers of people with a limited amount of time for each. In addition, closed-ended questions can be constructed to force respondents to make themselves comparable with others by expressing an opinion or belief on a scale from very strong to very weak: so-called **Likert scales** and similar scaling devices (Chapter 2, Panel 2.1). Without this, it would be very difficult to distinguish between those who forcefully express an opinion not very important to them and those who reticently express an opinion dearly held.

Chapter 2, Table 2.4 illustrates the different kinds of results which might come from asking 'Yes/No/Don't know' questions, as opposed to asking a scaled question. With the unscaled questions there seems to be little difference in 'satisfaction' between males and females, but with a scaled question large differences show themselves. However, to use scaled questions it is necessary to use larger samples, for the reasons explained in Chapter 6, Section 6.10. The strength with which an opinion or feeling is held is virtually impossible to determine with open-ended questions, where the different ways respondents use for expressing themselves add a complicating factor. Of course, scaling does not entirely solve this problem.

Researchers have to frame questions in terms which are likely to be understood by respondents. This includes avoiding ambiguity, except in those kinds of research where the object is to see how different kinds of people resolve an ambiguous stimulus differently, as in some psychological, 'projective' research. Sometimes it is necessary to produce questionnaires or interview schedules in various language versions. This can introduce confounding factors into the research: differences between languages are not just differences between words, but also differences between ideas (Temple 2005). A directly translated question may not be the same question as the original (Meadows and Wisher 2000). Differences in the results may reflect this, rather than whatever it was that they were supposed to reflect. For example, in the national survey of minority ethnic mental health Nazroo (1997) found that those respondents who were asked questions in South Asian languages appeared to be more mentally healthy than were either other minority groups interviewed in English, or the 'white' respondents. These South Asians were the more recent arrivals so this might be taken as evidence that the longer you live in Britain the more mentally unhealthy you become. But, equally, the finding might be an artefact of the way the ideas in the interview were conveyed differently in different languages.

Producing 'user-friendly' questions by phrasing them in colloquial terms also has problems. Several questionnaires still used commonly in health services research use 'feeling blue' instead of 'sad' or 'depressed', and are very out of date in this respect (for example, Jenkinson 1994: 69). Yet using the term 'sad' for its more usual meaning might cause confusion for those young people for whom it meant 'pathetic' or 'despicable' in 2007. Generally 'user-friendly' language is more exclusionary than standard English. The same is true with regard to colloquial Hindi as compared with the educated Hindi which is much more widely understood among subcontinental populations.

Leading respondents to appropriate answers

Similar problems may arise with expert terms. For example, it would be no good asking people if they had angina because there will be people who have been diagnosed with angina, but who don't know this, people who have been diagnosed and do know it and, of these, some will have been correctly and some incorrectly diagnosed. And there will be people who have not been diagnosed with angina who actually have it, some saying 'Yes' and some saying 'No', and some people who haven't been diagnosed, haven't got angina but say they have. To make matters worse, as with most illnesses, people don't just have it or not. They have heart conditions ranging from very mild to very severe. Somewhere on this continuum a line is drawn between 'angina' and 'not-angina'. Different doctors are likely to make such 'casing' decisions differently (see Chapter 9, Section 9.4).

Payne and Saul (1997) were particularly interested in whether, in Sheffield, the people most in need of coronary care services were those who received them most frequently. To find this out they had to know who suffered from angina. It was impossible to use medical records, since part of the problem was that doctors were not picking up all the cases. It would have been much too expensive to send teams of doctors out into the community to examine people. Instead they sought information directly from people in the community, using a sample survey technique (see Chapter 6). It would have been silly just to ask: 'Do you have angina?', but people do know sufficient about their own bodily experiences to be able to provide the kind of information which an expert can use to judge whether they have angina or not. Payne and Saul used the *WHO Angina Questionnaire* (Rose, McCartney and Reid 1977). This asks people questions about their experience of what doctors usually take to be the symptoms of angina. What Payne and Saul actually found was that poorer people were much more likely to report the symptoms of angina than richer people, and much less likely than richer people to have been diagnosed by local doctors or, even if they had been diagnosed with a heart condition by local doctors, to be less likely to be receiving coronary care.

The *WHO Angina Questionnaire* had been subjected to criterion validation (see Chapter 2, Section 2.7) by its results being compared with medical examinations of the respondents. Using standard instruments such as this allows direct comparisons to be made between the results of two different pieces of research using the same data collection instrument. Experimental researchers, in particular, tend to use standard questionnaires for this reason. But the same principle is applied in various repeated 'state-of-the-nation' surveys such as the *General Household Survey*, the *Labour Force Survey* or the *British Crime Survey*. These have some new questions on each occasion but there are also standard questions. A major objective is to measure trends over time. With differently worded questions it would be difficult to say whether any differences from time to time were real or merely due to asking different questions.

There are two reasons, then, for using standard questions in survey and experimental research:

- To ensure *comparability* between different pieces of research
- To *share 'tried and tested' questions* among researchers.

To these ends, those who design British government surveys draw on and contribute to a central question bank and use standardized terms for new questions (GSS 2003; see the *Further reading* of this chapter).

The term **leading question** is usually used pejoratively to refer to questions which lead the respondent towards giving a misleading response. This is usually if the phrasing of the question implies that the questioner will think better of the respondent for answering one way rather than another, provoking an acquiescence or a social desirability bias. For example, 'Do you ever get drunk?' is probably a leading question in this sense, and 'Do you ever get rat arsed?' is certainly one. But these questions wouldn't necessarily 'lead' everyone in the same direction. Some people would be ashamed of getting drunk, others proud. So the idea of a leading question is a problematic one. The *WHO Angina Questionnaire* example shows how researchers have to lead respondents towards giving the information required. So all questions lead: they lead to an answer. The important issue is whether they lead to the truth.

The lead of a question may not be immediately obvious. For example, it makes a difference whether questions are framed positively or negatively. Panel 10.2 shows the difference in administration and wording of two Scottish NHS consumer satisfaction questionnaires.

The Lothian Survey showed much higher rates of dissatisfaction with the NHS than the all-Scotland Scottish Users' Survey. But Cohen and his colleagues (Cohen, Forbes and Garraway 1996) found that people from Lothian who were polled in the all-Scotland survey were no more dissatisfied than people in Scotland as a whole. They concluded that the differences had to do either with one survey being conducted face to face, and the other as a self-completed, self-return, anonymous questionnaire, or it had to do with the different ways the questions were posed. There were important differences in responses to only some questions, which suggested that it wasn't the mode of administration making a difference to the results. The main differences were associated with questions which were framed positively in one survey but negatively in the other, as in the examples in Panel 10.2. Cohen, Forbes and Garraway conclude:

> Whereas only 5.6% of respondents in the Scottish Users' Survey agreed with the statement: 'I was not encouraged to ask questions', 23.9% of the Lothian respondents disagreed with the statement 'You were encouraged to ask questions about your treatment'. Thus substantially different conclusions can be obtained if patients are presented with a negative statement about care and asked to agree that something 'bad' happened, as opposed to presenting them with a positive statement and asking them to disagree that something good happened.
>
> (Cohen, Forbes and Garraway 1996: 843)

Here a fourfold difference in dissatisfaction is attributable to a difference in the way that questions were asked about similar issues. However, this is a problem only when comparing the results of the two different surveys.

PANEL 10.2 Differences in questioning strategy and wording between an NHS consumer satisfaction survey in Lothian and one covering the whole of Scotland (NHS Scottish Users' Survey)

Lothian Survey: a self-completed postal questionnaire survey

The *questionnaire* asked:
'Thinking generally about your experience in hospital last year, please tell us if you agree or disagree with the statements below'
One of the statements was:
You were encouraged to ask questions about your treatment.
And the questionnaire asked:
'The National Health Service in Scotland published a booklet called "Framework for Action". They listed some of the things which upset patients. In your experience of hospitals in Lothian are any of these a cause for concern?'
One statement was:
Doctors have no time to listen

NHS Scottish Users' Survey: a survey in which a questionnaire was filled in by an interviewer face to face with the interviewee

The *interviewer* asked:
'Thinking about the information you were given at the hospital, did any of these things happen at your visit?'

The interviewer then showed interviewees a card with a number of negative statements including:
I was not given enough information;
I was not encouraged to ask questions;
I was not encouraged to get involved in decisions about my treatment;
There was not enough time for me to be involved.

Source: Based on Cohen, Forbes and Garraway (1996: 843).

Results from the same survey questions administered in the same way at different points in time would be adequate for showing time trends in consumer satisfaction.

Interviewer effects and respondent reactions

Interviewer effects include some which are directly equivalent to the expectancy effects referred to in the context of experiments in Chapter 3, Section 3.6. In survey interviews, too, what interviewers expect and how they would prefer the results to come out may influence the results. A classic example here is Kinsey's huge research programme on human sexuality. Kinsey believed that child sex abuse was extraordinarily rare but that sex with animals was common. Although there was a standard schedule of questions, Kinsey frequently departed from these, apparently asking many supplementary questions about bestiality and cutting short respondents who claimed to have been sexually abused as children, who he regarded as deluded. Not surprisingly, the *Kinsey Reports* give a picture of Americans who rarely engaged in child sexual abuse and often had sex with animals (O'Connell Davidson and Layder 1994: 83–113).

> **PANEL 10.3** Some circumstances lead to large interviewer effects: that is, when there are large differences between the responses elicited from the same kinds of people by different interviewers, using the same questions
>
> Interviewer effects are greatest when:
>
> - Sensitive or emotional topics are investigated;
> - Open, rather than closed questions are used;
> - Questions are ambiguous or difficult to understand;
> - Interviewers have received little or no training;
> - Interviewers adjust their performance to the demeanour of the interviewee
> - Interviewers disclose themselves personally to interviewees.
>
> *Source*:   After Groves (1989).

Interviewer effects also include the effects created inadvertently by the interviewer's gender, ethnicity, social class, age, accent, demeanour and so on. We could force the comparison with experiments further and say that respondents may also show *Hawthorne effects*, answering questions in a way most unlike they would do otherwise, because they know they are being researched (Chapter 3, Section 3.6). But since the context of questioning and answering is a *social relationship* between questioner and respondent it is better to think in terms of interviewer effects and respondent reactions together – see Panel 10.3.

Whatever a respondent does, he or she will set themselves up as being a particular kind of person. It is an issue for a respondent, then, as to what kind of person they are going to represent themselves as being at the time of the research. Everyone is quite capable of representing themselves in different ways in different situations, so this doesn't necessarily suggest attempts to mislead, though some people may use the opportunity to tell outrageous untruths, or to fantasy role-play being the kind of person they usually aren't. There are at least two audiences for these performances. One is the interviewer or, in the case of a postal questionnaire, the person the respondent imagines will read it when completed. The other is the respondent himself or herself. The answers tell the respondent what kind of person they are. When I fill in market research questionnaires I am inclined to lie when I wouldn't like the look of myself given by answering correctly. Sometimes there are additional members of the audience. A one-on-one interview overheard by others adds another audience to posture to or hide things from (Walby and Allen 2004: Table A6). A focus group (see Section 10.5) provides a very complex audience to perform in front of (Green and Hart 1999).

The **demand characteristics** of an interview situation are what it is that the respondent thinks the situation demands – or, rather, what it is that the respondent thinks the situation demands if he or she is going to come across as sensible, competent, moral and otherwise OK, or as put-upon, neglected and abused, or as strong and resilient, or whatever impression he or she would prefer to make. Part of the demand structure will have been put in place intentionally by the researcher explaining what is necessary, and indeed in the phrasing of each question. But part will consist of all the *cues* which the respondent will pick up as to what would be appropriate and inappropriate behaviour and what answers will lead the respondent to be viewed as he or she would prefer. The usual bias here is towards *social desirability*, but some respondents will want to shock and scandalize their interviewer.

The sources of such cues include the characteristics of the interviewer. Research suggests that white respondents are less likely to express racist views in the hearing of a black interviewer (Finkel, Guerbock and Borg 1991). So far as government surveys in the UK are concerned, most interviewers are female and males are more likely to express weaknesses to female interviewers (Walby and Allen 2004: Table A4. See also Nathanson 1978; Padfield and Proctor 1996). Again, drug users seem more likely to describe themselves as having a problem they can't handle and as being in need of treatment when interviewed by social worker interviewers than when interviewed by someone representing themselves as an 'ex-user' (Davies 1997). Other cues will come from the behaviour of the interviewer, and yet others from the venue of the interview. Interviews in pubs seem to produce higher estimates of alcohol consumption than interviews at home (Crawford 1987). Respondents are always likely to be looking for 'a lead' from the interviewer or from the questions (see also Chapter 8, Panel 8.1).

Controlling the interview situation

The way in which survey researchers try to manage such problems is through controlling the circumstances of the research directly by *standardization* – by the equivalent of experimental control (see Chapter 3), and by monitoring closely what happens, to see if control has been effective – by *statistical control* (see Chapter 7, Section 7.2). Controlling the circumstances mainly means training interviewers to give a standard, courteous, non-judgemental performance. This may mean getting them to learn a script to recite, though they usually find they have to depart from the script from time to time (see Transcript 10.1, p. 224). Attention may be given to the clothing, cleanliness, hairstyle and so on and to the furnishings and layout of any venue. Standardization doesn't rule out using interviewers who are ethnically or gender matched to respondents, but there is conflicting evidence as to whether ethnic or gender matching produces more accurate results.

In surveys with several interviewers, monitoring is likely to include separate analysis of the results for each interviewer to see if there are any consistent differences between them. Even with one interviewer, it is not uncommon to analyse separately the results of interviews conducted early in the programme compared with those conducted later, since interviewers may significantly change their style as time goes on. If there are worries about particular categories of respondents responding to the research situation in a way that might produce misleading results, then again the results for them can be compared with those for others: recall the example of those who were interviewed in South Asian languages in the National Survey of Minority Ethnic Mental Health (Nazroo 1997). All this is the exercise of statistical control over the results in order to detect any distorting factors at play.

Increasingly, however, those who conduct large-scale surveys are regarding this as inadequate, since it can only be inferred from the results as to what might have happened in the interview. Thus it is becoming common practice to tape or video-record at least a sample of interviews for each interviewer and subject these to detailed analysis. With telephone interviewing, this can be done unobtrusively.

The research interview as fact-producing interaction

Transcript 10.1 is an example of an interview involving the use of a questionnaire. The questionnaire here is from the large-scale *American National Health Interview Survey*. The actual interview was not part of the survey as such but conducted in order to investigate the interview process.

TRANSCRIPT 10.1   The research interview

1 **Interviewer**: During those two weeks did she [daughter] miss any time from a job because of illness or injury?

2 **Mrs E** [pause, looking to Mr E]: I don't know. I don't know if she did have one day when she didn't go to work, when she didn't feel too well. I think one day, she didn't.

3 **Interviewer**: One day?

4 **Mrs E**: Mm hm
[portion omitted, during which it appears that the daughter may have missed two weeks' work]

5 **Interviewer**: What condition caused her to miss work, and stay in bed during those two weeks?

6 **Mrs E**: [smiles, looks to Mr E]

7 **Mr E**: I think she had . . .: She had a sore throat.

8 **Interviewer**: Sore . . .

9 **Mr E**: Sore throat or cold, yes.
[portion omitted]

10 **Interviewer**: When did [your daughter] last see or talk to a doctor or assistant about her sore throat?

11 **Mrs E**: Well, she didn't talk to one, to a doctor about the sore throat at this time, but in the fall, I believe it was in October [looks to Mr E] she had flu. She was run down. And she was. I believe she was ill for about a week. She had flu, and she had a fever. And she went to Dr C. Twice she went to Dr C.

12 **Interviewer**: This was, uh, you stated in the fall . . .

13 **Mrs E**: In the fall of the year.

14 **Interviewer**: Has she seen the doctor about uh her sore throat?

15 **Mrs E**: No, not this week, no. Not this last time.

16 **Interviewer**: What was the cause of her sore throat?

17 **Mrs E** [shrugs] She had a cold. I don't know.

18 **Interviewer**: Did the sore throat result from an accident or an injury?

20 **Mrs E**: No.

Source: Suchman and Jordan (1990: 236, numbering added).

This transcript illustrates how a carefully constructed set of questions proves awkward to use in actual interviews, and how the interviewer has to depart from the script and use *ad hoc* methods in an attempt to find answers. One question sounds quite daft (**18**): How could a sore throat be caused by an accident or injury? But the question the interviewer is trying to find an answer for is something like '*whatever the condition which caused the person to see the doctor*, was it caused by an accident or injury?' In many circumstances it wouldn't have been a daft question. Even though it is a silly question in this context, the interviewer has been instructed to ask all the questions of all the respondents.

A more important point is that the transcript shows how 'an interview' isn't just one person asking questions, and another answering them, but a *co-operative activity* in which interviewer and interviewee work together to establish the truth of the matter of interest. The interviewer here is just as important as the interviewees in providing the answers. Indeed it is the interviewer who makes a fact of the daughter's sore throat, while the interviewees leave it as ambiguous as to whether she had a sore throat or the flu or both. The interviewer needed something to be established as a matter of fact by point **10** in the transcript in order to pose the questions she poses at points **14**, **16** and **18**, all of which require her to ask a question about an illness or injury which has already been established as real and relevant to the survey. The daughter seems to have had three, perhaps four, episodes of illness, one involving time off work and perhaps a different episode associated with seeing the doctor. But in the survey results she will appear as having had just one episode of illness, necessitating two weeks' absence from work and causing her to consult a doctor.

A further feature illustrated by the transcript is of the *co-operative bias* shown by many respondents. Mr and Mrs E don't seem at all sure about the facts of the matter, but since the interviewer wants some facts they willingly serve some up. The interviewers for the *American National Health Interview Survey* are experienced and highly trained. Even with well-designed questionnaires and experienced interviewers, what are supposed to be highly structured interviews, in a series attempting to engage each respondent in the same way as each other, interviews often show messy sequences like this when transcribed.

This example shows how the performance of the interviewer and the interaction between interviewer and interviewees can influence survey results in a way not intended by the survey designers. We can only see this, of course, because the interview was recorded and transcribed. Usually such effects disappear. They may leave their traces on the results, but it may be difficult to see them for what they are.

Random and systematic errors in survey research

However, for the *American National Health Interview Survey* things are not as bad as might first appear. This is a large-scale survey which attempts to build up a picture of how things are in aggregate. For this it is not essential to produce entirely accurate data from each individual respondent. A large percentage of the errors in such surveys will be 'one-offs' and each affect so few people that they won't affect the overall results much at all, and a large percentage will be random errors where what is recorded wrongly for one respondent will be compensated for by an error in the opposite direction for another. Much more worrying to survey researchers than random error is undetected systematic error where some feature of the research creates a bias always in *one direction* (see the example in Panel 10.2 from Cohen, Forbes and Garraway 1996 above). However, if systematic errors are detected the results can be adjusted accordingly. For example, once it is known that the WHO *Angina Questionnaire* over-estimates the prevalence of angina, as it does, and by how much it usually does so, this is no more of a problem than having a watch which is consistently ten minutes fast.

10.5 Group interviews

Some of the issues discussed above can be revisited by considering situations where interviews are conducted not with individuals or couples, but with larger groups of people.

Focus groups have a long history in market research for testing new commercial and political products and advertising campaigns. Their popularity in the business world persists despite mounting evidence of their poor showing as a way of predicting what products will sell and a string of product launch disasters based on focus group research (Walvis 2003; Rushkoff 2005). Seemingly without reference to this, focus groups have recently become popular in mainstream social research (Barbour and Kitzinger 1999; Bloor *et al.* 2000; Krueger and Casey 2000). They consist of a group discussion focused on topics provided by the researcher and sometimes involve the use of stimulus material, such as problem scenarios for participants to discuss, videos for them to comment on, or set piece debates. The group discussion will probably be audio or video recorded and the write up is most likely to be qualitative rather than quantitative, although there are exceptions. Typically group size is between 8 and 12. Focus group method raises three important methodological issues.

First, there is an issue of the *representativeness* of the group and *generalizability* of the findings (see Chapter 6, Section 6.2). Are the people who are recruited to be focus group members representative of anyone but themselves? Would the information derived from the focus group apply to anyone but them? In Chapter 6, this was discussed in relation to selecting samples for surveys of individuals, but the same principles apply. For *statistical representativeness* and *empirical generalization*, large samples are needed. Ideally these are selected on *probability principles*. But in market research and political opinion polling it is typical that participants are selected on *quota sampling* principles (Chapter 6, Section 6.13) to create a representative mix, either within groups or of groups within a research programme. Large numbers of focus groups tend to be run for the same research programme by market research and opinion-polling companies. With regard to sampling it is important to note that, while a focus group might involve 10 participants, it is still only *one* interview for the kind of statistical analysis used by survey researchers. If statistical representativeness and empirical generalization are the aim, there are no merits in the claim that conducting 20 focus groups of 10 people each is equivalent to interviewing 200 individuals separately.

With *theoretical sampling* and *theoretical generalization* (Chapter 6, Panel 6.3; Chapter 12, Section 12.5) the researcher has reason to believe that the people of interest fall into a number of different types in ways that are relevant to the research, and decides to investigate each type. For example, in her study of the response of medical students to a new problem-based learning curriculum Lloyd-Jones (2002) suspected that this would differ according to various differences among students influencing their peer-group membership and their study habits. Therefore she arranged different **group interviews** with, for example, overseas students and UK students, students living at home and students living on campus and so on. It might have been better for her to have conducted individual interviews, but as a single-handed researcher with limited time available, group interviews increased the range of types of people she could interview and allowed her to cover the dimensions of diversity which seemed most relevant to her research topic.

Second, these are *group* interviews. A number of people are involved and encouraged to vocalize, so there are plenty of opportunities for all of them to influence each other as to what is said. This is like the problem of the 'interviewer effect', but on a larger scale. From the viewpoint of the orthodox survey researcher, the focus group looks like a hopelessly uncontrolled environment, in the sense that it will be difficult to work out what in the results reflects whatever was the research topic, and which derive from the 'chemistry' of the group. Mortimore and Atkinson (2000) of MORI Polls report: 'not all groups work as they should. On one occasion, two strangers seduced each other as the group was going on. Everyone pretended not to notice.' The Activity at the end of Chapter 11 offers you an opportunity to look at interaction within a focus group.

The influence of the participants on each other is a problem if the object of the research is to discover what each one thinks or believes individually and independently of the others. In groups there are often very strong pressures towards conformity, even if this means conformity to one or other of two opposing views taken by members. Lloyd-Jones (2002) also collected some information from individually completed questionnaires. This allowed her to judge how far the group situation had influenced what people said. Thus she controlled responses elicited in a group situation against individually elicited responses. Mutual influence also raises issues of *reliability*. In one-to-one interviews it is always an issue as to whether the same interviewee would have given the same response on a second occasion. Group discussions twist and turn and group dynamics ebb and flow, so it must be the case that what anyone says is closely determined by the state of the group at the moment when they say it. In a different group, or in the same group run on a second occasion, they might have said something very different.

Sometimes, however, the researcher's interest will be precisely in how people express themselves in group situations. David Morgan (1988: 12, original emphases) says: 'The hallmark of focus groups is *the explicit use of group interaction to produce data and insights that would be less accessible without the interaction found in a group.'* For example, focus group members might be recruited from within an existing organization – a school, perhaps, or a firm. Then the way they discuss issues in the focus group is likely to provide some insight into how these same issues are discussed in the everyday circumstances of the organization. In the group they may 'talk the talk' of the organization, in ways that would not happen in one-to-one interviews. If a researcher cannot directly observe what happens under naturally occurring circumstances (Chapter 12) a focus group may be the next best approach.

But in these circumstances there are likely to be important topics which are unmentionable in the group, but which might be disclosed one-to-one.

Focus groups, and other group interviews, raise issues of confidentiality and participant welfare which are not raised to the same extent by individual interviews. In one-to-one situations, interviewers are able to promise confidentiality and are in a position to keep the promise. Where information is shared with other participants there is no guarantee that they will respect each other's confidentiality later even if they are made to promise this at the outset. Again, in a one-to-one interview it is easier to minimize the chances of any distress being caused to the interviewee – only two people are involved. Ensuring this in a group situation means controlling the behaviour of a number of people towards one another. This may call for very skilful group facilitation. It is sometimes argued that in group situations participants find it easier to articulate their views because they feel supported by the group. This has been claimed with regard to research with minority ethnic groups (Chiu and Knight 1999) and children (Kitzinger and Farquhar 1999) and similarly where sensitive issues are the topic (Farquar and Das 1999). But at the same time participants take risks in disclosing themselves in a group situation which are not present in a private one-to-one interview. This is particularly so if groups are composed of people who will be in contact with each other later. Issues of confidentiality and participant welfare are discussed further in Chapter 16.

Action research is discussed in more detail in Chapter 14 (Section 14.5). The main purpose of action research is to effect some worthwhile change while studying how this does (or does not) come about. Here focus groups may be used as part of the change process – for example, as ways of getting groups of people to define what they want to happen, commit themselves to action, or to sort out misunderstandings between them. When focus groups are used in health promotion research, part of the aim is often that the members will learn more about healthy behaviour and will become more committed to healthy life-styles.

Third, unlike most other kinds of group interviews, in a focus group the facilitator *focuses* group discussion on a set of issues for discussion, rather than just asking questions. There is an expectation that what participants know and believe will be transformed by hearing what other people say, and by their own responses. This is probably not very different from most one-to-one interviews. These often ask people questions they have not thought of before, and thinking up an answer on the spot may change and add to what they originally thought. However, in the focus group research, this becomes explicit and the data will show how people stake out and argue positions, how they are convinced by others, negotiate compromises, and so on. In this regard focus groups are not very different from some of the group interviews and task groups used in psychology to study, leadership, group decision-making, group problem-solving, or group dynamics in general. However, in these examples it is likely that the researcher will use a structured observation technique (Chapter 12, Panel 12.1) and produce quantitative data rather than, or in addition to, qualitative data, and most such psychological research on groups involves some of the usual control devices of experimentation (see Chapter 3).

In a **'Delphi' group** the participants will be experts in their field and the object will be for them to reach a consensus about the issues discussed. The participants might, for example, be a group of doctors developing some guidelines for the treatment of a medical condition (see Chapter 15), or a group of economic forecasters producing a report for a government department or a merchant bank. **'Nominal groups'** involve participants coming to some agreement about the ranking of options or preferences. This might involve voting for different versions of the same package design in market research, or ranking the importance of various options for service development in consumer research in public services. Whether Delphi groups and nominal groups are regarded as 'focus groups' varies from author to author. But in both cases the interest is in the results of the group discussion rather than in the process of the discussion. The same is true of focus groups used to trial different versions of a questionnaire for later use in a survey.

While much group interviewing in psychology and some in market research and opinion polling generates quantitative data, as does nominal group technique, focus groups usually produce qualitative data and are best regarded as within the genre of qualitative interviewing discussed below.

10.6 Making close relationships with respondents: qualitative interviewing

So, one approach to the possibility that the research situation may be distorting the truth is to try to exert more *control*: either directly or by collecting information about the situation, as described earlier. The other approach goes entirely in the opposite direction. If the research situation is artificial and distorting then it should be made less 'researchy' and more like 'real life'. People who hold this view prescribe that interviews should be more like ordinary conversations, with no pre-set questions, and respondents allowed to decide topics and ask questions themselves. **Loosely structured interviews** is probably a better term for this than '*in-depth*'. First, because psychoanalysts and police investigators also conduct in-depth interviews, but certainly not on the same egalitarian terms as being suggested here; second, because what is 'deep' and what is 'shallow' depends on the analogy in use: a brain-scan might be regarded as in-depth in some ways and superficial in others. For a loosely structured interview there will usually be a list of topics the researcher hopes to cover, though in no particular order, and with no particular wording. Since each interviewee is regarded as being different it makes sense to treat each one of them differently.

Margaret Andersen describes the way she, as a white and middle-class researcher interviewed poor African-American women:

> it is impossible even to count the exact number of interviews in my project and to report the amount of time they took. Many of the women included in this research refused to be interviewed formally, but were willing to talk with me for hours. One woman asked that the tape recorder be turned off at various places in our conversation. With the tape recorder turned off, she spoke freely about information she thought should remain confidential, although it revealed important yet sensitive information about race and gender relationships in the community. Another woman told me her long and intriguing life history and talked openly about class and race relations in the community, but refused to be taped. We sat in my car for most of the afternoon, in subfreezing winter temperatures. Other important information and ideas in this project came from many days and hours of informal discussion with these women at the local senior centre . . .
>
> Several talked at length about how my 'personality' made them more trusting, open and willing to speak with me. These comments made me think about what I was doing – consciously and unconsciously – to elicit their reported trust . . . In sum, what seems to have made these interviews possible was my direct violation of the usual admonitions to social science researchers. During the interviews I answered questions about myself, my background, my family, and my ideas. In the interviews and during the field research, the women and I exchanged our feelings and ideas about many of the ideas we were discussing. At times, I showed the emotion I felt during very moving moments in their accounts of their experiences.
>
> (Andersen 1993: 47–50)

For the orthodox social survey researcher, interviewers getting over-involved with respondents looks like a problem. There are three reasons for this. First, there is the worry that if respondents get to know too much about interviewers they will begin to care too much what they think about them, and answer questions accordingly. In focus group research the equivalent worry is that respondents will care too much about the opinions that others in the group form of them. Second, the worry is that the more interviewees get to know about the interviewer, the more likely they will be to adjust their performance in ways they imagine will impress or please them. In focus group research an additional concern here is the way in which *participant roles* emerge in the group – someone, for example, emerging, and playing up to the role of group fool, someone else as the champion of a particular view and so on. Third, there is the concern that interviewers will make better relationships with some respondents than others, and hence introduce a confounding differentiating factor into the research (Figure 10.1, box 9). However, for those who believe that the problem lies in the artificiality of the research situation the policy is again entirely opposite. The argument is that only by developing intimate, trusting and empathetic relationships will respondents feel able to disclose the truth (counter to the evidence of research in this topic, see Section 10.4). This is sometimes applied to encounters between researchers and interviewees which last for only an hour or so, but the preference is for longer and more intense encounters. For the orthodox survey researcher the personal characteristics of the interviewer are regarded as something to be controlled out of the way by standardizing their performance (see Section 10.4). But here the personal characteristics of the interviewer may be regarded as either an asset or a disqualification. Thus it is may be argued that only women can successfully interview women, and only black people can successfully interview black people, and that the more the interviewer and interviewee share in the way of characteristics and previous experience the more successful the interview is likely to be (Oakley 1981). In their studies of what respondents to surveys preferred, Graham, Lewis and Nicholas (2006), and Graham, Grewal and Lewis (2007) actually found that respondents were unlikely to express preferences for the ethnicity or gender of the interviewer, but these responses themselves might have suffered from social desirability bias, and it is not clear how the gender or ethnicity of interviewers affected the answers to Graham *et al*. It is important also to distinguish between what respondents like about an interview, and how efficient the interview is in eliciting valid and reliable information: the two may not be the same. Thus the findings by Graham, Lewis and Nicholas (2006: 33), that respondents preferred interviews which allowed them self-expression, might mean that such interviews elicited more truthful accounts, or it might mean that such interviews allowed respondents more opportunity to express themselves in ways that they thought would impress or please the interviewer; the two effects might be the same for some people, and different for others.

Interviewing for understanding

One-to-one qualitative interviews are usually conducted with the aim of producing a picture of the interviewee as a person with their own way of understanding the world, although usually as having a way of understanding which can be taken as characteristic of people of the same category or in the same social circumstances: the kind of mind-reading research referred to in Chapter 1, Section 1.4. And the main interest is in incorrigible matters (Section 10.2). The relationship which the interviewer wants to make is a befriending one, on the assumption that people are more likely to disclose themselves 'authentically' to friends, as in the quotation from Andersen (1993) above. The psychology of person perception and of the development of inter-personal relationships tells us that how others are to us is very much a product of how we behave to them (Blumstein 1991). Thus it is possible for someone to appear differently in the context of different intimate relationships. Making a befriending relationship with a respondent may then elicit data as to what they say in the context of a relationship with one friend (the interviewer), but not what they are like in relation to another friend (someone other than the interviewer). Again, being 'friendly' over any period of time is a learning process for both parties. Thus the respondent will learn what to say and do which seems to please the interviewer, and hence consolidate the relationship. Moreover as Madeline Grumet (1991: 69) says: 'telling a story to a friend is a risky business; the better the friend, the riskier the business.' So 'friends' may be the last people someone will disclose some intimacies to. It is a common experience that people will disclose some things to a stranger which they will not disclose to a friend, and vice versa, and probably people differ in this regard. Thus all in all, although the befriending interview will produce more and richer data than the social survey interview, it will remain a question as to how much of the extra data are an artefact of the relationship made between interviewer and interviewee.

What kind of problem this is depends on whether a researcher subscribes to the view that inside every person there is a real person hidden beneath a misleading exterior, which has to be disclosed by making an empathetic relationship with them. On that assumption, the considerations above are really fundamental, since there will never be any way of knowing whether the researcher has been successful. Alternatively, we might assume that people are always who they are in the context of relationships they make, whatever these may be. On that assumption, the more impersonal relationship of the social survey interview tells us how people behave in that context, and the more personalized relationship of the qualitative interview tells us how people behave in that kind of relationship: they are no less 'themselves' in the former than in the latter; they simply show different aspects of themselves. Rather than assume that adopting a befriending relationship will elicit truthful accounts it can equally be argued that for some respondents a befriending relationship is precisely the kind where they feel more comfortable about telling lies. If they value the 'friendship', they may be most motivated to lie in order to elicit the good opinion of the interviewer (Sikes 2000).

Some researchers seem to evade this problem by conducting research not as a way of getting to understand people as they are, but as a way of changing people (Lather 1986 – see also Chapters 14 and 16). This doesn't evade the problem, it merely changes the success criterion, which is now whether the person really changed or not. To judge that, it is necessary to know how they really were at the beginning and how they really were at the end, and that takes us straight back into the problems discussed in the previous paragraphs.

10.7   The accountability of interview research

Table 10.4 gives a synoptic contrast between survey interviewing and qualitative interviewing. Many of the points have already been dealt with and the important points for this section concern differences in the way in which the research is made accountable.

To be able to judge the credibility of research, readers need to be given information as to how it was conducted. It is relatively easy for survey researchers to show readers what was done to produce the results. Social survey interviews are protocol-driven – there are rules to follow, often written down, and the questions are printed out. In CAPI and CATI the rules are forced on the interviewer by the way the software works (Section 10.4). Protocols can be shown to readers. Limits of publication space often mean that readers have to apply for copies of the questionnaire. But for most recent large-scale surveys copies are available via the World Wide Web. Sometimes the raw data can be made available too, after anonymization. Survey researchers orient to confounding variables as a set of problems to be solved and are therefore able to tell readers how they addressed such problems, and with what results. The interview transcript presented in Transcript 10.1 showed that not everything that might have influenced the results will be made available to readers, but there is usually enough for readers to make a considered judgement as to whether the differences and similarities shown between respondents in the results were due to the reasons attributed by the researchers, or due to other reasons.

By contrast, it is much more difficult for those who do qualitative interviews to make themselves accountable to readers. Margaret Andersen (1993), quoted earlier, says she did not know how many interviews she conducted, and for the many which were unrecorded she would be unable to provide an accurate account of what she and the respondent said, or in detail how her own behaviour produced particular responses. Since each interview will be different there is no interview protocol or list of questions which will serve as a summary of all of them. Some agencies which fund research do make it a condition than transcripts of qualitative interviews are archived so that other researchers can consult them (Chapter 15: Section 15.6 and the *Further reading* of this chapter). But 20, 1-hour-long, qualitative interviews can convert into 1,000 pages of transcript. The central issue running through this chapter is the question of what in the results is an *artefact* of the research and what reflects the *reality* of whatever it was that the researcher set out to capture. All the matters which survey interviewers take pains to control are allowed free play in the qualitative interview or focus group. Without analysing transcripts in detail, it is extremely difficult to see how the researcher's behaviour shaped the data and whether this was in a misleading way. You will be able to examine this in more detail in Chapter 11, Section 11.4. It is perhaps worth drawing a parallel here between the reader confronted with some statistics of medical diagnoses or statistics of crime on the one hand (Chapter 9), and the reader confronted with some claims about the findings from a study based on qualitative interviews, with only minimal indications of what happened in the interviews. In both cases the reader's problem is in not knowing how the data were produced, and hence not knowing how much credence to give the results.

This is not a case against qualitative interviewing. Sometimes, as Andersen implies, this is the only kind of interviewing to which respondents will agree. Such interviews produce interesting results and give us access into the lives of other people, in ways that other approaches do not. But it is a case for saying that the results of well-conducted research using qualitative interviews should be regarded with less confidence than those from well-conducted survey research. Probably the appropriate analogy to draw here is between qualitative interviewing in social research and the kind of interviewing a biographer does with the subject of the biography, their associates and confidants. Many famous people are the subjects of several biographies, which give rather different pictures of the person concerned (Plummer 2000). In the same way, it is to be expected that qualitative interviews conducted by one person would give a picture different from those conducted with the same people by another researcher: and it would be very difficult to say which one was more accurate (see also Chapter 11).

TABLE 10.4 A comparison between interviewing for social surveys and qualitative interviewing

	Interviewing for social surveys	Qualitative interviewing
The sample (see also Chapter 6)	Typically a large representative sample of people	Rarely a large and rarely a representative sample (Figure 10.1, box **5**)
The interviews	Organized to be as similar for each respondent as possible with the same instructions, the same questions and the same sequence	Different for each respondent although probably involving the same set of key topics for discussion Respondents will be allowed to raise their own issues (Figure 10.1, boxes **6**, **7**, **8**, **9**)
The interviewer	Will attempt to behave in a standardized way, disclosing as little as possible about his or her personal characteristics: an impersonal relationship	Will adjust his or her performance to each interviewee. Will use his or her own characteristics as a resource for making a relationship with respondents: a more personal relationship (Figure 10.1, boxes **6**, **7**, **8**, **9**)
The data collection instrument	Typically a questionnaire dominated by forced choice questions asking for brief responses from each respondent Sometimes a questionnaire which has been tested and validated in other studies	Typically just a list of discussion topics, probably a tape recorder
Comparability	The interviews will have been designed to ensure that point-by-point comparisons can be made between all respondents in terms of a standard vocabulary	Point-by-point comparisons may not be possible if each interview is different, with different topics being discussed at different levels of detail and not using a standard vocabulary

The data and analysis	Most of the analytic decisions will be made before the interviews are conducted and the questions designed on that basis, thus the data will be 'pre-structured' before it is collected The data will be framed in the categories and expressed in the language decided by the researcher	There will be many on-the-spot intuitive analytic decisions made during the interviews but the data from the interviews will be loosely structured, and most of the explicit analytic decisions will be made after the interviews have been conducted The data will quite likely be framed in categories and expressed in the language of the respondents (see Chapter 11)
Control measures	Care is likely to be taken to control confounding variables such as interviewer effects and erratic or idiosyncratic behaviour by the interviewer Data will be analysed to detect any such distorting effects – as described in the main text	Little in the way of control measures
Accountability	*Readers*: are usually able to access the questionnaire used, and any details about its validation They are usually given details of the analyses undertaken to scrutinize for confounding variables *Subjects* of the research: will be given a standardized explanation, and may or may not be sent a copy of the completed research	*Readers*: are often asked to take it on trust that the researcher did not do anything untoward in conducting the research Readers may not know what questions were asked, and often have to be satisfied with selected quotations from the interviews *Subjects* of the research: some qualitative researchers believe that their prime accountability should be to the subjects; thus subjects may be treated as co-researchers, may be allowed to vet the material before publication and may be allowed to be the final arbiters as to what is published (see Chapter 14)

ACTIVITY 10   Designing 'ethnic' questions

PANEL 10.4   The 'ethnic question in the census 2001 and 1991

2001 Census	1991 Census
What is your ethnic group? Choose ONE section from A to E, then tick the appropriate box to indicate your cultural background	**Ethnic group – please tick the appropriate box**
	White ☐
	Black-Caribbean ☐
A White	**Black-African** ☐
☐ British ☐ Irish	**Black – Other** (please describe) ☐
☐ Any other White background	
please write in	**Indian** ☐
	Pakistani ☐
B Mixed	**Bangladeshi** ☐
☐ White and Black Caribbean	**Chinese** ☐
☐ White and Black African	**Any other ethnic group** (please describe) ☐
☐ White and Asian	
☐ Any other Mixed background,	'If the person is descended from more than one ethnic or racial group, please tick the group to which the person considers he/she belongs, or tick "Any other ethnic group" and describe the person's ancestry in the space provided.'
please write in	
C Asian or Asian British	
☐ Indian ☐ Pakistani	
☐ Bangladeshi	
☐ Any other Asian background	
please write in	**(2001 continued . . .)**
D Black or Black British	**E Chinese or other ethnic group**
☐ Caribbean ☐ African	☐ Chinese
☐ Any other Black background	☐ Any other, please write in
please write in	. . . .

In 1991 the 'ethnic question' in the Census proved controversial (Panel 10.4). Simply asking an 'ethnic question' led to some Census enumerators being physically attacked. In 2001 the 'ethnic question' aroused little hostility, though this was probably not due to the change of question wording. The categories used in 2001 for the Census are now used across all government agencies and government funded schemes for ethnic monitoring purposes.

1   Do you think that the 2001 question is an improvement on the 1991 question? If so, how: if not, why not?

2 Comment on the usefulness of the 2001 question for producing data to classify people:

   (a) For an investigation into ethnic differences in levels of educational achievement

   (b) For an investigation into racial harassment

   (c) For an investigation into how people experience their own ethnicity.

3 Try designing a different approach for the purpose of:

   (a) Collecting information about the 'race/ethnicity' of the perpetrator of a 'racial attack'

   (b) Collecting information as to how people experience their ethnicity – remember that from this point of view ethnicity is relational and people may regard their ethnicity differently according to whom they are comparing themselves with.

You may use as many questions as you like and forced choice or open-ended questions, but remember that if you use open-ended questions, you will have to close them down again by classifying the respondents' replies into a single framework.

On the classification of ethnicity in surveys and government statistics, see Kertzer and Arel (2002).

Further reading

There is no shortage of books on designing questionnaires; de Vaus (2002) and Fink (2003c) provide excellent advice. Arksey and Knight (1999) is a guide to conducting interviews of all kinds. Bourque (2003a) is about telephone interviewing, and Bourque (2003b) about self-administered questionnaires and postal surveys. Madge and O'Connor (n.d.) describe web-based and synchronous on-line interviews. Fielding (2003) offers four volumes of papers on interview research. Bulmer (2002) consists of four volumes of key articles on questionnaire research. Behling and Law (2000) is about translating questions into other languages

Berg (1995), Mason (2002), or Flick (1998) give treatments of qualitative interviews in particular, and see also Chapter 11. Bloor *et al.* (2000) and Kruger and Casey (2000) are comprehensive manuals on focus groups and Barbour and Kitzinger (1999) provides a selection of papers featuring focus groups used in a wide diversity of research. Several of the papers are cited in this chapter.

UK Government surveys now all use a set of harmonized concepts – for example, what counts as a 'household' – and, if possible the same questions to ensure comparability between surveys (GSS 2003). The standardization is continually updated on the ONS web site; keyword search 'Harmonized Concepts and Questions.'

The CASS question bank (http://qb.soc.surrey.ac.uk/) provides access to the questionnaires used in a wide variety of large-scale surveys, sometimes directly, sometimes via links or addresses. It also carries methodological descriptions of the surveys and a series of fact sheets about survey methodology well illustrated with examples from actual surveys. CASS gives access also to the UK Data Bank (www.data-archive.ac.uk), which stores data from most large-scale surveys in the UK and, for some, allows data extraction and manipulation using its own on-line tools. The PEAS project is an on-line training programme on the analysis of survey results (www.napier.ac.uk/depts/fhls/peas/).

The Neighbourhood Centre web site provides standard questions for local surveys (www.neighbourhoodcentre.org.uk/bank/bank.html).

Commercial software is available providing templates for creating questionnaires and other instruments, some for easy uploading onto the WWW, with some supplied free as loss leaders (http://sourceforge.net/project/showfiles.php?group_id=114508). While actually made for producing teaching materials, the free software on the Hot Potato site works quite well for questionnaire construction (http://hotpot.uvic.ca/).

11 Analysing the Results of Qualitative Interviews

By the end of this chapter, you will:

- Understand the implications for conducting interviews of coding in advance or coding in arrears, and hence more about why survey questions are different from the questions in qualitative interviews
- Know what is meant by thematic analysis
- Know what is meant by, and have practised, linguistic analysis of, the Conversation Analytic (CA) kind
- Be able to make a point-by-point comparison between thematic and linguistic analysis in terms of their underlying assumptions, procedures, strengths and limitations.

And you will know the meaning of the following terms:

Account • adjacency pairs • characterization • coding • corrigibles and incorrigibles • discourse analysis • grounding • intuitive data processing • locution and illocution (or speech act, or performative) • preference order • pre-structured data • recipient design • respondent validation/member-checking/fallibility testing • sequential analysis • speech exchange • theme • triangulation of sources.

At the end of the chapter there is an Activity which will test your understanding of analysing speech data.

11.1 Introduction

Chapter 10 looked at asking people *questions*. This chapter is about analysing the *responses*. Where researchers use forced choice questionnaires, the way the questions are posed *follows* from the decisions about how the responses will be analysed. The data are *pre-structured* by the way the questions are designed and most of the important analytical decisions have already been made before any questions are asked. By contrast, where researchers use open-ended questions on a questionnaire, many of the important analytic decisions are made *after* the data have been gathered. Where researchers engage in semi-structured or qualitative interviews, most of the

239

important analytic decisions are made *while* the data are being collected, and *after* the data have been collected. The kinds of analytic decisions made while the data are being collected are those which lead to the interviewer deciding what question to ask next, when to speak, when to remain silent and so on. Respondents to an interview will be making the same kinds of decision. As you saw in Transcript 10.1 in Chapter 10, Section 10.4, even in highly structured interviews with forced choice questions, interviewers and interviewees will be engaged in this kind of *intuitive data processing*. In the highly structured interview this is not supposed to happen very much. But in the qualitative interview it is regarded as an important facility for making relationships between interviewer and interviewee and for allowing the interviewee's ideas and understandings to be articulated without being distorted by a more structured framework. This chapter will throw more light on this intuitive data processing (Section 11.4, and see Chapter 12) but its main topic is the more explicit process of analysing the results of qualitative interviews after the data have been collected.

We will look at three main ways of analysing such data:

- As a set of *reports* about states of affairs and matters of facts – Section 11.2
- *Thematic analysis* as a way of describing what things mean to people – Section 11.3
- *Linguistic analysis*, which treats the interview as a display of the use of language in context – Section 11.4.

11.2   Analysing interviews as reports on states of affairs

Corrigibles and incorrigibles

There are many things which researchers cannot investigate at first hand, and can find out about only by asking people questions. These include some which, in principle, could be verified as matters of fact – *corrigibles*, and some which in principle are unverifiable because they are matters of self-knowledge – *incorrigibles* (Ayer 1956). The former include matters such as how many cigarettes someone smoked in a week. The latter include opinions, attitudes, beliefs, understandings and so on. The incorrigibles are incorrigible because it is built into the definition of, say, an 'opinion' that it is something which is first and foremost known by the person who holds it, and known by others only insofar as that person discloses it. We could not logically say 'I know what your opinion really is, even though you don't know yourself'. Between the corrigible and the incorrigible is an area of disagreement as to those matters about which an individual must be regarded as the authoritative source of information, as against those intimate details of their own lives about which they can be regarded as mistaken. For example, someone who adopts a psychodynamic point of view can logically say: 'You are out of touch with your true feelings' and imply that he or she is a better judge of those 'true feelings' than the person who allegedly has them. For a researcher who assumed that feelings were the kinds of stuff about which feelers themselves could not be mistaken, this would be an illogical claim. The border is not something which doing research can decide. Rather it is something which is decided by an *a priori* decision – that is, independently of doing the research. For this section, we will concentrate on what are conventionally regarded as verifiable facts and corrigible. Section 11.3 strays into the field of incorrigibles.

Some possible facts about George

I interviewed George as part of a local census of roofless people, people crashing out with friends and relatives and people living in hostels and night shelters. This used a questionnaire with forced choice questions. Against the warning in Chapter 6, Section 6.12, a few people were selected for longer loosely structured interviewing, largely to collect some 'quotable quotes' for the research report. George was one of these people.

In an early draft of the final report George appeared as follows:

It is notable how often homelessness is preceded by one or more traumatic events. For example:

then my wife died, unexpectedly and that threw me. It was stomach cancer, which was common in her family but I didn't see it coming [so] it was a great shock, and I reacted badly. I began hitting the drinking very hard, but not for the same reasons as earlier . . . and then when I was just getting over that I got made redundant, which knocked the stuffing out of me. And what with the drink and the [lack of] money I just ended up here in [hostel] which is just one better than being on the street, but only just.

(George: male, aged 69: resident in hostel for single homeless men)

George is made to stand here as an example of how predisposing events of particular kinds may lead to homelessness. But is it true that these events actually happened to George, and in the order described? Asking this is prior to asking whether this is a sequence of events which *caused* George's homelessness.

Some things George reports could in principle be checked for their veracity. These are matters for which there are socially organized processes for producing authoritative versions of the truth. For deaths, the identity of the deceased, the date of death and the cause of death are all produced as factual matters by a process of death certification. Illness leading up to death and family histories of conditions may be inscribed in medical records. Redundancies are recorded in personnel files, and often in social security records. Place of residence may be given a factual status by tenancy agreements, rent-books and, in the case of hostels, hostel records. As discussed in Chapter 9, there are problems with these kinds of data.

For reasons most unusual in research of this kind, I actually knew about the timing of some events in George's life. In fact George's wife died several years after separating from George, and moving 150 miles away. He became aware of her death several years after it happened and long after he became homeless. George was not made redundant but dismissed for persistently failing to turn up for work, and before he learned of his wife's death.

Factual facts and interesting stories

My reconstruction of George's CV suggests that we cannot take his story of the events leading up to his homelessness as a straightforward factual account of what happened. This illustrates something referred to earlier (Chapter 8, Panel 8.1) which is the way people take 'facts' and turn them into meaningful stories and invent facts to plug the gaps in stories which would otherwise be less credible. This does not necessarily involve them in lying. It may do (Sikes 2000), but we could rarely know whether someone had the intention to deceive us, or genuinely believed the untruth he or she was telling (Miller and Stiff 1993). The more important point is that 'facts' are told in some context and the context is likely to shape what is told as 'the facts' (Peneff 1990). As you saw in Transcript 10.1 in Chapter 10, Section 10.4, the facts about the daughter's illness were shaped first by the structure of the questionnaire, and then by the efforts of the interviewer to find some facts in answer to the pre-set questions. In loosely structured interviews, interviewees and interviewers have even more latitude to turn facts into interesting stories, and hence further to depart from what might have been inscribed as the facts in an independent record.

But what kind of problem is this? It is a really serious problem if the purpose of the interview is to draw information from informants to build up a picture of some factual state of affairs. As noted in Chapter 8, survey researchers often try to elicit accurate information about antecedent events in order to identify causal factors, by asking respondents to draw on their memories. I was doing much the same in the quotation from the draft report earlier. In these circumstances the data are likely to suffer from **retrospective** or **recall bias** (Chapter 8, Panel 8.1) and from other biases determined by the **demand characteristics** of the interview – that is, from the way in which people will modulate and finesse what they say in order to shape it to what they understand to be the context of the interview (Chapter 10, Section 10.4, and Section 11.4 below). One way of evading some of the problem is to collect data *prospectively*, before something has happened (Chapter 8). But that resolves only problems of accuracy in timing and sequence, and only some of them, because people may give factually misleading accounts before and after. And remember that if administrative data are used for establishing time sequences, much of this, too, is interview data or data from self-completed questionnaires, though the interviews may be medical consultations, or the questionnaire may be an application for housing benefit (see also Chapter 9).

Triangulating between sources and judging credibility

I was able to correct the historical sequence of events in George's life through independent sources of information, much of which happened to be in my filing cabinet since I had represented George in his claim against 'unfair dismissal'. But, of course, the usual reason for relying on informant accounts is that there are no easily available independent sources. However, sometimes survey researchers will adopt the strategy of collecting most of their information from informants via a questionnaire, and checking a random sample of responses against some independent source. This is often done in health services research where levels of illness in a community are estimated from questionnaire responses, but a level of confidence is assigned to the responses by medically examining a sub-sample. As noted in Chapter 2 and Chapter 10, Section 10.4, many standard data collection instruments have been produced though a process of *validation* like this, but only for instruments producing quantitative data.

Validation is a matter of **triangulating** evidence from different sources about the same events. Historians often do this, cross-checking news reports against official records and against contemporary diaries and memoirs (see Chapter 13, Section 13.7). Triangulation raises the problem of what to do when sources disagree. In their study of dual-career families, Rona and Robert Rapoport (1971, 1976) carried out something which is variably called **respondent validation, member-checking,** or **fallibility testing,** which is allowing respondents to comment on the results prior to publication. They found that couples often disagreed with each other as to what was 'the truth' about events which had happened in their relationship. Where accounts are discrepant, *and as long as we assume that there is only one correct account of the truth,* then some decision has to be made as to which account to believe. Then in analysing the accounts and trying to reconcile them, the analyst has to have some *theory of witnesses* as a guide to deciding which account is the more credible. Researchers rarely make their theory of witnesses explicit. It is usually a fairly commonsensical and *ad hoc* set of assumptions about which people were in the best position to know the truth, which are the kinds most likely to tell the truth, what are the likely reasons why someone may have a distorted view of the truth and so on. Researcher bias in favour or against particular kinds of people may play a part in the decision as to which person to believe (Chapter 14, Sections 14.4 and 14.5).

The above is problematic only if researchers are trying to use informant accounts as evidence about some factual matter. That is what I was doing in the way I used the quotation from George: using George's words to imply a cause–effect relationship between antecedent and consequent events. Worse, I was offering George's words as a generalization about cause and effect to apply to other homeless people too. This was entirely unjustifiable, and would have been so even if George had himself provided an accurate CV (see Chapter 6 on representativeness).

However, I might instead have said something like this:

It is notable how often homelessness people *attribute* their homelessness to sequences of traumatic events:

> then my wife died, unexpectedly and . . .

(George: male, aged 69: resident in hostel for single homeless men)

Here the interest is not in what caused what, for which it is necessary to pin down the facts of what happened and when. Rather, the interest is in how someone understands – or, at least, describes – what happened. Here it doesn't matter whether what George says is true in an historical sense. Not only does its factual accuracy not matter, but it is actually very interesting if what he says departs from what might be taken as a factual account. But now we face another problem. Is what George said in the interview to be taken as evidence of what he usually, ordinarily, generally, believes: of how he understands his situation in some general sense? Or is what George said in an interview to be taken as evidence just of what was going on in the interview, without begging questions as to what he might think, feel or say in other situations? These two different orientations lead to two different ways of analysing data. The first usually leads to a *thematic* analysis, or something similar, the second to a *linguistic* analysis. These will be demonstrated in Sections 11.3 and 11.4.

11.3 Thematic analysis of qualitative interviews

What I shall call 'thematic analysis' is a version of content analysis. That term is more usually used for the analysis of written and broadcast materials, but content analysis doesn't have to be quantitative (Chapter 13, Section 13.2). Thematic analysis will be familiar to anyone who has studied literature as a subject – the theme of 'betrayal' in Shakespeare's plays; the theme of 'renewal' in the poetry of T.S. Eliot and so on. The analyst looks for themes which are present in the whole set or sub-set of interviews and creates a framework of these for making comparisons and contrasts between the different respondents.

Sometimes themes are inspired by a set of theoretical ideas already espoused by an analyst. For example, someone may already be suspicious that teachers have stereotyped views about girls and boys, may look for evidence of this, and label (or 'code' or 'index') different utterances by teachers as examples of different kinds of themes such as, 'Proactive boys', 'Passive girls', 'Girls as non-mathematical' and so on. Sometimes themes just seem to float up from the data. But wherever themes come from, the mechanics of thematic analysis are similar:

- Deciding what themes will be
- Deciding what will count as evidence of a theme
- Coding a transcript to indicate that this passage is an example of this theme, and that passage is an example of another theme; sometimes this just means writing a code word for the theme in the margin of a hardcopy transcript (see below), but nowadays it often means assigning a database fieldcode to a passage so that the analysis can be automated (Fielding 2001)
- From then on the analysis is in terms of which kinds of people said what, which relates to a particular theme, and how saying something with regard to one theme relates to saying something with regard to another theme.

Some writers use the term *code* – in the sense of something to be cracked – rather than theme, but this tends to confuse something which is allegedly in the data with the technical process of indexing the data: coding it to show what is where. One of the many uses of the term 'discourse' is an alternative to 'theme' (Chapter 13, Section 13.1).

Coding a transcript thematically

TRANSCRIPT 11.1   Transcript coded for themes in a thematic analysis

Speaker and utterance number	Speech	THEME
RG1	So, hmm, you were aware that you had a drinking problem. That was the wor-d you used wasn't it?	ADDICTION
G1	Yea [2 seconds]	
G2	I mean it took me a long time to accept it, to really accept it that is as, hmmmm a problem to be solved sort of problem. An derrr then I said, well [Georgie] boy you gotter do somethink about this. Sssss so I spose I got myself dry for about err year	CHARACTER TRAIT: PERSONAL DETERMINATION
RG2	Uhhm	
G3	Well occasional lapses, but nearleee dry. It was o.k.	
RG3	Yeahh	
G4	Hmmm, then my uh, wife died [3 seconds]	VICTIM OF CIRCUMSTANCES: LOSS OF RELATIONSHIP
G5	Unexpectedly and derr that threw me. It was stomach cancer which was common in her family, but which I didn't see it coming [untranscribable] it was a great shock, and I yh reacted badly. I began to hit the drinking very hard, but not for the same reasons as ear[lier]	
RG4	[ear]lier. Hhh, earlier you said drinking was about stress. Stress at work.	
G6	Yea. I told you. But I got to handle that see. That was behind me. Then this thing with [wife's name]. And then when I was just getting over that, I got made redundant, which knocked the stuffing out of me.	VICTIM OF CIRCUMSTANCES: LOSS OF RELATIONSHIP/ LOSS OF JOB

Speaker and utterance number	Speech	THEME
G7	[Omitted passage on redundancy and how badly it affected many people. How it was caused by bad management and greedy unions, ending on 10 second silence]	VICTIM OF CIRCUMSTANCES: LOSS OF JOB/ACTS OF OTHERS
G8	And what with the drink and the [lack of] money I end up here [in the hostel] which is just one better than being on the street but only just.	
	[5 minutes' more interview talk. **RG5–RG9 G9–G14**]	VICTIM OF CIRCUMSTANCES: FINANCIAL CRISIS
RG10	So in more general terms, what do you think makes people homeless?	
G15	Oh, oh, mmmm, there's lots. Everyone's got their own. Hmmmm hhhhhher. I mean some it's really a lack of character. I mean little things which anyone else could hmm, anyone with a bit of character could cope with. But me (attributed to self)? ?? hhhhm, all though my life my luck's been against me. It's almost as if I was heading for the bottom all the time and now I've pretty well reached it. At least there's nothing to be afraid of any more [2 seconds]	FLAWED CHARACTER (attributed to other people) GOOD CHARACTER (attributed to self)???
G16	That's what I tell myself [3 seconds]	VICTIM OF CIRCUMSTANCES: GENERAL AND FATE/LUCK
G17	I mean, everything I've tried to do, just when I was succeeding has been snatched away from me. It's been me getting it together, and then the slap in the gob. The mistake was trying to get it together. Ider bin much happier if I'd just accepted I was a loser from the start [2 seconds]	
G18	Hmm? [3 seconds]	
G19	Someone up there's laughing at me	

RG – Roger Gomm, **G** – George, [2 seconds] – 2 seconds' silence; [ ] encloses over-lapping speech.

Transcript 11.1 here is coded thematically. The inspiration for the themes is attribution theory (Kelly and Michella 1980). This is the idea that people have many options available to them as to what to attribute as the cause of

Agentive and non-agentive attributions: coding frame for a thematic analysis   TABLE 11.1

Causes of misfortune	
Non-agentive attributions: victim of circumstances	*Agentive attributions: victim of own behaviour*

• Loss of relationship
• Loss of job or other valued activity
• Disability/limiting illness
• Addiction
• Financial crisis
• Discrimination on basis of: Age
                            Gender
                            Race
                            Other
• Bad luck, fate or supernatural agency
	• Loss of relationship
	• Loss of job or other valued activity
	• Disability/limiting illness
	• Addiction
	• Financial crisis
	• Criminal offence
	• Supernatural punishment
	• Flawed character
	• Other eventuality (specify)
	• Other eventuality (specify)

Causes of advantage	
Non-agentive attributions: beneficiary of circumstances	*Agentive attributions: self-made good fortune*
• Good will/philanthropy of others • Good luck: being in the right place at the right time • Good luck –treated as an agency, e.g. 'Lady Luck' • Supernatural intervention	• Good character accounting for good fortune (specify character traits) • Other – specify

their misfortunes or advantages, including their own character and actions, the actions of others, luck, the will of God and so on. Particular people tend to use only some of these options, or some in some situations and others in others. Some tend to attribute all the good that happens to them to their own actions, and all the bad that happens to them to the actions of others, or to discorporate entities such as 'fate' or 'society'. Some people show the opposite tendency, rarely crediting themselves as the cause of good happenings, and usually blaming themselves for bad occurrences. The extreme version of this is symptomatic of clinical depression (Beck 1970). In the literature of addictions it is a common idea both that addicted people tend to think of themselves as *non-agentive* (as the victims of forces they cannot control), and that people who think of themselves in this way are rather unlikely to be able to throw off their addiction (Davies 1997).

The coding in Transcript 11.1 derives from a model like that shown in Table 11.1. The coding labels are at the bullet points.

To show how this coding scheme might generate similarities and contrasts between different respondents, consider how this passage from an interview with Lara might be coded and compare Lara with George:

It's because I'm a shit. I was a shit to my ol' man and a shit to my kids. I've let down every employer who's been good enough to employ me even if I haven't ripped him off as well. Which is probably that I was born that way.

(Lara: female aged 35, living rough)

These procedures may look radically different from asking people questions using forced choice questionnaires. They are different, but not radically so. The thematic framework in Table 11.1 constitutes a kind of questionnaire, answered by the analyst while reading transcripts of interviews. The 'questionnaire' asks the analyst: 'Is this an example of this theme, this theme, this theme or this theme?' The major difference is that with forced choice questionnaires all the *permissible* responses from interviewees are decided in advance, whereas with thematic analysis the range of *interesting* responses is decided after the interview data are available. Insofar as themes suggest themselves to the researcher as a result of reading the data, this is sometimes described as grounding theory/concepts/categories, and so on in data, meaning the opposite of imposing theory/concepts/categories on the data (see also Chapter 12, Section 12.6). However, the contrast is not so sharp as the words imply. The difference is really one of *timing*. Even with thematic analysis there comes a point at which the analyst imposes a structure on the data. It will only be one of many structures he or she might have imposed.

Forced choice questions aim to provide *measurements of variables*. There is also something rather 'variable-like' about a theme. It is fairly easy to imagine converting the themes in Table 11.1 into forced choice questions, using them and counting the responses. Indeed there are many 'attribution questionnaires' generating numerical data used in psychology, psychiatry and in the study and treatment of addictions.

Delaying the making of analytic decisions until after interviews have been conducted may mean that different interviews take different paths, so that it may be impossible to find examples of variants on the same theme in all the interviews. This leads to puzzles as to whether what was missing from an interview was unimportant to the interviewee, or important but just didn't come up in the interview. For example, if an interviewee doesn't attribute blame for the breakdown of his marriage to himself, his wife, social circumstances or to other people, does this mean he doesn't usually attribute any particular cause, or that the interview didn't make it appropriate for him to do so? This is the obverse problem of that arising from asking a forced choice question along the lines of: 'To what do you attribute the breakdown of your marriage: to your own character or actions/to those of your wife/. . ./don't know?' The forced choice question may lead a respondent to give an answer to a question he doesn't usually pose to himself; an answer made up on the spot to satisfy a researcher's question, but that may happen in a qualitative interview, too (see Section 11.4).

It wasn't particularly difficult to use the coding framework in Table 11.1 with the interview with George. But sometimes it is quite difficult to know which codes, if any, to attach to a particular passage of speech. Since nothing is going to be counted this isn't so much of a problem as it would be in research generating numerical data. Nonetheless, there are still opportunities for coding to be slipshod, or for analysts to code in such a way as to massage the data so that it shows what they want it to show. Because of the sheer bulk of the data from qualitative interviews, readers are sometimes not shown the coding at all – or, more often, have to be satisfied with some examples of speech which exemplify the coding. Only rarely do thematic analysts subject their coding to blind independent scrutiny and conduct inter-rater reliability tests to measure the degree of agreement between different people doing the same coding (see Chapter 2, Section 2.10 and Panel 2.6). Armstrong *et al.* (1997) have suggested that this should be standard practice in this kind of research.

The coding demonstrated above is only the beginnings of a thematic analysis. It is quite common to subject the same data to analysis using several different coding frames. The analyst is likely to go on to ask questions such as: 'what themes tend to cohere with what other themes; which never occur together; what kinds of people provide the examples of these themes and not those?' and other questions. Eventually the analysis will be written up; qualitatively rather than quantitatively. For example, the paragraphs below might have resulted from continuing the thematic analysis begun above, applying it to the transcripts of other interviews as well:

> In summary then, in the study two distinctively different groups of homeless people can be identified. First there were a group who might be called 'self-blamers' who mainly attributed their misfortunes to personal failings. They had very low self-esteem, and seemed to be inhibited from trying to improve their situation, partly because they had no confidence that they could do so, and partly because they did not seem to believe that they deserved anything better:

> > It's because I'm a shit. I was a shit to my ol' man and a shit to my kids. I've let down every employer who's been good enough to employ me even if I haven't ripped him off as well. Which is probably that I was born that way.

> > (Lara: female aged 35, living rough)

> These were in the minority, however and were more likely to be women than men. Much more usual was the person who attributed homelessness and other misfortunes to bad luck, and to the machinations of other people. In one sense they had a high opinion of themselves, since they often explained how they had made determined efforts to deal with problems, and it was despite this that adversity had nonetheless beset them: they were 'persons of character but victims of circumstances'. In representing the forces acting against them as extremely powerful they also represented themselves as having shown admirable character traits such as perseverance, determination and so on. However, in this sense they 'lived in the past'. They faced the present and the future having learned lessons from the past to the effect that the forces acting against them were just too great for them to prevail. As one of them said:

I mean, everything I've tried to do, just when I was succeeding has been snatched away from me. It's been me getting it together, and then the slap in the gob. The mistake was trying to get it together. Ider bin much happier if I'd just accepted I was a loser from the start.

(George: male aged 69: resident in hostel for single homeless men)

What do themes stand for?

The paragraph above describes types of people: people with particular ways of thinking, understanding the world, acting and so on. The data source would have been an hour-long interview with each person, and only some of what they said would have entered the final analysis. Yet the implication is that by looking through that 1-hour window, the analyst was able to discover what each person was like, 24 hours a day, 7 days a week and over some period of their life-span. The credibility of this rests on a number of assumptions:

- That people think, feel and act much the same in most or all of the situations in which they find themselves, such that studying them in one situation will tell us about them in other situations.
- Or, failing this, that the qualitative interview is an especially effective way of finding out about how people are in general, underneath some misleading appearances, or despite their acting in ways uncharacteristic for them in some situations. (Note the remarks about the importance, and the problematic, of making close relationships with interviewees in Chapter 10, Section 10.6.)
- That the themes in a thematic analysis are not merely convenient headings for use in writing up the results of an interview study, but actually stand for something about the way the minds of interviewees are organized. I have used the term 'theme' where others might have used terms more strongly implying that what was being discovered was the structure of people's minds: terms such as 'world-views', 'perspectives', 'typification schemes', 'actor social theories', 'interpretive frameworks', 'schemes of relevance', 'cognitive frameworks', 'representational structures' or 'discourses'.

Whichever term were used, the implication would be that George would have a mind organized such that being 'a person of character but a victim of circumstances' is a persistent characteristic of the way he thinks about himself and understands his experience.

These assumptions cannot be tested while all we have from each interviewee is a small sample of their speech, elicited in what may be a highly unrepresentative situation when judged against the spectrum of situations in which they usually find themselves. Commonsense suggests, anyway, that had a different person done the interview, then the interview talk might have been different (see Chapter 10, Sections 10.4–10.6). And had a different thematic framework been used, then the themes claimed to be persistent features of the respondents' consciousness would have been different themes. Whether a different interviewer, asking different questions, analysing the results in terms of different themes, would nonetheless produce similar findings must be an open question. But this seems rather unlikely.

This kind of mind-reading approach has been the traditional approach in qualitative sociological research. While it was being abandoned by many 'mainstream' qualitative researchers in the 1980s (Hammersley 1992) the tradition was renewed by feminist researchers thereafter (Oakley 1981). But the idea that underneath appearances there is a 'real person' is also held by attitude researchers and personality researchers in psychology who believe that they have the psychometric tests to delve beneath appearances to find out what people are really like underneath (Procter 2001a). There is a wide-spread belief in there being 'real people beneath misleading appearances' but less consensus as to what they are like, and what are the best methods for finding out about them.

Section 11.4 turns to a different kind of analysis which doesn't require such assumptions. It is far less interested in people and much more interested in situations. It is sceptical about the underlying and interested in the superficial on the grounds that all there is which can be researched is on the surface, to be observed. This orientation runs from the dramaturgical approach adopted by Goffman (Burns 1992: 106–40), to ethnomethodological approaches. For this chapter it will be represented by Conversation Analysis (CA).

11.4 A linguistic or sequential analysis of a qualitative interview

Ethnomethodology and Conversation Analysis (CA)

The term '**ethnomethodology**' was coined by Howard Garfinkel (1967) to designate the study of the methods (the methodology) that people (ethnos) use to make their lives sensible. An ethnomethodologist would not be interested in what life meant to George in particular, or even in what life meant to George as an exemplar of homeless people, or people with 'drink problems'. Rather an ethnomethodologist would be interested in a transcript of an interview with George for what it might tell us about how people in general go about making sense – or, what is the same thing, how people make what they do sensible to other people. One of the tenets of ethnomethodology is that action is always **occasioned** and **situated**. It is what it is, when it is, where it is. Thus ethnomethodologists would say that an interview with George is an interview with George. It cannot tell us much about what happened to George previously, or what George would be like in another situation. What such a transcript does best is to stand as evidence of what happens when a researcher interviews a respondent (Cicourel 1982).

Conversation Analysis (CA) is a development of ethnomethodology to deal with spoken language data. The 'conversation' does not mean that attention is restricted to what we call 'conversations'. Rather it deals with all kinds of **speech events** or **speech exchange systems**, including interviews. From prag-matic linguistics (Levinson 2000) comes the idea that speech should be analysed for what people are doing with speech, rather than what they mean by what they say, as explained below.

Locutions and illocutions

In everyday life, and in psychological and sociological research, there are at least three ways of reading or hearing words. One is in mind-reading mode as evidence of the thoughts, mind, mental state, mood, personality, ways of understanding and such like mentalistic characteristics of the speaker. People who engage in this kind of analysis are wont to say that what they are studying is what things 'mean' to people, or how they 'experience' their lives. They pursue the topic of meaning by asking a question something like:

> What must have been in that person's mind in order that they said this or did that?

Thus the topic of meaning is approached by building *models of the minds* which are supposed to lie behind and give rise to what was said, as in the thematic analysis above.

Another approach to language is in *locutionary*, or referential fashion. This is hearing words as intended to refer to something. So a locutionary reading of

> **G2** I mean it took me a long time to accept it, to really accept it that is as, hmmmm a problem to be solved sort of problem. An derrr then I said, well [Georgie] boy you gotter do somethink about this. Sssss so I spose I got myself dry for about err year

is as a report by George which refers to something which happened to him earlier in his life. This was the approach adopted in Section 11.2 of this chapter. For this reading we dis-attend to when George said this in the sequence of the interview, and hear it instead in terms of a different sequence of events: the sequence of George's life. Treating language in a locutionary way usually directs our attention to the question of whether the speech is an *accurate* report about whatever it is that it refers to (see Section 11.2).

The third way of hearing words is as *illocutions*, or 'speech acts', or 'performatives'. What is important is not what someone means by the words, but what is accomplished by saying them. The classic source for speech act theory is J. L. Austin's *How to Do Things with Words* (1962). What Austin says people do with words is to issue commands, give compliments, ask questions, make promises, provide excuses and such like. For example, as a locution, *I'm very busy* is a report on the state of one's commitments. *We're going to lunch*, as a locution, reports on an intended action. But put the two phrases together one after the other:

> We're going to lunch
> I'm very busy.

Now the two are hearable in an illocutionary way: the first as an invitation; the second as a refusal to accept the invitation with a reason for the refusal: a so-called 'reasoned refusal'.

Turn-taking

An illocutionary reading of the utterances in Transcript 11.1 would pay attention to what George and the interviewer are doing with words in the context and sequence of the interview. For this reason the term *sequential analysis* is often used. One thing they are doing is to create and sustain the kind of social situation we recognize as 'a research interview', with people playing the social roles of interviewer and interviewee. Part of this is done by taking turns in the interview, which is structured in a turn-by-turn fashion. This may seem obvious, but it is actually very important. The principle of turn-taking is one of the most fundamental principles for understanding how people organize their interaction one with another:

> Turn-taking is used for the ordering of moves in games, for allocating political office, for regulating traffic at intersections, for serving customers at business establishments, and for talking in interviews, meetings, debates, ceremonies, conversations, etc. – these last being members of a set which we will refer to as 'speech exchange systems'. It is obviously a prominent type of social organization, one whose instances are implicated in a wide range of . . . activities.
>
> (Sacks, Schegloff and Jefferson 1974: 710)

As you will see, taking note of turn-taking in the transcript of the interview with George gives an interpretation of what is going on, which is different from that derived from the thematic analysis.

Adjacency pairs

In a speech exchange, whatever is said by the first party is likely to shape what is said by others. This is often referred to in terms of *adjacency pairs* (Schegloff and Sacks 1973). Everyday speech consists of a large number of paired utterances where the second may be predictable from the first, or at least where a later utterance may be predictable from an earlier one.

Even if a 'second' cannot be predicted it is usually unsurprising. Thus:

- A first which is a greeting will most likely be followed by a second which is a greeting
- A question will most likely be followed by an answer (or an apology for not being able to give an answer, or a reason for not giving an answer, or a joke about questions and answers, and so on)
- A complaint will most likely be followed by a denial, a justification, an excuse or an apology
- A compliment will most likely be followed by a combination of a thanking and a diminisher such as 'thank you, no, no but you are too kind', or a return such as 'you're looking very pretty yourself'.

What is predictable is not the locutionary meaning of an utterance, but its illocutionary meaning (sometimes called its illocutionary 'force' or 'intention').

Thus we can predict with a fair degree of accuracy that a question will be followed by an answer, or by one of the other illocutions which often follow questions. But we are much less able to predict what the answer will be.

Of course, the second party's utterance cannot always be predicted from the first party's utterance. Sometimes verbal interchanges do take surprising directions. Sometimes people make sure that what they say is unpredictable when making jokes, catching others out and so on. Nonetheless, illocution-wise everyday language is probably more predictable than most other things studied by social scientists. That this is so relates to the fact that people have to be able to predict responses in order to have coherent conversations with each other. If I could not, to some degree, predict that what I intend as a question will elicit an answer, then I could not engage in questioning. Indeed almost by definition what a question is is that kind of utterance which elicits an answer. And what an answer is is that kind of response which is elicited by a question.

Not only is speech fairly predictable in illocutionary terms, but people do predict in order to determine the sense of another's responses. Thus if I ask a question, *however the other person responds* I am most likely to regard the response as being one of the kind which usually follows questions – or, in the last resort, to regard the response (or no response at all) as evidence of a mishearing or a misunderstanding, a rudeness or an evasion on behalf of the other person. Thus by the act of asking a question I severely limit the number of categories for classifying the response of the other. Whatever they say after my question it is an utterance following a question. In the interchange below, for example, what the second speaker says does not at first seem to be a response to a request for information:

Speaker 1 What's the time?
Speaker 2 About 180 degrees

But since the provision of information is what is most to be expected following a request for information, we can probably work out that what Speaker 2 means is 'turn around there's a clock behind you'.

Accounts and self-presentation

Whatever we say, even if we stay silent, we nonetheless give off evidence which other people will take as evidence of our character. This is no mystery to ordinary folk, who always engage in some degree of impression management. Goffman's book *The Presentation of Self in Everyday Life* (1959) suggests that people know they are likely to be judged by others and respond to this by putting on a show. Many of the examples which Goffman gives might suggest that people are poseurs and seek either to mislead others about what they are really like, or that they fool themselves. These assumptions, however, do not necessarily follow from the idea of self-presentation. It requires just as much of a performance to show to others what one believes to be the truth about oneself as it would to mislead other people.

In sociology and psychology, the terms 'account' and 'accounting' mean that people monitor the impressions they make on others, and adjust their behaviour in order to *give an account* of themselves as being the kind of person they would prefer others to think they are; those particular people in that particular situation:

I'm sorry it's such a mess, but we've got the builders in.

We're not usually so behind, but it's this latest 'flu thing.

These are accounts (Buttney 1993). They are instructions to another not to judge by appearances, which give an undesired impression, but to take some additional information into consideration in order to reach a different judgement. As these examples suggest, accounting often has to be done under difficult circumstances where all else which is assumable or observable looks discrediting. Indeed the more discrediting the circumstances seem to be, the more an account seems to be called for. People who don't give accounts when all the evidence seems against them are likely to be regarded as 'brazen', 'uncouth' 'not respectable', 'unrepentant', 'insensitive' and so on. George, as a person with a known drink problem, living in a hostel for homeless single men, is the kind of person who has to work harder than others to give an account of himself as being other than a worthless derelict.

Accounts in word form may take any of the forms below:

- *Self-commendations*: attribute meritorious characteristics to oneself, or describe the results of one's own actions as benign
- *Denials*: refuse to accept that anything is wrong or refuse to accept that anything which is wrong is any fault of one's own
- *Disclaimations*: a particularly common kind of denial; they take forms such as:

    'I know it might sound racist to say this but . . .', followed by something which might be interpreted as racist.

- *Blames*: attribute moral fault to others, or attribute blame to circumstances such as 'the recession', 'capitalism', or 'modern society'; blames are common adjuncts to excuses, justifications and denials
- *Justifications*: may accept that something unfortunate has happened, but refuse to accept any moral fault by providing good moral reasons for one's own actions
- *Excuses*: accept moral faults, but offer mitigations for them: 'I was feeling under the weather when I was rude to you'
- *Apologies*: accept blame for what is wrong, perhaps completely, but perhaps for only part of it
- *Self-blames*: accept one's own culpability often associated with apologies; self-blames without excuses are particularly self-blaming
- *Promises of remedial or reformatory action*: often associated with self-blames, apologies and *expressions of remorse*.

There is no precise way of dividing these up, or of allocating particular utterances precisely as being one kind of account or another. They are better thought of as lying on a dimension (or 'cline') running from self-commendation through denial ('nothing to blame me for') down to self-blame ('it's all my fault, I can't excuse myself').

A linguist would say that the list is a *preference order* (Levinson 1983: 332–45). People would prefer to give an account of themselves which attracts commendation, failing that they would prefer to give an account which denies any moral fault, but failing that a justification, and so on down the list. Giving an account which is not acceptable to others may be worse than not giving an account at all. Thus, where an excuse would not be believable it is preferable to own up and promise to make amends. One's past moral faults may then be balanced out by one's present and future moral actions and there are brownie points to be had for 'coming clean' (Snyder and Higgins 1990).

We can now apply some of these ideas to the transcript.

Producing characters through interviews

I want to focus on the beginning of the transcript: **G1–G5** (p. 259). From now on, ignore the 'thematic' codes. The general question I am going to ask about this sequence is:

> What does this sequence tell us about a social situation in which a researcher interviews another person who lives in a hostel for homeless men and has a known and self-confessed drink problem?

To say that a speech exchange is an 'interview' is to say that it is a form of social organization in which one person plays the role of the interviewer, who asks questions and determines the topics to be discussed, and the other person plays the role of the interviewee, who is to answer questions and otherwise provide information on the understanding that the information given will be 'on the record'. It is not too difficult to see this social structure in the transcript. Even if the speakers were not identified in the transcript you would have no difficulty in deciding who was playing which role. Moreover, once we know what this social structure is, we have little difficulty in allocating most of the silences as between the speakers. If it is the prerogative of the interviewer to ask (most of) the questions then (most of) the silences will be attributable to the turn of the interviewee and interpretable as failures to answer questions adequately.

To be interviewed is to be required to give some kind of account of oneself. To be interviewed as a homeless person with a drink problem is to be required to give an account of oneself in stigmatizing circumstances. None of this requires any particular account to be given, but it does seem likely that in such an interview such stigmatizing circumstances will frequently be oriented to and this will be seen in transcripts in the form of excuses, justifications, self-blames, apologies and promises of reform. There is little difficulty in seeing the transcript in terms of George accounting for his discrediting situation, sometimes by giving answers to questions which haven't actually been asked. Thus **G4** seems to be a response to the accusatory question: 'Why didn't you *stay* dry?'

At **G3**, George says:

Well occasional lapses, but nearleee dry. It was o.k.

Why does George say this at precisely this point in the interchange? We must look for the answer in what came before. What came before was:

G2 I mean it took me a long time to accept it, to really accept it that is as, hmmmm a problem to be solved sort of problem. An derrr then I said, well [Georgie] boy you gotter do somethink about this. Sssss so I spose I got myself dry for about err year

Here, George is telling a story about how he did what 'everybody knows' is difficult for an alcoholic: staying dry. And the story he tells is one of some success. It is a self-commendation. The most predictable responses to stories like this are either congratulations, or they are commiserations that the effort was not more successful than it was. Or it might be some combination of the two; for example, perhaps: 'Well done, that must have been difficult, but it shows you can do it.'

But what George actually gets as a response to his story of determined effort is a non-judgemental, non-committal:

RG2 (0.5) Uhhm

Let's use a coarse-grain size of analysis and say that, following a self-commendation, the most predictable response is a positive evaluation.

Positive and negative evaluations are important forms of illocution. They may be explicit ('Thanks: jolly good') or executed in the form of other kinds of utterances, for example by matching one story with another; for example: 'Yea I felt exactly the same when . . .' The possibility for a negative evaluation may be evaded by a rapid change of topic, or a negative evaluation may be executed by saying nothing at all; for example:

- The teacher asks the pupil a question. The pupil gives an answer. The teacher says nothing. What is the most usual interpretation of this nothing-saying by the teacher?
- Marion tells William some good news. William does not indicate that he has heard it, but launches into a story of his own. What is Marion likely to feel about this?
- Claudette tells a joke. No one laughs. Unbeknown to Claudette everyone has agreed not to laugh when she tells a joke. The joke's on her. What principle is being exploited by Claudette's friends?
- George tells a story of his determined effort to overcome a problem. **RG** says 'Uhhm'.

A rule for covering all these situations is that where an evaluation is expected, the absence of a positive evaluation is usually taken as a negative evaluation. Thus a highly typical classroom sequences runs:

1 Teacher question
2 Pupil answer/failure to answer
3 Teacher evaluation of pupil's answer/failure to answer.

This is so common that virtually anything a teacher says or does in the third slot is heard as an evaluation of the pupil's answer, even if – perhaps especially if – what the teacher says is nothing at all. Teacher silence at this point is usually to be heard as an indication that the pupil's answer was wrong or incomplete. The silence offers the pupil an opportunity to extend or amend the answer (Coultard and Montgomery 1981). Similarly whether people find jokes funny or not, common politeness requires people to laugh on the punch line. No laugh – no positive evaluation – is hearable as a negative evaluation of the joke and/or of the joker – it wasn't funny. Perhaps it wasn't taken as a joke, but as an insult.

In **G2**, George tells a story for which it is reasonable to predict that the other party to the interchange will give a positive evaluation. Nothing recognizable as a positive evaluation is forthcoming. The minimal utterance by **RG** and **RG**'s status as interviewer, leave the turn with George and the topic still the same: George's drink problem. What does George do? He does one of the things we might expect. He amends his story as if its first version had been regarded as an exaggeration or an untruth. He diminishes his claims of success a little (**G3**):

Well, occasional lapses, but nearleee dry. It was o.k.

Something you might realize from the example of teachers' questions and pupils' responses is that positive evaluations often also serve as *topic change markers:* as in 'yea, thanks that's great. Now another thing.' Silence or minimal responses, whether taken as negative evaluations or not, usually indicate that the topic has not been exhausted. In the case of teacher questions and pupil answers, the teacher silence is likely to imply that the pupil's answer was wrong and the pupil should correct it, or that it was incomplete and the pupil should complete it. Either way the turn stays with, or returns to the pupil for him or her to offer a completion or a correction. Something like this seems to be happening in the transcript. **RG**'s minimal and non-responses are responded to by George as if they meant: 'what you have said so far is incomplete, insufficient, incredible or otherwise inadequate: redeem yourself.'

As the interview unfolds George's responses slide down the preference scale of accounts, from a self-commendation at **G2**, which is then amended to become less self-congratulatory at **G3**, is replaced by an excuse at **G4**, with excuse piled on top of excuse from **G5** to **G8**. At **G15** George is back to self-commendations, characterizing himself as someone 'fighting against the odds' – the 'person of character, but victim of circumstances' theme of the thematic analysis (see Transcript 11.2).

TRANSCRIPT 11.2 Transcript coded for illocutions: sequential analysis

Speaker and utterance number	Speech	ILLOCUTION
RG1	So, hmm, you were aware that you had a drinking problem. That was the wor-d you used wasn't it?	Question
G1	Yea [2 seconds]	Response No positive evaluation/no topic change signal from **RG** leaves the silence with George, and implies that his response was inadequate or incomplete
G2	I mean it took me a long time to accept it, to really accept it that is as, hmmmm a problem to be solved sort of problem. An derrr then I said, well [Georgie] boy you gotter do somethink about this. Sssss so I spose I got myself dry for about err year	Self-commendation
RG2	Uhhm	No positive evaluation of the self-commendation
G3	Well occasional lapses, but nearleee dry. It was o.k.	Amendment of self-commendation to be less self-congratulatory
RG3	Yeahh	No positive evaluation of **G3**
G4	Hmmm, then my uh, wife died [3 seconds]	Excuse No positive evaluation of excuse
G5	Unexpectedly and derr that threw me. It was stomach cancer which was common in her family, but which I didn't see it coming [untranscribable] it was a great shock, and I yh reacted badly. I began to hit the drinking very hard, but not for the same reasons as ear[lier]	Elaboration of excuse
RG4	[ear]lier. Hhh, earlier you said drinking was about stress. Stress at work.	Topic change, which might be heard as rejection of the **G5** excuse on

Speaker and utterance number	Speech	ILLOCUTION
		the grounds that a different excuse had been made earlier
G6	Yea. I told you. But I got to handle that see. That was behind me. Then this thing with [wife's name]. And then when I was just getting over that, I got made redundant, which knocked the stuffing out of me.	Excuse
G7	[omitted passage on redundancy and how badly it affected many people; how it was caused by bad management and greedy unions, ending on 10 second silence.]	(Several more excuses)
G8	And what with the drink and the [lack of] money I end up here [in the hostel] which is just one better than being on the street but only just. [5 minutes more interview talk. **RG5–9 G9–14**]	Rounding up of narrative – implies this topic is exhausted new topic introduced by new question from RG]
RG10	So in more general terms, what do you think makes people homeless?	Question
G15	Oh, oh, mmmm, there's lots. Everyone's got their own. Hmmmm hhhhhher. I mean some it's really a lack of character. I mean little things which anyone else could hmm, anyone with a bit of character could cope with. But me hhhhm, all through my life my luck's been against me. It's almost as if I was heading for the bottom all the time and now I've pretty well reached it. At least there's nothing to be afraid of any more	Self-commendation in terms of response to the challenges life has thrown at him/self-characterization as victim fighting against the odds

RG – Roger Gomm, G – George, [2 seconds] = 2 seconds silence [ ] encloses overlapping speech.

But by **G17** George is characterizing himself as a pathetic victim, someone foolish even to consider he could beat the odds against him:

I mean, everything I've tried to do, just when I was succeeding has been snatched away from me. It's been me getting it together, and then the slap in the gob. The mistake was trying to get it together. Ider bin much happier if I'd just accepted I was a loser from the start

Then, towards the end of the interview, and beyond our transcript, George is at the bottom of the preference scale with a self-blaming account:

G32 Yah, well you know Roger this old guff that people like me give you, its all about refusing to confront, what's in the personality, of hhh, y'h average alcoholic. I mean you talk to an alco, and what you probably get is a lot of excuses and justifications and when it's really down to a failure of will power, which is hhhhh, which is something we don't want to confront. I mean that's my story
(5 seconds)
G33 In a nutshell.

Aha, at last, George is revealing his true authentic self which he has been dissimulating previously. But why should we assume this? It would perhaps be better to think of George trying out various ways of presenting himself, none of which seem to elicit any validation from **RG** and at **G32** trying yet another tack. It is worth noting here perhaps, that what George says in **G32** is cast in the genre of Alcoholics Anonymous meetings of which George attended from time to time. Other research has suggested that something which people with drug and alcohol problems learn from their contacts with members of the helping agencies is that they get a better deal from them by describing themselves in this way. In professional circles it is described as 'showing insight' (Davies 1997). Thus there is a case for regarding **G32** as 'off-the-peg' drink-problem talk appropriate for an alcoholic to use in talking to members of the helping professions, and not as George finally disclosing his 'true self'.

Rather than puzzling about which is the 'real George' it might be better to consider instead how it is that characters are *realized* or *produced* in an interview, or in any other kind of speech exchange. The term 'produced' is used here in the same sense as in dramatics where it refers to a producer and the production enabling an actor to realize a character in a play. In the same way, in an interview, an interviewer and an interviewee enable or disable the realization of characters. For example, if you are part of the audience for a lecture, this offers only limited opportunities for producing yourself as a character, except by breaking all the conventions of playing the rather passive role of audience member. As you have seen, how George comes across depends on what the interviewer does and how George responds to this. How his interviewer – that's me – behaves depends on how he thinks such interviews should be conducted. As far as I can remember, I thought it was important to say as little as possible, but to make encouraging and non-judgemental noises in order to 'draw interviewees out' on interesting topics. That was the basis of my on-the-spot intuitive data analysis which determined what I said next. You might say that it all went horribly wrong. I would agree. But, whatever I might have said differently, I would still have been involved in the production of George as a character. Note also that George is also partly responsible for how I come across as an interviewer.

11.5   Thematic and linguistic analysis compared

One of the main devices George uses to give himself character is that of telling stories in which he is the leading character. So far as the transcript is concerned, a reasonable synopsis of the overall plot would be that this is a story of someone beset with such a sequence of misfortunes that 'anyone' under the same circumstances might turn to drink and become homeless. As you saw from Section 11.2 of this chapter, this sequence of events is not an accurate one in historical terms. Having looked at the transcript in terms of the interaction between interviewer and interviewee, you may now be suspicious that the 'one thing on top of another' impression is created by George piling excuse on excuse in response to what seems to be a rather unsympathetic interviewer. With a more sympathetic response, George might not have depicted himself as beset with so many adversities. Nor perhaps, would he have finally ended up with a self-blame.

This story line is picked up by the thematic analysis in Section 11.3. It is the grand theme of 'persons of character as victims of circumstances'. But the assumptions underlying the thematic analysis force us to accept that the stories people tell about themselves have their foundation in some general ways in which the tellers understand themselves and their lives. The linguistic analysis, however, suggests that such stories are devices adopted in particular circumstances as seem appropriate to perform immediate tasks, such as to entertain, to commiserate, to show solidarity, to persuade, to show good character traits; or, in George's case, to find some kind of personality to occupy which would provoke a positive evaluation from his interviewer. Another way of saying this is that what George says is **audience directed** or **recipient designed** in terms of what George understands to be the **demand characteristics** of the interview (Chapter 10, Section 10.4).

In addition, from the linguistic point of view, what we hear when we hear people telling stories is that they know how to tell stories: that is, they know how to use *narrative conventions* to tell plots and depict characters; to know what is a credible out-turn from an antecedent state of affairs; and to know what motivations people usually assume to lie behind what actions. For example, George does not have to spell out in **G8** that being made redundant and being short of money are conventionally regarded as stressful and among the candidate causes for homelessness. Nor should he have to say, in so many words, that staying dry is difficult for an alcoholic, and that succeeding to some degree is a matter for commendation.

The result of a thematic analysis is usually the delineation of a *type of person* or of a range of types of persons. These are usually the types of person who are assumed to be as they are because of their social location or biographical experience – because, for example, they have been socialized as doctors they think the way they do; because they were abused as children they are anorexic adults, or because their teachers have a poor opinion of them they have gained a view of themselves as stupid and this explains why they engage in disruptive behaviour. The typification is likely to be in terms of mentalistic characteristics, such as personality traits or ways of understanding, together with a causal theory as to how they got that way. In an analysis like this the generalizations run from someone who is interviewed to a much larger number of people, allegedly of the same sort, who have not been studied. Thus the generalization would be from the 15 homeless people I interviewed to other homeless people. The generalizing claim – Section 11.3 – would be that some of them would be of the 'self-blaming type', and some of the type who are 'persons of character but victims of circumstances' and that, for both types, homelessness (or some other set of adversities) gave them these characteristics (or that these characteristics explain the state they are in).

The linguistic analysis, however, is framed around the idea of a *type of situation*. In this case, the situation is the type of speech exchange system called 'a qualitative interview'. Thus what has been found more generally about linguistic behaviour in such situations might be applied to, or tested against, the interview with George. What is discovered about the interview with George might be claimed to be true also of other, as yet unstudied qualitative interviews. But there are also likely to be some things which are true of qualitative interviews which are also true of other speech exchange systems: perhaps of job interviews, academic tutorials, radio interviews and so on. Here the generalizing movement is from one kind of speech exchange system to another. Just as I used teacher–pupil exchanges in classrooms to inform my analysis of the transcript of a qualitative interview, so ideas arising from the analysis of a qualitative interview might be used to inform the analysis of, say, classroom interaction, counselling sessions, or medical consultations. Carrying this sequence on, we reach the most general level which is about the general properties of spoken communication, and includes such general ideas as turn-taking, adjacency pairs, preference orders, accounts and accounting, narrative conventions and many others not dealt with here, which seem utilizable for explaining speech interaction in a wide range of circumstances.

A final difference relates to the researcher's **accountability**. Those who do thematic analysis typically work on a large data set, even if it is drawn from only a few tens of interviews. Considerations of space usually prevent them sharing much of their analysis with their readers, so readers have to take much of it on trust. The linguistic or sequential analysis has demonstrated the crucial importance both of what is said by the interviewer and what was said previously by the interviewee, for understanding any particular utterance by the interviewee. Whereas those who conduct surveys with forced choice questionnaires usually tell readers what the questions were, thematic analysts rarely show what it was that the interviewer said which shaped the interviewee's response.

By contrast, conversation analysts, and others of similar ilk, typically work intensively on small segments of data and provide their readers with all the data which they have analysed. I have followed this practice here. You may not agree with my analysis, but since I have provided you with all the data, you are in a position to analyse it yourself and come to your own conclusions. My analysis may not be valid, but at least it is objective.

ACTIVITY   Analysing data from a focus group (Transcript 11.3)

This Activity shows some of the differences between the two party-speech exchange system of the one-on-one qualitative interview and the orchestrated, multi-party speech exchange system of the focus group: 'orchestrated' because there is a facilitator to allocate turns when this is necessary, to designate topics and so on. The activity asks you to try to analyse a short extract from a focus group. This was actually run as a telephone conference. Participants were not in face to face contact with each other. This doesn't seem to show itself in the extract here, though elsewhere in the transcript it does. The speakers are older, housebound women and the general topic is their experience of hospitalization.

For the George transcript, we got some mileage out of imagining George having a problem of giving an account of himself while occupying a stigmatising status. For this transcript I suggest you think of these women as having the general problem associated with complaining. If one makes a complaint which others find unjustified, one produces oneself as having the character of an ingrate or whinger, or as a busybody if the complaint is on behalf of someone else. And if one reports not making a complaint when others think one should, then one characterizes oneself as a sucker, a coward or someone of unreasonable fortitude, or as cowardly, uncaring or irresponsible if the complaint would have been on behalf of someone else. Thus either reporting oneself complaining, or reporting states of affairs which might be complained about, but were not, is hazardous for the character until one knows what other people think. Bear this in mind while you analyse the transcript.

I suggest you analyse it by coding utterances as 'speech acts' (illocutions). Use your own vocabulary, but always to indicate what was being *done* with the words at the moment they were uttered, rather than trying to reconstruct what was in the minds of the women. Thus **3.10** is a self-characterization – a self-commendation, perhaps.

TRANSCRIPT 11.3   Extract from focus group for analysis in Activity

Turn number and speaker	Utterances	Your notes
3.10 **Mrs Bloor**	When things are not right I'm afraid I'm not one to stand by. I'm a right busybody when I like? hhh	
3.11 **Mrs Roberts**	You have to be	
3.12 **Mrs Bloor**	So when the poor old thing couldn't feed herself I called the nurse over and told her straight [0.5]	
3.13 **Mrs Farmer**	You could starve to death [in that place]	
3.14 **Mrs Roberts**	[No one gives you] hhh any help if you can't get your food down [you]	

Turn number and speaker	Utterances	Your notes
3.15 **Mrs Farmer**	[I] didn't get a proper feed 'til the Chaplain came and helped me mm?	
3.16–3.18	[talk establishing Chaplain's name and character]	
3.19 **Mrs Bloor**	So I told her straight =	
3.20 **Mrs Farmer**	= Quite right too Minnie	
3.21 **Mrs Bloor**	I don't think that was out of turn [do you?]	
3.22 **Mrs Roberts**	[They] need telling a thing or two. Like dead man's meals, like the way you have to eat what someone before you ordered, in your bed before you. I told them off about [that]	
3.23 **Mrs Bloor**	[That's] right Mavis [but]	
3.24 **Mrs Roberts**	[My] husband used to say: you're a terror when your dander's up =	
3.25 **Mrs Bloor**	= But it's all right for us because we can stand up for ourselves. But there are some of the old dears that get in there, well they really don't know what time of day it is, really, so they really get put upon [0.5] hhh	
3.26 **Mrs Farmer**	Like the one I was telling you about when the nurse gave her her pills and she dropped them and she said 'O well I don't suppose it matters' and walks AWAY =	
3.27 **Facilitator**	= Did you do anything about that?	
3.28 **Mrs Bloor**	If the doctor gives you the pills, you're SUPPO :::: SED to have them. Isn't that RIGHT? [2.0]	
3.29 **Mrs Farmer**	Well, you don't like to interfere too: much do you I mean .hhhh [0.5]	
3.30 **Mrs Bloor**	No you don't want to be too:: interfering	
3.31 **Mrs Roberts**	Not if it isn't any of your business [you don't]	
3.32 **Mrs Bloor**	[no you]don't. That's VERY true.	
3.33 **Someone**	hhhhhhhh [5.0]	

Turn number and speaker	Utterances	Your notes
3.34 Mrs Bloor	And some of them in there, that has sort of [0.2] lost their marbles, they complain about every little thing [0.2]	
3.35 Mrs Roberts	Every lit::tle thing.	

[ ] means overlapping speech; [0.5] means 0.5 of a second silence; [5.0] means 5 seconds silence; = means that there was no gap between one utterance and another. Upper case as in SUPPO:::SED indicates words spoken more loudly than the surrounding speech. Colons as in SUPPO:::SED indicates that the preceding sound was prolonged; .hhhh is a sounded in-breath; hhhhh is a sounded out-breath; ? indicates an interrogative tone. For other transcribing symbols not used here see Sacks, Schegloff and Jefferson (1974), or Heritage (1984).

Further reading

I used the term 'thematic analysis' to cover analyses with the aim of finding out what was, and generally is, in the minds of interviewees. It is not necessarily the term you will find in other books, where instead of themes researchers write about the interviewees' perspectives, social theories, typification schemes, world-views, schemes of relevance, interpretive frameworks, or use other words implying that people's minds have structures and that these are knowable from analysing what they say in an interview. What I have called 'thematic analysis' is not restricted to the analysis of interviews, but is also applied to talk in non-interview situations and in the analysis of texts (see Chapter 13). Miles and Huberman (1994), Searle *et al.* (2004) or Gbrich (2006) demonstrate a much wider range of approaches than was possible in this chapter.

Most modern texts on the analysis of qualitative interviews are strongly influenced by the ideas of linguistic analysis. Silverman (2006) is a very accessible text, linguistically sensitive without having a through-going commitment to CA.

CA now has a huge literature. Hutchby and Wooffitt (1998) is a comprehensive introduction. Membership categorization analysis (MCA) is a common adjunct of CA, dealt with in Chapter 13. The term 'discourse analysis' is sometimes used for something very similar to CA, though with roots more firmly grounded in linguistics; for this see Brown and Yule (1983) or Stubbs (1983). Levinson (2000) or Horn and Ward (2005) are again similar though headlined as 'Pragmatics'. Sometimes, however, the term 'discourse' is used as a modern synonym for what would previously have been called 'ideology'. Discourse analysis in this sense uses procedures and makes assumptions much more like those I have called 'thematic analysis', particularly where the enterprise is called 'critical discourse analysis' – for example, van Dijk (1993). In CA, 'narrative analysis' is an interest in the linguistic devices people use for telling stories and depicting characters, and for the uses people make of storytelling to accomplish interactional effects, such as entertaining people or making complaints. But the term may also refer to the idea that the way people tell stories in one context is evidence about how they think in general: for example Holloway and Jefferson (2000) or Clandinin (2007); or that the stories they tell are elements of an ideology which oppresses them (Mumby 1993). See also Chapter 13, Section 13.1.

There are several computer software packages for analysing qualitative data – Computer-Aided Qualitative Data Analysis (CAQDA), including *Ethnograph* (www.qualisresearch.com/), *Atlas/ti* (www.atlasti.com/), QSR Nvivo and NUD*IST (www.qsrinternational.com/products.aspx). Bazeley (2007) is a handbook for using Nvivo and Richards (2005) is an excellent general, hands-on introduction to computer-aided qualitative data analysis, even though it is tied to NUD*IST. It has a related web site with downloads free for those who buy the book. Atlas/ti offers free tutorials on how to use the Atlas package and the On-line qualitative data analysis (QDA) site at the University of Surrey gives step-by-step guides for all the major CAQDA software, and some profiles of the packages which help users to choose between them (http://onlineqda.hud.ac.uk/). A highly recommended text is Lewis and Silver (2007). Lewis (2001) gives a shorter introduction.

12 Observing Naturally Occurring Events

By the end of this chapter, you will:

- Understand the idea of ecological or naturalistic validity and how study-ing naturally occurring events are an attempt to achieve this . . .
- . . . but recognize that researchers will vary in their assumptions of what is there to be naturalistically observed
- Understand that a picture of things as they 'naturally' are is produced by a large number of selection decisions and interpretations on behalf of the researcher
- Know the problems qualitative researchers have in making any empirical generalizations
- Know how the ideas of theoretical sampling and theoretical generaliza-tion feature in some qualitative research
- Have practised observation of naturally occurring events.

And you will know the meaning of the following terms:

Breaching (or disruption) experiment • constant comparison • ecological (or naturalistic) validity • ethnography/ethnographic research • generalizing within the case • grounding theory in data/grounded theory • multiple realities • observer expectancy effects • participant and non-participant observation research • Rashomon effect • reflexivity • sympathetic bias (or over-rapport)

At the end of the chapter there is an Activity which will test your under-standing of observing and disrupting turn-taking.

12.1 Introduction

Experiments, surveys and interviews are all events set up by researchers to generate research data. They attract the criticism that they give only a distorted picture of what usually goes on – for example, that:

- Experimental situations are so unlike 'real life' that their results cannot easily be generalized beyond the experiment (Chapter 3, Section 3.10), and that this problem persists even when attempts are made to make experiments more naturalistic (Chapter 4, Sections 4.2, 4.3). Experimentalists have their own response to this charge (Chapter 4, Section 4.5).

- The opinions, attitudes and so on 'discovered' in surveys using forced choice questionnaires are actually conjured up and brought into being by the questions the researchers ask and the way they ask them (Chapter 10, Section 10.6).
- The data generated by an interview are just a record of the interaction between interviewer and interviewee, with only a doubtful relationship to whatever it was the interview was supposed to be about (Chapter 11, Section 11.4).

An antidote prescribed for these problems is for researchers to study 'naturally occurring' situations which would have happened whether researchers had been around or not, and which are as influenced as little as possible by research activity. The case in favour of naturalistic observation is often expressed using the terms **naturalistic** or **ecological validity**, meaning that a study will be valid insofar as it accurately captures how things would be irrespective of research activity. There is a close analogy here with the critique of studies of animal behaviour under conditions of captivity, coming from researchers who prefer to study animals in their natural habitats.

Research based on naturalistic observation is often called **field research** or **ethnographic research**, though the latter is also used for studies combining observation with qualitative interviews. The term **ethnographic data** is often a general-purpose term for any qualitative data. However, sometimes the term 'ethnographic' is used in contradistinction to 'ethnomethodological', the former attempting to study meaning by getting into the minds of the people observed, the latter looking for what it is that makes actions meaningful. This is the distinction between thematic analysis and conversation analysis (CA) in Chapter 11 (see also Chapter 1, Section 1.4). In the social sciences what observers most usually 'observe' is speech and other communicative behaviours, so the analysis of data collected from naturally occurring events is often very similar to the analysis of interviews as described in Chapter 11.

Researchers cannot simply go and look at 'naturally occurring' events and write an account of these 'telling it like it's at'. Their report will be a report by them, based on what was observed by them, excluding what they did not observe, informed by the sense they made of their observations. If the results of surveys are shaped by the way the questions are asked, and the results of interviews reflect the performance of the interviewer then, equally, the results of a study involving the observation of naturally occurring events will be determined by the way the researcher did the observing. Various aspects of this are discussed in this chapter.

An observation study is as much a process of *excluding* data as accumulating them and entails selection decisions at many levels (Figure 12.1). This is true of all kinds of research, of course, though the selection decisions may be made in different ways and at different stages. At the end of a study involving observation there will be a research report which is, among other

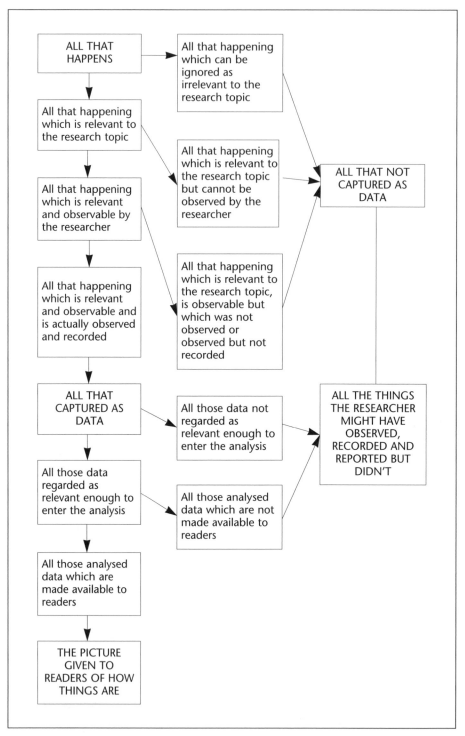

Figure 12.1   *Levels of selection in an observation study: what influences whether data are selected in, or selected out?*

things, a result of making such selection decisions. There is an important general question:

> Are the findings of the study the result of the observer collecting sufficient relevant data, and excluding all irrelevant data, *or* did the study result from the exclusion of relevant data which, had it been included, would have produced a different picture of how things 'naturally are'?

There is something analogous here to the problem of non-response in survey research (Chapter 6, Section 6.9), though in a more acute form.

12.2   Inside looking out or outside looking in

All those who favour naturalistic observation would agree, first, that this is sometimes the only way of studying some kinds of people and some kinds of activities, *and*, second, that it is a way of doing research where the researcher makes the minimal possible impact on what is being researched, and hence can claim to be giving an account of what ordinarily happens: that is, an account with a high level of ecological validity.

Beyond this, researchers divide. One way of getting at the distinction is to consider whether the appropriate position for the observer is as an insider looking out or an outsider looking in.

Insiders looking out

To claim to study things naturalistically is to make some assumptions about how things 'naturally' are. Chapter 11 dealt with the analysis of qualitative interviews, making a distinction between two very different ways of looking at the same interview data which derive from radically different views about the nature of social phenomena. What I called 'thematic analysis' proceeded from the assumption that social events happen as they do because the participants have particular ways of understanding the world. 'Actor theories', 'interpretive frameworks', 'perspectives', 'typification schemes' and many other terms, are used to express this idea of 'ways of understanding'. From this point of view, 'how things naturally are' is people interpreting their experiences in terms of their particular ways of understanding and acting on the basis of this. The answer to the question 'Why did s/he do that?' is 'because this is what the situation meant to her/him'. It is a matter of research interest as to how and why people acquired such ways of understanding. These are usually attributed either psychologically – to their upbringing or to the more immediate psychodynamic context of a family or an organization – or sociologically – to their being in a particular location in a social structure which shapes their experience and understandings: for example, being female in a patriarchal world.

But here the first target for research is finding out what these ways of understanding are. For this reason, many researchers regard it as sensible to combine naturalistic observation with qualitative interviews. They observe people to see what they do. They then interview them to discover *why*. This is where the 'why' question is answered in terms of meaning, and 'meaning' means what must have been in the mind of the person in order for them to have done what they did. Some regard the approach to interviews here as 'naturalistic' in the sense that interviews should be more like conversations or chats, and the relationship between interviewer and interviewee modelled on a friendship relationship (Chapter 10, Section 10.6).

This is research which seeks explanation through understanding, where 'understanding' means being able to see the world from the point of view of the people being studied. So if what is important is the way some groups of people understand the world, then why not join them, learn their ways of speaking and acting, experience their experiences, learn to understand things as they understand them and then report back as a 'member' of the category of persons being studied? This is what I mean by 'observing as an insider looking out'. It is best exemplified by participant observation research: joining in with the activities being researched (see Section 12.4). The justification for this approach may not entirely rest on it producing explanations for what happens in social life. It may be extended with the argument that the purpose of such research is also to foster human understanding by enabling readers of the research to understand things from the viewpoints of others (see also Chapter 14, Sections 14.4 and 14.5).

All this assumes that the important topics for research are found in what members know or experience, which a researcher can discover by learning to be a member. But there are limits to members' knowledge, as discussed below.

Outsiders looking in

I conducted research on educational assessment in participant observation roles as lecturer, as an examiner and as a chair of an examination board (Gomm 1986). To preserve confidentiality (Chapter 16, Section 16.5) I anonymized transcripts and field notes of events in which I had participated so that I became 'examiner 3' or 'lecturer 1'. I often found it very difficult to work out who was me in a transcript without looking this up in my secret code book, although there was rarely any difficulty in deciding what roles people were playing. Even if I did know who was me, it was no good relying on my experience of having been there and done that to answer questions such as 'why did you say that, then?' or 'what did that mean to you at the time?' The only way I could find of explaining what was going on was to look at the data from an outside point of view and treat myself as just one among others, all equally mysterious. Similarly, I was the interviewer in the transcript with George (Chapter 11). I might have been interviewed after the interview. I could have answered questions as to what I was trying to achieve, how I thought the interview went, what it felt like to do the interview, what kind of person George was and so on. But it would have been pointless to ask *me* how my performance produced what George said, when he said it and how that produced particular versions of George. For that, I would have had to look at the transcript and analyse it as if I had been 'any old interviewer' (Chapter 11, Section 11.4). And, of course, had I been interviewed thus, I would have given answers to interviewers' questions, shaped by the way the questions were asked of me.

For many social activities people do not know how they do them, or notice what they have done. This is why it is often held that in participant observation research the early stages of learning to be a member are the important ones (Schutz 1964). What experienced members do without thinking about it is strange and difficult for the newcomer. And because it is strange and difficult it is noticeable. For example, as a newly appointed teacher I felt thoroughly inadequate in the face of my more experienced colleagues' ability to give definitive-sounding descriptions of pupils. Pupils seemed so diverse and individual to me. But I soon learned the trick. It was to locate any particular pupil in terms of two dimensions, one running from bright to dull, and another running from well-behaved to naughty (Becker 1952). There were some helpful local phrases for doing this, for example 'puddings' were good girls who weren't very bright, 'bitches' were bright but unruly girls. Had I not been a sociologist I would probably not have noticed the mechanics of this. Even though I was a sociologist I soon fell into the same habits of description without thinking much about what I was doing. On these considerations the *last thing* a naturalistic observer should want to do is to become a *fully* experienced member of the group who are being studied, because fully experienced members are the kinds of people who take for granted the things which researchers ought to regard as puzzling.

Many anthropologists have remarked that it is much more difficult to do anthropology in your own society than in one exotic to you, because doing so requires an effort to unlearn what you have learned to take for granted (Barnard 1994: 154). Garfinkel (1967: 9) makes the same point by saying that it is the purpose of ethnomethodology to render the mundane anthropologically strange. Dr Spock in the first series of *Star Trek* is only one of a large number of aliens and androids who serve to make what humans take for granted look anthropologically strange in sci-fi works. As you saw from the exercise in conversation analysis in Chapter 11, Section 11.4, ethnomethodologists adopt an outsider's point of view in doing naturalistic observation on the assumption that it wouldn't help the analyst to experience the interview as if they were George or as if they were me. That probably wouldn't have been possible, and anyway, it would be impossible to know whether one person had indeed re-created another person's experience in their own mind.

The outsider-looking-in position is preferred by those who assume *both* that it is important to study naturally occurring events *and that* the people involved would not themselves be able to provide information for a satisfactory explanation, and hence where becoming one of them would not be enlightening. This includes psychologists studying, for example, group dynamics or children's play through one-way mirrors or on video-tape.

12.3 Windows of observation, sampling and generalization in observation research

To avoid a horrible mix of metaphors, put the notion of insiders looking out and outsiders looking in to one side, and try thinking about observation

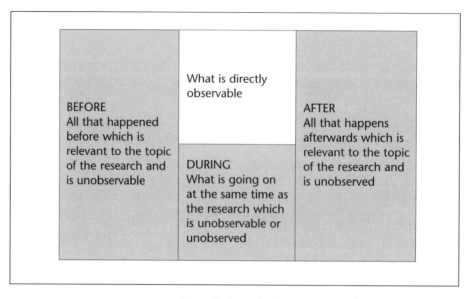

Figure 12.2   *The window of observation in observation research*

research in terms of there being a 'window' of observation: a set of circumstances making it possible for observers to observe some things but not others. An important issue is how far what is unobservable can be legitimately inferred from what is observable, sometimes called *generalizing within the case* (Gomm, Hammersley and Foster 2000). For example, what does knowing what someone does when we can see them tell us about what they do when we can't see them?

As Figure 12.2 suggests, the duration of a study is important in shaping the window for observation. For example, a large number of ethnographic studies of schools purport to explain why some categories of pupils do better than others in national examinations, attributing this to the way teachers treat different kinds of pupils in different ways: working class as opposed to middle class, girls as opposed to boys, black and Asian pupils as opposed to white. But the groups studied have often been in the lower school years, and the researchers left the scene long before the pupils studied received their results in 16+ examinations. Thus what was observed to happen in earlier school years was used as a basis for explaining what was assumed to be going to happen in the future – what was actually happening to pupils some years older than those studied. This had particularly embarrassing consequences for feminist researchers who had conducted studies of lower-school pupils explaining that the ways that teachers treated girls led to girls achieving less than boys at 16+. By the time the girls they had studied were 17, girls nationally were achieving more than boys (Foster, Gomm and Hammersley 1996). What those observed achieved, we do not know.

One way of avoiding this problem entirely is for the researcher to disclaim any interest in what comes before or after the period of study and to claim merely to give an accurate account of happenings during the research period. Ethnomethodologists assume that the past is what is created as the past in the present – for example, by people telling stories about the past for some immediate purpose (Chapter 11, Section 11.4), while the future is something which people appeal to in the present as a way of justifying their actions as actions which will 'lead to' or 'avoid' some future happening. All the 'past' and all the 'future' *relevant to the study* are observable.

Timing and duration shape the study as a *time sample*. What is an appropriate time sample depends on the topic of the research. If the topic implicates a long-term causal sequence, such as the events leading up to differences in educational achievement at 16+, then that suggests the need for a series of time samples, perhaps one each for 11 years for the same cohort of pupils. If the topic were 'pupil–teacher interaction in 1999 in year 9 of an inner urban comprehensive school', and the study was conducted only in the summer term, there might be questions as to how typical the summer term was of other terms in the school for the year 9 pupils.

It is the size and the shape of the window of observation that provides the basis for drawing general conclusions from the study. This idea is elaborated in Table 12.1. This distinguishes between 'time', 'place' and 'people' sampling. But any decision made on one of these dimensions will have implications for the others.

Of all the dimensions in Table 12.1 the one which generates the most discussion is what I have called the 'angle of view' of the researcher. This includes discussion of the relative merits of participant as against non-participant observation.

12.4 Participant observation and non-participant observation research

Covert electronic surveillance apart, there are some areas of social life which can be studied naturalistically only by the researcher becoming a member of an otherwise closed social group: as a participant observer. These include both stigmatized and deviant groups and elite groups where the presence of an outsider would be so disruptive that observing things 'as normal' would be impossible.

Many studies of deviant gangs and religious cults have been conducted by researchers who join up as members. Sometimes such participation has been *covert* or known about only by a few insiders and not the rest. Covert participant observation has the difficulty that researchers cannot ask the kinds of questions they might want to ask for fear of 'blowing their cover' (Patrick 1973). Rosenhan's pseudo-patient experiment (1973 and see Chapter 4, Section 4.2), involved infiltrating 'sane' people as patients into various American mental hospitals to see what would happen to them. This could not have been done overtly. When they asked questions of staff and noted down the responses, this was treated as a symptom of their insanity rather than blowing their cover, but this is a rather odd example. Covert research has the advantage that the researcher can be fairly sure that what he or she observes is not a 'Hawthorne effect' (see Chapter 3, Section 3.6) created as a reaction

TABLE 12.1 Sampling, representativeness and generalizations from observation research

What shapes the window of observation?	Examples (from ethnography in the sociology of education)	Limits on confident generalizations from sample observations
Time: The historical moment of study Questions: What changes and what stays the same? How and in what ways is what happens at one historical moment representative of what happens at others previously or later?	In what ways do the earlier ethnographies of schools such as Hargreaves (1967) or Lacey (1975) provide insights into the life of schools in the 2000s?	What is observed at one time cannot form the basis for confident generalizations about what has happened or will happen at another time, unless either the observations constituted a statistically representative sample of some unchanging phenomenon, or the researcher can specify the characteristics of time, place and people which caused the events to happen, and can specify where else in time these same circumstances will occur (Chapter 4, Section 4.7).
Time: The duration of the research study Question: How and in what ways was the time period of the study representative of other time periods relevant to the topic of the study?	How far does a study of one year in the life of a year 9 class represent their 9 years of compulsory education?	
Time: Timing of observations within the study Question: How and in what ways were the episodes observed representative of the episodes not observed?	Several American studies of 'progressive' primary school education in England were conducted by observation Tuesday to Thursday. They gave a very misleading picture of laissez faire practices, because they missed the sessions on Monday when tasks were set for pupils and the sessions on Fridays when the pupils' progress was reviewed (Berlak et al. 1975)	What is observed at one time cannot easily be attributed as caused by something unobserved happening at an earlier time, nor as the cause of something which will happen in the future, without knowledge of causation derived from experimental (Chapters 3 and 4) or natural experimental research Chapter 7).

Place: Social location of the study

Question: How and in what ways is this location representative and unrepresentative of other locations?

Place: Settings within the location studied

Question: How and in what ways were the settings actually observed representative or unrepresentative of the settings not observed?

Place: Angle of view within the settings observed

Question: Would an observer differently located physically and/or socially have produced essentially the same description?

How far would a study of interaction in a boys' public boarding school throw light on interaction in a custodial institution for young offenders?

Can observations of English lessons and Maths lessons stand as representative of all lessons?

Would a researcher playing the role of a teacher observe more or less or differently compared with an observer sitting in the back of the class?

Would either provide the same data as a fly-on-the-wall video camera?

What is observed in one location cannot form the basis for confident generalizations about what will happen in other locations, unless *either* the observations constitute a statistically representative sample of the population of locations to which the generalization is addressed, *or* the observer can specify the characteristics of time, place and people which caused the events to happen and can specify that much the same will happen in another location with the same constellation of factors (Chapter 4, Section 4.7).

TABLE 12.1   continued

What shapes the window of observation?	Examples (from ethnography in the sociology of education)	Limits on confident generalizations from sample observations
People: Social composition of the location studied Question: How in its social composition is the research location representative or unrepresentative of other locations?	Are studies of ethnic differences in pupil–teacher interaction in schools with large percentages of ethnic minority pupils relevant to understanding ethnic differences in pupil–teacher interaction in schools with small percentages of minority ethnic pupils (Gomm and Hammersley and Foster 2000)?	What is observed *from* one social location cannot form the basis of a confident generalization about what would be observable from a different location, without some additional evidence.
People: Characteristics of those observed Question: How representative or unrepresentative of those unobserved are those observed?	How far will what was observed of these 15 teachers in this school also be true of these 35 teachers who were not observed?	What is observed to happen among some people, cannot form the basis for a confident generalization as to what would happen among some other group of people, *unless* the people are a statistically representative sample of the population to which the generalization is addressed, *or* unless the researcher can specify the time, place and people characteristics which caused what was observed to happen, and can specify that much the same is likely to happen where this constellation of factors occurs elsewhere (Chapter 4, Section 4.7).
People: Characteristics of those most closely studied within research location Question: How representative or unrepresentative of those who are less frequently or less intensively observed are those who are more frequently or more intensively observed?	How far will what was true for a set of detailed case studies of 25 pupils, stand for what was true of 100 pupils observed but not made the topic of case studies? How far will the comments of a handful of pupils who have a close relationship to the observer throw light on the understandings of the pupils less close to the researcher?	

to the subjects' knowledge of being under observation. It raises important ethical issues which will be discussed in Chapter 16.

Researchers may use pre-existing memberships to do participant observation research. Roth's study of a tuberculosis sanatorium (1974) was done while he was a patient there. There are many studies of schools conducted by teachers and of healthcare settings by nurses. There are some situations in which some researchers can never participate as members or quasi-members. Males are excluded from all female groups. Lay people cannot take the participant role of a doctor or nurse. Participant observation studies of schools have by necessity been conducted by researchers occupying the role of teacher rather than pupil, even where pupil behaviour is the topic of the research.

Where researchers place a strong emphasis on the need to understand the experiences of those they research, they may argue that only researchers with particular social characteristics and previous experiences are qualified to do the research: for example, that only black women can understand black women (Collins 1990) or only people with disabilities can understand what it is like to be disabled (Beresford and Evans 1999). The end-point of this argument is that the only person who can understand anyone is that person themselves. This leads to research which consists of the researcher 'ghosting' the autobiographies of those studied, or of the researcher's own autobiography being presented as a research report (Stanley 1992). If you are willing to accept that an autobiography is based on a series of naturally occurring events then autobiographies must count as naturalistic observation research (see also Chapter 13, Section 13.7).

Against the assumption of the need for empathetic understanding, it may be argued that the more understandings researchers share with those they research the more likely it is that their research will be restricted to being a re-description of a rather narrow, local and unsociological way of understanding the world and that they will come to share the same biases and prejudices as those they research; what Miller (1953) called *over-rapport* or Becker (1967) called *sympathetic bias* (Lidz 1989).

Participant observation research requires the researcher to find a role to occupy in the setting studied. This is at least so that they can fade into the background and not disrupt 'things as usual' except in the ways that ordinary members influence each other. It may be so that the researcher can experience what it is like to do the kinds of things done by those researched. Some settings naturally include people standing around with clip boards. Hospitals and clinics have an abundance of such roles. There is not much 'participation' to being a participant observer in these circumstances.

Finding a role in other settings can be much more challenging. Humphreys (1975), studying male homosexual liaisons in public toilets took on the role of 'watch queen': the person who keeps look-out in return for satisfying his voyeuristic tendencies. This absolved Humphreys from actually engaging in homosexual acts. Julia O'Connell-Davidson (O'Connell-Davidson and Layder 1994) in her study of prostitutes and their clients conducted her research from the position of the prostitutes' receptionist (see also Chapter 16). As these examples indicate, there can be dangers in being a participant observer, including those of being drawn into illegal activity. Both Patrick (1973) and Yablonsky (1967) ran close to breaking the law in their research with gangs of young men, and Yablonsky narrowly avoided being seriously injured when gang-members found out about him being a researcher.

The role occupied as a participant shapes what is and what is not available for study. For example, Dingwall's study of health visitor education (1977) was conducted with him playing the role of a health visitor student. In his student role his experience was close to that of the other students, or at least of the other male students. But because he played the role of a student he was usually excluded from activities privy to staff. Something which Dingwall purports to describe is the way health visitor tutors and other staff *view* the world. His main resource for this was listening to staff talk to students in lectures and tutorials.

My own study of health visitor education (Gomm 1986, 2000c) was conducted by participant observation as a lecturer, an examiner and a chair of examination board. These were roles I occupied anyway. Whereas the staff world was closed to Dingwall it was open to me. From my participant role I did not feel able to say anything at all about what it was like to be a health visitor student. I found that the world-view of staff *conveyed by staff to students* several years later and in different colleges was remarkably similar to that in Dingwall's account. But I could also say that what staff said when students weren't around was something different again. Thus it could hardly be said that what Dingwall had discovered was the way staff *viewed and understood* the world. Interestingly what health visitor tutors said to me *in interview* was very similar to what they told the students. The difference between this and what they said to me as a colleague and to each other gave me a healthy sense of scepticism with regard to the capacity of interviews to capture what people 'really think' (see Chapter 11, Sections 11.3, 11.5). Dingwall's research is a good piece of ethnographic research, but it has to be read as research conducted from a particular observation point, as indeed does my own study (see Figure 12.2)

A common experience for an overt participant observer is that the people researched make efforts to direct the researcher's interpretations, usually with the aim of being helpful. I can almost guarantee that when I visit a school or a clinic or a youth club in a research role, someone will tell me that today is 'not a typical day' with the implication and that I should not rely on what I am seeing, but listen to them instead (see also Chapter 11, Section 11.4 on accounts). In addition, participant observation researchers often make closer relationships with some of the people they are studying than with others. There is a danger, then, that the researcher comes to see events through the eyes of only some participants and with their prejudices. Much of William Foot Whyte's classic ethnographic study *Street Corner Society* (1981) is 'through the eyes' of Doc, his key informant and there are some indications that Doc was not entirely truthful (1981; see also *Journal of Contemporary Ethnography* 1992). Labov (1973) warns that the kinds of people who make close relationships with researchers are most unlikely to be typical of the category of people being researched. Similarly, making close relationships with some participants will often restrict a researcher's relationships with others. In my research on an island off the Kenya coast, before I realized it, I was 'captured' by one of two political factions in the village, who housed me in their part of the village and gave me an honorific kinship title in their clan. This made it extremely difficult to interact with the other faction. Being co-opted to one faction or another is a common problem in evaluation research (see Chapter 14, Section 14.3):

> [Tenge] said something to the effect that even if I pulled my weight as a worker I would still as an evaluation researcher have been 'beamed in' by the bosses to check up on them. So that 'this would go against the trust we have to have in each other'. [Tenge] said that they would prefer to select their own evaluation researcher who 'would stand up for the staff against the "suits"' [management].
>
> (Note on negotiations to operate as participant observer evaluation researcher in drugs project, 1989)

Participating can get in the way of observing. It usually rules out using audio or video. If the medium of recording is written notes, it is sometimes difficult both to participate and take adequate notes. Hammersley, for example, found that he had to make frequent trips to the toilet in order to write up his notes of observations of staffrooms, with a cover story about a medical condition (personal communication). Note-making entails on-the-hoof analysis with split-second decisions on what to record and what to ignore. Most of what is preserved as a record of what happened will be that field note. With electronic recording researchers do have to make decisions about where to site the recording apparatus, when to switch it on and when to switch it off, but electronic records can be reviewed at leisure. There are benefits of having the hard data produced through electronic recording. But there are the disadvantages that this is likely to be more disruptive of 'things as normal'. In their video-tapes of market traders Pinch and Clark (1986) found examples of traders orienting to the fact of being recorded, with jokes about selling goods 'as advertised on TV'. However, as this example shows, some at least of the disruptive effects of electronic recording produce data themselves, so that the effects of recording can be seen in the data. This is less likely where note-taking is the medium of recording. Electronic recording also limits the angle of view of the observer to that in the view-finder of the camera, or within the range of the microphone.

12.5 Representativeness in qualitative research

Table 12.1 frequently uses the term 'representative'. There are two main kinds of representativeness: statistical or empirical and theoretical.

Statistical representativeness and empirical or statistical generalization

Chapter 6 dealt in detail with the idea of *statistical* representativeness. What is statistically representative depends on the definition of the 'population' of which a sample is supposed to be representative. Typically those who do naturalistic observation study smallish, naturally occurring groups of people, who for this reason are unlikely to be a statistically representative sample of a wider population. It is doubtful, for example, whether any school class of 15–16 year olds in the UK is a representative sample of all 15–16 year olds in the population. However, if the 'population' is a population of classes (rather than of pupils) within a particular school, then it is conceivable that a researcher might be able to select a statistically representative sample of these. Panel 12.1 and Table 12.2 give an example of the systematic sampling of points in *time* to produce a statistically representative sample of teacher behaviour within a lesson.

Qualitative researchers are rarely able to study statistically representative samples. Nonetheless, they often write as if they had managed to do something like this, and in two ways. First, even the most qualitative of qualitative researchers still use quantitative terms such as 'most', 'many', 'few' or 'rarely'. Such usage presupposes some '100%' in terms of which something is 'many' or is 'rarely'. There are many ethnographic studies of classrooms which make claims that teachers *more often* do something with regard to that kind of pupil, or *rarely* do that with regard to this other kind. For example, that they pay less attention to certain types of pupils, or are more likely to criticize some other kinds (see Chapter 14, Section 14.4). Most of these claims are made on the basis of *unstructured* observation, usually using written field notes rather than hard records (Foster, Gomm and Hammersley

---

PANEL 12.1   Structured observation to produce numerical data from naturally occurring situations

There is no inherent contradiction between studying naturally occurring events and recording observations in numerical form. An observation schedule is just another kind of questionnaire. The one in Table 12.2 would ask the observer the question: 'At this point in time, was the teacher doing this, or this, or this . . .?' Using an observation schedule like this requires a great deal of preparation in deciding what will count as being an action of a particular kind. If the observations are made in real time rather than in viewing a video, then using the schedule requires some split-second decisions to be made. As Scarth and Hammersley (1993) comment, this observation schedule is rather difficult to use, since it is difficult to decide what counts as a *question* and what as a *statement* when spoken questions do not come conveniently marked with a question mark.

Despite the difficulties of this particular example, the use of structured observation illustrates the merits of taking an outsider-looking-in approach. No insider would ever view a situation in this way, and no insider would ever be able to provide the information captured by a structured observation of this kind. From tape-recording lessons Hammersley and Scarth (1986) found that teacher talk made up over 90% of all talk, but the teachers interviewed immediately after their lessons rarely gave estimates greater than 60%. Again it is a common finding that males often believe females spoke more than males in a discussion or a lesson, when a transcript shows the opposite (Spender 1980).

TABLE 12.2   Observation schedule for observing teachers' behaviour in the classroom

Conversation QUESTIONS	Silence SILENT INTERACTION
Task	
Q1 recalling facts	Gesturing
Q2 offering ideas, solutions (closed)	Showing
Q3 offering ideas, solutions (open)	Marking
Task supervision	
04 referring to supervision	Waiting
Routine	
Q5 referring to routine matters	
STATEMENTS	STORY READING
Task	
S1 of facts	Not observed
S2 of ideas	Not coded
Task supervision	
S3 telling child what to do	Adult interaction
S4 praising work or effort	Visiting pupil
S5 feedback on work or effort	Not interested
Routine	
S6 providing information, direction	
S7 providing feedback	
S8 of critical control	
S9 of small talk	Silence

The observer has a pad of sheets like this with boxes against each category. An observation is made at each 25-second sampling interval, the time being recorded in the appropriate box (Boydell and Jasman 1983: 104)

1996: 107–38). These claims are rarely restricted just to the instances the researcher has observed, but are usually generalized to situations they have not observed. But, for this, it is really necessary both to have an accurate count and to count what is a representative sample of instances. Something we know about human beings is that they are impressively *incompetent* in making accurate judgements about the frequencies and durations of events (Gilovich, Griffin and Kahneman 2002), unless using some kind of aid to structure their observations. One of the routes through which expectancy effects flaw the results of experiments is through biased time measurements *even when experimenters are using some aid to structure observation* (Chapter 3, Sections 3.6, 3.7; Barber and Silver 1968). There is no reason to believe that researchers engaged in naturalistic observation are any better at judging frequencies and durations, *without observation aids*, than are experimental researchers when using such aids.

Much of anthropology consists of studies of a few families, perhaps in only one village, yet the write-up may be as if what was discovered would be true of a population numbering tens of thousands. This is a second way in which qualitative researchers behave as if their observations have the quality of statistical representativeness. The claim to generality is often indicated in the title of a book, such as *The Swazi* or *The Nuer*. Similarly, many ethnographic studies in the sociology of education, while based on observations of a few classes in a particular school, imply general claims that the findings will apply to large categories of pupils in many different schools. Thus Paul Willis' (1977) *Learning to Labour* has the sub-title *How Working Class Kids Get Working Class Jobs*. It is actually a study of 12 pupils who seem to be very untypical even of the other working-class pupils in their own school. Mary Fuller's studies of the education of African-Caribbean girls seems to be based on a sample size of 5 in a single school (for example, Fuller 1982). Both were widely cited and influential studies and, irrespective of the authors' intentions, were taken as pictures of the general state of affairs in British education at the time they were published, and for some time afterwards.

The first column of Table 12.1 contains a series of questions. The empirical or statistical generalization from small-scale to large-scale assumes that the researcher knows the answers for all these questions and that the answer to each is that what was observed was indeed representative of a larger population in a statistical sense. But qualitative researchers often do not have answers for these questions.

The Rashomon effect

Margaret Mead's *Coming of Age in Samoa* (1948) is the most famous of all ethnographic studies. Translated into at least 16 languages, it has never been out of print since its publication in 1928. It gives a picture of adolescent life in Samoa as being without the difficulties associated with adolescence in America or Europe and of a free-and-easy pre-marital sexuality engaged in with the tacit consent of parents. *Coming of Age* was subjected to caustic criticism by Derek Freeman (1983), a researcher who had been conducting research in Samoa on and off since the 1930s. Freeman gives a picture of Samoan society in the 1930s (and earlier and later), as one with a strong puritan morality, severe punishments by parents of their children's pre-marital sexual adventures, chaperonage of young people to prevent sexual liaisons and rape as a common crime.

Putting the two studies side by side creates what Heider (1988) calls the *Rashomon Effect*. This is named after a film by the Japanese director Akria Korosawa, which presents several incompatible versions of the same events, leaving viewers wondering whether they have viewed a murder or a suicide, a seduction or a rape. As Heider says, when we read two accounts of the same society by two different anthropologists we often get incompatible pictures like this (Naroll 1973).

Looking again at Table 12.1, it shows that incompatible accounts are exactly what is to be expected when two ethnographic researchers look through different 'observation windows' by basing their research on different, statistically unrepresentative samples of time, place and people, but both claiming that what they have discovered is true for the same larger aggregate of people, times and places: for example 'Samoa'. Or, looking at Figure 12.1, we can see that this is to be expected when researchers or their circumstances, make different selection decisions influencing the inclusion and exclusion of particular kinds of data. Thus although Freeman's research was based on a rather larger population than Mead's, both were geographically restricted: Mead's on an island in Eastern Samoa, Freeman's on islands in Western Samoa, some hundreds of miles distant from each other. Mead's account is almost entirely based on what was told her by the group of 31 adolescent girls she befriended, only 12 of whom claimed to be sexually experienced. Freeman's is based on talking to adults remembering their adolescence. Both project their picture of Samoan society backwards into a past period when they could not have observed what happened, though Freeman draws much more extensively on what historical records were available, particularly court records of sexual offences, including those for Eastern Samoa. The duration of Freeman's research was much longer. Freeman is a fluent speaker of Samoan; Mead was only a novice. Mead as a female had access to situations that Freeman could not access: vice versa for Freeman as a male. Neither could directly observe the sexual behaviour of young people. Although Freeman's account of 'Samoan society' in the 1920s and 1930s seems more believable, some such discrepancies are inevitable if researchers study statistically unrepresentative bits of a society and then gross these up to stand for the society as a whole. The same might be said of school ethnographies where some study, of, say, some of the working-class pupils in a particular school is grossed up so that these pupils stand for most working-class pupils in most schools.

It is important to distinguish the Rashomon effect from the idea of *multiple realities*. The Rashomon effect arises when two different researchers make contradictory claims about what is represented as a single reality. Other researchers avoid the problem by saying that different participants will have different views as to what is going on, and that their account is either only from the viewpoint of one kind of participant, or that it is an attempt to document the contradictory views of many kinds of participants (for an example see Chapter 14, Section 14.3). But there is still a potential for something like a Rashomon effect on a smaller scale, for it would be possible for two researchers to make incompatible claims about the viewpoint of the *same* group of people.

Theoretical representativeness, theoretical sampling and theoretical generalization

In qualitative research, as in experimental research, theoretical representativeness and theoretical sampling are much more important than statistical or empirical representativeness. Theoretical sampling entails a classification of phenomena into a set of types, such that what is observed can be classified as one type or another. For example Cicourel and Kitsuse (1963) believed that the process of schooling in the US was becoming more bureaucratized with the careers of pupils being increasingly monitored and directed by specialist staff – counsellors – using tests and performance measures. To study this

TABLE 12.3   *Theoretical sampling frame implied by Cicourel and Kitsuse's (1963) study of Lakeside High*

	Elite schools	
	Large	*Small*
With specialist counselling staff	Type 1 – Lakeside High studied by Cicourel and Kitsuse	Type 5
Without specialist counselling staff	Type 2	Type 6
	Non-elite schools	
	Large	*Small*
With specialist counselling staff	Type 3	Type 7
Without specialist counselling staff	Type 4	Type 8

ethnographically they did not choose a school of a common type but one of a type which they believed would be more common in the future (Lakeside High). This was a large school with a specialist staff of counsellors doing what in other schools might have been done by classroom teachers. It was also a school taking pupils only from affluent backgrounds. These characteristics could generate a classification of 8 types of school (Table 12.3).

The ethnographic study of Lakeside is of the processes through which pupils come to be classified into those who are expected to go to elite universities and do well there, and those who are labelled as less clever, and the way in which these definitions determined the educational treatment they received. Thinking of Lakeside as being only one type of school out of 8 possible types addresses some of the problems raised by Table 12.1. If the social composition of the school, if its size and the presence and absence of counsellors makes a difference to the way pupils are processed as successes and failures, then Lakeside cannot represent schools with a non-elite social composition, of a small size, or without counsellors. Cicourel and Kitsuse are reticent about generalizing their findings to schools of types other than the 'elite-large-with-counsellors' category. Any generalization based on a study of Lakeside would be a theoretical generalization. It would entail theorizing that different ways of processing pupils were associated with the variables school size, elite or non-elite composition and presence and absence of specialist school counsellors and that, if this were so, the same kind of processing would occur in schools showing the same constellation of variables. As noted in Chapter 4, Section 4.6, this is the kind of generalization which makes an attempt to specify the circumstance under which it is claimed to be true.

Frequencies of occurrence are not important here. Lakeside might be the only school of its type in America, but it would be interesting nonetheless. And there might be no real schools in some of the other categories. That would make it impossible to study examples of the type, but they would still be theoretically interesting categories. Particle physics, for example, largely proceeds by generating theoretical frameworks which logically predict the existence of particles, and then trying to see whether they actually exist or not.

Sociological researchers often have limited choice over where and when they can do research, or do not develop a theoretical framework until long after the research is under way. In both these circumstances researchers do not use a theoretical sampling frame to select an example of a theoretical category to study; instead they decide where it is in such a framework that what they are already studying actually fits. In terms of conducting natural experiments (Chapter 7) researchers often do not start by asking 'where can I find the right naturally occurring constellation of variables for my experiment?' but by asking 'what constellation of variables is there here, and what natural experiment could I do with them?'

12.6   Structuring observation and grounding theory

Figure 12.1 includes the term 'relevant' several times. But qualitative researchers often begin research with the very broad question: 'What of interest is going on here?' As the research proceeds, and as they hit on something interesting, they ask more specific questions. This is somewhat grandly described as **progressive focusing**, though often it is a rather desperate attempt to reduce the complexity of what is observable to something which is manageable. In this process the definition of 'relevant data' shifts throughout the research study, so that selection decisions made early may turn out to have been the wrong ones with regard to what was relevant at the end. A common response to this problem is to do 'vacuum cleaner' observation at the beginning in the hope of sucking up anything that might turn out to be relevant later. It is an old joke among ethnographers that one thing which is reliable is that 90% of the data collected will turn out to be useless, but that you never know which 90% until the end of the research.

The justification for starting research with a vague question again invokes the idea of ecological validity (see Section 12.1). The notion is that, to achieve ecological validity, it is necessary first to find out what things are like, and then to develop a theoretical framework to explain that – **grounding theory in data** – rather than assuming what things are like in advance and forcing observations to fit these preconceptions. It is, of course, impossible to begin research with *no* preconceptions, but there is still a persuasive argument that sometimes it is useful to start research with a more, rather than a less, open mind.

But at some stage in the research, researchers have to structure their observations to focus on what has emerged as relevant to the more specific questions driving their research. There are three closely linked reasons for this.

The first is that observations have to be observations of *something*, and the something they are treated as observations of derives from a framework of ideas developed by the researcher. Thus it is necessary for researchers to develop clear criterial rules for what counts as an observation of this, and what of that. These are the same kind of 'coding' decisions dealt with in

Chapter 11. Thus what counts as an instance of a teacher ignoring a pupil, or what counts as an instance of a male behaving in a patriarchal way?

Second, this is a way to control for the effects of the *observer's observation behaviour*. Any text on the psychology of perception details (1) how attention is *selective* – people see only some of what there is to see; (2) how perception is *constructive* – people tend to see what they expect to see; and (3) how memory is *reconstructive* (see Chapter 8, Panel 8.1). People re-organize their memories in the light of subsequent happenings. This is the psychology lying behind the experimenter expectancy effects, discussed in Chapter 3. The potential for observer expectancy effects in naturalistic observation research is much greater than the equivalent in experimental research (Sadler 1981). Structuring the way observations are made can control for these to some extent. Again the problems are more acute where field notes are the medium of recording and coding decisions have to be made on the spot, rather than on an audio or video record where the same record can be analysed again and again in different ways (see also Panel 12.1), and where others can be involved in checking the criterial rules for classifying instances (Chapter 2, Section 2.10).

Third, adopting a structure for observation is the only way to test out the *theories* being developed by the researcher in this kind of research.

Theoretical sampling and constant comparison in a hospital study

As an example of observation structured for theory testing purposes, consider Anne Other's ethnographic study of hygiene procedures in a district general hospital (1999). This is an extremely important topic given the prevalence of hospital-acquired infections (ONS 2007). Her initial impression was that the lower the status of the staff the more assiduously they followed the laid-down hygiene procedures, such as wearing gloves for patient contact, changing gloves in between patients or, alternatively, scrubbing up in between patients. Conversely, it seemed to her that the higher the status of the staff the less likely they were to do this. This was in contradistinction to the results of a recent test of knowledge administered by the infection control staff of the hospital studied. This showed that the higher the status of the staff, the better their understanding of cross-infection. It seemed that those who knew most did least and those who knew least did most in the way of preventing cross-infection.

Initially this was just an impression, and one which was gained from observing situations in which there were many other variables at play, such as the busyness of the ward, the topicality of cross-infection as a problem, the recency of training events, wards running out of gloves (which was common), the composition of bedside congregations of staff, open multiple-bed wards and single-bed side wards and so on.

In these terms any observation of staff hygiene behaviour was a type in a very complex theoretical sampling frame (see Section 12.5), such that, for instance, what was observed with regard to health care assistants on the open wards under the observation of senior nurses might not be true of the behaviour of health care assistants working alone in single-bed side wards. Or what was true of day-shift behaviour might not be true of night-shift behaviour. Thinking of the many variables which might influence hygiene behaviour gave Other a structure for her observations. She wanted observations to cover all of the diverse factors which might have been relevant, either to modify her theory, or to 'eliminate them from her enquiries'. The framework also indicated what had to be recorded in addition to the hygiene behaviour: personnel, place, time, audience and so on and whether the member of staff made physical contact with a patient or a patient's belongings. Most of the required observations cropped up without her having to go out of her way to look for them, though for some, such as nightshift observations and those in intensive care she had to make special arrangements. Over a 3-month period she accumulated over 5,000 observations representing most of the important constellations of factors. This wasn't a statistically representative sample but the large number of observations made it possible to make frequency statements with some confidence. She wasn't claiming that all senior staff were negligent, merely that they were *more likely* to be negligent than junior staff. But for this kind of statement a large sample size is still necessary.

Only up to a point did her observations substantiate her initial impression. She did not find that senior staff were *less* likely than junior staff to follow hygiene procedures; merely that as a group there were no more likely to do so. This illustrates a tendency for people's impressions to mistake what is interesting for what most often happens:

> had I not attempted to produce quantitative data I might well have allowed my initial impressions to influence my later observations, noticing examples which supported them, and ignoring examples which did not.
>
> (Other 1999: 4)

Other also found that while some senior and some junior staff were lax, others were punctilious, so that her generalizations would not apply to whole categories of staff. The generalization would not hold in the intensive care wards where everyone was careful to abide by hygiene protocols. Something which appeared to affect the hygiene behaviour of all staff was having an audience of other staff. All kinds of staff were less likely to follow the rules when no other staff seemed to be around to observe them. For these observations Other had to adopt strategies to avoid being seen to be observing. As she says:

> A reasonable case can be made that I under-recorded such instances, since in order to make observations of behaviour un-observed by staff, I, as a member of staff, had to be around observing!
>
> (Other 1999: 5)

Again, senior nursing staff sometimes made a great show of following hygiene procedures. This was either where a consultant was present, who nonetheless might not wash his hands between patients, or as part of a dressing-down of a junior member of staff for not following the procedures, or as part of inducting new staff or students.

The structuring of observations in this way gave Other's theory abundant opportunities to be falsified. This forced her to move from the claim that senior staff were less likely to follow hygiene procedures to the claim that they were no more likely than junior staff to do so. Had she not structured her observations in that way, her findings would have been vulnerable to the suggestions that what she observed could be put down to, say, the over-busy state of the ward at the time of the observation. Given the 'audience effect', staff were actually less likely to follow hygiene procedures when the ward was less busy. Or her findings might have been vulnerable to the suggestion that she observed only particularly punctilious juniors and particularly negligent seniors. But her observations included virtually every member of staff on the shifts she observed. She herself draws attention to the dangers of being biased:

> towards findings which show the great and the good as no better than they should be, and towards those which show inferiors as misunderstood and put-upon (Becker 1967).
>
> (Other 1999: 15)

This is a particularly strong bias within sociology with its tradition of favouring 'underdogs' and drawing attention to social inequities (Hammersley 2000b). Hence Other felt it was particularly necessary to counteract the possibility of a personal bias of this kind.

The theory Other was testing was a low-level one without much explanatory power: a theory about what was actually happening. She found a partial explanation in listening to the senior nurses talk. From this, it became evident that they believed that cross-infection was brought into the hospital by outsiders; patients, relatives and agency staff, and spread by the poor hygiene practices of junior staff. In this respect their ideas matched a folk model, common world-wide, attributing pollution, infection and other troubles to 'dirty' 'immoral' low-status outsiders such as immigrants, or travelling people (Douglas 1966). On this Other remarks:

> it seemed important to make special efforts to substantiate the claim across a wide range of circumstances in the face of the possibility that Mary Douglas' ideas about pollution, which seemed so seductively appropriate, were distorting the way in which I observed what was going on.
>
> (Other 1999: 17)

Other's account remains unpublished (see Chapter 16: Section 16.8), but something rather similar was found by later by Jenner and her colleagues (2006). Like Other they found that there was little relationship between knowledge of the risks and of the procedures to reduce them, and the practising of those procedures. They also found that staff descriptions of their own behaviour did not tally with what they were observed to do, even when they knew they had been observed: another example of it being unwise to rely on people's own descriptions of their behaviour.

The example of Other's study illustrates much of what is referred to as the development of **grounded theory**. The theory, such as it is, is rooted in the data. The observation is structured by a theoretical sampling frame, which allows for a process of constant comparison. This involves the comparison of what happens under one set of circumstances with what happens under another set of circumstances different in only one regard: akin to imposing statistical control (Chapter 7, Section 7.2). This allows inferences to be drawn as to what are the consequences of the differentiating factor. For example, when everything else is the same what difference does being knowingly observed make as compared with not knowingly being observed? Note that the theoretical sampling frame, and hence the programme for constant comparison, may emerge over the life-time of the research.

Other's research does not represent the final stage of a grounded theory approach, which is taking the theory and applying it to what happens in another location, and perhaps in another kind of setting entirely. The study which gave rise to the idea of grounded theory was by Glaser and Strauss (1964). It was about how people behaved when they were uncertain as to whether their doctors considered them to be in a terminal state. The same ideas have been transferred fairly successfully to research in other hospitals, and also to other situations such as students in a state of uncertainty as to whether they have passed or failed their examinations, or parents uncertain as to whether their newborn child is handicapped or not. This last stage of 'grounded theory' is precisely the opposite of 'discovering the theory in the data', since it entails taking a theory developed to explain data from one set of circumstances and applying its ideas to another. But that is how theories with a general application are developed.

Grounded theory and grounded theory

These remarks indicate that discovering theory in the data is not the only legitimate approach in qualitative research. Good arguments can be made for entering the field with a theory which is already well developed and testing it against the findings. What is important is to adopt a strategy which gives the theory the best possible chances of being disproved. Much social psychological research proceeds in this way.

As Lyn and Tom Richards remark, the term grounded theory is 'widely adopted as an approving bumper sticker in qualitative studies' (cited in Bryman and Burgess 1994: 6). There are many studies based on naturalistic observation which include no attempts to test ideas rigorously by looking assiduously for data which would falsify the ideas and consist instead of researchers having ideas and then cherry picking the data to find good examples to illustrate these. Many such studies claim to be exercises in grounded theory, but they aren't (Bryman and Burgess 1994: 4–6).

A distinction should be made between 'grounded theory' as a general approach, and the proprietary brand associated with Strauss and Corbin (1998). This, in addition to being a method of theoretical sampling and constant comparison within the case (as described above) is a highly prescriptive approach to data analysis and to recording the process of research through various kinds of 'memos'. In my experience many student researchers get lost in the detail prescribed. Glaser and Strauss came to disagree radically as to the proper practice of grounded theory (Glaser 1992, 1998). Glaser's version is far less prescriptive, allows for both quantitative and qualitative data and the testing of theories derived from other contexts and is closer to the description given above.

12.7 Accountability and reflexivity

The accountability of research by naturalistic observation can be very high where researchers use electronic records, which can be made available in part or in total to readers and where the claims made are restricted to what the readers can see is in the data. Ethnomethodological studies often achieve this level of accountability. These studies are replicable to the extent that readers can subject the same data to their own analysis. By contrast, the accountability of participant observation research conducted over a long period of time, where the medium of recording is field notes, is very low, because the reader has to rely on the researcher both to describe what was found and to describe everything that was going on from which someone else might have collected different data and of which they might have made a different kind of sense. Such research is, of course, unreplicable. However, researchers can make themselves more accountable by being explicit about their observation strategy and their coding rules, answering readers' questions such as 'where and when was she in order to observe that?' and 'how often?' and 'by what criteria did he recognize this as an instance of that?'. Strauss and Corbin (1998) suggest a system of writing different kinds of 'memos' as a way of recording the process of the research, in addition to field notes. This, in addition clarifying the researcher's thoughts at each stage, will provide a basis for writing up an account of how the research was done. Most ethnographic researchers keep a research diary or research log for this purpose.

The term **reflexivity** is used in a wide variety of ways. Its basic meaning in research is that researchers adopt a third-party viewpoint on their own research activities: they treat themselves, as it were, as research subjects in their own research. In that sense, my analysis of my own performance as George's interviewer in Chapter 11 (Section 11.4) is a reflexive account.

Often, however, reflexivity takes the form of extended philosophical discussions in the field of epistemology – about how anyone can know anything about anything – or in the field of ethics – about the moral implications of doing research in general and this research in particular (see Chapter 16). And sometimes reflexivity is interpreted as the need to tell 'the inside story' of the research, its thrills and spills, sometimes extending to telling how the author became a researcher, or what it is like to be a female researcher, how it felt to do the research and so on. These accounts can make interesting reading. But there is an issue here as to whether they put the reader in a better position to evaluate the research. Such accounts are often based on field diaries or other kinds of records made about the process of the research at the time at which it was conducted, but as Bryman and Burgess say:

It is important to remember that it is *post hoc* reflections which are provided, with the result that projects are tidied up by their authors before being presented to a wider public. (1994: 8) (see also Chapter 13, Section 13.6)

Researchers making themselves accountable to readers are also researchers making themselves accountable to themselves. The field research I did in Kenya in the late 1960s was done through unstructured observation research. In the year 2007 I have my yellowing field notes. I have the publications (for example, Gomm 1975) and I have my memories. What I do not have is access to the situation from which I drew the data. For many of the questions posed by Figure 12.1 as to how selections were made I do not have satisfactory answers. Thus I find it difficult to have any great confidence in my account of spirit possession on the South Kenya coast. And if I don't have any great confidence in it, why should anyone else?

ACTIVITY   Observing and disrupting turn-taking

This is an activity which can be done in an hour or so, or longer if it interests you. It starts from the comments by Sacks, Schegloff and Jefferson (1972) in Chapter 11, that turn-taking is a basic constituent of a wide range of forms of social organization, from traffic at roundabouts, to lunch queues, to deciding who should go first through a door. There are many situations in life where, momentarily at least, it is an important organizational consideration as to whose turn it is – because someone has to take the turn, or if no one does, something has to be done about this – and where it is an important moral consideration – because people will have ideas as to who has the right or obligation to take the turn. Because turn-taking is a moral matter, whenever turns are being taken people are vulnerable to be evaluated as being particular kinds of personality – 'pushy', 'reticent', 'polite' and so on.

1 Observation

Find a situation in which turn-taking is implicated: for example, turn-taking by precedence order in a queue, goes in a game, sorting out who goes first through a crowded doorway, who gets served first in the restaurant. Observe how people offer each other turns, take turns when offered, how people otherwise know when it is their turn, how long people wait without complaint for another to take a turn, how they grab turns, complain that someone has taken their turn and such like. You will be observing the minutiae of social organization as social organization is done. Against this background observe how people come across as being particular kinds of personalities according to expectations about how people should behave in this kind of turn-taking situation. People are realized as the characters they appear to be in terms of how things are being organized.

2 Breaching experiment

For this, you need to be braver. Garfinkel (1967) developed a strategy for studying what usually happens by disrupting it and seeing how people try to put it together again – so-called disruption or breaching experiments. The best-known is the lodger experiment. Students were asked to behave in their own homes as if they were a guest or a lodger, for example asking permission to have a glass of water, or asking questions to which, as a family member, they would be considered to know the answer. In behaving like this they threw into stark relief unstated and unnoticed expectations about how family members should behave. A common way in which families restored the disrupted social order was by invoking the idea of mental illness, such that there was again a 'normal family' but one with a mentally ill member.

For your breaching experiment try disrupting a turn-taking situation. Don't take a turn when it is obviously your turn. Offer no explanation for this. Record what happens. What does this tell you about the way the local social organization is put together? How does this cast you as being a particular kind of character? If nothing seems to happen, consider why it does not and the conditions necessary under which not taking a turn would have observable consequences.

Before you do this, consider carefully where you are going to do it. The lodger experiment sometimes provoked violent reactions.

Further reading

On doing ethnographic research in sociology see Hammersley and Atkinson (2007) or Silverman (2004a). Atkinson *et al.* (2007) provides a wide variety of approaches to ethnography (classic and new) in a wide variety of settings. Hughes and Sharrock (2009) is a four-volume set of new and classic studies produced through participant observation. Hammersley (1998) provides a readers' guide to ethnographic research and Hammersley (1992) a discussion of the problems of the genre. Miles and Huberman (1994) is a handbook containing a wide range of techniques for analysing qualitative data, and see also the *Further reading* for Chapter 11. Emerson *et al.* (1995) is a thorough treatment of ethnographic fieldnotes and there is a good chapter on this in Bernard (2005), which also includes advice on other aspects of ethnographic research in anthropology.

Strauss and Corbin (1998) is a guide to doing grounded theory their way. An on-line description of their approach is given by www.scu.edu.au/ schools/gcm/ar/arp/grounded.html. Glaser's version is supported by its own research institute (www.groundedtheory.com/) and publishing house: the *Sociology Press*.

Many of the data observed under naturally occurring circumstances are speech data, so books on this listed at the end of Chapter 11 are equally good as guides to analysing talk in naturally occurring situations.

Ethnographic research is a very literary enterprise. To a great extent its credibility rests on the ability of the researcher to tell a good story. Atkinson (1990) examines the literary devices used by ethnographers to present convincing pictures of real scenes and real people and real research going on. This point is picked up again in Chapter 13.

13 Analysing Written Documents

By the end of this chapter, you will:

- Know more about the differences between data which are produced by speaking and data which are produced by writing
- Know enough to be able to conduct a simple content analysis
- Be able to analyse a text by interrogative insertion
- Be able to conduct a simple version of analysis by membership categorization
- Be able to conduct the analysis of a problem–solution discourse
- Understand what is meant by rhetorical analysis and be sensitive to the ways in which writing constructs an impression of the author
- Know the difficulties of using written documents as sources of evidence about what is referred to in the writing.

And you will know the meaning of the following terms:

Category bound activity (CBA) • content analysis • discourse analysis • interrogative insertion • membership categorization device (MCD) and membership category (MC) • narrative analysis • problem–solution discourse • rhetoric • standardized relational pairs (SRPs) • textual interaction • triangulation • trope.

At the end of the chapter there is an Activity which will test your understanding of deconstruction and reconstruction of written text.

13.1 Introduction

Very similar techniques can be used for analysing both speech (Chapter 11) and written materials. But in applying them it is important to bear in mind the way the original data were produced. For example, in his interview (Chapter 11, Section 11.4), George told a series of stories or narratives. But these were told through the medium of a two-party, face to face, exchange where the performance of the interviewer was important in shaping what George said. Had George written his life story instead, he would have written it with some kind of audience in mind. But otherwise, the audience would not have had an opportunity to shape the writing.

Again, speech is usually produced with each utterance building on the last, in an open-ended and emergent way. At the beginning, speakers do not know what will be said at the end. But in writing, authors can usually change the beginning to be consistent with the end. And again, speech erodes away as it is spoken. Speakers have to rely on their imperfect memories (Chapter 8, Panel 8.1) of what has been said in order to make what they say next relate to what was said previously. With text, writers can read back, and so can readers.

It is not surprising, then, that sequences of speech are usually marked by inconsistency, incompleteness and incoherence. Most of this is noticed only if the speech is recorded and transcribed, and our impressions of incoherence come mainly from *reading* later what was produced as speech, rather than *hearing* it as it was produced. The sequential analysis of the interview with George showed that whatever he said could be made out as consistent with whatever was going on at the moment immediately before and as he said it (Chapter 11, Section 11.4). It would be wrong, therefore, to regard inconsistencies in George's speech as evidence of his inconsistent mind or of the incoherence of his self-image.

By contrast, in writing, authors do have an opportunity to impose a beginning-to-end consistency on the text and to compose the text as an artful display of the kind of person they want readers to think they are, and or as a persuasive version of the truth. Many documents go through several drafts, involving several people, with distinct stages of composition, editing, styling and printing. Some are written into a template or according to a given pattern.

The important distinction, then, is not between speech and writing but between communications produced in different ways for different purposes. Telephone text messages are more like spoken conversation than book writing, and a spoken lecture can be more like a chapter in a text book than a conversation. Broadcast speech is often 'de-ummed' with the hesitancies edited out. Interviewers' questions may be dropped in later, and interviewees' nods and grunts replaced from a series of 'Yeses' and 'Nos' recorded before or after the interview. The whole interview may be introduced by a 'reverse': an introduction composed after the interview. Thus broadcast speech can be more like written text (Heritage 1985). In transcribing interviews researchers often clean them up, making them read more like text than speech, thereby risking misrepresentation by detaching the data from the context in which they were produced (Chapter 11, Section 11.5).

This chapter will centre on written documents which have been produced in a way that allows authors to revise them before releasing them to readers. From time to time I will refer to these as *texts*. I prefer to restrict this term to written materials, but some authors use it to include speech, pictures, films and anything which has been composed to convey a meaning, or even anything which can be interpreted as meaningful, however it was composed. For example, Fiske (1993) refers to, and analyses a holiday beach as, a 'text'.

The chapter deals with the use of documents as sources of evidence about events (Section 13.7), with content analysis, analysis by interrogative insertion, membership categorization analysis (MCA), problem–solution discourses and rhetorical analysis. But beware: there are no fixed meanings for some of these terms. You will find other authors using the same terms in different ways, and yet others giving different titles to the same kinds of analysis. There is no chapter in this book on the analysis of visual images, but some of what is said about text in this chapter will be relevant (see also *Further reading* at the end of this chapter).

The term 'discourse'

The term **discourse analysis** is sometimes used to refer to the analysis of speech or texts or broadcasts. But it can refer to radically different enterprises (Hammersley 2008: Chapter 6). There are three main possibilities:

- Discourses are assumed to have an *existence independent of individuals and of their speech and writing*. Thus a piece of writing is treated as a manifestation of a more general way of thinking, understanding or doing things: as an aspect of culture. Here the term 'discourse' has replaced the more traditional term 'ideology'. Today writers tend to write of 'patriarchal discourses' rather than of 'patriarchal ideologies'. Much of such writing goes under the title of critical discourse analysis (Wodak and Meyer 2001), where the assumption is usually that the ideas and practices constituting the discourse favour the powerful and mislead the powerless.
- Discourses are seen as *evidence of ways individuals or groups interpret the world*. They are manifested, patchily, in particular pieces of speech or writing but have an existence independent of them. Here the term 'discourse' has been added to the already over-loaded set of synonyms, including, 'perspective', 'world-view', 'interpretive scheme' and such like. Speech and writing are here studied mainly in an attempt to gain insight into the minds of speakers and writers (for example, Riessman 2008).
- Discourses are the *words and the way they are arranged*. The interest here is in how particular kinds of communication are put together, how these formats convey the meanings they convey, and the uses to which such communications are put. This is the meaning for conversation analysis (CA) and pragmatic linguistics (Chapter 11) and for some other approaches dealt with in this chapter (see Sections 13.3–13.6).

Similarly, the term **narrative analysis** is used for a wide range of approaches to speech or writing which has plots and characters (narratives), but again falling roughly into the three kinds of approach suggested above.

13.2   Content analysis

Indexing a book is a kind of content analysis. Though the name dates back to the 1960s the technique has a long history in biblical scholarship in the Jewish and Christian traditions, cross-referencing various parts of the bible in order to discern its hidden meanings, and especially in the scrutiny of other texts with a view to censoring them for heresy (Krippendorff 2004).

Today, content analysis refers first and foremost to the quantitative analysis of documents or broadcast media – something gets counted. But the same approach is adopted by qualitative researchers using what I called 'thematic analysis' in Chapter 11, Section 11.3. And most quantitative content analysis begins with a qualitative analysis of the data to discover what they might contain which could be counted.

Representativeness

Usually a content analyst wants to make some claims about the representativeness of the data entered into the analysis (Chapter 6, Section 6.1). If the interest is in producers and the products, this is fairly straightforward. For example, in a study of the way newspapers present stories about HIV/AIDS, the analysis might be conducted on all HIV/AIDS stories in a sample of all national newspapers, selected by systematically sampling the dates in January and February in a particular year, with a sampling interval of 8 (see Chapter 6, Panel 6.1). That would result in 7 days' worth of newspapers, each batch on a different day of the week. And it would be a 'blind' sample preventing the analyst from cherry picking newspapers for particularly juicy, but possibly unrepresentative, stories. Such a sample would probably be representative only of the time period from which it was drawn. If the interest was in changes in the newspaper presentation of HIV/AIDS, then it would be necessary to sample from a much longer time period.

But it may be that the analyst is most interested in the influence of these stories on those who read them. In that case, logically, more widely read stories, in more widely read newspapers should feature in the analysis more than little-read stories in minority newspapers. Published readership figures could be used to weight a sample in favour of those papers with the bigger readership, or papers with readerships below a certain level could be excluded. Data on readership numbers is continually produced from research by JICREG (www.jicreg.co.uk/data/index.cfm). For example, in her study of images of women in women's magazines Majorie Ferguson (1983) restricted her content analysis largely to *Woman*, *Woman's Own* and *Woman's Weekly*: the three largest-selling women's magazines in the period. Actually, more women read other women's magazines, though each of these had lower sales, and Ferguson's study does include content analysis of less well-read journals. But these figures are not a particularly good basis for selecting a sample to represent articles and stories proportional to the numbers of people reading them, because they don't tell us who actually read the publications they purchased, or what they read in them. Most people only read a tiny proportion of their newspapers, but different tiny portions each.

Content frames and coding

Panel 13.1 gives an example of a content analysis framework. A 'content frame' is essentially a questionnaire which is filled in by the analyst. The general question asked by this frame is 'What's in the stories about innocence and guilt?' For each column there is a more specific question to answer. This is only one of many themes which might be examined in analysing the same news stories. The frame is filled in for two examples.

Reliability and validity

Reliability is an important consideration. Would other people concur on the way the analyst used the content frame and coded the examples? For this, inter-rater reliability checks (Chapter 2, Section 2.10) should be conducted for at least a sample of the news stories. This might go some way towards showing whether or not the analyst had been consistent herself (intra-rater reliability).

In classifying and coding stories there are particular difficulties in knowing how far to go in 'reading between the lines' and coding for what seems to be implied rather than what is explicitly said: a problem of *construct validity*

PANEL 13.1   Content analysis frame for preliminary analysis of newspaper stories on HIV/AIDS

(Code NI ('not indicated') where the story features HIV/AIDS but contains no information for any columns.)

Characters	Who gets HIV/AIDS	Who's at risk?	Why/ How?	Who's in the right?	Who's in the wrong?	NI

Coded example 1

THE SADDEST little girl in the world sat alone with her Cabbage Patch doll yesterday because her friends won't play with her. Pretty four year old [. . .] is a victim of AIDS. The tragic tot, believed to have caught the disease from her drug-taking mother, is banned from school, shunned by friends and victimized by ignorance.

Characters	Who gets HIV/AIDS	Who's at risk?	Why/ How?	Who's in the right?	Who's in the wrong?	NI
Child	X		Drug-taking parent	Innocent child		
Parent	X				Drug-taking parent	
Friends of child		?				
Parents of friends, school authorities					'Ignorant public'	

Source: *Daily Express* (3 June 1985).

Coded example 2

CHARLES GIVES BLOOD TO STEM AIDS SCARE

PRINCE CHARLES gave a pint of blood yesterday to try to stop a panic over the killer disease AIDS. The number of donors has fallen dramatically as fears of catching the gay plague have spread . . . So the Prince made a surprise visit to a blood donor centre to prove there is no danger . . . Afterwards staff joked about the Royal pint, saying 'Look it's not blue' . . . Prince Charles's blood, which was anonymously bottled, was then added to other pints given by ordinary people.

Characters	Who gets HIV/AIDS	Who's at risk?	Why/ How?	Who's in the right?	Who's in the wrong?	NI
Homo-sexuals	X		Homo-sexuality		X	
Prince Charles				X (celebrity)		
Health care Staff				X		
Blood donors					'Ignorant public'	

Source: *Daily Express* (2 March 1985).

The examples have been coded. If the analysis is done manually, then the next stage would be to draw up an index, so that all the examples, say, featuring children as innocent victims would be listed together; all those featuring celebrities listed together and within that category, all those featuring celebrities as victims would be distinguished from celebrities featured in other ways. Celebrity children would, of course, need their own index label. All this is much easier done electronically where the codes are field codes in a database, and indexing is thereby automated. Then the computer can print out a list of all the examples for any mixture of codes.

Coding is crucial (Fielding 2001) but is usually an awkward and tedious process because when the codes are most useful is while the analysis is in progress, but only when the analysis is complete is the analyst is in a good position to decide on an appropriate set of codes. The example here suggests two different sub-themes within the theme, one about who contracts HIV and one about public attitudes to HIV. If the analyst wants to separate these out, maybe a different coding scheme would be more appropriate.

(see Chapter 2, Section 2.4). For example, does the Prince Charles story actually blame homosexuals for contracting HIV? This becomes even more difficult where pictures are involved, and even more so with television and film, where camera angles and soundtrack music can contribute to the message (Wollen 1998; Fiske and Hartley 2003).

Moving from the examples to the entries in the content frame loses information or *degrades* or *reduces the data*. Unlike the situation where someone takes notes as an observer, nothing is actually lost (Chapter 12, Section 12.1). The news stories are still there and can be looked at again. But much of the detail drops out of the analysis. For example, the way in which an 'innocent child victim' is characterized as 'a tragic tot', 'pretty' and playing with a Cabbage Patch doll, is likely to disappear when this example is combined with other examples of innocent child victims. But some data degradation is necessary if generalizations are to be made about large numbers of news stories. This is particularly so if the data are going to be translated into numbers.

The results of quantitative content analysis

Table 13.1 gives an example of what part of a numerical display of the results of this content analysis would look like.

Quantifying the results of content analysis raises some issues. First there are problems of classification. Is everything which is counted as being the same, really the same? When a result is quoted as a total of, say, 36 instances, readers may have no way of knowing whether they themselves would count all 36 as being sufficiently similar to be added together. These are issues of *reliability* and *construct validity* again.

Second, there is an issue about units of analysis. In Table 13.1, the basic unit is the news story. But dividing one news story from another is not always easy. Some sections of newspapers consist of a single headline, followed by a number of different, unrelated or only loosely related stories. Here if there are two paragraphs referring to HIV, is this one story or two? Again, sometimes the same story appears in different forms in the same newspaper. The 12 April 2002 edition of the *Sun*, featuring a foot injury to a footballer called David Beckham, might have been counted as having between 10 and 17 'Beckham' stories, or one Beckham story spread over 7 pages. Sometimes the unit used is column-centimetres. This does mean that long stories count for more than short ones, and that stories in big type (presumably regarded as more important) count more than stories in small type. But in this analysis of HIV stories, using column-centimetres as a measure would cause some problems, if attempts were made to count the number of centimetres devoted to a 'theme'. In the 'tragic tot' story, is the whole story to be counted as an example of a child being infected by a parent, or only the eleven words explicitly stating this?

Third, there are decisions to be made about how to combine data and compose '100 per cents'. In Table 13.1, stories which feature both children infected with HIV and spouses/partners infected with HIV will count twice. Longer and more complex stories will contribute more to the overall analysis than shorter and simpler ones, and columns will add up to more than 100%. If newspapers of different kinds are combined in the analysis then, just because they are bigger, the bigger newspapers are likely to contribute more to the results than smaller ones, unless each newspaper is tallied separately. If the interest is in the percentage of all stories of whatever kind constituted by stories about HIV/AIDS there is also some difficulty of deciding what is 100% of all stories, whatever their topic. Often this is done by

TABLE 13.1   *Table for presenting some results of a quantitative analysis of news stories about HIV/AIDS*

Themes	No. of stories of HIV/AIDS with theme	Stories with theme as percentage of all stories featuring HIV/AIDS	Stories with theme as percentage of all stories, all topics
Children infected by parents/carers/older siblings			
(1) Parents'/carers'/older siblings' sexual behaviour implicated			
(2) Parents'/carers'/older siblings' drug-taking behaviour implicated			
(3) Both of parents'/carers'/older siblings' sexual and drug-taking behaviour implicated			
(4) **Total**			
(5) Children infected as victims of blood transfusion service			
(6) Children infected as victims of rape (not by parents/carers/older siblings)			
(7) Children infected 'innocently' by other means			
(8) **Total children infected as 'innocent victims'**			
(9) Children infected from own drug-taking behaviour			
(10) Children infected from own sexual behaviour			
(11) **Total children as victims by infection**			
(12) Children victimized by HIV/AIDS infection of another: for example, orphaned.			
(13) **Total children in adversity because of HIV/AIDS**			
Spouses/partners infected by spouses/partners			
(14) Implicating spouse/partner's sexual activity			
(15) Implicating spouse/partner's drug-taking activity			
(16) Spouse as victim of blood transfusion service			

estimating the number of words/column inches in a typical edition of a news-paper, then counting the number of words/measuring the column inches in the stories of interest, and expressing the latter as a percentage of the former. But again, combining different newspapers for this purpose could be mislead-ing. The problems here are similar to those associated with handling the responses of open-ended questions in questionnaires (Chapter 10, Section 10.4).

Effects on readers

These considerations, however, become rather trivial if what is of interest is not what is in the newspaper for the analyst to discover, but what is in the newspapers which influences newspaper readers. Newspaper readers do not read by conducting content analyses. There is no basis for assuming *a priori* that what the analyst finds in the stories is what the readers will find there and what will influence their thinking. But a very large number of content analyses of mass media products assume just this.

To study the influence of any kind of media on audiences it is necessary to add to content analysis other kinds of investigations where representatives of the audience are the research subjects. These can include experimental stud-ies, questionnaire research, face to face interviews, focus groups, observation studies, or asking people to author news stories themselves and comparing these with those that appear in the papers (Gunter 1999).

This kind of research usually raises an issue about **direction of effect** (see also Chapter 8). For example, do newspaper readers learn to see the world in the way described to them by newspapers, or do journalists describe the world in a way they know their readers will believe, or both – and, if so, which is the stronger influence?

Experimental approaches are usually the best way to settle questions about direction of effect, but only about direction of effect under experimental circumstances (Chapter 3, Section 3.10). There is a strong tradition of exper-imental research on topics such as whether media exposure to violence leads to violent behaviour. But the experimental conditions adopted are so unlike real-life circumstances that the results may not have much bearing on life outside the lab. Natural experiments (Chapter 5) are common in media research, dividing people into comparison groups such that one group has had first-hand, direct experience of the issue of interest plus information provided by the media, while the other gets its knowledge only from media sources (for example, Hartman and Husband 1981; Philo 1990; Philo *et al.* 1994). Comparing the knowledge, attitudes, beliefs and opinions of the two groups gives an estimate of the influence of the media net of direct experi-ence. This approach might explain otherwise curious findings such as that in NHS consumer satisfaction research – that the people who express most dissatisfaction are the people who have had least recent contact with the NHS (Bosanquet and Zarzecka 1995). This might be explained in terms of an unre-lentingly negative picture of the NHS given by the mass media, unmodified by direct experience for those who express most dissatisfaction. But there is still a direction of effect problem here. Perhaps the people who express most dissatisfaction are those who, uninfluenced by the media, avoid visiting doctors or who use private health care facilities.

At first sight, HIV/AIDS might seem to provide the ideal conditions for a natural experiment on media influence. In the 1980s, from when the examples above were drawn, hardly anyone had any direct experience of HIV/AIDS and the media were the main source of most people's knowledge. Thus it might be argued (as by Vass 1986) that what people thought about HIV/AIDS must have been put in their minds by the mass media. But the way the mass media handled such stories at the time was in terms of very traditional formats used for hundreds of years for telling about epidemic diseases (Herzlich and Pierret 1985) and about crime and other undesirable phenomena. These formats divide people into innocent victims and those afflicted because of their own moral shortcomings. They associated disease with immorality, and sourced disease or crime from strangers within the country, or from foreigners outside, much as Other found among senior nurses with regard to hospital-acquired infections (Chapter 12, Section 12.6). There is an argument here in favour of saying that the way the popular media handled the topic of HIV/AIDS was strongly influenced by journalistic need to communicate in ways readers would find meaningful.

By itself, the analysis of the content tells us nothing for sure about what is conveyed to readers by a text or to listeners or viewers by a broadcast. Nor does it necessarily tell us about the thoughts in the author's mind, except something about the author's thinking about how to convey something to an audience. For example, many journalists who write for right-wing newspapers write under other names in left-wing minority journals. Many people write documents with styles and contents determined by their employers which they themselves would not otherwise choose. And just whose thoughts, ideas and beliefs does a TV programme express when so many people have been involved in its production?

But what content analysis can do is to show how communications are put together and what the communicative conventions which authors use to produce particular effects are. The examples in this section give a glimpse of one kind of communicative convention – *news angles* (Galtung and Ruge 1981; Hall *et al.* 1978: 51–138) or 'news conventions' which journalists use to judge the newsworthiness of events and to write them into what are distinctively newspaper news stories. Thus celebrities – Prince Charles here – are always good copy. People with problems are nearly always divided into innocent victims on the one hand and those who are to blame for their own misfortunes on the other. And there are no better innocent victims than children, unless they are dogs, cats, or horses. There are many content analyses of news which use news angles as the categories in the content frame (for example, Best, Dennis and Draper 1977; Hall *et al.* 1978; Hartman and Husband 1981; van Dijk 1991).

The advantage of content analysis, as described above, is that it allows for generalizations to be made about large quantities of data. But to do this it is necessary to extract the data from their immediate context. There is a risk then of losing sight of how the stories are put together to convey meanings. The approaches described below are all attempts to analyse how meaning is produced through the forms taken by writing. Since the attention is given to the way the texts are constructed, the analysis is often called *deconstruction*: taking them apart to see how they work.

13.3   Analysis by interrogative insertion

This kind of analysis shows one of the ways in which a written text hangs together coherently. Most written texts are presented as monologues, but interrogative analysis treats the text as a dialogue between the writer – whose words you can see – and an invisible reader, who the writer imagines is asking questions. Few writers actually write this way, except when they write the answers to those FAQs (Frequently Asked Questions) now common on many web sites. But the skilful writer does put questions into the mind of the reader, and then answers the questions the writer wants the reader to ask.

Interrogative insertion goes like this:

1   **Writer:** PRINCE CHARLES gave a pint of blood yesterday.
2   **Reader:** *Why did he do that?*
3   **Writer:** To try to stop a panic over the killer disease AIDS.
4   **Reader:** *How would giving a pint of blood do that?*
5   **Writer:** The number of donors has fallen dramatically as fears of catching the gay plague have spread. So the Prince made a surprise visit to a blood donor centre to prove there is no danger . . .
6   **Reader:** *What was special about it being a member of the royal family giving blood?*
7   **Writer:** Afterwards staff joked about the Royal pint, saying 'Look it's not blue' . . .
8   **Reader:** *Would anyone know they were being transfused with Prince Charles' blood?*
9   **Writer:** [No] Prince Charles's blood which was anonymously bottled was then added to other pints given by ordinary people.

This suggests that this is a story written by someone who thinks readers are more interested in Prince Charles than in HIV. At 7 the writer answers an imagined reader's question (**6**) about Prince Charles's celebrity status, rather than a further imagined question about HIV and public attitudes to it: such as '*Do you think Prince Charles's action will be successful?*' or '*What other measures are being taken to allay fears among blood donors?*'

Interrogative insertion gives an indication of the **recipient design** of a text. That is both how the text was written for a particular readership imagined by the author, and how the text was written to shape the mind of the reader to find each passage in turn appropriate. Recipient design is also a feature of spoken communication. In Chapter 11, Section 11.4 George tried, rather unsuccessfully, to recipiently design his speech for me as the interviewer.

This kind of analysis also shows us why we sometimes find written texts incoherent and disjointed, when we 'can't see what the author is getting at'. This is often when we can't ourselves see what 'reader's question' each passage is answering. *Interrogative insertion* has a practical as well as a research usage. If your writing is disjointed try inserting 'reader's questions'. You will locate the problem where you can't do this, or where the reader's question the text seems to be answering, appears 'out of the blue' and doesn't relate to anything previously.

If writers can lead readers to expect answers to particular questions, then they can also give them expectations that they then thwart in order to make a joke, or say something surprising:

> **Writer**: There's a name for people who won't pay standing charges.
> **Reader**: *And what is this pejorative name?*
> **Writer**: British Gas customers.
>
> (British Gas poster, August 2002)

'There's a name for' sets the reader up to expect an insulting name. The joke, such as it is, comes from violating this expectation by giving a name which isn't insulting (according to British Gas, anyway).

Red-herrings in detective stories are produced by writing in ways that distract the reader from seeing the information given as relevant to answering the overall 'who dun it?' question, or by encouraging readers to see irrelevant information as relevant to this. In many detective stories this is done by putting the 'reader's questions' in the voice of one or many of the characters, which is why so many fictional detectives have rather unintelligent side-kicks.

13.4   Membership category analysis

Consider this newspaper headline:

> MUM'S WARNING TO BEWARE OF DAUGHTER
>
> (*Stevenage Comet*, 20 June 2002)

This is newsworthy because it violates taken-for-granted expectations about the way mothers behave towards their daughters, which *does not* include warning others to beware of them. By 'taken-for-granted' I mean what we assume unless we are told otherwise: a kind of default understanding. The same default understanding might lead us to read this headline as misleadingly phrased; as referring to one mother warning people about *another* mother's daughter, but it does not.

Membership category analysis (MCA) attends to the way in which authors and readers (and speakers and listeners) draw on common ideas about social organization: about what kinds of people there are, about how these kinds of people relate to each other and about the kinds of things which different kinds of people do (Lepper 2000). MCA is an important part of Conversation Analysis (CA) discussed in Chapter 11, Section 11.4. Table 13.2 provides some of the basic ideas of MCA.

The headline suggests some rather odd behaviour for the mother. But in the story below it is consistent with more usual expectations for the behaviour of mums towards daughters. It is about a mother's resistance to her autistic daughter being removed from a special educational unit and placed in mainstream education. Her 'warning' can be paraphrased as:

Beware of my daughter if she is placed in mainstream education. She will be violent towards your children and that won't be good for her either.

Hence the story itself fulfils expectations for SRPs and CBAs where 'Mums' and 'daughters' are categories belonging to the MCD 'family', while the headline does not (Table 13.2).

You have no difficulty in understanding the Prince Charles story given earlier, because you are a highly competent reader of such stories, but how do

Some ideas from MCA TABLE 13.2

Idea	Explanation	'Mum's warning to beware of daughter'
Category	Any person can be labelled in many ways, so readers assume that the way they are labelled is important	'Mum' and 'daughter'[a]
Category modifiers	Finesse the meaning of a category	No examples in this headline, but note *'Saddest little* girl' and *'tragic tot'* in the earlier example
Membership categorization device (MCD)	Categories are (usually) written and read as grouped together in collections (MCDs)	'Mum' and 'daughter' imply the MCD 'family'
Consistency rule	If one member of a collection is identified then, unless there are indications to the contrary, the next person is likely to be a member of the *same* collection	Although the headline does not explicitly say so, we read the daughter as this mum's daughter. We read them as of the same MCD 'family'
Standardized relational pairs (SRPs)	Pairs of categories are linked together in taken-for-granted ways	Our default expectation is that 'mums' will support and defend their daughters Warning others against your own daughter violates this expectation That is why this is newsworthy
Category-bound activity (CBA)	Activities may be read as tied to or 'bound to' certain categories	Warning others against their own daughters is not an activity commonsensically tied to 'mums': not a CBA for mums This is why this is newsworthy

Note: [a] Note how the categorization device 'Mum' raises our expectations for a loving relationship to a greater extent than would the MCD 'Mother'. This heightens the contrast between our default expectations for the CBA and SRP and the actual activity described.

you do it? Let's say that the term 'Prince Charles' allocates someone to the membership category 'celebrities'. Let the opposite MCD be 'ordinaries'. The important thing about celebrities is that they are not ordinary, and when they do ordinary things, they are doing something rather special: the CBAs for celebrities are different from the CBAs for ordinaries. Paradoxically 'an ordinary family Christmas' for the royal family is a most extraordinary ordinary family Christmas. The more like the Christmas of ordinary people it is, the more remarkable it becomes. You know this already and on this basis you know, that when Prince Charles gives a pint of blood, this isn't the same thing as an ordinary person giving a pint of blood. You do not have to be an ardent royalist to do this reading. It doesn't rely on your beliefs and attitudes, but upon public knowledge of categories which are available to those who believe in them and approve of them, and to those who do not.

So the story juxtaposes the social meaning of activities for members of the category 'celebrities' on the one hand and 'ordinaries' on the other. Giving a pint of blood, in order to allay public fears about blood donoring is only a sensible motivation (CBA) for celebrities. To describe this as the motivation of an ordinary would be to describe him as misguided or foolish. Then there are the references to 'blue blood' and the only point of mentioning that Prince Charles's blood was anonymously bottled is that it was celebrity blood.

This may all seem very obvious. But if you were an anthropologist raised in an entirely different culture, you would find the story very difficult to understand until you had cracked the code of MCDs and CBAs. Garfinkel (1967: 9) says the task of sociology is to *render the ordinary anthropologically strange*. This means viewing what is familiar from an alien point of view. MCA is one of the ways of making visible the very important taken-for-granted notions on which the communication of meaning relies. MCA is also a way of understanding how authors do *characterization*. Even when writing purports to be about real people and real-life events, in the text the characters have only the existence granted to them by the writer. It is the writer who provides them with personalities, moods and motives. This point will be picked up in the next section.

13.5 Problem–solution discourses

The anthropologist Gregory Bateson (1972) suggested that most statements have two kinds of implications. They have *report* implications, about how things are, and *command* implications, about what ought to be done about them. This is very like the distinction between locutions and illocutions (Chapter 11, Section 11.4). Consider this advertisement:

> Sensitive teeth?
> Sensodyne
>
> (Toothpaste poster advertisement, August 2002)

Here the 'report' is in a conditional form: '*if you have* sensitive teeth'. And the 'command' is not a command as such but a suggestion: '*why not try* Sensodyne?'.

Components of a complete problem–solution discourse   TABLE 13.3

Components	'Readers' questions	Example: extracts from a student health visitor case study (Gomm 1986)
SITUATION	What was the situation?	'I was visiting a family where the mother was pregnant and had a history of miscarriages' 'There was a two year old child . . .'
PROBLEM	What was the problem?	'The toddler reacted by being 'clingy' and unwilling to let her mother out of her sight' 'Mrs Green was herself rather anxious about this pregnancy and I felt she was conveying this anxiety to the child'
RESPONSE	What was done about the problem?	'I suggested that Mrs Green should make sure that she put some time aside each day to play with Louise, and that it might be a good idea for the play to be about babies to prepare Louise for the forthcoming event'
RESULT AND EVALUATION	What was the result of the response? (Result) and *Was the result benign or adverse?* (Evaluation)	[on a later visit] 'I was pleased to see that Mrs Green and Louise were playing at bathing baby, so I knew my advice about involving her in the birth of a sibling had had some effect'

Michael Hoey (1983) elaborates the same basic idea and suggests that a very large variety of texts can be read as what he calls 'problem–solution discourses' (PSDs). He includes as examples, advertisements, Mr Men books, detective novels, instruction manuals and government reports. For the advertisement above, the first line is the 'problem' and the second the 'solution'. But most PSDs have other components – or, if they do not, their absence is noticeable and gives rise to particular effects.

The first column in Table 13.3 gives the major components of a *full* problem–solution discourse (PSD).

The example is taken from a case study by a student health visitor submitted as part of her assessment towards qualification. These case studies are some 2,000 words long. Each consists of a large number of PSDs intertwining and threaded through the episodes of visiting the families concerned. They are written in a distinctive health-visitorly way. For example, the *situation* is a health visiting situation – a health visitor visiting a pregnant woman. Elsewhere in the case study, the student will have described a very large number of things which health visitors are supposed to take note of as relevant to the practice of health visiting. The *problem* is the kind of problem that health visitors claim the expertise to deal with: anxious mothers, clingy toddlers. And the *response* is the kind of response which is stock-in-trade for health visitors.

Put another way, and recalling Section 13.4, the student describes herself engaged in approved-of, category-bound activities for health visitors. What she describes herself as doing is, she hopes, what her examiners will agree that a health visitor faced with this problem, in this situation, should do. The mother is displayed in terms of an important CBA for pregnant mothers in health visitor lore – being anxious – and a health visiting SRP for mother and child: mothers conveying their anxiety to their children. The child is displayed in terms of another health-visitorly CBA for children – being upset by their prospective displacement by the birth of a sibling. The same situation could have been told very differently by a GP, a double-glazing sales person, a police officer and so on.

As you can see from the second column in Table 13.3, interrogative insertion is part of Hoey's approach (Section 13.3). Hoey argues that readers expect these kinds of questions to be answered, and where they are not they feel a sense of incompleteness. The readers for this particular example are health visitor examiners. It is recipiently designed for them. They will certainly read such case studies to see whether the student has indeed answered all these questions in a health-visitorly way.

The example ends with a positive evaluation: 'I was pleased to see . . .' and 'I knew my advice . . . had had some effect.' Positive evaluations are the usual finishing point of PSDs. For the toothpaste advertisement, the *result* and the positive *evaluation* are provided by a picture of a woman happily eating an ice-cream. In writing, writers can supply their own positive evaluations without requiring a confirmation by another at the time. Compare the health visiting example here, with its written-in positive evaluation, with George's first story in Chapter 11, Section 11.4. There the story fell flat because of the absence of a positive evaluation by the interviewer.

In the student case study, if there had been no evaluation at all then any reader, let alone examiners, would feel that the discourse was incomplete. Recall the news story of Prince Charles (Section 13.3). There was no 'result' or 'evaluation' component to the story and the question of whether his intervention had any effect was left hanging.

Negative evaluations, where they occur in text, are often followed by another PSD which tells of a different response (to the same problem, though perhaps re-conceptualized), the result of the new response and then a positive evaluation. The cause of the negative evaluation is then the 'problem' in the new PSD. For example:

Negative evaluation/(new) problem: 'There was no evidence that Mrs Green accepted my advice.'
Response to new problem: 'So I introduced her to another mother who had had similar problems, who I knew would reinforce my suggestions about play to prepare the toddler for the birth of a sibling.'
Result/Positive evaluation: 'On visiting just before the birth I was pleased to see that Mrs Green and Louise were playing at bathing baby.'

Positive evaluations are not always possible. If the action which did not lead to a positive result was described as taken by the author, or someone with whom the author feels solidarity, then a negative evaluation is likely to be followed by an *account* mitigating the blame for failure – as described in Chapter 11, Section 11.4. In health visitor student case studies, something like the following often appears after a negative evaluation:

> 'There was no evidence that Mrs Green accepted my advice and I realized that I would have to develop my relationship skills further'

In the language of accounts (Chapter 11, pp. 254–6) this is an *acceptance of blame* mitigated with a promise of reformatory action, and scores some brownie points for honest self-appraisal and willingness to learn, which always goes down well with teachers. In the language of PSD it is, of course, a *response* to an unstated but implied *problem*: the problem of inexperience. In her aural examination, a student who wrote the above would likely be asked 'What did you do to improve your relationship skills?' and 'Was it successful?' – completing the written PSD through verbal interaction.

If the action which did not lead to a positive result was taken by someone else, then the negative evaluation, and the whole story, can stand as a complaint that someone has done other than they should have done. For example:

> **Situation/Problem**: THE SADDEST little girl in the world sat alone with her Cabbage Patch doll yesterday . . . Pretty four year old . . . is a victim of AIDS
> **Response/negative evaluation**: The tragic tot, believed to have caught the disease from her drug-taking mother/. . . her friends won't play with her/[she] is banned from school, shunned by friends and victimized by ignorance.

Here the response is the response of friends, their parents and the school authorities. As this shows, the components of a PSD do not necessarily appear neatly distinguished from each other, nor necessarily in the order given in Table 13.3.

Many news stories can be regarded as *incomplete* PSDs, mentioning a problem without mentioning a satisfactory solution. There is usually more 'bad news' in newspapers than there is 'good news'. The format of bad news is that of a PSD missing a positive evaluation component.

Now consider the following example:

> [the consultant psychiatrist] considered he had three options. Firstly, he could allow the patient home untreated, putting at risk not only the residents of the [residential] home, but his residential place. Secondly, he could call on several nurses to be on hand while he attempted to inject haloperidol. He had little doubt that [the patient] would have put up a determined resistance, leading to risk of physical injury to [the patient] and the staff, loss of rapport, and an insult to [the patient's] self-respect. Thirdly, he could give him 10mg of liquid haloperidol disguised in a cup of tea.
>
> (Kellett 1996: 1249)

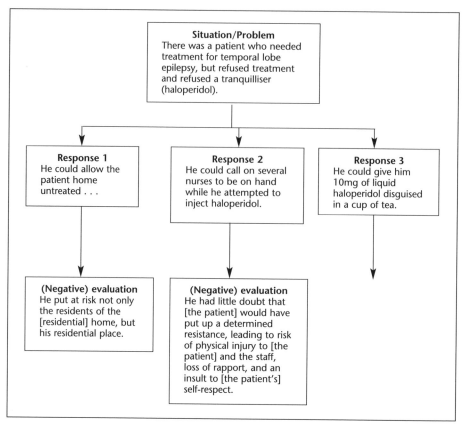

FIGURE 13.1   *The consultant's decision as a problem–solution discourse*

Figure 13.1 shows how Hoey (1983) might have shown this in PSD terms. You can probably guess which option was taken: the one without the negative evaluation. The whole structure of the passage serves to rule out the other two options as unacceptable. It also follows a common 'rule of three' found in many texts where three things are mentioned in ascending or descending order of desirability, undesirability, size, or something – as in *Goldilocks and the Three Bears*. Although Hoey does not himself use MCA (Section 13.4) we could say that, to be convincing, the passage relies on its intended audiences' notions about the SRP 'doctor–patient' as the basis for the negative evaluations (Table 13.3). The story appeared in the *British Medical Journal* and the SRP can be regarded as rules for good conduct for doctors which include: not putting patients, or others, at risk, not undermining patients' self-respect, maintaining rapport with patients, and treating their illnesses successfully – later in the story, we are told that the option chosen improved the patient's condition. The author of this passage does not explicitly describe the consultant's personality, but does give the consultant a character. First, the consultant is displayed as a judicious man, carefully considering all the options before making a decision. Second, he is shown as motivated by good professional reasons for ruling out some of the possibilities.

But it is the third option (*Response 3*) which is ethically most suspect: tricking patients into taking medication they have previously refused. The story goes on to tell how doing this led to disciplinary proceedings against the consultant and against the nurse who it was who administered the medication hidden in a cup of tea. Against the reasonableness of the consultant's reasoning the disciplinary proceedings seem unreasonable. The whole story then can be read as a defence against a complaint of professional misconduct. In the language of accounts (Chapter 11, Section 11.4) it is a justification, which might be paraphrased as 'after due consideration of all the options available, the consultant took the one most likely to be the least harmful'. The 'good character' given by the author to the consultant is important therefore in strengthening the defence of the action taken.

This analysis draws attention to the *pragmatics* of writing. That is to the purpose for which the text is composed and how that purpose is likely to influence the way in which one event is told as leading to another, and what personalities and motives the characters had. A barrister acting for an aggrieved patient might have told the 'same' events very differently, perpetrated by the same consultant but characterized with a different personality and motives. Because it considers how a text works in interaction with a reader, Hoey's approach is called '**textual interaction**'.

13.6   Rhetorical analysis

Sometimes people use the term 'rhetoric' as if it were the opposite of 'truth'. But it takes just as much rhetoric to convince people of the truth as it does to convince them of the verity of a lie. When someone draws a distinction between 'the rhetoric and the reality' what they really mean is that they are going to undermine one kind of rhetoric by using another, usually by drawing attention to the tricks and artefacts of the first, but not to those they use themselves. Indeed, contrasting 'rhetoric with reality' is itself a rhetorical device, or **trope**: a way of doing things with words.

Rhetorical analysis sometimes refers to a very broad-ranging analysis of speech or writing in terms of the traditional vocabulary for figures of speech – such as metaphor, or irony, metonymy, or synecdoche, or using alternative schemes (Burke 1966). There are some excellent analyses of these kinds in the social sciences (Edmundson 1984; van Maanen 1988; Atkinson 1990), but in this book there is insufficient space to explain the very large vocabulary such analyses use. Instead, I will focus on what is at the heart of the idea of rhetoric, which is the way communications convey impressions of their authors. I shall take it for granted that spelling, punctuation, use of vocabulary and sentence construction are important. This is a matter of appropriateness. For example, someone who presents their own diary which is correctly spelt, well punctuated and full of difficult words correctly used may not be believed if they claim that at the time they wrote it they had received no education.

A key question in rhetorical analysis is 'What makes this document believable, to *some readership*?'. The phrase 'to some readership' is important.

TABLE 13.4   *Credibility markers in feminist, anti-racist and other socially critical texts*

Markers	Examples
Markers of correct moral position	*Writing from a commitment to 'women's emancipation'* *Or 'work such as mine which is firmly grounded in the anti-racist struggle'*
Markers of alliance with oppressed groups	*Although we take responsibility for the finished product, this research has at every stage been produced through intensive consultation with disabled people*
Markers of privileged understanding of oppression	*Writing as a black woman . . .*
Deconstructions of alternatives as unbelievable	*[Our] experiences have been named for us by men: but men have used what Sheila Rowbotham has called 'the language of theory' and not the 'language of experience' (1973). Our experience . . . is removed from experience altogether by being cast in abstract and theoretical terms. We need a women's language, a language of experience, and this must necessarily come from our exploration of the personal, the everyday, and what we experience – women's lived experience (Stanley and Wise 1993: 146).*

What is believable to one audience may undermine the confidence of another. Rhetorical skill inheres partly in recipiently designing a communication for a particular audience. Since research reports are themselves documents I will use them as an example here.

Chapter 14, Section 14.4 deals with feminist, anti-racist and other kinds of **partisan research**. A quick scan of this literature shows that it is marked with 'believe me' signals, or **credibility markers** of the kind which imply 'believe me, I'm on the right side', and 'don't believe them, they're on the wrong side'. Table 13.4 gives some examples.

Signals like this are likely to convince some people of the good moral character of these authors and hence of their believability. But for other readerships they smack of over-involvement, bias and hence of unbelievability.

The equivalent 'believe me' signals in more mainstream social science writing are not quite so easy to see (Table 13.5), for such authors often give no explicit characterizations of themselves at all. Or, if they do, these are separated from the main text and put in a foreword, a footnote or a pen-picture at the end, which rarely give any more information than their institutional position and the other things they have written. But the absence of self-characterization is itself rhetorical. It goes with the notion that too much personal involvement in research is likely to lead to biased and erroneous results, and with the idea that who the researcher was should be irrelevant with regard to the truthfulness of the account. Thus the absence of self-characterization excludes from the report what (allegedly) should have been excluded in doing the research – the personal characteristics of the researcher (though these

Credibility markers in mainstream social science research TABLE 13.5

Markers	Examples
Markers of objectivity	Reports: • Rarely include material on the authors' subjective feelings or personal lives • Rarely level blame • Often include descriptions of measures taken to exclude personal bias
Markers of methodical practice	Reports are usually dominated by descriptions of the methods used
Markers of logicality	Authors show themselves taking pains over ensuring that conclusions follow logically from evidence
Markers of circumspection	Authors limit what they claim, since making grandiose claims throws doubt on the credibility of the report as a whole.

were almost certainly not excluded in reality). The use of the third-party format, as in 'it was found that' (rather than 'I found') serves to give the impression that the truth is speaking for itself, undistorted by human agency. Implicitly rather than explicitly, the research comes across as believable because it is told as the result of a disinterested technician competently following the kinds of methods which that audience will believe usually lead to the truth (Halliday and Martin 1993).

Most researchers deploy another rhetorical strategy, which is to co-opt other writers to agree with them. This can be done as simply as prefacing their own ideas by writing 'As so and so said . . .' thus underpinning their own credibility with that of others. Different readerships will find different co-optees more or less acceptable. Some readers of this book will be upset to find so many biologists, physicists and medical researchers in the bibliography of a book on *social science* methods. Each genre of research has its own set of particularly authoritative figures who get enrolled as allies and supporters of the author. Many classic studies get bent into new shapes in this way. Again, a bibliography of a research study is a rhetorical device insofar as it shows how well-read the author is, and whether the author has read the works of which the readers approve.

The research reports of quantitative research usually read as if they were stories of how the research was actually done. But we are rarely told about the aborted questions which didn't get into the questionnaire, or the blind alleys pursued by the researcher, still less about conflicts of personality, or early analyses of data which didn't make sense. Research always seems a much more trouble-free activity than it really is. These reports are better read as sets of instructions as to how someone else *could* do the research to reach the same conclusions, but told rather misleadingly in story format; what Kaplan (1964) calls the 'reconstructed logic of research'.

Many researchers who do qualitative research, particularly using participant observation, give much richer accounts of themselves doing the research, so that readers can visualize, in realistic detail, the researcher being there, finding things out. It all seems so believable. TV companies sometimes screen programmes to show how another programme was made. And it is easy to be lulled into the belief that these programmes about making programmes get straight to the truth without the intervention of directors directing cameras or editing tapes. But, of course, behind the shots of camera crews taking shots there is another hidden camera crew, and screened discussions of how a programme was edited are themselves edited. And, in the same way, the 'inside story' of a piece of ethnographic research is just another story. It probably won't be untrue, but it might have been told in a large number of other ways.

Why for example, do Rex and Moore (1967), towards the beginning of their study of ethnic relations in Sparkbrook, tell readers about cats foraging in gardens? This is an inconsequential detail with regard to ethnic relations but consequential in the sense that it gives an impression that they really were there, on location, doing the research (Edmundson 1984: 38).

Rhetoric in unavoidable. However authors write, they will convey some impression of themselves to readers, and in turn will make their accounts more or less believable. But in evaluating research reports, of whatever kind, it is important to see the rhetoric for what it is.

This brief consideration of the rhetoric of research reports should have sensitized you to the rhetorical features of other kinds of documents. For example, how advertisers associate a product with what they imagine an audience will value, how newspapers use quotations (often invented) to suggest that what they report is not made up by journalists, how those who write press releases include material which will serve as quotable quotes, how the consultant in the example earlier was given a good character to strengthen the defence, or how political speeches include markers of solidarity with the audience, such as 'speaking as a parent myself'.

13.7 Writings as evidence

The sections above treated writing as evidence of itself, of how writing is written. Writings were treated as a *topic*. But social scientists frequently make use of writings as a *resource* of evidence about the events or experiences the writing refers to. Now you have considered writings as a topic, you will see the difficulties associated with using writings as a resource, if the object of doing this is to derive accurate information about something from what has been written about it.

Historians in particular have little choice but to use ready-made written documents as resources of evidence, and this is true of other social scientists where they cannot gain direct access to what is being described. There are two levels of problems here. The first is whether a document is itself *authentic*. This a particular problem for historians and they have developed a wide variety of ways of authenticating documents, often grouped together under the rather misleading term 'textual criticism' (Howell and Prevenier 2001). Then there is the issue of whether what is said in the document is *true*. Panel

---

PANEL 13.2   Questions to ask about witness evidence

1 *Capacity to observe accurately*:
   - Would the witness' physical and temporal location have allowed him/her accurately to observe what was claimed?
   - Were the conditions of observation conducive to accurate observation?
   - Was any special observation knowledge or skills required, and if so did the witness have them?
   - Were his/her senses adequate for the observation?
   - Was s/he in an emotional state conducive to accurate observation?
   - Was his/her presence likely to have influenced what was observed?
   - Did s/he have any prejudices or preconceptions which might have led to misinterpretation of what was observed?

2 *The language of reportage*:
   - Is the meaning of a statement different from its literal meaning? Are the words used in senses not used today or only used in particular sub-cultures? If so, can they be translated adequately into modern/mainstream terms?
   - Is the report meant to be ironic, or hyperbolic, or under-stated, or otherwise not literally intended?

3 *The accuracy of the report*:
   - Was the witness biased? Was s/he under time pressure? Was s/he under duress?
   - Was the report made contemporaneously, or did it rely on memory?
   - For what audience was the report intended, and what effect might the witness want to create in them which might distort the truth?

4 *Probability*: Do the statements seem probable; in line with what we already know about the subject of the report; consistent with other evidence?

5 *Non-contradiction*: Are there internal contradictions in the report?

6 *Any other validating or invalidating evidence?*

Source: Loosely based on Shafer (1980: 157–8).

13.2 gives a list of questions to be asked about witness evidence. It is based on one of the bibles of historical research methods: Shafer's *A Guide to Historical Method* (1980). Shafer has in mind written documents containing eye-witness accounts. The same list would serve for evaluating a piece of ethnographic research such as Margaret Mead's *Coming of Age in Samoa* (Chapter 12, Section 12.5) and point **3** might be elaborated by applying the ideas of rhetorical analysis (Section 13.6). The list will serve equally as questions to ask about the verbal responses of a subject being interviewed. Then some of the questions could be elaborated with reference to research findings concerning interviewer effects (Chapter 10).

Using ready-made writings thus gives rise to questions about the accuracy and completeness of the evidence they provide. The first step in evaluating this must always be to consider the kind of writing it is, the purpose for which it was produced and the audience to which it was directed. For example, once we realize that the story of the consultant's decision was being told as a defence against a charge of professional misconduct, we know that we must treat with some suspicion the description of him judiciously weighing the options *before* making his decision. Perhaps this is what he did. But it is also exactly the kind of *post hoc* reconstruction of events we would suspect to appear in a justification.

As in Chapter 10, Section 10.2, it is worth making a distinction here between, on the one hand, what are conventionally regarded as 'matters of fact' – such as the date, time and sequence of events or who was present – and, on the other hand, incorrigibles such as feelings and beliefs and experiences. Where it is possible for there to be an accurate datum, it is possible to **triangulate** different sources of evidence to decide on which are accurate. This is also called **validation** (see also Chapter 9, Section 9.5; Chapter 10, Section 10.2; Chapter 11, Section 11.2). Various modes of triangulation or validation are shown in Panel 13.3.

PANEL 13.3 *Different kinds of triangulation*

Meta-analysis	See Chapter 15
Data source triangulation (Using two or more sources of data about the same phenomenon collected in much the same way)	• Data collected at different phases of the research • Data collected from different subjects – simply 'sampling' • Data collected at different points in time – 'time sampling' • Data collected from different settings • Observer triangulation – data collected by different members of a research team.
Respondent validation (fallibility testing, member checking)	Subjecting the researcher's interpretations to the judgement of the subjects of the research, as to their validity.
Methodological triangulation [cross-method triangulation]	Using data collected by different methods about the same phenomenon
Theoretical triangulation	Comparing the accounts of the same phenomenon given by research(ers) with different theoretical understandings.
Reasons why lines of triangulation may contradict each other:	• *One is valid and another invalid* • *Both are valid, but one describes something exceptional/unusual and the other something more common* • *Both are valid, but the phenomenon in question is variable and each refers to versions of it in different places, or at different times, or in different sub-groups or in different kinds of situation* • *Both are valid, but the qualities they express are not of the kind about which anyone can be right or wrong* • *Both are wrong*

The problem with triangulation is always that of deciding which of several discrepant possibilities is the accurate one (Chapter 10, Section 10.4). This usually has to be decided in an *ad hoc* manner as appropriate to the puzzle at hand, speculating about which authors were in the best position to know the truth and which were most likely to tell the truth – much after the manner in which the police and the courts decide between the accounts of different witnesses (Platt 1981; Plummer 1983: 99–109; Panel 13.2). Nor is it necessarily safe to assume that because several accounts concur that they must be the accurate ones. Several sources might be erroneous in the same way. A large number of news stories can be generated from a single misleading press handout, errors are copied from one text to another, or several writers may share the same prejudices. Discrepancies can be an interesting topic of research in their own right. Why do some people say one thing, and others another?

When it comes to using writing as evidence about incorrigibles such as feelings or experiences then there are no conceivable ways of judging the accuracy of written descriptions of these. Feelings are felt, and experiences are experienced, and they are so at the moment when they are felt and experienced. Remembering transforms a feeling or an experience into a memory (see Chapter 8, Panel 8.1). Writing down the memory transforms it yet again. When social scientists write that their research 'captures the experience' of some group of people they commit a category error: they mistake one kind of thing for another. What they must mean is that they have collected some *stories* which people tell about their experience. Whether these stories are spoken or written they will be *tellings* of experience, shaped by the linguistic and social conventions available for telling experiences and told in order to have some effect on an audience in terms of presenting the teller as being a particular kind of person. The difference between writing and speaking here is that writers have a longer period of time to compose what they want to convey. As Ann Oakley says of autobiographies:

> Autobiographies are the most partial ways of representing life, since their writers are usually striving in the very act of writing to make sense of their own lives in a way which offers them the most congenial justification for living them as they did.
>
> (Oakley 1993: 414)

And as Ken Plummer writes of letters:

> [E]very letter speaks not just of the writer's world, but also of the writer's perceptions of the recipient. The kind of story told shifts with the person who will read it – witness the different letters produced by Robert Burns to his mistress, his friends and his wife on the same day.
>
> (Plummer 1983: 23)

This is not to say that the analysis of writings about feelings and experiences is not worthwhile. First, the stories show us a *cultural repertoire* which people use and how they use it and for what purposes, which is suitable material for analysing in the ways suggested in this chapter. For example, rather than analysing autobiographies for telling us about the lives of the people who wrote them, we can analyse them for what they tell us about the practice of autobiography writing, or how, for example, the genre of scientists' autobiographies differs from that of feminist autobiographies.

Second, they provide a glimpse of a process through which people try out versions of themselves, by characterizing themselves in particular ways and writing themselves into particular story lines. In this sense, what people write about themselves, as in autobiographies, or how they construct themselves as authors in writing about someone or something else, is a stage in a process of becoming someone. But it is not one which stops when the writing is done. Another piece of writing, another conversation, allows for another self-characterization. In this regard there is something rather disrespectful in social scientists (or literary biographers) claiming that they have pinned down the essence of someone else on the basis of a small sample of their speech or writing.

ACTIVITY   Deconstruction through reconstruction

This is an activity based on a research technique pioneered by Richard Winter and Michael Hoey (Hoey 1983: 3–16).

Find a piece of writing which is more or less self-contained and runs to about 1,000 words. Avoid writings which consist of numbered lists and ideally choose a piece with largish print and double-spacing. Make two photocopies. Take one of these and cut it up into sentences. Then trim the edges of the cut-up pieces so that they cannot be re-assembled jigsaw style, or paste each sentence on a strip of card for the same purpose.

Give the cut-up pieces to someone else and ask them to re-assemble them.

When they have completed the task, check it against the uncut copy and ask them what clues they used to accomplish it, with 'how did you know that it went there?' questions.

You will find that people use a large variety of different sorts of clues. They will follow 'way-markers' such as 'There are three main points about . . .' They will know what kinds of sentences are likely to precede a sentence beginning 'However'. They are unlikely to explain to you that they used interrogative insertion (Section 13.3), but they might say: 'that went there because it seemed to complete what was said in that earlier sentence'. This is much the same as saying that it answered a question which an earlier sentence provoked the reader to ask. They are even less likely to explain how they used MCA (Section 13.4), but in deciding to whom a pronoun referred, they may explain that it had to be that person, because what was described of him was consistent with the personality, situation, or role of a person named earlier. They probably won't know about PSDs (Section 13.5) but they are quite likely to use their intuitive sense of what makes a complete PSD to recognize a passage as, say, a *response* which they predicted would follow a *problem* described earlier. Or they may grasp the overall purpose of the writing, or recognize the genre and use this as a guide to re-assembly.

That people can re-assemble a cut-up document is witness to the fact that writing has a structure – or rather, *many structures* – and that people know about these. This is the knowledge which allows them to create texts which others find meaningful and find meanings in texts written by others.

Further reading

As a source for a large number of different ways of analysing writing you might try Titscher *et al.* (2000). For content analysis, Neuendorf (2002) is a very detailed text, with 'how-to-do-it' advice and an associated web site which you can visit without buying the book (http://academic.csuohio.edu/ kneuendorf/content/). The same site gives a listing and commentary on software packages suitable for text analysis, including freeware, as does www.textanalysis.info/inforet.htm.

Berger (2000) is a thorough introduction to mass media research. Koenig's *Frame Analysis* web site offers resources and advice on analysing texts along the lines of Goffman's seminal *Frame Analysis* (1974) (www.ccsr.ac.uk/ methods/publications/frameanalysis/).

For MCA, Lepper (2000) gives a very full treatment. Hoey's approach belongs to a field of linguistics sometimes called 'textual interaction', referring to the interaction between reader and text provided for by the writer (Hoey 1983, 2000; Scott and Thompson 2000). But beware this term since it also applies to a field of computing where it is computers that generate or interpret text.

Edmundson (1984), Atkinson (1990) and van Maanen (1988) are all books on the rhetorical analysis of social science texts, and Halliday and Martin (1993) is on the rhetoric of natural science writing. Wodak and Meyer (2001) explain and illustrate what is meant by critical discourse analysis.

This chapter has not dealt with semiology or semiotics. This is partly because semiology is mainly about visual images, though it does have things to say about written texts, and partly because it is such a large and diverse tradition, with almost every writer introducing a new vocabulary. Some versions of semiology are rigorous (Eco 1976) others such Barthes (1993) seem whimsical. For an entertaining introduction to semiotics try Fiske (1993). The chapter on semiotics in Howells (2003) is also a good introduction, and the whole book introduces a wide range of approaches to the analysis of visual images; see also Rose (2001) and Van Leeuwen and Jewitt (2000). Williamson (1994) is an engaging approach to analysing advertisements, inspired by Barthes, but without the jargon or heavy theorizing.

Kenneth Burke's scheme for analysing texts (1966) is quite widely used though not described in this chapter. Nor does the chapter deal with the forms of structural analysis associated with the analysis of myths and folktales which are often extended to other kinds of narrative. They are covered in Titscher *et al.* 2000.

On using ready-made documents as a resource of evidence Platt (1981) remains a sensible source of advice on the evaluation of authenticity and accuracy, as are various texts on the methodology of historical research such as Howell and Prevenier (2001). Plummer (1983, 2000) are useful sources on using documents in life-history research. Diaries including those which subjects are asked to keep for the purpose of research are a special kind of document, and are well dealt with in Alaszewski (2005).

14 Evaluative and Emancipatory Research

By the end of this chapter, you will:

- Know the arguments in favour of value-neutral and value-led research
- Understand the difficulties of producing value-neutral research.

And you will know the meaning of the following terms:

Action research • catalytic validity • emancipatory research • naturalistic fallacy • participatory research • partisan research • practitioner research • sympathetic bias • value-led research • value-pluralism • value-relevant • value-neutral research.

At the end of the chapter there is an Activity which will test your understanding of performance indicators (PIs).

14.1 Introduction

A piece of research can be evaluated for its quality in terms of how well it was conducted or how credible are its results. But the term 'evaluation' is also used in a narrower sense to mean making *moral judgements*. This is the important sense of the term for this chapter, that is about the ways in which value judgements are involved in research, apart from those which have to do with the way researchers treat those they research. This latter is usually termed 'research ethics', and is dealt with in Chapter 16.

Value judgements may be explicitly made, where those who make them lay out a moral case for what they are doing. Or they may be made without people recognizing that values are influencing their judgements. So far in this book values have usually appeared in relation to the way experimental and survey researchers take such pains to avoid the researcher's hopes and desires, preconceptions and prejudices biasing research findings. But matters of value cannot be entirely excluded from research. For example, to be worried about values of one kind influencing research findings is to be signed up to some other values, such as the value of truth.

Options for managing values

I shall assume that all researchers are committed to the value of finding out the truth, and to some values about not harming the people involved in the research (see Chapter 16). But otherwise researchers might:

- Try to exclude issues of value entirely from decisions about what topics to choose, what methods to use, how the data are interpreted, and how they are made public – **value-free research**.
- Allow issues of value to be involved in selecting topics for research and in deciding how to make the findings public, but exclude values from influencing the way the research is done and the conclusions reached – **value-relevant but value-neutral research**.
- Specifically select topics for research on the basis of their moral or political values, do the research in such a way as to maximize the chances of findings which promote these values and use the findings in ways that will have the moral or political consequences they desire – **value-led** – or, sometimes, **partisan research**.

There is one step further down this path. This is where researchers conduct research not so much to produce findings but in an attempt to make the world a better place in the very act of doing the research. Thus the research may be directed towards improving the knowledge of the people who are the subjects of the research, or their self-image, or their public reputations, or of winning some resources for them, or of helping them to win some political conflict. When it is done by feminist, or anti-racist or disability researchers it is often called *emancipatory* research (making the claim that it frees some people from some kind of oppression), or *empowering* research (making the claim that it increases the capacity of those researched to improve their situation).

Without the use of terms such as 'emancipation' or 'empowerment', much the same kind of activities are engaged in by the people employed by political parties whose job it is to find the information which will help their party to win, and which can be 'spin-doctored' and published to improve the party's ratings, or to smear the opposition, and by the public relations departments and consultants employed by large corporations to manage the company's public image and to enhance its relationships with governments and international agencies such as the EU or UN. People employed in this capacity are also often called 'researchers' and call what they do 'research'.

14.2 Value-relevant, value-neutral research

The naturalistic fallacy

Philosophers warn against the naturalistic fallacy, which is fallaciously arguing from 'is' to 'ought'. It is fallacious to say: 'It is raining and therefore you ought to get the washing in.' A complete and logical formula would be: 'It is raining *and* it is a bad thing for washing to get wet, *and* it is your moral responsibility to prevent this, *therefore* you ought to get the washing in.' The naturalistic fallacy entails the missing out of the moral component of an argument, hiding it away so that it might be accepted as if the argument was entirely factual. A more common form of the naturalistic fallacy in the social sciences is: 'It is a fact that these people are disadvantaged, therefore something should be done about it.' But the fact of disadvantage is not in itself an argument for alleviating it. For that, a moral justification is necessary.

It is probably impossible to do research which is entirely value-free. It might seem that whether the sun goes round the earth or vice versa is an issue which is easily abstracted from moral and political concerns. But that was not what Galileo found. It is particularly difficult at the front end of research (where topics for research are chosen), and at the rear end (where findings are published). Researchers might wish to pursue knowledge for knowledge's sake, but those who fund research programmes usually want something which will suit their interests. Governments usually want research which will be relevant to whatever they define as the most pressing social and political problems. Companies prefer to fund research which will have some relevance to their profitability. For example, Conversation Analysis (CA), which you encountered in Chapter 11, has been has been very heavily funded by telephone and computer companies in connection with the development of voice recognition and generation by machines. Market research is the major application of survey technique and focus groups. Much psychological research is involved in the design of products and marketing campaigns. Thus the pattern of options available for the researcher is partly determined by the values and interests of the kinds of people and agencies who control research funding. Options may also be limited by the kinds of people who can deny a researcher access to a particular research location. There are very few published sociological studies of corporate boardrooms, for example, and none from within the state security services. (For influences on publication see Chapter 15, Sections 15.3 and 15.4, and Chapter 16 Section 16.8.)

The Weberian position: value relevance and value neutrality

The mainstream position on values and social science is that based on the thinking of Max Weber (1949: 89–99; see also Bruun 1972). Weber is sometimes represented as being an advocate of 'value-free research'; but that was not his thinking. Weber recognized that if research was to have any benefits, someone would have to make value decisions as to the best ways to put the findings to practical use. Therefore what he prescribed was research which was 'value-relevant but value-neutral'. By 'value-relevant' he meant that researchers might, and often should, select research topics according to value decisions about the kind of research which would be of social benefit. By 'value-neutral' he was referring to setting up a kind of exclusion zone for values, to insulate the way the research is conducted, and the way the data are interpreted, from being influenced by what the researcher, or the research funders, *desire* the findings to show.

Throughout this book there have been examples of devices used to maintain and police such an exclusion zone: blinding to control experimenter expectancy effects (Chapter 3, Section 3.6); blind methods of selecting participants as with randomization (Chapter 3, Section 3.3) or with probability sampling (Chapter 6, Section 6.4); standardized performances for survey interviewers, the separate analysis of interviews from different interviewers to check that none of them was conveying their values to respondents and thereby influencing responses (Chapter 10, Section 10.4); inter-rater reliability tests to check that coding decisions are not biased in analysing data (Chapter 2, Section 2.10); and a falsification programme to avoid researchers simply cherry picking data to produce the results they want to see (Chapter 12, Section 12.6); see also Panel 4.1. These are all modulations on standard practice within scientific research in general.

Puzzles, problems and the attribution of blame

There are always multiple options for framing a topic of research. Some will frame in more moral assumptions than others. Physicists and engineers sometimes draw the line between themselves by saying that physicists pose and solve physicists' *puzzles* and engineers accept and solve other people's *problems*. The point being made is that physicists are usually able to select topics for research less influenced by wider moral, political and commercial considerations. Their puzzles are generated by the theoretical development of the subject. By contrast, the kinds of topics worked on by engineers are framed by the practical interests of other people. Hence doing engineering assumes that some people have a moral and political right to have their problems solved (by engineers), which may sometimes be to the disadvantage of some other people.

In everyday social affairs the idea of causation is nearly always double-barrelled. Whenever it is said that *this* is the cause of *that*, the implication can be drawn at the same time that someone is morally responsible for either causing it, or has an obligation for doing something about it (see Chapter 13, Section 13.5). Such implications will probably commit the naturalistic fallacy (see above) but that does not stop people making them.

At first sight the causes of heart disease in later life might merely appear to be a biological issue. An evolutionary biologist might frame this as a puzzle, abstracting the topic as far as possible from any immediate practical concerns of solving it as a problem. The biologist might argue that evolution proceeds by favouring those characteristics which maximize reproductive success. In the evolutionary past there have been no reproductive advantages in developing mechanisms which keep the heart in good repair beyond the age at which people are most fertile, and therefore there has been no mechanism for favouring the transmission of any genes which do this, and therefore it is understandable that human hearts wear out. This wearing out is 'heart disease'.

This solves a biological *puzzle* but it hardly addresses the *problem* of heart disease as most people would like it addressed: that is, in terms of finding a solution to something which they find undesirable. As soon as we move from puzzle to problem we make a moral judgement that heart disease is a bad thing, and that reducing its incidence would be a good thing. And we narrow the objectives of research in such a way that successful research is the kind of research which has morally desirable pay-offs. However, all phenomena have multiple causes, and no research can investigate all of these at the same time. Thus among the causes which make heart disease more likely for some people are their dietary behaviour and their smoking behaviour and the poverty or the affluence of their mothers and themselves immediately before birth and in their early years. These are all topics which have been investigated by social and psychological research as applied to medicine. Framing 'the problem' of heart disease around each of these bits of the causal network points in the direction of different kinds of 'solution'. But, in turn, each of these tacks might itself be framed in different ways. Thus dietary and smoking behaviour might be conceptualized as behaviour chosen by the people concerned, perhaps under conditions of imperfect knowledge of the consequences of what they are doing to their health. This constructs them as morally responsible for their health, and predicates some kind of health education intervention as a solution. Alternatively their dietary and smoking behaviour might be attributed not to individual choices but to the blandishments of the food processing and tobacco industries. This points towards some solution in terms of the state regulation of industry and advertising. Or, in the case of smoking, the researcher might draw attention to the socially structured stresses and strains of life for which people find smoking a relief, to the fact that poorer people seem to suffer these more, and to a solution in terms of some redistribution of incomes or advantages.

Note what is happening here. Different framings construct different people as the 'goodies' and 'baddies' in the situation, and carry different implications as to who is to blame for the problem and different implications for who should change their ways. Reframing the problem around the idea of poverty in the early years of life has different moral and political implications again. Now it appears that the current pattern of heart disease was in part determined by social conditions 50–90 years ago. No one living can be held responsible for doing anything about that. But this framing has implications for the present day. It directs attention to current patterns of socio-economic inequality as they impact on maternity and infancy and to whatever it is that governments should be doing in the here and now to prevent heart disease and other health problems in the future.

The above was written as if problems were framed in such a way as to lead to proposals for solutions. But it is equally apposite to suggest that the way problems are framed *follows from* the kinds of solutions people would prefer. Thus it is understandable that health educators prefer research which points towards a solution lying in health education interventions, drug companies in research which suggest pharmaceuticals as the solution, tobacco companies prefer research which will show that people freely choose to smoke and that advertising influences only which brand they choose. Governments prefer research which attributes problems to individual behaviour rather than failures of government policy, while opposition parties, of whatever political persuasion, often take the opposite view. Socialists prefer framings of problems which have socialist solutions, feminists framings which have feminist solutions and so on. The advancement of occupations and of political groups relies on finding problems for the solutions they have on offer, as much as it does on finding solutions for problems (Spector and Kitsuse 1987).

Social science research which gets tied to particular occupational groups tends to incorporate the values and interests of the occupational group in ways that are not always immediately apparent. Nurses, for example, have developed their own genre of research and have called it 'nursing research'. It is not surprising that it tends to portray nursing as an important occupation and doctors as less important than people believe they are. Although not always the case, it is common in nursing research for the term 'the role of the nurse' to mean 'the role nurses think nurses *ought* to play'. This prescriptive rather than descriptive use of terms then allows states of affairs to be described in a slanted way, as descriptions of how things deviate from what nurses would prefer. Partly to avoid such problems, sociologists have asserted their independence from occupational groups of practitioners or from the state. Criminology became the sociology of deviance (for sociologists, at least). Medical sociology became first the sociology of medicine and then the sociology of health and illness. Educational sociology became the sociology of education. These all represent attempts to move towards framing topics for research as puzzles rather than as problems. There has been a counter-movement with practitioners trying to seize back control of research in their fields with various 'practitioner–researcher' movements (Section 14.5).

'Cause' in social affairs is often taken to mean 'blame', so, whatever a researcher says, it is likely that someone will claim that the research is wrong if the blame seems to fall on them. The claim may be that it is wrong in a factual sense. But the motivation for the complaint is likely to be that the research has the wrong moral and political implications, those which the complainant does not like. In an often-cited paper called 'Whose side are we on?', the sociologist Howard Becker drew attention to what is an occupational problem for sociologists: that whatever sociologists say it is likely to be complained about as being biased in someone else's favour (Becker 1967). You have now seen why this is an occupational problem. Becker's paper is often misquoted as an argument in favour of researchers siding with 'underdogs' as against the 'establishment'. But, as Becker himself has made clear, he takes a Weberian line on values and social research and prescribes that research should be value relevant and value neutral (Becker 1971; Hammersley 2000a). Becker's (1963) own approach to the sociology of deviance is instructive here. He attempts as far as possible to approach deviance as a sociological puzzle, rather than as a social problem. His central question is *not* 'Why do people commit deviant acts and how can we stop them?', but 'Why is it that some people find the activities of some other people so objectionable that they attempt to stop them acting thus?' Becker's framing of the issue for research is much more threatening to 'respectable and right-minded people' than it is to the groups labelled as 'deviant'. But subverting respectability and improving the reputations of deviant groups was a side effect rather than a central objective of Becker's approach. Becker's own answer to his question 'Whose side are we on?' is that sociologists shouldn't be on anybody's side, but they will always be accused of siding with someone and against someone else.

The researcher's moral expertise and political mandate

Becker's position also represents another part of the rationale for attempting a value-neutral approach when investigating value-relevant issues. In order, knowingly, to allow his or her own values to influence the research, a researcher must assume some special skill in deciding moral or ethical issues. To do research in an attempt to change the world for the better, researchers have to assume both that they have a superior grasp of what is 'for the better' and that they have some kind of mandate to use research to change the lives of other people. Researchers who adopt the value-relevant, value-neutral position, argue that what researchers are particularly good at is doing research. That should include following the moral codes designed to minimize the chances of harm coming to those involved in the research (see Chapter 16). Their personal morality should decide what research topics they select and what kinds of sponsorship they will accept. But otherwise, it is argued, researchers have no special expertise in deciding moral issues such as who should have an obligation for what with regard to whom, or whether this state of affairs is fair or unfair. Similarly, so the argument goes, no one has given researchers, as researchers, any mandate to prescribe social morality or political action. This does not mean that as individuals they are disbarred from philanthropy or political activism, but that that is in their role as citizen, or town councillor, or university dean: Max Weber himself was heavily involved in the German politics of his time. The mandate for influencing political affairs is what is held by duly elected governments, duly appointed administrators, or people playing their role as active citizens. It is noticeable, for example, how in writing articles about global warming or the loss of bio-diversity, natural scientists often take pains to separate out what they are saying as scientists and what they are saying as concerned citizens (Halliday and Martin 1993). Value-neutral social researchers often adopt the same literary convention (see also Chapter 13, Section 13.6).

Looked at in this way, for a researcher to do research deliberately to provide a persuasive case for or against some public policy would be to act without a mandate, and to abuse a privileged position. The argument is buttressed by the assumption that to design research so that it would have the maximum political impact would almost inevitably distort the truth of the findings.

Section 14.4 will explain why those researchers who engage in value-led or partisan research find this rationale unsatisfactory. But in the next section I want to deal with the way in which researchers who do highly value-relevant 'evaluation research' manage the values embedded in the topics they study.

14.3 Evaluation studies and evaluation criteria

Evaluation studies are one of the most common kind of applied social research. Some of them remain unpublished because they are primarily of interest to the future planning of a particular agency, and some because their findings are embarrassing for those who commissioned the research. They are frequently commissioned by government departments, social services departments, education authorities, health authorities and philanthropic trusts to investigate the success or failure of a policy or a project.

Here there is no clear boundary between social scientific research and other kinds of investigations with similar purposes, such as inspections by one of the many official inspectorates such as OfStEd for schools, or the prison inspectorate, by bodies such as the Audit Commission and its Scottish counterpart, official inquiries, judicial reviews, performance indicator measurement, internal agency reviews, clinical audit and such like. Many such exercises rely more on the expert judgements of those conducting them than on rigorous use of social scientific methodologies. Where such methodologies are used they range from experimental and quasi-experimental designs (see Chapter 3 and Chapter 4), to surveys of consumer satisfaction (see Chapters 6 and 9), to interview studies (see Chapter 10) and naturalistic observation (for example, see Chapter 12, Section 12.6, though this was not a commissioned evaluation study). Research associated with 'evidence-based practice' looms large, in health care, social work, education and the criminal justice system. Usually this prioritizes experimental and quasi-experimental research, using methods described in earlier chapters.

Value pluralism and evaluation criteria

The methods used in evaluation studies are diverse and discussed in other chapters. But what they have in common is the need to define evaluation criteria. Evaluation studies always ask questions such as 'Is it as good as it could be?', or 'Does doing this have better outcomes than doing something else?' In order to answer such questions it is necessary to have criteria for defining 'good' or 'better'. What it is that an agency or a policy ought to achieve is nearly always subject to some disagreement. For example, ideas about what a welfare-benefits system ought to be achieving are likely to be quite different according to the view of the Treasury, the Department of Work and Pensions, people thinking of themselves as taxpayers or various benefits recipients. Even where there is less radical disagreement, no agency can coherently pursue more than a few goals and the goals it prioritizes must be chosen from many others it might otherwise pursue. No agency can ever satisfy all of the people all of the time. Similarly no evaluation study can ever measure performance against more than a limited number of standards.

Thus evaluation researchers face a problem of value-pluralism, which raises questions about:

- Whose values, desires, preferences and so on should inform the criteria for evaluation?
- Which among the many matters which might be evaluated should be featured in an evaluation study?

Sometimes evaluation researchers are employed to do research which leads to the formulation of evaluation criteria. For example, on the assumption that what is 'good' is what is approved of by a clientèle, they might be commissioned to conduct a survey, or run some focus groups to discover what clients want most from an agency, or what the public wants most from a policy; thus providing information for setting criteria. Then the evaluation is conducted in terms of client satisfaction according these goals. As you saw from Chapter 10, the results of such research are likely to depend on what questions people are asked and how they are asked them. The sample surveys of consumer satisfaction now conducted annually with reference to the British National Health Service (NHS), define evaluation criteria by the questions asked. For example:

> Thinking generally about your experience in hospital last year, please tell us whether you agree or disagree with the statements below:
>
> • You were encouraged to ask questions about your treatment Agree Disagree Don't Know
>
> (Cohen, Forbes and Garraway 1994)

And the responses given are taken to indicate the extent to which these criteria have been met. In this case, what percentage of patients felt they were encouraged to ask questions about their treatment is a measure of success or failure, or of greater or lesser success comparing area with area, and or of progress or regress comparing the same area in succeeding years.

Sometimes evaluation researchers have only limited choice about the criteria to use. Much evaluation research is commissioned by bodies who already have fairly clear ideas what they mean by 'good', 'bad', or 'better': that, for example, in a neighbourhood watch scheme, 'good' means reducing property crime by 10% over a 5-year period. For a hired-hand researcher, accepting these notions of 'good' and 'better' may come with accepting the contract to do the research.

Turning a value statement into a factual standard

It is an expression of values to say:

> This agency should be offering a service to all clients irrespective of their ethnicity, but according to their need for the service and capacity to benefit from it.

But it can be made a matter of fact as to whether the agency is actually doing this. In this example there would be some tricky decisions to make as to how to define 'need' and 'capacity to benefit' in identifiable ways: how to *operationalize* these terms. In principle, to turn value statements into standards for judging matters of fact is the same as making decisions as to what questions to ask to elicit information about alcohol consumption, or where to draw the line between 'often' and 'rarely'. But it is important not to forget, first, that the criterion did originate from a value judgement; second, that this was *someone's* value judgement, about which others might disagree; and, third, that in judging performance against some criteria the researcher will not be judging the performance against others which might be more highly valued by someone else.

Pluralistic evaluation

Evaluation researchers may start with a more open-ended brief. Then they often agonize over the question of whose values should inform an evaluation, among the many 'stake holder' groups associated with the service. One response among evaluators to this problem of value pluralism is **pluralistic evaluation**, which goes under a wide range of other names as well, such as Fourth Generation Evaluation (Guba and Lincoln 1989). This approach accepts that different kinds of people want different kinds of outcomes from an agency or policy, and frames the evaluator's task as clarifying these diverse wants and discovering who has and who has not had their requirements satisfied. Smith and Cantley's (1985) study of a Scottish, psycho-geriatric day hospital provides an illustration of this. Smith and Cantley did not themselves take a value position of what would count as 'success' and 'failure' in the hospital. Instead, they investigated the ways in which different groups defined 'success' and whether they were satisfied: each in terms of their own notion of 'success'. For example, everyone agreed that 'patient flow' should be properly managed, but there were disagreements as to the proper management of patient flow.

As Panel 14.1 suggests Smith and Cantley have made the decision that as researchers they have no particular expertise or mandate to decide what a day hospital ought to be achieving, or how it ought to do it. What they do in their

---

PANEL 14.1   Pluralistic evaluation: different notions of 'success' in a psychogeriatric day hospital

Everyone agreed that admissions and discharges – patient flow – should be properly managed, but with disagreements as to what proper management would be:

- *Consultants* judged patient flow in terms of 'not silting up' hospital beds and favoured an active discharge policy to keep on creating spaces in the hospital. Their view on the intake policy was that there should always be room to admit the patients they wanted admitted.
- *Day hospital staff* also favoured an active discharge policy, but also a selective intake policy operated by them: hence there were disagreements with the consultants.
- *GPs* were most interested in patient flow as a means of getting admission for their patients, but were less enthusiastic about discharges for their own patients, unless to long-term residential care.
- *Social workers* were in favour of discharges home to the care of relatives, but slowed down discharges in order to create suitable arrangements at home.
- *Relatives*, on the whole, were opposed to discharges, seeing these as a withdrawal of a valued service and creating an additional burden for them.
- *Patients* looked at matters in an entirely individual way: those who wanted to continue coming to the day hospital were unhappy about their own discharge; those who wanted to stop coming wanted to be discharged.

Sources: Smith, Cantley and Ritman (1983); Smith and Cantley (1984, 1985).

research is to make the value positions of various different groups 'objective' by bringing them into the open, without themselves taking sides.

The result of a pluralistic evaluation is to produce information which reflects back to an agency or service the diversity of view points of different stake holder groups, so that these can be reconciled – or not, as the case may be. Some evaluation researchers themselves go so far as to conduct debates and negotiations in order to produce consensus within agencies they have evaluated (Dukes 1996). But it could be argued that in doing this they have gone beyond a researcher role, and have taken on the mantle of an organizational development consultant. Indeed, much of what is described as 'evaluation research' is better described as organizational development, when the object is for members of the organization to discuss issues, learn from them and plan better ways of doing things for the future. The kinds of *group facilitation techniques* used in the brokering of mutual understanding and consensus are not 'research methods' in the usual sense of the term and are therefore beyond the subject matter of this book.

Sympathetic bias in evaluation research

Often an evaluator's report will have important consequences in the form of the renewal or non-renewal of funding for a project. While not often written about, there is much anecdotal evidence that evaluator–researchers sometimes omit some criticisms from their written reports and give them verbally and confidentially to project teams and management. I have done this myself. This means that published reports are often more complimentary than the project deserves, which may cause problems for someone trying to emulate a 'successful' project elsewhere on the basis of a published report alone. Pluralistic evaluation demands that researchers take everyone's views into consideration and deal with them in an even-handed way. But some groups will always be much easier to relate to than others.

So far in this chapter I have dealt with those researchers who attempt to maintain some value neutrality with regard to their research, whether the research is of the kind designed to produce general knowledge, or evaluation research designed to judge the value of some practice, or the success of some agency or policy. However some researchers reject the idea of value neutrality.

14.4   Socially critical and emancipatory research

The term 'critical' used to mean 'objective', 'rational' and 'disinterested', as in the sub-title for this book. But these days in social science it often means 'socially critical' and 'critique' means complaining about social affairs from a particular point of view. The field of critical research includes Marxist or Marxist–feminist (Lather 1986), feminist (Mies 1991), anti-racist (Ben-Tovim *et al.* 1986) and disability rights researchers (Barnes and Mercer 1997), among others, although each of these fields is internally very diverse. The term 'critical' is sometimes very narrowly used to refer to the writings of the Frankfurt School, and even more narrowly to the writings of Jürgen Habermas, one of its members (Cuff, Sharrock and Francis 2006). But I shall use the term more broadly to encompass a wide range of *socially* critical positions.

Partisanship

Unlike researchers who attempt value neutrality, these researchers believe that, as researchers, they do have a particular expertise in making moral judgements about social arrangements and attempting to change them. They usually draw their mandate for this from representing themselves as researching on behalf of a constituency of oppressed people such as women, black people, working class people, gays, disabled people and so on, who deserve to have their concerns articulated by a researcher – another moral judgement here. Sometimes they are members of such a category themselves (see also Chapter 13, Section 13.6).

Writing of feminist research Mies says that research must be subordinated to the political aims of the women's movement, and that research: 'is not just the study but the overcoming of women's oppression and exploitation' (1991: 61).

Similar manifesto statements can be found from critical thinkers who align themselves with other social groups. The best known of these is that from Marx, to the effect that the object of philosophy is not to understand society but to change it, meaning to change it for the better. The philosopher Martin Heidegger's insistence that scholarship should primarily be directed towards helping the German people to fulfil their historic destiny is a similar mission statement (Sluga 1993). Thus whether the orientation is feminist, marxist or fascist, the research it proposes is value-led and evaluative. The mission of each establishes a 'regime of truth', which determines what will count as relevant and credible knowledge. This will be different according to values leading the research. Although most such theories make some claims to be aiming to change society for the better for nearly everyone, there is usually some group whose interests are prioritized. Thus this kind of research is sectarian and it is often termed **partisan research**.

A value-neutral researcher such as Becker (Section 14.2) would be particularly interested in the political processes through which 'private troubles' are converted into 'public issues' to quote the famous phrase of C. Wright Mills (1959). The interest would be in this as a sociological topic: some puzzles to solve. By contrast, critical researchers are interested in taking an active part in putting 'private troubles' on the public agenda: that is, in drawing attention to what they define as 'social evils' which ought to be remedied. There is a huge quantity of sociological research which is 'issue-raising' in this way, in fields such as poverty research, educational inequality, domestic violence, gender and ethnic inequality and various kinds of discriminatory behaviour by employers, the police, the courts and other public agencies. The feminist Carol Erhlich (Stanley and Wise 1983: 24–38) approvingly calls this 'muck-raking research'.

Inequality as a moral category

Writers of this kind very frequently present what are matters of moral judgement as if they were matters of fact. This is particularly the case with the idea of inequality. The term 'inequality' sits rather unhappily between the straight-forward and factual 'difference', and the much more problematic and morally loaded 'unfair' or 'inequitable'. In much social research differences are treated as evidence of inequity without researchers justifying the moral judgement they make to convert a difference into an inequity. They routinely commit the naturalistic fallacy (see p. 323 above).

Ethnographic studies in the sociology of education provide many examples where differences in treatment of pupils by teachers are treated as inequalities, and these inequalities as inequities, as if researchers could observe unfairness without making a moral judgement to do so. To use the idea of unfairness or inequity means dividing people into categories of similar deservingness and judging whether all those in the same category are treated the same. Arguments in this field have a 'scissors–paper–stone' quality where each ethical proposition about who deserves what can be countered by another which, to someone at least, will seem more persuasive (Western 1990). For example, in deciding whether different pupils deserve 'the same treatment' should we regard or disregard the fact that some try harder than others? If a teacher gave the same marks to two pupils turning in work of different quality on the grounds that each had invested the same amount of effort, there would be a complaint that the pupil whose work was best was being unfairly treated. But if two different marks were given, then there might be an argument that the pupil who achieved least, achieved least because circumstances prevented her from investing as much effort as her more fortunate colleague, and that therefore the marking was unfair to her. These are very difficult, and probably irresolvable moral issues which teachers have to grapple with. Many researchers who have carried out ethnographic studies of schools seem to solve them at a stroke, by simply assuming that, however teachers treat pupils differently, it is unfair.

Disciplinary actions by teachers have attracted much attention. Contrasts are usually drawn between the treatment of black pupils as opposed to white, working class as opposed to middle class, girls as opposed to boys. Sometimes it is the girls and sometimes it is the boys who are depicted as the disadvantaged group. There are two versions of what constitutes 'unfair' behaviour in the field of discipline. One is that some disadvantaged group of pupils is subjected to too *much* control by teachers (Clarricoates 1980; Gilbourn 1990; Wright 1986, 1992). Evidence is cited of allegedly 'the same' naughtiness or inattention being disciplined if committed by the disadvantaged group and ignored among the favoured group. The other is that it is the favoured group who are 'kept on task' while the disfavoured group is ignored: that the disfavoured group receives too *little* control (Sharp and Green 1975; Stanworth 1983). Thus in one study we will read that the educational needs of girls are neglected because teachers spend too much time controlling boys (Spender 1982; Stanworth 1983; Licht and Dweck 1987) and in another that when girls step out of line this is heavily checked, while similar behaviour for boys is ignored as natural male high spirits (Clarricoates 1980). In one study it is a scandal that African-Caribbean boys are subjected to heavy control (Wright 1986) and in another it is a scandal that teachers don't know how to control them and they are allowed to waste valuable learning time (Green 1983).

In addition, not only do such studies issue complaints when teachers treat different kinds of pupils differently when they should treat them the same, they also complain when teachers treat different kinds of pupils the same when they should treat them differently; hence critiques of teaching which is 'colour-blind' or 'gender-blind', or where teachers do not take into consideration that pupils come from different social classes. Where teachers are supposed both to treat everyone the same and everyone differently it is extremely easy to describe whatever they do as wrong. These moral judgements are made in the context of an argument that it is these unfair actions by teachers which cause differences in educational achievement. As noted in Chapter 12 observational studies of these kinds have no way of linking observations in a classroom to educational outcomes (Foster, Gomm and Hammersley 1996: Chapter 5, 2000). As you saw from Chapter 7, Section 7.3, the effects of social class or gender on educational achievement cannot be seen directly by looking in a classroom.

To issue judgements of this kind, a critical researcher has to assume that he or she knows what the teacher ought to do, and is better able than the teacher to make the everyday moral decisions that teaching entails. It is worth remembering the remarks made in Chapter 12 about the necessarily selective nature of ethnographic observation. If researchers start out with the intention to find unfairness, then they will easily find examples. This is an expectancy effect on a grand scale (Chapter 3, Section 3.6). The position taken on such research by those of a value-neutral persuasion is not that unfairness towards a gender, or a social class or an ethnic group is a figment of the critical researcher's imagination. Rather it is that such research rarely provides sound evidence *one way* or *the other*. The partisan tendency in educational research in particular has been severely criticized by OfStEd (Tooley 1998) not so much for being partisan, but for the research being poor in quality and without sound evidence to back the claims made.

Political impact

Some research has been politically influential, particularly the early poverty surveys of Booth (1902) and Rowntree (1901), the national birth cohort studies (Chapter 8, Section 8.3) and studies such as Peter Townsend's *Last Refuge* (1962) which was an exposé of institutional care for older people; it is rumoured that John Lea and Jock Young's *What is to Be Done about Law and Order* (1993) influenced Tony Blair in taking a tough line on criminal justice issues.

Up until the 1960s the mass media tended to be rather deferential to the establishment and there was a greater role for sociological studies to put issues on the public agenda, or to present sympathetic pictures of stigmatized groups. But nowadays it seems that at least one new social issue is placed on the agenda every week by journalists, and each week's television and radio contains a rich diet of personal accounts of what it is like to be black, or gay, or a victim of domestic abuse or child abuse, to be mentally ill, or to have learning difficulties and so on. Doing social research these days does not seem to be such an effective way of influencing the political process as does doing journalism. Of course, there is no sharp boundary between the two. Social concern documentary makers employ researchers, and social researchers from academia are sometimes interviewed on screen. But the principles of putting together a piece of social research, and those of constructing a 'hard-hitting' social documentary, are rather different: audience impact and entertainment, rather than truth, are the principal concerns of the latter.

Partisanship versus pluralism

Panel 14.1 is useful in distinguishing value-neutral and critical approaches. Smith and Cantley (1985) lay out the viewpoints of the majority of people in each category. They try to be even-handed between them. No doubt they fail in some regards, under-representing minority views within each category, perhaps. Probably it was easier for them to elicit accurate information from some kinds of people compared with others. By contrast, critical researchers would make a moral judgement as to which of all the stake holders was the most deserving. They would probably choose the elderly patients and concentrate almost entirely on the way in which the hospital failed to satisfy their interests. The views of other participants might then be displayed as 'misunderstanding' the 'needs' of the patients and as evidence of an ideology. 'Ageism' would be the most likely ideology referred to here (Blytheway and Johnson 1990).

Smith and Cantley's decision to be even-handed is as much a moral and political decision as is the critical researcher's judgement to be partisan. Each follows from a different view as to proper conduct for researchers. Each also follows from different views as to the implications of being even-handed or of taking sides. From the value-neutral position, taking sides seems likely to produce a partial and distorted view of the truth, favouring one set of views or interests as against others. For a partisan researcher, current knowledge is viewed as already biased against certain kinds of people – say, older people with mental health problems. Therefore being even-handed simply perpetuates this bias. What is needed, it is argued, is research which strongly advocates for the interest of disadvantaged groups and strongly expresses their point of view to redress the balance.

This idea of redressing the balance is often expressed in terms of research having a function of 'giving voice' to people who otherwise would not be heard, or who are so stigmatized that few people would otherwise believe what they say. Research here is being thought of in terms of making a contribution to the democratic process so that minority viewpoints can be broadcast. There is a logical relationship between this and the notion that the object of social research is to foster mutual understanding by enabling different kinds of people to understand things from each other's point of view (Chapter 10, Section 10.5). In this regard, researchers act as if public relations consultants to various groups of people, choosing the group to advocate for according to the researcher's own political and moral predilections – feminists for groups of women they regard as silenced and oppressed, anti-racists for minority ethnic groups similarly regarded, researchers employed by the Institute of Directors (IoD) on behalf of those 'misunderstood' to be undeserving 'fat cats', and researchers employed on behalf of the Tory party to correct 'media distortion' of Tory party policy. There is virtually no group in society which does not believe that it is seriously misunderstood by others: quite rightly, too, if being 'misunderstood' means that other people's views about them are other than they would prefer.

14.5 Participative research, action research and practitioner research

Participative research

In the *Mass Observation* programme of the 1930s, 1940s and 1950s (Hubble 2006) members of the public were enrolled to collect information about ordinary life in Britain and again when the project was relaunched in 1981. The *Cambridge Group for the History of Population and Social Structure* founded by Peter Laslett and Tony Wrigley in 1964 relied heavily on amateur historians to extract information from parish registers and similar sources (Laslett and Smith 2005). But participative research usually means more than co-opting volunteer research assistants.

Feminist and disability rights researchers, in particular, are inclined to regard the traditional distinction between researcher and researched as elitist and exploitative. One of the arguments made in favour of focus group research (for example, Wilkinson 1999) is that it reduces the power of the researcher over those researched, because the researcher is confronted by the power of the group. This may sometimes be so. But power is not necessarily a matter of numbers. In therapeutic and educational contexts it is sometimes argued to the contrary that a skilled group worker can harness the power of the group to give her more persuasive power than she would have in one-to-one encounters. At least this was the message of the 'green bible' of group work (Wilson and Ryland 1949). This is why group work is so highly favoured in health promotion, drug rehabilitation, or anger management programmes.

The terms *'collaborative'* or *'participative research'* usually mean something more than allowing those researched to participate in group discussions facilitated by a researcher. They usually mean research where those who are the *subjects* of the research become co-researchers.

In social work and health this might also be called **user-led** or **user-controlled** research (Beresford and Evans 1999). The terms **emancipatory** and **empowering** are often used in this respect. There are published evaluation studies of this kind, for example involving people with learning difficulties (Whittaker, Gardner and Kershaw 1990), with mental health problems (Nettle 1996) and other disadvantaging characteristics (Barnes and Mercer 1997). Government policy to increase patient and public participation in the NHS has led to many small-scale evaluation studies by service users which contribute to the evidence for the annual 'health check' of each NHS Trust (www.cppih.org).

But sometimes collaborations of this kind take the form of group dialogues in which participants share their feelings and experiences; there are no 'findings' as such and the object is to *raise the consciousness* of those participating. 'Raising consciousness' refers to enabling people to come to understand themselves in terms of some given framework of ideas, such as Marxism, feminism, or anti-racist theory.

Helping members of oppressed groups to articulate their view of the world, or express their political demands more forcefully, is another kind of enterprise. A particularly vigorous area of this kind of work has been that of anthropologists assisting in the advocacy of the tribal land claims of indigenous peoples in Australasia, Canada and South America (Maddock 1998). One of the major programmes of the Joseph Rowntree foundation is its *Voice* programme. Projects funded thus have the aim of helping otherwise inarticulate groups to clarify their concerns and make cases on their own behalf: for example, Deborah Marks' work with school excludees (1995). Again, helping women to write their own autobiographies is regarded as a feminist research strategy (Stanley 1992).

The major interest in the activities above is in having an immediate and benign effect rather than in producing general knowledge. The effects sought might be:

* *Therapeutic* – in improving some group's image of themselves and their morale through doing the research
* *Educative* – in improving the knowledge and skills of those doing the research
* *Political* – in improving the public image of a group, or building them into a cohesive political force, or in helping them win some political battle.

Many of these activities are primarily of interest to those immediately involved rather than to other people. Since the kinds of people likely to participate in participative research are likely to be rather unusual kinds of people, it is doubtful if generalizations can be based on this kind of research anyway. Published success stories, however, are important in building a movement, and published stories of failure important in reminding members of the movement how powerful are the forces they have to strive against.

The practices and skills centrally involved in this kind of research are those such as counselling, group therapy, education (particularly political education), organizational development and political activism. This raises questions as whether it is apposite to call these kinds of activities 'research' at all, and why anyone should want to do so, for often exactly the same activities are carried out without being called 'research'. So why would people want to represent what might otherwise be called political activism, or group therapy, as being 'research'? There seem to be two kinds of reason for this.

Action research

The first is on the basis that this is an extension of experimental method. This argument may be advanced when these activities are called *action research*. Then reference will probably be made to the psychologist Kurt Lewin who in the 1930s allegedly coined that term (Lewin 1997). Lewin clearly saw the difficulties of generalizing from highly controlled experiments as discussed in Chapter 3, Section 3.10 and Chapter 4. His picture of action research is as a way of doing experiments under natural conditions. Lewin reports only one such 'change experiment' (1997: 148). This divided delegates to a congress on race relations into groups who received different kinds of support after the congress, and investigated which groups were more successful in fostering good race relations on their return to their home areas. The fact that Lewin desired to make a particular change didn't stop him setting up one comparison group who received no support at all, because had he not done this he would have been unable to discern whether offering post-congress support had any effect. And, except for the way in which 'field experiments' have to differ from controlled ones (Chapter 4, Section 4.2), Lewin otherwise followed an orthodox experimental approach.

Like Lewin, some people who say they are practising action research model their practice on experimental methods, building in controls where possible, taking care to define the situation prior to the action and to describe it accurately after the action (for example, Barker 1992; Titchen and Binnie 1994). They see their main objective as contributing to a general stock of knowledge about what interventions are likely to have what consequences under what circumstances, and adopting their interpretation of action research as a means of getting round the problem of the artificiality of experimental situations. Apart from the name, there is very little difference between these and the 'design experiments' and the n-of-1 experiments discussed in Chapter 4, Section 4.5.

By contrast, there is much of what is called 'action research' which seems much more interested in making an immediate and local change, where the only aspect of 'experimentalism' is that of doing something and seeing what happens. There may be no controls, little attempt to produce an accurate picture of the situation before the action and the situation after it, and hence great difficulty in knowing what effects the action taken actually had. Typically, the evidence presented will be in the form of personal testimonies by those involved. Many of the articles published in the journal *Educational Action Research* take this form. 'Educational' in this title does not mean that the research is necessarily conducted in educational institutions, but that its main purpose is to provide opportunities for people to learn from doing the research. What people are supposed to learn from doing the research is not how to do research, but about themselves and their situations.

Sometimes a different kind of validity criterion is suggested for this kind of research – **catalytic validity** – where the research is judged as valid or not in terms of whether it effects a desirable change (Lather 1991; Kincheloe and McLaren 1994). However, it is idle to propose this as a validity criterion without setting up the control structures which would allow judgement to be made as to whether a desirable change had occurred because of the action taken.

In some circles, at least, the term 'research' is prestigious. This may be a second reason why people want to label what would otherwise be called 'practice' as 'research'. This may go with the notion that making a distinction between researchers and others is indefensibly elitist. In these terms, participative research in which, say, the tenants of a council estate become co-researchers, represents a democratization of research: a kind of 'people's research'. To be interesting to them the 'research' has to address their immediate concerns and to have some tangible pay-offs: for example, winning a campaign against damp housing (Hunt 1993). Thus again 'research' becomes more like 'practice'. Nonetheless, writing about the research continues to be published in academic journals in very difficult theoretical terms, which most members of disadvantaged groups would find very hard to understand.

Practitioner research

In its more orthodox forms, research not only divides researchers from research subjects, but also divides researchers from practitioners. Applying the term 'research' to what otherwise would be called social work, or nursing, or community work, or teaching, turns what practitioners would ordinarily do as practice into research. There have been strong movements for *practitioner research* in education (Elliott 1991; Middlewood, Coleman and Lumby 1999), health (Nichols 1997) and social work (Fuller and Petch 1995), all favouring action research. Doctors continue to control 'medical research' and nurses, 'nursing research'. Millions of pounds has been spent by central government in the NHS to facilitate 'clinical audit' through which groups of practitioners monitor their own performance and mount research investigations with a view to improvement. The results have actually been rather disappointing (Thomas 2002; Audit Commission 2003). See also Chapter 4 on design experiments, which are very often conducted by practitioners addressing problems identified by practitioners.

The need for practitioners to do the research is argued on the grounds that it is practitioners who really know what research needs to be done to provide the knowledge that will be useful in their field. This usually turns out to be research which looks very much like practitioners doing their thing and studying it at the same time. Practitioner research also has the advantage of 'cutting out the middle-man' so that there is an immediate feedback of results from the practitioner as researcher to the (same) practitioner as practitioner. Very often the desired results are in terms of learning for professional development (Middlewood, Coleman and Lumby 1999; Blenkin, Kelly and Rose 2001) and/or improvement in the organization where the research was conducted (Coghlan and Brannick 2000), rather than the production of findings for widespread dissemination. Another advantage of re-labelling 'practice' as 'research' is that it enables a nurse, a teacher, or a social worker to gain a research degree by submitting a study of their own practice.

These kinds of research are claimed to produce effects, such as greater community cohesion, enhanced self-images, better political understanding, more empathetic relationships between practitioners and clients, or further-ing the cause of women's liberation. To this extent, then, they should be amenable to appraisal in terms of whether the methods used did indeed produce the effects claimed. As noted in Chapter 3, Section 3.5 and in Chapters 7 and 8, the only way to bring off a convincing claim that doing something had a particular effect is by using a research design which includes devices for controlling variables. However, with few exceptions (notably clin-ical audit and design experiments and some self-proclaimed action researchers), these kinds of research tend to reject the idea of control. Thus many such studies in action research (participative or practitioner) fail to produce convincing accounts that the 'action' taken had the effects claimed for it.

ACTIVITY 14   Appraising a performance indicator

Performance indicators are increasingly used to evaluate the performance of public services. There are well over 400 performance indicators for the NHS (www.healthcarecommission.org.uk and navigate to 'performance ratings') and about 200 for social services (www.csci.org.uk/ and navigate to 'star ratings'). For education, scores on Standard Achievement Tests (SATs) and in national examinations are used to judge the relative performance of schools. In 2004 the Welsh stopped publishing school results in ways that allowed schools to be league tabled, because the raw results reflected the socio-economic background of intakes rather than the quality of schools. By contrast the English Department for Education and Skills (DfES) began to publish the GCSE results for schools in a way that showed the relationship between pupils' SATs scores in earlier years and their 16+ examination results (DfES 2007). This 'value-added' approach is supposed to provide a measure of progress attributable to school-level factors – school effects. But there is considerable doubt as to whether it does so (Gorard 2006b). Put simply, the pupils in schools with the higher social class intakes on average recorded greater progress, so the value-added measures will only truly measure value added in terms of contrasts between schools with similar social compositions.

Table 14.1 lays out some questions which need to be asked in order to appraise any performance indicator. For this activity:

(a) Re-read Chapter 7, Section 7.3.

(b) Visit the DfCSF web site, look at the secondary school league tables and read the explanation given there (www.dcsf.gov.uk/performancetables/).

(c) Use the questions in Table 14.1 to appraise the use of 16+ examination results as data for performance indication:

   (i) in comparing the performance of schools one with another, both with-out and with reference to previous SATs scores;

   (ii) in comparing the performance of the same school year on year, both without and with reference to previous SATs scores.

TABLE 14.1   Questions to ask about performance indicators

1 *Values* On what, and on whose values, is performance measurement based? Who decides what measures and by what justification? What performance indicators (PIs) would be appropriate to other values held by other people?

2 *Costs* Is the cost of collecting and processing the data justified by the benefits of having them, and where do the costs and the benefits fall?

3 *Incentives* Does the measurement provide incentives to improve performance? What is counted as 'improvement' and by whom? (See **1**.) Or does it divert effort into achieving less worthwhile objectives (according to someone's judgement)?

4 *Performance* Are changes on the PI clearly attributable to the actions of those whose performance it is supposed to evaluate, and are they able to respond effectively to what the PI shows?

5 *Independence* Is the production of PI data protected from the influence of interested parties: can the data be massaged or rigged?

6 *Simplicity* Is the meaning of the PI easily understood by whosoever is the audience for the information?

7 *Even-handedness* Is there provision for judging performance according to what is feasible for practitioners/ agencies to achieve in their different circumstances?

8 *Validity* Does the PI measure what it purports to measure? (See also **4**.)

9 *Reliability* Are the same means of measurement used in the same way by different people/agencies? (See also **5** and **7**.)

10 *Sensivity and robustness* Are changes in performance speedily and attributably reflected in changes in the indicator, and is the indicator unaffected by irrelevant factors? (See also **4**.)

11 *Transparency:* Is the method through which the PI data are produced transparent and open to inspection?

12 *Timeliness and availability:* are the PI data available at a time when they are needed to the people who are supposed to respond to them?

Further reading

Hammersley (2000b) is a book of essays on various aspects of values and social research, advocating value neutrality. Partisan or value-led research is marked by vigorous internal disputes about ethics, politics and research strategy so that it is difficult to find works which adequately represent even the feminist, anti-racist and disability versions. However, Lather (1986) is a widely cited essay advocating value-led research from a Marxist, or Marxist–feminist point of view. Stanley and Wise (1983, 1993) are arguments for partisan feminist research, Ben-Tovim *et al.* (1986) for partisan research of the anti-racist kind and Barnes and Mercer (1997) for disability research.

Reason (1994) puts the case for participative research. Hart and Bond (1995) is a good introduction to action research by enthusiasts for this approach and Reason and Bradbury (2007) is exhaustive. The University of Sydney hosts an 'electronic reader' on action research with accumulating content (www.scu.edu.au/schools/gcm/ar/arr/arow/default.html).

Clinical audit research is supported by the Clinical Audit Support Centre (www.clinicalauditsupport.com). Teacher researchers are supported by the British Educational Research Association (www.bera.ac.uk) and the Scottish Research in Education Centre (www.scre.ac.uk/). Many Universities support local practitioner researcher networks among teachers, social workers, or nurses.

Gomm, Needham and Bullman (2000: pp. 306–13) suggests critical questions to ask about qualitative research in general and action research in particular. Spencer *et al.* (2003), from the Cabinet office, offer a more extensive model of quality in qualitative evaluation research.

15 Systematic Reviews, Meta-Analysis and Syntheses from Diverse Sources

By the end of this chapter, you will:

- Understand how a systematic review differs from a narrative review
- Know what is meant by statistical meta-analysis, its use and the problems with the method
- Know about the *Cochrane Collaboration* and the *Campbell Collaboration* and how to access them
- Know of the *Qualidata* archive, and how to access it
- Understand the principle behind using Bayesian statistics in synthesizing evidence from diverse sources
- Know what is meant by qualitative comparative analysis (QCA) and meta-ethnography, and how they differ from one another.

And you will know the meaning of the following terms:

Boolean algebra • citation bias • compositional bias • conflicts of interest • fixed effects and random effects • forest plot • fuzzy logic • inclusion criteria • multi-method studies • prior probabilities and posterior probabilities • publication bias • secondary analysis • substantive as opposed to statistical significance • vote counting

Within the chapter there is an Activity which will test your understanding of confidence rating.

15.1 Introduction

Secondary analysis refers to the reworking of data already collected. Chapter 9 touched on the secondary analysis of administrative data. This chapter will concentrate on secondary analysis where there is an attempt to synthesize the results of more than one research study using approaches which are formalized. Terms vary but those to be used here are *systematic reviews*, *meta-analysis*, *meta-ethnography*, and *qualitative comparative analysis (QCA)*. This is *triangulation* on the grand scale (see also Chapter 9, Section 9.5; Chapter 10, Section 10.2; Chapter 11, Section 11.2; and especially Chapter 13, Section 13.7).

Although by no means restricted to these fields, the chapter also gives a brief introduction to *Bayesian statistics* as they are used in synthesizing data from various sources.

> Cumulation has always been a problem in the social and behavioural sciences: 'There are never enough bricks and there are too few good synthesizers who wish to search out the bricks and thus put the wall together. These worthy people are usually too busy working on their own data!'
>
> C. Wright Mills (1959: 65)

Somehow, or other, individual studies do not seem to build into coherent bodies of knowledge in the way that happens in the natural sciences. A recognition of this is what led psychologists first (Glass 1976; Rosenthal 1979) and then other human scientists to begin to look for special procedures for synthesizing knowledge.

15.2 Systematic reviews

The movement for 'evidence-based practice' in health care, social work, the criminal justice system, education and other public services has generated a great demand for research demonstrating which practices are effective in producing desired results (see also Chapter 4, Section 4.4; Chapter 14, Section 14.3). Often the evidence which does exist is scattered across a number of different studies, which may be small in scale and of variable quality and which may give discrepant results so that studies just don't 'add up'. The response has been to develop techniques to weigh studies against each other in terms of the confidence with which their findings can be accepted – *systematic reviews* – and to *combine* data from different studies to reach an overall judgement – *meta-analysis*. But an additional purpose of both is communication between researchers and practitioners, always a difficult channel. Systematic reviews enormously reduce the effort required of practitioners and other service decision-makers in finding and evaluating research evidence to inform their decisions. In practice, most practitioners won't even read the reviews except in bullet point form, or as embedded in recommendations and guidelines for good practice.

The *Cochrane Collaboration* (www.cochrane.org/index.htm) unites a number of academic centres together for the purpose of conducting systematic reviews and meta-analyses, mainly in medicine but also in other human service fields. It is named after Archie Cochrane who was important in pointing out in the 1950s that most of medicine was practised without sound evidence as to its effectiveness, or in the face of evidence of its ineffectiveness and dangerousness (Cochrane 1972). For health care in the UK, large numbers of systematic reviews, usually with accompanying meta-analyses (Section 15.4), are conducted under the auspices of the National Institute for Clinical Excellence (NICE) and its Scottish counterpart which from time to time arouse controversy by refusing to endorse a treatment for inclusion on the NHS menu – on grounds of unsafety, ineffectiveness, or low cost-effectiveness.

> **PANEL 15.1** The usual characteristics of a systematic review
>
> - They review research studies addressing a similar research question and adopting a similar methodology
> - Or, if the object is methodological, they review research studies using a range of methods, or the same methods applied with different degrees of rigour, to see how these differences generate difference in results
> - They attempt a *comprehensive* review including published and unpublished studies, and the unpublished data from published studies, thus trying to overcome publication bias (see Panel 15.3)
> - They use quality criteria as:
>   - *Inclusion criteria*, to screen out what are regarded as lower-quality studies
>   - A basis for *weighting* studies in terms of the credibility of their findings
> - The quality criteria or inclusion criteria are:
>   - *Methodological* – how confident can we be about the results of each study as judged by the methods used (see Panel 15.2, and Chapter 4, Section 4.4)?
>   - *Temporal* – how up-to-date are the studies?
>   - *Absence of bias* due to conflict of interest (for example, Cho and Bero 1996 found that 98% of drug company sponsored research, published in medical journals, was favourable to the interests of the company, while this was true of only 79% of studies without such sponsorship)
>   - For particular topics, *other quality criteria* may be used in addition.
> - The review may include a *meta-analysis* or *vote-counting exercise* (Section 15.3).

The Campbell Collaboration (www.campbellcollaboration.org/) is a similar network for producing systematic reviews for education, social work and criminal justice interventions.

The characteristics of systematic reviews are shown in Panel 15.1. Reviews of research other than those called 'systematic' are not necessarily unsystematic, but they do not follow a standard formula. The purpose of other reviews may be to give a broad overview of a field of knowledge, as in the kind of 'literature review' typical of PhD theses and in the early chapters of monographs, or to compare and contrast different approaches. Often, other kinds of review articles are propagandist, with the reviewer being rather picky about the research chosen, ignoring or lambasting research with gives unwelcome findings, and lauding research which supports some case the author is making. Others are exercises in self-promotion by the reviewer. Reviews other than the systematic kind are often lumped together as *narrative reviews*, a not very helpful residual category. But the term 'narrative' does suggest, correctly, that such reviewers are free to use the review to tell whatever story they wish, however they wish to tell it.

Rating the quality of studies for a systematic review is often done by groups of experts (see Panel 15.2), and cross-checked with an inter-rater reliability test (Chapter 2, Section 2.10).Usually the studies are 'masked' as to authorship which is the equivalent of blinding when studies rather than human beings are the subjects (see also Chapter 3, Section 3.6). Sometimes

---

PANEL 15.2 Scale for measuring the quality of randomized trials

Please read the article and try to answer the following questions . . .

1 Was the study described as randomized (includes the use of words such as 'randomly', 'random' and 'randomization')?
2 Was the study described as double blind?
3 Was there a description of withdrawals and drop-outs?

Scoring the items:
Either give a score of 1 point for each 'Yes' or 0 points for each 'No'. There are no in-between marks.

Give 1 additional point if:	for question **1**, the method to generate the sequence of randomization was described and it was appropriate (table of random numbers, computer generated, etc.)
and/or:	if for question **2** the method of double blinding was described and it was appropriate (identical placebo, active placebo, dummy, etc.)
Deduct 1 point if:	for question **1**, the method to generate the sequence of randomization was described and it was inappropriate (patients were allocated alternately, or according to date of birth, hospital number, etc.) and/or: for question **2**, the study was described as double blind but the method of blinding was inappropriate (e.g. comparison of tablet versus injection with no double dummy) and/or: for question **3**, the number and reasons for withdrawals and drop outs were not described.

The Jadad Scale was devised by Jadad *et al.* (1996: 10–11) to be used by groups of experts to screen studies for inclusion in systematic reviews and to assign weightings to them. Their validation of this instrument showed that studies with lower-quality scores typically reported larger effects.

---

the order in which judges read the studies is randomized. For various practical (see Chapter 4, Section 4.1) and ethical reasons (Chapter 16, Section 16.4) RCTs are not particularly common in education, social work or the criminal justice system, so that more inclusive standards have to be adopted for systematic reviews in these fields. For quality criteria which might be used with regard to survey work see Chapters 6 and 8; for case and population control studies see Chapter 7, Section 7.4).

Publication bias (see Panel 15.3 and Rothstein 2005) is really only a subsection of what might be called the 'research knowledge distribution bias', referring to the fact that, at any one time, research has only tackled certain topics in certain ways. For example, third world cash crops such as coffee or cocoa have been studied much more than third world subsistence crops such as sorghum or yams, or, until the 1970s, sociological research on inequality tended to focus on inequality between males, and to ignore gender inequality. This kind of bias shows itself most clearly in what has been published. If systematic reviewers attempt to synthesize all that is known about a topic

PANEL 15.3 Publication bias

- All the research which is easy to find is not a representative sample of all the research which has been conducted
- All the research which is published is not a representative sample of all the research which has been conducted
- All the research which has been conducted is not a representative sample of all the research which might have been conducted

Publication bias derives from:

- Pre-publication circumstances, including the topicality of particular research questions, the differential availability of research funding and the differential accessibility of different settings or social groups
- The availability of publishing outlets for different topics
- Manipulation of the publication system – for example, by dominant figures' editorial control; by drug companies publishing only research favourable to their drugs
- The biases of particular journals for articles which accord with their editorial line
- The biases of referees who conduct pre-publication reviews recommending publication or not[a]
- The biases of research sponsors, including government ministries, who may veto publication
- Limitations of space (which prejudices the publication of qualitative research and limits the amount of data published by any researchers)
- The preference of publishers for
  - novel findings, rather than findings which confirm what was already thought to be the case
  - definite findings, rather than tentative ones
  - positive findings (e.g. that an intervention is effective), or for
  - controversially negative findings (i.e. that something widely thought to be so, is not so)

  and against publishing material which is similar to that published earlier.
- A further bias may be superimposed on publication bias if the quality criteria for inclusion in a systematic review inadvertently rule out most studies with findings pointing in one direction, and rule in most studies pointing in the other
- The most usual effect of publication bias has been to increase the chances of publication for research finding that an intervention is effective, as against the chances of publication for research which finds that the benefits of an intervention are unproven (Song *et al.* 2001).

Note: [a] The journals from which studies are drawn for systematic review publish articles after 'peer review': that is, review by experts in the field. Nearly always, reviews and reviewers are anonymous to avoid bias in favour or against people on a personal or gender basis, although it is often easy to see through the masking.

they are starting from a corpus of material which is already likely to be biased by omissions. To counter this, systematic reviewers attempt to find not only everything which is published (within a given time frame), including material in journals published in lesser-used languages (Juni *et al.* 2002) but also unpublished studies and the unpublished data and calculations on which published material is based. This is much easier than it used to be now electronic searching is possible and now that most scholars in a field are connected to each other via the internet – in small-world networks (see Chapter 5, Section 5.9). With internet publishing the size of publications is not a limitation (Song *et al.* 1999). However limits are still set by the fact that most internet publishing is accompanied by a hardcopy version to which size limits do apply. The huge increase in academic journals from the 1970s onwards ended the situation of an earlier period when a relatively small number of dominant figures in each field could exercise a stranglehold on what got published, usually in ways that disadvantaged their rivals. With internet publishing, this would be impossible.

'Snowballing' involves following the citations in one article to the citations in another and so on. It is similar to the sampling technique of the same name where what is being sampled is people (see Chapter 6, Panel 6.3). In the latter application, sampling is, or should be, adopted when what is required is a sample of people who are like each other and *un*representative of the general population (delinquents, for example). But the sample required for systematic reviews is a representative one, and this approach will produce a corpus with *citation bias*: an exaggerated form of publication bias. These kinds of bias are an even greater problem with regard to meta-analysis, and will be dealt with further below.

Those who conduct systematic reviews usually give a detailed account of the *strategy* they used to search for sources. This is so that others can check the representativeness and comprehensiveness of the material reviewed. They sometimes list the sources they have excluded as well as their inclusions.

15.3 Statistical meta-analysis

This section will deal with meta-analysis in its narrower usage as applying to the synthesis of results from several quantitative studies all using a similar methodology, sometimes termed *statistical* meta-analysis to distinguish it from the meta-analysis of qualitative materials.

Table 15.1 shows some results which might have come from a number of studies of the effectiveness of a custodial regime for young offenders. The outcome of each study is given as an odds-ratio (OR). The results of all of them are combined to give a pooled OR of 1.20, which is given with its confidence limits 1.3 to 1.28 (see Panel 15.4).

ORs become more meaningful when displayed visually with their confidence limits, as in Figure 15.1, which is called a 'Forest Plot'.

In order to be entered into calculations to produce a pooled estimate, studies have to be commensurate, or be processed to become so. There are problems here, summarized in Table 15.3. As you can see, these problems are a case for the development of instruments for common use with regard to particular research questions.

TABLE 15.1   Meta-analysis of five studies of the effectiveness of a custodial regime for young offenders: invented data

a	b	c		d		e		f	g	h	j
Study no.	Total no. subjects	No. subjects in each arm		No. not reconvicted after 2 years		No. reconvicted after 2 years		% Diff. (%)	Odds-ratio	95% Confidence interval	
		Prgrm	control	Prgrm	control	Prgrm	control			l.c.l	u.c.l
1	846	424	422	84	86	340	336	-0.6	0.97	0.69	1.35
2	3,489	1,149	2,340	231	936	918	1,404	-19.9	0.38	0.32	0.45
3	9,003	4,503	4,500	899	450	3,604	4,050	10.0	2.25	1.99	2.54
4	4,091	2,051	2,040	412	346	1,639	1,694	3.1	1.23	1.05	1.44
5	6,087	3,043	3,044	607	305	2,436	2,739	9.9	2.24	1.93	2.59
Pooled	23,516	11,170	12,346	2,233	2,123	8,937	10,223	2.8	1.20	1.13	1.28

How to read this table

The table shows five studies using a similar programme (**Prgrm**) with young offenders while in custodial care. Young offenders in the same institutions, but not following the programme were the controls. Outcomes are whether a young offender was re-convicted within the period 2 years after release. Column **f** shows the difference in percentages of reconvicted offenders for each treatment. A positive score favours the programme. Column **g** shows the odds ratio and **h** and **j** the lower (**l.c.l.**) and upper (**u.c.l.**) confidence limits for the odds ratio (see Panel 15.4 and Table 15.2). The final row of the table shows the results of pooling all results of all the studies.

PANEL 15.4   The confidence intervals of odds ratios (ORs)

TABLE 15.2   Outcome of study 1 in Table 15.1

	Intervention group (prgrm)	*Control group*
Happened (didn't get reconvicted)	(a) e.g. 84	(b) e.g. 86
Didn't happen (did get reconvicted)	(c) e.g. 340	(d) e.g. 336

The formula for the odds ratio (OR) is **(a/b)/(c/d)**. For study **1** in Table 15.1 this is:

$$(84/86)/(340/336) = 0.965 = 0.97$$

Conventionally the figures are entered so that if the results favour the intervention this generates an odds ratio of more than 1.

Panel 6.2 explains confidence intervals (CIs) and shows the way they are calculated for survey findings. CIs for ORs have a similar meaning. Those in Table 15.1 are the 95% confidence limits. Those in the first row indicate that, although the best bet for the odds ratio is 0.97, there is a 95% chance that the figure lies between 0.69 and 1.35 and only a 5% chance that it lies outside, on either side of that range.

The calculation of CIs for ORs involves conversion into and then out of logarithms. This gives the distribution of the error a more normal distribution (see Chapter 2, Panel 2.8) and is why one whisker in Figure 15.1 is longer than the other (though this would not be so if the figure was drawn on a log scale). It also makes manual, and even spreadsheet calculation, tedious.

If you don't have access to one of the major statistics software packages such as SPSS, then the SISA website has a useful calculator for CIs for ORs and for other statistics (http://home.clara.net/sisa/two2hlp.htm).

A pooled estimate is supposed to provide the best estimate of the effect of following the programme, rather than the control regime, as derived from all the studies together. A pooled OR is shown in Table 15.1 and Figure 15.1. Procedures for pooling fall into two types.

The *fixed effects* or *inverse variance approach* assumes that each study is measuring an effect which is really of the same size, but which shows as a different sizes in different studies because of sampling error. What is pooled is the inverse of the variance of each study, which weights the contribution each study makes to the pool in a way that offsets the effects of sampling error.

The *random effects approach* assumes that underlying each study there is a version of the same phenomenon, but which varies in size. Pooling involves conversions of the original outcome data, both to deal with sampling error (as above), and in accordance with a model of how the effect size 'really' varies (Sutton *et al.* 2001). This is the kind of statistical

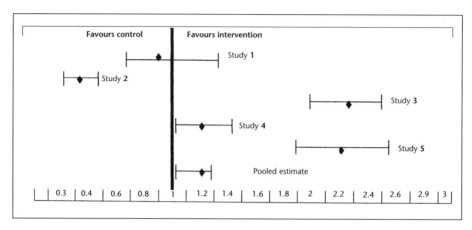

Figure 15.1   *Odds ratios and 95% confidence intervals for effects of young offenders'*
programme; data as shown in Table 15.1: Forest Plot

How to read this figure
Think of the vertical line down the middle as a line of no differential effect. If an intervention has the same effect as the control condition, then the OR will lie plumb on this line with its whiskers on either side – as is nearly the case with study **1**. The diagram has been marked up to show whether a result 'Favours intervention' or 'Favours control'. Where this is not done, it is usual for ORs above 1 to favour intervention. Where the CIs span the central line it remains unclear as to whether the results favoured the controls or the intervention. If, as is the case with studies **2**, **3**, **4**, and **5**, the confidence interval lies clearly on one side or another, whiskers and all, then this is a claim that the outcome clearly favours one or the other. The further away from the mid-line the more definite the judgement. If the 99% confidence intervals were used the intervals would be longer and there would be less of a chance of reaching a definitive judgement.

black magic that makes non-statisticians very worried. Which approach to use, and within each, which of various formulae to use, is controversial. Luckily the pooled estimates reached by different measures are often very similar.

The meta-analysis above has resolved a situation where there were a number of studies showing different results. The pooled estimate shows a small benefit for the programme in terms of numbers of offenders not being re-convicted: around 2 or 3 fewer reconvictions for every 100 offenders on the programme. Statistically this is a very small difference. But if one regime is much cheaper, or if there are other major advantages or disadvantages associated with one rather than the other, quite small statistically significant differences might be of considerable, practical, or **substantive** significance. But given the possibility of a pooled estimate being misleading, it would be unwise to base practical decisions on small statistical differences.

But what has the meta-analysis really resolved? Meta-analysis treats a number of studies as if they were all parts of one large study. If we were evaluating one large study we would be asking the kinds of questions indicated in Chapter 3, Figure 3.2, and discussed throughout that chapter.

Commensurability problems in statistical meta-analysis   *TABLE 15.3*

Problem	Response
Studies measuring different base-line and outcome data, and or with different research designs	This is not usually resolvable within the framework of a statistical meta-analysis, but see Section 15.4
Studies measuring different base-line data but similar outcome data, or vice versa	• Some way may be found to impute data to some studies to replace incongruent data, or the researcher may work with a range of models making different assumptions for replacements for incongruent data.
Studies measuring similar base-line and outcome data with different scales (Chapter 2, Section 2.3)	• The lowest-common-denominator (LCD) measure will probably be used – usually a nominal level measure such as an OR – but it may not be clear where an ordinal or interval scale should be cut to yield nominal measures
	• Scales may distribute data differently including having floor and ceiling effects, and skewed distributions – usually dealt with by transforming data into z-scores to give normal distributions (Chapter 2, Panel 2.8) or other transformations; this should be done before transforming to nominal measures
	• More rarely, measures produced by different instruments can be converted directly from one to the other if both were involved in a criterion validity test (Chapter 2, Section 2.7) as with many aptitude tests and intelligence tests
	• Different scales may cover different ranges – either mismatches will have to be deleted, or shorter ranges extended with imputed data
Outcome data measured at different stages	• Shorter-term measures may have to be projected forwards, or longer term measures projected backwards, to estimate outcomes at a common time point in relation to intervention.

Are there outcome differences between the two conditions in each study attributable to:

1   Pre-existing differences between subjects (not successfully eliminated when subjects were divided into groups, and greater than those which can be adjusted for using a fixed or a random effects approach)?
2   Chance at the point of allocating subjects to conditions making the groups non-equivalent?
3   Differential drop-out from the two arms?
4   Participants' knowledge about their involvement?
5   Bias or inconsistency in measurement and recording?
6   Infidelity to treatment protocols?

In a meta-analysis some of these questions will be addressed by the quality control procedures. If the only studies allowed into the analysis are RCTs, then that minimizes the possibility of confounding via **1** and **2** (Chapter 3, Section 3.3). If only studies reporting results on an intention to treat basis, and with few lost subjects are included, that deals with **3** (Chapter 3, Section 3.4). Only including blinded trials deals with **4** (Chapter 3, Section 3.6). **5** and **6** are much more difficult to deal with via selection on the basis of quality criteria, since it is likely that even the original researchers won't know about them – or, if they do, won't admit to them. Note that all these questions are much more difficult to answer the further we relax the controls present in a blinded RCT.

Those are the kinds of questions we ask of *differences in outcome between conditions* in the *individual studies* entering a meta-analysis. They re-occur in relation to *differences between studies*, as questions about the diversity of results *within* the meta-analysis which enter into the final pooled estimate. As with individual experiments, the difference of outcome attributable to a failure of randomization to create two exactly equivalent groups is managed by calculating CIs (or conducting significance tests) for the pooled estimate and through the procedure of conversion into inverse variances. The CIs or the significance levels give an estimate of the magnitude of the difference which *might* be still be attributed to chance differences in allocating subjects to conditions. But the effect size differences in studies contributing to a pooled estimate are also likely to include other differences between studies.

Single studies with markedly different outcomes to the remainder of the set stand out and raise suspicions. A consistent bias across a majority of studies will not. Meta-analysis tends to be practised on the hopeful assumption that research artefacts in each study will balance each other out in a large set and hence in the pooled estimate. More effectively, sensitivity analyses may be conducted.

Sensitivity analysis for the effect of differences between studies usually takes the form of calculating the pooled estimate as many times as there are studies, minus 1, each time with one study left out. Similarly, sometimes studies are divided into groups according to their methodological rigour and pooled estimates calculated separately. If, for example, a group of studies without blinding shows a much larger effect than a group with blinding, then that is presumptive evidence that failure to blind spuriously inflates effect size (as, indeed, shown by Schulz *et al.* 1995 and Pidal *et al.* 2007). The association between poor control and spuriously enhanced effect size is not inevitable however. Glass and Smith (1978) in a classic early meta-analysis found that it was the better-controlled studies which showed the strongest inverse correlation between between class size and educational achievement.

Sometimes a blanket recommendation that some intervention should become standard practice is issued on the basis of the pooled estimate favouring the intervention, when the meta-analysis itself will have usually contained some studies where it was implemented unsuccessfully. In our example (Table 15.1), two studies showed the controls with better outcomes than those experiencing the intervention: in study **2** substantially so. Was there something odd about the circumstances of study **2**? Was the programme badly implemented there? Or is a result such as that part of the normal variation which would be expected if the programme was rolled out more widely?

ACTIVITY   Updating belief

It is worth doing this short Activity here as a preparation for what is to come.

1   Look at Table 15.1. What level of confidence does this evidence give you that the programme is superior in preventing reconvictions by comparison with the control conditions? Rate your confidence on a 10-point scale where 10 = 100% certain superiority, 5 = undecided either way and 0 =100% certain that the control condition is superior.

2   Now rework the data in Table 15.1 to calculate for each study the percentage success rate for both conditions, and describe the overall pattern.

3   Imagine that for study **3** there was some ethnographic research suggesting that resources were poached from the control condition to resource the programme, and that for studies **3** and **5** there were data from a self-report questionnaire with young offenders from both the control and the programme groups admitting to roughly the same levels of offending after discharge, though all the surveys had a low response rate (Chapter 6, Section 6.9). How would this information and your thoughts on question **2** above change the level of confidence you had originally. Rate this again on the same 10-point scale.

These points will be picked up later in the chapter.

In terms of reconvictions, the performance of the programme was very consistent whereever it was implemented, but the performance of the regimes which served as control was very variable. It happened that 64% of all cases were drawn from two studies in which the control regime had very high rates of reconviction (**3** and **5**). These comparisons gives a pooled estimate its greatest steer towards favouring the intervention. Differences in the control conditions between studies can be very important in meta-analysis. The ideal situation in meta-analysis is a set of studies where the control conditions are identical. But this is rarely the case except with placebo-controlled drug trials.

If we delete studies **3** and **5** from the set, the pooled estimate (crudely estimated) drops to an OR of 0.63 (95% CI 0.37 to 0.70) favouring the control condition and we can see that the results of studies **3** and **5** were not so much due to the good performance of the experimental programme as to the poor showing of the regime used as its control. This should have shown up on a sensitivity analysis dropping each study from the set in turn.

Variations in outcomes for the same intervention in different trials, over and beyond what might be expected by chance are often the subject of what is sometimes called *second-level meta-analysis* to further specify the conditions under which an intervention is most, and or least, likely to be successful (Detsky *et al.* 1992). Rather than being the end of the process, a table such as Table 15.1 can be the beginning of a programme asking what works, for whom, under what circumstances, and drawing in data from studies other than experimental ones (see Section 15.4).

Publication bias and statistical meta-analysis

Publication bias is even more of a problem for meta-analysis than it is for systematic reviews (Section 15.2). The calculation of a pooled estimate makes most sense on the assumption that the studies assembled constitute a representative sample of all the studies of this kind which might be conducted. Then, as with any other representative sampling procedure, taking samples and adding them together will give a grand sample which has characteristics similar to the population from which each sample was drawn; though it is notable that survey researchers are much more chary of combining samples drawn in slightly different ways than are meta-analysts of experimental research (Chapter 6, Section 6.6). Those who conduct systematic reviews and meta-analyses do attempt to construct a 'grand sample' which is representative of all the work which has been published plus whatever relevant unpublished material they can find. But a representative sample of all that is not necessarily a representative sample of all the studies which could be made. Pre-publication and publication bias makes sure of that (see Panel 15.3).

Various kinds of *sensitivity analysis* are used to estimate the effect of publication bias on the mix of studies which enter into the meta-analysis. The estimate is of the number of unpublished studies which would need to be found, giving a statistically non-significant result in order to overturn a previous statistically significant result. Note that these are not estimates of the number of unpublished studies that actually exist. Rosenthal's 'file draw' or 'fail-safe N method' is the best known of these (Rosenthal 1979; Song *et al.* 2001).

In some respects meta-analysis is superior to the first-hand studies that it draws on. The number of subjects in all the studies combined is larger, the range of circumstances represented by many studies, rather than by one study is greater. There is a possibility that the errors and biases in individual studies will be balanced out by being combined so long as they are random errors. But this is only a possibility. There is also a possibility, though a lower one, that the errors and biases in individual studies will combine to create a more misleading picture than some individual studies do. Some meta-analyses are analyses of sets of studies:

- unrepresentative of all the studies which might be conducted (publication bias)
- each conducted in circumstances which are unrepresentative of normal practice (Chapter 4, Section 4.5)
- each on subjects who are unrepresentative of all the subjects who might be subjected to the intervention in practice (Chapter 4, Section 4.5).

There is a danger then that meta-analyses may exaggerate rather than ameliorate the problem of external validity associated with experimental research (see Chapter 3, Section 3.10).

Nonetheless statistical meta-analysis is a legitimate and valuable research practice. It is the best means available to synthesize quantitative data on effectiveness coming from different studies. The problem is not so much with the method as with the over-confidence with which the results may be regarded, particularly when incorporated into bureaucratic procedures of deciding what shall be good practice and regulating it within public services.

15.4 Bayesian Synthesis

Statistical meta-analysis is restricted to quantitative studies. It is on its safest grounds when dealing with blinded RCTs. But often there are relevant studies which are surveys, or are various kinds of qualitative research. Bayesian analysis offers a way of translating the findings of any kind of research, quantitative or qualitative, into numbers which can be combined to express the confidence with which a conclusion drawn from several diverse sources can be held.

The statistical techniques described elsewhere in this book are 'frequentist' or 'Fisherian': frequentist because they usually involve estimating the frequency with which some result might have arisen by chance, Fisherian after R. A. Fisher, probably the single most important figure in the development of this branch of statistics in England.

There is another tradition of statistics associated with the eighteenth-century clergyman the Reverend Thomas Bayes and the contemporary French mathematician Laplace. Bayesian statistics have always been important in business and clinical decision-making such as diagnostic medicine (Dowie 1996). Recently there has been a great deal of interest in other fields. One of these is synthesizing evidence from various sources.

The Bayesian approach involves making an estimate of the probability of some proposition being true (the 'prior probability' – sometimes just 'the prior'), and then updating this probability in the light of additional evidence to yield the 'posterior probability'). This is what you were asked to do in the Activity on p. 355. A story sometimes used to illustrate the Bayesian approach is that of a new born child (of immense intelligence apparently) who on her first day of life watches the sun rise, and wants to estimate the probability of this happening again. She invents a simple computer consisting of a bag and a supply of black and white pebbles: black for 'it won't', white for 'it will'. Since she has only one day's experience she hedges her bets and puts one black and one white pebble in the bag – a 50:50 probability. Thereafter, every time she observes the sun rising (or perhaps every day when there is no evidence that it didn't) she puts a white pebble into the bag. This means that if she takes a random sample of pebbles from the bag, on day 11, she should get a sample showing something like a 10:1 ratio, and on day 101, a sample showing something like a 100:1 ratio, and so on, each an updating of her original estimate.

In the Activity on p. 355 you were asked to update a probability estimate (your prior) which was based on the statistical meta-analysis, updating with reference to some qualitative research findings. This resulted in your posterior probability. In practice, priors might come from research, or from the consensus of experts, and they might be 'flat priors' where every possible (including highly unlikely) probabilities are updated. Applying Bayes' Theorem in practice to any but the simplest issue involves hard calculus, and Bayesian statistics didn't take off until the advent of cheap powerful computers and the requisite software.

As you will have seen from the Activity on p. 355 what a Bayesian analysis does here is to convert a subjective opinion into a statistic – a belief in the probability of something being true. Usually Bayesian calculations involve a consensus judgement by a group of experts in the relevant field. The fact that Bayesian analysis relies explicitly on subjective judgements makes it controversial. But while the judgements are subjective in the sense of being private and unaccountable, the role of subjectivity is minimized in that the process through which the judgements were elicited, and most of the evidence on which they were based, are objective. It is true of all science that however hard we try to be objective there will always be a residuum of our beliefs about which we cannot give a clear account (Polanyi 1958). Bayesians also point out that if you continually update your beliefs in this way it doesn't matter what the prior was. It would make only a marginal difference to the posterior estimate on day 101 as to whether the child prodigy had started with a prior of 50:50, or 100:0.

Consensus statements have long played a part in the social sciences, particularly in applications in management science and medicine, using techniques such as Delphi groups and nominal groups (see Chapter 10, Section 10.5). These can yield quantitative measures of agreement between judges (from **vote counting** for example, or kappa scores for levels of inter-rater agreement (see Chapter 2, Section 2.10).

Producing a confidence measure, through polling experts, does mean that such judgements depend on just which group of experts is assembled to make the judgement, raising issues about their competence and their biases. So just as the mix of studies is important to a meta-analysis and may be somewhat arbitrary, so also will be the mix of experts for a consensus exercise and any **compositional bias** will carry forward into the prior estimate for a Bayesian synthesis. But, of course, whatever approach is taken it is always true that the verdict you get is likely to depend on who is involved in the deliberations. Consensus statements can, and often are, produced without Bayesian synthesis.

Surveys results can be used to elicit prior and posterior probabilities and Bayesian synthesis allows qualitative research to be included alongside quantitative research in research syntheses. What gets incorporated is merely a probability figure. This ignores almost all of the richness and subtlety that qualitative research produces. Comparative qualitative analysis and meta-ethnography are two alternative approaches in which much more of the original in primary studies survives the synthesis.

15.5   Qualitative Comparative Analysis (QCA)

The term QCA is closely associated with Charles Ragin (Ragin 1989, 1994: Chapters 4–6; Ragin and Hein 1993). The approach will accommodate both qualitative and quantitative studies. It is a variant of what is sometimes called *cross-case analysis* or *comparative case method*, though those terms have been more often used for the analysis and synthesis of cases *within* a single research programme. At base, the approach couldn't be simpler. It involves gathering a relevant body of literature in the hopes of covering the full range of variation of the phenomenon of interest, and analysing it to identify the dimensions of its variation. No explicit quality criteria are used as filters, though the studies will be evaluated as time goes by, and the process of analysis doesn't have to wait until all the literature is assembled. Rather, this can go on until something akin to *theoretical saturation* (Chapter 12, Section 12.6) is reached and each additional study yields less new information.

Ragin and Hein (1993) adopt a procedure similar to that shown in Chapter 4 (Section 14.7). In their comparative analysis of the politics of race relations they identify the important ways in which ethnopolitical situations can vary and code each example accordingly. For example, code *A* stands for whether the dominant ethnic group is in numerical majority or minority, and code *B* stands for whether the dominant ethnic group is culturally homogeneous or not, and so on through the alphabet to code *N*. This identifies whether ethnic political dominance is at the level of the nation, as was the case in South Africa, or at a local government level as in Belgium. Thus each example can be given a profile such as: *AbCDEFgHIjKLMN*, where, for each letter, upper case designates the first modality – for example upper case 'A' means the dominant ethnic group is also in the numerical majority. A lowercase letter designates the opposite.

Treated as binary distinctions, this coding would generate a matrix of 16,384 possible combinations – more, if each dimension were finessed. This matrix is essentially the same as a *theoretical sampling frame* described in Chapter 12 (Section 12.5).

The first point of interest is in combinations that *don't* occur in reality – or, more correctly, for which there are no published studies. Publication bias aside, this will say something about how the conditions identified relate to each other. A second matter of interest is which variables are inevitably found together. Where this occurs they can be combined. Questions can be posed in the form of 'which outcomes are associated with which profiles?' For example, 'which profiles are most associated with uprisings of subordinated ethnic groups?'

Ragin's own approach becomes more difficult for many readers since his further analysis uses the algebra of symbolic logic, closely related to set theory: **Boolean algebra** (Ragin 1989). And his latest work has extended his use of symbolic logic into the field of '**fuzzy logic**' (Ragin 2000, see also Cooper 2005). This is a recognition that many social – and, indeed, many natural – categories are not composed of entities which are exclusively members or not and that members of a category do not necessarily all share the same characteristics. Rather, the members of a category have a 'family resemblance' to each other, the first and the second resembling each other in one way and the first and the third resembling each other in another way and so on. Ragin (2000) claims that fuzzy logic much better captures phenomena which are complex in the sense described in Chapter 5 (Section 5.7–5.11).

But without symbolic logic, fuzzy or otherwise, in a chapter called '*How to make evaluations cumulate*' Pawson and Tilley (1997: 115–52) do some synthesizing of information from various studies, and in Chapter 4, Tables 4.5 and 4.6 of this book you can see something similar again (see also Gomm 2000e: 171–91). Simply called 'comparative method', this has been part of stock-in-trade of social scientists since Compte and certainly since Durkheim (Fletcher 1972: 351–6).

15.6 Meta-ethnography and similar syntheses of qualitative data

The foundation text on meta-ethnography is Noblit and Hare (1988), which is mainly about synthesizing case studies within the same research programme. And most of the commentary on this method has actually been about the re-analysis of existing qualitative data, rather than about synthesis as such: see, for example, the special edition of *Sociological Research Online* (12(3), 2007) (www.socresonline.org.uk/home.html). However, most re-use entails attempts to bring existing qualitative data sets into line with each other and so involve synthesis at least to this extent. Despite the name, meta-ethnography covers interview as well as observation studies.

Of all areas of research, ethnography produced though loosely structured interviewing and by participant observation is probably the most difficult to synthesize. This is not only because many of the studies are so small scale and idiosyncratic, but because there is such a strong bias within this field for novelty – new settings, new concepts and new paradigms. In the 1960s Naroll and Naroll (1963) drew attention to **exoticism bias** in anthropology: a tendency to focus on what was different about the people studied, as compared with other subjects of anthropological work, and much the same might be said of studies of sub-cultures within Britain and America; again a steer against cumulation. Rashomon effects have been a common outcome of anthropologists independently studying the same society (Naroll 1973; see Chapter 12, Section 12.5).

Unlike quantitative researchers who can publish a large percentage of their data, or at least the results of processing it, qualitative researchers typically publish only illustrative selections. Therefore, other people's qualitative data have not usually been available for synthesis or re-analysis. Now the data from all ESRC-funded qualitative research has to be archived at the ESDS QUALI-DATA archive at the University of Essex, which also includes the data from some earlier classic studies (www.esds.ac.uk/qualidata/). But the field notes and other records of qualitative research are typically huge and often untidy.

As the Rashomon effect (Chapter 12, Section 12.5) suggests, there are some points where if one study is right, another must be wrong. For example, it is either true or false that a large number of cases charged as rape were heard by the courts in Samoa at the time of Margaret Mead's study. But a great deal of qualitative research deals with incorrigibles, where the attempt is to capture and convey what it is like to live a particular kind of life. Here there may be no way of deciding that one alternative is more true than another, or whether both versions are within the normal range of variation for the society in question.

Sometimes what is of interest in qualitative research is what confirms, illuminates, or undermines that are otherwise being treated as matters of fact – as in the Activity on p. 355 where qualitative information about the 'poaching' of resources from the control regime threw some doubt on what was shown by the quantitative data. But much of the re-use and or synthesis of qualitative data treats what is to be re-used as interpretations, and the process as one of *translation*: that is, of providing a (meta-)framework into which interpretations from different sources can all be translated.

An issue here is the question of whose prior interpretations are the focus. Some writers (Wood 2000; Weed 2005) write as if what is to be translated are the interpretative frameworks of the original researcher. There are concepts in qualitative research with a wide-ranging applicability which can be used to bring two or more pieces of qualitative research on to the same ground, for example deviancy amplification, stigma, moral career, timetables. These are terms which belong to the vocabulary of scholars not of the people they study.

Other writers behave as if what is important is to transcend the interpretations of the original researchers, get back to the interpretations of the people he or she studied and then translate them into some further, allegedly better and more generally applicable interpretative framework. For example, in order to chart changing attitudes to food, particularly its moral significance, Bishop (2007) drew on data from *The Edwardians* (Thompson 1975; Thompson and Lummis 2005) and the now historical data from *Mothers and Daughters* (Blaxter and Patterson 1982, 1983; Blaxter 2004), both from the Qualidata archive. Her main interest was in the interpretations of food by the subjects of the research. But the data only supplied what was *created* as the subject's interpretations by the different designs of each research projects, the choices of sample, the way questions were asked, the modes of recording the answers and so on. Thus she used what she could find of the commentaries by the researchers, as aids 'to see through', as it were, the research process to find the original ideas these women had about food.

This is just applying to a research study the kinds of thinking we would apply in evaluating a witness statement (see Chapter 13, Panel 13.2). It will always be difficult to know how successful this 'archaeological' task has been, but that is no reason not to attempt it. However, this was only the first phase of Bishop's study (and of others similar in kind). The next stage is to find a common framework in which to re-describe ideas about food held by women of different eras, including today's. Without an over-arching framework it would be difficult to give a coherent account of changes in attitudes and beliefs about food. To date Bishop has not published such a (meta-)framework, but she quotes Warde's framework as a step on the way:

Warde (1997) defines four antinomies that characterize food discourses: novelty/tradition, health/indulgence, economy/extravagance and convenience/care. During the periods the grandmothers describe, themes of tradition, economy and care were dominant. Tinned food as protection from want was surely more prominent for the grandmothers than would be typical today. In the 21st century, some of these discourses have shifted, with novelty, health, indulgence, convenience and extravagance more prominent.

(Bishop 2007: para 6.9)

What meta-ethnography turns out to be is a procedure of *thematic analysis*, similar to that described in Chapter 11, Section 11.3, but of completed research studies rather than of interviews or observations. And the search is for themes which can be organized into a *framework* – a 'meta-framework' – which will accommodate all the interpretations in all or most of the studies being considered.

This really is business as usual for qualitative researchers. Something like it occurs towards the beginning, and or the end, of many qualitative studies as a researcher puts her work in the context of studies by other people, but without this being termed meta-ethnography.

The kinds of synthesis described above attempt to treat a number of studies as if they were components of one single study, when they have not been designed for that purpose. As Table 15.3 showed, there are problems here even when the studies are very similar in design and addressed to much the same research question. Problems become much worse where, for example, the studies included are addressed to different research questions, use different methods of data collection, measure (or don't measure) different entities, ask different questions of their subjects and/or record the answers in different ways; raising all the problems of triangulation discussed elsewhere in this book (Chapter 13, Panel 13.3). This was the case for Bishop (p. 361 above), where the two data sets derived from asking different questions in the context of research programmes with different interests. You may recall how different frequencies of responses can be generated by what look like the same question asked in different ways (for example, Chapter 2, Table 2.4 and Chapter 10, Panel 10.2).

Our knowledge of research methodology can help to *evaluate* the likelihood of such effects, but can only help to *correct* them to a limited extent.

15.7 Multi-method research

Multi-method, (or multiple-method)research is an attempt to gain the benefits of using a variety of research methods without creating acute problems such as those discussed above. It is building triangulation into the research design (Chapter 13, Panel 13.3). It is only recently that including more than one method of research in the same programme has gained this title. It has always been quite common to combine a questionnaire with an experiment, use longer interviews together with a closed-question questionnaire survey, case studies with surveys, or interviews with observations. The main purposes of the combinations have been to get more than one purchase on the phenomenon and to triangulate data from one approach with data from another. Thus observations can be used to check whether people actually do what they say they do; or a questionnaire study alongside an experiment, can provide information on the experience of an intervention which odds ratios (ORs) or effect sizes cannot.

The trick of designing multi-method studies is to avoid in advance the kinds of problems which arise when attempts are made to synthesize studies which have not been designed for this purpose. It means:

(i) identifying some core issues where all methods will be addressed to the same questions
(ii) identifying those aspects of the study where one method can be used to supplement another, and planning a strategy to use the two in tandem (for example, asking interview questions about events which cannot be directly observed)
(iii) identifying those issues for which one method of study is more appropriate than the other methods, and planning to use that method for that purpose.

There will be occasions when two (or more) methods produce discrepant results, and then only *ad hoc* reasoning, with or without Bayesian synthesis, is likely to resolve the issue (Chapter 11, Section 11.2; Chapter 13, Section 13.7; this chapter, Section 15.4).

Further reading

For health service research, the Cochrane Collaboration web site carries the *Cochrane Handbook for Systematic Reviews* (2006) (www.cochrane.org/resources/handbook/).

The Campbell Collaboration web site provides similar advice for social services, educational, and criminal justice research (www.campbell collaboration.org/guidelines.asp). The EPPI Centre (http://eppi.ioe.ac.uk/cms/) also includes advice on conducting systematic reviews.

The literature on statistical meta-analysis is heavily concentrated in medical research, though applicable to any other kinds of experimental research. Here, Sutton *et al.* (2001) is a good introduction with useful references. Lipsey and Wilson (2000) is a more generic primer and the *Wilderdom* web site has a useful tutorial not tied to any field of study (www.wilderdom.com/research/meta-analysis.html). Rothstein (2005) provides a more than adequate treatment of publication bias, and how to deal with it.

Gorard and Taylor (2004) is about combining different methods in research. It includes accessible material on the use of Bayesian analysis in this context. Textbooks on Bayesian analysis tend to assume a knowledge of higher mathematics. For the newcomer, Yudkowsky (2003) is an easier introduction to Bayesian thinking overall.

For qualitative comparative analysis (QCA) there is a University of Arizona web site with explanations and software downloads for QCA analysis (www.u.arizona.edu/~cragin/fsQCA/index.shtml). Otherwise, see the Ragin references in the text (Section 15.5). The later references are heavy with fuzzy logic. Cooper (2005) is an interesting exemplar of this mode of analysis, addressing a social mobility issue and using data from one of the longitudinal studies (Chapter 8).

For meta-ethnography, Noblit and Hare (1988) is still a very readable introduction. More up-to-date are the articles in the special edition of *Sociological Research Online* (12(3), 2007) on re-using research data, though it is possible that not all the authors would regard their work as meta-ethnography (www.socresonline.org.uk/home.html).

The major repository for qualitative research data, field notes, field diaries and such like, is *Qualidata*, which is increasingly archiving reworkings of its original holdings as well (www.qualidata.essex.ac.uk/dataResources/introduction.asp). In addition, the *Mass Observation* repository gives access to the Mass Observation data, which methodologically chaotic but a rich and interesting social and cultural history resource (www.massobs.org.uk).

16 Research Ethics

By the end of this chapter, you will:

- Understand the way different ethical prescriptions for research follow from adopting value-neutral or value-led approaches to research (see Chapter 14)
- Have considered some of the ways in which harm might come to the subjects of social research, and ways of avoiding this
- Have considered some of the ethical dilemmas faced by researchers
- Have acquired one of the codes of research ethics in use in social research and used it to appraise the ethicality of a piece of research.

And you will know the meaning of the following terms:

Accountability • anonymization • confidentiality • informed consent • privacy • randomized controlled experiments • research ethics • sympathetic bias.

At the end of the chapter there is an Activity which will test your understanding of ethical research and its appraisal.

16.1 Introduction

'Research ethics' refer to rules of morally good conduct for researchers. Just as research cannot tell us what is the good life, research itself cannot tell us what is morally good research. Research ethics are grounded in moral and political beliefs which are *external* to the research itself.

Research ethics are not first and foremost a matter of individual morality. Rather, they are a communal discipline upheld by communities of researchers and others, who police research conduct. Individual researchers thus have to commit themselves to communal ethics, or suffer censure from their colleagues and sanctions from other agencies. There are communities within the community (Chapter 14); different groups of researchers subscribe to different values. Nonetheless, there is enough common agreement, or enough social pressure, for most to sign up to professional codes of conduct such as those issued by the British Sociological Association (BSA) and other organizations listed in the Activity at the end of this chapter.

To practise as a doctor, nurse or lawyer, clinical or educational psychologist requires registration with a professional body and breaches of professional codes can result in deregistration, including disciplinary action for research misconduct. There is no such ultimate sanction for research misconduct for people who are not registered as professionals, with the partial exception of the registration of people who are licensed to conduct psychometric tests. Despite their codes it can hardly be said that the associations of researchers function as powerful disciplinary bodies: their codes are offered as 'guidelines' rather than as by-laws with powerful sanctions for misconduct.

Other agencies, however, also play a role in regulating research. For example, researchers are subject to the Data Protection Act and its regulations about the extraction, curation, confidentiality and use of data about individuals (SRA 2005). Some Acts of Parliament include specifications for research which have to be followed, particularly with vulnerable groups (see for example Sections 30–34 of the Mental Capacity Act 2005).

Accepting a research grant is accepting a contractual obligation to follow ethical guidelines. Grants given by the ESRC, the main funding body for social research in the UK, require researchers both to follow its ethical guidelines (Panel 16.1) and to place their unpublished data in central archives to improve its availability for peer review. Grants managed by universities are subject to the universities' research ethics committees. Therefore for university-based researchers, following ethical guidelines becomes part of their contract of employment or student registration and breaches could be a cause for dismissal. Research conducted within the NHS has to be approved by local research ethics committees under the overall control of the National Research Ethics Service (NRES) (www.nres.npsa.nhs.uk/), within what is called the 'Research Governance Framework for Health and Social Care' (DoH 2005; for the Scottish equivalent, see Scottish Executive 2006). Research involving clients and staff of social services departments falls within

---

PANEL 16.1   The Principles of Ethical Research laid down by the Economic and Social Research Council (ESRC)

- Research should be designed, reviewed and undertaken to ensure integrity and quality
- Research staff and subjects must be informed fully about the purpose, methods and intended possible uses of the research, what their participation in the research entails and what risks, if any, are involved. Some variation is allowed in very specific and exceptional research contexts for which detailed guidance is provided . . .
- The confidentiality of information supplied by research subjects and the anonymity of respondents must be respected
- Research participants must participate in a voluntary way, free from any coercion
- Harm to research participants must be avoided
- The independence of research must be clear, and any conflict of interest or partiality must be explicit.

Source: ESRC (2005: 1). Detailed guidance is provided for each of these points.

the same frameworks (Research Governance in Social Care Advisory Group 2005). Such research committees include lay members, so that there a measure of public participation in research supervision.

Irrespective of who does it, all research in the NHS falls under the research ethics code for medical research (MRC 2005), which includes a requirement that patients have been involved in the design of the research. There is a Europe-wide code of ethics for social researchers (Respect Project 2004). Counting all the committee memberships in the UK at any one time, there are now probably more people involved in the ethical supervision of research than actively involved in doing research.

Access to many research locations involves the negotiation of local agreements about the conduct of the research. Breaching such agreements may lead to permissions being withdrawn. And, then, there is the criminal law and the civil law on tort, privacy, confidentiality, defamation, slander and copyright and intellectual property rights, within the bounds of which researchers are supposed to stay. The Nuremberg code, passed in the aftermath of the revelations about Nazi atrocities in research, and the Helsinki code adopted by the World Health Organization (WHO) both cover social research in medical settings (Eby 2000), and the European Declaration of Human Rights which is incorporated into British law as the British Human Rights Act, is also relevant (Sprumont 1999).

All these codes of practice are broadly speaking similar; they differ in the detail. As yet, there have been no publicized cases of researchers found to have practised unethically under one code while claiming that they acted ethically under another. This is almost bound to happen. In the last resort, the codes which are backed with sanctions such as the withdrawal of funding, or loss of employment will prevail unless their decisions are overturned at employment tribunals or in the civil courts.

16.2 The ethic of producing truthful and transparent research

Researchers may disagree as to what the 'truth' is, and how to get at it, but they are all subject to a moral requirement to do research truthfully. Knowingly falsifying research is an important form of deviance for all researchers. It may be very difficult for others to know whether researchers have intentionally falsified research, or have inadvertently allowed expectancy effects (Chapter 3, Section 3.6) or other sources of bias to flaw their judgements (Chapter 4, Section 4.4; Chapter 14, Sections 14.4, 14.5).

Researchers require each other to take 'all reasonable precautions' to prevent the production of misleading results, just as health and safety law lays a duty on employers to take all reasonable precautions to keep their workforce safe. Different kinds of researchers would interpret this in different ways. Among quantitative researchers there is an array of devices used as preventatives against inadvertent bias and against error arising from slipshod methods: for example, blinding (Chapter 3, Section 3.6), the blind selection of subjects in experiments and surveys (Chapter 3, Section 3.3; Chapter 6, Section 6.4); the independent scrutiny of data and its protection from post-hoc revision, inter-rater reliability tests (Chapter 2, Section 2.10) and so on.

Many qualitative researchers regard all this as interfering with their capacity to get at the truth. They ask others to trust them to get it right without the aid of all these disciplinary mechanisms. From the viewpoint of a researcher committed to controlled experiments, this sounds rather like the company boss who says 'we don't need a health and safety policy here; it would destroy our happy family atmosphere'. But there is no doubt that, for some research topics, over-regulation may grossly distort whatever it is that the researcher is trying to study. This relates to the debate between the merits of control as against the merits of naturalism running though most of the chapters in this book (see particularly Chapter 10) and the notion of ecological validity discussed in Chapter 12).

With regard to truthfulness, the most important disciplinary mechanism is making the research available for scrutiny by others (Chapter 1, Section 1.8). Quantitative research lends itself relatively easily to accountability. Qualitative research can be more difficult to give accounts of, and hence more difficult to audit by others (see Chapter 10, Section 10.7; Chapter 12, Section 12.7). Though it probably isn't, much ethnographic research could be pure invention and no third party would be in a position to detect this. Again, then, qualitative researchers ask for more trust from their readers than do quantitative researchers. A great deal hinges here on the relationship between what is claimed and the account given to support the claim. It makes a difference whether a researcher says 'it seems to me that . . .' or 'this is definitely so'.

There are always temptations for researchers of any kind to 'lose' data which go against their main conclusions, or to push data further than they will go. But it is worth noting that falsified and biased research does not necessarily lead to false conclusions. Gregor Mendel, who was the first to work out the mechanism of genetic inheritance (Stern and Sherwood 1966: 173–5), and Isaac Newton who established the subject of optics and discerned the mechanics of planetary motion and the role of gravity (Westfall 1973), both invented or massaged their data to make it fit their theories. Their conclusions were correct, but did not follow from their data. So their conclusions were really speculations, and had no right to be regarded as any more than that, until properly supported by evidence. Cyril Burt's false data (Chapter 7, Section 7.2) supported conclusions which subsequent research has modified considerably. But it still seems true that genes determine something about intelligence and personality, if not as much as hereditarians once believed.

Thus falsifying data, or skewing the analysis, doesn't necessarily lead to error, just as the police planting evidence doesn't necessarily lead to the conviction of the wrong person. There is a difference between convicting the wrong person and wrongful conviction. The latter implies a 'due process' which is a general-purpose set of procedures, not necessarily successful in every case, but adopted in an attempt to ensure fair and accurate disposals in the majority of cases. In the same way, the commitment to the 'due procedures' of bias control and peer accountability may inhibit the discovery of the truth in particular cases, but there are dangers in making exceptions for particular cases or for particular kinds of research. What once was the exception may drift into becoming the norm.

Temptations to make special cases, and to 'fit up' the opposition as it were, are experienced by those researchers who commit their research to the furtherance of a political cause (Chapter 14, Section 14.4). Consider this example from Back and Solomos (1993), committed anti-racist researchers:

> [while] we are rejecting a 'value free' perspective we still have to show why our account is a plausible explanation of processes and events. While we recognize that accounts provided by research are partial, this does not absolve us of the need to provide an analysis which is persuasive.
> (Back and Solomos 1993: 196; cited in Hammersley 2000b: 10)

On this, Hammersley comments:

> by using the terms 'plausible' and 'persuasive' in place of 'valid', they seem to imply that what is required is simply that research findings be convincing enough to have the correct political effect. At the same time, these authors expect lay people to treat their research as objective.
> (Hammersley 2000b: 10)

In the famous words of the otherwise unknown Senator Hiram Johnson in 1917, 'the first casualty when war comes is truth' (Knightley 1975: Preface). Hammersley's point is that in 'declaring war' on social evils, partisan researchers such as Back and Solomos are tempted to compromise a commitment to the truth with a commitment to win the war. The literature of critical research is indeed rich with militaristic metaphors about struggles and battles and forces and sides (see Chapter 14, Section 14.4). And things do look different from the partisan viewpoint. For them, the war started long ago. The opposition have already produced huge quantities of (allegedly) false knowledge; truth is already a 'casualty', and what is needed to secure the truth is counter-propaganda.

With regard to their accountability, researchers divide. The more orthodox position associated with the idea of value neutrality (see Chapter 14, Section 14.2) is that researchers should first and foremost be accountable to the research community, and only secondarily to other social groups. This makes sense as an expediential strategy on two kinds of grounds. The first is the argument that researchers need to be free of other influences in order to see the truth; hence the proscriptions against getting too emotionally involved with research subjects in order to avoid **sympathetic bias** (Chapter 14, Sections 14.3–14.5; see also Chapter 4, Section 4.4) and the demand not to be regulated by companies or politicians whose interests might bias the research.

The second is that being accountable to the research community is being accountable to the group who have the expertise to discern good research from bad, truth from error. In the metaphor of adversarial legal systems the research community is supposed to play the role of the disinterested jury. In practice it will often be far from disinterested. Some will prefer some findings rather than others, because these support or undermine their own line of thought. It is in medicine that this problem of 'jury bias' has been most seriously addressed, with specially commissioned independent reviews of research on particular treatments, most notably those of the Cochrane Collaboration network and the National Institute for Clinical Excellence(NICE) and its Scottish counterpart (Chapter 15, Sections 15.2 and 15.3).

By contrast, feminist, anti-racist and disability researchers take the position that they should make themselves accountable first to the oppressed group among whom they do research, and only secondarily to the research community (Lather 1986). This stance makes sense on the assumption first, that research should be about improving the circumstances of the oppressed, rather than accumulating knowledge in academia, and second that it is the oppressed who really know the truth and are in the best position to evaluate the research: no disinterested jury here. In practice, however, such researchers publish in academic journals and make their careers that way. Thus they do make themselves significantly accountable to that part of the research community which reads their work, and in publishing in academic journals they certainly don't make themselves directly accountable to many people suffering from severe oppression.

Associated with this division is another about the proper conduct of researchers towards those whom they research. The more orthodox position is that researchers should behave so as to do subjects no *harm*, while critical researchers prescribe that researchers should behave so as to do *some good* to categories of people they favour.

16.3 Doing no harm and doing some good while doing research

Table 16.1 gives a synopsis of the more important possibilities for doing harm and doing good, *while* doing the research. Section 16.8 looks at the possibilities for doing harm or good in publishing the results.

In what follows, it is worth keeping in mind that the vast majority of social research does none of the subjects any significant harm or good. In their extensive review of the literature and their own study of social research participants Graham, Lewis and Nicholas (2006) and Graham, Grewal and Lewis (2007) found that:

> research generally emerged as a positive experience for most people in the studies reviewed. A number of studies highlighted that interviews which were painful could nevertheless be, overall, a positive experience. Recounting a painful experience could itself provide an important opportunity for catharsis and a chance to reflect.
>
> (Graham, Lewis and Nicholas 2006: 2)

The fact that most social research has no substantial benign effects for those researched is sometimes elevated into a serious sin. This is based on the assumption that social researchers, as researchers, could actually do some good to people.

The last column of Table 16.1 suggests that deciding on ethical conduct involves balancing harms and benefits. Ethical considerations usually throw

TABLE 16.1   Doing good and harm to subjects in doing research

Possibilities	Possible harm	Possible good	Trade-offs
Physical harm and good	Outside the field of health research, social research rarely presents any particular risks to the physical health and safety of subjects. A possible exception is the kind of action research (Chapter 14, Section 14.5) which involves political activism.	Health research may have have benign effects on the physical health and safety of some subjects. Action research campaigning against damp housing, or environmental pollution probably has had benign health effects.	In randomized controlled trials used in testing treatments in medical research (Chapter 3) members of one group are more likely to experience improvement or deterioration of their health than the other, but which may be unknown in advance.
Psychological harm and good	The risks of emotional harm are greatest where subjects are vulnerable and the research involves close, emotionally charged relationships between researcher and subjects and/or between research subjects. High-risk situations include some psychological experiments (Section 16.6) qualitative interviews or focus groups on sensitive topics, participative research and action research (Section 16.7). High-risk groups include children, people with mental health problems and victims of abuse.	The possibility of improving people's emotional state while doing the research depends on the kinds of relationship it is possible for researchers to make with subjects, and research subjects with each other. There are greater opportunities in clinical trials of psychotherapeutic treatments, in-depth interviews, focus groups, participative and action research (Section 16.7).	The situations with the greatest risks of doing emotional harm to people are similar to those in which there are the greatest opportunities to do emotional good to them. In some situations it is possible that some subjects will improve their emotional state at the expense of some other subjects: for example in a focus group or a consciousness raising group.

TABLE 16.1 *continued*

Possibilities	Possible harm	Possible good	Trade-offs
Educative effects	In most social research participants have little opportunity to learn much of significance to them, but harm might come via the emotionally charged relationships some participative research, or in a poorly managed focus group (Chapter 10, Section 10.5).	In participative research and action research, it may be the prime objective of the research to improve the knowledge and of skills of the participants (Chapter 14, Section 14.5).	What people learn about themselves as research subjects may not be congenial to them (see Section 16.6). This may be true in action research where the action fails to have the desired results (Chapter 14, Section 14.5).
Self-determination	The right to self-determination for subjects of research is a common item in codes of research practice, usually phrased in terms of the need to obtain the subjects' 'informed consent to participation'. However, much research simply would not work if subjects were fully informed about the details of the research (Sections 16.5, 16.6). Hence this is a right which is often breached in research, though rarely with any tangible harm arising.	In participative and action research (Chapter 14, Section 14.5) it may be among the primary objectives of the research to enhance the participants' ability to take charge of their own lives.	Much research, particularly in psychology, relies on deceit. Hence there is a conflict between the subject's rights to self-determination and the researcher's need to mislead them. See Section 16.6. In overt participant observation research constantly reminding people as to the fact that they are being researched will increase any 'Hawthorne effect' (Chapter 12, Section 12.4). Covert observation research is a direct breach of the right to self-determination (Chapter 12, Section 12.4; see also Section 16.5).

Privacy and confidentiality	While people's right to privacy is an important right, breaching it does little tangible harm without an accompanying breach of confidentiality. Breaches of confidentiality may have serious consequences if the information falls into the wrong hands.	Breaches of confidentiality may forewarn other people of dangers to themselves or may give them an edge in some conflict in which they are engaged where the researcher supports their cause.	In participative/action research with political aims, the gains of the subjects may be at the expense of someone else (Chapter 14, Section 14.5). Conflicts between: the rights of subjects not to have their privacy breached and the researcher's need to study people unbeknown to them; the researcher's obligations to prevent harm coming to other people and the rights of the subjects to confidentiality.
Material, political and reputational gains and losses	Research may influence policy and practice against the subjects' interests or consolidate a stereotyped view of them.	Research may influence policy or practice in the research subjects' favour or improve their public reputation. In participative research may inaugurate a research career.	Gains for the subjects may be at the expense of someone else.

up *ethical dilemmas*. General principles and codes of practice may provide steps on the way to resolving these, but in the last resort most ethical dilemmas have to be dealt with in an *ad hoc*, best-of-the-worst kind of way. The conflicts here may be between:

- One ethical principle and another for example, maintaining confidentiality towards one person, as against preventing harm coming to another; telling the whole truth as against protecting someone's interests
- Serving the interests of one group of people as against serving the interests of another
- The researcher's desire to find something out and the researcher's obligations to inform the subjects fully. For example, much psychological research would be impossible without deception.

16.4   The ethics of the lottery: randomized controlled experiments

Randomized controlled experiments (see Chapter 3) are widely used in psychology. As randomized controlled *trials* (RCTs) they are regarded as the 'gold standard method' in testing the effectiveness of treatments in medicine. As the demand for 'evidence-based practice' grows in social work, criminal justice interventions, counselling and education, it is likely that RCTs will be used more widely in these contexts in the future (Oakley 2000). When used in studies of effectiveness, the interest is in some intervention which is designed to do people good: to cure their illness, for example. And there is often a suspicion that there is a risk that the intervention might do some harm: drug side-effects for example. Such trials, then, ask research subjects to give their 'informed consent' to be entered into a lottery with various hazards.

The first aspect of the lottery is that if researchers already knew who, if anyone, would benefit, and who, if anyone, would be harmed and in what kinds of ways, precisely, there would be no need for the research. Thus researchers are not fully in a position to facilitate *fully* informed consent by the subjects, except in the sense that subjects can be informed that they will face risks of unknown kinds and magnitude. Properly conducted RCTs do involve a risk assessment, but however well this is done there will be a residuum of risk unknowable in advance. All RCTs include a provision to 'withdraw' subjects who seem to be in distress, but this will not protect against harmful effects which show only in the long term.

The second aspect of the lottery is that subjects will not know to which comparison group they will be allocated. With a control group and a treatment group those in the control group may be deprived of a treatment which would improve their health, but be protected from any adverse side-effects of the treatment, while those in treatment group might receive a treatment beneficial to them, and/or might experience unpleasant or occasionally even fatal side-effects.

People's attitudes to the ethics of RCTs as lotteries tend to polarize between those who feel that any element of lottery is unfair and unethical, and those who feel that in situations of uncertainty some blind and disinterested decision-making is fairer than choosing people according to their known characteristics when various biases and prejudices might play a part (Elander 1991; Featherstone and Donovan 1998). But apart from gut feelings it is important to view RCTs in a broader context and consider the implications of not proceeding in this way. Here the question is whether the risks and deprivations suffered by the losers in the lottery are justified by the benefits gained for much larger groups of people. No one would argue these days, surely, that medical treatments should be implemented without prior research to establish their benefits and risks. And, increasingly, people are asking why social workers, counsellors and educationalists should be allowed to launch into what are *ad hoc* uncontrolled experiments on their clients and students as a routine aspect of their work, without some prior research evidence about the future effects of what they are doing (Oakley and Fullerton 1996). Some legitimate doubts can be framed about the appropriateness of RCTs in these other fields because of the complexity of the interventions concerned (Chapter 3, Section 3.10; Chapter 4, Section 4.1; Chapter 7, Section 7.1). But there is no doubt that the RCT is the best design for judging the effects of many interventions. Randomization in RCTs is not adopted because it is the *fairest* way of allocating risks between research subjects. It is adopted because it is the most *efficient* way of controlling out prior subject variables, and hence essential for producing less ambiguous results (Chapter 3, Section 3.3; Chapter 15, Sections 15.2, 15.3). If an effect was so large and so unambiguous that it was not necessary to use randomization in the research to detect it, then the research would probably be unnecessary. No one has to conduct RCTs to discover that heavy blows to the head with large hammers do a lot of damage, for example.

Thus the argument here is that if a large number of people in the future are to benefit from practitioners' knowledge about the effectiveness and risks of particular interventions, then RCTs are the best way of producing such knowledge and the risks to the experimental subjects are justified, so long as they are willing to play the role of public benefactors and are fully appraised of the fact that an RCT will be a risky business for them (see Panel 16.2)

I have used the example of medical trials because here there are the highest risks. But the same might apply with regard to a particular method of teaching. It might be argued that if a method of teaching was particularly effective it would be an unfairness to the controls to deprive them of this. But if it proved otherwise, then the unfairness might be to the experimental group. Trying to solve this by treating all the same actually makes the problem worse. For if the method is used and is ineffectual everybody suffers; and if the method is not adopted but would have been an improvement, then everyone loses, too. The gamble is on the unknown effectiveness of the method, which is what the research is supposed to clarify.

As used in psychology, randomized controlled experiments have less dire ethical implications, unless of course there is also some risk of harm to research subjects (see Section 16.6).

The remarks about RCTs in medicine above assumed that they were properly conducted. In practice, many medical trials are rather badly done, with poor briefings of the subjects and negligible support for them while they are research subjects (Bosley 1999). But there is a difference between the ethics

> ## PANEL 16.2   Informed consent
>
> In codes of ethics for social researchers, informed consent is one of the most important principles. Put crudely, participants to research need to be told what they are letting themselves in for, before they make a decision to co-operate. For informed consent the social researcher should:
>
> > Explain as fully as possible, and in terms meaningful to participants, what the research is about, who is undertaking it and financing it, why it is being undertaken, and how it is to be disseminated [and] not as a once-and-for-all prior event, but as a process, subject to re-negotiation over time.
> >
> > (British Sociological Association 2002)
>
> Ideally, informed consent would be part of a contracting process with a written agreement between the researcher and each subject, laying out the terms and conditions of the research (for examples, see Hart and Bond 1995: 199–201). There are particular difficulties about deciding whether consent has indeed been 'informed' with subjects who are very distressed, have mental health problems or learning disabilities, or those for whom informed consent is made by others on their behalf, such as children.
>
> In practice, providing for informed consent depends on researchers having some idea of the trajectory and outcomes of the research, on the possibilities of subjects understanding the purposes of the research, on the feasibility of doing the research in the full knowledge by the participants of what is going on and/or of constantly being reminded that they are being researched and, in much ethnographic research, on decisions about who among the many people who float into view are to be regarded as research subjects with a right to be informed.
>
> Justifications for not gaining informed consent rest on the practical issues above and on the estimation either that no harm will come to the participants in the absence of their consent, or that any such harm is more than compensated by some good done to other people.

of a particular research strategy competently used and those of using the method without due care and attention.

16.5   Privacy, confidentiality and covert research

The canonical case for discussing the ethics of covert research is Laud Humphreys' (1975) *Tearoom Trade*: his study by naturalistic observation of male homosexual liaisons in public toilets. It is inconceivable that this research could have been done by observation other than covertly. At the time at which it was conducted, homosexuality was illegal in the US and highly stigmatized. It is unlikely that Humphreys could have conducted an interview study instead. Reiss (1964) is an interview study, but of a group of what we would now call 'rent boys', while Humphreys was interested in the engagement of otherwise 'respectable' people in homosexual acts. How else, in the 1970s, could he find them except by going to the places where such acts were committed and disguising his intentions for doing so?

So if the research was to be done, it had to be covertly. The research is not a straightforward breach of the subjects' privacy, for they were knowingly and consentingly observed. But the consent was gained under false pretences. They did not give fully informed consent, since they did not know Humphreys' purposes for observing them. Apart from observing homosexual acts, Humphreys also collected the men's car registrations. From these he traced their addresses, and then arranged interviews with them not about their homosexuality but about other aspects of their lives. They remained unaware of the linkage between the being observed and being interviewed. Thus they did not give fully informed consent to the way in which Humphreys used the interview data, either. In addition, by having a list of names and addresses Humphreys put his subjects at risk of being investigated and prosecuted by the police should the addresses have fallen into the wrong hands. Though this did not happen, it is this risk of a breach of confidentiality that Humphreys most regretted in retrospect.

So far, then, Humphreys' research looks entirely unjustifiable in an ethical sense, and it would certainly breach today's research ethics codes of practice. But it looks less unjustifiable when we consider the following. Humphreys was an ordained Episcopalian minister and an active civil libertarian who had spent times in gaol for his political activities in supporting civil rights. He was deeply committed to liberalizing the law on homosexuality and in removing the stigma attached to it. The purpose of his research was to provide evidence that male homosexuals were not derelicts and vicious perverts but often 'family men' and pillars of their local communities. The evidence he collected showed just that, and the *Tearoom Trade* probably did have some influence in the subsequent liberalization of the law in the US, though homosexuality still remains illegal in some states of the union (Galliher, Brekhus and Keys 2004).

This case raises a host of ethical dilemmas. First, should we judge the ethicality of research by reference to the motivations of the researchers? Probably the answer to this is 'Yes, up to a point'. Second, in judging the ethicality of research how much weight should we place on the conduct and how much on the outcomes? In this respect, the Humphreys' case has a format very familiar in fiction. Think of all those cop movies where 'our hero' disregards the constraints of ethical policing, but by so doing rids the streets of hoodlums and serial killers. By this 'Dirty Harry' clause we might perhaps judge research which was unethical in its commission as nonetheless ethical because of its outcomes.

Anne Other's research cited in Chapter 12, Section 12.6, is a similar case. She was refused permission to conduct her research on hygiene behaviour in a hospital by a local research ethics committee, who decreed that she should gain informed consent not only from the staff, but also from all the patients – or, in the case of their incapacity, from their next of kin. Other regarded the latter requirement as a 'wrecking' strategy to make quite sure her research was not carried out. She is not the first researcher to suspect that NHS research ethics committees, dominated as they are by doctors and nurses, are sometimes used as a way of preventing researchers prying into their affairs. And, she thought, it would have wrecked her research to have announced the fact and the purpose of her research to the staff. Thus she conducted her research covertly and 'unethically'. Having done the research without ethical clearance, as a nurse she is vulnerable to disciplinary action by the disciplinary committee of her profession, and might well be struck off and prevented from earning her living as a nurse. Anne Other is not her real name. By contrast, in another part of the country, Jenner and her colleagues, not long afterwards, gained ethical permission for an observation study of staff hand hygiene practice, without having to gain informed consent from the patients (Jenner *et al.* 2006).

Even where observational research is overtly engaged in, it may be difficult and impractical to secure and maintain the subjects' informed consent (see Panel 16.1). Much ethnographic research is open-ended (Chapter 12, Section 12.6). If researchers do not know where it will lead, then how can they forewarn the subjects adequately? And if they are forever reminding subjects that research is going on, then this will influence the way people behave, when the object of most ethnographic research is to observe 'things as usual'. It is sometimes very difficult for researchers to explain the concept of the research adequately to the subjects. Like many anthropologists I found it very difficult to explain the idea of anthropological research to the people I studied in Kenya. We settled in the end on the understanding that I was studying history, a concept they did understand, but this was hardly true. And, then, many settings for ethnographic research are full of people coming and going: a village, a market place, a hospital ward. Do they all have a right to know that research is being conducted in the setting? If they do, then much research by naturalistic observation must of necessity breach these rights since it would simply be impracticable to uphold them.

When the raw data of grant-aided research is archived it continues to be covered by the assurances about confidentiality given at the time of collection. But archiving makes it impossible fully to inform research subjects as to how in the future information about them might be used and who might see it, even if those who see it are bound to treat it confidentially (Backhouse 2002).

Anne Other's main defence against a charge of research deviance would be in terms of 'public interest'. After all, hospital-acquired infections are a major source of death and unnecessary suffering in hospital (ONS 2007). She could claim that only by studying hygiene behaviour covertly could the causes of the problem be adequately investigated. The public interest defence is widely used, or over-used, by journalists for breaches of privacy and confidentiality. With the passing of legislation to protect whistle-blowers from recriminations from those they blow the whistle on (HMSO 1998), Other's own position is stronger these days than it would have been in the past. Thus with both the case of Humphreys and that of Other, we are forced to balance the rights of people studied to the privacy and to the confidentiality of their affairs, as against the value of the findings made in breach of these rights.

Such value as the findings might have may not be to the benefit of the people studied. And this is not a straightforward balance.

First, we rarely regard everybody as having equal rights to privacy and confidentiality. These days, no doubt, most readers of this book would say that homosexuals in public toilets should have their privacy respected. But in the climate in which Humphreys was working, a very large constituency would argue that they had no such rights since what they were doing was evil and illegal. Similarly, there is relatively little controversy today about researchers who breach the rights of privacy and self-determination of people stealing from their employers (Ditton 1977) or people engaged in racially discriminatory behaviour (Bowler 1993). In her study of prostitution Julia-O'Connell Davidson felt that it was necessary to inform the prostitutes of her research intentions, but not their clients (O'Connell Davidson and Layder 1994), though it is unclear as to whether this was a decision made on moral or expediential grounds.

Second, rights of self-determination, privacy and confidentiality do not mean much unless we specify the degree of harm which follows from their breach. In fact, very little harm follows from breaches of privacy alone. It is never entirely clear what rights to privacy people have, or should be granted. For example, as the current law stands, there is an obligation to inform people that their image may be captured via a security camera but there are no procedures for them to give or withhold permission for this, nor to arbitrate how the information is used, though that is circumscribed by the Data Protection Act. Rights to privacy always seem to relate to the social role someone is playing, the ownership of the space they are occupying, or of the documents on which details of themselves are inscribed, and the legality of their activities. Thus pedestrians in public spaces seem to have little in the way of rights to privacy, people in their homes have many, but people in their homes may have their privacy legally invaded if there is a reasonable suspicion that they are engaged in illegal activities. Researchers' behaviour seems roughly to mirror the legal situation, though they have no legal right to bug phones, use secret cameras, or demand entry to private places.

Breaches of privacy are relatively trivial if they are not accompanied by breaches of confidentiality. Nearly all published research is anonymized as to place and persons, with some exceptions. I shall deal with these in relation to the ethics of publication in Section 16.8. Some researchers take care to use pseudonyms or code numbers to anonymise people in their research notes. It is a possibility that a court might subpoena a researcher's notes – under national security legislation, for example. Although there has been no legal case to date, Wolf (1991: 220) found his PhD thesis on an identifiable chapter of individually anonymised Hells Angels, cited in a court case about the renewal of a firearms permit. Similarly, breaching a subjects' rights to self-determination has serious consequences only where this may lead them into actions which will do them harm. In all these regards, then, no tangible harm came to research subjects from Humphreys' or Other's research in their breaching of the subjects' rights to privacy and self-determination, mainly because no confidentiality was actually breached.

However, there is also a public interest defence for breaching the subjects' rights to confidentiality. This is one which researchers rarely use, and where others might regard them as being unethical in *not* doing so. Particularly in the field of deviancy studies, researchers get to know and sometimes to observe criminal acts and other acts of harm done by their research subjects.

In English and Scottish law (national security and child welfare apart) there is no legal requirement to inform the police that a crime has been committed, but it might be argued that, as good citizens, researchers should do just this. Even feminist and anti-racist researchers will often allow racist and sexist language to be used in their presence and for apparently discriminatory acts to take place without challenging these (for example, Bowler 1993). Other stood by while zillions of MRSA bacteria were transmitted from patient to patient and did nothing to prevent this happening. There is an issue here of *when* to be ethical. To act immediately would be to jeopardise the research. In the case of covert research this might sometimes lead to personal danger, as in Fielding's study of the National Front (1981). Most researchers prefer to be ethical in their publications rather than on the spot, for being ethical on the spot may mean that there is no publication.

16.6   Psychological harm, self-determination and deceit

If the Humphreys' study is the canonical case for discussing the ethics of covert research, then it is Stanley Milgram's studies in obedience (1963, 1974, 1992) which constitute the canonical case for considering psychological harm arising from research. Milgram's research involved a suite of experiments all with a similar structure. Subjects were told that they would be participating in an experiment to investigate whether pain would improve the way people learned. From the subjects' point of view the experiments seemed to consist of a random selection between two subjects: one to be a 'learner', and one to be a 'teacher'. In fact, the 'learner' was a confederate of the experimenter, a stooge. The only subject in each case was the 'teacher'. The subject was shown the learner being strapped into an apparatus which would deliver an electric shock and then taken into another room (in most versions of the experiment) and seated at the consol of an impressive 'electric shock machine' with calibrated shock levels, the higher levels being marked 'Danger: do not use'. The subject, as 'teacher', was asked to read lists of words over a microphone, allegedly to the stooge as 'learner' in another room, and then to test him on his accuracy of recall. In the event of an error, or a silence, the subject was to administer an electric shock, stronger for each successive error. In most versions of the experiment the 'learner's' apparent responses were supplied on a light-up screen, with pre-recorded protests and sounds of distress relayed over a loudspeaker to standardize the stimulus for all subjects. Pre-recorded responses were arranged so that if the subjects followed their instructions they would continue until they reached the highest shock level – '450 volts', despite the 'learner's' requests to stop, his reports of having a heart condition, his refusal to continue and eventually ominous silence. Variations on this basic design included the presence or the absence of the experimenter in the same room as the 'learner' stooge, and the venue of the experiment in a prestigious university building or in a shabby downtown office. A more radical departure required the subject directly to apply shocks to the 'learner' by pressing his hand on an electrode; the 'learner' acting out the pain of the experience.

The whole suite of experiments included 900 subjects, but in the basic experiment, 26 out of 40 subjects continued to the highest shock level, while 14 refused to go any further than between '300' and '375' volts, after the 'learner' complained about the pain and refused to supply any more answers.

All this is impressive as an experimental design in its control of variables. Despite their staged nature, the experiments do achieve some degree of naturalism if compared with the circumstances of the 'death' laboratories of Nazi Germany or Stalinist Russia. Milgram's findings carried a valuable lesson for understanding atrocities committed by the Nazis, or by American servicemen in Korea and Vietnam; for example see Browning's (1993) study of a Nazi death squad in wartime Poland. The experiments made it impossible to attribute such behaviour to deranged psychopaths or to the stresses of war. They showed that ordinary men, under rather minimal conditions of compulsion, would follow instructions to inflict pain on harmless strangers. These were findings which were widely regarded as valuable, but the way they were obtained is ethically very dubious.

Most psychologists would not raise ethical objections to the experiment simply on the grounds that it involved trickery (but see Baumrind 1964 on Milgram's experiments and Milgram's replies 1964, 1992). A very large amount of psychological research could not be done without directly misleading subjects as to the purpose of the research, or by allowing them to misinterpret what was going on by withholding important information. Almost all of the psychology of perception, for example, involves tricking the senses.

In Milgram's experiments the major ethical problems are associated with the obvious psychological distress caused to the subjects. They displayed this at the time as perspiration, hysterical laughter and nervous tics. More importantly, however, those subjects who complied, learned something unpleasant about themselves. The experiment showed them that they did not have the moral fibre to resist the instructions of someone else, despite the fact that the experimenter had no serious sanctions he could use to enforce compliance. And it showed them that they were the kinds of people who would inflict pain and maybe death on a fellow human being who had done them no harm. It might be argued that what they learned about themselves was true, but whether it is always beneficial for people to know the truth about themselves, and who has a right to tell it to them, are difficult questions to answer.

In provoking an ethical controversy, the Milgram experiments led to a revision of the code of practice for American psychologists (Harris 1988), mirrored in the British codes, requiring experimenters to 'debrief' their subjects. This means both to explain to them how they had been misled, and to provide such care and counsel needed for their psychological welfare. In fact, Milgram did debrief his subjects immediately after the experiments but he did not provide any follow-up. Milgram notes that 80% of the subjects said that they were glad to have been involved in the experiment (1992: 130–3), but this in turn might be regarded as another 'obedient' response. And there remains a question as to whether the value of the findings of the research justified the infliction of distress on the subjects.

It is unlikely that Milgram's experiments would gain ethical approval today. But that is from the wisdom of hindsight, to which Milgram's experiments contributed. Milgram himself expected most subjects to refuse to continue at a much earlier stage. He might, however have aborted the series before completion, as Philip Zimbardo did with his prison simulation experiment (Haney, Banks and Zimbardo 1981: www.prisonex.org). This involved no deception but the allocation at random of volunteers to the roles of 'prisoners' or 'guards' in a simulated live-in gaol. Within a few days prison 'guards' were behaving with considerable cruelty towards the 'prisoners'. As with the Milgram experiments, it was the perpetrators of cruelty who were the most psychologically disturbed by the experience. Zimbardo and his colleagues provided a counselling service for the experimental subjects. Like Milgram, they had not expected the results they produced and were not therefore able to put subjects in a position where they could exercise *informed* consent.

The BBC's emulation of the experiment in 1992 was also abandoned because of the distress caused to the participants (Wells 1992). It is very unlikely that a re-run would gain ethical approval as research today, although the ethical standards for so-called 'reality TV', such as *Big Brother*, are much more lax than those for research. Zimbardo (2007) himself now regards the prison simulation as unethical. None the less, he claims that the experiment indicated lessons which, if learned, would have prevented thousands of cases of abuse in military units, boarding schools, prisons and similar institutions, including what happened at Abu Ghraib in Iraq (Zimbardo 2004).

The ethical problem in these two experiments is about causing psychological harm to people who do not deserve it. But Diana Scully considered that she faced the opposite problem of doing psychological good to people who did not deserve that benefit. Her study involved conducting loosely structured interviews with men who had been convicted of rape:

> The type of information sought in this research required a supportive, non judgemental neutral façade – one that I did not always genuinely feel. Frankly, some of the men were personally repulsive ... additionally the stories they told were horrible and a few of the men were not overtly co-operative. Indeed, some of the interviews require immense effort to remain neutral. But the fact is that no one tells his or her secrets to a visibly hostile and disapproving person.
>
> (Scully 1990: 18, cited in O'Connell Davidson and Layder 1994: 141)

Apart from these issues of practicality, Scully 'worried that some of these men might interpret neutrality as a signal of agreement or approval' (1990: 19) – that they would feel better about themselves as a result of the interviews, and that the interviews might reinforce their propensity towards violent sexuality.

Avoiding doing research subjects psychological harm, or avoiding doing them good when they don't deserve it, requires some percipience. Researchers have to be able to guess what people will find upsetting or supportive. To some extent, this can be taken as given by the topic and the subjects of the research. Much interview research is done about sensitive topics, such as victimization or bereavement, or with subjects who have a mental illness problem. Here it is a reasonable assumption that the interviews will need to be handled with care, subjects pre-briefed as to their rights to discontinue, and interviewers willing to switch from extracting information to offering support. But any interview about any topic can trigger distress occasionally. Handling distress in an interview context is rarely a skill taught in research methods courses. It is not something which can simply be accomplished by making a befriending relationship with subjects. Our friends and other intimates are usually those who hurt us most.

Some feminists (Grumet 1991; Stacey 1991), against the grain in feminist research, have suggested that befriending relationships can lead to a sense of false intimacy and hence are unethically exploitative and create a false promise of a future relationship which the researcher will not fulfil. The literature on counselling suggests that what some might see as supportive, educative and empowering relationships are seen by others as manipulative and indoctrinating (Masson 1988). And the research literature on research interviewing suggest that it is the distant and detached – or better still, the absent interviewer – who is least upsetting, and who elicits most disclosure on sensitive topics (Chapter 10, Section 10.4).

In their study of dual-career families (Chapter 11, Section 11.2) the Rapoports (1976) interviewed couples several times. It is likely that these interviews themselves became important components of marital dynamics, having some effect on how the couples viewed themselves and each other. It seems highly likely that the way the interviews twisted and turned sometimes favoured one of a couple rather than the other. Something like this seems inevitable. But the difficulty here is knowing what effect the interviews did have. Only if researchers know this can they actually address this as an ethical problem, and do something practical about it. Discovering the effects of the researchers' actions on the subjects in this case would be a much more challenging research topic than the research the Rapoports actually conducted. Much the same is true of most research with regard to the retrospective estimation of the effects of the researcher on the morale, self-images and social relations of the subjects. It is true of almost all research with regard to knowing this in advance.

16.7 Doing good while doing research

Researchers who believe that research should be designed to do those researched some good usually have in mind benefits such as improved self-image, improved competences and knowledge, greater understanding of their social and political situation, more cohesive communities, or some tangible improvement in their situation. As you might guess from Scully's feminist research on rapists, such benefits are supposed to be supplied only to those whom the researcher believes deserves them, and what counts as greater social or political insight depends on what beliefs the researcher subscribes to.

This ethical position is usually accompanied by the idea that it is unethical for researchers to take the commanding role in directing the research. The ethical grounds for this are nicely captured by Heron (1981):

> For persons, as autonomous beings, have a moral right to participate in decisions that claim to generate knowledge about them. Such a right ... protects them ... from being managed and manipulated ... the moral principle of respect for persons is most fully honored when power is shared not only in the application ... but also in the generation of knowledge ... doing research on persons involves an important educational commitment: to provide conditions under which subjects can enhance their capacity for self-determination in acquiring knowledge about the human condition.
>
> Heron (1981: 34–5)

This then, is the kind of ethical argument advanced for participative or collaborative research where the 'subjects' are both co-researchers and principal beneficiaries.

It is worth noting that following this ethic would rule out the acquisition of a great deal of 'knowledge about the human condition', particularly in psychology with its reliance on deceit, and also in sociological studies of crime, racial and sexual discrimination, many of which have been done covertly. But then being morally good always has costs, and it has to be decided whether the good which would come from following these principles is worth the cost in general or in particular cases. I shall restrict my remarks to some of the difficulties of putting these principles into operation.

Here is a prescription for doing good, by the researcher *not* being in control:

> The study of an oppressive reality is not carried out by experts but by the objects of the oppression. People who before were objects of the research become subjects of their own research and action. This implies that scientists who participate in this study of the conditions of the oppression must give their research tools to the people.
>
> (Mies 1983: 126)

There are two problematic aspects of this. First, most such research is open-ended. No one will be able to predict where it will end up. Open-ended research is always a high-risk enterprise. Where the research is designed to effect political change, or to change people, then the risks are that much higher. Any book on counselling or group work practice issues warnings about this. This raises problems of informed consent. If the future cannot be predicted, then no one can be adequately informed. Involvement in the kind of political activism associated with community action research (Hunt 1993) can be a bruising experience, and involvement in the kind of consciousness raising associated with some feminist research (Patai and Koertge 1994) even more so.

However, second, if the researcher devolves control and responsibility to the subjects of the research as co-researchers, then what is there to ensure that *they will* behave in an ethical way? Enthusiasts for this approach write of the need to establish ethical ground rules to which all will subscribe (Romm 1997). But if the participants won't follow the rules, then apart from persuasion, the only sanction the 'professional' researcher has is to say 'goodbye'. I found myself in this position when doing participatory action research on claimants' unions in the 1970s. Because of the vicious infighting between members I eventually withdrew. As they told me in no uncertain terms, I had no right to tell them how to behave, and this was actually written into the agreement I made to ensure their 'informed consent' (see Panel 16.2). Again, in evaluating a piece of 'user-controlled' consultation research which had been conducted to inform the planning for the closure of a mental hospital, I was forced to the conclusion that the group of inmates doing the research had wrongly represented their own ideas for community care as those desired by all the inmates. The latter illustrates a violation of Heron's prescription that 'persons . . . have a moral right to participate in decisions that claim to generate knowledge about them'. But, as always, talk about 'rights' is idle if there are no mechanisms to ensure that one group of people accepts another's rights as their obligations.

The idea of participatory research sits rather awkwardly with the idea of the professional regulation of research ethics, for participatory research is a deprofessionalized practice. Nonetheless professional researchers who engage in it do publish their work in the professional journals and are thereby vulnerable to judgement according to professional codes of practice. This is even more so if they receive research grants from most of the major funders. It might be argued that to regard the professional researcher as the one ethically responsible for the research would be patronizing and demeaning of their non-professional co-researcher subjects. But equally other people might say: 'You're the professional researcher; the buck stops with you.'

Some participatory research achieves its objectives fairly well. There must often be some doubt about this because the notion that accountability is primarily to the subjects makes them, as both subjects and researchers, advocate, judge and jury in their own case. In this kind of research, the most usual evidence of success is in the form of the personal testimonies of those still involved at the end of the research. Publication of these angles the reader into a moral bind. Any independent ethical judgement by the reader is an impertinence committed by an outsider who has no right to make it and, as someone who is not oppressed, as having insufficient understanding to make it. Hence the only moral response allowable for a reader is to agree with the ethical appraisal of the writer(s). However, this is not a bind that readers have to accept.

As with the ethical consideration of all kinds of research, it is important to judge the risks and the harms of such research against the benefits of its outcomes. But since costs and benefits are likely to fall to different people such judgements are not easy to make. In evaluating a piece of action research of the community development kind I found that a large sum of public money had funded the activities of a group of around 15 local activists, who gave glowing accounts of the success of the project. What was left out of account was the non-benefit to the other 5,500 members of the community who were supposed to be beneficiaries but had hardly been involved at all. It was difficult to see how the project could have been structured to include meaningful participation for more than the number who actually did get involved, but it was quite easy to imagine how the money could have been spent otherwise to benefit more people. Participatory research is usually research which is designed to bring a direct benefit to a small group of people, and only secondarily to generate knowledge for use by others.

16.8 The ethics of publication

The fate of the vast majority of published research is to sit on library shelves unread. In this, research is no different from any other kind of publication. However, researchers might be said to have some moral obligations to manage the effects of what they publish. This includes the decision not to publish at all.

The most obvious obligation is that of publishing truthful research, and of publishing, or otherwise making available, sufficient information to allow for scrutiny by others (Chapter 1, Section 1.8). Beyond this, it is worth distinguishing between the effects of publication on those from whom the information was derived, and the effect on practices, policies and public opinion which might affect much larger groups of people.

Effects of publication on the people researched

The most obvious risks of harm to the subjects of research from publication are avoided through anonymizing persons. This is automatic in most quantitative research where information is expressed in numbers. It is a more important concern in qualitative research where accounts have to be written to ensure anonymity, as is usual. In addition, if published qualitative accounts do not require individual case studies, what is said by one person may be presented under several different names. Where there are case studies of people, sometimes minor details about them are changed to disguise identity further (Dingwall 1977). Anonymity might not be adopted in specially commissioned evaluation studies where the performance of identifiable individuals is subjected to judgement (these are rarely published, however), in performance indicator (PI) and other studies where the purpose is to make agencies publicly accountable and in other research concerning well-known institutions or events: thus Eileen Barker's (1984) study is published as a study of the 'Moonies' and not of an unnamed religious cult. Barry Turner's studies of disasters (for example, 1994) identifies the disasters in question and John Wakeford's study of public schools (1969) names the schools to which the data apply.

The naming of institutions becomes more necessary the more the researcher derives from documents. Without the naming, the sources cannot be cited and no one can check the author's interpretations of these. Nor can an agency be located in terms of larger data sets if the geographical location of the agency is disguised. In the same vein, the accountability of case studies is undermined by the anonymization of the site. For example, the Commission for Racial Equality (CRE) study *Set to Fail* (CRE 1992; see also Troyna 1991) charges an anonymous school as discriminating against South Asian pupils in the way it divided pupils into sets and entered them for examinations. But the analysis of the data was biased towards this finding and ultimately the verity or otherwise of the charge rests on data that was missing from the published study (Gomm 1993). Since the school was anonymous it is impossible for another researcher to remedy this. The anonymity of the school protected it from public censure, but it also prevented anything being done about its private shame if that were undeserved.

As noted in Chapter 14, Section 14.3, evaluation researchers sometimes tone down their criticisms if the people evaluated may suffer career setbacks from adverse comments in the report, in return for their undertaking to do better in the future. I would not identify the name of the mental hospital of the user-led consultation referred to earlier, because I have no wish to harm the reputations of those who conducted it. But, in my keeping this secret, you have no way of knowing that I didn't invent the whole thing. As you can see, there is a conflict between anonymization and accountability.

Some researchers agree in advance to allow those they study to amend and veto publication, on the grounds that they have the right to control the publication of information derived from themselves. This is particularly the case with research commissioned by organizations and governments, though there the veto is usually with the funder rather than with the people studied. In their study of dual-career families (1976) the Rapoports allowed their subjects a veto, with the result that subjects vetoed the publication of some of the most enlightening data. Without actually making such an agreement with the police he studied, Lidz (1989: 51) felt it would be a betrayal of their trust to publish information about false arrests, perjury, planting evidence, racism and brutality.

There are two different issues here. One is the expediental one of eliciting co-operation. The other is the ethical one about the subjects' rights to determine what is published about them. Participatory research always implies some such control over what is published. On the assumption that people really truly know the truth about themselves, such practices might be defended as improving the truth value of the research. But on the assumption that people are likely to use their veto to foster benign images of themselves there is a conflict here between the researcher's obligation to tell the truth and the subjects' rights to be represented as they would prefer to be. Leaning too far in the direction of saying what respondents want said about them, may put the researcher in the position of perpetrating untruths through publishing them (Ozga and Gerwirtz 1994; Sikes 2000).

Effects of publication on policies, practices and public perceptions

In the past, it was rarely the case that policy-makers drew on psychological or social research to formulate policies in a rational way (Bulmer 1982). Nor has there been any close relationship between the practices of practitioners in human services and a knowledge base accumulated via research (for example, Lomas 1994; Hargreaves 1996; Macdonald 1999). In the last 10 years or so there has been a large drive towards generating, collating, evaluating and disseminating research findings which could be used as the basis for making practice and policy decisions (Chapter 4, Section 4.4; Chapter 14, Section

14.3; Chapter 15, Sections 15.1–15.3; and see the web site of the Evidence Network, www.evidencenetwork.org/). In health care it would be true to say that research knowledge now features in a large swathe of practical decision-making. This is much less true of other areas of human services, partly because the research effort in these fields is tiny as compared with health. But even in healthcare, policy decisions are usually made with an eye to political expediency and budgetary possibilities as well as, or instead of, research evidence (Davies 2000).

Nor is it clear how social science research influences public thinking. Little of it is reported in the mass media. That which is, may be treated in a hostile or garbled way (Fenton *et al.* 1998; Hammersley 2000c; Gaber 2005). Perhaps the best model of the influence of social science research on public thinking is one of a haphazard process of percolation, rather like rumour dissemination, with fragments of social science entering through school sociology and social studies mixing with television 'social concern' documentaries, and being remembered by people in ways that are modified by their other beliefs and experiences (Chapter 8, Panel 8.1): a process ripe for computer simulation (Chapter 5, Sections 5.5, 5.6).

This being so, it is extremely difficult for researchers to know what effects their publications will have. For example, it is doubtful as to whether Margaret Mead in 1928 (1948) could have predicted that what was received in America as a sympathetic picture of the Samoan people, would be regarded by Samoan opinion leaders 50 years later as highly offensive (Freeman 1983).

This preamble is to indicate that it is difficult for social researchers to predict what kinds of effects publishing their research might have on wider society, though the best odds are on 'none at all'. This is not necessarily a matter of great concern to researchers who adopt a value-neutral stance. For most of them, the primary purpose of social research is to produce high-quality knowledge about the social world. It is someone else's business as to how this knowledge might be used. For critical researchers, however, the primary purpose of doing research is to improve the world, and to do it as quickly as possible. For them, then, publication can seem a way of publicizing how unfair social arrangements are, and how they might be improved. If the world is an evil place, then the only ethical publications are those which attack it. The problem with this strategy is that hardly anyone, except other social researchers, read such publications, and among social researchers socially critical research is mainly read by those who are already committed to the particular cause.

Much critical research is published as a corrective to ideas and images which critical researchers believe to be supporting the *status quo*. For researchers of these persuasions an important ethical question is whether anything they are about to publish might be taken to support some state of affairs or way of thinking of which they disapprove. Again, much is invested in designing publications to give 'voice' to the views and concerns of groups of people whose ideas are rarely heard and in the promotion of positive images of groups who are misunderstood and stigmatized in order to challenge stereotypes which are alleged to exist about them. Sometimes doing both leads to some rather vicious stereotypes of other kinds of people, for example of teachers (for example, Carrington 1983), or of health service personnel (Bowler 1993), or police officers and judges (for example, Young 1971). Dingwall, attacking such publications from the value-neutral position suggests that an important ethical consideration in judging research should be that

> it displays its adherence to an ethic of fair dealing ... does it convey as much understanding of its villains as its heroes? Are the privileged treated as having something serious to say, or simply dismissed as evil, corrupt or greedy without further inquiry?
>
> (Dingwall 1992: 172)

Here there are directly contradictory ethical prescriptions among researchers. And they are predictable ones given the different assumptions about the purpose of research. For Dingwall, research is primarily about presenting evidence and argument and allowing readers to decide whether to believe this or not. For him, producing stereotypes of 'baddies' is not just unethical, it is misleading. Sculley's feminist research on rapists was primarily designed on the grounds that rapists could not be understood via the stereotypical picture usually conveyed of them. Milgram's research undermines the stereotype of those who commit atrocities; Humphreys' was designed to dissolve the contemporary stereotype of homosexuals. All these manage to do this while adhering to an ethic of 'fair dealing'. Much critical research, by contrast, is designed as a foray in an ongoing battle, where stereotyping the opposition is fair game and rhetorical tricks are fair play in eliciting the reader's belief. Here, to paraphrase Karl Marx, the object of social research is not to understand the world but to change it for the better. How to do this remains unclear, but it is certainly not by producing socially critical work for low-circulation academic publications.

ACTIVITY   Ethically appraising research

For this Activity, you should download or otherwise obtain one of the following codes of research practice, according to your own sphere of interests – or, if you are a university student, the code from your university research ethics committee:

Association of Social Anthropologists
(www.theasa.org/ethics.htm).
British Educational Research Association
(www.bera.ac.uk/publications/pdfs/ethical.pdf).
British Psychological Society
(www.bps.org.uk/about/rules5.cfm).
British Society of Criminology
(www.lboro.ac.uk/departments/ss/bsc/council/CODEETH.HMT).
British Sociological Association
(www.britsoc.org.uk/about/ethic.htm).
Economic and Social Research Council
(www.esrcsocietytoday.ac.uk/ESRCInfoCentre/Images/ESRC_Re_Ethics_Frame_tcm6-11291.pdf).

Medical Research Council
(www.mrc.ac.uk/PolicyGuidance/EthicsAndGovernance/MRC002578).
Social Research Association
(www.the-sra.org.uk/ethic.htm).

1   Either:
    (a) sketch out the design of a piece of research which you might conduct
        given the time and resources to do so
    or
    (b) find a published research article.

In either case, review the research in terms of what ethical issues doing it and
publishing the results raises, and how you might, or the author did, resolve these
issues, using the code of practice you found as a framework for doing this.

Further reading

If you are going to conduct research you must be familiar with one of the
codes of ethics available as shown in the Activity at the end of the chapter.
The subject of ethics has become increasingly important in the twenty-first
century, with new university courses and centres, and a great outpouring of
publications. This includes publications on research ethics. Among the many
books, Israel and Hay (2005) is a good general introduction which gives
particular attention to the points of conflict which may arise between social
researchers and the ethics committees which regulate research. Mauthner *et
al.* (2002) deals with ethics in qualitative research and contains interesting
material on the ethical considerations of dealing with sensitive and disturb-
ing issues. Williams (1995) discusses the ethics of action research when
conducted by practitioners. Masson (2004) outlines the legal context for
research with children. Wiles *et al.* (2004) discuss the difficulties of offering
informed consent with vulnerable groups such as children, people with learning difficulties, or people with mental health problems. Research participants
give their views on the ethics of research in two studies one by Graham, Lewis
and Nicholas (2006) and the other by Graham, Grewal and Lewis (2007).
Graham *et al.* (2006) is a literature review of a wide range of interview
research; Graham *et al.* (2007) is a study interviewing samples of participants
from five major government surveys, including one qualitative survey.

Value-led researchers tend not to separate their discussions of research
ethics from their discussions of research in general, so any research text of
this kind will contain ethical discussion, though Reason (1994) addresses
ethics directly. Feminists often write about having an ethical epistemology: an
ethical theory of knowledge, contrasting this with the objective theory of
knowledge adopted by value-neutral researchers. For discussions of this kind,
see Addelson (1993, 1994); Stanley and Wise (1993: 200–3); Walker (1989).

References*

Addelson, K. (1993) 'Knowers/doers and their moral problems', in Alcoff, L. and Potter, E. (eds), *Feminist Epistemologies*, New York, Routledge: 265–94.

Addelson, K. (1994) *Moral Passages: Towards a Collectivist Moral Theory*, New York, Routledge.

Agar, M. and Wilson, D. (2002) 'Drugmart: heroin epidemics as complex adaptive systems', *Complexity*, 7(5): 44–52.

Alaszewski, A. (2005) *Using Diaries for Social Research*, London, Sage.

Alwin, D. (1997) 'Feeling thermometres versus 7-point scales: which are better?', *Sociological Methods and Research*, 25(3): 318–40.

Andersen, M. (1993) 'Studying across difference: race, class and gender in qualitative research', in Stanfield, J. and Dennis, R. (eds), *Race and Ethnicity in Research Methods*, London, Sage: 39–53.

Arksey, H. and Knight, P. (1999) *Interviewing for Social Scientists: An Introductory Resource with Examples*, London, Sage.

Armstrong, D., Gosling, A., Weinman, J. and Matineu, T. (1997) 'The place of inter-rater reliability in qualitative research: an empirical study', *Sociology* 31(3): 597–606.

Atkinson, J. M. (1978) *Discovering Suicide: Studies in the Organisation of Sudden Death*, Basingstoke, Macmillan.

Atkinson, M. W., Kessell, N. and Dalgaard, J. (1975) 'The comparability of suicide rates', *British Journal of Psychiatry*, 127: 427–56.

Atkinson, P. (1990) *The Ethnographic Imagination: Textual Constructions of Reality*, London, Routledge.

Atkinson, P., Delamont, S., Coffey, A., Loftland, J. and Loftland, L. (2007) *Handbook of Ethnography*, London, Sage.

Atkinson, R. and Flint, J. (2001) 'Accessing hidden and hard-to-reach populations: snowball research strategies', *Sociological Research Update*, Issue 33.

Audit Commission (2003) *Achieving Improvements through Clinical Governance: A Progress Report on Implementation by NHS Trusts*, Report by the Auditor and Comptroller General, HC 1055, Session 2002–03, London, The Stationery Office online (www.cgsupport.nhs.uk/PDFs/clinical_governance_report.pdf).

Audit Commission (2005) *Crime Recording 2005: Improving the Quality of Crime Records in England and Wales*, London, Audit Commission (www.audit-commission.gov.uk).

Aust, R. and Smith, N. (2003) *Ethnicity and Drug Use: Key Findings from the 2001/02 British Crime Survey*, London, Home Office *Findings* 209 (www.ukcia.org/research/EthnicityAndDrugUse2001-2002.pdf).

Austin, J. (1962) *How to do Things with Words*, Oxford, Clarendon (Oxford, Oxford University Press edns, 1975, 1980).

Axelrod, R. (1987) 'The evolution of strategies in the iterated prisoner's dilemma', in Davis, L. (ed.), *Genetic Algorithms and Simulated Annealing*, London, Pitman.

---

* Web sites accessed January 2008.

Ayer, A. J. (1956) *The Problem of Knowledge*, Harmondsworth, Penguin.

Babbie, E. and Halley, F. (2007) *Adventures in Social Research: Data Analysis Using SPSS 14.0 and 15.0 for Windows*, London, Sage.

Back, L. and Solomos, J. (1993) 'Doing research, writing politics; the dilemmas of political intervention in research on racism', *Economy and Society*, 22(2): 178–99.

Backhouse, G. (2002) 'How preserving confidentiality in health research can be compatible with preserving data for future use', *Medical Sociology News*, 28(3): 32–5.

Bak, P. and Tang, C. (1989) 'Earthquakes as a self-organized critical phenonenon', *Journal of Geophysics*, B49: 15635.

Bak, P, Tang C. and Weisenfeld, K. (1987) 'Self-organized crticiality: an explanation of 1/f noise', *Physics Review Letters*, 59: 381–4.

Barabasi, A. L. (2002) *Linked: The New Science of Networks*, Jackson, TN Perseus Publishing.

Barabasi, A. L. and Bonabeu, E. (2003) 'Scale free networks', *Scientific American*, May: 50–9.

Barber, T. and Silver, M. (1968) 'Fact, fiction and the experimenter bias effect', *Psychological Bulletin Monograph Supplement*, 70(6:2): 1–29.

Barbour, R. and Kitzinger, J. (1999) *Developing Focus Group Research: Politics, Theory and Practice*, London, Sage.

Barker, E. (1984) *The Making of a Moonie: Brainwashing Or Choice?*, Oxford, Blackwell.

Barker, W. (1992) 'Health visiting: action research in a controlled environment', *International Journal of Nursing Studies*, 29(3): 251–9.

Barnes, C. and Mercer, G. (1997) *Doing Disability Research*, Leeds, The Disability Press.

Barthes, R. (1993) *Mythologies* (trans Annette Lavers), London, Vintage.

Baruch, R. (1997) *Randomized Experiments for Planning and Evaluation: A Practical Guide*, London, Sage.

Bateson, G. (1972) *Steps Towards an Ecology of Mind*, Harmondsworth, Allen Lane.

Baumrind, D. (1964) 'Some thoughts on ethics of research: after reading Milgram's "Behavioural Study of Obedience"', *American Psychologist*, 19: 421–3.

Bazeley, P. (2000) *Qualitative Data Analysis with NVIVO*, London, Sage.

Beck, A. (1970) *Depression: Causes and Treatment*, Philadelphia, University of Philadelphia Press.

Becker, H. (1952) 'Social class variations in teacher–pupil relationships', *Journal of Educational Sociology*, 52: 451–65.

Becker, H. (1963) *Outsiders: Studies in the Sociology of Deviance*, New York, Free Press.

Becker, H. (1967) 'Whose side are we on?', *Social Problems*, 14: 239–47.

Becker, H. (1971) 'Reply to Riley's "Partisanship and objectivity"', *American Sociologist*, 6: 13.

Behling, O. and Law, K. (2000) *Translating Questionnaires and Other Research Instruments: Problems and Solutions*, London, Sage.

Ben-Tovim, G., Gabriel, J., Law, I. and Stredder, K. (1986) *The Local Politics of Race*, London, Macmillan.

Beresford, P. and Evans, C. (1999) 'Research note: research and empowerment', *British Journal of Social Work*, 29: 671–7.

Berg, B. (1995) *Qualitative Research Methods for the Social Sciences*, 2nd edn, Boston, Allyn & Bacon.

Berger, A. (2000) *Media and Communication Research: An Introduction to Qualitative and Quantitative Approaches*, London, Sage.

Berlak, A., Berlak, H., Bagenstos, N. and Mikel, E. (1975) 'Teaching and learning in English primary schools', *School Review*, 83(2): 215–43.

Berlekamp, E., Conway, J. and Guy R. (1982) *Winning Ways for Your Mathematical Plays. Vol 2: Games in Particular*, London, Academic Press.

Bernard, H. (1994) *Research Methods in Anthropology: Qualitative and Quantitative Approaches*, London, Sage.

Bernard, H. R. (2005) *Research Methods in Anthropology: Qualitative and Quantitative Approaches*, 4th edn, London, Sage.

Best, G., Dennis, J. and Draper, P. (1977) *Health, the Mass Media and the National Health Service*, London, Unit for the Study of Health Policy, Guy's Hospital Medical School.

Bishop, L. (2007) 'A Reflexive Account of Reusing Qualitative Data: Beyond Primary/ Secondary Dualism', *Sociological Research Online*, 12(3) (www.socresonline.org.uk/ 12/3/2.html).

Blackwell, L., Swann, S., Lynch, K. and Smith J. (n.d.) *The ONS Longitudinal Study: Quality Issues for 30 years of data linking*, London, Centre for Longitudinal Studies (www.celsius.lshtm.ac.uk/publications/general.html).

Blair, P., Fleming, P., Benakey, D., Smith, I., Bacon, C., Taylor, E., Berry, J., Golding, J. and Tripp, J. (1996) 'Smoking and sudden infant death syndrome: results from 1993–95 case control study for confidential inquiry into still births and deaths in infancy', *British Medical Journal*, 313: 195–8.

Blanden, J., Gregg, P. and Machin, S. (2005) *Intergenerational Mobility in Europe and North America: A Report Supported by the Sutton Trust*, London, Sutton Trust (www.suttontrust.com/reports/IntergenerationalMobility.pdf).

Blaxter, M. (2004) 'Mothers and daughters: accounts of health in the grandmother generation, 1945–1978 [computer file]', Colchester, Essex: UK Data Archive [distributor], July, SN: 4943.

Blaxter, M. and Patterson, E. (1982) *Mothers and Daughters: A Three-Generational Study of Health Attitudes and Behaviour*, London: Heinemann Educational Books.

Blaxter, M. and Patterson, E. (1983) 'The goodness is out of it', in Murcott, A. (ed.), *The Sociology of Food and Eating*, Aldershot: Gower.

Blenkin, G., Kelly, A. and Rose, J. (2001) *Action Research for Professional Development: An Early Years' Perspective*, London, Paul Chapman.

Bloor, M. (1991) 'A minor office: the variable and socially constructed character of death certification in a Scottish city', *Journal of Health and Social Behaviour*, 32: 273–87.

Bloor, M. (1994) 'On the conceptualisation of routine medical decision-making: death certification as an habitual activity', in Bloor, M. and Taroborrelli, P. (eds), *Qualitative Studies in Health and Medicine*, Aldershot, Avebury: 96–109.

Bloor, M., Frankland, J., Thomas, M. and Robson, K. (2000) *Focus Groups in Social Research*, London, Sage.

Bloor, M., Samphire, M. and Prior, L. (1987) 'Artefact explanations of inequalities in health: an assessment of the evidence', *Sociology of Health and Illness*, 9(3): 231–64.

Bloor, M., Venters, G. and Samphire, M. (1978) 'Geographical variations in the incidence of operations on the tonsils and adenoids: an epidemiological and sociological investigation: parts 1 and 2', *Journal of Laryngology and Otology*, 96: 791–801, 833–95.

Blumstein, P. (1991) 'The production of selves in personal relationships', in Howard, J. and Callero, P. (eds), *Self-Society Dynamic: Cognition, Emotion and Action*, Cambridge, Cambridge University Press: 305–22.

Blytheway, B. and Johnson, J. (1990) 'On defining ageism', *Critical Social Policy*, 29: 27–39.

Booth, C. (1902) *Life and Labour of People in London*, 18 vols, London, Macmillan.

Boreham, R. and Shaw, A. (eds), (2001) *Smoking, Drinking and Drug Use among Young People in England in 2000*, London, Office of National Statistics, Stationery Office.

Boring, E. (1923) 'Intelligence as the tests test it', *New Republic*, 35: 35–7.

Bosanquet, N. and Zarzecka, A. (1995) 'Attitudes to health services 1983 to 1993', in Harrison, A. and Bruscini, S. (eds), *Health Care UK 1994/95*, London, King's Fund Policy Institute: 88–94.

Bosley, S. (1999) 'Trial and error puts patient's at risk', *Guardian*, 27 July: 1, 7, 8.

Bottomley, K. and Pease, K. (1986) *Crime and Punishment: Interpreting the Data*, Milton Keynes, Open University Press.

Bouchard, J.-P. and Mezard, M. (2000) 'Wealth condensation in a simple economy' (www.science-finance.fr/papers/0002374.pdf).

Bourque, L. (2003a) *How to Conduct Telephone Surveys*, 2nd edn, London, Sage.

Bourque, L. (2003b) *How to Conduct Self-Administered and Mail Surveys*, 2nd edn, London, Sage.

Bowler, I. (1993) '"They're not the same as us": midwives' stereotypes of South Asian descent maternity patients', *Sociology of Health and Illness*, 15(2): 157–78.

Bowling, A. (1997) *Research Methods in Health: Investigating Health and Health Services*, Buckingham, Open University Press.

Bowling, A. (2007a) *Measuring Health: A Review of Quality of Life Measurement Scales*, 3rd edn, Buckingham, Open University Press.

Bowling, A. (2007b) *Measuring Disease: A Review of Disease Specific Quality of Life Measurement scales*, 2nd edn, Buckingham, Open University Press.

Boydell, D. and Jasman, A. (1983) *The Pupil and Teacher Record: A Manual For Observers*, Leicester, Leicester University Press.

Brainerd, C. and Reyna, V. (2005) *The Science of False Memory*, Oxford, Oxford University Press.

Brandt, L. (2003) 'From kissing frogs to demonic possession: people can be led to believe they experienced the improbable', *Eurekalert*, February (www.eurekalert.org).

British Medical Journal (1998) 'Dealing with research misconduct in the United Kingdom', Special Section, 316: 1726–33.

British Sociological Association (2002) *Statement of Ethical Practice for the British Sociological Association: March 2002*, London, BSA (www.sociology.org.uk/asbsoce.pdf).

Broad, W. and Wade, N. (1982) *Betrayers of the Truth: Fraud and Deceit in the Halls of Science*, London, Century Publishing.

Brown, A. (1992) 'Design experiments: theoretical and methodological challenges in creating complex interventions in classroom settings', *Journal of Learning Science*, 2: 141–78.

Brown, C. and Gay, P. (1985) *Racial Discrimination: 17 Years after the Act*, London, Policy Studies Institute.

Brown, G. and Yule, G. (1983) *Discourse Analysis*, Cambridge, Cambridge University Press.

Browning, C. (1993) *Ordinary Men: Police Battalion 101 and the Final Solution in Poland*, New York, Harper Perennial.

Bruun, H. (1972) *Science, Values and Politics in Max Weber's Methodology*, Copenhagen, Munksgaard.

Bryman, A. and Burgess, R. (1994) 'Developments in qualitative data analysis', in Bryman, A. and Burgess, R. (eds), *The Analysis of Qualitative Data*, London, Routledge: 1–17.

Buchanan, M (2000) *Ubiquity, The Science of History or Why the World is Simpler than We Think*, London, Weidenfeld & Nicolson.

Buchanan, M. (2003) *Smallworld: Uncovering Nature's Hidden Networks*, London, Phoenix.

Buck, N. (2001) 'Identifying neighbourhood effects in social exclusion', *Urban Studies* 38: 2251–75.

Budd, T., Sharp, C. and Mayhew, P. (2005) *Offending in England and Wales: First Results from the 2003 Crime and Justice Survey*, HORS 278, London, Home Office.

Bulmer, M. (1982) *The Uses of Social Research: Social Investigation in Public Policy-Making*, London, Allen & Unwin.

Bulmer, M. (2002) *Questionnaires*, 4 vols, London, Sage.

Burke, K. (1966) *Language as Symbolic Interaction: Essays on Life, Literature and Method*, Los Angeles, University of California Press.

Burns, T. (1992) *Erving Goffman*, London, Routledge.

Buttney, R. (1993) *Social Accountability in Communication*, London, Sage.

Byrd, D. (1981) *Organizational Constraints on Psychiatric Treatment: The Outpatient Clinic*, Greenwich, CT, JAI Press.

Byrne, D. (1998) *Complexity Theory and the Social Sciences*, London, Routledge & Kegan Paul.

Campbell, M. (1991) 'Children at risk: how different are children on the child abuse registers?', *British Journal of Social Work*, 21: 259–75.

Campbell, T. and Stanley, J. (1996) *Experimental and Quasi-experimental Designs for Research*, Chicago, Rand MacNally.

Carrington, B. (1983) 'Sport as a sidetrack: an analysis of West Indian involvement in extra-curricular sport', in Barton, L. and Walker, S. (eds), *Race, Class and Education*, London, Croom Helm: 40–65.

Casti, J. (2001) 'Would-be business worlds: an interview with John. L. Casti', *Complexity*, 6(2): 13–15.

Chainey, S. and Smith, C. (2006) *Review of GIS-Based Information Sharing Systems*, Home Office Online Report 02/06, London, Home Office (www.homeoffice.gov.uk/rds).

Charlton, J., Kelly, S., Evans, B., Jenkins, R. and Wallis, B. (1992) 'Trends in suicide deaths in England and Wales', *Population Trends*, 69: 10–16.

Chambers, R. and Skinner, C. (2003) *Analysis of Survey Data*, London, John Wiley.

Child, D. (2006) *The Essentials of Factor Analysis*, 3rd edn, London, Continuum.

Chiu, L.-F. and Knight, D. (1999) 'How useful are focus groups for obtaining the views of minority groups?', in Barbour, R. and Kitzinger, J. (eds), *Developing Focus Group Research: Politics, Theory and Practice*, London, Sage: 99–112.

Cho M. and Bero, L. (1998) 'The quality of drug studies published in symposium proceedings', *Annals of International Medicine*, 124: 485–9.

Cicourel, A. (1966) *Method and Measurement*, New York, Free Press.

Cicourel, A. (1982) 'Interviews, surveys and the problem of ecological validity', *American Sociologist*, 17(1): 11–20.

Cicourel, A. and Kitsuse, J. (1963) *The Educational Decision-Makers*, Indianapolis, Bobbs-Merrill.

Clandinin, D. (ed.) (2007) *Handbook of Narrative Research Methods*, London, Sage.

Clarricoates, K. (1980) 'The importance of being Ernest . . . Emma . . . Tom . . . Jane: the perception and categorisation of gender conformity and gender deviation in primary schools', in Deem, R. (ed.), *Schooling for Women's Work*, London, Routledge: 26–41.

Cochrane, A. (1972) *Effectiveness and Efficiency*, Oxford, Nuffield Provincial Hospitals Trust.

Coghlan, D. and Brannick, T. (2000) *Doing Action Research in your own Organization*, London, Sage.

Cohen, G., Forbes, E. and Garraway, M. (1994) *Lothian Health Survey-Summary of Initial Findings*, Edinburgh, University Department of Public Health Sciences.

Cohen, G., Forbes, J. and Garraway, M. (1996) 'Can different patient satisfaction surveys yield consistent results? A comparison of three surveys', *British Medical Journal*, 313(7061): 841–4.

Collins, P. H. (1990) *Black Feminist Thought*, London, Unwin Hyman.

Colton, D. and Court, R. (2007) *Designing and Constructing Instruments for Social Research and Evaluation*, San Francisco, CA, Jossey-Bass.

Commission for Racial Equality (CRE) (1992) *Set to Fail: Setting and Banding in Secondary Schools*, London, Commission for Racial Equality.

Coolican, H. (1994) *Research Methods and Statistics in Psychology*, 2nd edn, London, Hodder & Stoughton.

Coolican, H. (2004) *Research Methods and Statistics in Psychology*, 4th edn, London, Hodder Headline.

Cooper, B (2005) 'Applying Ragin's Crisp and fuzzy set QCA to large datasets: social class and educational achievement in the national child development study', *Sociological Research Online*, 10(2) (www.socresonline.org.uk/10/2/cooper.html).

Coulthard, M. and Montgomery, M. (1981) 'Originating a description', in Coulthard, M. and Montgomery, M. (eds), *Studies in Discourse Analysis*, London, Routledge & Kegan Paul: 1–12.

Cox, C. and Marks, J. (1980) *Real Concern: An Appraisal of the National Children's Bureau Report on 'Progress in Secondary Schools' by Jane Steedman*, London, Centre for Policy Studies.

Crawford, A. (1987) 'Bias in a survey of drinking habits', *Alcohol and Alcoholism*, 22(2): 167–79.

Cuff, E., Sharrock, W. and Francis, (2006) *Perspectives in Sociology*, 5th edn, London, Routledge.

Curtis, J. and Sparrrow, N. (2002) *The Failure of the Polls in 1997: Learning the Lessons for the Future*, London, ICM Research (www.icmresearch.co.uk/reviews/2002/failure-of-the-polls-1997.htm)

Daston, L. (1992) 'Objectivity and the escape from perspective', *Social Studies of Science*, 22(4): 597–618.

Davie, N. (1999) 'Revealed: how the police fiddle crime figures', *Guardian*, 18 March.

Davie, R. (1993) 'The impact of the National Child Development Study', *Children and Society*, 7(1): 20–36.

Davies, C. (2000) 'Understanding the policy process', in Brechin, A., Brown, H. and Eby, M. (eds), *Critical Practice in Health and Social Care*, Milton Keynes and London, Open University/Sage: 211–30.

Davies, J. (1997) *Drugspeak: The Analysis of Drug Discourse*, Amersterdam, Harwood Academic.

Dawkins, R. (1993) 'Viruses of the mind', *Free Enquiry*, Summer: 34–41.

Dawkins, R. (2006) *The Blind Watchmaker*, Harmondsworth, Penguin.

de Heer, W., de Leeuw, E. and van der Zouwen, J. (1999) 'Methodological issues in survey research', *Bulletin de Méthodologie Sociologique*, 64: 25–48.

de Leeuw, W. (1999) 'Item non-response: prevention is better than cure', *Survey Methods Newsletter*, 19(2): 4–8.

Demark, S., Drew, D. and Grimsley, M. (2000) 'Minding the gap: ethnic, gender and social class differences in attainment at 16, 1988–95', *Race Ethnicity and Education*, 3(2): 117–43.

Dennett, D. (1995) *Darwin's Dangerous Idea: Evolution and the Meanings of Life*, Harmondsworth, Allen Lane/Penguin.

Department for Education and Skills (DfES) (2005) *Youth Cohort Study: The Activities and Experiences of 17 Year Olds in England and Wales*, London, DfES (www.dfes.gov.uk/rsgateway/).

Department for Education and Skills (DfES) (2007) 'Secondary schools (GCSE and equivalent: achievement and attainment Tables 2006' (www.dcsf.gov.uk/ and navigate to 'School performance tables').

Department of Health (DoH) (2005) *Research Governance Framework for Health and Social Care*, 2nd edn, London, The Stationery Office (www.dh.gov.uk/en/PublicationsandstatisticsPublications/PublicationsPolicyAndGuidance/DH_4108962).

Department of Health (DoH) (2006) *Tackling Health Inequalities: 2003–05 Data Update for the National 2010 PSA Target*, London, Department of Health (www.doh.gov.uk).

Design-based Research Collective (2003) 'Design-based research: an emerging paradigm for educational inquiry', *Educational Researcher*, 32(1): 2–14.

Detsky, A., Naylor, C., O'Rourke, K., McGreer, A. and L'Abbé, K. (1992) 'Incorporating variations in the quality of individual randomized trials into meta-analyses', *Journal of Clinical Epidemiology*, 45: 225–65.

de Vaus, D. (2002) *Surveys in Social Research*, 4 vols, 5th edn, London, Sage.

Dex, S. and Joshi, H. (2005) *Children of the 21st Century: from Birth to 9 Months*, London, London University Institute of Education.

Dhiri, S., Brand, S., Harries, R. and Price, R. (1999) *Modelling and Predicting Crime Trends in England and Wales*, London, Home Office Research Study 199.

Dingwall, R. (1977) *The Social Organisation of Health Visitor Training*, Beckenham, Croom Helm.

Dingwall, R. (1992) 'Don't mind him – he's from Barcelona: qualitative methods in health studies', in Daly, J., McDonald, I. and Willis, E. (eds), *Researching Health Care: Designs, Dilemmas, Disciplines*, London, Routledge: 161–75.

Dingwall, R., Eekelaar, J. and Murray, T. (1983) *The Protection of Children*, Oxford, Blackwell.

Dingwall, R. and Murray, T. (1983) 'Categorisation in accident departments: "good" patients, "bad" patients and children', *Sociology of Health and Illness*, 5(12): 121–48.

Ditton, J. (1977) *Part-Time Crime: An Ethnography of Fiddling and Pilferage*, London, Macmillan.

Docherty, T. (ed.) (1993) *Postmodernism: A Reader*, London, Harvester Wheatsheaf.

Doll, R. and Hill, A. (1964) 'Mortality in relation to smoking: ten years' observation of British doctors', *British Medical Journal*, June: 1399–410, 1460–7.

Doll, R., Peto, R. Wheatley, K., Gray, R. and Sutherland, I. (1994) 'Mortality in relation to smoking: 40 years' observations on male British Doctors', *British Medical Journal*, 309: 901–11.

Donkin, A., Huang Lee, Y. and Toson, B. (2002) 'Implications of changes in the UK social and occupational classification in 2001 for vital statistics', *Population Trends*, No. 107: 23–29 (www.statistics.gov.uk) (journal articles).

Doran, T., Drever, G. and Whitehead, M. (2004) 'Is there a north–south divide in social class inequalities in health in Great Britain? Cross sectional study using data from the 2001 census', *British Medical Journal*, 328: 1043–5.

Douglas, J. (1964) *The Home and the School: A Study of Ability and Attainment in the Primary School*, London, McGibbon & Kee (Panther edn, 1967).

Douglas, M. (1966) *Purity and Danger: An Analysis of the Concepts of Pollution and Taboo*, Harmondsworth, Penguin.

Douglas, M. (1987) *How Institutions Think*, London, Routledge & Kegan Paul.

Dowie, J. (1996) 'The research practice gap and the role of decision analysis in closing it', *Health Care Analysis*, 4: 5–18.

Drever, F. and Bunting, J. (1997) 'Patterns and trends in male mortality' in Drever, F. and Whitehead, M. (eds), *Health Inequality: Decennial Supplement*, London, Office for National Statistics Series DS, 15: 95–107 (www.statistics.gov.uk/downloads/theme_health/DSIS_HlthInequals_v2.pdf).

Dreyer, F., Whitehead, M. and Roden, M. (1996) 'Current patterns and trends in male mortality by social class (based on occupation)', *Population Trends*, 86: 15–20.

Drogoul, A., Corbra, B. and Lalande, S. (1995) 'Manta: new experimental results on the emergence of (artificial) ant societies', in Gilbert, R. and Conte, R. (eds), *Artificial Societies: The Computer Simulation of Social Life*, London, UCL Press.

Dukes, E. (1996) *Resolving Public Conflict: Transforming Community and Governance*, Manchester, Manchester University Press.

Durkheim, E. (1952) *Suicide: A Study in Sociology*, trans F. Spalding and G. Simpson, London, Routledge (original French edn, 1897).

Dwyer, T. and Ponsonby, A. L. (1996) 'Sudden infant death syndrome: after the "back to sleep" campaign', *British Medical Journal*, 313: 180–1.

Eby, M. (2000) 'Producing evidence ethically', in Gomm, R. and Davies, C. (eds), *Using Evidence in Health and Social Care*, London, Sage: 108–28.

Eco, U. (1976) *A Theory of Semiotics*, Bloomington, IN, University Press.

Edmundson, R. (1984) *Rhetoric in Sociology*, Basingstoke, Macmillan.

Effective Health Care (1998) 'Cholesterol and coronary heart disease: screening and treatment', *Effective Health Care*, 4(1): 1–18.

Elander, G. (1991) 'Ethical conflicts in placebo treatments', *Journal of Advanced Nursing*, 16: 947–51.

Elkin, E., Frankston, S., Lebowitz, B., Kapust, L., Hollis, A. and O'Conner, M. (2007) 'The use of the Color Trails Test in the assessment of driver competence: preliminary report of a culture fair instrument', *Archive of Clinical Neuropsychology*, 25 (5): 631–5.

Elliot, D. (1999) *Report of Task Force on Weighting and Estimation*, National Statistics Methodology Paper, 16, London, Office for National Statistics, (www.statistics.gov.uk/methods_quality/publications.asp).

Elliott, J. (1991) *Action Research for Educational Change*, Buckingham, Open University Press.

Elton, L. (2004) 'Goodhart's Law and performance indicators in higher education', *Evaluation and Research in Education*, 18(1&2): 120–8.

Emerson, R., Fretz, R. and Shaw, L. (1995) *Writing Ethnographic Fieldnotes (Chicago Guides to Writing, Editing & Publishing)*, Chicago, University of Chicago Press.

Epstein, J. and Axtell, R. (1996) *Growing Artificial Societies – Social Science from the Bottom Up*, Cambridge MA, MIT Press.

ESRC (2005) *Research Ethics Framework*, London, Economic and Social Research Council (www.esrc.ac.uk/ESRCInfoCentre/Images/ESRC_Re_Ethics_Frame_tcm6-11291.pdf).

Eve, R., Horsfall, S. and Lee, M. (1997) *Chaos, Complexity and Sociology: Myths, Models and Themes*, London, Sage.

Farquhar, C. and Das, R. (1999) 'Are focus groups suitable for "sensitive topics"?', in Barbour, R. and Kitzinger, J. (eds), *Developing Focus Group Research: Politics, Theory and Practice*, London, Sage: 47–63.

Farrington, D., Coid, J., Harnott, L., Jolliffe, D., Soteriou, N., Turner, R. and West, D. (2006) *Criminal Careers and Life Success: New Findings from the Cambridge Study in Delinquent Development*, Home Office Research Findings, 281, London, Home Office (www.homeoffice.gov.uk/rds/).

Featherstone, J. and Donovan, J. (1998) 'Random allocation or allocation at random? Patients' perspectives in a randomised controlled trial', *British Medical Journal*, 317: 1117–80.

Fenton, N., Bryaman, A., Deacon, D. and Birmingham, P. (1998) *Mediating Social Science*, London, Sage.

Ferguson, M. (1983) *Forever Feminine: Women's Magazines and the Cult of Femininity*, London, Heinemann.

Ferrie, E., Brynner, J. and Wadsworth, M. (2002) *Changing Britain, Changing Lives: Three Generations at the Turn of the Century*, London, University of London Institute of Education, Befordway Papers, 18.

Ferrie, J. (ed.) (2004) *Work, Stress and Health: The WhiteHall II Study*, London, Council of Civil Service Unions/Cabinet Office.

Field, A. (2000) *Discovering Statistics: Using SPSS for Windows*, London, Sage.

Fielding, J. (2001) 'Coding and managing data', in Gilbert, N. (ed.), *Researching Social Life*, 2nd edn, London, Sage: 227–51.

Fielding, N. (1981) *The National Front*, London, Routledge & Kegan Paul.

Fielding, N. (2003) *Interviewing*, 4 vols, London, Sage.

Fink, A. (2003a) *How to Sample in Surveys*, 2nd edn, London, Sage.

Fink, A. (2003b) *The Survey Kit*, 10 vols, 2nd edn, London, Sage.

Fink, A. (2003c) *How to Ask Survey Questions*, 2nd edn, London, Sage.

Fink, A. (2003d) *How to Manage, Analyze, and Interpret Survey Data*, 2nd edn, London, Sage.

Fink, A. (2005) *How to Conduct Surveys: A Step by Step Guide*, 3rd edn, London, Sage.

Finkel, S., Guerbock, T. and Borg, M. (1991) 'Race-of-interviewer effects in a preelection poll: Virginia 1989', *Public Opinion Quarterly*, 55: 313–30.

Fischbaker, C., Bhopal, R., White M., Unwin, N. and Alberti, K. (2000) 'The comparative performance of the Rose Angina questionnaire in South Asian population', *Journal of Epidemiology and Community Health 2000*, 54: 786.

Fiske, J. (1993) *Reading the Popular*, London, Unwin Hyman.

Fiske, J. and Hartley, J. (2003) *Reading Television (New Accents)*, 2nd edn, London, Routledge.

FitzGerald, M. and Hale, C. (1996) *Ethnic Minorities, Victimisation and Racial Harassment*, London, Home Office Research Study (www.homeoffice.gov.uk/rds/).

Fletcher, R. (1972) *The Making of Sociology: 2 Developments*, London, Nelson.

Flick, U. (1998) *An Introduction to Qualitative Research*, London, Sage.

Flick, U. (2004) 'Triangulation in qualitative research', in Flick, U., von Kardoff, E. and Steinke, I. (eds), *A Companion to Qualitative Research*, London, Sage.

Flynn, J. (1999) 'Searching for justice: IQ gains over time', *American Psychologist*, 54: 5–20.

Foster, J. (2000) *Data Analysis Using SPSS for Windows Versions 8.10–10.0*, London, Sage.

Foster, P., Gomm, R. and Hammersley, M. (1996) *Constructing Educational Inequality*, Lewes, Falmer.

Foster, P., Gomm, R. and Hammersley, M. (2000) 'Case studies as spurious evaluation: the example of research on educational inequalities', *British Journal of Educational Studies*, 48(3): 115–30.

Fowler, F. (2001) *Survey Research Methods*, 3rd edn, London, Sage.

Franke, R. and Kaul, J. (1978) 'The Hawthorne Experiments: first statistical interpretation', *American Sociological Review*, 43(5): 623–43.

Freeman, D. (1983) *Margaret Mead and Samoa: The Making and Unmaking of an Anthropological Myth*, Cambridge, MA, Harvard University Press.

Frette, V., Christensen, K., Malthe-Sorenssen, A., Feder, J., Jassans, F. and Meakin, P. (1996) 'Avalanche dynamics in a pile of rice', *Nature 1996*: 179: 49–52.

Fuller, E. (ed.) (2005) *Smoking, Drinking and Drug Use by Young People in England in 2000*, London, Health and Social Care Information Centre.

Fuller, M. (1982) 'Young, female and black', in Cashmore, E. and Troyna, B. (eds), *Black Youth in Crisis*, London, George Allen & Unwin: 87–99.

Fuller, R. and Petch, A. (1995) *Practitioner Research: The Reflexive Social Worker*, Buckingham, Open University Press.

Gaber, A (2005) 'Media coverage of Sociology', *Sociological Research Online*, 10(3) (www.socresonline.org.uk/10/3/gaber.html).

Galliher, J., Brekhus, W. and Keys, D. (2004) *Laud Humphreys: Prophet of Homosexuality and Sociology*, Wisconsin, University of Wisconsin Press.

Galtung, J. and Ruge, M. (1981) 'Structuring and selecting news', in Cohen, S. and Young, J. (eds), *The Manufacture of News: Deviance, Social Problems and the Mass Media*, London, Constable: 52–63.

Garfinkel, H. (1967) *Studies in Ethnomethodology*, Englewood Cliffs, NJ, Prentice-Hall.

Gbrich, C. (2006) *Qualitative Data Analysis: An Introduction*, London, Sage.

Geertz, C. (1973) 'Thick description: towards an interpretive theory of culture', in *The Interpretation of Cultures: Selected Essays of Clifford Geertz*, London, Hutchinson: 3–30.

Gephart, R. (2006) *Ethnostatistics and Organizational Research Methodologies*, London, Sage.

Gilbert, N. (1993) *Analysing Tabular Data: Loglinear and Logistic Models for Social Researchers*, London, UCL Press.

Gilbert, N. (ed.) (2001) *Researching Social Life*, 2nd edn, London, Sage.

Gilbert, N. (2007) 'Simulation: an emergent perspective', Guildford, Centre for Research on Social Simulation (http://alife.ccp14.ac.uk/cress/research/simsoc/tutorial.html).

Gilbert, N. and Troitzsch, K. (1999) *Simulation for the Social Scientist*, 1st edn, Buckingham, Open University Press.

Gilbert, N. and Troitzsch, K. (2005) *Simulation for the Social Scientist*, 2nd edn, Buckingham, Open University Press.

Gilbert, R. and Conte, R. (eds) (1995) *Artificial Societies: The Computer Simulation of Social Life*, London, UCL Press.

Gilbourn, D. (1990) *Racism and Anti-Racism in Real Schools*, Buckingham, Open University Press.

Gilbourn, D. and Gipps, C. (1996) *Recent Research on the Achievements of Ethnic Minority Pupils*, London, OfStEd.

Gillespie, R. (1991) *Manufacturing Knowledge: a history of the Hawthorne Experiments*, Cambridge, Cambridge University Press.

Gilovich, T., Griffin, D. and Kahneman, D. (eds) (2002) *Heuristics and Biases: The Psychology of Intuitive Judgement*, Cambridge, Cambridge University Press.

Gladwell, M. (2000) *Tipping Point: How Little Things can make a Big Difference*, New York, Little Brown.

Gladwin, T. (1971) *The East is a Big Bird*, Boston, Havard University Press.

Glaser, B. (1992) *The Basics of Grounded Theory Analysis*, Mill Valley, CA, Sociology Press.

Glaser, B. (1998) *Doing Grounded Theory: Issues and Debates*, Mill Valley, CA, Sociology Press.

Glaser, B. and Strauss, A. (1964) *Awareness of Dying*, Chicago, Aldine.

Glass, G. (1976) 'Primary, secondary and meta-analysis of research', *Educational Research*, 5: 3–8.

Glass, G. and Smith, M. (1978) *Meta Analysis of Research on the Relationship of Class-Size and Achievement*, San Francisco, Far West Laboratory.

Goddard, E. (2001) *Obtaining Information about Drinking through Surveys of the General Population*, National Statistics Methodology Series 24, London, Office for National Statistics (www.statistics.gov.uk/methods_quality/publications.asp).

Goffman, E. (1959) *The Presentation of Self in Everyday Life*, Harmondsworth, Penguin (Anchor Books edn, 1956).

Goffman, E. (1968) *Asylums: Essays on the Social Situation of Mental Patients and other Inmates*, Harmondsworth, Penguin.

Goffman, E. (1974) *Frame Analysis: An Essay on the Organization of Experience*, New York, Harper & Row.

Goldberg, D. and Huxley, P. (1992) *Common Mental Disorders*, London, Routledge.

Goldblatt, P. (ed.) (1990) *Longitudinal Study: Mortality and Social Organisation 1971–1981* OPCS series LS, 6, London, HMSO.

Goldthorpe, J., Lockwood, D., Bechofer, E. and Platt, J. (1968a) *The Affluent Worker: Industrial Attitudes and Behaviour*, Cambridge, Cambridge University Press.

Goldthorpe, J., Lockwood, D., Bechofer, E. and Platt, J. (1968b) *The Affluent Worker: Political Attitudes and Behaviour*, Cambridge, Cambridge University Press.

Goldthorpe, J., Lockwood, D., Bechofer, E. and Platt, J. (1969) *The Affluent Worker in the Class Structure*, Cambridge, Cambridge University Press.

Goldstein, H. (1987) *Multilevel Models in Education and Social Research*, Oxford, Clarendon.

Gomm, R. (1975) 'Bargaining from weakness: spirit possession among the coastal Digo', *Man* (n.s.), 10: 530–43.

Gomm, R. (1976) 'Discovering anthropology', *Cambridge Anthropologist*, 3(1): 27–41.

Gomm, R. (1986) *Normal Results: An Ethnographic Study of Health Visitor Student Assessment*, Milton Keynes, PhD thesis presented to the Open University.

Gomm, R. (1993) 'Figuring out ethnic equity: a response to Troyna', in Gomm, R. and Woods, P. (eds), *Educational Research in Action*, London, Open University/Paul Chapman: 199–215 (also in *British Educational Research Journal*, 19(2): 147–63).

Gomm. R. (2000a) 'The basics of experimental design', in Gomm, R., Needham, G. and Bullman, A. (eds), *Evaluating Research in Health and Social Care*, London, Sage: 47–70.

Gomm, R. (2000b) 'Reading the results of experimental research', in Gomm, R., Needham, G. and Bullman, A. (eds), *Evaluating Research in Health and Social Care*, London, Sage: 86–105.

Gomm, R. (2000c) 'Uncertain minds or uncertain times? Expressions of uncertainty in professional discourse', in Gomm, R., Needham, G. and Bullman, A. (eds), *Evaluating Research in Health and Social Care*, London, Sage: 230–8.

Gomm, R. (2000d) 'Controlling for age and socio-economic circumstances', in Gomm, R., Needham, G. and Bullman, A. (eds), *Evaluating Research in Health and Social Care*, London, Sage: 170–95.

Gomm, R. (2000e) 'Would it work here', in Gomm, R. and Davies, C. (eds), *Using Evidence in Health and Social Care*, London, Sage: 171–91.

Gomm, R. (2008) *Key Concepts in Research Methods*, Basingstoke, Palgrave Macmillan.

Gomm, R. and Davies, C. (eds) (2000) *Using Evidence in Health and Social Care*, London, Sage.

Gomm, R., Hammersley, M. and Foster, R. (eds) (2000) *Case Study Method: Key Issues, Key Texts*, London, Sage.

Gomm, R., Needham, G. and Bullman, A. (eds) (2000) *Evaluating Research in Health and Social Care*, London, Sage.

Goodhart, C. (1975) 'Problems in monetary measurement: the UK example', in Courakis, A. (ed.), *Inflation, Depression and Economic Policy in the West*, London, Marshal (cited in Elton 2004).

Gorard, S. (2005) 'Flaws in social mobility claims', *The Times Educational Supplement*, 13 May.

Gorard, S. (2006a) *Using Everyday Numbers Effectively in Research*, London, Continuum Publishing Group.

Gorard, S. (2006b) 'Value-added results are of little value', *Journal of Educational Policy*, 21(2): 233–41.

Gorard, S. and Taylor, C. (2004) *Combining Methods in Educational and Social Research*, London: Open University Press.

Gould, S. J. (1992) 'The case of the creeping fox terrier clone', in *Bully for Brontosaurus*, Harmondsworth, Penguin: 155–67.

Graham, J., Lewis, J. and Nicholas, G. (2006) *Ethical Relations: A Review of the Literature on Empirical Studies of Ethical Requirements and Research Participation*, Manchester, ESRC Research Methods Programme, Working Paper, 30 (www.ccsr.ac.uk/methods/publications/documents/WP30.pdf).

Graham, J., Grewal, I. and Lewis, J. (2007) *Ethics in Social Research: The Views of Research Participants*, London, GSR Analysis for Policy (www.gsr.gov.uk/downloads/professional_development/ethics_in_gov/ethics_social_research_participants.pdf).

Gray, J., Goldstein, H. and Jesson, D. (1996) 'Changes and improvements in schools' effectiveness: trends over five years', *Research Papers in Education*, 11(1): 35–51.

Gray, J., Jesson, D. and Sime, N. (1993) 'Estimating differences in the examination performances of secondary schools in six LEAs: a multilevel approach to school effectiveness', in Gomm, R. and Woods, R. (eds), *Educational Research in Action*, London, Paul Chapman: 118–40.

Green, C. (1992) 'Of immortal mythical beasts: operationalism in psychology', *Theory and Psychology*, 23(3): 291–320.

Green, J. and Hart, L. (1999) 'The impact of context on data', in Barbour, R. and Kitzinger, J. (eds), *Developing Focus Group Research: Politics, Theory and Practice*, London, Sage: 21–35.

Green, P. (1983) 'Teachers' influence on the self-concept of pupils of different ethnic origins', PhD thesis, University of Durham.

Gregory, I. (2005) *A Place in History: A Guide to GIS in Historical Research*, 2nd edn, ESRC (www.ccsr.ac.uk/methods/publications/ig-gis.pdf).

Gregory, R. (1981) *Mind in Science: A History of Explanations in Psychology and Physics*, London, Weidenfeld & Nicolson.

Groves, R. (1989) *Survey Error and Survey Costs*, New York, John Wiley.

Grumet, M. (1991) 'The politics of personal knowledge', in Withering, C. and Noddings, N. (eds), *Stories Lives Tell: Narrative and Dialogue in Education*, New York, Teachers' College Press: 67–78.

Gschwert, P. (2005) 'Analysing quota sample data: the peer review process', *French Politics*, 3: 88–91.

GSS (2003) *Harmonised Concepts and Questions for Government Social Surveys*, London, General Statistical Service, Office for National Statistics (www.statistics.gov.uk/methods_quality/publications.asp).

GSS (2005) *Guidelines for Measuring Statistical Quality*, London, General Statistical Service, Office for National Statistics (www.statistics.gov.uk/methods_quality/publications.asp).

Guba, Y. and Lincoln, E. (1989) *Fourth Generation Evaluation*, London, Sage.

Gunter, B. (1999) *Media Research Methods, Measuring Audiences, Reactions and Impact*, London, Sage.

Guy, W. and Levitas, R (eds) (1996) *Interpreting Official Statistics*, London, Routledge.

Hage, J. and Meeker, B. (1988) *Social Causality*, London, Unwin Hyman.

Hague, P., Hague, N. and Morgan, C.-A. (2004) *Market Research in Practice: A Guide to the Basics*, Kogan Page.

Hall, S., Critcher, C., Jefferson, T., Clarke, J. and Roberts, B. (1978) *Policing the Crisis: Mugging, the State and Law and Order*, Basingstoke, Macmillan.

Halliday, M. and Martin, J. (1993) *Writing Science: Literacy and Discursive Power*, Lewes, Falmer.

Hammersley, M. (1992) *What's Wrong with Ethnography?*, London, Routledge.

Hammersley, M. (1998) *Reading Ethnographic Research: A Critical Guide*, 2nd edn, London, Longman.

Hammersley, M. (2000a) 'Whose side was Becker on? ', in Hammersley, M., *Taking Sides in Social Research: Essays on Partisanship and Bias*, London, Routledge: 60–89.

Hammersley, M. (2000b) *Taking Sides in Social Research: Essays on Partisanship and Bias*, London, Routledge.

Hammersley, M. (2000c) 'Media representation of social and educational research: the case of a review of ethnic minority education', paper presented to British Educational Research Association conference, Cardiff University, September.

Hammersley, M. (2008) *Questioning Qualitative Inquiry: Critical Essays*, London, Sage.

Hammersley, M. and Atkinson, R. (2007) *Ethnography: Principles in Practice*, 3rd edn, London, Routledge.

Hammersley, M. and Gomm, R. (2000) 'Bias in social research', in Hammersley, M., *Taking Sides in Social Research: Essays on Partisanship and Bias*, London, Routledge: 151–66.

Hammersley, M. and Scarth, J. (1986) 'The impact of examinations on secondary school teaching', unpublished report, School of Education, Open University.

Haney, C., Banks, C. and Zimbardo, P. (1981) 'A study of prisoners and guards in a simulated prison', in Potter, D., Anderson, J., Clark, J., Coombes, R., Hall, S., Harris, L., Holloway, C. and Walton, T. (eds), *Society and the Social Sciences: An Introduction*, London, Open University/Routledge & Kegan Paul: 226–39.

Harding, S. (1995) 'Social class differentials in men: recent evidence from the OPCS longitudinal study', *Population Trends*, 80: 31–7.

Hardy, M. and Bryman, A. (eds) (2004) *Handbook of Data Analysis*, London, Sage.

Hargreaves, D. (1967) *Social Relations in a Secondary School*, London, Routledge & Kegan Paul.

Hargreaves, D. (1996). *Teaching as a Research-Based Profession: Possibilities and Prospects*, London, Teacher Training Agency.

Hargreaves Heap, S. and Varoufakis, Y. (2004) *Game Theory: A Critical Introduction*, London, Routledge.

Harris, B. (1988) 'Key words: a history of debriefing in social psychology', in Morawski, J. (ed.), *The Rise of Experimentation in American Psychology*, London, Yale University Press: 188–212.

Harris, J. and Grace, S. (1999) *A Question of Evidence? Investigating and Prosecuting Rape in the 1990s*, Home Office Research Studies 196, London, Home Office (www.homeoffice.gov.uk/rds/).

Hart, E. and Bond, M. (1995) *Action Research for Health and Social Care: A Guide to Practice*, Buckingham, Open University Press.

Hartman, R. and Husband, P. (1981) 'The mass media and racial conflict', in Cohen, S. and Young, J. (eds), *The Manufacture of News: Deviance, Social Problems and the Media*, London, Constable: 288–302.

Hatamian, T. (2001) 'Mathematical fortune telling', *Complexity*, 6(5): 27–40.

Hawking, S. (1988) *A Brief History of Time: From the Big Bang to Black Holes*, London, Bantam Press.

Hayek, F. (1967) 'The theory of complex phenomena', Chapter 4 in *Studies in Philosophy, Politics and Economics*, Chicago. Chicago University Press.

Heath, A. and Payne, C. (2000) 'Social mobility', in Halsey, A. and Webb, J. (eds), *Twentieth Century Britain Social Trends*, 3rd edn, Basingstoke, Macmillan.

Hedeker, D. and Gibbons, R. (2006) *Longitudinal Data Analysis*, New York, John Wiley.

Heider, K. (1988) 'The Rashomon effect: when ethnographers disagree', *American Anthropologist*, 90: 73–80.

Hemminki, E., Topo, P. and Kangas, I. (1995) 'Experience and opinions of climacterium by Finnish women', *European Journal of Obstetrics Gynecology and Reproductive Biology*, 62: 81–97.

Heritage, J. (1984) *Garfinkel and Ethnomethodology*, Cambridge, Polity Press.

Heritage, J. (1985) 'Analyzing news interviews: aspects of the production of talk for an "over-hearing" audience', in van Dijk, T. (ed.), *Handbook of Discourse Analysis*, London, Academic Press.

Her Majesty's Stationery Office (HMSO) (1998) *Public Interest Disclosure Act 1998*, London, HMSO.

Hernstein, R. and Murray, C. (1996) *The Bell Curve: Intelligence and the Class Structure in American Life*, Glencoe, Free Press.

Heron, J. (1981) 'Experimental research methods', in Reason, P. and Rowan, J. (eds), *Human Inquiry*, New York, Wiley: 153–66.

Herzlich, C. and Pierret, J. (1985) 'The social construction of the patient: patients and illnesses in other ages', *Social Science and Medicine*, 20(2): 145–57.

Heyerdahl, T (1950) *Kon-tiki*, New York, Rand McNally.

Heywood, I., Cornelius, S. and Carver, S. (2006) *An Introduction to Geographical Information Systems*, 3rd edn, Englewood Cliffs, NJ, Prentice-Hall.

Himmelweit, H., Humphreys, P. and Jaeger, M. (1985) *How Voters Decide*, Milton Keynes, Open University Press.

Hoey, M. (1983) On *the Surface of Discourse*, London, George Allen & Unwin.

Hoey, M. (2000) *Textual Interaction: An Introduction to Written Discourse Analysis*, London, Routledge.

Holloway, W. and Jefferson, T. (2000) *Doing Qualitative Research Differently: Free Association, Narrative and the Interview Method*, London, Sage.

Horn, L. and Ward, G. (2005) *The Handbook of Pragmatics*, Oxford, Blackwell.

Horowitz, A., Vidio, T., Schmitz, M. and Davis, D. (2003) 'Rethinking twins and environment: possible social sources for assumed genetic influences in twin research', *Journal of Human and Social Biology* 44(2): 111–29.

Howell, M. and Prevenier, W (2001) *From Reliable Sources: An Introduction to Historical Methods*, Ithaca, NY, Cornell University Press.

Howells, R. (2003) *Visual Culture*, Oxford, Polity Press.

Hubble, N. (2006) *Mass Observation and Everyday Life*, Basingstoke, Macmillan.

Hughes, J. and Sharrock, W. (eds) (2009) *Participant Observation*, 4 vols, London, Sage.

Humphreys, L. (1975) *Tearoom Trade: Impersonal Sex in Public Places*, Chicago, Aldine.

Hunt, S. (1993) 'The relationship between research and policy: translating knowledge into action', in Davies, J. and Kelly, M. (eds), *Healthy Cities: Research and Practice*, London, Routledge & Kegan Paul: 71–82.

Hurry, J. and Lloyd, C. (1997) *A Follow-Up Evaluation of Project Charlie: A Life Skills Drug Education Programme for Primary Schools*, London, Paper 16, Drug Prevention Advisory Service, Home Office.

Hutchby, I. and Wooffitt, R. (1998) *Conservation Analysis*, Cambridge, Polity Press.

Iordananova, R. (2006) 'How can identical twins be genetically different?', *Eureka Alert*, July (www.eurekalert.org).

Israel, M. and Hay, I. (2005) *Research Ethics for Social Scientists*, London, Sage.

Jadad, A., Moher, R., Carroll, D., Jenkinson, C., Reynolds, C., Gavaghan, D. and McQuay, H. (1996) 'Assessing the quality of reports of randomized clinical trials: is blinding necessary?', *Controlled Clinical Trials*, 17: 1–12.

Jankowicz, D. (2003) *The Easy Guide to Repertory Grids*, New York, John Wiley.

Jenkins, R., Smeeton, N., Markiner, M. and Shepherd, S. (1985) 'A study of the classification of mental ill-health in general practice', *Psychological Medicine*, 15: 403–9.

Jenkinson, C. (ed.) (1994) *Measuring Health and Medical Outcomes*, London, UCL Press.

Jenner, E., Fletcher, B., Watson, P., Jones, F. and Miller, L. (2006) 'Discrepancy between self-reported and observed hand-hygiene behaviour in health care professionals', *Journal of Hospital Infection*, 63: 418–22.

Jesson, D., Gray, J. and Tranmer, M. (1992) *GCSE Performance in Nottinghamshire: Pupil and School Factors*, Nottinghamshire County Council, Education Advisory and Inspection Service.

Jones, S. (1992) 'Was there a Hawthorne effect?' *American Journal of Sociology*, 98(3): 451–68.

Journal of Contemporary Ethnography (1992) (Special Issue) 'Street Corner Society Revisited', 21: 3–132.

Juni, P., Holmstein, F., Sterne, K., Bartlett, C. and Egger, M. (2002) 'Direction and impact of language bias in meta analyses of controlled trials: empirical study', *International Journal of Epidemiology*, 31: 115–23.

Jussim, L. and Harber, K.D. (2005) 'Teacher expectations and self-fulfilling prophecies: knowns and unknowns, resolved and unresolved controversies', *Personality and Social Psychology Review*, 9(2), 131–55.

Kalton, G. (2000) 'Developments in survey research in the past 25 years', *Survey Methodology*, 26(1): 3–10.

Kamin, L. (1974) *The Science and Politics of IQ*, Potomac, Erlbaum.

Kamin, L. (1981) 'Separated identical twins', in Eysenck, H. and Kamin, L., *Intelligence: The Battle for the Mind: H. K. Eysenck versus Leon Kamin*, London, Pan: 106–13.

Kaplan, A. (1964) *The Conduct of Inquiry: Methodology for Behavioural Science*, San Francisco, Chandler.

Kazi, M. and Wilson, J. (1996) 'Applying single case evaluation in social work', *British Journal of Social Work*, 26: 699–717.

Kellett, J. (1996) 'An ethical dilemma: a nurse is suspended', *British Medical Journal*, 313(7067): 1249–50.

Kelly, H. and Michela, J. (1980) 'Attribution theory and research', *Annual Review of Psychology*, 31: 457–503.

Kertzer, D. and Arel, D. (eds) (2002) *Census and Identity: The Politics of Race, Ethnicity and Language in National Censuses*, Cambridge, Cambridge University Press.

Kincheloe, J. and McLaren, P. (1994) 'Rethinking critical theory and qualitative research', in Denzin, N. and Lincoln, Y. (eds), *Handbook of Qualitative Research*, London, Sage: 105–17.

Kish, L. (1965) *Survey Sampling*, London, Wiley.

Kitzinger, J. and Farquhar, C. (1999) 'The analytical potential of "sensitive moments" in focus group research', in Barbour, R. and Kitzinger, J. (eds), *Developing Focus Group Research: Politics, Theory and Practice*, London, Sage: 156–73.

Kline, T. (1993) *An Easy Guide to Factor Analysis*, London, Routledge.

Kline, T. (2005) *Psychological Testing: A Practical Approach to Design and Evaluation*, London, Sage.

Knightley, P. (1975) *The First Casualty*, London, Purnell.

Korovessis, C. (2001) 'Sampling minority ethnic groups in the UK population', *Survey Methods Newsletter*, 21(1): 12–19.

Krejcie, R. and Morgan, D. (1970) 'Determining sample size for research activities', *Educational and Psychological Measurement*, 30: 607–10.

Krippendorff, K. (2004) *Content Analysis: An Introduction to its Methodology*, 3rd edn, London, Sage.

Krueger, R. and Casey M. (2000) *Focus Group Research: A Practical Guide to Applied Research*, 3rd edn, London, Sage.

Kunz, R. and Oxman, A. (1998) 'The unpredictability paradox: review of empirical comparisons of randomised and non-randomised clinical trials', *British Medical Journal*, 317: 1185–90.

Labov, W. (1973) 'The linguistic consequences of being a lame', *Language in Society*, 2(1): 81–115.

Lacey, C. (1975) *Hightown Grammar*, Manchester, Manchester University Press.

Laslett, P. and Smith, R. (2005) *The World We Have Lost, Further Explored*, 4th edn, London, Routledge.

Lather, P. (1986) 'Research as praxis', *Harvard Educational Review*, 56(3): 257–77.

Lather, P. (1991) *Getting Smart: Feminist Research and Pedagogy with the Post Modern*, London, Routledge.

Laycock, G. (1985) *Property Marking: A Deterrent to Domestic Burglary? Crime Prevention Paper*, 3, London, Home Office.

Lea, J. and Young, J. (1993) *What is to be Done About Law and Order?*, London, Pluto Press.

Lepper, G. (2000) *Categories in Text and Talk: A Practical Introduction to Categorization Analysis*, London, Sage.

Levinson, S. (1983) *Pragmatics*, Cambridge, Cambridge University Press.

Levinson, S. (2000) *Presumptive Meanings: The Theory of Generalized Conversational Implicature*, Boston, MIT Press.

Lewin, K. (1997) 'Action research and minority problems', in Lewin, G., *Resolving Social Conflicts: Selected Papers on Group Dynamic and Field Theory by Kurt Lewin*, Washington, DC, American Psychological Association: 143–152 (Harper Bros edn, 1948).

Lewis, A. (2001) 'Computer assisted qualitative data analysis', in Gilbert, N. (ed.), *Researching Social Life*, 2nd edn, London, Sage: 302–23.

Lewis, A. and Silver, C. (2007) *Using Software in Qualitative Research: A Step by Step Guide*, London, Sage.

Liberman, A. (2007) *Longitudinal Research on Crime and Delinquency*, New York, Springer-Verlag.

Licht, B. and Dweck, V. C. (1987) 'Sex differences in achievement orientations', in Arnot, M. and Weiner, G. (eds), *Gender and the Politics of Schooling*, London, Huitchinson: 95–107.

Lidz, C. (1989) '"Objectivity" and rapport', in Glassner, B. and Moreno, J. (eds), *The Qualitative–Quantitative Distinction in the Social Sciences*, Boston, Kluwer Academic: 43–56.

Liebovitch, L. and Scheurle, D. (2000) 'Two lessons from fractals and chaos', *Complexity*, 5(4): 34–43.

Lipsey, M. (1995) 'What do we learn from 400 research studies on the effectiveness of treatment with juvenile delinquents?', in McGuire, J. (ed.), *What Works? Reducing Re-Offending*, Chichester, John Wiley: 63–78.

Lipsey, M. and Wilson, D. (2000) *Practical Meta-Analysis*, London, Sage.

Little, T., Bovaird, J. and Card, N. (2007) *Modelling Contextual Effects in Longitudinal Studies*, London, Lawrence Erlbaum Associates.

Lloyd-Jones, G. (2002) A *Multiple Case Study of the First Year Student Perspective in a Medical Undergraduate PLB Curriculum*, Liverpool, University of Liverpool, unpublished PhD thesis.

Logan, C. (1972) 'Evaluation research in crime and delinquence: a reappraisal', *Journal of Criminal Law, Criminology and Police Science*, 63(3): 378–87.

Lomas, J. (1994) 'Teaching old (and not so old) Docs new tricks: effective ways to implement research findings', in Dunn, E., Norton, P., Stewart, M., Tudiver, F. and Bass, J. (eds), *Disseminating Research/Changing Practice*, London, Sage: 1–15.

Lomborg, B. (1996) 'Nucleus and shield: the evolution of social structure in the iterated prisoner's dilemma', *American Sociological Review*, 61: 278–307.

Luhmann, N. (1990) *Essays on Self-Reference*, Columbia, Columbia University Press.

Macdonald, G. (1999) 'Social work and its evaluation: a methodological dilemma?', in Williams, E., Popay, J. and Oakley, A. (eds), *Welfare Research: A Critical Review*, London, UCL Press: 89–103.

Macdonald, G., Sheldon, B. and Gillespie, J. (1992) 'Contemporary studies of the effectiveness of social work', *British Journal of Social Work*, 22(6): 615–43.

McGuffin, P. (1999) 'Getting personal', *Medical Research Council News*, 80: 20–3.

McPherson, K., Strong, P. and Epstein, A. (1981) 'Regional variations in the use of common surgical procedures: within and between England and Wales, Canada and the United States of America', *Social Science and Medicine*, 15A: 2773–85.

Maddock, K. (1998) 'The dubious pleasures of commitment', *Anthropology Today*, 14(5): 1–2.

Madge, C. and O'Connor, H. (n.d.) *Exploring the Internet as a Medium for Research: Web-Based Questionnaires and On-Line Synchronous Interviews*, Manchester, ESRC Research Methods Papers, 9 (www.ccsr.ac.uk/methods/publications/documents/WorkingPaper9.pdf).

Makse, H., Havlin, S. and Stanley, H. (1995) 'Modelling urban growth patterns', *Nature*, 377: 608–12.

Mandelbrot, B. (1983) *The Fractal Geometry of Nature'* New York, W.H. Freeman.

Mant, J. and Jenkinson, C. (1997) 'Case control and cohort studies', in Jenkinson, C. (ed.), *Assessment and Evaluation of Health and Medical Care*, Buckingham, Open University Press: 31–46.

Marks, D. (1995) 'Accounting for exclusion: giving a "voice" and producing a subject', *Children and Society*, 9(3): 81–98.

Marmot, M. and Wilkinson, R. (2000) *Sources of Inequality: Social Determinants of Health*, Oxford, Oxford University Press.

Marsh, C. (1988) *Exploring Data: An Introduction to Data Analysis for Social Scientists*, Cambridge, Polity Press.

Marsh, L., Irwig, L., Schwartz, J., Simpson, J., Chock, C. and Brooks, P. (1994) 'n of 1 trials comparing a non-sterodal anti-inflammatory drug with paracetamol in osteoarthritis', *British Medical Journal*, 309: 101–6.

Marshall, G., Rose, E. D., Newby, H. and Volger, C. (1988) *Social Class in Modern Britain*, London, Unwin Hyman.

Martin, J. (1998) '2001 census output areas: from concept to prototype', *Population Trends*, 94: 6.

Martin, J. (1999) 'An overview of imputation methods and their application to survey data', *Survey Methods Newsletter*, 19(2): 9–11.

Mason, J. (2002) *Qualitative Researching*, 2nd edn, London, Sage.

Masson, J. (1988) *Against Therapy: Emotional Tyranny and the Myth of Psychological Healing*, London, Fontana.

Masson, J. (2004) 'The legal context', in Fraser, S., Lewis, V., Ding, S., Kellet, M. and Robinson, C. (eds), *Doing Research with Children and Young People*, Buckingham, Open University Press: 43–58.

Matthews, F. and Brayne, F. (2005) 'Incidence of dementia in England and Wales', *PloS.Medicine*, 2(8)e193, Epub 2005.

Mauthner, M., Birch, M., Jessop, J. and Miller, T. (2002) *Ethics of Qualitative Research*, London, Sage.

Maynard, D. (1989) 'On the ethnography and analysis of discourse in institutional settings', *Perspectives on Social Problems*, 1: 127–46.

Mead, M. (1948) *Coming of Age in Samoa*, Harmondsworth, Penguin (first published, 1928).

Meadows, K. and Wisher, S. (2000) 'Establishing cross-cultural validity in health surveys', *Survey Methods Newsletter*, 20(2): 16–22.

Meltzer, H., Gill, B., Petticrew, M. and Hinds, K. (1995) *The Prevalence of Psychiatric Morbidity among Adults living in Private Households in Great Britain*, OPCS Surveys of Psychiatric Morbidity in Great Britain, Report 2, London, HMSO.

Mendes, J. and Dorogovtsev, S. (2003) *Evolution of Networks: From Biological Nets to the Internet and WWW*, Oxford, Oxford University Press.

Middleton, D. and Edwards, D. (1990) 'Conversational remembering: a social psychological approach', in Middleton, D. and Edwards, D. (eds), *Collective Remembering*, London, Sage: 23–45.

Middlewood, D., Coleman, M. and Lumby, J. (1999) *Practitioner Research in Education: Making a Difference*, London, Paul Chapman.

Mies, M. (1983) 'Towards a methodology of feminist research', in Bowles, G. and Klien, R. (eds), *Theories of Women's Studies*, London, Routledge & Kegan Paul.

Mies, M. (1991) Women's research or feminist research? The debate surrounding feminist research and methodology', in Fonow, M. and Cook, J. (eds), *Beyond Methodology: Feminist Scholarship and Lived Research*, Bloomington, IN, Indiana University Press: 60–84.

Miles, M. and Huberman, A. (1994) *Qualitative Data Analysis: An Expanded Sourcebook*, London, Sage.

Milgram S. (1963) 'Behavioural study of obedience', *Journal of Abnormal and Social Psychology*, 67(4): 317–78.

Milgram, S. (1964) 'Issues in the study of obedience: a reply to Baumrind', *American Psychologist*, 19: 849–50.

Milgram, S. (1967) 'The small world problem', *Psychology Today*, 2: 60–7.

Milgram, S. (1974) *Obedience to Authority*, New York, Harper & Row.

Milgram, S. (1992) *The Individual in a Social World: Essays and Experiments*, 2nd edn (ed. by J. Sabini), New York, McGraw-Hill.

Miller, G. and Stiff, J. (1993) *Deceptive Communication*, London, Sage.

Miller, S. (1953). 'The participant observer and "over-rapport"', *American Sociological Review*, 18: 97–99.

Mills, C. W. (1959) *The Sociological Imagination*, New York, Oxford University Press.

Mirrlees-Black, C. (1998) *Domestic Violence: Findings from the BCS Self-Completion Questionnaire*, London, Home Office Research Studies, 86 (www.homeoffice.gov.uk/rds/).

Moerman, D. (2002) *Meaning, Medicine and the 'Placebo Effect'*, Cambridge, Cambridge University Press.

Moher, D., Klassan, T., Jones, A., Pham, B., Cook, D., Jadad, A., Tugwell, P. and Moher, M. (2001) 'Assessing the quality of reports of randomised trials included in meta-analyses: attitudes, practice, evidence and guides', in Stevens, A., Abrams, K., Brazier, J., Fitzpatrick, R. and Lilford., R (eds), *The Advanced Handbook of Methods in Evidence Based Healthcare*, London, Sage: 409–25.

Morgan, D. (1988) *Focus Groups as Qualitative Research*, London, Sage.

Morrison, K. (2001) 'Randomised controlled trials for evidence-based education: some problems in judging what works', *Evaluation and Research in Education*, 15(2): 69–83.

Mortimore, P., Sammons, P., Stoll, L., Lewis, D. and Ecob, R. (1988) *School Matters: The Junior Years*, Wells, Open Books.

Mortimore, R. and Atkinson, S. (2000) 'Political polling in Britain: the history', *Poll Digest*, 15 December (www.mori.com/digest/c001215.htm).

MRC (2005) *Good Research Practice*, London, Medical Research Council (www.mrc.ac.uk/Utilities/Documentrecord/index.htm?d=MRC002415).

Mumby, D. (ed.) (1993) *Narrative and Social Control: Critical Perspectives*, London, Sage.

Muncie, J. and McLaughlin, E. (2001) *The Problem of Crime*, 2nd edn, London, Sage.

Naroll, R. (1973) 'Quality control in cross-cultural surveys', in Naroll, R. and Cohen, R. (eds), *A Handbook of Methods in Cultural Anthropology*, New York, Columbia University Press.

Naroll, R. and Naroll, F. (1963) 'On the bias of exotic data', *Man*, 63, February: 25.

Nathanson, C. (1978) 'Sex roles as variables in the interpretation of morbidity data: a methodological critique', *International Journal of Epidemiology*, 7(3): 253–62.

Nazroo, J. (1997) *Mental Health and Ethnicity: Findings from a National Community Study*, London, Policy Studies Institute.

NCFO (2003) *Gender Bias in College Admissions Tests*, Fair Test: The National Center for Fair and Open Testing (www.fairtest.org/facts/genderbias.htm).

Nettle, M. (1996) 'Listening in the asylum', in Read, J. and Reynolds, J. (eds), *Speaking Our Minds: An Anthology*, Basingstoke, Macmillan: 202–6.

Neuendorf, K. (2002) *The Content Analysis Guidebook*, London, Sage.

Nichols, R. (1997) 'Action research in health care: the collaborative action research network health care group', *Educational Action Research*, 5(2): 185–92.

Nicolls, W., Baker, R. and Martin, J. (1997) 'The effect of new data collection technologies on survey data quality', in Lyberg, L., Bierner, P., Collins, M., Dippo, C., De Leeuw, E., Schwartz, N. and Trewin, D. (1997), *Survey Measurement and Process Quality*, New York, John Wiley.

Nicholson, R. (1997) 'Helsinki declaration revising continues', *Bulletin of Medical Ethics*, 146, March: 3–5.

Noblit, G. and Hare, R. (1988) *Meta-Ethnography: Synthesising Qualitative Studies* (Qualitative Research Methods, 11), London, Sage.

Oakley, A. (1981) 'Interviewing women: a contradiction in terms', in Roberts, H. (ed.), *Doing Feminist Research*, London, Routledge & Kegan Paul: 30–61.

Oakley, A. (1993) 'Telling stories: auto/biography and the sociology of health and illness', *Sociology of Health and Illness*, 15(3): 414–18.

Oakley, A. (2000) *Experiments in Knowing: Gender and Method in the Social Sciences*, Cambridge, Polity Press.

Oakley, A. and Fullerton, D. (1996) 'The lamp-post of research: support or illumination?', in Oakley, A. and Roberts, H. (eds), *Evaluating Social Interventions*, Ilford, Essex, Barnados: 4–38.

Oakley, A., Rajan, L. and Robertson, P. (1990) 'A comparison of different sources of information about pregnancy and childbirth', *Journal of Biosocial Science*, 22: 477–87.

O'Connell Davidson, J. and Layder, D. (1994) *Methods, Sex and Madness*, London, Routledge.

O'Donoghue, C., Thomas, S., Goldstein, H. and Knight, T. (1997) '1996 DfEE study of value-added for 18 years olds in England', *DfEE Research Series*, March, London, DfEE.

ONS (2003) *UK Population: By Ethnic Group: Census Update*, London, Office for National Statistics (www.ons.gov.uk).

ONS (2006) *National Statistics Post Code Directory: November 2006 version notes*, London, Office for National Statistics (www.ons.gov.uk) [accessed August 2007].

ONS (2007) *MRSA: Deaths Continue to Rise in 2005* (www.statistics.gov.uk).

Other, A. (1999) 'Above infection: status and hygiene behaviour in a hospital setting', unpublished paper.

Owusu-Bempah, J. (1994) 'Race, self-identity and social work', *British Journal of Social Work*, 24: 123–36.

OPCS (1994) *Undercoverage in Great Britain 1991: Census User Guide no. 58*, London, OPCS.

Ozga, J. and Gerwirtz, S. (1994) 'Sex, lies and audiotape: interviewing the education policy elite', in Halpin, D. and Troyna, B. (eds), *Researching Education Policy: Ethical and Methodological Issues*, Lewes, Falmer, 34–59.

Padfield, M. and Proctor, I. (1996) 'The effect of interviewer's gender on the interviewing process: a comparative study', *Sociology*, 30(2): 355–66.

Parsons, E., Chalkley, B. and Jones, A. (1996) 'The role of Geographical Information Systems in the study of parental choice and secondary school catchments', *Evaluation and Research in Education*, 10(1): 23–34.

Patai, D. and Koertge, N. (1994) *Professing Feminism: Cautionary Tales from the Strange World of Women's Studies*, New York, Basic Books.

Patrick, J. (1973) A *Glasgow Gang Observed*, London, Eyre Methuen.

Pawson, R. and Tilley, N. (1997) *Realistic Evaluation*, London, Sage.

Payne, N. and Saul, C. (1997) 'Variations in the use of cardiology services in a health authority: comparison of artery revascularisation rates with the prevalence of angina and coronary mortality', *British Medical Journal*, 314: 257–61 (reprinted in Gomm, R., Needham, G. and Bullman, A. (eds), *Evaluating Research in Health and Social Care*, London, Sage, 2000).

Peneff, J. (1990) 'Myth in life stories', in Samuel, R. and Thompson, P. (eds), *The Myths We Live By*, London, Routledge: 36–48.

Pereira, R. (2002) 'The census coverage surveys: the key elements of a one number census', *Population Trends*, 108: 16–31.

Pett, M. (1997) *Non-Parametric Statistics for Health Care Research: Statistics for Small Samples and Unusual Distributions*, London, Sage.

Philo, G. (1990) *Seeing and Believing: The Influence of Television*, London, Routledge.

Philo, G., Secker, J., Platt, S., McLaughlin, G. and Burnside, J. (1994) 'The impact of the mass media on public images of mental illness: media content and audience belief', *Health Education Journal*, 53: 271–81.

Pidal, J., Hrobjarbsson, A., Jorgenson, A., Hilden, J., Alman, D. and Gotzsche, P. (2007) 'Impact of allocation concealment on conclusions drawn from meta-analyses of randomised trials', *International Journal of Epidemiology*, 2007:doi:10.1093/ije/dyn087.

Pinch, T. and Clark, C. (1986) 'The hard sell: "patter merchanting" and the strategic (re)production and local management of economic reasoning in the sales routines of market pitchers', *Sociology*, 20(2): 169–91.

Piquero, A., Farrington, D., Blumstein, A. and Loeber, R. (2007) *Key Issues in Criminal Career Research: New Analyses of the Cambridge Study in Delinquency Development*, Cambridge, Cambridge University Press.

Plass, C. (2005) 'Identical twins may have more differences than meets the eye', *Eureka Alert*, July (www.eurekalert.org).

Platt, J. (1981) 'Evidence and proof in documentary research', *Sociological Review*, 29(1): 31–66.

Plummer, K. (1983) *Documents of Life: An Introduction to the Problems and Literature of a Humanistic Method*, London, George Allen & Unwin.

Plummer, K. (2000) *Documents of Life 2: An Invitation to Critical Humanism*, London, Sage.

Polanyi, M. (1958) *Personal Knowledge: Towards a Post-Critical Philosophy*, London, Routledge & Kegan Paul.

Popper, K. (1963) *Conjectures and Refutations*, London, Routledge.

Potter, J. and Wetherell, M. (1987) *Discourse and Social Psychology*, London, Sage.

Price, J. and Evans, J. (2002) 'N-of-1 randomized controlled trials ("N-of-1 trials") singularly useful in geriatric medicine', *Age and Ageing*, 31: 227–32.

Prigogine, I. and Stengers, I. (1984) *Order out of Chaos*, New York, Bantam.

Prior, L. (1989) *The Social Organization of Death: Medical Discourse and Social Practices in Belfast*, London, Macmillan.

Pryke, M., Rose, G. and Whatmore, S. (2003) *Using Social Theory: Thinking Through Research*, London, Sage.

Pudney, S. (2006) 'Rarely pure and never simple: extracting the truth from self-reported data on substance misuse' (www.irc.essex.ac.uk/seminars/jess/2007/papers/pudney.pdf).

Punch, K. (2003) *Survey Research: The Basics*, London, Sage.

Radley, A. (1990) 'Artefacts, memory and a sense of the past', in Middleton, D. and Edwards, D. (eds), *Collective Remembering*, London, Sage: 46–59.

Ragin, C. (1987) *The Comparative Method*, Berkley and Los Angeles, University of California Press

Ragin, C. (1989) 'The logic of the comparative method and the algebra of logic', *Journal of Quantitative Anthropology*, 1, 373–98.

Ragin, C. (1994) *Constructing Social Research: The Unity and Diversity of Method*, Thousand Oaks, CA, Pine Forge Press.

Ragin, C. (2000) *Fuzzy Set Social Science*, Chicago, Chicago University Press.

Ragin, C. and Hein, J. (1993) 'The comparative study of ethnicity: methodological and conceptual issues', in Stanfield, J. and Dennis, R. (eds), *Race and Ethnicity in Research Methods*, London, Sage: 254–72.

Rapoport, R. and Rapoport, R. (1971) *Dual Career Families*, Harmondsworth, Penguin.

Rapoport, R. and Rapoport, R. (1976) *Dual Career Families Re-Examined*, London, Martin Robertson.

Rasulo, P., Madhavi, B. and Yar, M. (2007) *Inequalities in Health Expectation in England and Wales – Small Area Analysis from the 2001 Census*, London, Office for National Statistics (www.statistics.gov.uk).

Reason, P. (ed.) (1994) *Participation in Human Inquiry*, London, Sage.

Reason, R. and Bradbury, H. (2007) *Sage Handbook of Action Research: Participatory Inquiry and Practice*, 2nd edn, London, Sage.

Reiss, A. (1964) 'The social integration of peers and queers', in Becker, H. (ed.), *The Other Side: Perspectives on Deviance*, New York, Free Press: 181–210.

Respect Project (2004) *The Respect Code of Practice for Socio-economic Research across Europe*, Brighton, Respect Project (www.respectproject.org).

Research Governance in Social Care Advisory Group (2005) *Research Governance Framework*, London, Social Services Research Group (www.ssrg.org.uk).

Rex, J. and Moore, M. (1967) *Race, Community and Conflict*, London, Oxford University Press.

Richards, L. (2005) *Handling Qualitative Data: A Practical Guide*, London, Sage.

Riessman, C. (2008) *Narrative Analysis: Methods for the Human Sciences*, London, Sage.

Rispini, E. (2002) *Introduction to Longitudinal Research*, London, Routledge.

Riverside Publications (2004) *Stanford-Binet Intelligence Scales, Fifth Edition* (www.riverpub.com/products/sb5/).

Roe, S. and Man, L. (2006) *Drug Misuse Declared: Findings from the 2005/06 British Crime Survey: England and Wales*, London, Home Office Statistical Bulletin, 15/06.

Roeslisberger, F. and Dickson, W. (1939) *Management and the Worker*, Cambridge, MA, Harvard University Press.

Rogers, A., Pilgrim, D. and Lacey, R. (1993) *Experiencing Psychiatry: Users' Views of Services*, Basingstoke, Mind/Macmillan.

Romm, N. (1997) 'Becoming more accountable: a comment on Hammersley and Gomm', *Sociological Research Online*, 2(3) (www.socresonline.org.uk/socresonline/2/3/2.html).

Rose, D. and Pevalin, D. (2003) *A Researcher's Guide to the National Statistics Socio-economic Classification*, London, Sage.

Rose, G. (1982) *Deciphering Sociological Research*, Basingstoke, Macmillan.

Rose, G. (2001) *Visual Methodologies: An Introduction to the Interpretation of Visual Materials*, London, Sage.

Rose, G., McCartney, P. and Reid, D. (1977) 'Self-administration of a questionnaire on chest pain and intermittent claudication', *British Journal of Preventative Social Medicine*, 31: 42–8.

Rosenhan, D. (1973) 'On being sane in insane places', *Science*, 179: 250–8.

Rosenhan, D. (1996) 'On being sane in insane places', in Heller, T., Reynolds, J., Gomm, R., Muston R. and Pattison, S. (eds), *Mental Health Matters: A Reader*, Basingstoke, Mind/Macmillan: 70–8.

Rosenthal, R. (1966) *Experimenter Effects in Behavioral Research*, New York, Appleton-Century-Croft.

Rosenthal, R. (1979) 'The file draw problem and tolerance for null results', *Psychological Bulletin*, 86: 638–41.

Rosenthal, R. and Fode, L. (1963) 'The effects of experimenter bias on the perform ance of the albino rat', *Behavioural Science*, 8: 183–9.

Rosenthal, R. and Jacobson, L. (1968) *Pygmalion in the Classroom*, New York, Holt, Rinehart and Winston.

Rosenthal, R. and Jacobson, L. (1992) *Pygmalion in the Classroom*, expanded edn, New York, Irvington.

Rosenthal, R. and Rosnow, R. (eds) (1969) *Artifact in Behavioral Research*, New York, Academic Press.

Rosenthal, R. and Rubin, D. (1978) 'Interpersonal expectancy effects: the first 345 studies', *Behavioural and Brain Sciences*, 3: 377–415.

Roth, J. (1974) 'Turning adversity to account', *Urban Life and Culture*, 3(3): 347–59.

Rothstein, H. (2005) *Publication Bias in Meta-Analysis: Prevention, Assessment and Adjustment*, New York: John Wiley.

Rowbotham, S. (1973) *Woman's Consciousness, Man's World*, Harmondsworth, Penguin.

Rowntree, B. (1901) *Poverty: A Study of Town Life*, London, Macmillan.

Ruddock, V. (1999) *Measuring and Improving Data Quality*, National Statistics Methodology Papers, 14, London, Office for National Statistics (www.statistics.gov.uk/methods_quality/publicaitons.asp).

Runciman, W. (1998) *The Social Animal*, London, HarperCollins.

Rushkoff, D. (2005) *Get Back in the Box: Innovation from the Inside Out*, New York, Collins.

Rutter, M. (1999) 'Natural experiments to study psychosocial risks', *Medical Research Council News*, 80: 24–7.

Sackett, D., Haynes, R., Guyatt, G. and Tugwell, P. (1991) *Clinical Epidemiology: A Basic Science for Clinical Medicine*, London, Little, Brown.

Sacks, H., Schegloff, H. E. and Jefferson, G. (1974) 'A simplest systematics for the organization of turn-taking in conversation', *Language*, 50(4): 696–735.

Sadler, R. (1981) 'Intuitive data processing as a potential source of bias in naturalistic observation', *Educational Evaluation and Policy Analysis*, July–August: 25–31.

Sainbury, R., Ditch, J. and Hutton, S. (1993) 'Computer assisted personal interviewing', *Social Research Update*, 3 (http://sru.soc.surrey.ac.uk/SRU3.html).

Salisbury, H. (2003) 'Trends in crime', in Simmons, J. and Dodd, T. (eds), *Crime in England and Wales 2002/03* (British Crime Survey), London, Home Office: 3.4 and 3.5 (www.homeoffice.gov.uk/rds).

Sapsford, R. (2006) *Survey Research*, 2nd edn, London, Sage.

Savage, R. and Armstrong, D. (1990) 'The effect of a general practitioner's consulting style on patient satisfaction: a controlled study', *British Medical Journal*, 301: 968–70.

Scarth, J. and Hammersley, M. (1993) 'Questioning ORACLE: an assessment of ORACLE's analysis of teachers' questions', in Gomm, R. and Woods, P. (eds), *Educational Research in Action*, London, Paul Chapman: 184–98.

Schagan, I. (1993) 'Beyond league tables: how modern statistical methods can give a truer picture of the effects of schools', in Gomm, R. and Woods, P. (eds), *Educational Research in Action*, London, Paul Chapman: 109–17 (previously in *Educational Research*, 33(3), 1991: 216–28).

Schegloff, E. and Sacks, H. (1973) 'Opening up closings', in Turner, R. (ed.), *Ethnomethodology*, Harmondsworth, Penguin: 233–64.

Schelling, T. (1971) 'Dynamic models of segregation', *Journal of Mathematical Sociology*, 1: 143–86.

Schultz, K., Chalmers, I., Hayes, R. and Altman, D. (1995) 'Empirical evidence of bias: dimensions of methodic quality associated with estimates of treatment effects in controlled trials', *Journal of the American Medical Association*, 273: 408–12.

Schutz, A. (1964) *Studies in Social Theory: Collected Papers II*, ed. A. Brodersen, The Hague, Martinus Nijhoff: 91–105.

Schwartz, J. (2001) 'I tawt I taw a bunny wabbit at Disneyland: new evidence shows false memory can be created', *Eurekalert*, June (www.eurekalert.org).

Scott, J. (2000) *Social Network Analysis: A Handbook*, 2nd edn, London, Sage.

Scott, M. and Thompson, G. (eds) (2000) *Patterns of Text: in honour of Michael Hoey*, London, Benjamin Publications.

Scottish Executive (2006) *Research Governance Framework for Health and Social Care* (revised edn) Edinburgh, Scottish Executive (www.sehd.scot.nhs.uk/cso/Publications/ResGov/Framework/RGFEdTwo.pdf).

Scully, D. (1990) *Understanding Sexual Violence*, London, HarperCollins.

Searle, C., Gobo, G., Gubrium, J. and Silverman, D. (2004) *Qualitative Research Practice*, London, Sage.

Shafer, R. (1980) *A Guide to Historical Method*, London, Dorsey Press.

Sharp, C., Hutchinson, D. and Whetton, C. (1994) 'Children's attainment at key stage 1', *Educational Research*, 36(2): 107–19.

Sharp, R. and Green, A. (1975) *Education and Social Control*, London, Routledge.

Shayer, M., Ginsburg, D. and Coe, R. (2007) 'Thirty years on – a large anti-Flynn effect? The Piagetian test volume and heaviness norms', *British Journal of Educational Psychology*, 77 (1): 25–41.

Shields, J. (1965) *Monozygotic Twins Brought up Apart and Brought up Together*, London, Oxford University Press.

Shipman, M. (1988) *The Limitations of Social Research*, 3rd edn, London, Longman.

Shotter, J. (1990) 'The social construction of remembering and forgetting', in Middleton, D. and Edwards, D. (eds), *Collective Remembering*, London, Sage: 120–38.

Sikes, P. (2000) ' "Truth" and "Lies" Revisited', *British Educational Research Journal*, 26(2): 257–70.

Silverman, D. (2004a) *Doing Qualitative Research: A Practical Handbook*, 2nd edn, London, Sage.

Silverman, D. (ed.) (2004b) *Qualitative Research: Theory, Method and Practice*, 2nd edn, London, Sage.

Silverman, D. (2006) *Interpreting Qualitative Data: Methods for Analysing Talk, Text and Interaction*, 3rd edn, London, Sage.

Sluga, H. (1993) *Heidegger's Crisis: Philosophy and Politics in Nazi Germany*, Cambridge, MA, Harvard University Press.

Smith, D. and Tomlinson, S. (1989) *The School Effect: A Study of Multi-Racial Comprehensives*, London, Policy Studies Institute.

Smith, G. and Cantley, C. (1984) 'Pluralistic evaluation', in Lishman, J. (ed.), *Evaluation Highlights in Social Work Research*, 8, Aberdeen, University of Aberdeen: 140–62 (Jessica Kingsley edn: 118–36).

Smith, G. and Cantley, C. (1985) *Assessing Health Care: A Study in Organisational Evaluation*, Buckingham, Open University Press.

Smith, G., Cantley, C. and Ritman, V. (1983) 'Patient turn-over in a new psychogeriatric day hospital: pluralistic evaluation', *Aging and Society*, 13(3): 325–56.

Snyder, C. and Higgins, R. (1990) 'Reality negotiation and excuse-making: President Reagan's 4 March 1987 Iran arms scandal speech and other literature', in Cody, M. and McLaughlin, M. (eds), *The Psychology of Tactical Communication*, Clevedon, PA, Multilingual Matters Ltd: 207–28.

Song, F., Eastwood, A., Gilbody, S. and Duley, L. (1999) 'The role of electronic journals in reducing publication bias', *Medical Informatics*, 24: 223–9.

Song, F., Eastwood, A., Gilbody, S., Duley, L. and Sutton, A. (2001) 'Publication and related biases' in Stevens, A., Abrams, K., Brazier, J., Fitzpatrick, R. and Lilford, R. (eds) *The Advanced Handbook of Evidence Based Health Care*, London, Sage: 371–90.

Spector, M. and Kitsuse, J. (1987) *Constructing Social Problems*, New York, Aldine & de Gruyter.

Spencer, L., Ritchie, J., Lewis, J. and Dillon, L. (2003) *Assessing Quality in Qualitative Evaluation*, London, Cabinet Office.

Spender, D. (1980) *Man-Made Language*, London, Routledge & Kegan Paul.

Spender, D. (1982) *Invisible Women: The Schooling Scandal*, London, Writers & Readers Publishing Cooperative.

Sprumont, D. (1999) 'Legal protection of human research subjects in Europe', *European Journal of Health Law*, 6(1): 25–43.

SRA (2005) *Data Protection Act 1998: Guide for Social Researchers*, London, Social Research Association (www.the_sra.org.uk).

Stacey, J. (1991) 'Can there be a feminist ethnography?', in Gluck, S. and Patai, D. (eds), *Women's Words: The Feminist Practice of Oral History*, London, Routledge: 111–20.

Stake, R. (1994) 'Case studies', in Denzin, N. and Lincoln, Y. (eds), *Handbook of Qualitative Research*, Thousand Oaks, CA, Sage.

Stanley, L. (1992) *The Autobiographical I: The Theory and Practice of Feminist Auto/Biography*, Manchester, Manchester University Press.

Stanley, L. and Wise, S. (1983) *Breaking Out: Feminist Consciousness and Feminist Research*, London, Routledge & Kegan Paul.

Stanley, L. and Wise, S. (1993) *Breaking Out Again: Feminist Ontology and Epistemology*, London, Routledge.

Stanworth, M. (1983) *Gender and Schooling: A Study of Sexual Divisions in the Classroom*, London, Hutchinson.

Steedman, J. (1980) *Progress in Secondary Schools*, London, National Children's Bureau.

Steedman, J., Fogelman, K. and Hutchinson, D. (1980) *Real Research: A Rebuttal of Allegations*, London, National Children's Bureau.

Stern, C. and Sherwood, E. (1966) *The Origin of Genetics: A Mendel Source Book*, San Francisco, W. H. Freeman.

Stevens, A., Abrams, K., Brazier, J., Fitzpatrick, R. and Lilford., R. (eds) (2001) *The Advanced Handbook of Methods in Evidence Based Healthcare*, London, Sage.

Stimson, G. (1972) *The Drug Takers*, London, Tavistock.

Strauss, A. and Corbin, J. (1998) *Basics of Qualitative Research: Techniques and Procedures for Developing Grounded Theory*, 2nd edn, London, Sage.

Stubbs, M. (1983) *Discourse Analysis: The Sociolinguistic Analysis of Natural Language*, Oxford, Blackwell.

Suchman, L. and Jordan, B. (1990) 'Interactional troubles in face-to-face survey interviews', *Journal of the American Statistical Association*, 85(409): 232–41.

Suls, J. and Rostow, R. (1988) 'Artifacts in psychological experiments', in Morowski, J. (ed.), *The Rise of Experimentation in American Psychology*, London, Yale University Press: 163–87.

Sutton, A., Jones, D., Abrams, K., Sheldon, T. and Song, F. (2001) 'Meta-analysis in health technology assessment', in Stevens, A., Abrams, K., Brazier, J., Fitzpatrick, R.

and Lilford, R. (eds), *The Advanced Handbook of Evidence Based Health Care*, London, Sage: 391–408.

Sutton, J. and Smith, P. (1999) 'Bullying as a group process: an adaptation of the Participant Role Scale Approach', *Aggressive Behaviour*, 25(2): 97–111.

Sutton, J., Smith, P. and Swettenham, J. (1999a) 'Bullying and "theory of mind": a critique of the "social skills deficit" view of anti-social behaviour', *Social Development*, 8(1), 117–34.

Sutton, J., Smith, P. and Swettenham, J. (1999b) 'Social cognition and bullying: social inadequacy or skilled manipulation', *British Journal of Developmental Psychology*, 17: 435–50 (reprinted in Lewis, V., Kellett, M., Robinson, C., Fraser, S. and Ding S. (eds) (2004), *The Reality of Research with Children and Young People*, London, Sage: 44–60).

Swan, S., Shaw, G. and Schulman, J. (1992) 'Reporting and selection bias in case control studies of congenital malformations', *Epidemiology*, 3: 356–63.

Tarir, T. (2000) *A Primer in Longitudinal Data Analysis*, London, Sage.

Taylor, H. (1980) *The IQ Game: A Methodological Inquiry into the Heredity–Environment Controversy*, Brighton, Harvester Press.

Taylor, S. (1982) *Durkheim and the Study of Suicide*, Basingstoke, Macmillan.

Teddlie, C. and Reynolds, D. (2000) *International Handbook of School Effectiveness Research*, London, Falmer.

Temple, B. (2005) 'Nice and tidy: translation and representation', *Sociological Research On-line*, 10.3 (www.socresonline.org.uk/) (subscribers only).

Thines, G. (1987) 'Phenomenology', in Gregory, R. (ed.), *The Oxford Companion to the Mind*, Oxford, Oxford University Press: 614–16.

Thomas, M. (2002) 'The evidence-base for clinical governance', *Journal of Evaluation in Clinical Practice*, 8(2): 251–25.

Thompson, P. (1975) *The Edwardians: The Remaking of British Society*, London: Routledge.

Thompson, P. and Lummis, T. (2005) *Family Life and Work Experience Before 1918, 1870–1973* [computer file], 5th edn, Colchester, Essex: UK Data Archive [distributor], April 2005, SN: 2000.

Tilburg, T. van (1998) 'Interviewer effects in the measurement of personal network size', *Sociological Methods and Research*, 26(3): 300–27.

Tilley, N. and Laycock, G. (2002) *Working Out What To Do: Evidence-Based Crime Reduction*, Crime Reduction Research Series, 11, London, Home Office.

Titchen, A. and Binnie, A. (1994) 'Action research: a strategy for theory generation and testing', *International Journal of Nursing Studies*, 31(1): 1–12.

Titscher, S., Meyer, M., Wodak, R. and Vetter, E. (2000) *Methods of Text and Discourse Analysis*, London, Sage.

Tooley, J. (1998) *Educational Research: A Critique: A Survey of Published Educational Research*, London, Ofsted.

Townsend, P. (1962) *Last Refuge: A Survey of Residential Institutions and Homes for the Aged in England and Wales*, London, Routledge & Kegan Paul.

Troyna, B. (1991) 'Underachievers or underrated? The experience of pupils of South Asian origin in a secondary school', *British Educational Research Journal*, 17: 361–76.

Tudor Hart, J. (1993) 'Hypertension guidelines: other diseases complicate management', *British Medical Journal*, 306: 1337.

Tudor Smith, C., Nutbeam, D., Moore, L. and Catford, J. (1998) 'Effects of Heartbeat Wales programme over five years on behavioural risks for cardio-vascular disease: quasi-experimental comparison of results from Wales and a matched reference area', *British Medical Journal*, 316: 818–22.

Turkheimer, E., Haley, A., Waldron, M., D'Onofrio, B. and Gottesman, I. (2003) 'Socioeconomic status modifies heritability of IQ in young children', *Psychological Science*, 14(6): 623–8.

Turner, B. (1994) 'Patterns of crisis behaviour: a qualitative inquiry', in Bryman, A. and Burgess, R. (eds), *Analyzing Qualitative Data*, London, Routledge: 173–94.

Tzamourani, P. (2000) 'An experiment with a promised contribution to charity as a respondent incentive on a face-to-face survey', *Survey Methods Newsletter*, 20(2): 13–15.

Tzamourani, P. and Lynn, P. (2000) 'Do respondent incentives affect data quality? Evidence from an experiment', *Survey Methods Newsletter*, 20(2): 3–7.

van Dijk, T. (1991) *Racism and the Press*, London, Routledge.

van Dijk, T. (1993) 'Principles of critical discourse analysis', *Discourse and Society*, 4(2): 249–83.

van Leeuwen, T. and Jewitt, C. (eds) (2000) *The Handbook of Visual Analysis*, London, Sage.

van Maanen, J. (1988) *Tales of the Field: On Writing Ethnography*, Chicago, Chicago University Press.

Vass, A. (1986) *AIDS: A Plague in Us – A Social Perspective*, St Ives, Venus Academica.

Vickers, D. and Rees, P. (2006) 'Introducing the area classification of output areas', *Population Trends*, 125: 15–24.

Wadsworth, M. (1996a) 'The survey that shocked the nation', *Medical Research Council News*, Winter: 28–32.

Wadsworth, M. (1996b) *The Imprint of Time: Childhood History and Adult Life*, Oxford, Oxford University Press.

Wakeford, J. (1969) *The Cloistered Elite: A Sociological Analysis of English Public Boarding Schools*, London, Macmillan.

Walby, S. and Allen, J. (2004) *Domestic Violence: Sexual Assault and Stalking: Findings from the British Crime Survey*, London, Home Office Research Studies, 276 (www.homeoffice.gov.uk/rds).

Walker, A., Kershaw, C. and Nicholas, S. (2006) *Crime in England and Wales 2005/06I* (British Crime Survey), London, Home Office, *Home Office Statistical Bulletin*, 12/06 (www.homeoffice.gov.uk/rds).

Walker, M. (1989) 'Moral understanding: an alternative "epistemology" for a feminist ethics', *Hypatica*, 4(1): 15–28.

Wall, W. and Williams, H. (1970) *Longitudinal Studies and Social Science*, London, Social Science Research Council/Heinemann.

Walvis, T. (2003) 'Avoiding advertising research disasters: advertising and the uncertainty principle', *Journal of Brand Management*, 10(6): 403–9.

Warde, A. (1997) *Consumption, Food and Taste*, London, Sage.

Watts, D. and Strogatz, S. (1998) 'Collective dynamics of small-world networks', *Nature*, 393, 440–2.

Weber, M. (1949) *The Methodology of the Social Sciences*, eds A. Shils and H. Fihn, Glencoe, Free Press (original, 1904).

Weed, M. (2005) ' "Meta Interpretation": a method for the interpretive synthesis of qualitative research', *Forum for Qualitative Social Research*, (6(1) Art. 37 (www.qualitative-research.net/).

Wells, M. (2002) 'BBC halts "Prison Experiment" ', *Guardian*, Thursday, 24 January, www.guardian.co.uk.

Wertsch, J. (1987) 'Collective memory: issues from a socio-historical perspective', *Quarterly Newsletter of the Laboratory of Comparative Human Cognition*, 9(1): 19–22.

West, D. and Farrington, D. (1973) *Who Becomes Delinquent*, London, Hutchinson.

Western, P. (1990) *Speaking of Equality: An Analysis of the Rhetorical Force of 'Equality' in Moral and Legal Discourse*, Princetown, NJ, Princetown University Press.

Westfall, R. (1973) 'Newton and the fudge factor', *Science*, 179: 751–8.

White, C., Glickman, M., Johnson B. and Corbin, T. (2007) 'Social inequalities and adult male mortality by the National Statistics Socio-Economic Classification: England and Wales 2001–2003', *Health Statistics*, 36 (6–23) www.statistics.gov.uk (journal articles)

Whittaker, A., Gardner, S. and Kershaw, J. (1990) *Service Evaluation by People with Learning Difficulties*, London, King's Fund.

Whyte, W. F. (1981) *Street Corner Society: The Social Structure of an Italian Slum*, 3rd edn, Chicago, Chicago University Press, 1st edn, 1935).

Wiles, R., Charles, V., Crow, G. and Heath, S. (2004) 'Informed consent and the research process', ESRC Research Methods Working Paper, 16 (www.ccsr.ac.uk/methods/publications/#Papers).

Wilkinson, S. (1999) 'How useful are focus groups in feminist research?', in Barbour, R. and Kitzinger, J. (eds), *Developing Focus Group Research: Politics, Theory and Practice*, London, Sage: 64–78.

Williams, A. (1995) 'Ethics and action research', *Nurse Researcher*, 2(3): 49–59.

Williamson, J. (1994) *Decoding Advertisements*, London, Marion Boyars.

Willis, P. (1977) *Learning to Labour: How Working Class Kids get Working Class Jobs*, Farnborough, Saxon House.

Wilson, G. and Ryland, G. (1949) *Social Groupwork Practice: The Creative Use of Social Process*, Boston, Houghton Mifflin.

Wodak, R. and Meyer, M. (eds) (2001) *Methods of Critical Discourse Analysis*, London, Sage.

Wolf, D. (1991) 'High risk methodology: reflections on leaving an outlaw society', in Shaffir, W. and Stebbins, R. (eds), *Experiencing Fieldwork: An Inside View of Qualitative Research*, Newbury Park, CA., Sage: 220.

Wollen, P. (1998) *Signs and Meaning in the Cinema*, London, British Film Institute.

Wood, P. (2000). 'Meta-analysis', in Breakwell, G., Hammond, S. and Fife-Schaw, C. (eds), *Research Methods in Psychology*, 2nd edn, London, Sage: 414–25.

Wright, C. (1986) 'School processes: an ethnographic study', in Eggleston, J., Dunn, D. and Anjali, M. (eds), *Education for Some: The Educational and Vocational Experiences of 15–18 Year Old Members of Minority Ethnic Groups*, Stoke on Trent, Trentham Books: 127–80.

Wright, C. (1992) *Race Relations in the Primary School*, London, David Foulton.

Yablonsky, L. (1967) *The Violent Gang*, Harmondsworth, Penguin.

Young, J. (1971) 'The role of the police as amplifiers of deviancy: negotiators of reality and translators of fantasy – some consequences of our present system of drug control as seen in Notting Hill', in Cohen, S. (ed.), *Images of Deviance*, Harmondsworth, Penguin: 27–61.

Yudkowsky, E. (2003) *An Intuitive Explanation of Bayesian Reasoning* (http://yudkowsky.net/bayes/bayes.html).

Zipf, G. (1949) *Human Behaviour and the Principle of Least-Effort*, Cambridge, MA Addison-Wesley.

Zimbardo, P. (2004) 'Power turns good soldiers into bad apples', *Boston Globe*, 9 May (www.boston.com/news/globe).

Zimbardo, P. (2007) *The Lucifer Effect*, New York, Random House.

Index

Note: the more important entries are **emboldened.**